THE NEW SILK ROAD BECOMES THE WORLD LAND-BRIDGE:
A SHARED FUTURE FOR HUMANITY

VOLUME II

SCHILLER INSTITUTE

ISBN: 978-1-882985-03-6
Product code: SCHSP-2018-1-0-0-STD

Managing Editor: Megan Beets
Editors: Marcia Merry-Baker, Michael Billington, Ronald Kokinda, Dennis Small, Jason Ross

Copyright © 2018 Schiller Institute

Reproduction of all or part of these contents without explicit authorization of the publisher is prohibited.

CONTENTS

I. INTRODUCTION

A Shared Future for Humanity, *Helga Zepp-LaRouche* 2

Optimism and Vision: Two Speeches of Helga Zepp-LaRouche
    The New Silk Road, a New Model for International Relations 7
        Bad Soden, Germany, November 25, 2017
    The Belt and Road Initiative and the Dialogue of Cultures 20
        Zhuhai, China, November 29, 2017

The Schiller Institute: Decades of Fighting for a New, Just World Economic Order 25

II. PRINCIPLES OF PHYSICAL ECONOMY

Economic Principles of a New Paradigm: Lyndon LaRouche's Discoveries 36

The Strategic Defense of Earth for the Universal Progress of Man:
      What Does LaRouche's SDI Mean Today? 53

The LaRouche Doctrine: Draft Memorandum of Agreement
      Between the United States and the U.S.S.R., *Lyndon LaRouche* 64

III. PROGRESS REPORTS

Introduction 74
China: Development for a Shared Future for Humanity 76
Russia: In the New Silk Road 94
Central and South Asia: The Hub of the New Silk Road 106
Southwest Asia: Reconstruction for a New Renaissance 138
The Belt and Road: Transforming Southeast Asia 152
The Necessary Solution to the Crisis on the Korean Peninsula 166
The New Silk Road Reaches Africa 174
Europe: Western Terminal of the New Silk Road 196
The Future of the Americas Lies with the New Silk Road 272
The Arctic: The Ice Silk Road 316

IV. TRANS-ATLANTIC AT THE CROSSROADS

The United States Strategic Relation to the New Silk Road 326

Will Europe Finally Join the New Silk Road? 333

V. WITHOUT LAROUCHE'S 'FOUR LAWS,' FINANCIAL CRASH MEANS CHAOS

The Danger of a New Financial Crash without Glass-Steagall Bank Regulation 340

'Four Laws' for the New Paradigm 350

    'Glass-Steagall' Bank Separation 351

    'Hamiltonian' National Credit and National Banks 356

    Credit for Increased Productivity 364

    A Crash Program for Fusion Power, Plasma Technology, and Space 371

The Four New Laws to Save the USA Now!

    Not An Option: An Immediate Necessity, *Lyndon LaRouche* 379

VI. MOVING 50 YEARS AHEAD

2068—A Retrospective 384

Earth's Next 50 Years: The Space Silk Road 391

The Dialogue of Eurasian Civilizations: Earth's Next 50 Years, *Lyndon LaRouche* 400

Contributing Authors:
Dean Andromidas, Rainer Apel, Hussein Askary, Megan Beets, Christine Bierre, Michael Billington, Yannick Caroff, Claudio Celani, Benjamin Deniston, Elke Fimmen, Marsha Freeman, Paul Gallagher, Alexander Hartmann, Robert Hux, William Jones, Lyndon LaRouche, Jr., Borja Marugán, Marcia Merry-Baker, Jason Ross, Ulf Sandmark, Christine Schier, Dennis Small, Gretchen Small, Karel Vereycken, Helga Zepp-LaRouche

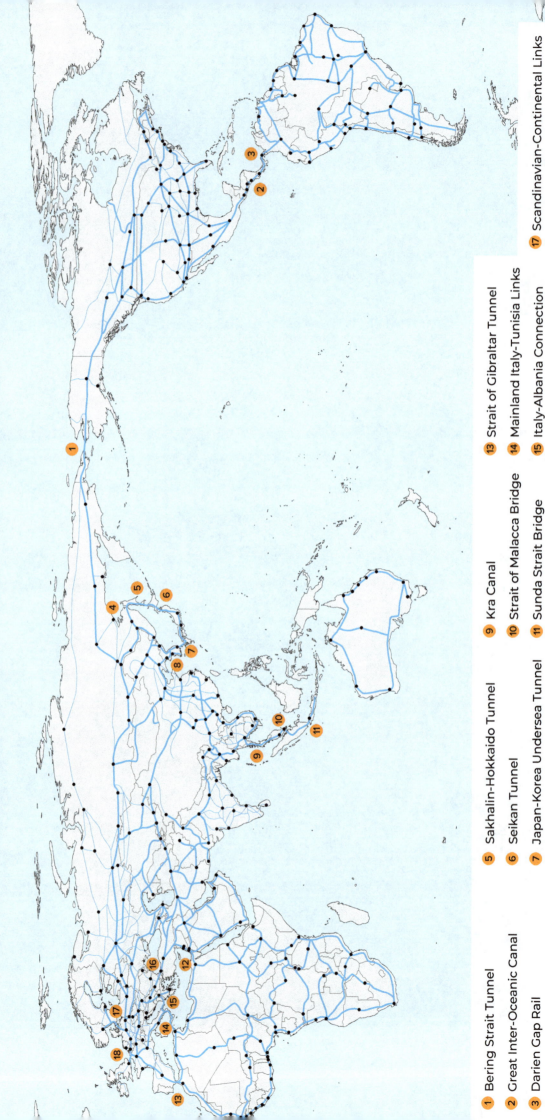

I. INTRODUCTION

"The 'Spirit of the New Silk Road' has changed the world for the better much more thoroughly than the trans-Atlantic sector has even remotely understood until now.... And because China is thus addressing the existential needs of billions of people, that policy is likely to be the greatest revolution in the history of mankind."

A SHARED FUTURE FOR HUMANITY

by Helga Zepp-LaRouche

The "Spirit of the New Silk Road" has changed the world for the better much more thoroughly than the trans-Atlantic sector has even remotely understood until now. Since Chinese President Xi Jinping placed the New Silk Road on the agenda in September 2013 in Kazakhstan, optimism on an unprecedented scale has swept over the developing countries in particular, a sense that poverty and underdevelopment can be overcome in the foreseeable future thanks to Chinese investments in infrastructure, industry, and agriculture. Geopolitically-oriented circles in the West have not understood that China is implementing a new model of international policy, which tackles the deficit which the legacy of colonialism and imperialism has bequeathed up to this day: the absolute lack of development. And because China is thus addressing the existential needs of billions of people, that policy is likely to be the greatest revolution in the history of mankind.

In the nearly four years that have elapsed since the release of the first 374-page comprehensive study *The New Silk Road Becomes the World Land-Bridge* in December 2014, numerous projects that were conceptualized in that report, have been carried out. Others, such as the Transaqua Project for the revitalization of Lake Chad and the development of a waterway system for 12 African countries, have been agreed upon by the governments involved and feasibility studies are being drawn up. Since then, the World Land-Bridge report has been published in English, Chinese, Arabic, and German, and a Korean version will soon be available.

China's Belt and Road Initiative has become the largest infrastructure program in human history. The "Belt and Road Forum" in May 2017 brought together 29 heads of state and government and more than 1,200 representatives from more than 140 nations, including this author (see articles on Schiller Institute activities later in this section). Hundreds of conferences and seminars on this subject have been held around the world, and more and more countries see that their economic opportunities lie in becoming a hub for the New Silk Road and the "Maritime Silk Road for the 21st Century." However, it is not only the enormous economic perspectives derived from economic cooperation on a win-win basis that

Helga Zepp-LaRouche in the CGTN studio in May 2017

have fundamentally changed the overall strategic situation, but also and above all Xi Jinping's idea of a "community of shared future for mankind."

What most people in the West can no longer even imagine, is that in Xi Jinping, a statesman who has assumed the political leadership of the most populous nation in the world, is also a profound philosopher. In his opening remarks to the welcoming banquet of the 2018 annual conference of the Shanghai Cooperation Organization (SCO), Xi invoked the spirit of Confucius, who was born in Shandong Province, the site of the summit. Shandong was the birthplace of Confucianism, which is an integral part of Chinese civilization, he said, and he believes that a just cause should be pursued for the common good, for the harmony, unity, and shared community of all nations. The future of the SCO, Xi implied, should be inspired by the spirit of Confucius! In Europe, one would have to go back at least as far as Adenauer and de Gaulle, Bismarck, and vom Stein to find a statesman who has based his policy on humanist philosophers.

With the Silk Road initiative and the idea of a community of shared future for mankind, Xi Jinping has developed a totally new model for relations among the nations of the world, which supersedes the previous geopolitical rivalries of the blocs with the higher idea of one single mankind, whose sovereign states cooperate with one another to their mutual benefit. As Xi Jinping explained in his report to the 19th National Congress of the Communist Party of China, he is pursuing the vision of initiating developments by 2050 that allow for the peaceful coexistence of all sovereign nations on Earth and a happy life for people.

Largely unnoticed or disregarded by the Euro-centric or Ameri-centric view of the mainstream media, is the fact that entirely new strategic orientations are developing in Asia as a result of this grand design, and that Asian countries are in the process of overcoming past historical antagonisms and working out a new type of cooperation. Numerous countries, which were played against each other until recently in geopolitical scenarios, now see a much more promising perspective in a strategic realignment of cooperation for mutual benefit and for a higher idea of the common development of all of mankind.

The historical breakthrough that President Trump and Chairman Kim Jung-un were able to achieve in Singapore on June 12, 2018 involving an agreement on full nuclear disarmament in return for security guarantees which China wants to help provide, as well as on the lifting of sanctions and North Korea's economic development, would have been unthinkable without the "spirit of the New Silk Road," that has triggered throughout Asia the optimistic mindset that genuine changes for the better are indeed possible. Trump's announcement that he will end the joint military maneuvers with South Korea represents an important step on the road to a peace treaty between the two Koreas. Laying the ground for this development, there was intensive cooperation among South Korea, China, Russia, India, and the United States, which could become a model for solving regional conflicts.

The economic modernization of North Korea pledged by Trump, Russia, and China, which will make it "prosperous and wealthy," corresponds to the intention discussed at the inter-Korean summit between President Moon Jae-in and Chairman Kim Jong-un in April 2018, and prior to that, at the Eastern Economic Forum in Vladivostok in September 2017. Both Koreas are to be included in the integration of the Belt and Road Initiative and the Eurasian Economic Union, including the connection of the fu-

I. INTRODUCTION

Leaders at the 2018 Shanghai Cooperation Organization meeting in Qingdao

ture trans-Korean railway to the Trans-Siberian Railway and to China's transportation network.

Another good example of this is the policy change in Japan and India. The Obama Administration's "Asia Pivot" was aimed at using the "Indo-Pacific" policy to line up countries in the Pacific region—Australia, Japan, New Zealand, and India—against China and above all against the dynamic of the New Silk Road. The United States and the European Union (EU) played the India card in particular, arguing that the "world's largest democracy" (India) should cooperate with the democratic West against the authoritarian China. However, following a two-day summit between President Xi Jinping and Prime Minister Narendra Modi in April 2018, the two most populous states in the world recalibrated their relations to each other. Speaking at the Shangri-la Dialogue in Singapore on June 1, 2018, Modi appealed to the world to rise above divisions and rivalries, and to opt instead to work together. He referred to the deep conceptions of Vedanta philosophy, going back to the Vedas and Upanishads of ancient India, namely, the idea of the "essential oneness of all," and the idea that every individual soul is that Being in full, and not part of that Being.

On the special relationship to China, Prime Minister Modi stressed that "No other relationship of India has as many layers as our relations with China. Our cooperation is expanding, trade is growing…. I firmly believe that Asia, and the world, will have a better future when India and China work together in trust and confidence, sensitive to each other's interests."

Modi concluded: "This world is at a crossroad. There are temptations of the worst lessons of history. But, there is also a path of wisdom. It summons us to a higher purpose: to rise above a narrow view of our interests and recognize that each of us can serve our interests better when we work together as equals in the larger good of all nations. I am here to urge all to take that path."

What is also missing from the radar screen of Western media and politicians is the change in policy in Japan. In the past, Japan was largely an integral part of the "Washington Consensus." But in recent years, Prime Minister Shinzo Abe has expanded his relations with Russia in a number of ways, while the perspective of joint economic development of the four South Kuril Islands claimed by Japan and of the improvement of bilateral relations has raised the possibility that a peace treaty could be signed between the two countries before Abe leaves office. At the same time, Japan's skepticism toward China and the Belt and Road Initiative has given way to a positive attitude. After Abe sent the Secretary General of the ruling Liberal Democratic Party, Toshihiro Nikai, as his personal envoy to the May 2017 Belt and Road Forum, Japan shifted to full cooperation with the New Silk Road policy as of June 2017. Moreover, Abe was also the first head of government to visit the newly elected Donald Trump in Trump Tower on November 17, 2016, and then on February 10, 2017 in Washington and after that at Mar-a-Lago, and that at a time when the trans-Atlantic neo-liberal fraction was still in a state of shock over Trump's election victory.

Perhaps the most important question for the future of the world is what relationship the United States will seek toward a rising China, in order to avoid the notorious Thucydides trap. The Chinese Ambassador to the United States, Cui Tiankai, said in a speech in New York that there have been 16 cases in history in which an ascending power surpassed the hitherto dominant power—in 12 of those cases, it led to war, and in four cases, the rising power overtook the previously leading power. China, of course, does not want to go to war, the Ambassador said, and it also does not want to overtake the United States as the world superpower, but it does seek win-win cooperation on a partnership basis. To that purpose,

Xi Jinping has developed a new model for relations among major powers based on the principles of absolute respect for the sovereignty of others, of non-interference in internal affairs, and respect for the respective other political and social system.

From this standpoint, it is most fortunate that President Trump and President Xi, from the very first visit of the latter to Mar-a-Lago in April 2017, established an exceptionally friendly relationship with one another. Xi returned the invitation to Trump's private residence with a "State visit plus" for Trump during his state visit to China that October. He also reserved the Forbidden City for an entire day for a personal tour for the U.S. President and First Lady Melania Trump. Despite all the tensions with China due to differences of opinion as to how to overcome the trade deficit, Trump has repeatedly called Xi a good friend. But it is above all the historic breakthrough with North Korea that would have simply been unthinkable without the relationship between Donald Trump and Xi Jinping.

However, while the populations of North and South Korea are enthusiastically viewing the common future now opening up, and while a completely new optimistic spirit is spreading throughout Asia, Africa, Latin America, and many countries in eastern and southern Europe, the mainstream media and many think-tanks and politicians are reacting to these fantastic strategic changes with such a negative attitude that one could assume that they are in a different universe. The rather special *Der Spiegel* journalist Roland Nelles described the day of the summit in Singapore as "bizarre" and the meeting of the two Presidents as "weird," which does less justice to the occasion than it affords a certain insight into Mr. Nelles' intellectual life.

For the West, it is evidently extremely difficult to grasp the new paradigm, which has developed out of the dynamic of the New Silk Road. Trapped in the old paradigm of geopolitical divisions and competition in the world, they can only see the projections of their own intentions through such spectacles. From the standpoint of geopolitics, politics can only be a zero-sum game—if one wins, the other must necessarily lose. They view Xi Jinping's concept of win-win cooperation with mistrust, as if it were impossible for a government to defend not only the common good of its own population, but also that of other cooperating nations.

In that respect, at the very latest, the comparison of the fiasco of the G7 summit in Canada in June 2018 with the tremendous success of the simultaneous summit of the Shanghai Corporation Organization should have provided the occasion for self-critical questions about the reasons for such a difference. The multifaceted erosion of the EU is not due to any alleged interference by Russian President Vladimir Putin, but to the lack of a policy that gives equal consideration to the interests of all member states. When a certain EU Commissioner, Günther Öttinger, after the March 2018 election in Italy, threatens that the markets would teach the Italians how to vote, one should not be surprised at the anger of the Italians and other southern European populations over the effects on them of Germany's "market-compliant democracy."

The mainstream media and most of the Western think-tanks had virtually ignored the groundbreaking dynamic of the New Silk Road for some four years, but then strangely enough during the Spring of 2018, the Australian secret services, the geopolitically-minded U.S. think-tanks CSIS and CFR, the Soros-financed European Council on Foreign Affairs, and the German think-tank MERICS all launched, as if on cue, an attack on China's New Silk Road policy as allegedly imperialistic.

The combination of non-reporting and ideological, manipulative characterizations makes it difficult for ordinary entrepreneurs or citizens to have a clear picture of the historically unprecedented potential that cooperation in this initiative opens up for the European and American economies. The events of the Spring 2018 should prompt us to reflect on the now undeniable inherent weaknesses of the neo-liberal model of globalization, and to revive the strengths of the best traditions of the West in our cooperation with China, and to develop a common model for shaping the future.

The world is changing dramatically, and the change is happening in Asia. President Xi Jinping, as we mentioned, opened the 2018 summit of the Shanghai Cooperation Organization in Qingdao with a reference to the thinking of Confucius which should inspire the organization's future. And indeed, Chinese Foreign Minister Wang Yi's remarks at the final press conference of the SCO summit reflected the spirit of Confucius: the SCO is building a new world order, he said, based on mutual trust, mutual benefit, equality, respect for the diversity and common development of civilizations. Its intention, he explained, is to transcend such outdated concepts such as the clash of civilizations, the Cold War, and thinking in the geometry of zero-sum games or exclusionary clubs.

The new era must be based on the best traditions of all the cultures involved. In China, Confucius stands for the ideal of self-perfection through lifelong learning and ennoblement of the character as a pre-condition for harmonious coexistence in the family, the nation, and among nations. And the notion of the "mandate of Heaven" implies that the duty of government is to ensure the common good. In Indian culture, this corresponds in principle to the concept of Dharma, the idea that universal laws set the rules for shaping relations on Earth, i.e., that the cosmic order is also valid on Earth. The five principles of the Pansheel Treaty and the concept of Ahimsa are culturally specific, and yet represent ideas that correspond to a positive image of man as the basis for the political order. In Islam there is a concept called "Istikhlaf," which means "giving a divine authority" to someone. According to the Quran, Allah (God) instructed all the angels, and even Iblis (Satan)—who, however, refused—to kneel in front of Adam, because Adam and his species will inherit earth and make it prosperous, which they are able to do because man is capable of knowledge which even the angels are not.

For European civilization, which America belongs to, the equivalent is the humanist tradition. An expression of this approach are the ideas of Nicholas of Cusa, the *coincidentia oppositorum*, that is, that human reason is capable of a higher level of thinking, on which the contradictions of the intellect are

A new paradigm must be based on a dialogue among the best traditions of each culture, for a new, truly global renaissance. Raphael's "School of Athens" reflects such a humanist tradition in Western culture.

resolved. Order in the macrocosm is only possible if all the microcosms develop in the best possible way and to their mutual benefit. The Treaty of Westphalia is built on this foundation, which gave rise to international law, just as is the philosophy of Gottfried Wilhelm Leibniz and Friedrich Schiller. In Russia, the same basic principle is expressed in the idea of Vladimir Vernadsky, that the significance of the Noösphere is constantly increasing over that of the biosphere, and that therefore the role of creative reason as a physical power increases.

The spirit of a new beginning, the cultural optimism about imminent breakthroughs in fundamental research, and an unprecedented dynamic toward the betterment of mankind's living conditions—all this characterizes the development in Asia, and this optimism has long since "rubbed off" on Latin America and Africa. We in Europe and the United States should recognize and exploit the tremendous potential it will mean for our economies if we join in this win-win cooperation. Provided we count on qualitative innovation as a source of social wealth, collaboration with the New Silk Road is by no means a threat; on the contrary, it offers us the urgently needed chance to re-discover our true identity.

"I think that the New Silk Road is a typical example of an idea whose time had come; and once an idea is in that way becoming a material reality, it becomes a physical force in the universe."

The New Silk Road

A NEW MODEL FOR INTERNATIONAL RELATIONS

Helga Zepp-LaRouche delivered the following keynote address to an international audience at a Schiller Institute conference, "Fulfilling the Dream of Mankind," held in Bad Soden, Germany, November 25 and 26, 2017.

Ladies and gentlemen, I want to greet you to this conference of the Schiller Institute. There are many honorable people in the audience, who we will introduce in the course of the event. But let me just greet especially the General Consul of Ethiopia.

So, let me start with an idea of Gottfried Wilhelm Leibniz. He said that we are actually living in the best of all possible worlds. This is a very fundamental ontological conception. It's the idea that we are living in a developing universe; that what makes the universe the best of all possible ones is its tremendous potential for development. It is in such a way created, that every great evil challenges an even greater good to come into being. I think when we are talking about the New Silk Road and the tremendous changes which have occurred in the world, especially in the past four years, it is actually exactly that principle working. Because it was the absolute manifest lack of development of the old world order which caused the impulse of China and the spirit of the New Silk Road having caught on that now many nations of the world are absolutely determined to have a development giving a better life to all of their people.

Now, I think that the New Silk Road is a typical example of an idea whose time had come; and once an idea is in that way becoming a material reality, it becomes a physical force in the universe. I personally have had the chance to see the evolution of this idea, which in many senses really started with this great gentleman—my husband, Lyndon LaRouche; who many decades ago—almost half a century ago—had the idea of a just New World Economic Order. This then became more manifest in the 1970s, in the 1980s, but especially in 1991 when the Soviet Union disintegrated, this idea of creating a just New World Economic Order became very prominent.

I personally had the chance to see how this spread after Xi Jinping in 2013 in Kazakhstan announced the New Silk Road. I visited China in 2014, and at that point it was still a very small number of officials discussing it; but then it very rapidly spread. There were industrial fairs in all cities in China; hundreds of international symposiums. The BRICS countries started to join the same spirit; the Shanghai Cooper-

I. INTRODUCTION

Helga Zepp-LaRouche

ation Organization. Altogether, more than 100 large nations and international organizations. It spread to the Belt and Road Forum at the beginning of this year in May, where 29 heads of state spoke, 110 nations participated. I think this determination of the Chinese people to effect a New World Economic Order was consolidated in a completely new way at the 19th National Congress of the Communist Party of China (CPC) in October.

This has generated a completely optimistic perspective. Xi Jinping announced that China will be by the year 2020 a country in which poverty is completely eradicated. I think this is wonderful! And it is absolutely to be believed, because China had an incredible economic miracle, and they lifted 700 million people out of poverty. They have now only 42 million people left, so why should they not succeed that there are no more poor persons by the year 2020? By 2035, China is supposed to be a great modern socialist country with Chinese characteristics; which in my view means predominantly Confucian characteristics. By 2050, China will be—according to Xi Jinping—a great modern socialist country with Chinese characteristics, prosperous, strong, democratic, culturally advanced, harmonious, and beautiful. So, the Chinese people by that time are supposed to be happier and have a safer and healthier life. But also, the peoples of the other countries of the world are supposed to have a better and healthier and happier life.

Now the Chinese media announced very proudly that this is a grand vision for the future. A new era has dawned. Xinhua wrote that China will make a new and greater contribution to the noble cause of peace and development for all of humanity. Well, it is very easy for the Chinese people to understand that, because the whole country is already united around this mission. The spirit of the New Silk Road has caught on also in the 70-plus countries which are cooperating [in it]. There are many people in the West who also have understood that; either because they have investments in China, or they know that the New Silk Road is the largest infrastructure program in history. It is already now 12 or maybe even 20 times larger than the Marshall Plan was in the postwar period; without the military connotation, however. It is basically causing complete enthusiasm among everybody who knows the project.

But there are naturally also those in the West who have complete opposition. You have right now the fight between the old paradigm of geopolitics against the New Paradigm of the one humanity. The representatives of the old paradigm say, "Oh, what Xi Jinping is saying is just empty propaganda. The real intention of the Chinese is to replace the United States as hegemonic. Xi Jinping is a dictator; he just wants to have a system which is a threat to the Western model of market-oriented democracy. Therefore, it is bad." The President of the EU Commission, Jean-Claude Juncker, even went so far to explain in his so-called "State of the Union" address that the EU is fully intending to block Chinese investments in Europe under all kinds of pretexts. You have many think-tanks like MERICS or the Rhodium Group, who basically see it only as a geopolitical challenge. Spiegel magazine of last week had a big cover story with Chinese letters on the cover—"Xǐng lái," which means "Wake Up!"—and an article about the awakening giant, saying that when Trump went to China just two weeks ago, he kowtowed; that this was his farewell speech handing over the leadership of the world. That the West must urgently wake up and unite against a rising China; that the Chinese achievements are a threat to the values and the system of the West.

Now, isn't it funny? One day the headlines are saying that the collapse of the Chinese banks and the Chinese economy will trigger a world financial collapse; and the next day, the same papers write that China is about to take over the world. So, obviously, some of these critics are completely freaked out about the fact that the old order—the idea that you can have a unipolar world and geopolitical control based on the Anglo-American special relationship in the tradition of Churchill and Truman in the postwar period and what the neo-cons started to build after the collapse of the Soviet Union—that that system is very clearly not working. As you can see in a revolt against the system; the Brexit, the defeat of Hillary Clinton in the U.S. election, the "no" to the referendum in Italy, the pitiful collapse of the Jamaica coalition talks in Germany. They collapsed because none of the participating parties had any vision for the future, or any substantive ideas.

So, there is no comprehension among these parties for the rapidly changing strategic alignment going on in the world. The common denominator between all of these phenomena is that the Western, neo-liberal, left-liberal establishment is completely unable and unwilling to reflect on the causes of the demise of this Western system. Which are: the absolutely ridiculous income gap where eight individuals have as much wealth as half of the rest of humanity, where the rich and poor gap is increasing in every country; the policy of regime change, of color revolution; the abysmal situation of the refugee crisis. Also, people have experienced that what we have been fighting for, for literally centuries, in terms of civil rights has almost vanished without discussion. You have a total surveillance by the NSA, the CGHQ—the British Secret Service; the Western values of democracy are in shambles. If the Democratic leadership decides one year before the party convention who should be the candidate, and then manipulates the election against Bernie Sanders for one year; is not a happy picture of democracy. You have the collusion of the Democratic Party of the United States with British intelligence and MI-6 to invent Russia-gate against Trump. You have the collusion of the Obama heads of intelligence against the elected President of the United States.

If you look at the famous human rights of the West, even the UN Human Rights Commission denounced what the Troika has been doing in countries like Greece, violating human rights completely. There is a deafening silence concerning the genocide in Yemen, conducted by the British and the Saudis. The way the EU has been treating the refugees has also been called by the United Nations a human rights violation.

When these people are criticizing China, what you can see is that they project their own intentions and viewpoints onto China and the New Silk Road. These people in the West who are attacking China cannot imagine the existence of a government which is truly devoted to the common good and a harmonious development of all people; because they think that the world is a zero-sum game, that if one wins, the other one has to lose. That they have to control the rules in order to be able to rig the game in their favor. If you can't do that, you are a loser.

This all leads to very absurd conclusions. For example, in 1995, Lester Brown, who was the president of the Earth Policy Institute, had a big scare story—Who Will Feed China?—saying that the growing number of people in China will mean a growing demand for food, which will overstretch demand on the food supply in the world. Naturally, this is just the old Malthusian idea that the number of people will grow more quickly than the amount of food. Now if you look at China today, they perfectly well can feed 1.4 billion people; and I can assure you, with excellent food which many countries should be envious of having such good food—like the British, for example. They are producing right now 30% of the world economy. So, the reality is quite different than the Western media portray.

In 2014, we published a study called "The New Silk Road Becomes the World Land-Bridge." That is exactly what is happening. What started with just

I. INTRODUCTION

The first volume of "The New Silk Road Becomes the World Land-Bridge," released in 2014, has been circulated widely around the globe, and is available in several languages.

the old Silk Road line between China and Europe, is now absolutely quickly developing into six major development corridors. There are already 40 rail lines every week from China to different European locations with cargo trains. The 16+1 countries—that is, the Eastern and Central European countries—are having a conference right now in Budapest, being completely on board of the collaboration with the New Silk Road. There is a new Balkans Silk Road. The President of Panama was just in China at the occasion that Panama switched their diplomatic relations from being tied to Taiwan; now they are allied with the mainland. The President of Panama said that all of Latin America will join the New Silk Road, and this is not directed against the United States because the United States is also invited to join. The New Silk Road has reached Africa; and there it has changed the mood in an unbelievable way. There is now a complete sense of optimism.

But the most important shift, naturally, is that of the United States and the relationship between China and the United States. At the recent trip of President Trump, where he made a two-day state visit, the obvious result was the most consequential. Because if the two largest economies of the world have a good relation, then world peace is moving in a very positive direction. Remember that the policy of Obama was the so-called "pivot" to Asia and the TPP, which was the idea of the encirclement of China and exclusion of China. There is still an element of geopolitics, so we have to watch whenever the term is being used—"India-Pacific"; which is the idea to make Japan, Australia, and India as a counterweight to China. But the major breakthrough occurred when Trump visited China, where Xi Jinping gave him the most unbelievable—what he called "state visit-plus-plus." Namely, for closing down the Forbidden City for one day; the Forbidden City is the largest conglomerate of palaces where the Chinese emperors lived since the 17th Century. It's incredibly beautiful; it's majestic, it's really breathtaking. So, Xi Jinping used the whole day to give Trump and the First Lady a course in Chinese history. They had a beautiful gala dinner; they had three Beijing operas. I want to read to you some of the statements made by President Trump, which I think you need to know because the Western media naturally would not report one single word about that.

So Trump, commenting the next day on this treatment, said, "Yesterday we visited the Forbidden City, which stands as a proud symbol of China's rich culture and majestic spirit. Your nation is a testament to the thousands of years of vibrant living history, and today it was a tremendous honor to be greeted by the Chinese delegation right here at the Great Hall of the People. This moment in history presents both our nations with an incredible opportunity to actually advance peace and prosperity alongside other nations all around the world. In the words of a Chinese proverb, 'we must carry forward the cause and forge ahead into the future.' I'm confident that we can realize this wonderful mission; a vision that will be so good and in fact so great for both China and the United States. So, we come from very different places and faraway lands. There is much that binds the East and the West. Both our countries were built by people of great courage, strong culture, and the desire to trek across the unknown into great danger that they overcame. The people of the United States have a very deep respect for the heritage of your country and the noble traditions of its people. Your ancient values bring past and future together in the present so beautifully. It is my hope that the proud spirits of the American and Chinese people will inspire our efforts to achieve a more just, secure, and peaceful world. A future worthy of the sacrifices of our ancestors and the dreams of our children."

President Donald J. Trump and Chinese President Xi Jinping, November 2017

Now I am sure that that is not what you read in *Bildzeitung* about Trump, nor do they ever report what President Trump is actually doing.

Now the Chinese Ambassador to Washington, Cui Tiankai, recently made the point that there were 16 times in world history when a rising country would surpass the dominant country up to that point. In 12 cases it led to a war, and in four cases the rising country just peacefully took over. He said that China wants neither, but we want to have a completely different system of a "win-win" relationship of equality and respect for each other.

Obviously, the most important question strategically, if you think about it, is can we avoid the so-called Thucydides trap. That was the rivalry between Athens and Sparta in the 5th Century BC, which led to the Peloponnesian War and the demise of ancient Greece. If this were to occur today between the United States and China in the age of thermonuclear weapons, I think nobody in their right mind could wish that; and therefore, we should all be extremely happy that Trump and Xi Jinping have developed this very important relationship. I stuck my neck out in the United States in February of this year, by saying if President Trump manages to get a good relationship between the United States and China, and the United States and Russia, he will go down in history as one of the greatest Presidents of the United States. Naturally, everybody was completely freaked out because that is not the picture people are supposed to have about Trump. But I think if you look at what is happening, you will see that Trump is on a very good way to accomplish exactly that.

So, he came back from this Asia trip with $253 billion worth of deals with China. I watched the press conference of the Governor of West Virginia, Jim Justice, where he said that now, because of China, there is hope in West Virginia. West Virginia is a totally depressed state; they have unemployment and a drug epidemic. But he said now we can have value-added production, we will have a bright future. So, the spirit of the New Silk Road has even caught on in West Virginia. Obviously the United States has an enormous

I. INTRODUCTION

demand for infrastructure, especially now after the destruction of all these hurricanes; which just to restore what has been destroyed requires $200 billion, not even talking about disaster prevention. So, this is all on a good way that China will invest in the infrastructure in the United States, and vice versa; U.S. firms will cooperate in projects of the Belt and Road Initiative.

There is a strategic realignment caused by all of this. The relationship between President Xi and Putin is the best in history. They have developed a close friendship, and there is right now quickly expanding, integration of the New Silk Road and the Eurasian Economic Union.

In a separate, but nevertheless related development, there was just now an historic visit of President Bashar al-Assad from Syria in Sochi, meeting with Putin. What happened is actually the exact opposite of what you would read in the media, where naturally you would say this dictator Putin and this horrible Assad. But what happened was the opposite. Putin introduced Assad to the Russian military leadership, and Assad thanked them for having saved Syria. Remember, when more than two years ago, Putin decided that the Russian military would intervene in Syria to defeat ISIS, the country was in complete disarray. It was hopeless—al-Qaeda, ISIS. Now, they are militarily defeated and the reconstruction can actually happen. Assad invited the refugees to return to help in the reconstruction of the country. The Silk Road will also be extended into Afghanistan, into Iraq, and hopefully all the other places around. This is a grand design of Putin, which involves the Astana process. He integrates Turkey, Jordan, and even trying to get Saudi Arabia on a different track. So, the idea to extend the New Silk Road into Southwest Asia, we pushed already a long time ago. But in 2012, we had a conference of the Schiller Institute in Frankfurt where we said the only way how you can stop terrorism and have development and peace in the Middle East is if all the big neighbors—Russia, China, India, Iran, the United States, and also European countries—join hands in the development. This is now, because of the Russian military intervention and the Chinese extension of the Silk Road, an absolute possibility. In the context of which, also the relationship between Putin and Trump has gotten on a much better track. In the aftermath of the Assad visit, they had a 1.5-hour telephone discussion; and people in Russia expressed afterwards on various levels—in the Duma, in the Federation Council—extreme optimism that the relationship between Russia and the United States can now become much more fruitful and better.

So, just think about it, because almost everything I'm saying goes against everything you hear in the Western media. But think: From who comes the motion for peace and development? Is it coming from those who attack Putin, Xi, and Trump? And those who side with Obama? It's obviously time for people to rethink how the Western viewpoint is on all of these matters. Or change the glasses which they have to look at the world.

Besides the change in the relations between the United States and China in Southwest Asia, the biggest change for the better as a result of the New Silk Road, is Africa. China has invested in Africa in railways, they have built a railway from Djibouti to Addis Ababa; they are building other railways from Kenya, they are supposed to go to Rwanda; hydropower dams, industrial parks. Especially in the past four years, the outlook of most Africans has completely changed; because they see for the first time that the suppression of colonialism and the denial of development through the IMF conditionalities, there is a possibility to truly develop the continent. They do not any longer want to be lectured about good governance, human rights, and democracy with no development; which is what the Europeans normally offer. But they want to be treated as equal partners.

Let me give tribute to that person who had that vision about African development more than 40 years ago. Again, my sweet husband. [applause] He wrote in 1980, as a supplement to the OAU Lagos Plan of Action, a paper with the title "Stop Club of Rome Genocide in Africa; A Critical Comment Appended to the Lagos Plan of Action." There he laid out a beautiful vision, a grand design for the development of Africa based on the LaRouche scientific method of physical economy; which in turn is based on Leibniz and Alexander Hamilton's credit policy. LaRouche naturally has added very much to that. He said, "The competent conception of economic processes flows originally from a moral principle, which is immediately accessible to any sane adult or adolescent in any part of the world; however literate or illiterate. To make my model individual existence of some value, how do I develop and inform my practice to produce something of benefit for the development of generations to come?" Lyn defines economic science as an inseparable facet of science, usefully called statecraft; which includes the development of the law and the cultural advancement of the people, of the development of the individual to master the lawful principles of the composition of the universe. He presented the total opposite of the Club of Rome, with [its] appropriate technologies and sustainable development; which is just another word for no development. By proposing to upgrade the labor force continuously to higher modes of production, by changing the proportions of employment from rural to urban productive occupations using higher energy-flux densities in the mode of production continuously. He took as a referent point for the development of Africa, the development of the United States, and showed how, for example, U.S. agriculture by the end of the 18th Century, 98% of the people worked in agriculture; and today, less than 4% producing obviously much more food than at the time, as the way for Africa to go. Including the development of roads, canals, railroads, the specialization of farmers, the increase of productivity in agriculture and industry, a shift away from labor-intensive to capital-intensive modes of production, better education, the development of the power of the population to produce the material alterations of nature with an increasing potential relative population density and higher energy-flux densities. He said, "The development of Africa must be directed to what nations of Africa are to become by the year 2000 and 2020." This was written in 1980; namely, two generations ago. He said, "The conception needed is one of the development of the productive powers of the entire population over the development period spanning two generations." Apart from the

Lyndon LaRouche published a 180-page special report in 1982 on the perspective for the economic development of the nations of the African continent, titled "Stop Club of Rome Genocide in Africa! Critical Comments Appended to the Lagos Plan of Action."

basic infrastructure—meaning a continental system of rail, waterways, highways—he proposed a string of new cities of 250,000 to a maximum of 2 million inhabitants. At the core of each new city would be an educational complex, pedagogical museums, libraries, cultural centers, parks, teaching and research institutions, including medical science and research institutions. He proposed a connected system of rapid transport for persons and freight; also, the transition from low-cost in one mode of transport to another. Also, inner city distribution of freight from warehouses in the city, daily deliveries of perishable goods such as foodstuffs. And around the core of the educational complex, then residential areas, industrial and commercial areas.

The cities were not only supposed to be functionally well designed, but beautiful; using the principles of Platonic ratios in architecture. Using for example, those methods used in Gothic cathedrals, or the architecture of the Golden Renaissance of Italy. It included the idea of many trees, flora, so that people would be happy and the climate would be moderated. He said, "The essential thing which the citizens of such a city must experience over the course of the city's gradual completion, is a sense of ongoing progress of perfection." To aid this process, there should be the technology transfer from the developed countries, financed by grants. He made the correct point that the technology transfer from Europe and the United States to Africa would stimulate the economy

I. INTRODUCTION

in the exporting nations, increase their tax income. The developing countries receiving grants would become the next generation's customer for purchasing on a credit basis. The exporting nations would develop prosperous customers for tomorrow, and have an accelerated turnover of capital stocks. And the exporting countries would increase their productivity and therefore, their national and per capita wealth.

Now, that is obviously the total opposite of what the IMF did, which lured countries into the debt trap which was exposed quite dramatically by John Perkins in his book *Confessions of an Economic Hit Man*. Now, Lyn, on the other side, said that the technology exporting nations must seek those portions of the labor force in the developing nations which can be upgraded immediately to productive employment using the most advanced technologies imported in the capital stock to be exported from the industrialized nations. The labor force is able to assimilate the advanced technologies, and that must be expanded; it requires methods of promoting the development potentials of the population at a large scale. So, the investment in infrastructure and the development of the population has to occur at the same time. He said, "Every infant born in any part of the world, has the potential for the development of his or her mental powers to the level sufficient for a direct competent use of modern technology. It is that potential development which is the only source of wealth. That development is a creditworthy asset in the eyes of a truly prudent lender."

So what occurs at the point where the economic development had absorbed most of the population of the world? By that time, we must have an increase in the rate of development of technology such that we no longer depend on the expansion of the economy in scale. When that transition to a New World Economic Order has been completed, we will have more and more members of society living and working as artists; as golden souls, as Plato describes them; as beautiful souls, as Schiller talks about it; as *junzi*, the Confucian idea of the noble man; or the people living on the level of the Paradise in Dante's Commedia; or as Vladimir Vernadsky says, that the Noösphere, that part of the physical universe which is dominated by creative activity of man, will take over more and more of the biosphere.

Actually, what is happening right now is going in this direction. What Xi Jinping has defined as a goal for 2050 for China and the rest of the world, is to have better and happier lives, poverty eradicated, people being able to devote their lives to meaningful

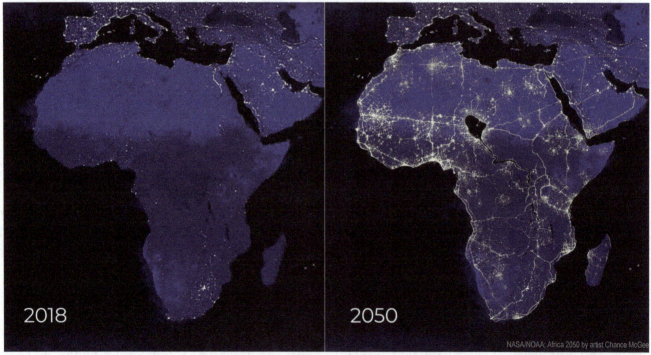

Africa at night as seen in 2018 and as projected in 2050 after its development into a continent of truly sovereign nations cooperating for the benefit of each other.

purposes, is actually going very much in this direction. Is this realistic? I practically can hear the howls of protest of the neo-liberals and neo-cons in the West alike. "What about Western values? What about our freedom? What about democracy?" Or better, market-conformed democracy as Mrs. Merkel likes to put it. We better reflect where these values have gotten us in Europe. Europe is completely disunited. We are faced with a financial crisis worse than that of 2008 about to erupt. The EU just completed guidelines eliminating the possibility for the separation of the banks, which China has just reconfirmed. The right-wing movements are rising; the refugee crisis has caused the reputation of Europe to go down the drain completely in the world. You have a very dangerous anti-immigration sentiment. The entire social and political fabric of Europe is disintegrating. Because Europe in its present form of the European Union is like a giant Babylon tower attempting an amalgamation of cultures, languages, and histories which is leading evermore to frictions between the supranational integration and the self-interest of these nations of Europe. Not to even mention the government crisis in Europe which is the worst since 1949; since the existence of the German Federal Republic.

Gottfried Wilhelm Leibniz (left) 1646-1716 and Confucius (right) 551-479 BC

Now, it is not the first time that Europe is in bad shape. This was addressed by Gottfried Wilhelm Leibniz in a policy memorandum of 1670, where he named the challenges of his time—a badly established trade and manufacturing, an entirely debased currency, uncertainty of law and the delay of all legal actions, a worthless education, an increase in atheism, terrible morals as if they were infected by a foreign plague, a bitter strife of religion which will weaken us and, in the end, may completely ruin us. So, that was the situation Leibniz saw. This was still the aftermath of the 150 years of religious war in Europe. He came up with the idea that the solution was a merger of the Chinese ancient natural theology and European culture. He called it a beautiful coincidence that the two most developed cultures in the world are like on two poles reaching hands between Europe and China. By creating a common exchange between them, civilization could reach the next superior stage in human history.

In the preface of the *Novissima Sinica*—"The Latest from China"—he expressed this intention. Leibniz followed very closely all the news from China; he had a very lively dialogue with many of the Jesuit missionaries, who informed him about all the developments in science and the famous rights controversy, where he sided with the people like Matteo Ricci, saying that there is a strong affinity between Confucianism and Christianity. He said Confucianism has much more to offer than any other known belief system of his time. He said, "We need the Chinese to send missionaries to Europe, so that we can learn from them natural religion that we have almost lost." He proposed an exchange of cultural ambassadors, which for his time was a very modern conception. He said, "There is in China a public morality, admirable in certain regards, conjoined to a philosophical doctrine, or rather a natural theology venerable by its antiquity, established and authorized for about 3,000 years. Long before the philosophy of the Greeks."

For Leibniz, the affinity of Confucius and Christianity, despite all differences in culture, proved that humanity has the universal characteristic of reason. The fact that the Emperor Kung-Xi and he—Leibniz—listened to the same mathematical solutions, proved for him the universal character of human reason and species. In the Chinese philosophy, he emphasized that the notion of the *li* refers to the supreme order of the universe in which harmony exists if each being exercises its lawful function in its proper place. And together with the notion *ren*, which approximates the Christian notion of agapē—love—is using different terminologies and different conceptions, but they have an analogy and affinity which is what Leibniz describes in his Monadology. According to Leibniz: "God has created the universe by the way of a pre-stabilized harmony, where the realm of the spiritual and the material world, the soul and the body are in total correspondence. This is so, because God—in His divine anticipation—has created the material and spiritual substance in such an ordered way and with such a precision that even if they follow their own lawfulness embedded in their nature, nevertheless there is such a cohesion as if there existed between them, a reciprocal inference. And as if God, apart from His general contribution, would act concretely in each single instant. Each monad, each uniform substance, reflects in germ the entire universe at large. But they only relate to each other because they take part in the absolute being of God."

Once one understands this inner cohesion between the Chinese ancient philosophy, especially in the Confucian expression and the idea of Leibniz, it is no surprise that he not only recognized the affinity, but concretely thought a reciprocal exchange of both cultures would merge into a superior, more advanced level of civilization. Among Leibniz's plans for this project were the creation of a world language, for which he thought the Chinese language and script were most appropriate; the creation of a world academy of sciences, where Chinese and Western scientists would work together; the creation of a world citizenship, which would allow for every human being to absorb all cultures of the world. The future role of Russia to mediate between China and the West; the development of Siberia in relation to the development of northern Africa. Peter the Great, with whom he was in contact, ordered in 1712 the expedition of Fritz Jonathan Bering, for whom the Bering Strait has been named. Further, the comparative study of languages to find the common origin of human language, which was later pursued by philologists like Humboldt and others. A chronological history of the West and China, and the only museum where I have seen that is the museum in Taipei, where you have a beautiful exhibition where you see above the history of China, and below what happened parallel in the Western culture; which gives you a completely different way of thinking about universal history. Also, the binary system, which was becoming the basis of computers and things like that. The development of a key which would make it easier to learn the Chinese language. I think everybody who has tried to learn Chinese would be very thankful for such a key. The development of a method to teach the difference between Western and Chinese culture. The principles of a new moral code for Western statesmen and politicians; but also, for the behavior among normal citizens among themselves, based on Confucianism. An analysis of Confucianism based on Western methods, with the purpose to show the closeness to Western Christianity.

If you look at these plans by Leibniz, it is absolutely amazing how similar they were to what Xi Jinping is doing with the New Silk Road policy today, which has aspects of all of these plans. So why then in the West, are so many people having a hard time to accept an offer of a "win-win" cooperation among all nations which would be so much clearly in the interest of all people?

Let me briefly go back to the end of World War II, to find the roots of this problem. Franklin D Roosevelt, in his famous dialogue with Churchill in Casablanca, had pledged the end of colonialism and the help of the United States to develop the developing countries. Churchill, on the other side, said the British did not fight World War II in order to end the British Empire. Now unfortunately, Roosevelt died at a very inconvenient moment, and Truman—who was a very small man—took over the White House. Remember what Lyn always said when he was in India about how shocked the people were about Roosevelt dying at this point. So, Roosevelt, who was allied with the Soviet Union in the Second World War, had gone. Churchill stepped into this vacuum, and basically then he made the famous March 1946 Iron Curtain speech in Fulton, Missouri, launching the Cold War. He proposed a new alliance, based on the special relationship between the United States and the British

Empire. That speech by Churchill in Fulton, shifted the American view on the USSR. Then followed the Truman doctrine in March 1947, which allowed such atrocities, for example, as Senator Joseph McCarthy to start a witch-hunt in America against everybody suspected of being a communist—a communist under every bed. Now this is what is happening with the anti-Trump witch-hunt today.

What happened in Europe? Recently there was an amazing article in the *Frankfurter Allgemeine Zeitung* (*FAZ*) covering an exhibition taking place in Berlin right now, on the occasion of the 50th anniversary of the scandal erupting about the Congress for Cultural Freedom (CCF). The Congress for Cultural Freedom, which lasted from 1950 to 1967, was the gigantic cultural warfare program by the CIA with the explicit aim to recruit lefty people, communists, into an anti-Soviet Cold War. They in reality wanted to destroy the axioms in the population which had made Franklin D. Roosevelt possible. Because Wall Street had been completely freaked out about Roosevelt implementing Glass-Steagall, the New Deal, having an alliance with the Soviet Union. So, that moment Truman started in cohesion with the British to have the idea to establish a paradigm shift in the population, with a left-liberal outlook which we have today. That is what the *FAZ* article said; it said the CIA did not plan to foster reactionary movements; they have created exactly that left-liberal outlook which is the politically correct view in Europe today. I think that is really noteworthy to reflect upon, because that is exactly what they did with the Dulles brothers under the command of the High Commissioner John Jay McCloy. If you look at this operation, which was huge; it involved 35 countries, 20 magazines. They controlled practically every art exhibition, cultural event. In Europe there were very few writers, poets, musicians, historians, critics, or journalists who were not connected to this project. Some witting; many unwitting. It was part of the Cold War to fight for the liberation of the human mind. The CCF acted like a cartel; they controlled the entire cultural industry, and based it on the myth of a freedom-oriented outlook.

Remember, the CIA, at the same time while they pretended to be for freedom, made a coup against Mossadegh, conducted the Bay of Pigs operation, the Phoenix Operation in Vietnam, and similar things.

It was in part funded with money from the Marshall Plan, which was diverted to the CCF; but also, all together 170 foundations. One of their key ideologues, George Kennan, in a speech in front of the National War College in December 1947, developed the strategy of the necessary lie; which would become an essential part of U.S. foreign policy, laid down in National Security Directive 68, and later another one for psychological warfare operations. This lasted for decades. So, the idea of fake news, of manipulating the population with lies, is not new, and it has not erupted only with Trump.

The aims of the CCF were very much those of the Frankfurt School. They wanted to destroy idealism, the Classical culture. Because Adorno, for example, argued that idealism leads to Nazism, because it leads to a radical view and that has to be rooted out; both in order to eradicate the remnants of Nazism, but also of the dictatorship of the Soviet Union. Adorno said for this, we have to eradicate beauty from art completely. Remember that Schiller said that art which is not beautiful is not art; and I fully agree with that, because art has to ennoble people and uplift their spirit. And when it's not beautiful, it does not do that.

In music, the CCF started a vicious campaign against Furtwängler; and instead of Classical composers, they pushed atonal 12-tone music, Alban Berg, Schoenberg, Weber; and eradicated the idea of polyphonic harmonic composition. The famous writer Susan Sonntag said, "We knew we expected to accept ugly music as pleasant." That is what happens when you go to the concerts—the Rheingau festivals or others—you always have Beethoven, Berg, and some other modern composer. You never can get a Classical concert.

They also made a list of allowed writers—Ibsen, Shaw, O'Neil, Wilder, Steinbeck. They forbade certain pieces by Shakespeare and Kleist, and they invented the famous Regietheater, which is the idea that you completely destroy the Classical composition of Schiller, Shakespeare, and each modern director can put his own interpretation in it up to the point where you cannot recognize these pieces anymore. A big role was played by the Museum of Modern Art in New York, which promoted the modern

I. INTRODUCTION

painting—Cubism, Futurism, Dada-ism, expressionism, abstract art, serialism, and so forth. A writer called Eva Cockcroft wrote in the ArtForum magazine, "The abstract expressionism was a weapon of the Cold War." The connection between the Cold War and this expressionism was absolutely no coincidence, because it was supposed to destroy the ability of the mind to understand anything. Harry Truman, of all people, liked to go to the National Art Gallery in the United States, looking at Holbein and Rembrandt. He said, "What a pure pleasure, and what a difference to our modern schmierfinken, our mucky pups."

Wilhelm Furtwängler (1886-1954), unequaled conductor, and fierce defender of the Classical principle in music.

So, the CCF influence did not end in 1967. It ended then, it came out with a big scandal, but it is working until the present. This is why people have this left-liberal ideology today; this is what is behind the interventionist policy, the color revolution, the export of democracy, the right to protect. This is what the Foreign Minister of Russia Lavrov calls "the post-Christian values." He said, "The Western values are no longer those values which were handed down from our grandfathers from generation to generation. But it has been replaced by 'everything is allowed'; a complete hedonism, where freedom is misunderstood as the right of everybody to live out all their pleasures in the here and now. Do whatever you like to do." That ugliness is what you see when you look at most movies nowadays, at the video games, the art, youth culture, which are all characterized by a cult of ugliness. So, in that sense, the CCF has done a very successful operation.

So, we do have a big cultural problem in the West. There is a huge drug epidemic in the United States, out-of-control violence, mass shootings in schools almost every week, terrorism. But the good news is that the solution to overcome these problems is readily available. When we founded the Schiller Institute—now more than 33 years ago—we said from the beginning that a just New World Economic Order must be combined with a renaissance of Classical culture. This is actually happening, because with the New Silk Road development being built since four years, the world has changed already, and many countries are reviving their Classical cultures. This is why the Schiller Institute, in all our conferences, always have a conference expressing this dialogue of Classical cultures.

We need obviously a completely new set of international relations. We must overcome geopolitics, and we must have a system of relations among each other with total respect for sovereignty, non-interference, respect for the different social systems, a "win-win" cooperation in the mutual interest of any of us, and the perspective of the one humanity. Nicholas of Cusa, who developed the method of the Coincidentia Oppositorum, the idea of the Coincidence of Opposites, argued that the One has a higher power, a higher order of magnitude than the Many.

So, the idea of harmony in the macrocosm is only possible when you have the best development of all microcosms. That development must not be static or linear, but it works like a contrapuntal fugue, where each development furthers the development of the next segment being unified to a higher concept of the composition.

What we have to build is a completely new set of international relations; where each nation is allowed to celebrate statecraft, meaning making possible the creative potential of all of its citizens. An interaction among nations where each focuses on the best cultural tradition and potential of the other. China is reviving Confucianism and its philosophy of philosophical Classical culture in poetry, music, and painting. In Europe, we must absolutely do the same.

The ancient Greek Classical period, which is what Greece is actually doing; they had recently a conference in essence of the ten oldest civilizations, and they revived exactly that spirit. In Italy, we have the Golden Renaissance; in Spain, the Andalusian renaissance and other great thinkers. In France, you have the tradition of Louis XI, Jeanne d'Arc, the École Polytechnique. In Germany, we have a tremendous wealth of philosophers and composers and poets; Schiller, Beethoven. In America, we have the American Constitution, the American System of Economy. All these treasures are there, and just need to be revived. If we undo what the CCF did, and revive the Classical culture of all nations, and enter a beautiful dialogue among them, mankind will experience a new renaissance and unleash an enormous creativity of the human species like never before.

So, it is very good to live at this moment in history and contribute to make the world a better place. And it can be done, because the New Paradigm corresponds to the lawfulness of the physical universe in science, Classical art, and these principles. Neo-liberalism and the left-liberalism are just as outdated and will disappear like the scholastics debating how many angels can sit on the top of a pin. What will be asserted is the identity of the human species as the creative species in the universe.

"As the ancient Silk Road led to an exchange of not only goods and technologies, but also ideas and cultures, so will the New Silk Road lead to a sharing of the best expressions of human creativity for the benefit of the one humanity."

The Belt and Road Initiative and the Dialogue of Cultures

ON THE BASIS OF THEIR HIGHER EXPRESSIONS

The following address was given by Helga Zepp-LaRouche at the "21st Century Maritime Silk Road Forum," held in Zhuhai, Guangdong, China on November 28-30, 2017.

You, the Chinese people, find yourselves at a very decisive moment in history, and I know, that after President Xi Jinping put the Belt and Road Initiative on the agenda, a little more than four years ago, and the tremendous success of the policy of a New Silk Road since then, that you are completely aware of the extraordinary role China is playing right now from the standpoint of the universal history of mankind. But let me share with you the view of a German, or actually, I see myself as an universal citizen, looking at what China is doing, from the outside, from an international perspective.

For all the centuries up to now, from the earliest manifestations of human civilization, tribes, ethnic groups, nations, or alliances of nations have pursued their alleged interests by various means, by negotiations, diplomacy, and if this did not work out, by armed conflict and war. Geopolitics, the idea that a nation, or group of nations, has the right to pursue their interest against another group of nations, has led to two World Wars in the 20th Century. It should be obvious to anyone, that in the age of thermonuclear weapons, war can no longer be a method of settling conflicts, if we as a human species are not to bring about our own annihilation. Humanity is distinct from all other species known in the universe so far, in that we are capable of creative reason. This means, that we can, unlike the animal species, consciously change the mode of our existence, continuously discover new universal principles in science and culture, develop a deeper and more profound knowledge about the physical universe, of which we are the most important part. So in a certain sense it is lawful, that mankind would come up with the idea on how to overcome geopolitics, and establish a system of self-governance, which would guarantee the long-term survivability of humanity.

The concept of a "community of a shared future of mankind" presented by President Xi Jinping, is exactly that idea. By putting the notion of the one mankind, defined from the standpoint of our common future, as the reference point as how to think about political, economic, social, and cultural issues, President Xi has established a higher level of reason, a conceptual basis for a peace order on the whole planet. It is no coincidence, that the concept for an entirely new paradigm in human history would come from China, as it is coherent with the 2,500-year-old Confucian tradition.

The economic dimension of this idea is expressed in the Belt and Road Initiative (BRI), the New Silk Road proposal, which Xi presented in September 2013 in Kazakhstan. In the very short time of four years, this initiative for win-win cooperation has become the largest infrastructure program in history, building six large economic corridors, numerous rail lines in Eurasia and Africa, ports, airports, industrial parks, power projects, water management etc., with more than 70 countries participating, and is all together already 12 times bigger than the Marshall Plan in Europe in the reconstruction period after World War II, and, is open ended. In Africa the "New Silk Road Spirit" has completely changed the outlook of the participating countries. For the first time after centuries of suffering of colonial oppression and a lack of financing, because of Chinese investments there is now the perspective of overcoming poverty and underdevelopment in the near future. This has created an unprecedented sense of optimism.

At the 19th National Congress of the CPC, Xi defined the goal for China to become by the year 2050 "a strong, democratic, civilized, harmonious and beautiful country"; he defined it to be the goal of politics to create a better and happier life for the people, and he called on the people of all countries to work together to build a community with a shared future for mankind, to build an open, inclusive, clean, and beautiful world that enjoys lasting peace, universal security, and common prosperity. Shortly after this remarkable event the extremely successful state visit of U.S. President Trump to China signified a historic step in the effort to reach this goal.

With this global perspective for the next 33 years, President Xi Jinping has put a vision on the agenda, which has inspired many people in many countries, especially in the developing sector, with an unprecedented spark of optimism. The response by some politicians in some Western countries and by the mainstream media, has been a variety ranging from complete censorship of what President Xi actually said, to the wildest ones concerning the real motives

Helga Zepp-LaRouche at the 21st Century Maritime Silk Road Forum

behind China's BRI policy. Some such statements went so far as to say that China's policy represented a threat to the liberal order of the West. Does that mean, that the idea of building a harmonious world, in which all nations can work together for the common aims of humanity, is a utopia, a dream, that can never become a reality?

I believe, that the universal history of mankind can provide the answer to that question, because it shows, that there are some profound characteristics, the ideal of the highest humanity, shared by the most noble expressions of different cultures. There is an amazing similarity among some of the most outstanding thinkers, coming out of completely different cultural backgrounds, coming nevertheless to the same insights into the nature of man and the purpose of his existence. These philosophers, poets, and scientists have in common a fundamental optimism about the role of man in the universe, that human creativity is itself a power in the further development of the physical universe, and that there is a cohesion between the harmonic development of all

I. INTRODUCTION

human mental and spiritual capacities, the harmonious development of both the state, as well as of states among themselves, and also the laws of the Cosmos.

In China this image of man and harmony in the state and among states is foremost associated with Confucius and his 2500-year-old tradition in Chinese culture, which accounts in my view for the gist of what is generally called "socialism with Chinese characteristics." Confucius had an image of man, that perceives man as fundamentally good, and who has the obligation to tirelessly improve himself intellectually and morally, which he can do by exerting his inner will power, and aesthetical education through poetry, classical music, and some other arts. If the individuals develop themselves to become *junzi*, there can be a harmonious development in the family; if the government is run by *junzi*, the common good is prospering.

The German poet of freedom, as he is called, Friedrich Schiller, after whom the Schiller Institute is named, has an amazing affinity with Confucius, despite the fact, that he lived and worked more than 2,000 years later. Likewise, he too developed the concept of the aesthetical education of man, as the only method for the political progress, with a special emphasis on poetry and beautiful art. His notion of the "beautiful soul" is very similar to Confucius's idea of the *junzi*. The beautiful soul, Schiller says, is someone who finds his freedom in necessity, does his duty with passion, and who has educated his emotions up to the degree, that he can blindly follow his impulses, since they would never command him to do something which would be opposed to Reason. Wilhelm von Humboldt, who created the best education system in the West, said about Schiller, that he created a very special category, uniting philosophy and poetry to a higher level, like nobody else.

Probably the closest almost contemporary philosopher of Confucius in European culture is Plato, who established likewise a school of thought, which continued, albeit with many interruptions in terms of influence, through the centuries into the present. He also had the idea of a harmoniously ordered universe, where development is embedded in the creation of the universe in such a way that it evolves from chaos to harmony, and where man can not only recognize

Plato, like Confucius, had the idea of a harmonious universe, which is developing in such a way that mankind can understand it, and tune his actions to its laws.

that harmony, but also tune his own action in accordance with the laws of the universe for the sake of everybody. In his famous work Timaeus, he writes:

"For God desiring that all things should be good, and that, so far as this might be, there should be naught evil, having received all that is moving not in a state of rest, but moving without harmony or measure, brought it from its disorder into order, thinking that this was in all ways better than the other. Now it neither has been nor is permitted to the most perfect to do aught but what is most fair. Therefore he took thought and perceived that of all things which are by nature visible, no work that is without reason will ever be fairer than that which has reason, setting whole against whole, and that without soul reason cannot dwell in anything. Because then he argued thus, in forming the universe he created reason in soul and soul in body, that he might be the maker of a work that was by nature most fair and perfect. In this way then we ought to affirm according to the probable account that this universe is a living creature in very truth possessing soul and reason by the providence of God."

This beautiful idea, that God created the best of all possible worlds, was explicitly elaborated by Gottfried Leibniz, in which each human being represents a monad, which has enclosed in it, in the small, all the characteristics of the universe at large, and that there is an inclusive, pre-established harmony in that universe. The world is the best of all possible worlds, because it is constructed in such a way, that every evil has the potential of generating an even greater good, which the human being can choose, because he or she has a free will. In that way, the degrees of freedom for the good increase, despite the existence of evil, out of which follows the obligation of man, to continuously ennoble himself in order to contribute to the progress of all of humanity and even the development of the entire cosmos.

To further this goal, Leibniz created academies and scholarly societies, in order to gather the entire intellectual, scientific, and cultural knowledge of all the people and put it to the service of all the nations. His conception was essentially the same as reflected in the new Center for International Knowledge Development (CIKD), which will serve as a platform for nations to share ideas, so that their development is not delayed by the lack of access to new knowledge. That spirit influenced many scientists in history to give the fruits of their inventive power, to that country which would make the best use of the discovery. One good example of that, is the collaboration of German scientists with China in the field of nuclear technology. Already Leibniz wrote to Tsar Peter the Great, "I aim at the benefit of the entire human species, and I [would] rather accomplish a great good for the Russians, than a little for the Germans or the other Europeans, because my inclination and passion is the general best."

Leibniz was completely enthusiastic about China, about which he tried to learn as much as possible from the Jesuit missionaries. He was fascinated about the fact, that the Emperor Kangxi had come to the same mathematical conclusions, as he himself, and concluded out of that, that there are universal principles accessible to all human beings and cultures. He even believed in the moral superiority of the Chinese and wrote: "In light of the growing moral decay it seems to be almost necessary, that one sends Chinese missionaries to us, who could teach us the application and practice of a natural theology. I therefore believe: that if a wise man were chosen to judge not the beauty of goddesses, but the excellence of peoples, he would give the golden apple to the Chinese." It is not surprising, that Leibniz had a conception of the more advanced countries helping the less developed countries, very similar to the New Silk Road idea.

In 1697 he published his book *Novissima Sinica*, about how Europe and China should cooperate, to develop all countries located between them. He wrote: "Maybe it is the aim of the highest providence, that those nations, which are highly civilized, but are located at the greatest distance, are uplifting also the peoples of the regions in between to a life more in accordance with reason."

Out of his optimistic idea of the best of all possible worlds follows for Leibniz the right of the individual to the pursuit of happiness, a notion which has nothing to do with the hedonistic idea of "having a good time," but means the right to have a fulfilled life by developing the fullest creative potential for the benefit of the whole society. It was explicitly this Leibnizian notion which is included in the American Declaration of Independence, that all people have the inalienable right to "Life, Liberty and the Pursuit of Happiness."

But not only Leibniz influenced the conceptions of the U.S. Constitution, the preface of which mentions explicitly the commitment to the common good, but also Confucius did. The intellectual father of the United States, Benjamin Franklin, was a convinced Confucian scholar. He published a treatise on the morals of Confucius in 1737 in the Pennsylvania Gazette, and he based his own moral philosophy which he summarized in the outline of thirteen virtues, entirely on the morals of Confucius. So maybe the "good chemistry" which President Trump emphasized to exist between him and President Xi, who himself expresses deep Confucian spirit, has something to do with the fact, that President Trump indicated repeatedly, that he wants to revive the "American System," which is associated with the philosophy of the young American Republic.

I. INTRODUCTION

Portait of Benjamin Franklin, intellectual father of the United States, and follower of Leibniz and Confucius

To sum up the argument why, despite some present opposition in the West to the conception of a "community of a shared destiny of mankind," there is nonetheless great reason for optimism that the beautiful vision will indeed become a reality, let me say this: In all great cultures there have been thinkers who understood the deep connections, between an optimistic image about the limitless moral and intellectual self-perfectibility of man, the pursuit of the common good as the precondition for the long-term survival of society, and the cohesion between human creativity and the laws of the physical universe.

For a very long time these philosophers influenced their cultures independently from each other, sometimes living at the same time, but not knowing about each other, since it took years to travel from one country to the other, sometimes influencing one another over the centuries and beyond national boundaries. There was Plato, who influenced the Arab philosophers Al Kindi, Al Farabi, and Ibn Sina, as well as the Christian thinkers, Augustinus, Nicholas of Cusa, or Leibniz.

But one can also find an affinity of their ideas in the Indian Vedic writings or the scholars of Timbuktu. Without the exchanges between the Caliph Harun Al Rashid and Charlemagne, much of the cultural and scientific heritage of ancient Greece, Egypt, Spain, and Italy might not have been saved after the collapse of the Roman Empire.

As the ancient Silk Road led to an exchange of not only goods and technologies, but also ideas and cultures, so will the New Silk Road lead to a sharing of the best expressions of human creativity for the benefit of the one humanity. Communication, travel, and knowledge about each other have sped up tremendously and will continue to do so. What in the past was only stated by the greatest philosophers with metaphysical arguments about man and the physical universe, can now be proven by modern science.

And there is no better proof of the cohesion of the microcosm of the human mind and the macrocosm of the universe at large than space research and travel. The fact that man can travel in space is the ultimate proof of the fact, that an immaterial idea, an invention, a scientific breakthrough, has an effect in the physical universe, and can elevate the human species beyond any barriers of sense perception. All the astronauts who have been in space, report the same thing: that looking at the Earth from outer space, one does not see national borders, one only perceives the one human species.

So there is profound reason for optimism, that despite the reluctance of some people in the West, that the beautiful vision of the One Dream of Mankind will come true.

Expedition 41 crew portrait on the International Space Station. From left: ESA astronaut Alexander Gerst, Roscosmos cosmonauts Elena Serova, Maxim Suraev and Alexander Samokutyaev, and NASA astronauts Reid Wiseman and Barry Wilmore.

"Over the past two decades, the Schiller Institute has organized hundreds of conferences and seminars on the theme of the Eurasian Land-Bridge, the New Silk Road, and then the Belt and Road Initiative.... It has been recognized, including by Chinese scholars, as a forerunner of the initiatives that the Chinese government has taken up."

THE SCHILLER INSTITUTE

Decades of Fighting for a New, Just World Economic Order

The Schiller Institute was founded in 1984 in international conferences near Frankfurt, Germany, and near Washington, DC, to lift international relations to a higher level, and replace the geopolitical order in the world, with a new paradigm based on the mutual respect and development of sovereign nation-states. It is named after the great poet and thinker Friedrich Schiller, for whom "the consummate work of art is the construction of true political freedom." That is true statecraft, the purpose of which must be to build a society compatible with mankind's identity as the only creative species known to us.

In that sense, economic development is not enough, it must be accompanied by a renaissance of the best cultural traditions and philosophies of each country and people.

The Schiller Institute, founded by Helga Zepp-LaRouche, was fundamentally inspired by the work of her husband, American economist and statesman Lyndon LaRouche, who has devoted his entire life to promoting the concept of mutually beneficial economic development for all nations and all peoples as the means to peace, an approach now increasingly known as "win-win cooperation." His concept has found a certain concretization in the Belt and Road

Lyndon and Helga LaRouche at the 1984 founding of the Schiller Institute

Initiative (BRI) called into being by Chinese President Xi Jinping in 2013.

For decades now, Lyndon LaRouche and the Schiller Institute have worked on concrete infrastructure and development plans for all regions of the world based on the principles of physical economy, associated with Alexander Hamilton, Gottfried Leibniz, Friedrich List, and Henry C. Carey, which LaRouche himself further developed and expanded.

I. INTRODUCTION

Lyndon LaRouche during his second trip to Moscow in June 1995, speaking at a seminar on physical economics sponsored by Moscow State University

Helga Zepp-LaRouche on a visit to China in 1996

His unique, fundamental discovery is the notion of "relative potential population density."

LaRouche has consistently warned that the trans-Atlantic financial system, starting in 1971, is inherently unsustainable, and will lead to a crash with devastating consequences. And indeed that system has only been able to survive by looting other countries and peoples, and it has not financed any real development in decades. Therefore, it needs to be urgently replaced.

Already back in 1975, shortly after traveling to Baghdad for meetings with Arab leaders, LaRouche proposed the creation of an International Development Bank to finance the industrialization of developing countries, and a moratorium on their unpayable debt in the context of a reorganization of the international monetary system. In 1979, the Fusion Energy Foundation, which had been founded by LaRouche, published a book on *The Industrialization of Africa*, and two years later, LaRouche developed a "Lagos Action Plan for Africa."

In 1983, LaRouche authored a visionary book titled *A 50 Year Development Policy for the Indian and Pacific Oceans Basin*, which proposed several projects that have now been taken up in the context of the BRI. Ibero-America, where the Schiller Institute was very active, was discussed in detail in a Schiller Institute book titled *Ibero-American Integration: 100 Million New Jobs by 2000!*, published in 1988.

Moving ahead in time, after the historic reunification of Germany, the Schiller Institute proposed a reconstruction plan for all of Central and Eastern Europe called the Paris-Berlin-Vienna "Productive Triangle." After the breakup of the Soviet Union, Lyndon and Helga were invited to speak at numerous seminars and conferences in Russia, where they strongly denounced the "shock therapy" imposed by Western financial institutions, and proposed instead a "Marshall Plan" of productive investments.

Over the intervening years, the "productive triangle" concept was expanded to include "development corridors" linking Western Europe to Eurasia and Asia, with high-speed rail lines and new cities and new industries to be built along those corridors, which came to be called the Eurasian Land-Bridge. Discussions with Chinese representatives in the first half of the 1990s then led to the Chinese Economics and Technology Ministry organizing a symposium in Beijing in 1996 ("Economic Development of the Regions along the Eurasian Land-Bridge"), at which Helga Zepp-LaRouche was one of the main speakers. There again, she warned of the systemic nature of the financial crisis that would soon become manifest.

The ideas she expressed there were published in a 1997 *EIR* Special Report titled *The Eurasian Land-Bridge: The New Silk Road*.

In the meantime, the Schiller Institute had elaborated an "Oasis Plan for the Middle East, Developing the Desert Is the Basis for Peace," which was never implemented due to the ruthless geopolitical operations in the region. But now, the BRI holds out the promise of overcoming the wars and conflicts by offering true economic development.

Over the past two decades, the Schiller Institute

ZEPP-LAROUCHE ADDRESSES THINK-TANK SESSIONS AT BELT AND ROAD FORUM

Lyndon LaRouche speaks a Schiller Institute conference in 1988, flanked at the podium by Helga Zepp-LaRouche and Fredrick Wills, former Foreign Minister of Guyana.

has organized hundreds of conferences and seminars on the theme of the Eurasian Land-Bridge, the New Silk Road, and then the Belt and Road Initiative.

In the United States, in virtually all European countries and in Ibero-America, at the Rhodes Dialogue of Civilizations and the Raisina Dialogue, among others, the Schiller Institute has resolutely promoted these programs. It has been recognized, including by Chinese scholars, as a forerunner of the initiatives that the Chinese government has taken up.

The Belt and Road Forum, held in Beijing in May 2017, which Helga Zepp-LaRouche attended, was a momentous event for the consolidation of the "new paradigm" and "win-win cooperation." Below is an article on the contribution by Helga Zepp-LaRouche to that forum.

For a more complete picture of the Schiller Institute's activities, please visit the website at: *newparadigm.schillerinstitute.com*.

Schiller Institute founder Helga Zepp-LaRouche was invited to participate in the "thematic sessions on think-tank exchanges" on May 14 and 15, 2017, as part of the Belt and Road Forum. On the first day, she was a discussant at the session on the "Belt and Road for Facilitating Strong, Balanced, Inclusive and Sustainable Global Economy," and on the second day, she spoke at the 5th Global Think-Tank Summit, "Gathering Wisdoms for Promoting Global Growth." Zepp-LaRouche addressed the issue from the highest cultural standpoint of the common aims of mankind, as seen in the quotes that follow:

> There has been a breathtaking dynamic of the New Silk Road in the three and a half years since it was pronounced by President Xi Jinping in 2013. The Belt and Road Initiative (BRI) has the obvious potential of quickly becoming a World Land-Bridge, connecting all continents through infrastructure, such as tunnels, bridges, reinforced by the Maritime Silk Road. As such, it represents a new form of globalization, but not determined by the criteria of profit maximization for the financial sector, but for the harmonious development of all participating countries on the basis of win-win cooperation.
>
> It is therefore important, that one not look at the BRI from the standpoint of an accountant, who projects his statistical viewpoint of cost-benefit into the future, but that we think about it as a "Vision for the Community of a Shared Future." Where do we want humanity as a whole to be in 10, 100, or even in a 1,000 years? Is it not the natural destiny of mankind, as the only creative species known in the universe so far, that we will be building villages on the Moon, that we will develop a deeper understanding of the trillions of galaxies in our universe, solve the problems of as yet incur-

I. INTRODUCTION

able diseases, or solve the problem of energy and raw material security through the development of thermonuclear fusion power? By focusing on the common aims of humanity we will be able to overcome geopolitics and establish a higher level of reason for the benefit of all.

The United States, Zepp-LaRouche pointed out, should take advantage of the BRI and "become an integral part of the World Land-Bridge." The European Union should do the same and join in a "Grand Design development plan for all of Africa with the BRI...."

To succeed,

...the New Silk Road must—as the ancient one did—lead to an exchange of the most beautiful expressions of culture of all participating countries.

Beyond infrastructure and industrial development, we need to:

...make the joyful discovery in other cultures of the beauty of their classical music, poetry, and painting, and, by knowing them, strengthen our love for mankind as a whole.

In building the World Land-Bridge, all nations will cooperate on studying how to apply the laws of the Noösphere to the establishment of durable forms of self-government. The development of the creative mental powers of all people in all nations will give all of mankind the sense of unity and purpose which will make our species truly human. If we organize our societies around scientific and artistic discovery, we will perfect our knowledge of how to continuously advance the process of self-development of mankind, intellectually, morally, and aesthetically, and we will find our freedom in necessity—doing our duty with passion!

CHINESE MEDIA COVER ZEPP-LAROUCHE AT THE BELT AND ROAD FORUM

While in Beijing to participate in the Belt and Road Forum (BRF), Helga Zepp-LaRouche was featured in a number of Chinese media reports with her assessment of the strategic changes underway.

- A special edition of *China Investment* magazine, in Chinese and English, was distributed to every participant at the BRF, which included an article by Helga Zepp-LaRouche. The magazine is supervised by China's National Development and Reform Commission.[1]

- She was a special guest on May 15 on the popular prime-time show "Dialogue—Ideas Matter" on CGTN. Asked first about China's global initiative, she said it offered a way to solve many problems at once, including regional cooperation, underdevelopment, and poverty. She stressed that this is not just about infrastructure and economics, but the beginning of a new era, where geopolitics is "replaced by a whole new set of relations among nations."

Helga Zepp-LaRouche on the CGTN show, "Dialogue—Ideas Matter."

---

1 http://www.larouchepub.com/eiw/public/2017/eir-v44n22-20170602/03-07_4422.pdf

She strongly urged President Trump to take up the Chinese offer to join the BRI, and replace competition with cooperation.[2]

- On the eve of the Belt and Road Forum, *Xinhuanet* ran an interview with Helga Zepp-LaRouche, in which she said she was confident that the New Silk Road "will lead to scientific and technological breakthroughs, with international cooperation in thermonuclear fusion technology, providing us with energy and raw materials security."

- Among the delegates to the BRF whom *People's Daily* chose to cover on May 14 was Helga Zepp-LaRouche, who praised the fact that all countries involved in the BRI will now have the opportunity to access the most advanced technologies and knowledge.

- In a six-minute interview in German to *People Television*, on the sidelines of the Forum, Helga Zepp-LaRouche deplored the deformed picture of the Belt and Road strategy painted by most European think-tanks and media. In fact, she said, it holds the key to solving the refugee problem, if a Grand Design for Africa and the Middle East is implemented.

  Concerning Germany, she noted that the Mittelstand companies have all the know-how required to make the BRI a success, and if the government would just drop its resistance, joint ventures between China and Germany could be launched in all parts of the world.

- A column in *Xinhuanet* entitled "Quotable quotes on the Belt and Road Forum from world intellectual, business personnel," begins with a quote from Helga Zepp-LaRouche, saying the BRI "not only brings economic prosperity to all participating countries, but also serves as a true basis for a peace order for the 21st Century."[3]

- *China Daily* published comments by Helga Zepp-LaRouche on May 15, in which she noted that many Western commentators were wrong in their assessments of the New Silk Road policy, and that China has unquestionably become "the engine for growth of the world economy."

- *Shanghai Daily* ran a lengthy interview with Helga Zepp-LaRouche, conducted during a visit to Shanghai following the BRF. The introduction notes that she "visited Shanghai for the first time in the summer of 1971. In 1977 she married American economist Lyndon LaRouche, and the couple have since worked together on development plans for a just new world economic order."

HIGHLIGHTS FROM SCHILLER INSTITUTE ACTIVITIES IN CHINA

Since President Xi Jinping announced the launching of the Silk Road Economic Belt in 2013, Helga Zepp-LaRouche, the founder and international chairwoman of the Schiller Institute, has participated in a number of events in China and has given numerous interviews there. Here in outline form are some of the Schiller Institute's main interventions over the intervening years.

February 2014

Helga Zepp-LaRouche traveled to Beijing and Shanghai, where she addressed some dozen think-tanks and university departments on the concept of the Eurasian Land-Bridge which she and her husband Lyndon LaRouche had developed. Their work was well known to many of the scholars whom Zepp-LaRouche met during her visit. Some of her friends who had followed the Schiller Institute since the 1990s held a banquet in Beijing in her honor.

The broader perspective of the Silk Road proposal presented by Mrs. LaRouche, which went far beyond transport infrastructure to a grand notion of building new cities and bringing civilization to the still unde-

---

2 http://newparadigm.schillerinstitute.com/belt-road-forum-may-14-15-2017

3 http://news.xinhuanet.com/english/2017-05/15/c_136285939.htm

I. INTRODUCTION

veloped areas of Central Asia, combined with a new renaissance of culture for all the peoples, sparked great interest in the various audiences.

April 2014
The CCTV program "Dialogue—Ideas Matter" conducted a half-hour interview with Helga Zepp-LaRouche in Beijing on February 20. This is a prime-time daily English-language talk show, which reaches viewers across China, and has more than 80 million subscribers around the world. Host Yang Rui began by noting that Mrs. LaRouche was known as the "New Silk Road Lady," and then asked her to elaborate on the concept of the New Silk Road.

August 2014
At an international conference on the "One Belt One Road" held August 25 and 26 at Lanzhou University in Gansu province in northwest China, co-sponsored by Lanzhou University and the China Soong Ching Ling Foundation, Helga Zepp-LaRouche spoke during the cultural exchange forum on the topic of "The Silk Road in the 21st Century is the cornerstone of peace and order."

September 2014
Helga Zepp-LaRouche addressed a forum in Beijing on September 5, on the subject of the global strategic significance of China's Silk Road program. The

Helga LaRouche on the show "Dialogue—Ideas Matter," September 3, 2014

event was sponsored by *China Investment* magazine, an arm of the National Development and Reform Commission, the main economic policy planning commission under the State Council of the Chinese government.

Two days earlier, on September 3, Helga Zepp-LaRouche participated in a panel on the show "Dialogue—Ideas Matter," which was aired live on the occasion of the 69th anniversary of China's victory over Japan. She joined Tao Wenzhao, a Research Fellow at the Chinese Academy of Social Sciences, in the studio.

On September 4, Helga Zepp-LaRouche gave a wide-ranging 25-minute interview on Radio China International to Zheng Chenguang, host of People in the Know, China's only high-end radio interview program in English.

December 2014
EIR published the first edition of the groundbreaking special report The New Silk Road Becomes the World Land-Bridge, of which Zepp-LaRouche was co-author. It presented a "conceptual road-map" to a New World Economic Order. The updated version is the one you are now reading. It was launched at conferences in Frankfurt, Germany, and in Washington, DC.

September 2015
The Chinese edition of the *EIR* Special Report *The New Silk Road Becomes the World Land-Bridge*

Helga LaRouche speaking at a forum in Beijing on the "One Road, One Belt," sponsored by China Investment *magazine, which is under the National Devolopment and Reform Commission of the State Council, September 5, 2014*

Helga LaRouche speaks at a Beijing symposium, presenting the Chinese edition of "The New Silk Road Becomes the World Land-Bridge."

was officially presented by Helga Zepp-LaRouche at a symposium in Beijing on September 29, sponsored by the Chongyang Institute for Financial Studies at Renmin University, which co-sponsored the translation of the Chinese-language report. The participation in this event made clear that this report had become an authoritative source for Chinese scholars in pursuing the "One Belt, One Road" project.[4]

October 2015

At an International Forum on Women in Beijing, sponsored by the Soong Ching Ling Foundation, Zepp-LaRouche was a featured speaker. The Foundation is dedicated to upholding the life and work of Soong Ching Ling, the wife of Sun Yatsen. Just one year earlier, two representatives of that foundation participated in a Schiller Institute conference near Frankfurt, Germany.

March 2016

The Arabic version of the report The New Silk Road Becomes the World Land-Bridge was launched in Cairo, Egypt at a conference organized by the Ministry of Transport, which featured Hussein Askary, the Arabic language editor of *EIR* and author of the expanded section on Southwest Asia in the report.

July 2016

A "Think-20 Forum" (T20) was held in Beijing July 29-30, whose purpose was to bring together scholars from around the world to provide ideas and suggestions on policymaking to the heads of state and government of the G20, which then met on September 4-5 in China. Helga Zepp-LaRouche spoke on Panel I on the theme "Global Governance: System Improving and Capacity Building."

She pointed out that whereas the system of trans-Atlantic monetarist finance was faced with near-term total collapse, the path to the future, including for the West, lay in orienting toward and cooperating with China's New Silk Road strategy, a concept which she and her husband Lyndon LaRouche had actively elaborated over decades. William Jones, the Washington bureau chief of *EIR*, was a speaker on Panel IV of the forum, dedicated to issues of North-South and South-South Cooperation.

May 2017

The major event of that month for the entire world was undoubtedly the Belt and Road Forum on May 14-15 in Beijing. Helga Zepp-LaRouche was invited to speak at the "think-tank exchanges," and gave a number of interviews on the occasion (see separate coverage on page 28).

After the forum, Helga Zepp-LaRouche traveled to Shanghai, where she was interviewed by *Shanghai Daily* about the importance of the BRI, and the Schiller Institute's role in working toward a new world system.[5]

Helga LaRouche speaks at the "Think-20" summit, Beijing, China, July 2016.

---

4 http://schillerinstitute.org/strategic/2015/1006-eir-silk_road_report-chinese.html

5 https://www.shine.cn/archive/opinion/chinese-perspectives/Belt-and-Road-initiative-instills-hope-for-peace-and-development-among-nations/shdaily.shtml

I. INTRODUCTION

She then gave a presentation on the BRI and the history of the LaRouche movement at the headquarters of the Phoenix Publishing House in Nanjing, which published the Chinese edition of the World Land-Bridge report.

November 2017

The Schiller Institute released a new report titled Extending the New Silk Road to West Asia and Africa, which highlighted the projects proposed or already being built in these two regions of the world that have been ravaged by conflict and wars, and presented the economic outlook and financing methods required to bring such programs to fruition.

Helga Zepp-LaRouche was a keynote speaker at the 21st Century Maritime Silk Road Forum held November 28-30 in Zhuhai, Guangdong. Her presentation was titled, "The Belt and Road Initiative and the Dialogue of Cultures Based on Their Higher Expressions." The event was organized by the provincial government of Guangdong.[6]

May 2018

William Jones, *EIR* Washington Correspondent and Schiller Institute representative, was invited to give one of the keynote speeches to a conference on Sino-American relations at Hangzhou's Zhejiang University on May 18-20.

---

6 https://www.youtube.com/watch?v=dGuANftvvHA&feature=youtu.be

---

Arabic Edition of the World Land-Bridge Report Launched in Egypt

In March of 2016, *EIR*'s Southwest Asia specialist and Arabic editor, Hussein Askary, made a highly successful one-week trip to Egypt to launch and promote the Arabic translation of *EIR*'s Special Report *The New Silk Road Becomes the World Land-Bridge*. Top government officials, economists, and numerous media representatives enthusiastically welcomed the ideas and the presentations made by Askary. The highpoint of his intervention was the very high-level and well-attended launching of the Arabic language report under the auspices of the Egyptian Ministry of Transport in a seminar on March 17 at the headquarters of the Ministry presided over and introduced by Minister Saad El Geyoushi personally.

Dr. Saad El Geyoushi, in his introductory remarks and his commentary on Askary's presentation, expressed total concordance with the idea of the New Silk Road, and his government's plans to integrate Egypt's transportation networks into the New Silk Road dynamic. He also took the opportunity to announce that the government intends to invest one trillion Egyptian Pounds (US$100 billion) in roads and railways, not only to develop Egypt's transportation network, but also to connect Egypt to Asia and most importantly to Africa to the south, in a 50,000-km network.

Among the participants at the event were top experts and advisors of the ministry and other institutions, as well several Egyptian television stations and newspapers. The Chinese channel CCTV-Arabic taped an interview with Askary, as did two other TV channels.

EIR's Hussein Askary (second from right) presents the Arabic edition of the World Land-Bridge Report at a high-level meeting in Egypt, March 2016

Chinese Edition of World Land-Bridge Report Endorsed by Chinese Scholars

The Chinese edition of the *EIR* Special Report, The New Silk Road Becomes the World Land-Bridge, was officially presented by Helga Zepp-LaRouche at a symposium in Beijing on September 29, 2015.

Introductory comments at the press conference were made by **Wang Wen**, Executive Dean of the Chongyang Institute, which sponsored the event, and Fu Jianming, Vice President of the Pheonix Publishing & Media Group, which published the Chinese version of the report in book form.

There was considerable coverage of the symposium in the economic press stressing the fact that this was the first analysis by American scholars of the Chinese project dubbed the "One Road, One Belt." There was also widespread recognition in the reports of the role of the Schiller Institute as key initiator of this project in the early 1990s.

The presentations by Zepp-LaRouche and by William Jones of *EIR* were followed by comments from eight leading Chinese scholars, who had read the report. A sample of their reactions:

Ding Yifan, former Deputy Director of the World Development Institute of the Development Research Center of the State Council of the P.R.C.: "I have known the Schiller Institute for a long time, and I have learned much from them. They have very specific ideas about the world economy.

The concept underlying LaRouche's view of the economy is that of the physical economy. LaRouche used the term negentropy to characterize the underlying laws of a healthy functioning economy."

He added that "Helga Zepp-LaRouche put forward the concept of the Eurasian Land-Bridge as a 'war avoidance concept.' The new concept of the Belt and Road has received great attention from the whole world.... We cannot allow capital to control everything. Instead, we must control capital."

Shi Ze from the China Institute of International Studies, who has been a featured speaker at several Schiller Institute events: "Geopolitics has led to the dangerous situation we have today. The aim of the [*EIR*] report is

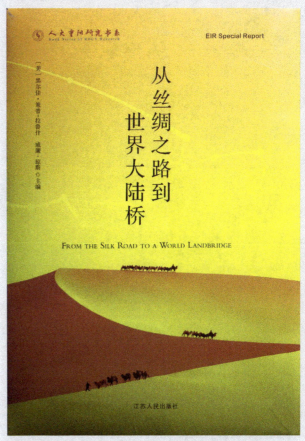

The cover of the Chinese edition of the World Land-Bridge report, released in September 2015

to develop a concept to replace geopolitics. And I found such a concept in this book.... On the other hand, is the economic aspect of the report, which places the stress on creating infrastructure. We have to look at the infrastructure needs of the other countries.... I am confident about the development of the Land-Bridge and I believe Mrs. LaRouche has made great progress in her idea."

Tao Qingmei of the Beijing Long Way Foundation: "This book reflects the views of U.S. experts and I really respect them. We should rethink the world on the basis of the new relationship between nations."

Liu Ying, Director of the Department of Cooperative Research at Chongyang Institute: This report, he noted, was written from a modern global perspective, including from a space perspective. "This report is about predicting the future rather than just explaining the past.

II. PRINCIPLES OF PHYSICAL ECONOMY

"Today, as the world enters a New Paradigm ... the necessity to fully comprehend and apply the insights of Lyndon LaRouche into a scientific approach to economic policymaking becomes indispensable for its success."

Economic Principles of a New Paradigm

LYNDON LAROUCHE'S DISCOVERIES

"The root of an economy is man. There is no economy among animals. An economy reflects a characteristic of people, of the human individual—the difference between an individual and the beast. That is, these cognitive powers by which we discover universal physical principles, derive new technologies or apply technologies based on these principles: We apply them to our problems. And therefore we find that through our physical efforts ... we are able to produce more wealth than it costs to keep us in the process of production.... Therefore it is the power of man to make discoveries and to use them, discoveries of universal physical principles, which increases the value of what is produced over the cost of production. Essentially, economy starts with purely physical values, dependent upon man's ability to discover universal physical principles, and to derive and apply technologies obtained through these discoveries. That is real economics."[1]

—*Lyndon LaRouche*

During the period of 1948-1952, Lyndon LaRouche made and elaborated an original, fundamental discovery in the science of economy, soundly refuting the destructive doctrines of British free-market economy, and firmly establishing economics as a physical science: the science of mankind's progress in and over the universe.

Over the subsequent 70 years, he has proven to be the most successful economic forecaster to date, due to the superiority of his method—demonstrating again and again that economics is a physical, not monetary, process, and is governed by knowable physical principles.

Over those decades, Lyndon LaRouche has shaped his life's work to bring about a change in humanity for the better, based on the potential of those discoveries. This has taken the form of forming an international movement, running eight campaigns for the U.S. Presidency, and establishing collaborations and friendships with world leaders—from heads of state for whose nations he created development policy proposals, to scientists, musicians, civil rights leaders, and many others.[2]

---

1 Lyndon LaRouche, Jr., "A Lesson in Economics." Schiller Institute Labor Day Conference, September 2, 2003.

2 See: "LaRouche's 40-Year Record: A New International Economic Order," https://larouchepac.com/new-economic-order,

Lyndon LaRouche delivered a series of lectures on his discovery in economics on various university campuses over the course of the late 1960s and early 1970s, and over that time period, recruited a large and growing political movement.

Today, as the world enters a New Paradigm, the first phase of which is manifesting itself in a renaissance of infrastructure building and worldwide poverty elimination, driven by the cooperative "win-win" policy of China's New Silk Road, the necessity to fully comprehend and apply the insights of Lyndon LaRouche into a *scientific* approach to economic policymaking becomes indispensable for its success. Just as the rejection of LaRouche's policies in the trans-Atlantic nations has led to the current collapse, the adoption of them today around the world will enable mankind to finally "grow up" out of its adolescence, and ensure human progress over the next 50-100 years.

Mankind: The Anti-Entropic Species

What is the nature of human knowledge? In other words: What is the experimental evidence which demonstrates, that the existence of the human species as we know it, depends upon some universal principle of human individual and social behavior, a principle which is lacking in all other living species?[3]

It is undeniable that over time, the human species has developed in a way which no other living thing has, *or could*. Our population and population density have far surpassed what is possible for biologically-similar species; simultaneously, our potential lifespan and standard of living have soared far beyond those of past eras; with the help of technologies, our power in and over nature has been revolutionized time and again, resulting in successive leaps upward in the productive powers of the labor force; and along the way, we have created new forms of existence—for example, new metals, super-heated plasmas, plastics—which would never have come about on Earth without our intervention, and which have transformed nature on a scale and at a rate even greater than that of the biosphere itself.[4]

This astounding process of growth not only is characteristic of the totality of mankind, but also is reflected at the level of the human individual. Over time, the power of the individual to change nature with his or her labor has been revolutionized. Along with that, however, the physical input required *per capita* to sustain and reproduce the population has increased tremendously—such that each person is much more "expensive" to support than before, even as the population grows. And yet, in a healthy economic process this does not lead to collapse; the system does not run down, or use itself up, as it might were man just another species of animal. Quite the opposite—the potential for future growth *increases*.

In his 1948-1952 work, and ever since, this uniquely *human* mode of development was identified by Lyndon LaRouche as a particular type of anti-entropic universal process, in which the individual is able to effect a leap in the productive and cognitive potential of the entire society. The cause of this anti-entropy

---

and Lyndon LaRouche, "On LaRouche's Discovery," *Fidelio*, Spring 1994.

3 "Science for Teachers: Visualizing the Complex Domain,"

21st Century Science & Technology, Fall 2003.

4 See the work of Vladimir I. Vernadsky on the biosphere and noösphere.

is rooted in a power specific to the individual human mind, above all other forms of life: the generation of *creative hypotheses*.

> ...[O]ur senses do not show us the reality outside our skins; they show us a shadow cast by the reality. We—our mind—can not "see" directly what has cast that shadow; we must craft an image in the human mind which experimental methods can prove to be the shadowy "other" image presented to natural or synthetic, sense-perceptual instruments.
>
> The most essential work of the individual human mind, on this account, is that of adducing what science identifies as universal physical principles, such as Kepler's uniquely original discovery of universal gravitation...[5]

Each new discovery of a universal principle is not a simple *addition* to previously-held beliefs, as one might add interesting objects to a collection; rather, it overturns those beliefs, and forces a recasting of our understanding of the way our universe is governed.[6] This new picture of the world contradicts and is incommensurable with, i.e., could never have come logically from, what came before. The *succession of new, revolutionary discoveries*, each of which redefines and opens up new possibilities in man's relationship to nature, has given rise to our upward evolution.

> These changes, from relatively lower, to higher ranks of species of effective change, are located in what is fairly identified as the discovery of what are, in effect, universal physical principles. These principled changes in quality correspond to leaps in what a competent physical science for today identifies as higher orders of universal physical principles.[7]

But how is it that a leap *within* the mind—a subjective, immaterial process, "contained" within an individual's cognitive processes—has such a great *physical* effect on the world outside our skins? This points to the fact that man's creative processes, his hypotheses, have a close likeness to the organization of nature itself—man in the image of the Creator. The proof of this can be found in physical economic terms:

> The introduction of the heat-powered machine, or analogous capital-intensive changes in the technology of production, must be comprehended as an indispensable feature of a change in human behavior, *a change in mankind's practical relationship to nature as a whole*. The economy of labor, accomplished by this means, is a reflection of the fact that the scientific discovery generating such changes in behavior, embodies an increasing correspondence between the behavior of mankind and the lawful ordering of our universe. *The economy of labor in the productive process must be comprehended as the greatest of all scientific experiments:* the experiment which proves empirically, as nothing else can, those *principles of scientific discovery* upon which the authority of all scientific knowledge entirely depends.[8]

To reiterate: All scientific progress depends upon the generation of a new hypothesis,[9] a unique, potential solution to a fundamental paradox that confronts us in our attempted mastery of the principles of nature. To test these hypotheses, to see whether the universe "agrees" with us, we design crucial experiments which will only succeed if our new notion is valid.

These experiments, when successful, become the basis for new families of technologies, and are sources of upshifts in our productive powers of labor:

> Each type of such refined experimental design for that same crucial hypothesis subsumes a set of machine-tool principles, or a *technology*; all of the

---

5 *Ibid.*

6 Two often cited examples by LaRouche are Kepler's discovery of universal gravitation, and Einstein and Planck's work on the quantum.

7 Lyndon LaRouche, Jr., "Hamilton in Today's World—& the Crisis Today: The Principle of Natural Economy—II," *EIR*, February 28, 2014.

---

8 Lyndon LaRouche, Jr., *So, You Wish to Learn All About Economics?* New Benjamin Franklin House, 1984.

9 Corresponding to the "idea" of Plato, "monad" of Gottfried Leibniz, or the "Geistesmassen" of Bernhard Riemann.

sets subsumed by crucial proof-of-principle design from that same hypothesis constitute a family of such sets, or a family of *technologies* derived from that proof of principle.[10]

In this way, mankind has the ability to increase the productive powers of his labor *willfully* by the introduction of new technologies—shadows, or generated applications of universal principles—into the productive process.

Each time the introduction of a set of new technologies causes an upshift in the productive powers of labor of the individual, the rate of output of that economy is increased, over and above the physical cost of production. This surplus LaRouche identifies as the only valid notion of profit. Economies in which the ratio of physical profit to the total cost of production is increasing over time—even while the cost of production is rising—are anti-entropic.

This fact has powerful implications for how we must measure economic value.

Metrics of Physical Economy

[A]ctual human behavior depends upon standards of measure which are specific to the fact that the human mind's characteristics do not correspond to linear or kindred measures, such as mere sense-perception, but, rather to the principled characteristics of human life, in its noëtic expressions, as a standard of measurement.[11]

LaRouche identified the potentially endlessly-increasing power of the human individual to exert power over nature as the sole source of progress in economics. He was therefore able to determine the proper, scientific measure for an economy as the accelerating rate of growth of the *potential relative population density*. Potential relative population density refers to the maximum number of people that could be supported on a given land area, given the currently-existing level of technology and accumulated improvements to the land ("relative"). For a primitive society ("hunter-gatherer") this would be approximately one person per 10 km^2, corresponding to a maximum world population of in the tens of millions. For an advanced society of today, based on nuclear fusion and the full use of the powers of the atomic nucleus, the world potential relative population density would be in the range of 100 billion people.

In elaborating this concept, LaRouche asks the reader to consider all of the economic activity of the society *as a whole*, as if it were a single agro-industrial firm. Consider—in physical terms—all of the necessary investments to support the activities of the *productive* part[12] of the labor force: from mining, processing, and transporting raw materials; to producing the machine tools for the factory floor and machines for the farmer's field; to the electricity grid which supplies power to the factory. Now consider all that is necessary to supply the needs ("market basket") of the households of those productive operatives: their food and electricity, transportation, and recreation. This LaRouche defines as the "energy of the system"—that which must be consumed to maintain the current process of production, supporting the entire society. Anything above and beyond that is "free energy" (**Figure 1**).

That free energy must be used to support the work and households of the non-productive but necessary workforce (e.g., doctors, teachers, administration), whose contributions serve to maintain and improve the current and future activities of the society. It is also funneled into "waste" activity (supporting the employable-but-unemployed,[13] and illegal or undesirable activities such as financial gambling and drug dealing). Anything above and beyond that is true physical profit, and can be reinvested into expanding and improving the productive process. This could take the form of, for example, replacing the machine tools of a factory with new, state-of-the-art

---

10   Lyndon LaRouche, Jr., "On LaRouche's Discovery," *Fidelio*, Spring 1994.

11   Lyndon LaRouche, Jr., "The Fuzz of the Impeachment: Our USA Now Enters a New Era," *EIR*, March 8, 2014.

12   The productive part of the labor force is defined by LaRouche as those engaged directly in agricultural or industrial manufacturing production or construction/maintenance. Others, such as administration, educators, and doctors play an indispensable role, but do not produce with their labor the physical goods needed to sustain society.

13   Whose unemployment is a waste of their potential contributions, and who ought to be employed in useful work for society.

technology; building a new concert hall or theater; or greatly expanding the nation's space program.

However, in an economy which is progressing, not only is the energy of the system—that which supports the current processes of production—growing, but the cost of production as a portion of that energy of the system is also growing. A primary factor in this is that *capital intensity*—understood most simply as the labor consumed (in the form of machines and other capital goods) to support the work of a given individual—increases as we base production on more numerous and increasingly advanced technological systems.

This, and related considerations, leads to the following yardstick, expressed in terms of inequalities: The requirement for the successful continuation of an economy is, that the ratio of "free energy" to "energy of the system," must not decline, despite the dependency of this ratio upon continuing increases of the absolute market-basket cost of "energy of the system," per capita and per square kilometer.[14]

Here we have a seeming paradox:

The apparent effect of re-investment of free energy to increase the energy of the system, is to increase the costs of the economy per capita, which might appear to be directly opposite to the result required. In a successful economy, it appears that a directly opposite net result occurs: the social costs of producing a "constant-content market basket" are reduced: economy of labor. To uncover the fallacy embedded within such a paradox, we are led to recognize that there is a "mixing of apples and oranges" in our counting procedure. Yes, the energy of the system does increase, but the cost of supplying this energy, as cost of labor, is reduced. There is an increase of the energy cost of the per capita activities of labor, but the labor cost of producing this energy is reduced sufficient to lower the average cost of per capita labor.[15]

In other words, an economically successful society must meet the requirement that the productive powers of labor *increase* over time such that the growing energy-of-the-system needs can be met and exceeded, at *lower* labor-cost than before. Therefore, what we must measure in economic science is not the ratio of free energy to total energy of the system *at any given time*, but how that ratio is increasing over time, and at what rate of acceleration (**Figure 2**). In such cases of growth, we have an anti-entropic economy, and a society whose potential relative population density is rising.

Now we must ask: What causes the required rate of increase in the ratio of free energy to energy of the system? How does an economy continually produce more than what it cost to be produced? We will address a number of these factors below, including the notions of energy-flux density and infrastructure.

First, however, we must dispense with the idea of money as a source of economic value, and restore the notion of "wealth" to an ontologically secure footing.

Figure 1
Total Productive Output

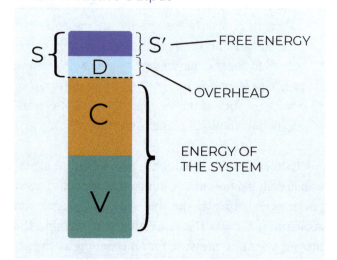

The total productive output of an economy is broken down into the energy of the system (C+V)—or that which is consumed directly by the productive process and its operatives—and profit (S). After subtracting that which supports the overhead portion of the economy (D), the remaining "free energy" (S') can be invested into future growth.

---

14 Lyndon LaRouche, Jr. "Leibniz From Riemann's Standpoint," *Fidelio*, Fall 1996.

15 LaRouche, *So, You Wish to Learn All About Economics?*

Figure 2
Anti-Entropic Economic Growth

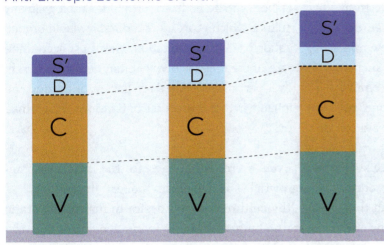

In a successful economic process, not only does the energy of the system (C+V) grow over time, but so does the ratio of profit (S') to C+V, and that at an accelerating rate.

The Noetic Root of Economic Value

> Money adds no value at all, unless the value is defined by the net *physical* gain of increase of the productive powers of labor by a society.[16]

As opposed to today's foolish notions that economic value is generated by money—financial "profit" created primarily out of thin air in the frenzy of the speculative market—money itself has no *content*. Simply increasing the price paid for a good or service, or assigning a monetary value to a newly-invented financial instrument, is no reflection of its actual value as part of the physical economic process, and adds no real value to the economy as a whole.

Examples of this abound in the unprecedented and growing values-reported of speculative financial instruments (see Section VI of this report), where prices might fluctuate wildly in mere microseconds, and create a nominal "profit" on the books, while nothing has been improved, or even *altered* in the real, physical world.[17]

Instead, economic value must be assessed top-down from the activity of the economic system considered as an *entirety*, not individual financial profits. Lyndon LaRouche wrote of this:

> [T]here is already no remaining basis for the widespread, but delusionary belief, that some intrinsic value is expressed by money. Value is expressed, not as a quantity per se, but only as the relative effects of the increase, or decrease of the physical potential relative population-density of the individual in society. The value of money lies not in the individual exchange, but in the functional unity (*unifying dynamic*) of the social process of a nation, or nations when considered as an individual, dynamic entirety.[18]

Examine this more closely.

What ought to be the desired effect or "product" of a national or global economic process *as an entirety*? The answer, in short, is *people*:

> A foolish economist measures the performance of an economy in the financial, or monetary, or, much less foolishly, the physical wealth enjoyed by either some, or all of the members of that society. The competent economist measures the wealth of the economy in the degree of self-improvement of the quality of the members of society as human. Making the same point more bluntly, it were said that the economic mission of society is to make the nation's people better than they are today. This is to be done through means employing the process of developing the people to higher levels of power in and over nature per capita. Or, we might better say, "The greatest wealth which the generation of the deceased has bequeathed to its heirs, is a society of a better quality of living people."[19]

---

16 Lyndon LaRouche, Jr., "Welcome President 'X': A New President for the U.S.A.," *EIR*, February 28, 2014.

17 Nothing altered *except* that available credit has been sucked into such meaningless varieties of money-making ventures, while becoming increasingly scarce or non-existent for capital improvements to industries, and maintenance of basic economic infrastructure.

18 Lyndon LaRouche, Jr., "Economy for Scientists: Economic Science, in Short," *EIR*, June 19, 2009.

19 Lyndon LaRouche, Jr., "Man's Original Creations," *EIR*, June 24, 2005.

It is important here to address a re-warmed, but prevalent myth that human population growth is dangerous, and therefore mankind must shift to a zero-growth model if we are to preserve human existence. It reality, there *is not* nor could there ever be such a thing as a "zero growth" society, because such a society would quickly pave the way for its own elimination. Even maintaining the so-called "status quo" of the current society over time requires an increase of output—growth!

Two primary factors are responsible for this: 1) the depletion of the best and most accessible resources means that more and more effort must be put into acquiring the same quantity of raw materials, or else the society will "run down"; and 2) aging infrastructure and capital goods (e.g., machinery) which the society relies on has a finite lifespan, requiring more and more maintenance—without which attritional effects on the economic process will occur.

In a 2009 paper, LaRouche spoke of this in terms of man's obligation to move to use of higher classes of energy-flux density (a term which will be discussed more below):

> [S]peaking now in the relatively simplest, but nonetheless competent terms of reference, the ability of mankind to maintain human life at even a constant level of population and standard of living, requires us to progress continuously to higher levels of effective *energy-flux density* in our methods of producing even currently achieved standards of living. *This requirement is typified by the obligation to proceed from relatively lower to higher sources of power, and to more advanced physical chemistries. This requirement is also expressed in the correlated form of an obligation to increase the capital intensity of productive and related modes of existence, per capita and per square kilometer of net inhabited territory.* This requires a steady rise in what is manifest as the net energy-flux density of not only the modes of production of society, but, also, of the conditions of life of the productive society as a whole.[20]

To underscore the point:

> [T]here can be no fixed form of technology in any culture which represents a durably viable organization of human habitation. Man must accept the fate of creating his own habitat, here or in whichever part of our immediate galaxy, or beyond, we inhabit, in that due course of times which overtake us.

Even were adherence to the myth of "zero-growth" sprung from honest intentions,[21] a healthy culture *does not* desire to maintain a static state of humanity. Each living generation has the moral imperative to create the potential for growth and progress of future generations, beyond simply maintaining the status quo.

> As I have emphasized, repeatedly, the still merely popular explanation for the meaning of human life, is an intrinsically depraved one: the notion that success is essentially the possession carried into mouldering in the grave. The truth is, that the increase must come from those gains in the power of mankind's productive powers which are expressed in the increase of the power of the human species (human reason) to exist in the universe, and are thus to produce the seeds of a greater future harvested by the soul of the deceased. The natural increase, for humanity itself, is expressed in the terms of the advancement of mankind's creative increase of the productive powers of human labor, each over the course of, implicitly, successive generations.

Taking this immortal mission as the economic goal of the "functional unity," or "unifying dynamic," of the society, referred to by LaRouche above, how, in practical terms, can future progress be ensured? And what, from *that* standpoint, is economic value?

It is here that we return to the effect of the revolutionary discovery, made by the individual and applied by the society, on the productive powers of labor. The creative process occurring inside the human

---

20   *Op. cit.*

21   See: "'Global Warming' Scare Is Population Reduction, Not Science." *EIR Special Report*, September 2015.

mind, noesis, does not exist within any other form of life. Our insights into new physical principles allow us to create forms of existence in the universe which had never occurred—nor were known to be possible—before. The original creations of humanity express two primary economic characteristics: 1) they could not have been factored into a "supply and demand" sort of monetary accounting, because they overthrow the linear system of that accounting—they had no existence in the previous economic stage; and 2) they make possible a leap upward in mankind's productive powers of labor (both per capita and per km^2). It is only contributions of this type which create new and expanded value in an economy, and generate an increase in *potential relative population density*. All other (financial) "profit" is a fraud.

> Therefore, what we must measure, to determine the performance of economies, is the relative rate of negentropy [anti-entropy] generated per capita. "Economic value" is properly measured only as per capita negentropy. Therefore, to measure "economic value," we must define a mathematical function in which the content of "work" measured is measured in "units of negentropy."
>
> In other words, if you do not assist in some necessary way, in transmitting negentropy to the economic process as a whole, you are economically useless. Any product produced and consumed, which does not satisfy this requirement, is economically useless.

We must now be more specific about what can effect the types of leaps in free energy which create anti-entropy. Central to this question is the shift to a higher energy platform.

Energy-Flux Density and Higher Forms of Promethean Fire

Mankind is a unique species in that what we call a resource is not fixed—resources change over time. What are today indispensable resources, played little to no role in our economic "metabolism" in previous eras. What determines something to be a resource (or not) is not anything self-evident about or intrinsic to the material itself; it is man's insight into a discovered principle of nature which taps into and utilizes specific powers or properties of that material in new ways, thereby *creating* a resource where it had not previously existed.

For example, before the discoveries of the powers of the atomic nucleus, uranium ore was a yellowish rock which played very little role in human activity.

Today, uranium is a highly valuable resource, which could support the growth of human civilization by an order of magnitude. A relatively small amount of refined uranium—the energy-equivalent of millions of tons of coal or fossil fuels—can supply the power needs of entire cities, including in places where shipping large amounts of oil or gas becomes impractical, like Earth's remote regions or burgeoning colonies on the Moon or Mars.

LaRouche discussed this changeover of resources in terms of man's use of different forms of "fire":

> It should now be common knowledge of civilized modern societies, that, from that "whatever ancient" time, on, man's essential evolution has always remained as being man's changing relationship to a succession of ontologically higher orders of the quality of expressions of what we may term, categorically, as equivalent to "fire": as "fire" is so defined from an overview of the chemistry of those rising states of relative energy-flux density, which, in turn, lead toward successive increases of relative physical-chemical modalities of man's use of the successively rising order of the categories of successive equivalents of "fire" (e.g., "the higher temperatures").[22]

We see in **Figure 3** that not only does the power per capita tend to rise exponentially over time, but that the primary resource used to supply that power has changed—a transformation in mankind's physical chemistry, or equivalent use of "fire." As alluded to by LaRouche above, the changeover of fuels is not random—a mere replacement of one thing with another more readily available. What creates the availability of

---

22 Lyndon LaRouche, Jr., "'Project Space': The Thesis," *EIR*, October 4, 2013.

Figure 3

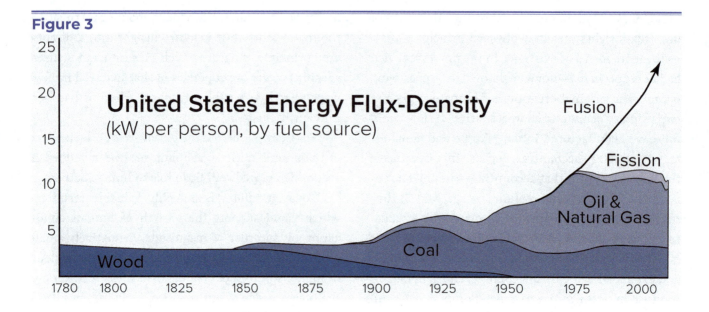

a material as a resource in the first place, much more than its physical abundance or accessibility, is the advancement of the human mind that transforms its usefulness.

The reflection of this ordered progress of growth is that each new resource is more energy-dense than its predecessor—it takes half as much coal to provide the same energy output as wood, and one millionth as much fission fuel to equal that of petroleum (**Table 1**)—and each puts *denser and higher temperature* "fire" within our grasp.

The hierarchy of energy densities in fuel sources is a primary factor in economic progress, as suddenly less of the labor force and corresponding capital goods are required to supply the same basic power needs of society.

And the impact of bringing a more energy-dense fuel into use is not felt in power production alone; more importantly, *new kinds of things* are achievable.

> ...[T]he impending upward jump [in the productive powers of labor] centers around the possibility of a fourfold or greater rise in the average effective temperature of heat-driven productive process. A fourfold leap in "average temperature" of productive processes, requires and makes possible new kinds of materials in general use, and redefines radically both the absolute and relative-cost meaning of the term "natural resources." The confinement of hot plasmas as sources of commercial energy, combined with the means to transform such plasma energy directly into industrial forms of directed-energy applications, suffices to signify the greatest and most rapid leap upward in productivity, in the history of mankind.[23]

For example, with the high heats and types of energies available to us in the nuclear domain,[24] we can manipulate matter on such a fine level that we could vaporize a cell without the next one noticing, fine-tune the properties of metal alloys down to the atomic level, and turn any known material into a plasma before separating it into its constituent elements. The general category of effect referenced is an increase in the *energy-flux density* of the power applied. This refers to the concentration of power at the point of work being done.

The most simple illustration of this for pedagogical purposes is the difference in work accomplished by a dull knife blade versus a sharp one. With the same pressure applied to both, the sharp knife accomplishes much more work, with much greater precision, because of the greater concentration of the power in the blade's edge. It is the *concentration* of power that opens up new domains of industrial and

---

[23] Lyndon LaRouche, Jr., "Wassily Leontief Acts to Block Effective Implementation of the SDI," *Fusion*, July-August 1985.

[24] Plasmas within a fusion reactor can reach the tens and hundreds of millions of degrees centigrade. For reference, the center of the Sun registers a mild 15 million degrees.

Table 1
Energy Density

How Much Fuel Would It Take to Meet New York City's Energy Requirements for One Year?*

Fuel Source	Tons
Wood	16,000,000
Coal	8,000,000
Petroleum	5,000,000
Uranium† (fission)	55
Deuterium-Tritium (fusion)	0.7
Matter-Antimatter	0.003

* based on 2015 consumption, disregarding conversion losses.
† uranium fuel, enriched to 5% U-235.

other productive capabilities to us.

This category of transformation characterizes the phases of human development throughout history:

> In the known history of cultures, this increasing of net productivity per capita and per square kilometer, is associated with a long-wave trend toward increase of the relative energy-flux density of the modes of heat-work employed, moving upward from the poorest quality of general resource, such as sunlight impinging on what is conventionally classified as our planet's surface, to the improvement of the net energy-flux density accomplished as the work of chlorophyll and the related role of increased use of that carbon atom which plays such a crucial role in the possibility of life, especially human life. We progress from burning of trash, to charcoal, to coal, to coke, to petroleum and natural gas, and then the leap into the much more powerful energy-flux densities of nuclear and thermonuclear power. It is the increase of the application of a certain energy-flux density, per capita, as distributed, in one or several particular portions, per square kilometer of territory, which is not only the only principled course for the improvement of the condition of human life, but without such increases in energy-flux density, human life on this planet must necessarily deteriorate, ultimately to the point of a large degree of genocide against the planet's population as a whole. A contrary policy, such as those of today's neo-malthusian fanatics, such as the World Wildlife Fund's Prince Philip, et al., would be clearly, and criminally, insane in its effects.[25]

Each energy platform is itself a reflection of higher domains of physical chemistry, which change mankind's relationship with and command over matter and energy. This implies something much more than a change of resource base; mankind assumes a new species characteristic, with a higher power to cause change in the physical world.

> Consequently, presently (today, for example) we are enabled to "map," as if quite literally, the evolution of mankind as mental, more than biological otherwise. The irony of this is, that it is human mental life which defines human biological evolution, rather than animal standards of comparison. Our action, as "chemists" in a certain proper sense of voluntary (willful), is the means by which we, unlike any other living species presently known to us, thus far, may evolve to higher states of existence by merely rethinking our practice, rather than being obliged to changing our already existing, physical-genetic modalities.
>
> Thus, we are left the fact, that it is the mind of man which determines the physical existence of the human species, rather than the other way (the animal way). In this respect, art and science are indivisible, as the imagination is more essential to progress in chemistry, than chemistry itself. The increase of the effective energy-flux density of the human society is the measure of its humanity in practice.[26]

In shifting to a new, higher power source, the economic process *as a whole* is lifted to a higher-order,

---

25 Lyndon LaRouche, Jr., "Economics as History: The Science of Physical Economy," *EIR*, July 11, 2009.

26 LaRouche, "Welcome President 'X': A New President for the U.S.A."

creating a top-down change in the potential output of every individual part, and therefore in the society's potential relative population density.

Another aspect of economy which increases productivity top-down is infrastructure.

The Role of Infrastructure

As with resources, what is meant by "infrastructure" is not fixed. In a series of writings and discussions over the course of 2010, LaRouche developed the notion of the *economic platform*, a concept closely linked with the evolution of human civilization.

> [W]hat we're moving for is a new conception of economy ... in which we will base ourselves on looking at infrastructure in a way which is different than the term is used these days by most economists. What we mean by infrastructure, we mean that the basic economic infrastructure of the planet, as typified by the development of, first of all, ocean travel, ocean transportation, which for a long time was the chief, most effective means of organizing society for some form of progress: maritime traffic was the basis. Then, with Charlemagne, he introduced a system of land-based water systems, a combination of rivers and canals, which was completed initially during his reign as emperor of what became known as France. That started a new system.... So therefore, what we have to understand, in looking at that aspect of history, in the progress from maritime systems, to inland waterway systems, to railway systems, to magnetic levitation systems, these steps are what we call "infrastructure"—and health care and other things go along with that. So infrastructure is not something you add, to enhance the economy: infrastructure, as defined in these kinds of terms, is the foundation of economy.[27]

Infrastructure, when viewed correctly, becomes the platform upon—or shapes the space-time within which—the economy operates, affecting and facil-

Infrastructure is not merely the "thing" that is built—e.g., bridge, dam, or train. It is a reflection of man's power to alter nature, to make it, and mankind itself, more productive than before. Here, the Hoover Dam holds back the Colorado River, providing water and electricity to thousands.

itating all human activities taking place within the given territory. As with resources, infrastructure systems reflect our species' mastery of discovered universal principles, and give us greater command over nature. Akin to a change in physical space-time, or an increase in energy-flux density of something, the introduction of a system of infrastructure, such as a magnetic-levitation rail network, will change the potential of the productive processes within that territory *without otherwise changing the specific activities of production*. LaRouche:

> Infrastructure enables mankind to increase the quality and quantitative feature of productivity of labor, as a qualitative step upward. And therefore, infrastructure, as such, when it's applied in this way, to mankind, introduces a qualitative leap upward in the possibility of productive economy. That is, agriculture and industry depend for their improvements, based largely on the factor of basic economic infrastructure, as I've just identified it.[28]

> ...[W]e should then recognize that the development of basic economic infrastructure had always been a needed creation of what is required as an "habitable" development of a "synthetic," rather than a presumably "natural" environment for the enhancement, or even the possibility of hu-

---

27 *LPACTV Weekly Report*, June 4, 2010.

28 *Ibid.*

man life and practice at some time in the existence of our human species.[29]

And elsewhere:

> [T]he function of "infrastructure" is not that of a supplement to production. It is the building up, to qualitatively higher levels of the equivalent of "energy-flux density," of the creation of the physical and related foundations on which the establishment and maintenance of a certain quality of range of direct productivity, as per capita, and as per square kilometer, is dependent.[30]

This scientifically-rigorous view by LaRouche of the nature of infrastructure systems is vital to understand from a policy-making standpoint, because the world today requires a rapid transformation of the productive potential of—especially—the inland regions of our planet. Such transformation will depend upon greatly increasing the productive powers of labor of the local populations, which, as LaRouche elaborates, depends upon the energy-flux densities and new principles made available via infrastructure systems.

> Ordinarily, the idea of "productive" is associated with the output of labor by production. That is an honest mistake in judgment. The fact of the matter is, that the precondition for the rise of cultures to revolutionary changes to higher qualities of regions of sustainable, potential relative population-density, depends on virtual leaps in potential relative, human population-density which, in turn, require a higher quality of physical-cultural "platform" within which to operate. Such platforms include the discoveries in astronomy on which trans-oceanic maritime cultures depend. They include the addition of the inland riparian cultures, featuring canal-systems linked to principal rivers. They include most extensive systems of transport, such as good quality of highway systems, and then continental railway systems. They include advances in the cultural level of forms of power, from relatively lower, to higher effective energy-flux-densities of the form of power employed.
>
> So, presently, the preconditions for the next great upward leap in the world's economy, now depend not only upon nuclear and thermonuclear power, as superseding types of qualitatively lower ranges of energy-flux-densities. They require a general upgrading of the methods of management of the planet....
>
> It is the great advances in basic economic infrastructure ... which constitute the platforms on which the potential for increase of relative potential population-density and quality of individual human life depend. In other words, the level of achievable productivity depends upon raising the "platform," through revolutions in infrastructure, on which successful general advances in potential relative population-densities depend. Without those advances in basic economic infrastructure, merely particular technological progress locally applied will fail in attempted performance of the truly vital mission of physical-economic program, failing for lack of the progress in advancement of the quality of the infrastructural platform on which the success of the society as a whole depends.[31]

There are many notable examples of the transformative effect of upshifts in infrastructure platforms on individual productivity. The New Deal projects of the Franklin Roosevelt administration in the United States give many: The 1930s electrification and flood control of rural areas such as the Tennessee Valley region of the United States increased productivity of farms manyfold, and allowed an opening up of the region to heavy, energy-intensive industries such as aluminum production, which were previously impossible; large-scale water management projects in the Western United States, such as the Hoover and Grand Coulee Dams, brought abundant electricity and water for irrigation which increased the output of enormous tracts of farmland manyfold. A more

---

29 Lyndon LaRouche, Jr., "What Your Accountant Never Understood: The Secret Economy," *EIR*, April 17, 2010.

30 Lyndon LaRouche, Jr., "The Folly of Chronic Wars," *EIR*, July 30, 2010.

31 Lyndon LaRouche, Jr., "The Economic Past Is Now Behind Us! Money or Credit?" *EIR*, September 10, 2010.

recent example is China's integration of its "Jing-Jin-Ji" region, and its growing network of national high-speed and light rail, which is integrating and transforming the social and economic potential of the entire territory and its more than 1 billion inhabitants.

These great infrastructure achievements must be seen as what they are: reflections of an elevated species characteristic of mankind, with increased control over nature, due to our wielding new, more powerful physical principles.

Looking ahead, civilization must move rapidly to a *new* infrastructure platform based on fusion power and space (see Section VI of this report). In such a platform, revolutionary technologies and the resources that they depend on will reorganize our use and habitation of the planet's surface. With magnetically-levitated rail in broad use for moving people and freight, the concentration of population will no longer lie predominantly along coastal areas, and will begin to fully develop the inland of continents. Prevalent use of fusion power will mean that with plasma technologies, such as the fusion torch, we can process materials from landfills and low-grade ore, creating new resource "deposits." This will eliminate the need to transport large quantities of ore or semi-processed raw materials over long distances. An increasing orientation to and habitation of nearby space will lead to the development of Earth's polar regions, with their unique magnetic and other interactions with cosmic phenomena.

All of this demands that as we consider infrastructure systems today, we think from the standpoint of future infrastructure requirements, rather than merely meeting current needs. Such a future orientation, in practice, must be coupled with a science-driver policy, to accelerate a breakthrough to knowledge of new physical principles.

Shaping Policy for the Future: A Science-Driver Mission

Astronaut Ed White performs the first American "spacewalk," June 3, 1965. With continued exploration and colonization of our Solar system, mankind will cease being an earthbound species, and assume a new role as an extraterrestrial being. Just as in the space program of the 1960s, previously impossible achievements will revolutionize economic potential on Earth and far beyond.

> Mankind's knowledgeable practice of our access to the principle of access to both knowledge in the present, and foreknowledge of the future, is the most essential of the known principles which distinguish the human individual's naturally given, distinctive aptitude. That is an aptitude, both to possess, and to act upon knowledge derived from the future, as such, and, thus, the opportunity to change that future willfully for the better.[32]

Fifty to one-hundred years from now, we will look back on today, and see that LaRouche's discoveries in the science of physical economy served as the indispensable guidepost for putting humankind on a trajectory which was *knowably* and *purposefully* anti-entropic. As LaRouche outlined many times, careful policymaking must put a priority on directing investment of economic profit ("free energy") into moving the society to a higher energy-flux density and infrastructure platform. These policy-making efforts must be centered around a science-driver program which places a premium on efforts toward discovering yet-unknown, higher energy-flux-density

---

32 LaRouche, "'Project Space': The Thesis."

physical principles—and also their implementation and application. Such an effort becomes the driver of all future economic progress, and organizes the talents of all generations within society:

> It is fair, and also necessary to say: that the human species makes its own future place voluntarily with respect to all other known living processes, but, also, absolutely, above each and every other species of living creature presently known to mankind. The fairly accurate description of that distinction, is that a human life, is governed, in its inherently natural design, by the necessity of an implicit progress of being a voluntarily upward-evolving species of the ontological characteristics of a human life, as distinct from all others presently known by us to exist, or have existed. The human species, therefore, always lives, actually, in the progressive development of its own future, to increase continually an ever-greater distance-in-principle from the beasts. This must be manifest, in fact, in practice: in a principle of constant anti-entropic change. No such example, is presently known among all other presently known species. Either you know the future, as a matter of principle, or your perception of your quality of life is a damaged one.
>
> The general principle of effect, of human progress in this mode of progress, demands use of the notion of a succession of future "eras" in the qualitative leaps of one human culture, each to another, qualitative higher state of social existence. This has been demonstrated for chemistry by insight into the principled ordering of mankind's general direction for its meaning of "progress," by a general rise in the qualities of energy-flux density of effects in the human process as a whole process.[33]

While discovery cannot be achieved by diktat, it has been demonstrated that just as the successful collaboration among the musicians in a string quartet produces something which is more than the sum of its parts, fostering a joint effort among great minds—as was done in a concentrated way during the wartime Manhattan Project, or the peacetime Apollo Project—can create the conditions for a higher density of revolutionary breakthroughs of completely new insights.

A national science driver program, in collaboration with other nations, can be supported through a Hamiltonian-style credit system (see Section VI of this report), which will underwrite the great scientific and economic efforts needed to pull the future into the present.

> [A] credit system permits sufficient fresh credit for physical investment in expansion and science-driven, advanced-technology enhancement of the productive powers of cooperating nations (as measured per capita and per square kilometer in each case) to begin a steeply accelerating process of increase of the physical productive powers of labor throughout most of the planet through *development of sources of public power which are of today's very high, and still rising energy-flux-density in character.*[34]

To that end:

The essential distinction by which this must be understood, is given in measures of progress ordered in a series of energy-flux densities in the relationship between the energetic and cognitive interdependency of the leaps upward in the ordering of living species generally, and in the weightier measure of leaps in the prowess of the development of the human mind. The relationship between increase of applied energy-flux-density and the leaps in the productive powers expressed as human productive progress, is crucial. The crucial feature, so identified is otherwise to be identified as the creative power of irony, as in progress in scientific principles for work, and in Classical musical rules of composition, as in Classical modes of poetry, drama, and song.

In his exceptional piece, on the subject of **Opinion on The Constitutionality of a National Bank**, [Hamilton] achieved a relatively highest point of insight into the nature of the human spe-

---

33   LaRouche, "The Fuzz of the Impeachment: Our USA Now Enters a New Era."

34   LaRouche, "Economics as History: The Science of Physical Economy."

cies: the essential wholeness of that species, a wholeness which is, in and of itself, the principle which regulates the process as a whole: the noëtic principle of the human mind.

This principle is located (for purposes of reference) in the nature of the actually noëtic characteristics shared by a congruence of both nature and the human mind. This pertains, specifically, to the essential feature of human creativity: the ability of the human species to order the leaps in power of the human species which we record, from experience, as the leaps in the mental-creative powers expressed as results of the progress of the human mind of both the individual, and the society of that individual: *The implied, as much as the expressed powers of the human mind. Especially, the power to foresee the future in the manner in which history necessarily unfolds. Those who cannot foresee the future, at least sometimes, do not yet know the present.*[35]

Today, the two, interrelated spear-points of such a needed effort are in the realms of the very small and the very large: nuclear fusion, and space exploration and colonization.

Comparing that role of scientific-technological progress of cultures on Earth in recent centuries, to the new qualities of progress required for exploration of nearby Solar space, should be employed as a way of generalizing the concept of typical human progress in such a way that both of the compared states are conceived as if they expressed a single principle of human development.[36]

A fusion- and space-driver program today cannot thrive in isolation from the rest of the economy. It must be supported by a rapid acceleration of the implementation of nuclear fission power and associated spin-off technologies. In other words, as we move society to the next energy-flux density platform, a natural acceleration of the consumption of current resources will occur as the result of upgrading of the entire system (people and capital goods/infrastructure) to a level which will be capable of implementing the coming breakthroughs in fusion.

Mankind's power within the Solar system and beyond that, corresponds to the development of the progressive power of the human mind in terms of ever-broader, and ever-deeper meaning of the universe as it becomes known to us. The bounds of sense-perception are thus breached for a belief in eternity, rather than the foolishness of mere sense-certainty.[37]

It is here that we arrive at the *economic* necessity of fostering a beautiful culture.

Culture and the Creative Imagination

It is thus, in the domain of culture ... that the essential secret of continued human civilized existence and progress now depend absolutely. Henceforth, economic science is the science of those transformations in individual and mass human culture on which the continued existence of civilized mankind depends.[38]

Return to LaRouche's initial 1948–1952 work. Central to his breakthrough in economic science was identifying that the anti-entropic nature of human society is dependent upon the poetic faculty within mankind—the ability to *communicate* newly-made discoveries, new ideas which do not yet exist in language. Therefore, uplifting the level of culture to one which coheres with a creative view of the nature of man is inseparable from an economically successful society.

A revolutionary discovery, one which overturns our previously-held beliefs about nature, does not emerge logically from the currently-reigning system of laws and principles. Therefore, it has no "name" within the current language-culture—the literal use

---

35   Lyndon LaRouche, Jr., "The Prospect for a U.S. Future: Build the Real American Party," *EIR*, April 18, 2014.

36   LaRouche, "Economics as History: The Science of Physical Economy."

37   The American Principle: Return to the Actual U.S. Constitution," footnote 8, *EIR*, May 9, 2014.

38   LaRouche, "Economics as History: The Science of Physical Economy."

Lyndon LaRouche and Norbert Brainin, first violin of the Amadeus Quartet. Brainin and LaRouche formed a decades-long friendship and collaboration around a shared mission of the defense and revival of the Classical principle in music. Of that principle, Brainin once said, "[The idea of] Motivführung is close to my heart; I've carried it around with me for a long time, and it never really resonated with anyone else; and the only person who immediately understood it, was Lyndon LaRouche, and that is the bond between us."

of language to describe a completely new concept will not function. Instead, the mind of the other person or persons must be induced to generate the new concept for themselves, *de novo*, as a result of their own, sovereign mental processes. This can only be done by a mode of communication that we associate with the artistic use of language found in great Classical poetry and music.

> The power of musicality expressed as Classical poetry, is the faculty of the creative imagination which produced the great, original scientific insights of impassioned amateur violinist Albert Einstein's wonderful assaults on the domain of the unknown in the practice of physical scientific investigations.[39]

The specific aspect of poetry (or music) which renders it fitting for the communication of completely *new* conceptions is that of ambiguity, or irony:

It is this function of ambiguity in both the composition and uttering of Classical poetry, and also Classical modes in composing and uttering literate prose, which touches the most crucial aspect of the role of the imagination in invoking the quality of creativity which is echoed by the act of discovery of validatable hypothesis in physical science.[40]

> In all respects, the leading role of human creativity, including physical-scientific creativity is located, not in mathematics, but in the dynamic role of that power of creative artistic imagination of Classical music, poetry, drama, and comparable expression of the Classical visual arts....
>
> It is this subjective element in human nature which is the locus of true creativity, in physical science and otherwise, and thus of the absolute superiority of man over beast. This is the ultimate secret of success in economy; this is the indispensable function of Classical artistic culture.[41]

Therefore, Classical culture cannot be an afterthought of economic science: it is the indispensable substrate of a successful and *happy* human civilization; one which is progressing upward in physical economic terms, fulfilling our essential, universal characteristic: creativity.

This is the reason that Lyndon and Helga LaRouche have repeatedly called for a global dialogue of cultures, leading to a new renaissance. Each nation will bring to the table the *best* of its culture and history, so that civilization as a whole may come to a more-perfect construction of the beautiful character of mankind, in the image of the Creator.

In addition to this being a natural and important part of the New Paradigm on Earth, the place where

---

39 *Ibid.*

40 *Ibid.*

41 *Ibid.*

such a dialogue of cultures will happen most naturally is in the colonization of our solar system. Here, though each astronaut comes from a particular cultural lineage, we will have the great privilege of establishing a rich, *human* cultural life in space and on other planetary bodies, with an active outlook for the outcome of one's life that reaches hundreds of years into the future.

This is the foundation of a truly human and scientific practice of economy, which fulfills the Leibnizian promise enshrined in the United States Declaration of Independence: the pursuit of happiness:

> The Classical artistic imagination to which civilized mankind aspires, inspires man's reach into a universal reality which is beyond currently prevalent practice during that period of time; but, the test of the reality of that imagination occurs in respect to the resulting increase, or failure, of the physical power of mankind to exist, per capita and per square kilometer of territory on the surface of the planet, which defines that which could be regarded as a validated innovation. It is the outcome of that aspect of both science and Classical art, which is the juncture of Classical artistic standards of beauty, as in the case of Brunelleschi's construction of the cupola of Santa Maria del Fiore, an outcome which is expressed in the increase of a culture's potential relative population-density. That which unifies science and art in that way, presents us with a rule-of-thumb for defining the unity of progress and beauty. It is that specific unity which produces, and attests to the beauty and eternal life of the human individual soul, and which underlies the motive-forces of all progress in the human condition.[42]

"Brunelleschi's Dome" in Florence, Italy. Brunelleschi completed the dome in 1436 with a design based on new insights into physical principles of previously impossible construction.

For further reading on Lyndon LaRouche's science of physical economy, and a catalogue of LaRouche's major works, visit: www.larouchepub.com.

---

[42] LaRouche, "Economics as History: The Science of Physical Economy."

"In the context of the New Paradigm, it is finally time that the full efforts of strategic capabilities of leading nations be brought together in a harmonious pursuit of their application to—and further development for—the defense and the progress of all mankind..."

The Strategic Defense of Earth for the Universal Progress of Man

WHAT DOES LAROUCHE'S SDI MEAN TODAY?

Preface: What Was the SDI, Really?

As presented by Helga Zepp-LaRouche in her introduction to this report, the emerging potential for a New Paradigm requires a new global security architecture. How will leading nations need to reshape strategic and military doctrines to fit this new historic era? What will be the role of national military capabilities in this new paradigm?

These questions have been brought into renewed focus following Russian President Putin's March 2018 national address, during which he outlined Russia's development of a new generation of strategic weapons—including nuclear-powered cruise missiles, ICBMs that can travel at 20 times the speed of sound while maintaining maneuverability, fast submarine drones capable of carrying nuclear weapons, laser weapons, and more.

This has shattered the Anglo-American neoconservative faction's delusional pursuit of a unipolar world "governed" under the threat of a first strike strategic nuclear capacity which could guarantee the elimination of any retaliatory threat. Russia has demonstrated that they have developed retaliatory capabilities, premised upon revolutionary technologies.

How should the U.S.A. and Western Europe respond? A new confrontational "arms race"? Or the option of the New Paradigm, with a new global security architecture?

The true purpose of military doctrines should be to ensure peace. The question becomes, what is the basis for peace?

We must look to Lyndon LaRouche's revolutionary work defining the relation between, on the one side, the fundamental scientific principles of economic progress, and, on the other, national and international strategic policy. LaRouche's unique insight was perhaps most famously presented in his conception of the Strategic Defense Initiative (SDI) policy.

This is elaborated in succinct precision in the accompanying 1984 article, "The LaRouche Doctrine: Draft Memorandum of Agreement Between the United States and the U.S.S.R."

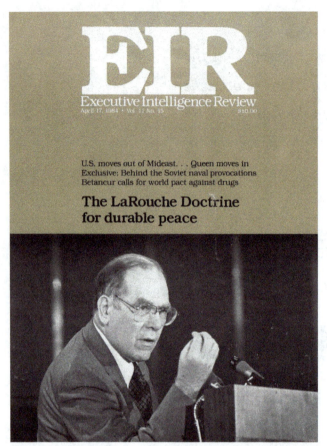

Cover of the 1984 issue of EIR featuring LaRouche's draft memorandum

As LaRouche defined there, his SDI was not merely a plan for defensive systems against nuclear missiles, it was a strategy for situating the necessary development of such systems in the larger context of a joint U.S.-Soviet scientific and technological driver program. This program focused on two objectives: generating high rates of capital goods exports to developing nations to end the legacy of colonial and neo-colonial suppression, and a Moon-Mars space colonization program to revive Apollo-era rates of high-technology growth.

Shared progress is the basis for peace. LaRouche's scientifically-derived global economic program for generating and implementing the fastest reasonable rates of technological advance throughout the entire world economy was—and is—the key, indispensable element required for a durable peace. Without that, any policy (even competent missile defense) can only bring limited, temporary benefits, at best.

In Article 5 of his draft memorandum, LaRouche addressed the specifics of the needed change in military doctrines, concluding,

If both powers and their allies were to deploy simultaneously the "strategic" and "tactical" defensive systems implicit in "new physical principles" [LaRouche's SDI program], the abrupt shift to overwhelming advantage of the defense would raise qualitatively the level of threshold for general warfare…. For a significant period of time, the defense would enjoy approximately an order of magnitude of superiority, man for man, over the offense, relative to the previous state of affairs. This would permit negotiation of a temporary solution to the imminence of a "Launch On Warning" posture by both powers: a solution which might persist for 10, 15 years, or longer. **The true solution must be found in the domain of politics and economics, and the further shaping of military relations between the powers must produce military policies by each coherent with the direction of development of the needed political and economic solutions.** [emphasis added]

We will let the reader study articles one through four in the accompanying draft memorandum for the scientific principles of economics on which a "political and economic" basis for peace can be secured.

Again, based on his assessment of the global situation from the standpoint of this scientific grounding, LaRouche defined two policy actions to be realized: high-technology capital goods export to developing nations and a Moon-Mars space colonization program.

Those objectives have not been fully realized, and remain the appropriate goals. Today, 35 years later, we are finally seeing progress on the first of these two key objectives, with China's Belt and Road Initiative bringing investment in infrastructure and industry throughout much of the developing world. While the current program may not completely conform to LaRouche's specifications, it is a significant start.

Regarding the second objective, space colonization, while actual progress has largely stagnated, the past three and a half decades have brought some interesting developments and considerations which further solidify the validity of the LaRouche Doctrine: the strategic importance of mankind's common destiny in space has only become clearer as we have realized how vulnerable life is on this small planet of ours.

The course of the evolutionary development of life on Earth has been fundamentally altered and shaped by catastrophic impacts of asteroids and comets, extreme climate change caused by changes in cosmic activity, and changes in our relation to our galaxy.

This poses a challenge to all mankind, one requiring the type of space colonization program proposed by LaRouche, one requiring strategic cooperation between the world's leading powers—i.e., one requiring the further development of LaRouche's original notions underlying his SDI policy.

The Strategic Defense of Earth

The more we have come to understand the Solar System and galaxy within which our small planet resides, the more we recognize the challenges and dangers inherent in our cosmic condition. From hypersonic impacts of colliding bodies, to various effects of high-energy cosmic radiation, to as-yet-unexplained cosmic forces, mankind's future wellbeing and survival depends upon a defense against these threats.

Here we will address three categories of cosmic challenges: the threat of asteroid and comet impacts, the effect of various forms of cosmic radiation, and the need for a better understanding of our galactic home.

There are many details and considerations involved in each of these categories, but here we will limit ourselves to a brief summary of each, and provide some indication of what broad steps could be taken to help address these challenges.

We will conclude with a reassessment of how these new considerations integrate with LaRouche's original conception of the SDI.

Asteroids, Comets, and the Impact Threat

Cosmic collisions have been an unavoidable aspect of existence in our Solar System since its initial creation. While somewhat rare relative to the timescale of an individual human lifespan, the tremendous speeds and energies involved can make these events truly catastrophic on anything from a local to a global scale.

Objects traveling in the Solar System, whether they are planets, asteroids, or comets, are typically moving at speeds in the range of 5 to 50 kilometers per second (20,000 to 200,000 km per hour). These speeds are hard to contemplate from the standpoint of the average person's day-to-day experience.

Imagine a rock the size of a city travelling faster than a bullet, or something the size of Mt. Everest hitting our planet at that speed. Depending upon the size of the object, the energy released from collisions at these speeds can far surpass any nuclear device mankind could conceive of presently (**Table 1**).

To ensure the defense of life on this planet, we must guarantee that mankind can be alerted to any potentially dangerous impacts with plenty of time to respond, and with the capabilities to change the trajectory of, or destroy, any threatening object. To better understand this challenge, these threats can be classified into three categories: asteroids, comets, and interactions from beyond our Solar System.

Near-Earth Asteroids

While the major repository of asteroids exists in the region between Mars and Jupiter, there are additional populations of asteroids throughout the Solar System, including in the more immediate neighborhood of Earth's orbit. These are generally called "near-Earth asteroids" or "near-Earth objects" (since some may be comets).

Though NASA has been able to find, catalogue, and track many of the largest near-Earth asteroids, there remain huge numbers of undiscovered smaller and medium-size near-Earth asteroids (likely in the millions). In the smaller size range, an impact could wipe out an entire city; in the medium-size range, an impact could devastate a continent.

Mankind needs better detection and tracking systems to find and track all potentially threatening asteroids, as well as the ability to defend the planet from the threat of an impact. The most effective defense is slightly altering an asteroid's orbit many years before a potential impact, but shorter term actions are needed.

Table 1

Events / Capabilities (Nuclear, Asteroid, Comet)	Energy Released (TNT Equivalent)
1945 Hiroshima Bombing Atomic fission bomb	0.014 Megatons (MT) (14 kilotons)
W-88 Thermonuclear Warhead Larger thermonuclear warhead of the Trident missile	0.475 MT (475 kilotons)
1908 Tunguska Event, ~30-50 Meter Object Believed to be the blast of either an asteroid or comet as it entered Earth's atmosphere (size is measured by diameter)	estimates range from 3-5 MT to as high as 30 MT
1961 Tsar Bomba Largest bomb ever tested (USSR; thermonuclear fusion bomb)	50 MT
140 Meter Asteroid Impact Lower size limit of potentially hazardous asteroids whose discovery by NASA is mandated by US Congress	100+ MT
Total Global Nuclear Arsenal Some estimates indicate about 30,000 nuclear warheads	roughly 5,000 MT (5 gigatons)
Chicxulub Impact (10+ kilometers) Comet or asteroid Impact event 65 million years ago associated with the extinction of the dinosaurs	96,000,000 MT (96,000 gigatons)

Comet and asteroid sizes are measured by their diameters. Values come from various sources.

Long-Period Comets

While the threat from asteroids mostly comes from objects within the inner Solar System, long-period comets pose a less frequent, but much more difficult challenge. In most cases, these objects are significantly larger than the near-Earth asteroid population, meaning an impact would likely be catastrophic for the entire globe.

They also orbit the Sun with extremely elliptical orbits, which can be as long as tens or hundreds of thousands of years—spending most of that time in the farthest depths of the Solar System (well beyond Pluto), where they are nearly impossible to detect with present systems.

This means a potentially threatening long-period comet would only be seen during its final approach (months, or possibly a couple years from impact)—not leaving enough time for mankind to mount an effective response to an object of the typical size of a long-period comet.

A robust survey and investigation of the outer Solar System is required, along with greatly improved capabilities for quickly traveling throughout the Solar System (e.g., as with fusion propulsion systems).

Interstellar Gravitational Interactions

Lastly, we should also identify the possibility of rogue planets passing through our Solar System. According to our present understanding of orbital mechanics and current theories of planetary system formation, it is expected that many planetary bodies are freely flying through interplanetary space (having been ejected from their home stellar systems through orbital interactions).

An object the size of a planet would not have to collide with anything in our Solar System to cause major problems. Its gravitational interactions alone could alter the Earth's orbit, creating extremely rapid and major climate change.

Defending the Earth from Impacts

As indicated above, there are two general aspects to addressing the threat of asteroid or comet impacts. The first is early detection. The United States, Russia, China, and leading nations in the EU and globally could bring together their most advanced technological and engineering resources to develop the best possible observation systems (and associated sensor technologies). Fundamentally, this technology overlaps with military and defense capabilities, so such

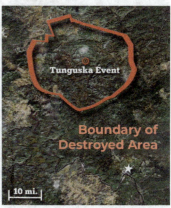

Washington, DC

San Francisco, CA

New York, NY

As an example of an impact from a "small" object, the 1908 Tunguska impact leveled 2,000 square meters of forest. The bottom images show the destruction area if a similar impact were to happen over Washington, DC, San Francisco, or New York.

cooperation would only succeed in the context of a new level of strategic trust.

The second consideration covers the active measures that could be taken to prevent an impact. There are many considerations involved here, but for the sake of brevity we will focus on the most fundamental point: expanding mankind's active and effective presence in the Solar System.

The more mankind develops cheaper and quicker ways to access space, advanced propulsion systems to travel the Solar System with ease, and industrial manufacturing on the Moon and in other locations, the greater capabilities mankind will have to be able to address any possible impact threat. The sharing, utilization, and further development of technologies and capabilities currently associated with military and defense activity will be critical—including technologies associated with, for example, hypersonic vehicles, thermonuclear explosive devices, and directed energy systems, along with the associated materials and manufacturing technologies.

Cosmic Radiation

Moving away from cosmic collisions between large objects, we have to examine the much smaller, but all-pervasive factor of cosmic radiation.

Of immediate interest (and potential concern) are categories of extremely fast moving, high-energy atomic particles coming from the Sun and the galactic environment more generally. These can have all kinds of short- and long-term effects on the Earth, from rapid electromagnetic pulses that can cripple large-scale power grids, to long-term climate changes that can alter the trajectory of life on this planet.

We need better monitoring, understanding, and, eventually, management of our Earth's cosmic radiation environment.

II. PRINCIPLES OF PHYSICAL ECONOMY

This artist's concept shows the Wide-field Infrared Survey Explorer, or WISE spacecraft, in its orbit around Earth. In 2013, the mission was brought out of hibernation to hunt for more asteroids and comets in a project called NEOWISE.

This starts with our Sun, which is, fundamentally, a massive thermonuclear fusion reactor—but do not assume it simply operates quietly and smoothly.

Solar Flares and Electromagnetic Pulses

On shorter timescales, the surface of the Sun is regularly graced with explosive events called solar flares. The frequency of these events changes with cycles of solar activity, and the intensity of each particular event varies over many orders of magnitude.

When a large solar flare erupts, it often ejects a massive, fast-moving cloud of plasma from the Sun's lower atmosphere. This is called a coronal mass ejection. When one of these large clouds of plasma is traveling in the direction of the Earth, it can generate major magnetic and electrical fluctuations and surges upon impacting the Earth's magnetic field.

For example, in 1859 a huge solar flare sent a massive coronal mass ejection directly toward the Earth. Upon impact with the Earth's magnetic field, it generated an amazing display of auroras and some of the largest geomagnetic field fluctuations ever recorded. The auroras were so intense they could be seen as far south as the Caribbean, and in the northeastern United States they were so bright a book could be read in the middle of the night.

However, the electrical surges generated by the magnetic fluctuations were not as beautiful. All across North America and Europe telegraph systems failed, some telegraph operators received electrical shocks, and sparks and fires were generated in certain systems. This was later named the Carrington Event (named after the astronomer who observed the initial solar flare).

While in 1859 the actual damage was minimal, with today's electrical transmission systems a similar event would be catastrophic for the higher latitude regions in the northern hemisphere (where the electrical surges are the strongest). Modern high-voltage electrical transmission systems are extremely vulnerable to these types of events, and if something similar to the Carrington Event happened today many key elements of the electrical transmission infrastructure would be destroyed. It is estimated that northern regions currently containing hundreds of millions of people could be left without power for months, or even years. With modern society's dependence upon electricity, this would be a humanitarian crisis on an unprecedented scale.

Efforts to harden and protect the electrical infrastructure on Earth will be critical to mitigating the effects of these events, and a better understanding of stars like our Sun will be important for forecasting future events and knowing what the Sun is truly capable of.

Climate Change

Longer and more sustained variations in solar activity have implications for the Earth's climate. Fundamentally, the Earth's climate system is largely controlled by cosmic forces.

While it is obvious that the heat and light from the Sun is its primary energy source, a growing body of evidence is now showing that galactic cosmic radiation plays a key role in controlling the behavior of water vapor and cloud formation—processes which have major impacts on the Earth's climate. On the longest timescales (over tens to hundreds of millions

Artist's illustration of events on the sun changing the conditions in Near-Earth space

of years), changes in the position of the Solar System through the galaxy has controlled the most extreme climate changes over the past billion years (through this galactic cosmic radiation effect). On shorter timescales, changes in the Earth's orbital characteristics have governed the shifts into and out of ice ages (currently on a roughly 100,000-year cycle).

While these changes are too long and gradual for our immediate attention, we do need to be concerned when we get down to timescales of hundreds of years. On these timescales the Sun cycles into and out of periods of prolonged weaker activity, called solar grand minima. The last major solar grand minimum corresponded with the Little Ice Age in Europe (and various records of a colder climate throughout the world).

While not as extreme as the typical depiction of a full-blown ice age, one of these mini-ice ages would have major effects on global agriculture and food production, and likely include shifts in weather patterns that would change drought and flooding patterns in various regions. This could affect the conditions of life for billions of people. For example, some studies indicate a new mini-ice age could shift the limiting boundaries for growing certain crops by hundreds of kilometers.

There is evidence that the Sun could currently be heading into a period of the type of prolonged weak activity that could cause a new mini-ice age, with some researchers warning this could happen by the middle of the current century.

This is more reason to put greater efforts into studying our Sun, and other Sun-like stars, to better understand and forecast the future cosmic conditions facing mankind.

Mankind's Response, and the Implications

Fundamentally, we need to understand the Earth's atmospheric (and climate and weather) systems from the standpoint of cosmic radiation. For example, the Earth's atmosphere is permeated by high-energy galactic cosmic radiation, which largely controls the ionization conditions of the atmosphere. This, in turn, has impacts on everything from cloud formation, to the behavior of water vapor, to the global electric circuit, to atmospheric temperature, and the related effects on weather and climate.

New generations of Earth-observing systems need to be developed to provide a full mapping of all of these conditions, and their changes in real time.

These measurements must stretch from the surface of the Earth through the atmosphere, through the ionosphere, and into all the substructures within the Earth's magnetic field.

These new readings must be compared with readings of interplanetary space stretching from the Sun and solar activity, on the one side, all the way out toward the edge of the Solar System, on the other.

Such an improved detailed mapping of all such processes, along with a better understanding of the causal activity behind them, will provide the basis for new revolutionary activities of mankind in the areas of earthquake and volcanic eruption forecasting and even weather control.

Earthquake and Volcano Forecasting

It has been well demonstrated that major earthquakes and volcanic eruptions are almost always preceded by various forms of precursor signals within the Earth's atmospheric and ionospheric systems. With a fuller understanding of the general activity of these systems a more precise identification of the specific signals preceding earthquakes or volcanic eruptions can become the basis for early warning systems to defend populations from the effects of these devastating events.

An international effort should bring leading scientists together and provide them with the monitoring systems needed for real-time earthquake forecasting. Any and all existing military or defense-related capabilities or technologies that can aid in providing the required monitoring capabilities must be brought forward and assessed.

Weather Control

As scientist have begun to understand the role of galactic cosmic radiation in controlling certain aspects of the atmospheric water vapor system, it has become clear to a handful of pioneering researchers that mankind himself can mimic some of these conditions using low-energy ground-based electrical systems. With this level of control, basic conditions affecting precipitation can be managed, and rainfall can either be induced where it is needed or prevented where it is undesired. With further development, basic weather systems, and perhaps major weather events such as hurricanes and cyclones can be managed and mitigated.

The effective implementation of weather control systems will also require new levels of strategic trust and agreement among nations globally. Any and all military-related investigations into weather management and control must be brought forward for transparent scientific investigation and assessment. An appropriate form of international consultation and oversight will be required to bring such an amazing revolutionary potential into its most fair and effective realization.

Our Galactic Home

For our third and final broad category pertaining to the Strategic Defense of Earth, we will look to the frontier questions about our galactic home.

A handful of groundbreaking studies have indicated that changes in the earth's relation to our galaxy have profound implications here on Earth. It was mentioned above that such changes control the most extreme ranges of climate change over the past billion years, but there is also evidence that these changes could somehow play a major role in the evolutionary development of life, and perhaps even certain forms of geophysical activity.

At the same time, fundamental questions about the basic organization and dynamics of our own galaxy point the way to possible revolutions in our basic scientific understanding of the universe—perhaps necessitating discoveries as revolutionary as those generated by Einstein, Planck, and their collaborators, as they led a complete transformation of our basic conceptions of space, time, energy, and matter with relativity and the beginnings of quantum theory.

Galactic Cycles and Earth Changes

Our Solar System's travels through our galaxy brings it into galactic environments and climates which vary dramatically. From the dense regions of activity within our galaxy's spiral arms, to calmer regions in between; from giant molecular clouds, to regions of intense new star formation, to territories populated by old ancient stars; from the populated

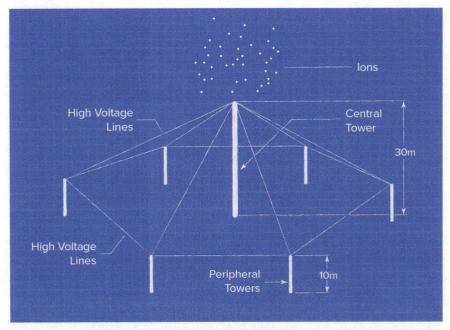

A schematic of the basic atmospheric ionization systems developed in Russia, and successfully utilized for weather modification in Mexico, Israel, and other locations.

regions in the middle of our galactic disk, to the diffuse regions above and below.

Regions within our galaxy defined by a climate of intense galactic cosmic radiation lead to higher rates of cloud formation within the Earth's atmosphere, and a significantly colder climate. In galactic environments characterized by lower densities of galactic cosmic radiation the Earth's climate system warms to the point where glaciation and ice caps simply do not exist anywhere on the planet.

While pioneering scientists have developed a basic grasp of the underlying physics governing these galaxy-driven climate changes on Earth, there are other processes on Earth which also appear to correspond to changes in our galactic relation. This includes variations in the rate of evolutionary development of life on Earth over the past half-billion years, and even some indications that geophysical activity somehow might be responding to changes in our galactic relation.

These correlations raise more questions than they provide answers. Regarding life and evolution, there are many studies showing that living systems are intimately connected with and respond to various forms of cosmic influences and radiation effects, although as a field of study it is still little understood.

Starting from this galactic perspective could provide a new basis for our basic questions about life in the universe. This, in turn, could have profound effects on our understanding of health and medicine.

Regarding planetary activity, we are at the very beginning of a new era of study investigating how stellar and planetary systems respond to and are governed by their galaxy. Much work can be done within our own Solar System, studying the records left behind on other planetary bodies, and smaller objects such as asteroids. Such considerations could lead to new fields of comparative interplanetary studies, looking for evidence of periods of simultaneous activity and changes on multiple planetary bodies corresponding to the same external galactic influences.

Galaxy Map and Dynamics

At the same time that we pursue a much better understanding of our own Solar System from the standpoint of its galactic relation, we must also look out to the galactic environment itself. As soon as we go to galactic scales, some of our most basic and trusted scientific theories quickly break down.

Some of these questions are already subject to extensive scientific investigations, as with the anomalous stellar motions theorized to be caused by some form of mysterious so-called dark matter, or with the evidence for ultra-dense phenomena referred to as so-called black holes—seemingly defining a regime of physics where our current theories literally break down.

Improved mappings of our galactic system, and the motions of its billions of stars, can provide an indispensible observational framework to better investigate these frontier questions. We can also improve our basic understanding of our own Solar System's motion within the galaxy itself.

New domains of questions will ultimately be confronted, as mankind comes up against evidence forcing new considerations of how galactic systems, and their stellar planetary systems within them, are created, evolve, and develop in an inherently anti-entropic universe.

The LaRouche Doctrine Revisited

We have covered a broad range of subjects, ranging from the very large of galactic systems in their entirety, to the very small of the microphysics of cosmic radiation; from the challenges posed by hypervelocity impacts, to the threats coming from explosive solar activity. What unifies all these areas?

Quite simply, these are the cosmic conditions confronted by all mankind. The very nature of the reality of this existence for all inhabitants of this planet defines these areas as the next frontiers to be addressed by the occupants of Earth.

The Strategic Defense of Earth encompasses the challenges that we are naturally facing together, collectively as a species.

In the context of the New Paradigm, with the associated requirements of a new security architecture, these become the forefront strategic challenges for the military and defense-related capabilities of nations. The technologies currently being developed for military and strategic dominance over supposedly rival nations, must now be refocused for the shared and common defense of all nations against these external cosmic threats.

We must come back to LaRouche's unique and indispensable contribution to this discussion. While aspects of peace are secured by the active defense against such catastrophic threats, the only long-term guaranteed basis for peace is the continual progress, growth, and development of mankind as a whole—progress which can be scientifically defined and understood by the work of Mr. LaRouche.

It is here that we returned to the harmonious convergence between, on the one hand, the requirements for the defense of Earth from cosmic threats, and, on the other, the critical role of space colonization and development—providing that absolutely necessary and required progress which is the inherent right of mankind.

As Mr. LaRouche stated in his 1984 draft memorandum:

> If this connection between military expenditures and civilian benefits is adequately realized, the return to society for such military expenditures will be many times the amount of the military expenditure. Two conditions must be fulfilled. First, it must be policy that new such technologies developed in the military area be rapidly introduced into the civilian area. Second, the rate at which economies can assimilate new technologies is limited by the relative scale of and rate of capital turnover within the capital-goods sector of production, most emphatically within the machine-tool-grade sub-sector of capital-goods production.
>
> Under these conditions, provided that all nations share in development of the frontiers of scientific research, in laboratories, and in educational institutions, all nations will be made capable of assimilating efficiently the technological by-product benefits of the military expenditures on systems derived from application of "new physical principles." To lend force to this policy, the powers agree to establish new institutions of cooperation between themselves and oth-

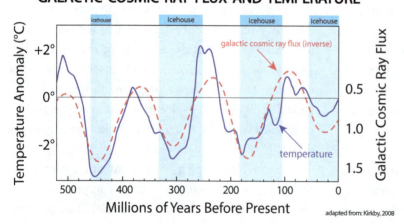

Comparison of changes in galactic cosmic radiation reaching the Earth and extreme climate change, as the Solar System traveled around the Galaxy over the past half-billion years.

Artist's depiction of the beginnings of a lunar base

er nations in development of these new areas of scientific breakthrough for application to exploration of space. To this purpose, the powers agree to establish at the earliest possible time institutions for cooperation in scientific exploration of space, and to also co-sponsor treaty-agreements protecting national and multinational programs for colonization of the Moon and Mars.

The powers jointly agree upon the adoption of two tasks as the common interest of mankind, as well as the specific interest of each of the two powers: 1) The establishment of full economic equity respecting the conditions of individual life in all nations of this planet during a period of not more than 50 years; 2) Man's exploration and colonization of nearby space as the continuing common objective and interest of mankind during and beyond the completion of the first task. The adoption of these two working-goals as the common task and respective interest in common of the two powers and other cooperating nations, constitutes the central point of reference for erosion of the potential political and economic causes of warfare between the powers.

Today, the core principles of LaRouche's program are as valid as they were then. Beyond recognizing the changes in the geopolitical landscape associated with the break-up of the Soviet Union and the emergence of the Belt and Road Initiative, the only significant addition that we have provided here are the considerations associated with the Strategic Defense of Earth from the types of threats and challenges defined above. These considerations completely integrate with the perspective defined by Mr. LaRouche more than 30 years ago.

Now, in the context of the New Paradigm, it is finally time that the full efforts of strategic capabilities of leading nations be brought together in a harmonious pursuit of their application to—and further development for—the defense and the progress of all mankind, as that destiny lies before us in the Solar System which is to be the new home and frontier for the immediate generations to come.

THE LAROUCHE DOCTRINE

Draft Memorandum of Agreement Between the United States and the U.S.S.R.

by Lyndon H. LaRouche, Jr., March 30, 1984

A critical part of the World Land-Bridge and the New Paradigm will be a new security architecture, focused on securing peace and stability globally. As background to the present discussion, we provide a reprinting of the following proposed legislation written by then-presidential candidate Lyndon LaRouche on March 30, 1984.

Article 1
General Conditions for Peace

The political foundation for durable peace must be: a) The unconditional sovereignty of each and all nation-states, and b) Cooperation among sovereign nation-states to the effect of promoting unlimited opportunities to participate in the benefits of technological progress, to the mutual benefit of each and all.

The most crucial feature of present implementation of such a policy of durable peace is a profound change in the monetary, economic, and political relations between the dominant powers and those relatively subordinated nations often classed as "developing nations." Unless the inequities lingering in the aftermath of modern colonialism are progressively remedied, there can be no durable peace on this planet.

Insofar as the United States and Soviet Union acknowledge the progress of the productive powers of labor throughout the planet to be in the vital strategic interests of each and both, the two powers are bound to that degree and in that way by a common interest. This is the kernel of the political and economic policies of practice indispensable to the fostering of durable peace between those two powers.

Article 2
Concrete Technological Policy

The term, technology, is to be understood in the terms of its original meaning, as supplied by Gottfried Leibniz, as the French translation of this same term, polytechnique, was understood by the Ecole Polytechnique under the leadership of Lazare Carnot and Gaspard Monge, and as the successive discoveries of Carl F. Gauss, Lejeune Dirichlet, and Bernhard Riemann provide an improved comprehension of the mathematical (geometrical) comprehension of Leibniz's original definition of "technology."

Technology, so defined, is understood to be the indispensable means not only for increasing the potential relative population-density of societies, but as also indispensable to maintaining even any present level of population potential. Potential relative population-density is measured in persons per square kilometer. The increase in potential relative population-density requires both an increase in usable energy supplies of a society, per capita, and also an increase of the energy-flux density of primary energy supplies, and in the form of application of such energy to various modes of production.

The foundation of development of productive powers of labor in agriculture (broadly defined) and industry (also broadly defined), is the development and maintenance of such elements of basic economic infrastructure as fresh-water management, transportation systems, energy production and distribution, general improvement of the habitability of land-areas, and urban industrial infrastructure of both industries and populations' daily life.

Next, in sequence, is the development of production of raw materials by agriculture and mining-refining. All other physical-goods production depends upon the scale of output and productive powers of labor in these two categories of raw-materials production. Most essential, economically, socially, and politically, is the increase of agricultural yields per hectare and per capita, effected through technological progress in both infrastructure improvement and in modes of production employed.

Since developments during the Fifteenth Century in Europe, all advances in technology, all advances in the productive powers of labor have been based on the development of the machine, or on the design of processes analogous to the functions of the heat-powered machine in terms of other sub-species of physical principles, such as chemistry, biology, the development of electrical energy supplies, and the emerging role of productive processes based on principles of plasma physics. "Technology," as com-

Lyndon LaRouche with Helga Zepp-LaRouche, touring the Seabrook Nuclear Plant in New Hampshire in 1979

prehended from the combined standpoints of Gauss, Dirichlet, and Riemann, treats each of these varieties of production-methods as subsumed by a common set of principles.

In all aspects of production excepting agriculture, and in respect to industrial goods required by agricultural production, advances in technology are transmitted into the productive process as a whole through the incorporation of improved technologies in capital goods, most emphatically capital goods of the machine-tool or analogous classifications. Therefore, the only means by which a national economy can sustain significant rates of technological progress, is by placing emphasis upon the capital-goods sector of production, and maintaining sufficiently high rates of turnover in that sector to foster high rates of technological innovation in the goods produced.

It follows that general increase of the productive powers of labor requires relatively high rates of investment of technologically progressive forms of such capital goods per capita in all spheres of production.

Therefore, the general advancement of the productive powers of labor in all sovereign states, most emphatically so-called developing nations, requires global emphasis on: a) increasing globally the percentiles of the labor force employed in scientific research and related functions of research and development: a goal of 5% of the world's labor force so employed is recommended as a near- to medium-term goal; b) increasing the absolute and relative scales of capital-goods production and also the rate of turnover in capital-goods production; and c) combining these two factors to accelerate technological progress in capital-goods outputs.

Therefore, high rates of export of such capital-goods output to meet the needs of developing nations are indispensable for the general development of so-called developing nations: Our common goal, and our common interest, is promoting both the general welfare and promoting preconditions of durable peace between our two powers.

The foreseeable direction of advances in technology over the span of the coming 50 years or longer is already clear in categorical terms of reference. There are clearly three general categories of scientific and technological progress on which humanity must rely into the period to come: a) very high energy-flux density, controlled thermonuclear plasmas, typified by the development of "commercial" fusion-energy production as the emerging, principal source of energy supplies for mankind, both on Earth and in exploration and colonization of nearby space; b) the application of energy supplies in the modes of coherent, directed-energy radiation, illustrated by the case of high-powered laser and so-called particle-beam modes; and c) new directions in biology, for which microbiotechnology is but a subordinated, but important aspect.

These three areas of technological breakthroughs define the role of powered, extended interplanetary and related forms of space travel, and of preconditions for life in synthetic, Earth-simulated environments of growing populations in colonies on the Moon, Mars, and elsewhere during the course of the coming 50 years.

Scientific cooperation in the development of these breakthroughs, and in respect to their applications to production and to exploration of nearby space, is an area in which the two powers must promote efficient cooperation between themselves, and with other sovereign states.

Article 3
Economic Policies

By supplying increased amounts of high-technology capital goods to developing nations, the exporting economies foster increased rates of turnover in their own most advanced capital-goods sectors of production. As a by-product of such increased rates of turnover in that sub-sector of the exporting nation's production, the rate of improvement of technology in such categories of goods is increased, with great benefits to the internal economy of the exporting nation. Thus, even were the exporting nation to take no profit on such exports, the promotion of higher rates of capital turnover in the capital-goods sector of that exporting nation would increase the productive powers of labor in the exporting nation's economy as a whole, thus supplying great benefit to the exporting nation's economy in that way.

The importer of such advanced capital goods increases the productive powers of labor in the economy of the importing nation. This enables the importing nation to produce its goods at a lower average social cost, and enables it to provide better-quality and cheaper goods as goods of payment to the nations exporting capital goods.

Not only are the causes of simple humanity and general peace served by such policies of practice; the arrangement is equally beneficial to exporting and importing nations. Only a profound ignorance of true interests of nations could desire any contrary policy of practice respecting "technology transfer."

Moreover, the general rate of advancement of the productive powers of labor is most efficiently promoted by no other policy of practice.

Article 4
International Monetary Policy

The only equitable and workable relations in financing of world trade among sovereign states with different economic and social systems is a system of credit based on fixed parities of national currencies, parities fixed by aid of a gold-reserve monetary order among states.

To prevent a gold-reserve system of fixed parities from becoming subject to disabling inflationary spirals, it is necessary to limit the extension of credit within the monetary system to "hard-commodity" categories of lending for import and export of physical goods. If such world trade emphasizes high proportions of efficiently employed advanced-technology capital-goods, the increase of productivity fostered by such trade has a secularly deflationary impact on prices.

In the present situation, in which world trade has been collapsing under pressures caused by pyramiding of refinanced external and domestic indebtedness of national economies, it is necessary to reorganize the present indebtedness, to the effect that low interest rates prevail in the anti-inflationary environment of a gold-reserve system, and that the schedule of repayments of existing, outstanding indebtedness does not consume more than 20% of the export earnings of any of these nations.

The general benefit of such monetary reforms is the creation, immediately, of greatly increased markets for trade in high-technology capital goods.

Article 5
Military Doctrines

Since the rupture of the wartime alliance between the two powers, U.S. military policy toward the Soviet Union has passed through two phases. The first, from the close of the war until a point beyond the death of Joseph Stalin, was preparation for the contingency of what was sometimes named "preventive nuclear war." The second, emerging over the period from the death of Stalin into the early period of the administration of President John F. Kennedy, was based on the doctrines of Nuclear Deterrence and Flexible Response as those doctrines were described in the keynote address by Dr. Leo Szilard at the second Pugwash Conference assembled in Quebec during 1958.

Until President Ronald Reagan's March 23, 1983 announcement of a new U.S. strategic doctrine, which overthrew the Nuclear Deterrence doctrine, from the time of the Kennedy administration, U.S. military doctrine toward the Soviet Union was more or less exactly that outlined by Szilard's keynote address at the second Pugwash Conference, of 1958. During the same interval, military negotiations between the Soviet Union and the U.S.A. have been premised on the assumption of continued U.S.A. adherence to the Nuclear Deterrence and Flexible Response doctrines.

From approximately 1963 until approximately 1977, it might have appeared, as it appeared to many, that the doctrines of Nuclear Deterrence and Flexible Response had succeeded in preserving a state of restive peace, something called "détente," between the two powers. This appearance was deceptive; during the period 1977-83, there was an accelerating deterioration in the military relationships between the two powers.

From the side of the United States, the impending breakdown of "détente" was signaled by the 1974 announcement of the so-called Schlesinger Doctrine. In fact, the Schlesinger Doctrine's perspective of "limited nuclear warfare" between the powers, or their so-called surrogates, was neither a violation of the Pugwash Doctrine, nor any innovation within that doctrine. Szilard, in outlining the doctrine in 1958, had already specified that the doctrine required provision for "limited nuclear warfare," as well as "local warfare" of a colonial-warfare variety.

The Schlesinger Doctrine's appearance was an embedded feature of Nuclear Deterrence and Flexible Response from the outset. If the Nuclear Deterrence doctrine were continued, it was already evident from the time of Szilard's 1958 address, "limited nuclear war" in the European theater was more or less an inevitable outcome.

Beginning shortly after the inauguration of President Jimmy Carter, the deterioration of the military situation accelerated. The Soviet Union's response was typified by the deployment of the SS-20 missiles in Europe, and the 1979 NATO response, prompted by Henry A. Kissinger, to deploy Pershing II and land-based cruise missiles as weapons to be deployed in an effort to induce the Soviet Union to eliminate the SS-20s deployment: the so-called double-track arms negotiations tactic.

As an arms-negotiation tactic, Kissinger's double-track gambit proved substantially less than worthless. Over the interval 1981-83, continuation of the Nuclear Deterrence/Flexible Response doctrine impelled both powers to the verge of the military postures of "Launch Under Attack" and the more ominous posture of "Launch On Warning."

In response to this direction of developments, the U.S. public figure Lyndon H. LaRouche, Jr. proposed that both powers develop, deploy, and agree to develop and deploy "strategic" defensive, anti-ballistic-missile defense based on "new physical principles." This proposal was issued publicly by LaRouche beginning February 1982; he proposed to U.S.A., Western European, and Soviet representatives that the development and deployment of such strategic defensive systems be adopted policy, as a means for escaping from the "logic" of Nuclear Deterrence.

Lyndon LaRouche and Ronald Reagan at candidates' debate in Concord, New Hampshire during the 1980 Presidential Campaign

During a period of not later than the 1962 appearance of Marshal V.D. Sokolovsky's Military Strategy, leading Soviet circles had recognized the dangerous fallacies of Nuclear Deterrence/Flexible Response doctrine from a military vantage-point, although no comparable assessment appeared as part of U.S.A. military doctrine until President Reagan's announcement of March 23, 1983.

In that sense, LaRouche's proposed strategic doctrine, as first announced publicly in February 1982, was congruent with the analysis first publicly offered by Marshal Sokolovsky in 1962. LaRouche's, and later, Dr. Edward Teller's and President Reagan's proposal of "Mutually Assured Survival," implicitly put both powers on the footing of identical military doctrines: LaRouche's doctrine, and President Reagan's, are properly judged to be U.S. versions of the Sokolovsky doctrine.

The leading objections raised, first, against LaRouche's proposal, and, later, the similar proposals of Dr. Teller and President Reagan, centered upon the observation that abandonment of Nuclear Deterrence/Flexible Response implied a new technological arms race centered around the development of layered ballistic missile defense. Examining the fallacy of that objection points toward the necessary changes in the military policy governing relevant negotiations between the two powers.

As key architects of Nuclear Deterrence, notably Bertrand Russell and Leo Szilard, emphasized most strongly during the 1950s and later, their purpose in proposing Nuclear Deterrence was to further Russell's feudalistic, utopian dream of creating an agency of world-government which would enjoy a monopoly of use and possession of means of warfare, including a monopoly of nuclear arsenals. Given the reality of Soviet development of nuclear arsenals, Russell et al. abandoned their earlier policy of "preventive nuclear warfare." They proposed to divide the world, at least temporarily, between what were proposed to be in effect, two world empires, an eastern and western division of the world between two "empires."

Nuclear Deterrence and Flexible Response were presented by Russell et al. as means for making general thermonuclear warfare between the two principal powers "unthinkable." The ability of either power to assure the annihilation of the other was argued to represent physical means for ensuring the preservation of the "two-empire" system. Flexible Response was added, to provide means for military adjustments, including local, and limited-nuclear warfare, without risking the escalation of such wars to general thermonuclear warfare.

History shows that such schemes are inherently unworkable. Exemplary is the case of the plan to divide the Persian Empire into two parts, Eastern and Western Divisions, during the Fourth Century B.C. Also exemplary is the effort of the Venice-centered European "black nobility" to orchestrate balance of power among the Ottoman, Austro-Hungarian, Russian, and German empires, during the interval 1453-1914 A.D. The very logic of such attempted arrangements ensures wars leading to the destruction of one or all of the contending powers. Such is proving to be the case for the doctrines of Nuclear Deterrence and Flexible Response, respecting the deteriorating situation between the Atlantic and Warsaw Pact alliances.

It is the nature of competently elaborated military capabilities of major powers that those capabilities must be developed and prepared to ensure the survival and victory of the power in case of war with the opposing power. At the point that continuation of the existing form of peace is perceived to ensure the destruction of one of the powers, that power must either launch war or must accept the destruction of the nation which it represents. Marshal Sokolovsky and his Soviet co-thinkers were obviously correct on this point, and so was LaRouche.

Lyndon LaRouche speaking at a Directed Energy Beam Weapons Defense Technologies conference in Washington, DC, April 13, 1983

The Nuclear Deterrence and Flexible Response doctrines were worse than merely incompetent. Had the threat of general warfare been perceived during the period beginning 1961-63, as Nuclear Deterrence seemed temporarily to remove that possibility, the powers would have been impelled to seek political and economic alternatives to such threats of general warfare. Instead, the political and economic impulses leading in the direction of warfare were permitted to aggregate. The political and economic impulses toward warfare were offset by adjustments in Nuclear Deterrence postures: including adjustments under the titles of détente generally, and arms-control agreements more narrowly. The unresolved political and economic issues seized upon the embedded logic of Nuclear Deterrence, to drive the powers to the verge of thermonuclear, general warfare.

The assumption prevailed, that as long as political and economic impulses toward general warfare did not surpass the "threshold" of Nuclear Deterrence, that such impulses toward war could be confidently maintained in existence, since neither power, it was assumed, would "dare to resort to the unthinkable" remedy of general thermonuclear warfare. So, under instruction of such deluded confidence in Nuclear Deterrence, the powers marched blindly toward the brink of general thermonuclear warfare.

If both powers and their allies were to deploy simultaneously the "strategic" and "tactical" defensive systems implicit in "new physical principles," the abrupt shift to overwhelming advantage of the defense would raise qualitatively the level of threshold for general warfare. This would be the case if defensive systems based on such "new physical principles" effectively deployed into the potential battlefield of Europe, as well as in the form of "strategic" defensive systems. For a significant period of time, the defense would enjoy approximately an order of magnitude of superiority, man for man, over the offense, relative to the previous state of affairs.

This would permit negotiation of a temporary solution to the imminence of a "Launch On Warning" posture by both powers: a solution which might persist for 10, 15 years, or longer. The true solution must be found in the domain of politics and economics, and the further shaping of military relations between the powers must produce military policies by each coherent with the direction of development of the needed political and economic solutions.

Articles 1-4 of this memorandum stipulate the leading, principled features of the required political and economic solutions. If each of the powers adheres to the republican military traditions exemplified by the work of Lazare Carnot and the Stein-Hardenberg reforms in Prussia, and defines its national interests according to the provisions of Articles 1-4, there need be no expectation of warfare between the powers: as warfare is the "continuation of politics by other means."

On the part of the United States of America, the government is committed to avoiding all colonial, imperial, or kindred endeavors in foreign policy, and to establish, instead, a growing community of principle among fully sovereign nation-states of this planet. This shall become a community of principle coherent with the policies of the articles of this draft memorandum. If any force should endeavor to destroy that community of principle, or any member of that community of sovereign nations, the United States will be prepared to defend that community and its members by means of warfare, should other means prove insufficient. With respect to the Soviet Union, the government of the United States offers the Soviet Union cooperation with itself in service of these principles, and desires that the Soviet Union might enter fully into participation within that community of principle.

Article 6
Weapons Policies of the Powers

The distinguishing kernel of most of the defensive weapons systems classed under the title of "new physical principles" is the development of applications of both accomplished and imminent breakthroughs in two of the three general areas of scientific progress to dominate the coming 50 years: controlled, high-energy plasmas, and directed-energy applications. The development of these military applications signifies an expansion of the varieties of research and development facilities and staffs occupied with such new technologies. The deployment of weapons systems of this class signifies development of production facilities oriented to these technologies.

The impact of this upon the economies is suggested by the reasonable estimate, that the U.S.A., Western Europe, Japan, and the nations of the Warsaw Pact, will spend aggregately about 1983 $3 trillion on development of "strategic" and "tactical" systems of this class by approximately the close of the present century, using U.S.A. costs as a standard of estimate. Although this amount is only a large ration of present levels of military expenditures by the same aggregation of states, to concentrate so large a ration of those military allotments upon the frontiers of present science and technology must have a very great impact upon the economies.

The best standard of comparison for estimating the impact of this upon the economies affected is the case of the impact of NASA research and development upon the U.S.A. economy, notably NASA's phase of intense development through 1966. The impact of the indicated program of high-technology military expenditures would be four to ten times as great as the NASA expenditure of that indicated period.

The impact of these technologies upon the civilian economies is suggested by the fact that the "second generation" of "commercial" fusion power might provide us with energy-flux densities in the order of as much as a half-million kilowatts per square meter, in contrast to between 40,000 and 70,000 kilowatts per square meter with best generating modes today. The industrial applications of high-powered lasers, including the important class of "tunable" such lasers, mean leaps in productive powers of labor, reasonably estimated to be as much as a twofold or threefold increase in productivity of U.S. operatives by the year 2000 A.D.

If this connection between military expenditures and civilian benefits is adequately realized, the return to society for such military expenditures will be many times the amount of the military expenditure.

Two conditions must be fulfilled.

First, it must be policy that new such technologies developed in the military area be rapidly introduced into the civilian area.

Second, the rate at which economies can assimilate new technologies is limited by the relative scale of and rate of capital turnover within the capital-goods sector of production, most emphatically within the machine-tool-grade sub-sector of capital-goods production.

The second of these conditions can not be adequately fulfilled unless the trend toward "post-industrial society," of the past 18 years, is sharply reversed. Although such an urgent change in policy of practice is chiefly a matter of domestic policy of sovereign nation-states, no sovereign nation-state can adequately pursue the needed policy-changes without very significant degrees of international cooperation.

To accomplish such a shift within sovereign states' economies, priorities must be set accordingly for investment allocations, in priorities for flows of credit, in relative costs of borrowing by priority categories of investment and employment, and in relative rates of taxation. Similar measures are required in international lending, including relative amounts available for financing international trade, and related extension of credit for investments of importing nations.

It should be general policy, that the goal for em-

Lyndon LaRouche and Helga Zepp-LaRouche visit NASA's Goddard Space Center in Greenbelt, Maryland, March 27, 1981

ployment of operatives in agriculture, mining and refining, industrial production of physical goods, and as operatives developing and maintaining basic economic infrastructure ought to be not less than 50% of the total labor force of nations, and that employment for science and for research and development ought to be not less than 5% of the total labor force of nations. It should be general policy that the percentile of the total labor force employed as operatives in production of consumer goods ought not to increase, but that the increase in supply of consumer goods per capita should be fostered by high rates of capital investment per operative in such categories of production. In this way, the percentile of the operatives employed in capital-goods production should rise—assuming that not less than 50% of the labor forces are employed as operatives.

Under these conditions, provided that all nations share in development of the frontiers of scientific research, in laboratories, and in educational institutions, all nations will be made capable of assimilating efficiently the technological by-product benefits of the military expenditures on systems derived from application of "new physical principles."

To lend force to this policy, the powers agree to establish new institutions of cooperation between themselves and other nations in development of these new areas of scientific breakthrough for application to exploration of space.

To this purpose, the powers agree to establish at the earliest possible time institutions for cooperation in scientific exploration of space, and to also co-sponsor treaty-agreements protecting national and multinational programs for colonization of the Moon and Mars.

At some early time, the powers shall enter into deliberations, selecting dates for initial manned colonization of the Moon and Mars, and the establishment of international space stations on the Moon and in the orbits of Moon and Mars, stations to be maintained by and in the common interest and use of space parties of all nations.

The powers jointly agree upon the adoption of two tasks as the common interest of mankind, as well as the specific interest of each of the two powers: 1) The establishment of full economic equity respecting the conditions of individual life in all nations of this planet during a period of not more than 50 years; 2) Man's exploration and colonization of nearby space as the continuing common objective and interest of mankind during and beyond the completion of the first task. The adoption of these two working-goals as the common task and respective interest in common of the two powers and other cooperating nations, constitutes the central point of reference for erosion of the potential political and economic causes of warfare between the powers.

Article 7
Arms Negotiations Policy

The pre-existing arms-control treaties and related agreements between the two powers are to be superseded by new agreements consistent with the preceding Articles of this draft memorandum.

The existing and future arsenals of so-called "strategic" thermonuclear weapons are to be destroyed as rapidly as deployment of "strategic" defensive weapons systems renders such thermonuclear weapons technologically obsolete as weapons for general assault for general warfare.

On condition that such agreements sought progress as presently anticipated, the powers shall act first to withdraw all thermonuclear weapons in excess of some specific kilotonnage from territories of nations other than their own.

No arms agreement shall be sought whose verifiable adherence requires on-site inspection by personnel of a foreign nation. Rather, both powers and other nations shall be encouraged to deploy such methods of defense by aid of weapons-systems based on new physical principles, that any "cheating" in deploying weapons of assault is virtually nullified by capabilities of the defense.

Progress in implementing the agreements on policy identified in this draft memorandum shall be the precondition for negotiating additional agreements as may be deemed desirable.

III. PROGRESS REPORTS

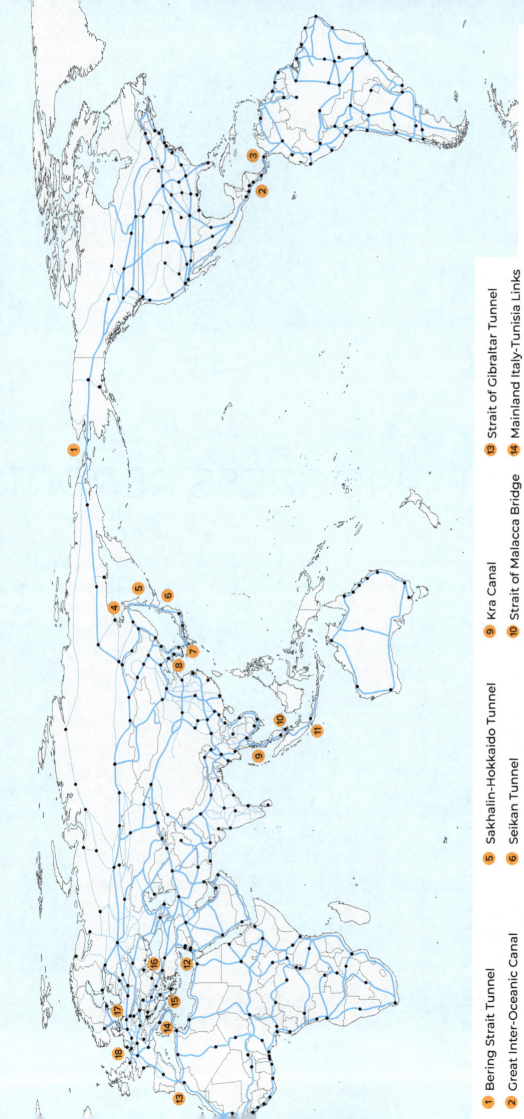

SIX DEVELOPMENT CORRIDORS
of the Silk Road Economic Belt

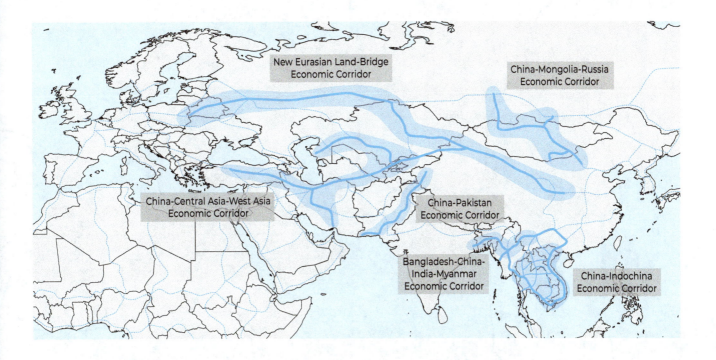

The overland system of the Belt and Road Initiative, the Silk Road Economic Belt, first announced by Xi Jinping in Kazakhstan in September 2013, has been subsequently filled out as a set of six fundamental "Development Corridors" across Eurasia. The map shows these corridors, representing road and rail connectivity between East Asia, Southeast Asia, Central Asia, South Asia, Southwest Asia, Eastern Europe, and Western Europe. As implied by the name, the corridors are not simply means of travelling or shipping goods from one place to another, but are more importantly aimed at opening up the entire continent—and especially the more impoverished landlocked regions—to economic and social development. In addition to transportation routes, developing a modern manufacturing base requires the provision of adequate power, water, educational facilities, health facilities, and access to cultural institutions in the arts, as well as athletic and entertainment facilities.

Although the six development corridors are all in Eurasia, the same concept governs the Silk Road projects in Africa and Ibero-America. The Chinese saying, "If you want to be rich, first build a road," is the guiding principle to the Chinese intention to extend their incredible success in nearly eliminating poverty within China to the entire world—although a road is now more often than not accompanied by a high-speed rail line.

Each of the corridors is discussed in the appropriate section of this report.

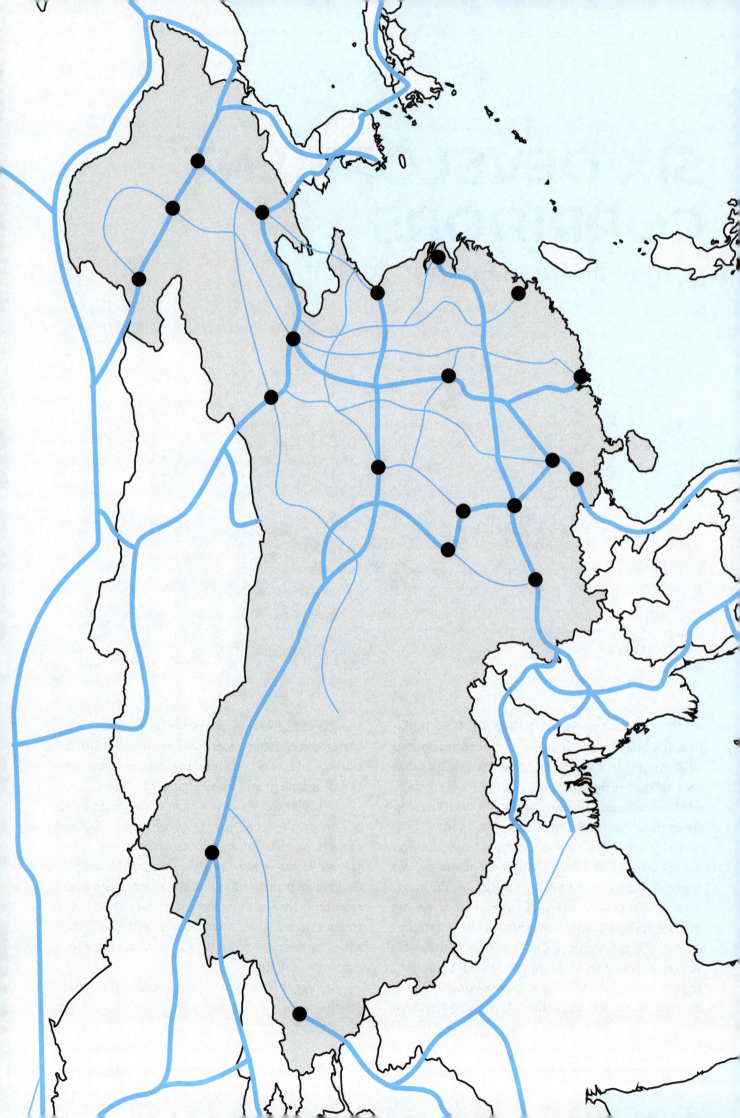

"In the first five years since the ... announcement by President Xi Jinping of the Belt and Road Initiative there have been magnificent achievements within China, and developments across Eurasia, Africa, and Central and South America. At the China Communist Party 19th Congress in October 2017, [Xi] presented his concept of a 'community of shared future for humanity.' China is well on the way."

Development for a Shared Future for Humanity
CHINA

In the first five years since the September 2013 announcement by President Xi Jinping of the One Belt-One Road initiative, and the Maritime Silk Road—now commonly known as the Belt and Road Initiative (BRI)—there have been magnificent achievements within China, and developments across Eurasia, Africa, and Central and South America. At the China Communist Party (CPC) 19th Congress in October 2017, President Xi Jinping put this progress in the context of looking ahead to 2050 and beyond, and defining still more goals for China, and for mankind. He presented his concept of a "community of shared future for humanity." China is well on the way.

The leading accomplishments are described below, by sector—rail and connectivity, water systems, innovation in industry and agriculture, energy, regional development—including new cities, achievements in space, and by 2020, the elimination of all poverty in China. All the while, China has expanded its foreign relations in the spirit of the New Silk Road, spurring increased economic activity globally. This perspective has come to be expressed explicitly in key goals of the United Nations. For example, in September 2016, the United Nations Development Program and China signed a memorandum of understanding for working together in using the BRI to carry out the UN 2030 Agenda for Sustainable Development. The UN General Assembly later ratified the same concept, and China was the first nation to submit a blueprint to the UN, for how to succeed in Agenda 2030.

A summary picture of concrete achievements of China in the past five years was presented in March 2018 by Premier Li Keqiang, in his Work Report at the opening of the 13th National People's Congress-CPC. Over that five-year period, China has expanded its high-speed rail system from 9,000 km to 25,000

A high-speed train in Guangxi Zhuang Autonomous Region of China.

III. PROGRESS REPORTS

Heads of State and Heads of Government at the opening session of the Belt and Road Forum, May 14, 2017.

km, which accounts for two-thirds of the world's total. The highway system has been increased from 96,000 to 136,000 km; plus, 1.27 million km of rural roads have been upgraded. The air traffic system has 46 new civilian airports. Work has begun on 122 major water connectivity projects. A new round of rural power grid improvement has been completed. The world's largest mobile broadband network is in operation in China, where Internet rates will soon be reduced, in order to foster what is called "Digital China." Under the program called "Health China," the medical system, including hospital insurance subsidies, is being expanded. In late 2018, China will launch its Chang'e-4 craft into space for a first-ever landing on the far side of the Moon.

Likewise, there are multiple foreign policy achievements between China and collaborating nations. These were recounted in March 2018, at the "Two Sessions" conclave (CPC and the Chinese People's Political Consultative Congress [CPPCC]) in several Work Reports, including by Foreign Minister Wang Yi, and by Commerce Minister Zhong Shan. Overall, more than 140 countries have participated in or responded to the BRI in the first five years of its initiation. The rapid increase in value of trade between China and these BRI nations is an indicator of their economic growth. For example, trade volume between China and BRI collaborators grew in value by nearly 18% in just one year, from 2016 to 2017, reaching a 2017 amount of 7.4 trillion yuan (about $1.2 trillion). Zhong said of the future, "We are big, but not strong enough. We aim to stabilize our position as a big trading nation by 2020, transform into a strong trading country by 2035, and finally become an economic and trade giant by 2050."

Thus, the domestic and international economic growth of China and BRI nations is proof-of-principle of the soundness of the Chinese model, whose nature and future were presented so eloquently by President Xi in his Work Report to the 19th China Communist Party Congress in October 2017. President Xi spoke in terms of successive phases of advancement.

First, Xi declared that in the period 2020 to 2035, China will have successfully completed its socialist transformation. To begin with, 2020 is the year when poverty will have been completely eliminated. The achievement of this goal marks the Centenary in 2021 of the founding of the Chinese Communist Party in 1921. Progress toward 2035 will include advances in high-speed rail transportation, new urban development, rural revitalization, and achievements in innovation. Plus, China will undergo transformation in terms of fundamental improvements in the environment, to reach a condition of a "Beautiful China."

From 2035 to 2050, China will reach new heights in every dimension of life, Xi said. China will become a global leader in terms of its comprehensive national strength and international influence. As of 2050, this achievement will crown another Centenary, the 100th anniversary of the founding of the People's Republic of China in 1949. By 2050, China, according to Xi's Work Report, will have a modern social governance system, and will have overcome the present economic and social discrepancies between the industrialized regions on the eastern coast, and the lands to the west and south, and between urban and rural areas. President Xi said that the "unbalanced and inadequate development" will be overcome.

Left: Modern housing being built in Nanpingtouwu village in China, 2018. Right: Modern road in the rural area of Longtoushan Town, Ludian County, in China, 2018.

Poverty Elimination

China is now the world leader in the goal of eliminating poverty. The year 2020 is set to mark the elimination of all poverty in China, whose population then will number in the range of 1.42 billion. Over a 40-year period, through to soon after the start of the BRI, China had already lifted 700 million people out of poverty.

As of 2015, the central government estimated that there were still another 70 million people who remained poor. This number was then further reduced, so that by 2017, only 30 million were poor. Many of these people were primarily in rural areas, often isolated and difficult to reach. But finally, programs were put into effect, so that 10 million people a year would be lifted out of poverty, from 2018 to 2020, and the goal of ending impoverishment will have been met on schedule.

President Xi laid out special anti-poverty plans in 2013. He put forward the notion of "Targetted Poverty Alleviation," which pinpointed those geographic areas and sociological groupings that were severely impoverished, in order for the government to deploy special measures. A "paired help" program was implemented in which a total of 320 departments were assigned to pair with 592 destitute counties, to help them out of poverty. In addition, 68 centrally administered state-owned enterprises assisted anti-poverty efforts in 108 impoverished counties in disadvantaged areas. Plus, the less developed areas in the west received support from many of the developed cities and provinces in the more prosperous eastern part of the country. They provided funds, skilled professionals, and innovative ideas and business investment to the west.

The areas and social groups targeted for poverty alleviation were specified in July 2017, at a press briefing by Hong Tianyun, Deputy Director of the State Council Leading Group Office of Poverty Alleviation and Development. He identified three geographical areas and three autonomous prefectures still suffering from extensive poverty. The areas were the Tibet Autonomous Region; the southern region of the Xinjiang Uyghur Autonomous Region; and the ethnic autonomous areas inhabited by the Tibetans, and other ethnic minority groups in Qinghai, Sichuan, Yunnan, and Gansu provinces. The three autonomous prefectures were Linxia Hui Autonomous Prefecture in Gansu, the Liangshan Yi Autonomous Prefecture in Sichuan, and the Nujiang Lisu Autonomous Prefecture in Yunnan.

Deputy Director Hong identified three social groups suffering severe or persistent poverty: those impoverished due to illnesses, in particular, serious and chronic diseases; those impoverished from natural disasters or market fluctuations; and the elderly poor.

Special interventions were deployed accordingly, coming on top of the poverty-reducing impact of economic changes which already had been occurring over preceding decades. These had included expansion of manufacturing, infrastructure-building, increased connectivity through transportation expansion and upgrades, and skills training. All these factors have boosted living standards.

Much of the poverty reduction in China has been an integral part of rural revitalization—a policy emphasized at the 2017 19th Party Congress. Reforms of land use have been made. While all land is owned by the government—either central, provincial, or local—new systems have been implemented so that long-term leaseholders (typically 30 years) can combine small plots to create larger land holdings, allowing for more effective utilization of larger farm machinery and modern methods. The leaseholders, if they leave to work in cities, can even sub-lease to others. There is a process of encouraging cooperatives in rural villages, through which the government can finance machinery, fertilizer, and other inputs. New farming methods, e-commerce sales, and food processing enterprises are also being developed. Output and living standards have increased dramatically. In this context, small businesses can take hold. Internet access has been vastly expanded, and the central government is promoting the "movement to the countryside."

The expansion of the social welfare system overall, has also provided income for the rural villagers who are too old or physically unable to work. In 2009, a nationwide pension system was established, which included the rural aged, but the effects are uneven, depending on the financial condition of local governments. China has built 100,000 day care and activity centers for the rural elderly, and 110,000 community centers for the elderly in urban areas. President Xi made a special commitment to provide more support for the elderly villagers "left behind" in rural areas, in his October 2017 CPC speech.

Expanding the medical services in the rural areas is also an important element in alleviating poverty. As of Fall 2017, it was reported that 80% of the Chinese population was not farther than 15 minutes from a medical clinic. But most of the remaining 20% are in rural areas. Steps are being taken to remedy this, including to recruit more medical practitioners to impoverished areas.

Overall, rural revitalization and the process of poverty alleviation have become an important interface between the central government and the provincial and local governments. Programs are carried out, beginning with lists of local households to raise up from poverty, through action plans specific to local opportunities, e.g., crops, jobs, training, and housing.

President Xi personally chaired a session of the Leading Group for Deepening Overall Reform at the 19th CPC Central Committee in November 2017, at which guidelines were set for deploying officials to work in poverty-stricken areas. In addition, a three-year action plan on the rural environment was created, to focus on practical actions such as garbage disposal and utilities, while at the same time preserving the landscape and the beauty of the countryside.

High-Speed Rail, Connectivity

Rail is the centerpiece of the goal of increased connectivity throughout China, interconnecting with key trans-Eurasian lines along the Belt and Road, and China is now the world leader in rail transport. By 2020, there will be 150,000 km of rail track crisscrossing the nation, 60% of which is double-tracked, and 70% electrified. Of this track, more than 30,000 km will be high-speed as of 2020, connecting 80% of the nation's major cities (**Figure 1**).

There will eventually be 38,000 km of high-speed rail, it was announced at the CCPPC in March 2018. On the newly built track, high speed means running at higher than 250 km per hour. One-third of the China Railway High-Speed (CRH) system runs in the range of 350 km per hour. The National Development and Reform Commission projects that by 2020, 60% of passengers will travel by high-speed rail. Travel time between major, adjacent cities will not be more than one to four hours.

The Danyang-Kunshan Grand Bridge in China, completed in 2010, is located along the route between Shanghai and Nanjing.

Connectivity planners initially built for a high-speed rail grid with four north-south lines and four east-west lines, but now they are preparing for eight lines in each direction, and there are considerations for having 10 lines in each direction.

In brief, the history of this remarkable commitment, is that in the 1990s, there was a debate as to whether China should develop wheel-rail technology, or go right into magnetically-levitated train technology. The decision was made to go with wheel-rail systems, because they could be built at a third of the cost of maglev.

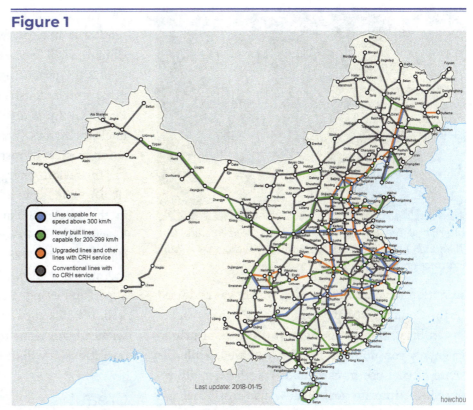

China's dense and growing high-speed rail network.

A delimited amount of maglev was built at the same time. But now, as manufacturing productivity goes up, and relative costs go down, China is looking at the most advanced kinds of maglev. In September 2017, it was announced that work will be underway on ultra-modern maglev, in which trains can travel at speeds up to 600 km per hour.

Initially, China borrowed wheel-rail technology from the German and Japanese systems, but the intensive construction campaign of high-speed rail in China has resulted in many technical innovations by Chinese engineers, including in wheel-rail dynamics, aerodynamics control, train body structure, and bogie pivot, which have made China the premier producer of high-speed rail in the world. In addition, the wide construction experience in China has made its engineers masters in bridging and tunneling, given the challenging terrain where high-speed rail has been built.

There are numerous feats and features of the Chinese rail system achievement. For example, there is the recent construction of a high-speed rail line between Xian in the north, and Chengdu in southwest China, which occasioned the first tunnel through the Qinling Mountains, which separate North China from South China. In fact, half of the Xian-Chengdu stretch was achieved by tunneling through the ridges, which slashed the travel time from 16 hours down to three hours. There is 4G network coverage for the entire length.

Powering Development—Nuclear in the Lead

With the world's largest population, plus rising economic activity and living standards, China is the world's largest energy consumer. As of 2015, the nation consumed 25% of the world's energy used daily.

In June 2014, President Xi Jinping called for an "Energy Revolution," to involve strategic planning to achieve revolutions in the efficiency of energy consumption, and in how power is produced. In 2016, the Chinese government issued its first set of specifics on how to do this, in its new "Energy Revolution Strategy (2016-2030)." Then, in April 2017, came the official government release by the National Development and Reform Commission of its Energy Revolution Strategy, titled, "Energy Production and Con-

Interior of the Experimental Advanced Superconducting Tokamak (EAST) in Hebei, capital of the east China Province of Anhui.

sumption Revolution Strategy," which was endorsed by the Communist Party Congress later that year.

In brief, the share of non-fossil fuels in primary energy consumption is to be increased, while the share of coal use in particular, is to be steadily reduced. An interim goal of 20% non-fossil-fuel use as of 2030, is the target set for primary energy consumption, with scenarios developed to go to 2050, when fossil-fuel energy is to account for less than 50% of total energy consumption. Of the coal facilities in use as of 2030, 80% of them are to be modernized, clean-burning facilities.

Moreover, another target is set for 2030, for a cap on primary energy consumption to be within 6 billion tons of coal equivalent, to be achievable not only by changes in power production, but by increasing the energy-intensity of how power is used in the various economic sectors—manufacturing, agriculture, transportation, housing, and so on. Already, as of 2017, there has been a one-third drop, since 2000, of the quantity of energy used per unit of gross domestic product, a crude but indicative measure.

The mix of the sources of new, non-fossil-fuel energy production includes the low-energy-density sources of wind and solar power. In 2016, for example, China added 77 GW of solar and 149 GW of wind power. The well-known problem, of course, is output curtailment, under unfavorable weather conditions. In addition, new hydropower is coming on line, which can have similar drawbacks. Also, liquified natural gas (LNG) use is being furthered, with increasing quantities of imports.

The leading advanced power source under promotion is nuclear fission, and research for fusion. China had 37 nuclear power reactors in operation as of 2018, producing 32.4 GW of electricity, and 20 more under construction. China General Nuclear Power Group is also at work on producing floating nuclear reactors, intended for use on islands, as well as for overseas infrastructure and humanitarian uses.

In fusion energy research and development (R&D), China is in a leading position. It participates in the International Thermonuclear Experimental Reactor (ITER) in southern France, which hopes to start testing in 2025. China's own research, centered in Anhui Province, with the Experimental Advanced Superconducting Tokamak (EAST), is proceeding well. It is designed as a test fusion reactor, which its science team plans to complete by 2023, and begin operations. It will be the world's first fusion reactor.

Creating New Water Supplies

China is conducting an outstanding program of creating new water resources, given the limitations of its resource base of land and water. The amount of arable land per capita in China is only 40% of the world average. The water resources per capita are one-fourth of the world average. China has tackled this challenge in terms of projects to redistribute the existing water supplies from areas of plenty, mostly in the southern and western areas of the Yangtze River Basin, to the dry lands in the northern areas of the Yellow River Basin, and China is developing plans for bringing water to the vast arid regions of the far western Xinjiang Uyghur Autonomous Region. There also are advanced hydrodynamic plans for re-directing the atmospheric vapor formations of the upper Yangtze Basin, to increase rainfall over the upper catchment area of the Yellow River to the north. In addition, there is the potential for new volumes of water supply, from nuclear-powered desalination on the coast, to serve the high-density population concentrations.

The projects for creating new and redistributing existing water supply include:

South-North Water Transfer Project (SNWTP). The SNWTP involves three main corridors of water diversion, from the Yangtze Basin in the south to the

Yellow River Basin in the north (**Figure 2**). It was conceived in the 1950s, and in 2002 the first phases were launched. When completed, the three canal routes will together move 44 cubic km/year of water northward. For comparison, the Yangtze disgorges on average, nearly 1,000 cubic km/year into the East China Sea, while the Yellow River's average is only 8 cubic km/year.

The Eastern Route. This conveyance system, which was partially opened in 2013, carries water some 1,150 km, from the Yangtze near its point of discharge into the East China Sea, northward to Tianjin, 108 km southeast of Beijing. There are pumping stations along the uphill grade, and the channel traverses the Yellow River by tunnel. The final stretch is an aqueduct to reservoirs near Tianjin. Much of the route follows the ancient Beijing-Hangzhou Grand Canal, which dates back to the 5th Century BC–6th Century AD, when it carried grain from south to north.

The Central Route. Completed in December 2014, this conveyance moves water from the Han River tributary of the Yangtze, from a reservoir at Danjiangkou in Hubei Province, to Beijing, and also to Tianjin. The existing dam at Danjiangkou was raised by 13 meters, allowing the water to flow by gravity along the 1,400 km canal route. Twin tunnels convey the water under the Yellow River. The flow enters Beijing through a 9-km tunnel, 15 stories below ground, before finally being pumped into a new reservoir near the Summer Palace. The goal, when the Central Route is fully built out, is to convey 13 cu-

Figure 2
The South-North Water Transfer Project

bic km/year by 2030. At present the flow is 9.5 cubic km/year. The Central Route, an engineering wonder, is now the longest canal in the world, subject to lower rank only when the "Transaqua" 2,500 km canal will be built in Africa, along the Congo River, for a diversion system to replenish Lake Chad.

The Western Route. This water diversion proposal is by far the most challenging so far. The idea is to run three canals from the headwaters of the Yangtze River in the Qinghai-Tibetan Plateau and western Yunnan Plateau, northward to the headwaters of the Yellow River. Crossing the divide between these two watersheds in the mountainous region will be a huge engineering feat, which is still in the planning stage. When completed, these canals will transfer 17 cubic km/year of water north to the Yellow River, vastly augmenting its flow. The source area of this water diversion proposal—the Qinghai-Tibetan Plateau, is known as the Sanjiangyuan, i.e., "The Source of Three Rivers" (Yangtze, Yellow, and Mekong). Also originating in southwestern China are the Brahmaputra and Salween Rivers. More projects for water resources upgrade are possible through international collaboration.

Water for Xinjiang. A fabulous plan to convey water from the Tibetan Plateau (known as the "water tower of Asia"), to green part of the Taklamakan Desert in Xinjiang, is under active consideration. The concept is to transfer part of the flow of the Yarlung Tsangpo River in Tibet, though a series of tunnels and man-made channels, including waterfalls, into

The head of the middle route of the South-North Water Transfer Project.

Xinjiang arid lands. The project would require large dams and pumping stations, and poses huge engineering challenges, as well as need for a huge investment. However, a water diversion project currently underway in Yunnan Province, which includes a 600 km tunnel, is seen as a demonstration project. It can "show we have the brains, muscle, and tools to build super-long tunnels in hazardous terrain—and the cost doesn't break the bank," said Zhang Chuanqing, at the Institute of Rock and Soil Mechanics, of the Chinese Academy of Sciences.

Heavenly River. The Tianhe (Heavenly River) Project is in the research and planning stages, to move water in its vapor condition, from above the headwaters of the Yangtze, northward to the headwaters of the Yellow River, and induce precipitation. Working on this fabulous idea, is a team connected to the Chinese Academy of Sciences, under the leadership of Wang Guangqian, president of Qinghai University. The idea is to influence water in the atmospheric boundary layer and troposphere. If successful, the process is expected to result in 5 cubic km of water into the North via the Yellow River annually.[1]

Finally, the most plentiful supplies of man-made "natural" water resources, given present-day technology, can come from nuclear-powered desalination. For China, this goes hand-in-hand with its commitment to add dozens of nuclear fission reactors to its power base, which, when located on the coast, can provide vast amounts of "new" water. One estimate (from 2015) is that by 2030, China will be able to produce 23 billion cubic meters of water yearly, in association with nuclear power generation, and do so at a reasonable cost.

There is also the international commitment by China to nuclear technology for water supplies. For example, in August 2017, a memorandum of understanding (MOU) was signed between China and Saudi Arabia, on advance desalting. The MOU stated support for "developing desalination projects using high-temperature and gas-chilled nuclear reactors," and was signed by the state-owned China Nuclear Engineering Group Corp. Also in 2017, Chinese state-

A water tunnel of 600 km, under construction in Yunnan, is part of a pilot project to test technical capabilities to construct the Tibet-Xinjiang tunnel.

owned and other firms created a new joint venture enterprise to build floating nuclear power and seawater desalination plants.

New Cities, Regional Development

An exciting manifestation of the growth of connectivity and productivity in China, is the deliberate establishment of new cities, as well as the enhanced development of whole regions of the nation. Among those new cities, designated as "state-level new areas," are Pudong (Shanghai), Binhai (Tianjin), Liangjiang (Chongqing), Nanshan (Guangzhou), and Tianfu (Chengdu). The newest one, begun in April 2017, is Xiongan—referred to as Jing-Jin-Ji, which stands for Beijing, Tianjin, and Hebei, because the megacity is planned in relation to the cities of Beijing, Tianjin, and a portion of Hebei Province. The new metropolis is starting out with an area of 100 square km (km^2), but will eventually grow to 2,000 km^2, with physical and social infrastructure being built from the ground up, to support a productive, beautiful mega-city for some 130 million residents.

The proposal for such a new complex as Xiongan was presented in 2014 by President Xi, who stressed many purposes of the new metropole including, for example, transferring some of Beijing's non-capital functions to the new area, and lowering Beijing's population density. In April 2018, the government released its official announcement of the plans for the Xiongan New Area, concluding by stating that

---

1 See the video presentation, "China's 'Heavenly River,' the Future of Water." (https://larouchepac.com/20161117/chinas-heavenly-river-future-water)

Xiongan will become "a model city in the history of human development." Xiongan will be a "new area of 'national significance,' following the Shenzhen Special Economic Zone and the Shanghai Pudong New Area."

The document characterized the initiative as "a strategy that will have lasting importance for the millennium to come, and a significant national event." Xiongan is to be a modern city by 2035, and by 2050, it will be a "significant part of the world-class Beijing-Tianjin-Hebei city cluster, effectively performing Beijing's non-capital functions and providing the Chinese solution to "big city malaise."

Another important purpose, is to create an additional center of innovation in the north of China. This will be the third such development zone in the north, which will have radiating effects.

Excellent transportation connections are being built. Xiongan will be reachable from Beijing by rail within 20 minutes. Xiongan will have special connections with the major port of Tianjin, providing a link to the northern Heilongjiang region, and from there to Russia and Mongolia, and their transport grids across Eurasia. As of 2018, construction was well underway on a new international airport south of Beijing, halfway between there and Tianjin. When fully completed, it is designed to handle 72 million passengers a year, 2 million tons of cargo, and 62,000 flights annually. A further expansion to seven runways, will allow it to handle 100 million passengers yearly. This compares with the present Beijing Capital International Airport, which is ranked second in the world, handling 83.65 million passengers, but it has reached the saturation point.

Regionally, there are many outstanding enhancement programs underway. For example, in the south of China there is the area of Guangzhou, which has historically served as the "port facing the world," and today has also become a regional center for high-tech innovation. The nine cities involved in the Guangdong Province are Zhuai, Foshan, Zhongshan, Dongguan, Huizhou, Jiangmen, Zhaoqing, and Guangzhou. Central to this region becoming such a major mega-center for innovation and finance, are the great connection projects of the Hong Kong-Zhuhai-Macau Bridge, and the Guangzhou-Shenzhen-Hong Kong Express Rail Link.

To the north, the entire Yangtze River Basin is a "Golden Waterway" of development. Separating north China from south China, the Yangtze east-west expanse traverses 11 provinces and municipalities that cover roughly one-fifth of China's territory, encompasses a population of 600 million, and generates more than 40% of the country's GDP. The Yangtze serves as a trade corridor from the coast to central and western China. While development has boomed in the past few decades in the coastal area, the Golden Waterway provides the means to bring development far inland. Transit was opened to large ocean-going vessels to go from the coast all the way to Chongqing in western China, once the Three Gorges Dam was completed in 2012, and subsequently the upper region was deepened from Yichag to Chongqing.

The Comprehensive Three-Dimensional Transportation Corridor Plan for the Yangtze envisions an integrated transportation corridor, with expansion of all modes—water, rail, road, air, and pipeline. By the end of 2020, the operating distances of these modes will reach 40,000 km of railways, 2 million km of roadways, 70,000 km of pipelines, and 3,600 km of urban rail transit. Civilian air transport will have 100 airports in service. The geography of development of the Golden Waterway has efforts underway in the Yang-

The Xiongan New Economic Zone.

III. PROGRESS REPORTS

The Hong Kong-Zhuhai-Macau Bridge

On July 1, 2018, the world's longest bridge, including the world's longest underwater road tunnel, will be officially opened for traffic. The 55 km bridge-tunnel connects the former British colony of Hong Kong to the former Portuguese colony of Macao and the neighboring Chinese metropolis of Zhuhai, crossing over the open sea at the mouth of the Pearl River, called the Lingdingyang channel.

Schiller Institute Chairwoman Helga Zepp-LaRouche visited the nearly completed bridge in November 2017, and said: "For me, the absolute high point was traveling over the new sea bridge. It is really a total masterpiece of engineering. They had to invent 120 new patented techniques to build this bridge. It was just incredible. It took them only eight years to build this unbelievable, very, very beautiful and modern bridge."

tze Delta region, and in the middle reaches of the river, efforts are combining cities along the river bank into an organized city cluster. Upriver, the products of the western cities of Chongqing and Chengdu now have an outlet to coastal markets and the entire Asia Pacific. This Yangtze Belt of relatively cheaper water transport comes in addition to the fact that Chongqing and Chengdu are already well connected by high-speed rail, across Asia, to European markets. Computer companies like Hewlett Packard have already made Chengdu the center of their production facilities for the European market.

Manufacturing—An 'Innovation Nation'

China's powerful manufacturing capacity is manifest in its production of heavy industrial inputs to supply its own large-scale development projects, and also to foster new factories in other nations of the BRI and Maritime Silk Road, including railroads, bridges, tunnels, ports, mass housing, and other infrastructure. The emphasis now is on building "the innovation nation."

In seeing what all that entails in China, it is worth understanding one clarification in advance: there is no "excess" or "over-capacity" in steel and other heavy industry, as is often casually asserted, in reference to China or worldwide. True, outmoded mills and factories may need to be shuttered or rehabilitated. But any apparent global "glut" of heavy industrial output and capacity, comes from the extreme lack of "demand" for construction inputs, because of the conspicuous lack of infrastructure and economy-building associated with the continuing backwardness in North America and most of Europe.

What leaders in China spell out, is that their nation has moved from a former export-oriented manufacturing base, to an economic model serving domestic consumption (plus foreign collaboration), and deliberately producing higher-value-added products, while stimulating innovative ideas that can lead to ever greater productivity. An expression of this is the "Make in China 2025" policy, which was announced in 2014. The idea is to orient the production process to supply goods and services for the "real economy" to meet domestic demand and goals, in the course of which innovation and quality are the drivers.

This tendency has been firmly established by President Xi Jinping. He said at the 19th Party Congress in late 2017, "Through devoting great energy to implementing the innovation-driven development strategy, we have seen much accomplished toward making China a country of innovators, with major advances made in science and technology, including the successful launch of Tiangong-2 space lab, the commissioning of the deep-sea manned submersible Jiaolong and of the Five-Hundred-Meter Aperture Spherical Telescope (FAST), the launch of the dark matter probe satellite Wukong and the quantum science satellite Mozi, and the test flight of the airliner C919." The results are already coming in. Thanks to Wukong, there are new discoveries in the area of dark matter. The Mozi now allows China to communicate by satellite without any danger of being hacked. The FAST telescope, which is in Guizhou, will be the most advanced of its kind.

China now accounts for 20% of global R&D. While the United States still accounts for 27% of R&D spending, this figure has dropped from 33%, and there is no doubt that, at current rates, China will surpass the United States.

In specific areas, a 2017 survey showed that China came first in computer science, mathematics, materials science, and engineering, while the United States led the way in physics, earth and environmental sciences, basic life science, and clinical medicine.

Overall in China, as of Winter 2017-18, there were 17 national high-tech innovation parks, and 146 regional ones across the country, which play a role in upgrading the various kinds of activities in the local economy. By early 2016, China had already put in place more than 5,000 high-tech start-up incubators, the highest number among all nations worldwide. In share of manufacturing output in the economy, recent production figures indicate the relative increase in output of higher-value-chain products, such as electronic and IT-related equipment and computers, relative to heavy industrial goods.

China is particularly well advanced in the move toward robotics, artificial intelligence, and precision medicine. One conspicuous reflection of this, is how the Chinese pay for things electronically on their smart phones, rather than with cards or cash. Facial recognition is largely replacing ID cards. Alibaba and Tencent have become equal players with Microsoft and Google in the electronic communications industry.

Shown is the construction phase of the Five-Hundred-Meter Aperture Spherical Radio Telescope (FAST), the world's largest filled-aperture radio telescope, located in the mountains of rural Guizhou Province. The design takes advantage of a large karst sink-hole. Construction began in 2011, and the project went operational in 2016. In August 2017, FAST discovered two new pulsars, and more since then. Called the "Eye of Heaven," the structure consists of a fixed 500-meter-diameter dish. FAST is funded by the National Development and Reform Commission, and managed by the National Astronomical Observatories of the Chinese Academy of Sciences, along with the government of the province.

Machine in China enabling rapid placement of elevated bridge trestles.

Agriculture Transformation Underway

The period of the initiation of the One Belt-One Road program in 2014 occurred during the third of three upward strategic shifts, roughly 10-plus years each, in Chinese agriculture, ecology, and food security since 1978. The policies in practice today are causing marked upgrades in the productivity of farming; improvements in the nation's ecological condition, e.g., reforestation; and in the nutritional content of the average diet. The experience of this progress also carries over into collaboration with other nations, especially in Africa and Central Asia, for food and agro-ecological advance. It also stands in dramatic contrast to the United States, which, over the same time period, suffered a downward de-structuring of its agriculture sector, in terms of the social condition of farm communities, ecology, and infrastructure.

The first policy period of structural improvement in Chinese agriculture was from 1978 to the 1990s. Up until the mid-1970s, episodic food shortages and rural impoverishment persisted in China; but, then, thanks to deliberate policy interventions, the nation became food self-sufficient as of 1984 in grains and basic food supply, and as of 1998, total grains output reached 500 billion kg for the first time. There was a relative surplus. The population at that time was 1.037 billion.

The next strategic shift period, from 1998 to 2003, implemented measures to maintain the food security level, but to also convert some grain area into forests and fishery ponds, and to convert some grain production capacity into supporting animal husbandry. The impact of this process of reducing grain area, led to a drop in grain output, which in 2003, fell to 430 billion kg, which created pressure toward food shortages, and had to be adjusted.

From 2003 to 2015, this problem was corrected, and more adjustments were made for continued advancement. Goals have been set, for example, to produce more animal protein for the diet, which will necessitate an ever-larger share of grain production to be committed for livestock feed. As of 2015, total grain production reached 600 billion kg for the first time. From 2016 onwards, the area producing corn has begun to be reduced, while at the same time, the share of corn output going for feed is increasing. The intention is for 70% of the national corn crop to go for animal husbandry.

There are other outstanding features of this transformation, one of which is crop genetics improvements. Dr. Yuan Longping, Director-General of the China National Hybrid Rice Research and Development Center in Hunan, is a veteran crop specialist, revered as the "Father of Hybrid Rice" for his breakthrough work on strains of high-yield rice in the 1970s, which now are in use the world over.

Today, measures are in effect to support more large-scale, high-technology agriculture, while at the same time, to raise up the income and social level of farm households. Plus, there are ecology- and beauty-enhancing projects, including furthering rural tourism.

In January 2017, drones were classified as agricultural machinery in China, and now are subsidized in targeted demonstration projects, as well as in growing commercial use. Here a worker is applying pesticide on a field in Shanghai, using a drone made by DJI.

Land Reclamation, Agriculture Expansion in a Village in Fuping

In Heibei Province, Baiyi Village is located in central Fuping (southwest of Beijing). Fuping has a population of around 2,400 people, and traditionally, only 76 hectares of arable land. A mountainous region, it also has well more than 1,000 hectares of non-arable land. More than half of the villagers in 2015, lived below the national poverty line. Agriculture experts then came in to carry out a study of what measures could be taken to reclaim Fuping's barren land. The villagers worked with them in their proposals, and transferred their land use rights on the barren plots, to become shareholders in the new joint project on combined land holdings. Much of the land was transformed into arable area, using water-saving irrigation facilities. By the end of 2016, 200 hectares of the mountainous region had been turned into arable land, with apple and peach trees, plantings of sweet potatoes and peanuts, and cassia trees (ornamental and herbal uses). The villager leaseholders earned a basic income of 1,000 yuan ($150) a month, per household.

Those who additionally work for the venture by tending the crops, can have an extra income of $450. When the project begins to fully pay off, the profits will be distributed between the investors and the villagers. By the end of 2020, when the land is expected to begin producing good yields, each villager can get profits of more than $900.

A timetable of goals was set at the October 2017 Communist Party Congress: by 2020, the institutional framework is to be in place for maintaining productive and fair agriculture and ecological practices; by 2035, there will be "decisive" progress in the agriculture sector; and by 2050, the agriculture sector will be strong and "beautiful," and farmers will be "well-off."

These deliberate measures are succeeding. Professor Mei Fangquan, Agricultural Information Institute, Chief Expert of the UN Global Food Security Committee, stressed the point in 2017, at a Schiller Institute co-sponsored conference in New York City. For China, he said, "Agricultural structural adjustment is the inevitable process of agricultural progress and modernization. Every adjustment is intended as an upgrade, into a higher stage of development."[2] This all goes hand-in-glove with government programs to end rural poverty, which accounted for a large share of the remaining 30 million people, as of 2018, whose relief from poverty by 2020, would mark the achievement of the national goal of poverty eradication.

To appreciate what is involved in how Chinese agriculture productivity and rural income improvement are rising at the same time, it is necessary to consider three factors. First, a form of what is called "parity" (of commodity prices with farming costs) is maintained for farm operations in China, meaning that farm income levels are maintained by various mechanisms, including government purchases, price-setting for farm commodities, and other means. This parity policy was once standard for U.S. agriculture under President Franklin Delano Roosevelt, for a period of the mid-1930s through World War II and some years afterward. Its elimination is part of what has given rise to the crisis for U.S. farm families in the 21st Century.

---

2   "Food for Peace & Thought: China-U.S. Agricultural Cooperation," July 7, 2017 (http://www.schillerinstitute.org/highlite/2017/0707-ny-ffp/main.html)

III. PROGRESS REPORTS

Second, China is making provision for infrastructure in rural areas in order to support agriculture including rail, water, electricity, Internet, housing improvements, and educational and cultural activity. For example, 1.275 million km of rural roads were built in the five-year period from 2012 to 2017, and about 99% of townships nationwide now have access to buses.

Third, China government officials (from various levels) have deployed into rural farm villages, working with rosters of individual households, to come up with betterment plans for villages and families. In some cases, for example, this has resulted in a land reclamation project, or a switchover to a different, more valuable crop or crops, such as specialty coffee beans, or putting in orchard groves, instead of cultivating subsistence roots. It can involve boosting yields of existing crops, by amalgamating small land holdings into larger leases, to allow mechanized field work, including very advanced methods, such as drone-applied pesticides.

There are even aesthetic teams at work, to provide government help to preserve and enhance the identity of old villages, through saving their special architectural and other features—e.g., old buildings and alleyways, shrines, riverbanks, and parks. In some hardcore cases of land degradation or similar problem, villagers are offered the opportunity to move to new homes in other farm regions or cities. For example, in the southwest province of Yunnan, a projected 650,000 people will have been relocated out of poverty-stricken communities by the end of 2020.

Beautiful China

Creating a "Beautiful China" was identified by the 19th CPC National Congress in October 2017, as a goal for the two-stage—2035 and 2050—economic development plan of the nation, to be achieved by the mid-21st Century. President Xi Jinping said then, that he expects that the "Beautiful China" goal will be attained by 2035. "The modernization that we pursue is one characterized by harmonious co-existence between man and nature. In addition to creating more material and cultural wealth to meet people's ever-increasing needs for a better life, we need also to provide more quality ecological goods to meet people's ever-growing demands for a beautiful environment."

For today's visitor to China, what stands out are the many lovely features of city design, parkland, and villages in the countryside. But much more is happening. Regulatory agencies are being established to manage state-owned natural resource assets, and monitor the condition of ecosystems.

Measures are continuing to lessen water and air pollution, which remain as some of China's worst problems, and to restore fertility to degraded soils. Besides such obvious interventions, as shutting down or retrofitting outmoded, smoky factories and coal-powered generating plants, there are additional, innovative projects.

For example, the "Miracle Oats" program is sowing a special variety of oats, which can uptake salt, and after several successive years of planting, the formerly barren, saline soil is returned to a productive condition. Dr. Ren Changzhong, Director of the National Oat Improvement Center, has worked to spread the cultivation of this oats in dry and salty soils in Jilin, Heilongjiang, and Inner Mongolia Provinces, in collaboration with the Canadian crop scientist Dr. Vern Burrows, who first developed the oat variety.

The most dramatic example of deliberate intervention to improve the environment, on a mass

Dr. Vern Burrows (with red book), the Canadian master crop scientist—known as "Dr. Oats"—received the China International Science and Technology Cooperation Award in 2016, for breeding up a successful oat variety that grows well in saline, dry conditions. Its cultivation in China since the late 1990s, is desalting large areas of cropland which had become unusable, in Jilin, Heilongjiang, and Inner Mongolia Provinces. Two crops a year can grow in the Baicheng City area of western Jilin.

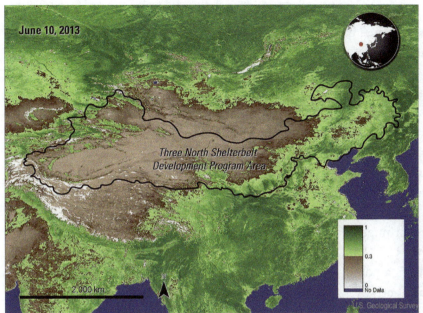

This 2013 image, created from Moderate Resolution Imaging Spectroradiometer (MODIS) data, was prepared in order to study long-term vegetation trends. The black line indicates the area of the Three North Shelterbelt Development Program (TNSDP), begun in 1978, to plant protective forests in arid and semi-arid areas of the northern portion of China. It is the world's largest afforestation program, covering more than 40% of China's land area. Billions of trees have been planted.

scale, is the anti-desertification program. More than 25% of the land of China, amounting to more than 2.5 million km², qualifies as desert, with varying kinds of problems, including wind erosion, salination, and rock erosion. After 1978, the government implemented the "Three-North Shelterbelt Program," which initiated planting millions of trees along the 4,500 km borderline of the desert lands of the north, to halt desert expansion. Some 66 billion trees have been planted in fewer than 40 years.

Known as the "Great Green Wall," the tree belt itself can enhance rainfall, but in some areas it also strains local water. Many good lessons have been learned, including from prior anti-desertification projects dating back to the 1950s. A famous, seminal project is the Saihanba Forest, about 400 km north of Beijing. In the mid-20th Century, this land was treeless and barren, due to severe lumbering in the early 1900s.

Then in 1961, tree experts found a single larch growing, proving a tree could again survive. The first planting program, covering 427 hectares, had only an 8% success rate, because seedlings brought in from other provinces died. Then, after seedlings were coddled locally, the program took off, to where today, there are 75,000 hectares of woods. The Saihanba Forest now functions as a shield against sandstorms, and purifies more than 130 million cubic meters of water for the Beijing-Tianjin area.

China is providing its expertise to Africa, for a Great Green Wall initiative to contain the Sahara, initially proposed by the African Union in 2007. In April 2018, the Chinese Academy of Sciences announced that, under its direction, the Xinjiang Institute of Ecology and Geography (XIEG) will offer its technological support for greening in the Sahel. XIEG Director Lei Jiaqiang said that his agency will systematically diagnose desertification and technical needs in the region, in collaboration with Nigeria, Mauritania, and Ethiopia.

China will train staff in Africa, and will directly participate in projects. Lei said, "We hope to bring China's wisdom in anti-desertification to Africa, and help enhance the capability of desertification prevention in African countries along the Great Green Wall."

Into the Heavens

China's strong initiatives in space reflect and lead its economic and strategic advances on Earth. After various successes in missile development and other precursors, China, in 2003, became the third nation to conduct a manned space mission. Astronaut Yang Liwei flew aboard Shenzhou 5. Ten years later, China conducted a successful soft landing on the Moon, in its Chang'e-3 mission, which was the first spacecraft to do so in nearly 40 years. The Chang'e-3 mission is still producing new information about the Moon.

Successful work then continued, to where in 2018, five years after the announcement of the One Belt-One Road, China has very important collaboration with other nations on space-related endeavors—the "Silk Road in Space"—and is taking the lead in several areas. Its BeiDou geo-positioning system is extensive. And there are important developments in its heavy-lift Long March rocketry capability.

As of 2018, China had agreements with 37 countries and four international space organizations. It is pushing ahead with the Belt and Road Initiative Space Information Corridor, and construction of the BRICS remote sensing satellite constellation.

Important talks have begun with Russia and the European Space Agency for further cooperation on deep space exploration. Standing aside from all this, is the United States, which, as of 2018, continued in its policy dictated by mistaken action of the U.S. Congress, to ban U.S.-China space cooperation, a policy which is inhibiting U.S. space research and activity.

Most exciting in China, is the work connected to the China Lunar Exploration Program (CLEP), which is underway in several phases. In June 2018, the relay satellite successfully entered its designated far-lunar orbit, which will enable communication between Earth, and the planned lunar lander.

Photos and communications can be sent from the lander, via the orbiter, back to mission control; and in reverse, commands can go from Earth to the lander. The projected launch for the lander is at the end of 2018 with the Chang'e-4 mission, whose destination is on the "dark" side of the Moon, which is a first. The reference is to the side of the Moon which faces away from the Earth. The lander and rover will carry out in-place and patrolling surveys.

Then in 2019, the third mission, the Chang'e-5, is scheduled, which involves a spacecraft that can make a return trip from the Moon, bringing back samples, including Helium 3—rare on Earth, but plentiful on the Moon.

The "Yutu" rover seen by the Chang'e-3 lunar lander. The 2013 Chang'e-3 mission landed on the Moon's near side. The 2018 Chang'e-4 lander and rover will carry out a much more difficult and unprecedented landing on the Moon's far ("dark") side.

In a fourth phase of the CLEP, Chang'e-6 will set up a robotic lunar research station. The south pole of the Moon is under consideration as the site. Scientists plan to land where there is sunlight most of the year, and most likely, the presence of water. This would be another first for China's lunar program, because no nation has ever landed on a lunar pole.

The significance of these lunar achievements lies not merely in their space engineering feats, but marks the potential of a whole new era of productivity of mankind in the universe. Helium 3, which has been collecting on the Moon for eons, will be the fuel for the nuclear fusion economy, with an array of plasma-based technologies, making for an industrial revolution beyond any ever before imagined. That, coupled with new knowledge gained from space exploration, truly puts humanity into the heavens.

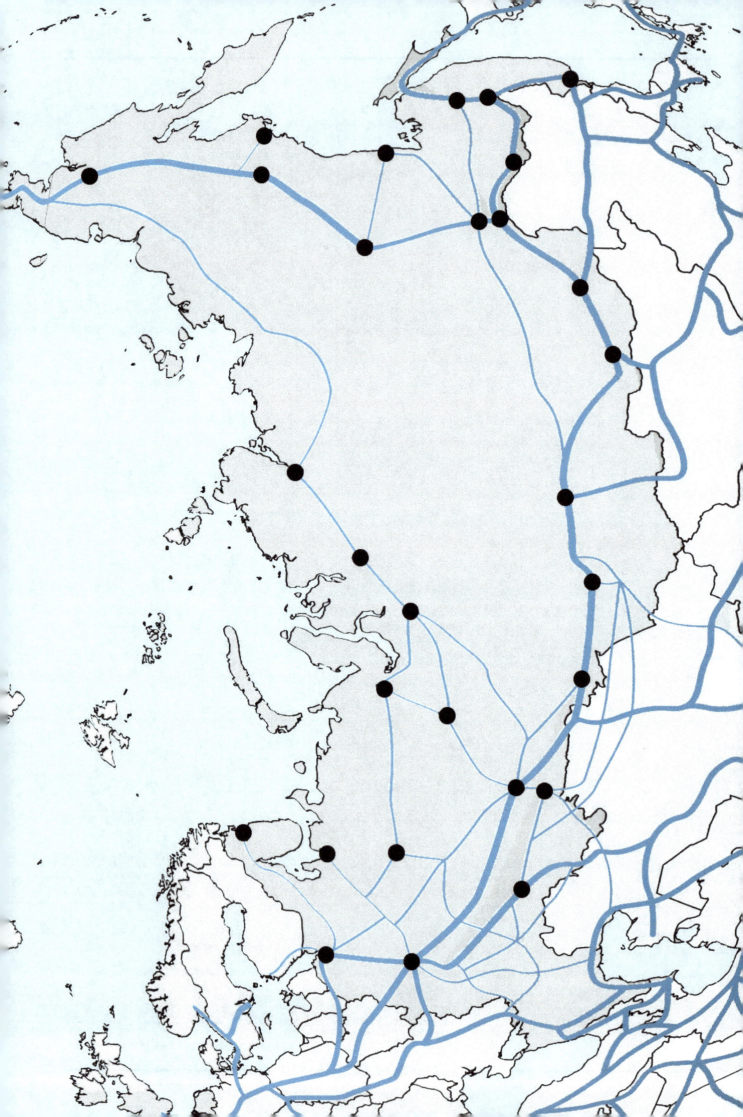

"The relationship between China and Russia ... has become the core relationship of the New Paradigm as it is rapidly transforming the physical and cultural map of the world. This cooperation has solidified and expanded significantly, both in terms of economic cooperation and in political and strategic cooperation on crucial issues around the world."

RUSSIA
in the New Silk Road

Russia and China—Transforming Eurasia

The relationship between China and Russia since the release of the *EIR* Report, "The New Silk Road Becomes the World Land-Bridge," in November 2014 has become the core relationship of the New Paradigm as it is rapidly transforming the physical and cultural map of the world. This cooperation has solidified and expanded significantly, both in terms of economic cooperation and in political and strategic cooperation on crucial issues around the world. Economic problems in Russia due in large measure to the collapse of oil prices and the sanctions regime imposed by the United States and the EU have led to postponement of several planned projects, but the relationship and the intention to proceed on both sides remains strong. Presidents Xi Jinping and Vladimir Putin have met with each other at many formal and informal events and state visits, including three meetings in 2017. Putin has visited China eight times since 2014. The two leaders have taken steps to link the New Silk Road and the Eurasian Economic Union (EAEU) launched by Putin in 2014, which now includes Russia, Belarus, Kazakhstan, Armenia, and Kyrgyzstan. During Putin's visit to Beijing in June 2016, Xi said: "President Putin and I equally agree that when faced with international circumstances that are increasingly complex and changing, we must persist even harder in maintaining the spirit of the Sino-Russian strategic partnership and cooperation." In July 2017, during a visit to Moscow by President Xi, Putin presented Xi with the Order of St. Andrew in the Grand Kremlin Palace, "for his outstanding contribution to strengthening friendship and cooperation between the people of Russia and China." The Order of St. Andrew the Apostle the First-Called, established by Peter the Great in 1698, is Russia's oldest state award. On June 8, 2018, President Xi Jinping awarded President Putin China's first "Medal of Friendship" at the Great Hall of the People in Beijing, calling Putin "my best and most intimate friend."

On February 6, 2018, Presidents Xi and Putin both sent greetings to a ceremony marking the opening of the "Years of Regional Cooperation and Exchange" held in Harbin, in Heilongjiang Province in China's Northeast. The years 2018 and 2019 have been designated as two years in which to strengthen cooperation between China's Northeast and the Russian Far East. A large number of events have been

Russian President Putin and Chinese President Xi Jinping, June 25, 2016

planned to take place over these two years, including conferences to further investments, trade, industry, agriculture, art festivals, and people exchanges.

The close relationship reflects the launch of the Belt and Road Initiative in 2013 and the EAEU in 2014, but is also influenced by the impact of western sanctions imposed on Russia after the coup against the elected government in Ukraine in 2014, orchestrated by the Obama Administration. That violent regime change campaign, openly funded by the "project democracy" networks in the United States, saw Obama's representative to Eastern Europe, Victoria Nuland, brag that the U.S. spent $5 billion to forge anti-Russian non-governmental organizations (NGOs) in Ukraine, supporting neo-nazi gangs attacking police and murdering supporters of the elected president, and finally driving President Yanukovych out of the country in February 2014, placing Nuland's hand-picked agents in power.

The subsequent revolt, primarily in Crimea and eastern Ukraine, against the neo-nazi putsch, was used as an excuse by Obama and the EU to attack and isolate Russia from the West, imposing sanctions against Russia which in many cases did as much damage to the European nations as they did to Russia—a fact increasingly being voiced by leading political and business interests within the EU. China, on its part, never accepted the fraudulent accusations against Russia, while at the same time the Obama Administration was also attempting to isolate China through a military "pivot to Asia" launched in 2012, to encircle China militarily, while trying to create an economic bloc, the Trans-Pacific Partnership (TPP), aimed at isolating China in the Pacific region, coercing Asian nations to choose between China and the United States.

The collaboration between Russia and China was given added strength by two critical events: first, the election of Rodrigo Duterte in the Philippines, who rejected Obama's confrontation with China in favor of cooperation with China's Belt and Road Initiative, while also establishing friendly relations with Russia; and second, the election of Donald Trump in the United States, who campaigned for establishing friendly relations with Russia, and, after he took office, established exceptionally close relations with China. Despite the hysterical anti-Russia campaign launched by British intelligence MI6 agent Christopher Steele and the corrupt chiefs of Obama's intelligence agencies, President Trump has (as of this writing) stood firm in his intention to break the British Imperial division of the world into East vs. West, by bringing the United States, Russia, and China together, both in fighting terrorism and in economic cooperation.

It is the intention of the LaRouche movement, including the publication of this report, to bring the United States into direct cooperation with China and Russia in the New Silk Road, participating in the reconstruction of the world economy as a whole.

The $400 Billion Gas Deal

President Putin visited China in May 2014, just weeks after the Ukraine coup and the imposition of Western sanctions on Russia. At that meeting, Putin and Xi agreed to one of the biggest energy deals in history. The $400-billion, 30-year framework to de-

Figure 1

— Gas pipelines in operation   --- Ongoing projects   --- Prospective gas pipelines   ⛏ Gas-Fields   Gas Production Centers: ① Krasnoyarsk ② Irkutsk ③ Yakutia ④ Sakhalin

liver 38 billion cubic meters of Russian gas to China annually secured the world's leading energy user with a major source of gas from Russia's huge gas reserves via thousands of miles of new pipelines across Siberia (**Figure 1**). "This is the biggest contract in the history of the gas sector of the former USSR," said Putin, after the agreement was signed in Shanghai between Russia's Gazprom and China National Petroleum Corp (CNPC). "Through mutual compromise we managed to reach not only acceptable, but rather satisfactory, terms on this contract for both sides. Both sides were in the end pleased by the compromise reached on price and other terms," Putin said.

In October 2017, Gazprom announced that 1,095 km of the eastern route, called the Power of Siberia gas pipeline, was completed, ahead of schedule, and was expecting to complete its 2,200 km of the 3,000 km total line by the end of 2019 and deliver gas from the Chayandinskoye field to Blagoveshchensk on the Chinese border. A second stage of 800 km will bring gas from the Kovyktinskoye field in the Irkutsk Region to Chayandinskoye, then on to China.

There is also a possibility that Japan and Korea could engage in the negotiations, possibly to build an extension from the Power of Siberia pipeline to take gas to the coast and on to Japan.

Moscow and Beijing plan to build another pipeline, Power of Siberia-2 or the western route, which will deliver another 30 billion cubic meters of Russian natural gas.

China began receiving 15 million tons of crude oil annually from Russia in 2012, when Russia completed the East Siberia-Pacific Ocean (ESPO) oil pipeline, started in 2006 (**Figure 2**). This pipeline delivers crude from fields at Tomsk Oblast and the Khanty-Mansi Autonomous Okrug in Western Siberia to Vladivostok, with a branch to Daqing in Heilongjiang Province in China.

A second, parallel pipeline to Daqing began construction in 2016, and began pumping oil on January 1, 2018, doubling the Russian oil going to China to 30 million tons annually. Russia overtook Saudi Arabia as the leading exporter of oil to China, the world's largest oil importer.

A pipeline bringing gas from Sakhalin Island to

Power of Siberia pipeline under construction

Figure 2
The East Siberia-Pacific Ocean Pipeline

Khabarovsk and Vladivostok was completed in 2011, and may be extended to China in the future. A possible pipeline to Japan to deliver some of this natural gas has been discussed between Prime Minister Shinzo Abe and President Putin, but there has been no agreement as yet.

The largest Chinese investment in Russia to date was completed in September 2017, when CEFC China Energy invested $9.1 billion to purchase a 14.16% stake in Russia's Rosneft oil company, buying most of the stake previously owned by the Anglo-Swiss Glencore and the Qatar Investment Fund. Rosneft chief Igor Sechin said he was "happy that it was specifically a Chinese corporation" which bought the stake.

Other major Chinese investments in Russia in 2017 include a $1.2 billion investment in the massive Yamal liquified natural gas (LNG) development in the Arctic; Beijing Gas's $1.1 billion investment in a Rosneft gas field in eastern Siberia; and Chinese consortium Fosun's $900 million purchase of 15% of Russia's largest gold producer, Polyus.

China-Russia Investment Fund

President Xi Jinping was hosted to a state visit in Moscow in July 2017. During the visit, the China Development Bank agreed to create a $10 billion investment fund with Russia's sovereign fund Russian Direct Investment Fund (RDIF) in projects along the New Silk Road and the Eurasian Economic Union. Called the China-Russia RMB Investment Cooperation Fund, it will be implemented in China by the Russia-China Investment Fund (RCIF), set up by the RDIF and China's sovereign fund, the China Investment Corporation (CIC). A number of smaller funds in the $100 million to $1 billion range have been established between Russian and Chinese entities and provinces. In September 2017, at the Eastern Economic Forum in Vladivostok, Vice Premier Wang Yang announced the intention to establish another China-Russia investment fund of $15.3 billion to facilitate Chinese companies investing in Russia's Far East in areas including manufacturing, resources exploitation, infrastructure, agriculture, and tourism.

High-Speed Rail, Moscow-Beijing

The long-term goal of connecting Moscow to Beijing via high-speed rail, a 7,000-km journey, is to begin with a high-speed connection of 772 km between Moscow and Kazan. The design, prepared by a Russian-Chinese consortium of designers commissioned by JSC High-Speed Railways, a subsidiary of Russian Railways, was approved in July 2017. Construction is scheduled to begin in 2018 with a targeted completion in 2020, which will reduce travel time from Moscow to Kazan from 14 hours to 3 hours and 30 minutes, travelling at an operating speed of 360 km/h and a maximum speed of 440 km/h. The estimated cost is more than $22 billion. In April 2016, Russian International Railway Group agreed to provide a loan of $6.2 billion over a 20-year period for the construction of the line. JSC is also calling on the BRICS New Development Bank (NDB) and the Asian Infrastructure Investment Bank (AIIB) for cooperation on the project. German interests are also interested in investing and in using German technology for the project. The economic and financial strains provoked by the Western sanctions have delayed the project.

Russian Far East

Russian Far East Development Minister Alexander Galushka said in August 2017 that Chinese investment in the Russian Far East had grown by one-third in 2016. More than two dozen projects worth more than $4 billion had been launched in the 13 Priority Development Zones (called TORs) in the Far East, in-

Figure 3

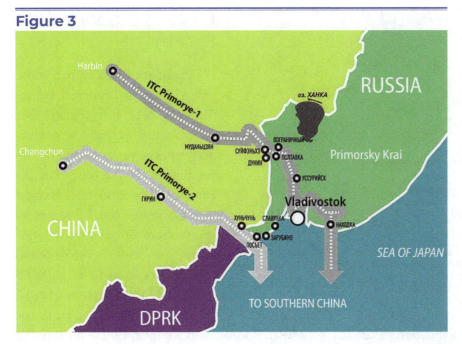

cluding the Free Port of Vladivostok, established in July 2015.

Among the priority projects for Russia-China cooperation are the Primorye 1 and Primorye 2 international transport corridors (**Figure 3**), part of the Greater Tumen River Development project. Because China has no seaports in its vast northeastern provinces, which were formally the industrial heartland of the nation but are now suffering from a "rustbelt" problem, it is crucial to the further development of the region to establish road and rail connections to the Russian seaports on the Sea of Japan and the Sea of Okhotsk. (Rail and road links to the nearby North Korean Port of Rason are also under development, but stalled by the sanctions against North Korea.)

Primorye 1 runs from Harbin, the capital of Heilongjiang Province, to Vladivostok, while Primorye 2 runs from Changchun, the capital of Jilin Province, to Hunchun just north of the North Korean border, then to the port in Zarubino, Russia. Zarubino, an ice-free port 150 km south of Vladivostok, has rail connections north to Vladivostok, south to the Rason port in North Korea, and west to Hunchun in Jilin Province, where it connects to China's extensive high-speed rail network. Plans for the development of the Zarubino Port have repeatedly been sidelined, but Russia's Summa Group intends to invest in a $3 billion expansion of the port, while China has long wanted to participate in building the port to facilitate shipping goods from northern China to the south via ship using the Russian port.

An agreement for joint development of Primorye 1 was signed on the sidelines of the Belt and Road Forum in May 2017 in Beijing. Both Primorye 1 and Primorye 2, although not fully developed, have been tested. Russia's Vostochnaya Stevedore Company and the Heilongjiang Sea Land Channel International transported timber along Primorye 1 for export to Italy, while Primorye 2 was tested for exports to Korea.

Customs problems along the border from China into Russia create a logistical bottleneck for these routes, which must be resolved.

China and Russia are near completion of the first rail bridge across the Amur (Heilongjiang) River, which is the border between the two nations in the Far East (**Figure 4**). The Chinese portion was completed in July 2016, and the Russian portion is expected to be completed by the summer of 2018. The bridge will connect Tongjiang in Heilongjiang Province to the Jewish Autonomous Oblast in Russia, providing for expanded exports from Russia to China and an enhanced capacity for China to reach the Russian ports on the Sea of Japan. The bridge will be 2.2 km, at a cost of more than $350 million, funded in part by the Russia-China Investment Fund.

A new highway bridge across the Amur is also under construction further upstream, to link the "twin" trading cities of Blagoveshchensk and Heihe. Ground-breaking was held on December 24, 2016, with expected completion in October 2019.

Russia's Norilsk Nickel, the world's second largest nickel company, together with China's Highland Fund and other Russian investors, launched the $1.5 billion Bystrinsky greenfield copper, iron, and gold mine in the Chita region of Siberia in October 2017. It holds one of the ten largest copper deposits in the world. China will be the primary customer for the output, which is expected to reach full capacity by 2020.

III. PROGRESS REPORTS

Figure 4
Bridges Across the Amur River

Population in the Russian Far East

In 2016, President Putin launched a program aimed at solving the severe underpopulation of the Far East, and spurring development of the unused lands. Called the "Far East Hectare" program, it is similar to the Homestead Act set up by Abraham Lincoln in 1862 to encourage western migration in the United States, offering settlers 160 acres of public land, which became the property of the farmer or developer after five years. Putin's plan offered one hectare (2.5 acres) of free land, with a similar five-year period before full ownership was granted, on condition that the plot is developed in some way. More than 145 million hectares of land has been allotted for the program.

The plan went into effect on February 1, 2017. Valentin Timakov, Director General of the Agency for the Development of Human Capital in the Far Eastern Federal District, told TASS on September 7, 2017: "We may talk of success judging by the results of the year. More than 100,000 applications have been made, more than 28,000 plots of land have been granted, and 8,000 are waiting for residents' signing."

He said that about one-third of the land has been granted to groups planning to create new communities. He also announced that loans to participants in the Far East Hectare program would be offered at reduced interest rates (although this is still in the 8-10% range). He further called for granting additional land to those who successfully develop their plots, and for regional governments to assist in building infrastructure.

Eastern Economic Forum

President Putin launched the annual Eastern Economic Forum (EEF) in 2015, bringing together international political and business leaders to focus on the development of the vast Russian Far East. The 2016 EEF brought together more than 3,000 participants from 56 countries, twice as many as in 2015, while 6,000 participants from more than 60 countries attended the Third EEF in September 2017. The Third EEF followed by a few days the tenth annual BRICS Summit in Xiamen, China, hosting the heads of state of the BRICS nations—China, Russia, India, Brazil, and South Africa—and several guests.

President Xi, addressing the Summit, said: "In the past ten years, our combined GDP [the BRICS countries] has grown by 179%, trade by 94%, and urban population by 28%. All this has contributed significantly to stabilizing the global economy and returning it to growth, and delivered tangible benefits to three billion and more people." The BRICS Bank, founded in 2014, like the Asia Infrastructure Investment Bank (set up with 57 founding member nations in Beijing in June 2015), provides funding for infrastructure development in the developing nations, without the "conditionalities" used by the International Monetary Fund (IMF) and the World Bank to impose Western political and economic demands on the borrowing nations.

In a message greeting those attending the Third Eastern Economic Forum following the BRICS Summit, President Putin said that Russia was committed to "provide the best possible conditions for doing business in the Far East; to launch new manufacturing capabilities, and to create additional jobs.... Russia's Far Eastern strategy is based on openness to collaboration and an interest in promoting the broadest possible international cooperation."

A significant aspect of the Forum was the attendance of Japan's Prime Minister Shinzo Abe and South Korea's President Moon Jae-in. These two

Bridge connecting mainland Russia to Russky Island

powerful economies intend to fully participate in the development of the "new frontier" in the Russian Far East, helping to bring the New Silk Road process into North Asia.

In 2012 Russia hosted the annual APEC meeting in Vladivostok. In preparation for that event the government undertook the construction of a bridge to connect the mainland to Russky Island, where the event was to be held, which was successfully completed in July 2012. It is the longest cable-stayed bridge in the world at 1,104 meters. It was a monumental accomplishment, given the region's severe climate, with temperatures reaching minus 37°C (-34.6°F) with high winds and thick ice flows.

More recently, Russia is building a pair of parallel bridges to span the Strait of Kerch, 12 miles in length of open sea, connecting Crimea's Kerch Peninsula to Krasnodar Krai, one for rail and one for vehicles. The road bridge officially opened on May 15, 2018, and the rail bridge is projected to open at the end of 2019.

The New York Times on November 11, 2017, in an article condemning the bridge and lying that Crimea had always been part of Ukraine (Crimea had been part of Russia since 1783, until the government in Moscow under Nikita Khrushchev transferred the administration to Kiev in 1954), nevertheless points to the amazing engineering feat that was being demonstrated by its construction: "The strait runs between two mountain ranges, sending fierce winds howling through its narrow confines. The alluvial flow from various rivers has carpeted the seabed with 80 meters of fine silt. Ice floes crash through during the spring thaw—indeed, an ice floe sundered a German military bridge constructed during World War II—and the area is prone to earthquakes."

While neither the Russky Bridge nor the Crimea Bridge were constructed under the auspices of the Belt and Road Initiative, they demonstrate the extraordinary engineering and construction capacities of the Russian Federation, while improving the connectivity crucial to the New Silk Road.

China-Mongolia-Russia Economic Corridor

One of the six "Economic Corridors" in the Belt and Road Initiative is the China-Mongolia-Russia Economic Corridor (**Figure 5**). The Corridor was formulated and signed by the three heads of state—Vladimir Putin, Xi Jinping, and then Mongolian President Tsakhiagiin Elbegdorj—at the 11th SCO meeting in June 2016 in Uzbekistan, involving 32 projects. This was the first multilateral cooperation plan to be implemented under the Belt and Road Initiative (BRI). The Corridor is a central part of the plan to unite the Eurasian Economic Union and the BRI, and will eventually be part of the planned Moscow-Beijing high-speed railway, through Mongolia's

Construction of the Crimean bridge, September 15, 2016

Figure 5
China-Mongolia-Russia Rail and Road Corridor

Prairie Road program. The Corridor will focus on transportation infrastructure, dry port construction, improving border and custom procedures, and cultural connectivity.

A paved road from China through Mongolia via Erenhot in Inner Mongolia, Ulan-Bator in Mongolia, and on to Ulan-Ude in Russia (meeting the Trans-Siberian Railroad), is expected to be opened to international traffic in 2018, along the route of the Trans-Mongolian Railroad, which was built during 1949-1961. Road maintenance on this route has proven to be extremely difficult due to the extremes of weather conditions, requiring high-quality road construction and maintenance.

A second transport route being upgraded as part of this corridor is the former Trans-Manchurian Railroad built by Imperial Russia at the turn of the 20th Century, connecting the Russian city of Chita (on the Trans-Siberian Railway) to Harbin, then branching east to Vladivostok and south to Beijing.

Tunnel Under the Bering Strait

The idea of a connection between Eurasia and North America across the Bering Strait has captured imaginations for the past 150 years. Even before Russia sold Alaska to the United States in 1867, there was support in the U.S. Congress for a telegraph line across the Bering Strait to Russia, a U.S. ally. In 1890, Governor William Gilpin of the Colorado Territory promoted a "grand scheme of a Cosmopolitan railway," reaching "north and west across the Strait of Bering; and across Siberia, to connect with the railways of Europe and all of the world" (**Figure 6**). There were several initiatives to launch the project in subsequent decades, both before and after the Russian revolution of 1917.

LaRouche's movement has campaigned for the Bering Strait connection since 1978. In 1995, *EIR* published an overview, written by American consulting engineer Hal B.H. Cooper, Jr. and Professor Sergei A. Bykadorov of the Siberian State Academy of Transport in Novosibirsk, of railroads in Siberia and the Russian Far East: existing lines, those started but not completed, and an ambitious vision of a far denser network to support the economic development of the continent and its resources.[1] **Figure 7** shows the Cooper-Bykadorov design for a web of the Trans-Siberian Railway, the Baikal-Amur Mainline, completion of the Near-Polar Mainline, and construction of a Bering Strait Connector, a North Siberian Mainline, and a Cross-Siberian Connector.

Within Russia, the Council for the Study of Productive Forces (SOPS, from its Russian acronym) took the lead in promoting the Bering Strait connec-

---

1 Hal B. H. Cooper, Jr., Sergei A. Bykadorov, "North Eurasian Rail Systems and Their Impact on Siberian Economic Growth," *EIR*, May 19, 1995.

Figure 6
Gilpin's 1890 Plan to Bridge the Bering Strait

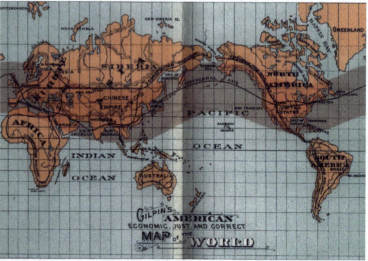

Figure 7
Cooper-Bykadorov Plan for Russian Rail

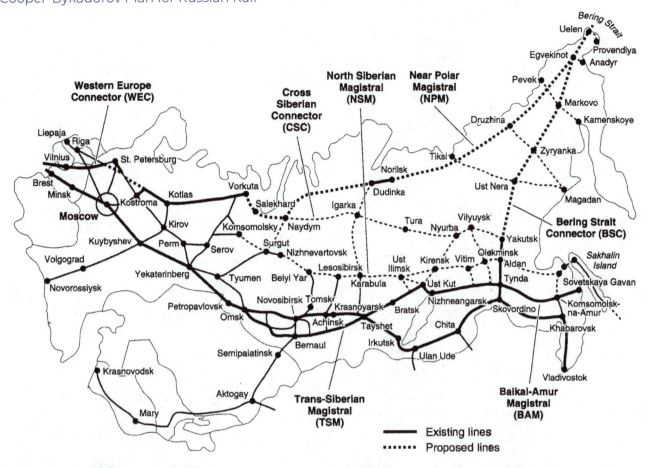

tion. From 1992 until his death in 2010, the head of SOPS was Novosibirsk-based Academician Alexander Granberg, Russia's leading specialist on regional development. In November 2009, Granberg endorsed a public call to "Put the 'LaRouche Plan to Save the World Economy' on the Agenda."

On April 24, 2007, SOPS co-sponsored a conference in Moscow called Megaprojects of Russian East: An Intercontinental Eurasia-America Transport Link via the Bering Strait.[2] Granberg told the meeting that Russia's leaders saw transportation infrastructure as essential for uplifting the country's vast outlying regions. He cited a presentation that Vladimir Yakunin, CEO of the state-owned Russian Railways company, had made earlier that month at a meeting chaired by Putin on rail transport, favoring construction of a 2,500- to 3,000-km railway from the Lena River to the Bering Strait.

Later in 2007, that railway to the coastal village of Uelen, with a spur to the gold-mining center of Magadan on the Sea of Okhotsk, would be incorporated into the Russian Railways Strategy for 2030 (**Figure 8**), as a "new railroad of strategic importance." SOPS invited LaRouche to address the Megaprojects conference. Although he was unable to attend, his contribution was read to the gathering: "The World's Political Map Changes: Mendeleyev Would Have Agreed!"

SOPS took the Bering Strait multimodal tunnel project to the Shanghai World Expo-2010, where it won a Grand Prize for innovation. As the Silk Road Economic Belt policy began to take shape after President Xi Jinping's late-2013 announcement, respected rail expert Academician Wang Mengshu voiced China's keen interest in the scheme. In May 2014, Wang told the Beijing Times that Chinese high-speed rail (HSR) plans now encompass the Bering Strait tun-

---

2 Rachel Douglas, "Russian-American Team: World Needs Bering Strait Tunnel!", *EIR*, May 4, 2007. The conference proceedings were published in the bilingual English-Russian Moscow periodical, FORUM International #7 (2007).

Figure 8
The Russian Railways Strategy for 2050

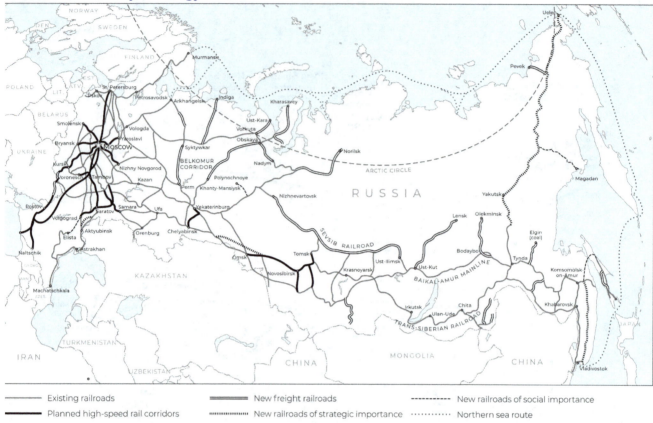

nel, which was being discussed with Russia. With HSR technology, Wang forecast, a passenger would be able to travel between China and North America by train in only two days. High-speed trains are already operating on the Beijing-Shenyang-Harbin line in northeast China. This route will be extended across the Amur River to the Trans-Siberian Railway, whence the Amur-Yakutsk Mainline and planned Bering Strait Connector lead to the Bering Strait.

Currency Agreements

The rapidly growing Russia-China cooperation has major consequences for the role of the dollar as the sole medium for world trade. Currency swap arrangements, allowing trade to be conducted in local currencies, have been expanding internationally over the past decade, but the scope of China-Russia trade, with each other and with others, makes their agreements that much more significant for the changing world currency policies.

In September 2015, the IMF finally agreed to include the Chinese renminbi (yuan) as one of the official reserve currencies, giving it just under 11% weighting in the SDR reserve currency basket—higher than the Japanese yen and the British pound. At the end of 2014, Russia and China concluded a three-year, $25 billion currency swap agreement, allowing some trade to take place in their own currencies, while similar swaps took place with the other BRICS countries. Gazprom began accepting renminbi for payment in 2015. Negotiations at the end of 2017 are aimed at extending the swap for another three years. Trade between Moscow and Beijing grew 2.2% in 2016 to $69.52 billion, while the goal is to reach $80 billion by 2018 and $200 billion by 2020.

Russia and China have also begun developing their own National Payments System, to guard against any move by the West to cut off use of the SWIFT system in a crisis or as part of their sanctions policies, and are moving toward honoring each other's national credit card systems.

Japan in the Russian Far East

Japan and South Korea are also greatly interested in the "new frontier" of the Russian Far East (Korea's role will be covered in a separate section later in this report). At the peak of the Obama Administration's attacks on Russia, including the imposition of sanctions on Russia by the United States and the EU, Japanese Prime Minister Abe essentially snubbed his erstwhile mentors in Washington, taking measures to work with Russia toward finally settling the conflicting territorial claims over the Northern Territories (the Kuril Islands), and opening up greater Japanese investment in Russia, especially in the Far East (**Figure 9**).

In May 2016, Abe held an extremely successful summit with Putin in Sochi on the Black Sea, despite intense pressure from the Obama White House to cancel the visit. Abe and Putin agreed on a path toward solving the territorial dispute that has prevented the signing of a peace treaty to end World War II between Russia and Japan. The agreement will eventually divide the four major contested islands between Russian and Japanese sovereignty, while immediately providing for Japanese visits to the two southernmost islands, and Japanese investments in fisheries and tourism in the two islands. The two leaders also discussed a wide range of potential Japanese investments in the Russian Far East, in oil and gas production, energy generation, medical facilities, transportation, ports, and more.

At the Sochi summit, President Putin invited Prime Minister Abe to attend the second Eastern Economic Forum in Vladivostok in September 2016, where the two leaders held a second summit. Putin then visited Japan in December 2016, meeting with Abe first in his home prefecture of Yamaguchi, then in Tokyo, where the two solidified their new close relationship.

With the election of Donald Trump, and especially with Trump's historic November 2017 visit to Japan, South Korea, and China, as well as Vietnam and the Philippines in Southeast Asia, the divisive policies of the Bush and Obama eras have been put to rest—at least temporarily—and a new paradigm of unity across Asia is emerging, providing for dramatic and rapid cooperation and development.

Russian President Putin and Japanese Prime Minister Shinzo Abe, Sochi, Russia, May 2016

During Trump's visit to Beijing, he and President Xi oversaw the signing of $253 billion in Chinese investment agreements in U.S. infrastructure, industry, and agriculture. This new U.S.-China relationship has also lifted a weight off of Japan's diplomatic shoulders, with Abe in December 2017 declaring that Japan will invest in joint development projects with China in third countries as part of the Belt and Road Initiative, marking a major phase change in Japan-China relations since the end of World War II.

Both the United States and Japan should, finally, join the Asian Infrastructure Investment Bank (AIIB) in the near future, correcting a serious mistake made by Washington and Japan in refusing to join at its founding in October 2014, as a result of Obama's attempted economic and strategic isolation of China.

Figure 9

The Kuril Islands-Northern Territories

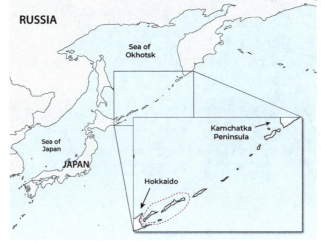

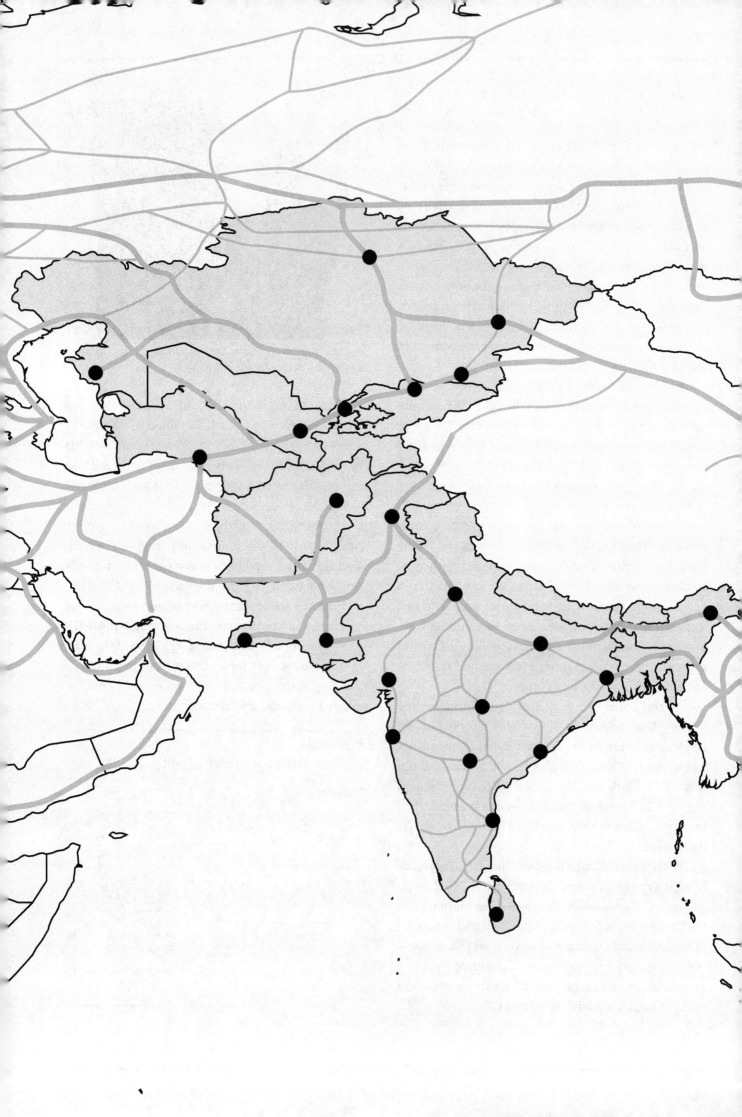

"Opening up the largely landlocked region to transportation networks ... was a major focus of the New Silk Road conception put forth by Lyndon and Helga LaRouche.... Fully exploiting the rich resources in the region ... depended on building transportation and other infrastructure necessary for a modern industrial economy."

CENTRAL ASIA
The Hub of the New Silk Road

The five Central Asian nations, Kazakhstan, Uzbekistan, Turkmenistan, Kyrgyzstan, and Tajikistan, were all part of the USSR until the 1991 demise of the Soviet Union. Afghanistan is also sometimes considered to be a Central Asian nation. Opening up the largely landlocked region to transportation networks, thus providing a basis for developing the domestic economies, was a major focus of the New Silk Road conception put forth by Lyndon and Helga LaRouche after the fall of the Soviet Union, and adopted by the Chinese under the name "Eurasian Land-Bridge" in the 1990s. Fully exploiting the rich resources in the region, especially oil and gas, also depended on building transportation and other infrastructure necessary for a modern industrial economy.

In the wake of the break-up of the USSR, Helga Zepp-LaRouche helped organize a major conference in Beijing, "International Symposium on Economic Development of the Regions Along the Euro-Asian Continental Bridge," featuring leading Chinese government and institutional speakers, with more than 450 experts and diplomats from 36 countries.

From this beginning, the aim was to bring the nations of Europe, Russia, China, and India together, and in so doing, lifting the underdeveloped nations in between to a higher level of existence.

In her presentation at that conference, titled "Building the Silk Road Land-Bridge: The Basis for the Mutual Security Interests of Asia and Europe," Mrs. LaRouche said in part:

> Any competent economic consideration must start from the point that already today, three-fourths of the world's population, 4.4 billion people, live in Eurasia, and that, given normal "development," without catastrophe, that population will grow to 7-10 billion. If, in the next years, we are to prevent seismic economic and demographic collapses, it is urgently required that we overcome the current underdevelopment of vast parts of the former Soviet Union, China, India, South and Southeast Asia, in basic infrastructure (water supply, modern transportation networks, energy production and distribution).

The first rail connection from China to Europe was opened in 1991, when a link between China's Xinjiang Autonomous Region and Kazakhstan was opened, after decades of delay due to the split between the USSR and China. But this route had to fer-

III. PROGRESS REPORTS

Figure 1
Railway and Road Corridors Across Eurasia

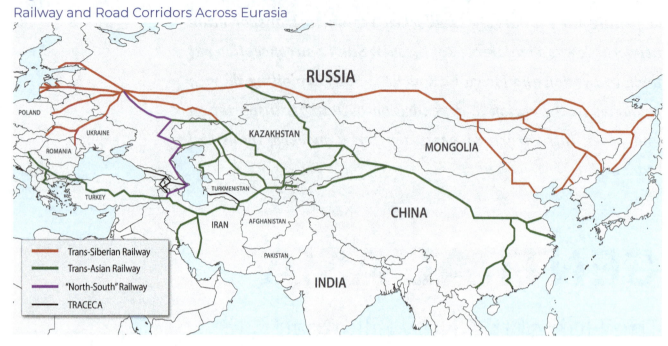

ry across the Caspian Sea from Kazakhstan to Baku in Azerbaijan before proceeding to Europe.

In addition to the road and rail connections that have been constructed or upgraded with Chinese assistance since the 1990s (**Figure 1**), the oil and gas reserves in the region have also been extensively developed, with a series of oil and gas pipelines feeding the massive growth in the Chinese economy, and providing funds for development in Central Asia (**Figure 2**).

In September 2017, the 5,000th train from China to Europe departed from Zhengzhou in Henan Province, arriving in Hamburg, Germany. The through route from China to Germany opened in 2011, arriving in Duisburg, which has since become a thriving dry port.

According to CGTN, there are (as of the end of 2017) 52 routes running between 32 Chinese cities and cities across Europe. Zhong Cheng, vice general manager of the China Railway Container Transport Company, told CCTV:

"It took us 55 months to increase from one train to the 1,000th, eight and a half months to increase to the second 1,000th train, five and a half months to increase to the third 1,000th train, and four and a half months to reach the fourth 1,000th train.

Kazakhstan's 'Nurly Zhol'

The most heavily travelled rail routes pass through Kazakhstan, both to Europe and to Southwest Asia. Not surprisingly, China's President Xi Jinping first announced his plan for the New Silk Road Economic Belt in 2013 in Kazakhstan. The Chinese vision was quickly embraced by Kazakhstan's President Nursultan Nazarbayev, who integrated the initiative with his own national vision for development, aimed at making Kazakhstan the major transit hub for Euro-Asian traffic as part of his "New Economic Policy," called "Nurly Zhol," or "Lighted Path." By 2020 it is expected that Kazakhstan will be servicing 15 routes between China and Europe.

Even years before President Xi's official declaration of the New Silk Road Economic Belt in 2013, China had already begun to invest heavily in the infrastructure to link China with Central Asia. The first rail connection between China and Kazakhstan was completed in 1991. After the break-up of the Soviet Union in 1991, there were some tensions between the two huge Eurasian nations over the investments in Central Asia. Due to the long period in which the Central Asian "stans" were part of the Soviet Union, there is significant Russian investment in the region,

Figure 2
Central Asia Oil and Gas Pipelines

and large numbers of Russia citizens living and working there. These tensions have been largely overcome as a result of the increasingly close relations between Russia and China, especially through cooperation between the Belt and Road Initiative (BRI) and the Eurasian Economic Union (EAEU), organized by Russia around the same time as the launching of the BRI. The EAEU now includes Russia, Belarus, Kazakhstan, Armenia, and Kyrgyzstan. Russian President Vladimir Putin and President Xi both have emphasized the close cooperation between the BRI and the EAEU.

The China-Pan Central Asia natural gas dual pipeline of 1,840 km (Lines A and B) was built in 2008-2010 to bring in 30 billion cubic meters (bcm) of gas from Turkmenistan, Uzbekistan, and Kazakhstan. A third pipeline of larger diameter, Line C, parallel to the first two, was built in 2012-2014 and delivers an additional 25 bcm. Line C includes gas from Kazakh gas fields.

Chinese banks have been encouraged by Beijing to lend money to the countries that are part of the land-bridge, and Kazakhstan has become a major beneficiary of Chinese loans. Especially, Kazakhstan has been a major recipient of Chinese investment in Central Asian oil over the past two decades. In Congressional testimony in 2014, a U.S. policy adviser provided some of the specifics:

"China's largest national oil company, China National Petroleum Corporation (CNPC), is the majority owner of two of Kazakhstan's major oil companies (it owns 85.42% of AktobeMunaiGas and 67% of PetroKazakhstan) and is involved in several oil exploration and production projects throughout the country. The company also provides oilfield services in Kazakhstan and plans to build a refinery there. China's sovereign wealth fund, China Investment Corporation, also invested almost $1 billion in Kazakh energy in 2009."[1]

The main transit hub between China and Kazakhstan on the border between the two countries, Khorgos, has already developed from a rather isolated outpost on the edge of the desert into a major dry port for the Belt and Road, although currently with more development on the Chinese side than on the Kazakh side of the border. Khorgos is now a major logistical corridor which can direct traffic to all four corners of the Eurasian heartland. Wade Shepard reported in Forbes in May 2017 that after just one year of full-fledged operation, it was handling more than one-fifth of its 2020 goal of 500,000 twenty-foot equivalent units (TEUs) per year. In May 2017, on the sidelines of the Belt and Road Forum in Beijing, COSCO, China's major shipping company, and the Port of Lianyungang, which was the terminus of the first of the Eurasian rail routes, signed a contract to buy 49% of the Khorgos Gateway dry port. This agreement is expected to lead to a rapid expansion of Khorgos Gateway and the Khorgos Eastern Gateway Special Economic Zone, a 600-hectare development area of which the Gateway is a part.

Trains passing through Khorgos must change rail gauge from the Chinese gauge of 1,435 mm to the gauge used across the former USSR, of 1,520 mm. The dry port is a montage of six sets of train tracks lined up side by side. When trains pull in, their platforms are lined up next to each other and the containers are transferred over from one to the other via giant 41-ton gantry cranes in a process that can be completed in as little as 47 minutes.

Kazakhstan is the world's ninth largest country, spanning 2.7 million square kilometers (km^2). But it has a population of only 16 million, less than that of Florida (20 million). Vast stretches of this largely

---

[1] Testimony of Dennis E. Shea, House Foreign Affairs Subcommittee, May 21, 2014.

arid and semi-arid country have remained sparsely populated. Nonetheless, the concentration of economic activity in the eastern and western ends of Kazakhstan (more than 1,500 miles across) has led to the development of a workable transport infrastructure. Railroads and highways crisscross the country; none are fully adequate, and many will become obsolete once the country begins to grow rapidly (**Figure 3**).

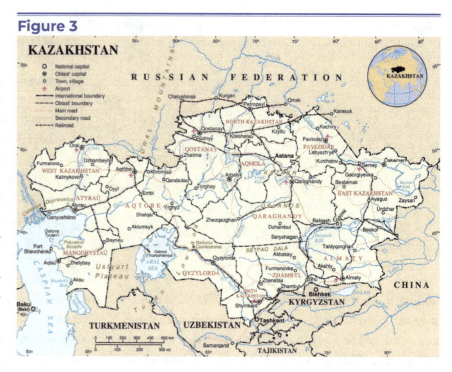

Figure 3

Kazakhstan has been led by President Nursultan Nazarbayev since its independence in 1990. His dedication to restoring the ancient Silk Road dates from that time. In his November 2014 State of the Union address, just a year after Xi Jinping's announcement of the New Silk Road in Astana with Nazarbayev at his side, the Kazakh President presented his Nurly Zhol:

> The Infrastructure Development Plan, which I want to make public today, will become the core of the New Economic Policy. It is intended to last for five years and is to run in parallel with the Second Five Year term of the Program of Accelerated Industrial and Innovative Development. More than 100 foreign companies intend to participate in its implementation. The total investment portfolio will amount to KZT6 trillion [about $18 billion at the December 2016 exchange rate between the U.S. dollar and Kazakh Tenge], with the state contributing 15% of the total. All the regions of Kazakhstan need to be closely connected by railroads, highways, and air services…. The New Economic Policy, "Nurly Zhol," will become a driver of growth in our economy during the coming years: 200,000 new jobs will be created by the construction of roads alone. And this means greater employment and growth of income for the population. "Nurly Zhol" will create a multiplier effect in other economic sectors: production of cement, metal, machinery, bitumen, equipment, and related services. Roads are lifelines for Kazakhstan. Life has always emerged and developed in our vast expanses around roads. Yet we must create a transport network such that car, railway, and airlines stretch in all directions from Astana.

Today, the integration of the Nurly Zhol and China's Silk Road Economic Belt is central to the development of Kazakhstan and Eurasia as a whole. Kazakhstan's Foreign Minister Erlan Idrissov, addressing a press conference on the Nurly Zhol and the Belt and Road on November 30, 2016, said:

> Implementation of the Nurly Zhol program will ensure the connection of the Kazakh regions to intercontinental routes, Western Kazakhstan-Western Europe [and] China-Iran, and will turn Kazakhstan into a major Eurasian transport and logistics hub that will connect the North with the South, the East with the West, the countries of the European Union, the Middle East, and Southeast Asia.

In addition to the transportation network, which Nurly Zhol addresses directly, Kazakhstan has immense mineral deposits of high quality. It is the world's leading uranium producer with 12% of world reserves, and the third largest chrome producer. Its deposits of copper and lead-zinc represent 10% and 13%, respectively, of world reserves. Kazakhstan is also well endowed with bauxite, coal, manganese, iron ore, phosphate, titanium, and tungsten. The mining industry as a whole was valued at nearly $30 billion in 2017.

The development of Kazakhstan's uranium production is impressive. From 2001 to 2015, production rose from 2,022 tons to about 23,800 tons per year (39% of world production), making Kazakhstan the world's leading uranium producer. Of its 17 mine projects, five are wholly owned by the government-owned Kazatomprom and 12 are joint ventures with foreign equity holders.[2] According to the World Nuclear Association, Kazakhstan has a major nuclear fuel pellet plant, and is building a nuclear fuel fabrication plant, through a joint venture with Areva of France, Kazatomprom of Kazakhstan, and China General Nuclear Power Corporation (CGN-PC), with 49% Chinese equity.

Kazakhstan Needs Nuclear Power

Although endowed with uranium, and soon to have a nuclear fuel fabrication plant, Kazakhstan does not have a single nuclear power plant. (A single Russian-built nuclear power reactor operated from 1972 to 1999, generating electricity and desalinating water.) Kazakhstan generates about 13 GW of electrical power, of which about 81% comes from coal and the rest from natural gas. It imports some electricity from Russia and exports a small amount to Kyrgyzstan, another power-starved nation.

Kazakhstan had plans for several new nuclear power plants, but in November 2016 these plans were postponed because it was thought that there would be no need until 2025. But there is an immediate need: As with roads, life has always emerged and developed around cheap, abundant energy. In September 2017, the energy minister said that Kazatomprom would undertake a new feasibility study in 2018.

Plans for building a high-temperature gas-cooled reactor (HTR) research project with the Japan Atomic Energy Agency (JAEA) and the Kazakhstan Atomic Energy Committee, focused on small cogeneration plants, have been under discussion since 2007, but have also been stalled. Kazakhstan's National Nuclear Center has proposed constructing 20 or more small reactors of 50-100 MW each to supply dispersed towns.

Water is also a serious issue for Kazakhstan, to enable its productive capabilities and to improve living conditions at the household level. Almost 90% of the country is considered arid or semi-arid, with low humidity. In terms of water resources, the country is among those at the low end of the scale in Eurasia. Kazakhstan's average annual surface water is 100.5 cubic kilometers (km^3), of which 56.5 km^3 is from precipitation within the country; the rest comes from China, Uzbekistan, Kyrgyzstan, and Russia. Surface water resources are also very unevenly distributed.

Although water is a major hurdle for Kazakhstan, desalination of water from the Caspian Sea could fully alleviate water shortages in the north, west, and parts of the south. Here again, nuclear power would greatly enhance desalination capacities.

In January 2018, President Nursultan Nazarbayev traveled to Washington, DC, with several members of his cabinet for meetings with President Trump and other officials, his first visit to the United States since 2006. President Nazarbayev emphasized the importance of Kazakhstan's role as a friend of the United States, Russia, and China, in helping to find solutions to the crises in Afghanistan, Korea, and Syria. Nazarbayev also spoke for the five Central Asian nations as part of the Central Asia plus the United States dialogue format, known as C5+1. The two leaders elevated their bilateral relationship to the level of "Enhanced Strategic Partnership." There are more than 500 U.S. companies operating in Kazakhstan, with total investments of more than $50 billion.

Uzbekistan

More than 2,000 years ago, many of the numerous trade routes across Asia passed through Central Asia. Caravans of hundreds of Bactrian camels, often led by Sogdian merchants, would wend their way to and from China, India, and Western Asia—what today some call the Middle East. From China, bolts

---

[2] "Uranium and Nuclear Power in Kazakhstan," World Nuclear Association, December 2016.

of silk went westward from about 100 B.C. to 1500 A.D. There were many and varied routes and modes of conveyance. Frederick Starr, in his book Lost Enlightenment: Central Asia's Golden Age from the Arab Conquest to Tamerlane, described it this way:

"...a 'Lapis Lazuli Road' from Afghanistan to Egypt and India, a 'Jade Road' from Khotan to China, an 'Emerald Road' stretching east and west from the Pamir mountains of Tajikistan and Afghanistan, or a 'Gold Road' or 'Copper Road' to the capitals of the Middle East."

Great Uzbek cities arose along the Silk Road trade routes: Tashkent (known as Chash, then), Ferghana (Farghona), Samarkand (Samarqand), Bukhara (Bukhoro), Khiva, and Termez. These were then the international transshipment points, the vital centers of trade, skilled craft work, and cultural exchange, even while political rule of the region shifted from the Iranian Sogdians to the Islamic Caliphate, and then to various embodiments of Mongol and Turkic rule. Uzbekistan was absorbed into the Russian Empire in the 19th Century and became part of the Soviet Union. This history is reflected in the Uzbek language, a Turkic language with influences from Persian, Arabic, Tatar, and Russian.

The Aral Sea in 1989 (left) and 2014 (right)

Uzbekistan and the New Silk Road

Uzbekistan is a nation of 30 million. The vast majority live in the eastern and southern part of the country; the vast arid zone of central and western Uzbekistan is virtually uninhabited. This was aggravated by the decision in the 1960s by the USSR to divert the rivers which flowed into the Aral Sea, the fourth largest lake in the world at one time, which straddles the Uzbek-Kazakh border.

The plan was to use the water to grow cotton in the desert. It was an economic and environmental disaster, leaving the Aral Sea a small fraction of its original size, furthering desertification, and driving much of the population to other regions to survive.

As during the golden age of Central Asia—7th to 14th Centuries—Uzbekistan's bilateral trade with China to the east remains crucially important. In the first decade following Uzbekistan's independence in 1991, the value of its annual trade with China did not exceed $140 million. It gained momentum in the early 2000s and amounted to $5 billion in 2017 (20% of its total international trade). China's BRI initiative is now interlinked with Uzbekistan's model for economic development.

Uzbek President Shavkat Mirziyoyev, who became President following the death of President Islam Karimov in 2016, visited China in May 2017, signing investment agreements worth $23 billion in energy, oil refining, agriculture, chemicals, transport, and communications. The chairman of the state oil

Figure 4

The Fergana Valley and the Kamchik Pass

and gas company Uzbekneftegaz, Alisher Sultanov, said in an interview that 10 separate deals worth $5 billion collectively were signed in the energy sector alone, mostly financed by Chinese banks and investment funds. Other projects include the modernization of 300 water pumping stations, and the building of an automobile tunnel under the Kamchik Pass, which divides the Fergana Valley from the rest of the country (**Figure 4**). China was largely responsible for a $1.5 billion railway tunnel along the same route that was completed last year.

China's Natural Gas and Other Investments

China's BRI-related investments in Uzbekistan span a range of sectors, none bigger than the development of Uzbekistan's natural gas reserves and gas transportation infrastructure, which have been a major source of China's huge appetite for energy. This features the Central Asia-China gas pipeline, of which Uzbekistan is the linchpin: All three lines, Lines A, B, and C, run from Turkmenistan through Uzbek territory, essentially parallel to each other, then through Kazakhstan to China, supplying 55 bcm of natural gas a year to China. This constitutes 20% of China's annual natural gas consumption (**Figure 5**).

Long-standing plans to build a fourth pipeline from Turkmenistan to China, Line D, was to take a different route, carrying gas from Turkmenistan's Galkynysh gas field 1,000 km to China through southern Uzbekistan, northern Tajikistan, and eastern Kyrgyzstan. It would be capable of transporting 30 bcm when completed, raising China's annual supply from Turkmenistan to 85 bcm. The three countries through which Line D would pass on the way to China were not to receive any of the gas, but would receive significant transit fees.

However, in March 2017, the project was put on an indefinite hold. The project is technically extremely difficult—the mountainous terrain of Tajikistan, where the longest section of Line D (410 km) was being built, necessitates costly and sophisticated engineering. These challenges include "the creation of 47 tunnels with a total length of 76 km. In 24 of these cases, the tunnels will be underwater," as Tajik President Emomali Rahmon himself emphasized at the ground-breaking ceremony on September 13, 2014, together with President Xi Jinping.

It is not only the difficulty of the project which has caused the indefinite postponement. Political and diplomatic problems between Kyrgyzstan and Tajikistan with China over contracts for the project are involved, which are also undermining plans for a rail connection along a similar route.

Turkmenistan

Turkmenistan's unique position in Central Asia today centers on its status as a major producer and exporter of natural gas. Turkmenistan exports 44 bcm of the 77 bcm it produces each year. Although Kazakhstan and Uzbekistan are also significant energy producers, Turkmenistan's population of 5.5 million is much smaller than Kazakhstan's 18 million and Uzbekistan's 30 million, and that reduces its domestic needs and enables a high level of export.

However, the postponing of the Line D pipeline to China has added to a serious economic crisis in Turkmenistan. Russia had cancelled a contract for Turkmen gas in 2016, and Turkmen gas supplies to Iran were suspended at the start of 2017 over a contract dispute. Added to the decline in oil and gas prices, the heavily gas-dependent Turkmenistan economy was facing a deep crisis as 2018 began.

It is not surprising that in response to this crisis Turkmen President Gurbanguly Berdimuhamedov has declared 2018 to be the Silk Road Year, under the slogan "Turkmenistan—the Heart of the Great Silk Road." Speaking at a news conference in Turkey's capital Ankara, Turkmen Ambassador to Turkey Isankuli Amanliyev said: "The key point in Turkmenistan's development policy in the transportation sector is establishing architectural bases of new geo-economic space which will connect Central Asia, Caspian Sea, Black Sea, the Baltics, Middle and Near East, South and Southeast Asia."

Turkmenistan had remained somewhat in isolation, by choice, since its emergence from the USSR in 1991 as an independent nation, but has recently emerged to establish more active relationships with its neighbors, and a particularly close relationship with China.

Figure 5
Gas Pipelines from Central Asia to China

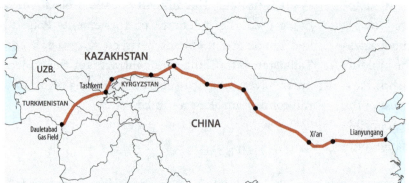

The A, B, and C gas pipelines from Turkmenistan to China, passing through Uzbekistan and Kazakhstan, run parallel to each other.

Its former isolation had resulted in stagnation in almost every sphere of its socio-political economy. This shift was born of the realization that it was necessary to ensure a beneficial life for the coming generations of Turkmenistanis. It was not entirely a result of the change of leadership in 2006, when Gurbanguly Berdimuhamedov became President. A significant part was played, and is being played, by China, through the Belt and Road Initiative.

The government practiced what was called "positive" (or "permanent") neutrality, a UN-recognized status, for almost 20 years, but has now begun to pursue new initiatives to build a prosperous Turkmenistan. These initiatives have largely remained confined to the development of its huge gas reserves and the natural gas trade. Besides the huge need for energy in China, delivered through the three existing pipelines, the nation's vast reserves of natural gas will be in high demand to meet the booming development process taking place in Pakistan and throughout the region through the Belt and Road process.

Connecting with Neighbors

How will the natural gas get to Pakistan? The Turkmenistan-Afghanistan-Pakistan-India (TAPI) gas pipeline project, which has been hanging fire for years, will bring to Afghanistan, Pakistan, and India an estimated 90 million standard cubic meters of gas per day from Turkmenistan's Galkynysh gas field in its eastern Mary province. The 1,800 km pipeline will traverse a path of 780 km through Afghanistan and about 830 km from west to east through Pakistan, to enter Punjab state, India. The Turkmenistan section of the pipeline was started in 2015, but the Afghan section is only now about to be launched, targeted for February 2018. (See more on TAPI in the section on Afghanistan.)

The Galkynysh Gas Field project, which supplies gas to TAPI and other pipelines, is an example of the close relations that have developed between China and Turkmenistan. The Galkynysh Gas Field, 75 km southeast of Mary, was discovered in 2006 and is one of the five largest gas fields in the world. It is actually a cluster of gas fields estimated to hold more than 14 trillion cubic meters of gas. It is owned by Turkmengaz State Concern, the state-owned national gas company of Turkmenistan. Gas production began in September 2013.

The first phase of development, requiring an investment of $8.5 billion, was funded through loans provided by the China Development Bank (CDB) and revenues of Turkmengaz. The second phase, now under consideration, will also be funded by the CDB, and is expected to come online in 2018. China is the most successful foreign investor in Turkmenistan and is the only one that has been given access to a major onshore gas field. China also provided a boundary security system and terrestrial trunked radio communications system at the Galkynysh project site.

Security—Afghanistan's Taliban

Yet there is another important reason for Turkmenistan to cultivate relations with its neighbors—the problem of the Taliban and Islamic State (Daesh). In recent years, activities by the Afghan Taliban along the Afghanistan-Turkmenistan border have caused the Turkmenistan government in Ashgabat to sit up. On the Afghan side, militant groups control extensive territory.

Of concern to the Turkmenistan government, Afghanistan has a significant Turkmen minority, which accounts for 3% of the country's population. In 2015, Afghan Turkmen in the Marchak district along Turkmenistan's border were surrounded by the Taliban, essentially cutting them off from Kabul, and they called for help from Turkmenistan.

In dealing with these security threats, Turkmenistan will have to seek closer cooperation with the Shanghai Cooperation Organization (SCO) and, in effect, with its neighbors. SCO is led by Russia and China and will soon be joined by India and Pakistan. Although Turkmenistan is the only Central Asian nation which is not a member of the SCO, President Berdimuhamedov took part in its 15th anniversary Heads of State summit in Tashkent in June 2016, as a guest, as he has at earlier summits.

Addressing the session, Berdimuhamedov said: "Cooperation with the SCO is an important component of the foreign policy course of our country aimed at providing stable and balanced regional processes, active economic and trade partnerships, and the creation of conditions for realization of large international infrastructure projects. That is why Turkmenistan considers the development of relations with the SCO as in inherent connection with both the advancing course of bilateral cooperation and with the general direction of its participation in regional processes."

Young Nation, Ancient Cultures

The vast majority of Turkmenistan's 5.5 million people—the smallest of the five Central Asian countries—are Sunni Muslims belonging to the Hanafi school within mainstream Islam. Nestorian Christians (properly called the Church of the East) entered the land of today's Turkmenistan in the 4th Century A.D.—as they spread widely throughout Asia—but by the beginning of the 14th Century, Christianity had been generally replaced by Islam.

What is today Turkmenistan was first delineated as the Turkmen Soviet Socialist Republic at the time of the consolidation of the USSR in the 1920s. Parts of the same territory, in the 7th Century A.D. for example, formed parts of Khorasan, Khwarezm, Sogdiana, and Tokharistan.

The region is steeped in history. In this land, Alexander's army and the armies of the Roman, Parthian, Persian, and Arab empires, and of the Mongols under Chinggis Khan, and of Timur the Lame, have passed through or held sway. For centuries, a part of today's Turkmenistan had formed part of the Persian province of Khorasan, and Khorasan had Merv (next to Mary, the modern city) as its capital. With the explosive expansion of Islam, beginning in the 7th Century, ancient Merv became one of the world's greatest cities, known as "the Queen of Cities"; it had already been a stop on the Silk Road for centuries. From Merv, caravans went westward to Iran and Turkey, and eastward to China. Its ruins now stand as silent witness to that glorious and eventful past. Thousands of years of civilization lie behind what is Turkmenistan today, at archaeological sites such as Kunya-Urgench (on the left bank of the Amu Darya), Dekhistan (a city by the Caspian Sea), Merv, and Old Nissa. The last named, Old Nissa, 15 km west of Turkmenistan's capital, Ashgabat, was the capital of the Parthian kings for 600 years, rivaling Rome itself.[3]

Ruins of the ancient city of Merv

The Driver: Belt and Road

Turkmenistan has a serious land problem: Only 5% of the land is arable. The Karakum Desert occupies more than 70% of the country (the desert sits atop a vast pool of unexplored gas reserves).

The arable land per capita is perhaps less than 0.5 hectares (1.2 acres), but in spite of this, much cotton is grown for export. Turkmenistan's small population and paucity of currently useful land might be expected to act as hindrance to its emergence as a prosperous and economically significant nation.

But its location, and China's push to develop connectivity with nations east, west, and south of the Caspian Sea, could make Turkmenistan a very important ingredient in the future of the Belt and Road.

---

3 John D. Grainger, *Rome, Parthia, India: The Violent Emergence of a New World Order, 150-140 BC* (Barnsley, UK: Pen & Sword Books, 2013), "Introduction."

Figure 6
The 'Silk Road Train'

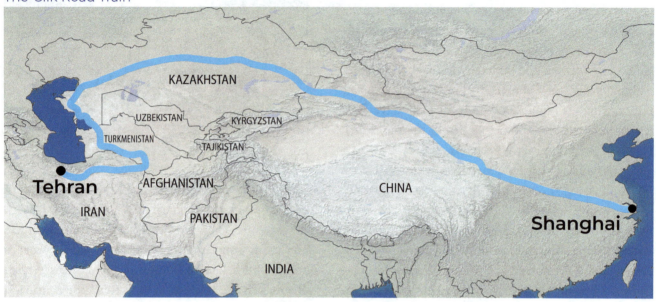

At the same time, Turkmenistan is "blessed" with not having direct access to the Ferghana Valley, whose fertile land and density of population of various ethnic groups have attracted Islamic extremists who promote sectarian strife, often exploited by Anglo-American policymakers with the intent to undermine Russia and China.

Major China-Iran Link

The first cargo train from China to Iran, the "Silk Road train," entered Turkmenistan from Kazakhstan and reached Tehran on February 15, 2016, having travelled 10,399 km with dozens of cargo containers. Welcoming the train at the Tehran Railway Station, Iran's Deputy Minister of Roads and Urbanism, Mohsen Pour-Aqaei, said on that occasion, according to *China Daily*, February 16, 2016: "To revive the Silk Road Economic Belt, the launch of the train is an important move, since about 700 kilometers of the trip has been done per day.... Compared to the sea voyage of the cargo ships from China's Shanghai city to Iran's Bandar Abbas port city, the travel time of the train was 30 days shorter" (**Figure 6**). The new line is expected to facilitate traffic between Central Asia and the Persian Gulf, including shipments of oil and agricultural produce. Large quantities of Kazakh grain are exported to Iran each year.

Developing Scientists, Diversifying Industry

Developments in the country and the region, some anchored in the China-led BRI and some stimulated by it, have opened up a new way forward for Turkmenistan. As the country becomes prosperous, increasing diversification of its economic development and fuller utilization of its manpower will take shape. Since President Berdimuhamedov took power in 2006, he has put special emphasis on education and especially science. He holds a Ph.D. in medical sciences (Moscow) and had a career as a dentist before being appointed minister of health.

To diversify its economy and add value to its abundant natural gas reserves, Turkmenistan has made plans to build four plants to convert natural gas to liquid synthetic fuel or gasoline. Two plants are under construction as of January 2018, with investments from Turkey, Japan, and South Korea.

Turkmenistan is now working with China to establish modern manufacturing facilities with its eye on import substitution and export. A plant for the production and maintenance of equipment for the oil and gas complex is being planned by Merdana Turkmen, a local company, together with the Chinese company Pekin Sancuan Sencyuri Teknoloji Ko. Ltd. Other manufacturing is being established in cellulose, filters, agricultural machines, gas generators, and granite and marble processing.

Turkmenistan, a producer of cotton and silk, has now engaged with China to help in developing its cashmere production from goat wool. These industries, although still nascent, indicate that Turkmenistan has begun a process with immense potential, because the country is in a perfect position to use its revenue from gas sales to develop its physical infrastructure and manpower.

The Golden Age Water Project

Like all Central Asian nations, Turkmenistan is short of water. The shortage of usable water is not only because the Karakum Desert is such a large part of the country. The discharge of drainage water from irrigation systems into natural depressions over many years has caused underflooding (the rise of shallow groundwater levels), waterlogging, salination of the soil, and pollution of groundwater over an area of 700,000 hectares (1.73 million acres, 37% of the arable land). It has also polluted the vital Amu Darya (Amu River).

To overcome this problem, in 2000 Turkmenistan began to plan a $6 billion project to construct two canals that cross much of the country, to collect the drainage water and discharge it into the Karashor ("black salt marsh") Depression, creating a large, new lake, to be called the Altyn Asyr ("Golden Age Lake"), just south of the point at which the boundaries of Turkmenistan, Uzbekistan, and Kazakhstan meet. The depression, 120 by 30 km (75 by 19 miles), reaches a depth of 28 meters below sea level (92 feet).[4]

"The lake will solve many problems," according to Paltamed Esenov, director of the National Institute for Deserts, Flora, and Fauna in Ashgabat, as reported in Science in 2008. Turkmen officials said that the project would reclaim 450,000 hectares of waterlogged agricultural fields and create a habitat for migratory birds and an inland fishery.[5] Today, the entire system is functioning and expectations for the project are being fulfilled. President Berdimuhamedov was present at the inauguration of the first stage in 2009, and the system is on its way to becoming a showpiece for specialists. According to the state news agency in October 2016, "The implementation of the innovative project of construction of 'Altyn Asyr' Turkmen Lake is a significant contribution to the resolving of global problems related to the conservation of the water resources of the planet."

And, one should add, the resolving of water problems has extensive social and economic implications. Now, thought is being given to establishing a center in Ashgabat for promoting the technologies used in the project for further projects in the region and worldwide, and especially for restoring the Aral Sea (Kazakhstan, Uzbekistan) and protecting the Caspian Sea.[6]

Uzbekistan, Kyrgyzstan, Tajikistan on the New Silk Road

China has identified the importance of building a railroad linking Kashgar in Xinjiang Autonomous Region to Uzbekistan by way of Kyrgyzstan, which lies between them. The line would run from Kashgar in Xinjiang through the Arpa valley via Kyrgyzstan's Kara-Suu, and on to the Uzbekistan city of Andijan in the Ferghana Valley, then to Tashkent (**Figure 7**). At present, there is no direct rail link between China and Uzbekistan through Kyrgyzstan, which "considerably complicates the freight transport between the two countries," according to Sofia Pale of the Russian Academy of Sciences.[7]

---

4 Igor S. Zonn and Andrey G. Kostianoy, "The Turkmen Lake Altyn Asyr," posted on ResearchGate, January 2013. This is a chapter from the book these writers have edited, The Turkmen Lake Altyn Asyr and Water Resources in Turkmenistan (Springer, 2014).

5 Richard Stone, "A New Great Lake—or Dead Sea?," Science, May 23, 2008, http://science.sciencemag.org/content/320/5879/1002.full?rss=1 This source provides details on the two canals: "For about half its length, the 432-kilometer Dashoguz Collector follows the bed of the ancient Uzboy River. The 720-kilometer Great Turkmen Collector starts in the Lebap region in the east and links up with the Dashoguz Collector 75 kilometers upstream of Karashor."

6 "Turkmenistan's Scientific Approach in Resolving Water-Environmental Tasks: Delegation of specialists travel to the Turkmen Lake Altyn Asyr," State News Agency of Turkmenistan, October 2, 2016, http:// science.gov.tm/en/news/20161003news_2016-10-03-1/ and "Turkmen Lake: Water Conservation—A key priority of the environmental policy of Turkmenistan," State News Agency of Turkmenistan, January 5, 2015, http://www.turkmenistan.gov.tm/_eng/?id=4376

7 Sofia Pale, "Kyrgyzstan and the Chinese 'New Silk Road,'" New Eastern Outlook, September 3, 2015.

Figure 7
Proposed Rail Link from Kashghar to Tashkent

The Kyrgyz trading town of Kara-Suu, located close to the Uzbek border, serves as a vital link to Uzbekistan: It is situated on the interregional highway that links the Kyrgyz capital of Bishkek, Osh, and the capital of China's Xinjiang province, Urumqi. In October 2017, the first pilot truck caravan tested this route by road, from Tashkent to Kashgar, ahead of implementation of the TIR system in China (TIR, International Road Transport, an international harmonized system of Customs control that facilitates trade and transport while protecting the revenue of each country through which goods are carried). There is an expectation that this route and the TIR will spur investment and economic growth for the communities along the route and beyond, and should revive efforts to build the needed rail link.

Political Roadblocks

Kyrgyz President Almazbek Atambayev showed a great deal of enthusiasm for the railroad in 2012, and in early 2015, after prolonged talks, a route linking China, Kyrgyzstan, and Uzbekistan was agreed. China is to build the 500 km segment in Kyrgyzstan, investing $6 billion. Kyrgyzstan hopes to gain about $200 million per year from the transit of goods through its territory. On the Uzbekistan side, Uzbekistan said in September 2016 that it had finished 104 km of the 129 km Uzbek stretch of the railway.

Kyrgyzstan, however, is not of one mind about the project. There are questions about profitability, and about the role of Chinese workers in the project.

But the real source of resistance may lie in the realm of politics and geopolitics. There are concerns that the railroad may result in "the strengthening of Uzbekistan's dominance in the region and even the probability of violation of Kyrgyzstan's territorial integrity," according to the Russian Academy of Sciences' Sofia Pale. And within Kyrgyzstan, "There are unspoken contradictions between representatives of the ruling elites of the northern and southern regions of the country, and the construction of the railway could shift the balance of power in the direction of one of the competing camps."

Pale is referring to the two elites, a northern (ethnic Kyrgyz) and a southern (ethnic Uzbek). The project will run through the south of Kyrgyzstan, causing the northern elite to fear that a shift in the internal power balance may result. She also refers to the fear that a strengthened southern region could attempt to secede and that it could be encouraged to do so by Uzbekistan.

Kyrgyz President Atambayev travelled to Beijing in January 2017, where the rail line was discussed, but reportedly no progress was made, reportedly due to disagreements on the funding, the gauge to be used, and the route.

Many Kyrgyz propose that a north-south railway—Russia-Kazakhstan-Kyrgyzstan-Tajikistan—uniting the two parts of the country, must be built first; they argue that if the China-Kyrgyzstan-Uzbekistan railroad is built first, the north-south line may never be built. These political considerations are also intertwined with geopolitical tensions—remaining tensions between Russia and China with respect to Central Asia, and tensions aggravated by the Anglo-American manipulations in the Tulip Revolution of 2005, one of the regime-change "color revolutions," which forced President Askar Akayev out of office and into exile. Kyrgyzstan will have to resolve these internal conflicts, and it is likely that China—if not also Uzbekistan, in particular—needs to take a hand in overcoming Kyrgyzstan's fears. Kyrgyzstan's situation is compounded by its weak financial condition, including heavy indebtedness. It has virtually no capital to invest.

Nonetheless, China's BRI is deeply involved in

Tajik President Emomali Rahmon at the site of the Rogun Dam, October 29, 2016

Kyrgyz industrial development. Kyrgyzstan is a victim of the collapse of the Soviet Union and its own lack of skilled manpower. There is a great deal of idle manufacturing capacity, particularly in the antimony and silicon processing plants, various medium-sized factories, and cotton and textile production lines in the South. Chinese Foreign Minister Wang Yi, while visiting Kyrgyzstan in May 2015, discussed relocating forty or so manufacturing operations from China to Kyrgyzstan. Kyrgyz Economy Ministry officials evaluated the proposal as a win-win project, reasoning that China would gain an important manufacturing base in Kyrgyzstan, while the Central Asian nation would benefit from the revival of idle industrial capacity.

Meanwhile, in Tajikistan a major hydroelectric project is underway, the Rogun Dam on the Vakish River in the Pamir mountain range, with primary input from French and Italian firms. The 335-meter clay core rockfill dam will be the tallest in the world, doubling the nation's energy production. The cofferdam was completed in June 2017. Two diversion tunnels are under construction. The dam will have six turbines of 600 MW each, with installed capacity of 3,600 MW. China is not involved in the construction, but has financed power lines in the country for other hydroelectric projects on the Vakish River.

And China and Uzbekistan have together developed a very important rail link between Tashkent and the Ferghana Valley. This is the Angren-Pap railway, inaugurated on June 22, 2016 by President Xi Jinping and the late Uzbek President Islam Karimov. The highlight of this rail link is the 19.2 km Qamchiq Tunnel, the longest in the 1,520 mm rail gauge region and the key element of the project. The tunnel eliminates the need for Uzbek trains to transit Tajikistan to reach the Ferghana Valley, and provides an all-weather alternative to the road over a pass at an altitude of 2,267 meters. The rail line, built by China Railway Tunnel Group, also includes 25 bridges and six viaducts with a total length of 2.1 km.

In November 2015, He Huawu, chief engineer of China Railway Corp, proposed a Silk Road high-speed railway connecting Urumqi, the capital of Xinjiang, to Tehran, Iran. Speaking at a forum on the BRI hosted by the China Civil Engineering Society, he proposed a 3,200 km route from China's Urumqi and Yining to Almaty in Kazakhstan, then to Bishkek in Kyrgyzstan, Tashkent and Samarkand in Uzbekistan, Ashgabat in Turkmenistan, and then to West Asia through Tehran. This massive project, still on the drawing boards, would dramatically transform the entire Central and West Asia region.

BRI Draws in Japan and Russia

These linkages with China, developed from the Chinese BRI, have attracted other international companies. For instance, the Japanese behemoths Mitsubishi Corporation and Mitsubishi Hitachi Power Systems, Ltd in October won a turnkey contract to construct the Turakurgan thermal power plant in the Namangan region of the Ferghana Valley. It will have two units, each generating 450 MW, with steam and gas turbines, the first of which is slated to come online is December 2019.

Similarly, Russia's oil company, Lukoil, announced in November 2016 an investment of $500 million for the development of the Gissar gas and gas condensate fields in the Kashkadarya Region of Uzbekistan (situated in the basin of the Kashkadarya River on the western slopes of the Pamir Alay Mountains, bordered by Turkmenistan and Tajikistan).

The Cultural Dimension

One of the most important contributions of the BRI is the exchange of cultural traditions among the countries that are becoming interlinked through railroads. In some cases, as in the case of Uzbekistan and China, the task involves reviving the long-lost cultural exchanges that took place when the Silk Road and other trade routes were alive in the past. In the 20th Century, Tashkent, the capital of Uzbekistan, served throughout the Soviet period as a center for Chinese studies. Beginning in 1957, people from all over Central Asia came to Tashkent to learn Mandarin.

Since becoming independent in 1991, Uzbekistan has received support from the Chinese government to continue that effort. The Confucius Institute in Tashkent, which opened in 2005, is not only the first Confucius Institute in Uzbekistan, but also the first in Central Asia. Like other Confucius Institutes around the world, its mission is to promote the teaching of Mandarin and develop cultural and educational exchanges between China and the host country.

Now the study of Chinese is viewed in Uzbekistan as advantageous for business and for professional employment abroad, and many students hope to get stipends to study in China.

Security Concerns

The BRI, with major support from Russia, also contributes to resolving the serious security concerns in the region, fortified in recent years by the formation and strengthening of the Shanghai Cooperation Organization (SCO). Since the early 1990s, following the demise of the Soviet Union and emergence of these Central Asian nations as independent countries, a well-organized effort was launched from abroad, particularly from Saudi Arabia and some Gulf Sunni countries, to spread Wahhabism, a heretical deviation from Islam, in its most virulent form, throughout Central Asia. Fighters were trained, arms were provided, and an organization of some sort was set up to undermine the newly independent and politically weak nations. That not only posed an existential threat to the Central Asian countries, but rang alarm bells in Moscow and Beijing.

The Uyghur secessionists, seeking to break Xinjiang Province off from China, have joined hands with these foreign-funded and foreign-promoted terrorists. Uyghur militants were suspected of involvement in a terrorist attack on the Chinese embassy in Bishkek, the Kyrgyz capital, on August 30, 2016. Meanwhile, the opium explosion in Afghanistan, under the watch of NATO and the United States since 2001, has not only created a brigade of armed smugglers who often work in collusion with the terrorists to protect each other, but has corrupted a vast section of the

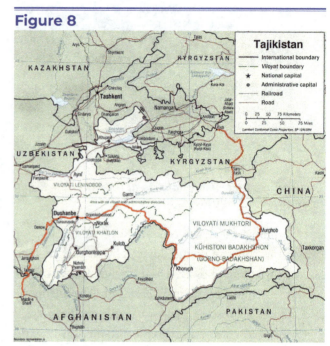

Figure 8

Pamir Highway, a major route for Afghan heroin into Central Asia, China, and Russia

security apparatus and bureaucracy in Central Asia.

The deluge of drug-generated cash has also strengthened the Islamist extremists. The Pamir Highway, sometimes called the "heroin highway," winding its way up through very high-altitude terrain, is used to bring Afghan heroin to Osh in Kyrgyzstan on the edge of the Fergana Valley (**Figure 8**). Osh has been recently dubbed the "drug capital of Central Asia." Russia, badly affected by the flood of heroin northward into its territory, has long placed troops along Tajikistan's 1,344 km border with Afghanistan. Seven thousand Russian troops patrol the border and Moscow has announced that the number will go up to 9,000 by 2020. Currently, Russia has military bases in Kazakhstan, Kyrgyzstan, and Tajikistan. The Collective Security Treaty Organization (CSTO), which currently has six member-states—Armenia, Belarus, Kazakhstan, Kyrgyzstan, Tajikistan, and Russia—has held several exercises aimed at facing off a veritable drug invasion from the south. Despite this, heroin continues to flow into Central Asia, Russia, and beyond into Europe.

Since the appearance of the Saudi-funded jihadis, violence has been used to weaken the political developmental process, endanger economic growth, and threaten the social ingredients necessary for future economic growth. In this context, China's Belt and Road provides hope for strong future development through mutually beneficial projects and industrialization. China's investments in infrastructure and in developing cadre of skilled manpower in these countries go hand-in-glove with the Russian efforts to provide on-the-ground security using its vast security apparatus and with the work of the SCO. The success of Russia's efforts is of equal importance to that of the BRI.

SOUTH ASIA

Afghanistan

If any nation can be declared to be the most in need of the New Silk Road, it is Afghanistan.

One often hears in the West the report that China's Belt and Road is doomed to failure because it is investing in unstable and corrupt nations, where there is little chance for a profitable return on the investment. But China's leaders are looking at the situation in exactly the opposite way. If nations are to escape from the backwardness and instability to which they have been condemned by centuries of colonial looting and "technological apartheid," then investment in connectivity, infrastructure, mechanization, and industrialization is the only path. In China's win-win view, they may not make monetary profit in the short term, but they will build modern nations which will be friends and trading partners forever.

Chinese Foreign Minister Wang Yi made this point clearly while in Angola in January 2018—a point which is particularly applicable to Afghanistan: "China will continue to support Angola in its efforts to diversify and modernize its economy through 'accelerated industrialization' ... on behalf of peace and unity on the African continent." Asked by a journalist about Angola's $40 billion in foreign debt, much of it to China, and whether China's financing was only increasing the debt burden of African countries, with political conditions attached, Wang was blunt: "Such a claim, which is made with ulterior motives, is an outright false accusation.... China's financing is in response to Africa's demands for self-development.

A country has a huge need for capital in its primary stage of economic take-off and industrialization and Africa is no exception. China also passed through this process; these are temporary problems.... Like African countries, China also had memories of a bitter past when, with its economic lifeline controlled by foreigners, it was unfairly treated and even exploited and oppressed. Therefore, when providing aid to and engaging in cooperation with Africa, China will not repeat what Western countries did and will never impose its own views on others." He added that China follows the principle of mutual benefit and win-win results. He cited two Chinese sayings: "Only the feet know if the shoes fit," and "People have a sense of natural justice." The African people are in the best position to decide who is Africa's true friend and most reliable partner.

In Afghanistan, if the BRI is to achieve what it has set out to achieve—that is, economic development on a foundation of connectivity—Afghanistan must become a prime center in Asia. Located at the cusp of three distinctly separate—and yet integral—parts of Asia, Afghanistan over the millennia has been the corridor through which cultural and trade exchanges across Asia, from one end to the other, have taken place. The same corridor was traversed by many invading armies. Afghanistan nestles between South Asia, on its south and east; Central Asia, on its north; and Southwest Asia, with Iran on its western border. China's BRI has connected the northern part of Asia to the Eurasian landmass through Central Asia and Russia.

Without Afghanistan's full participation, the BRI could still have access to Southwest Asia and beyond through Turkmenistan and Iran, but then South Asia would remain separated and un-linked to the BRI westward land routes through Central Asia. In addition, Afghanistan's strategic geographic position, bountiful mineral reserves, and other natural resources make it an important nation in intra-regional trade and energy networks, both as a provider and a transit hub.

At Last, Rail Links to Neighbors

So, when a Chinese train pulled into the railway station in August 2016 in the northern Afghanistan town of Hairatan, bordering Uzbekistan, hopes rose. The train delivered more than a load of textiles and freight, it brought expectations. That train's 13-day, 700-km journey was full of zig-zags, travelling through Kazakhstan and Uzbekistan to reach the Afghan border.

Hairatan, located in Balkh province and situated on the Amu Darya (Amu River), is both a dry port and a river port on the Afghanistan-Uzbekistan border, and is linked to Termez in Uzbekistan's railway network. The extension of the Termez-Hairatan railway link into Mazar-i-Sharif, the second largest city in Afghanistan with a population close to 700,000, had long been identified as a top government priority, and it is now in place. The Hairatan–Mazar-i-Sharif rail link was established in 2012, and since 2015 is maintained by the Uzbek national railway, UTY (**Figure 9**).

On its east, Afghanistan borders Pakistan along the poorly marked and wholly disputed 2,640 km Durand Line. The border was established after the 1893 Durand Line Agreement was reached between the Government of the British Raj (the British Government of India) and Afghan Amir Abdur Rahman Khan, for fixing their respective spheres of influence, in the context of the "Great Game" between the British and Russian empires. The demarcation was never accepted by Afghanistan. It is astonishing that even today, no functional rail link exists between the two neighboring countries, Afghanistan and Pakistan, with such a long common border.

To its north, Afghanistan and Turkmenistan have recently opened a major rail link. A railroad from Atamyrat in Turkmenistan to the Ymamnazar border crossing point (85 km) and Afghanistan's customs facilities at Aqina (3 km) was officially opened on November 28, 2016 by Turkmenistan's President Gurbanguly Berdimuhamedov and Afghanistan's President Ashraf Ghani. Construction had begun in June 2013. This route is also known as the Lapis-Lazuli Railroad, a reference to this historic export corridor along which Afghanistan's lapis lazuli and other semiprecious stones were exported to the Caucasus, Russia, the Balkans, Europe, and North Africa more than 2,000 years ago. Forty-six rail cars of the first cargo train—loaded with flour, grain, cement, urea for fertilizer, and sulphur—came to Aqina, traveling over two railway bridges along the 88 km Atamyrat-Ymamnazar (Turkmenistan) –Aqina (Afghanistan) section.

Plans are afoot to extend this railroad to Tajikistan. That project is known as the TAT Railway (for Turkmenistan, Afghanistan, Tajikistan), which will link Turkmenistan through northern Afghanistan to the Tajik border. The length of the extended railroad will be roughly 640 km.

A short, Soviet-built line also connects Afghanistan to Turkmenistan, from a freight terminal at the Afghan border town of Towraghondi, north of Herat.

Looking west, construction of a 191 km railway linking Afghanistan to Iran—from Herat to Khaf—is progressing. Herat is the most important city in west Afghanistan, where Iran has made notable investments over decades. Tehran has completed its segment which, from the Iranian town of Khaf (connected to Iran's main railroad), heads slightly south and then east. The line will cross the border through arid and rugged terrain. On the Afghan side, according to local officials, construction work has begun.

By establishing rail links with Turkmenistan and Iran, in particular, Kabul is indicating its priority to link up regionally in Afghanistan's north and west. But recently, discussions have begun in another direction, for a rail connection between Afghanistan and Pakistan. Beijing has shown interest in developing this link, and in May 2016, Pakistani media reported, quoting Masood Amin, adviser to the Afghan Ministry of Public Works, that a survey for a Jalalabad-Peshawar railway (150 km) would start soon. Jalalabad and Peshawar both lie near a line drawn between Kabul and Islamabad.

But as a nation ravaged by foreign invasions and a still ongoing civil war of almost four decades, Afghanistan remains perhaps the most insecure nation in Asia, heavily dependent on aid money for its daily sustenance. It simply does not have the means to carry out large capital investments until it is made secure. As a result, Afghanistan has no internal railroad network. At present, it is planning to link some of its border towns with its neighbors' railroads, but a fuller plan for a national railway, drawn up by the Afghanistan Railway Authority, is still only on paper.

Access to Chabahar Port in Iran

In May 2016, leaders of Afghanistan, India, and Iran signed the Chabahar Port agreement in Tehran. Afghanistan is expected to have multi-modal (sea and land) access through the strategic Chabahar Port in Iran, to South Asia, East Asia, and Africa, by 2018. Work on the port began in 2016 as a joint venture of India's Kandla Port Trust and Jawaharlal Nehru Port Trust.

Afghanistan's Garland Highway (or Ring Road) can be reached from Chabahar Port using the existing Iranian road network and the Zaranj-Delaram road, constructed by India in 2009 (Figure 9). The road connects Zaranj on the Iran border with the Ring Road at Delaram. Track began to be laid in January 2018 for a rail link between Chabahar Port and Zahedan, Iran, close to the intersection of the Iran, Afghanistan, and Pakistan borders and about 200 km from Zaranj. The Indian state-owned IRCON has an agreement with the Construction and Development of Transportation Infrastructure Company (CDTIC) of Iran to build the link at a cost of $1.6 billion, as part of the transit corridor to Afghanistan.

A Ring Road in Poor Repair

With no railway network that crisscrosses and unites Afghanistan, efficient movement within the country depends entirely on the 2,210 km Ring Road, a highway that lies inside Afghanistan like a garland (Figure 9). It is the only transport system that not only connects many Afghans within the country, but also connects with Pakistan, Tajikistan, and Iran. Construction of the Ring Road began in Herat province bordering Iran. From there it goes south, passing through Nimruz, Farah, and Helmand provinces before reaching Kandahar. The road continues through the eastern provinces to Kabul, continues north to Balkh province, which borders Uzbekistan, then

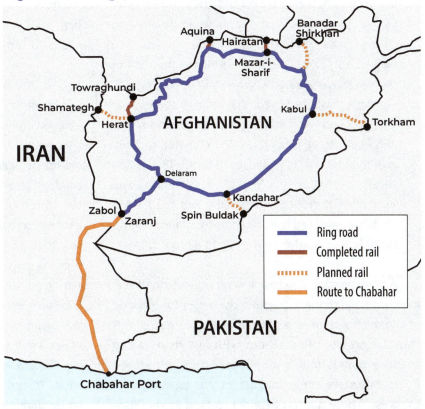

Figure 9
Afghanistan Ring Road, Rail Links, and Access to Chabahar

turns west, returning to Herat and completing the garland (Figure 9).

But the last segment, connecting Aqina on the Turkmenistan border with Herat, still has 233 km of road missing. There are some entirely unpaved stretches of dirt track. The ongoing armed conflict engulfing most of Afghanistan has significantly damaged the condition of the Ring Road and the regional road networks. The U.S. Special Inspector General for Afghanistan Reconstruction (SIGAR), John Sopko, in his October 2016 report, pointed out that the billions of dollars spent by USAID and the U.S. Department of Defense have done little to restore the full functionality of these roads. He wrote:

> SIGAR selected and assessed the condition of 1,640 kilometers of U.S.-funded national and regional highways, or approximately 22% of all paved roads in Afghanistan. The results indicate that most of these highways need repair and maintenance. For example, SIGAR performed inspections of 20 road segments and found that 19 segments had road damage ranging from deep surface cracks to roads and bridges destroyed by weather

or insurgents. Moreover, 17 segments were either poorly maintained or not maintained at all, resulting in road defects that limited drivability. MOPW [Ministry of Public Works] officials acknowledged that roads in Afghanistan are in poor condition. In August 2015, an MOPW official stated that 20% of the roads were destroyed and the remaining 80% continue to deteriorate. The official added that the Kabul to Kandahar highway is beyond repair and needs to be rebuilt. USAID estimated that unless maintained, it would cost about $8.3 billion to replace Afghanistan's road infrastructure, and estimated that 54% of Afghanistan's road infrastructure suffered from poor maintenance and required rehabilitation beyond simple repairs.

A transportation network across the difficult terrain is crucial to make possible the better integration of the diverse ethnic peoples that make up Afghanistan. Larger than France, but with less than half of France's population, it is dominated by the Hindu Kush mountain range and its extending ranges to the west. These natural barriers created by the Hindu Kush range, and the lack of transportation networks, have kept Afghanistan's ethnic groups largely divided: Pushtuns, Tajiks, Uzbeks, Tatars brought to Afghanistan by Chinggis Khan, and others, with different languages and of diverse ethnic origins.

TAPI Gas Pipeline

In the 1990s, a plan was proposed to bring gas from Turkmenistan to India passing through Afghanistan and Pakistan. TAPI, for Turkmenistan-Afghanistan-Pakistan-India Pipeline, was negotiated with the Taliban in Afghanistan, who were then the official government (**Figure 10**). When Taliban leader Mullah Omar expressed his support for the al-Qaeda bombing at U.S. embassies in Africa in 1998, the plan was scrapped, but after the U.S. invasion of Afghanistan in 2001, the plan was revived.

The chaos in the region repeatedly stalled the development, but an agreement was reached in 2012, with the Asian Development Bank (ADB) arranging the financing. The construction was to be carried out by Galkynysh—TAPI Pipeline Company Limited, a consortium of the state gas companies of the four countries. Construction began in Turkmenistan in 2015, with a target for completion in 2019. The capacity will be 33 bcm of natural gas per year, with 5 bcm going to Afghanistan and 14 bcm each to Pakistan and India.

Mineral Extraction Awaits Stability

In addition to inadequate transportation, the organized opium cultivation that profits many, from bankers to bandits, has turned Afghanistan into a center of permanent conflict and insecurity. Thousands of tons of opium are produced annually under the watch of thousands of NATO troops. The cash generated from opium cultivation not only feeds the world's cash-short banks and other vultures, but provides insurgents with arms and cash to carry out destruction and prolong Afghanistan's instability. Unless this menace is completely eradicated, the BRI, or any other plan to build up Afghanistan, will have no effect whatever.

On the other hand, once Afghanistan is stabilized, it could become a truly prosperous nation, while playing a major role as the hub and meeting point of Central Asia, South Asia, and Southwest Asia in the China-led BRI. Unlike many Central Asian nations, but like South Asian nations, Afghanistan is not an oil producing country. The country imports petroleum products such as diesel, gasoline, and jet fuel from Pakistan and Uzbekistan, with limited volumes from Turkmenistan and Iran. But Afghanistan is rich in mineral wealth and also has the potential to become an exporter of agricultural products.

U.S. hydrologists and mining engineers are working with Afghans southeast of Kabul in conducting tests to determine where mining is feasible. It could take up to 10 years for new mine operations to be established. The deposits are mainly of copper, but also include gold, iron ore, uranium, and precious stones such as emeralds. Afghanistan's Mes Aynak site, 40 km southeast of Kabul, reportedly has $100 billion in copper resources underground. In 2008 Kabul awarded a 30-year concession for mining to Metallurgical Corp of China (MCC), a Chinese joint venture. The copper mine development will produce annually approximately 200,000 tons of copper cathode or an equivalent amount of copper concentrate.

Figure 10
TAPI Gas Pipeline

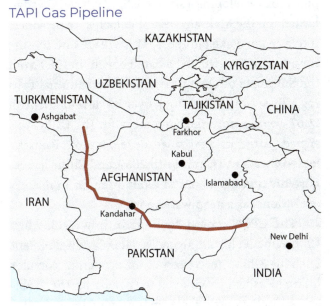

MCC proposed to build a coal-fired power plant and supply 50% of the power generated to Kabul and the surrounding community, and build a railroad to Xinjiang. Kabul considers Mes Aynak, which is expected to generate about 7,000 jobs, to be a crucial project. Mes Aynak also offers the opportunity to serve as a major anchor project for the development of upstream, downstream, and side-stream linkages as well as ancillary infrastructure that will drive economic growth.

The project, however, has not taken off. Mes Aynak is host to a trove of archeological ruins in a settlement that includes Buddhist statues, stupas (shrines), and a monastery complex dating from the time of the ancient Silk Road, when this area was a part of Gandhara, the Indo-Aryan culture which existed for several millennium in the region now occupied by Pakistan and Afghanistan. Gandhara provided major cultural impulses eastward along the Silk Road, including Greco-Buddhist sculptural styles. The settlement reached the peak of its prosperity in the 5th Century BC. There are also remains at a lower level that date to the Bronze Age, about 3,000 BC. International efforts are afoot to prevent or greatly delay the exploitation of the copper deposits, which would possibly destroy remains that had not been rescued. The motivation, however, is a combination of bad and good intentions.

Another major mining project that is yet to take off is the plan for an iron ore mine at Hajigak in Bamiyan Province, west of Kabul. Hajigak is Asia's largest untapped iron ore deposit. Seven of its 16 zones have been studied in detail. While concessions have been discussed with the Indian consortium SAIL-Affisco, consisting of seven companies with support from India's government, contracts have not been signed and no work is underway. Stability is a key to progress in mining.

Eradicate Opium, Modernize Agriculture

Wheat is Afghanistan's most important crop, followed by barley, corn, and rice, grown mostly in the northern plains, a region that extends eastward from the Iranian border to the foothills of the Pamir mountain range near the Tajikistan border. There is also abundant cotton, nuts, grapes, and other fruits.

However, the absence of adequate irrigation networks, and the lack of dams and reservoirs to facilitate such irrigation networks, has limited Afghanistan's agriculture. Much of the water flows into neighboring countries or is wasted in the deserts. The agricultural sector will also require agro-machinery such as tractors, harvesters, and hoeing machines. The manufacturing and maintenance of such machinery will introduce industries that will train skilled workers and technicians.

The most fundamental benefit of a successful, modern agricultural sector lies in that it builds the nation. Such an agricultural sector requires power, water, sufficient manpower, development of agro-industries, and a transportation network throughout the country. A successful agricultural sector needs concerted effort, and if the importance of the agricultural sector is fully understood, and developed in depth, it provides a shield against external manipulation. The process itself develops skilled manpower. Basic agricultural institutions include research and extension services that create agronomists who live in the country, work to develop high-yield varieties of seeds, and improve undernourished land. Development of water resources—including irrigation and water supply for the agro-industries and the population in general—produces engineers and technicians who build dams, canals, and flood plains. These actions themselves protect the soil, the land, and the environment in general.

Pakistan—China-Pakistan Economic Corridor

One of the most ambitious of the BRI development corridors in Asia is the China-Pakistan Economic Corridor (CPEC), a proposed road-based transport system that will link China's western province of Xinjiang to Pakistan and will then extend southwestward through Pakistan to reach the Arabian Sea. That is its basic form. It will not be a single highway, but a network. It begins as a single road at the border with China, and then branches out into a number of routes traversing the length of Pakistan while covering the country from west to east (**Figure 11**).

But it is also more than a network of roads—it includes two dozen projects for the construction of power plants and power transmission lines. Of equal importance is CPEC's objective to reach the Arabian Sea, near the Gulf of Oman, thereby connecting the land route to the other arm of China's BRI project for connectivity and trade, the Maritime Silk Road.

To achieve that end, China has put special emphasis on developing a sleepy fishing village, Gwadar, located on the Makran coast of Balochistan province, into a major Pakistani port. This village and its surrounding region, which Pakistan bought in 1950 from the Sultanate of Oman, remained a traditional fishing village until China took over its development in 2007, years before the agreement for the CPEC was signed. After its first-stage development, Pakistan leased Gwadar to China until 2059, and China has reportedly invested about $1.6 billion so far to make it operational as a deep-water port.

The CPEC project took off in July 2013, when China and Pakistan signed a landmark agreement enabling China to construct an economic corridor linking Kashgar in Xinjiang to Gwadar on the Arabian Sea. In the north, the economic corridor will enter Pakistan from China through Gilgit-Baltistan—the part of the disputed state of Jammu and Kashmir that is under Pakistani administration—and will wind its multiple ways through all four Pakistani provinces to reach the Arabian Sea in the south. CPEC, in its proposed form, is expected to be wholly functional around 2028. Of the many constituent projects that make up the CPEC, a few are already finished and numerous others are now under construction. In November 2016, the CPEC's potential was signaled when Chinese cargo travelled by road to Gwadar Port for maritime transshipment to Africa and West Asia.

The estimated cost to develop this highway system—and the associated infrastructure and energy projects necessary to make the CPEC a success—was put at $46 billion in 2014. China's state-owned banks are financing Chinese companies to build, maintain, and operate the highways and associated infrastructure and energy projects in Pakistan over the next few years. Of that amount, $33.8 billion will be invested in energy projects and $11.8 billion in building the highways and

Figure 11

China-Pakistan Economic Corridor

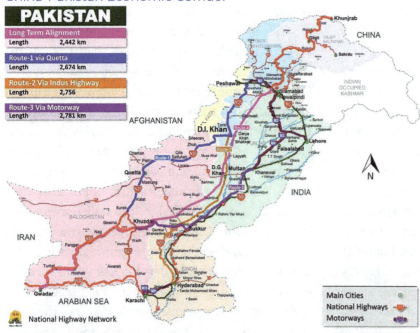

The China-Pakistan Economic Corridor comprises multiple routes from the border with China to the deep-water port at Gwadar.

associated infrastructure, such as upgrading railroads and even setting up a desalination plant.

But the $46 billion investment figure is not an amount etched on granite. Since 2014, China has come up with projects worth another $8.5 billion. Pakistan's Planning Minister, Ahsan Iqbal, in an interview with Reuters in November 2016, said that "some $4.5 billion of the additional investment will be spent on upgrading tracks and signaling on the railway line from Karachi to Peshawar (about 1,340 km) and increase the speed on the line to 160 km per hour from the current 60-80 kph." Another $4 billion will go toward a liquefied natural gas (LNG) terminal and transmission line. "This has now all been approved, so this is an additional $8.5 billion to the $46 billion we had already, so we are now close to $55 billion," Ahsan said. By January 2018, the figure had risen to $57 billion.

A Win-Win Project

In 2013, when China's President Xi Jinping proposed the CPEC, it became evident that this economic corridor would be significantly different from the China-Central Asia corridor or the China-Russia-Europe corridor, both based on railroads. Broadly speaking, the CPEC project has two major elements. First, Gwadar Port is important in China's future plans. Gwadar will enable China to bring oil and gas overland from the Persian Gulf to develop its western regions and avoid further crowding of the already crowded Malacca Strait that connects the Indian Ocean to the South China Sea. Gwadar is just 400 km from the Strait of Hormuz, a major world oil supply line, and is 1,500 km from Kashgar, China.

When the CPEC becomes fully operational, a significant part of China's oil imports from the Persian Gulf—which amount to about 60% of China's overall oil imports today—will come in through this route. The distance from the Strait of Hormuz to Kashgar via the CPEC is 2,000 km, as opposed to the 12,000 km maritime distance from the Strait of Hormuz to the eastern Chinese port of Shanghai via the Strait of Malacca. Oil or LNG landing at any port in China, if its destination is China's west, must then be carried westward overland for an additional thousands of kilometers. The CPEC cuts distance and time. Gwadar Port will also enable China to carry out two-way trade more efficiently with the nations along Africa's eastern coast, as well as with the Persian Gulf countries west of Pakistan.

The second element of the CPEC is that it will improve Pakistan's stability by helping it to strengthen, and in some cases build, its physical and industrial infrastructure. Pakistan, in many ways, is at a different developmental level than the Central Asian states, although it is not as rich in natural resources as the "stan" countries. Factors behind this difference include the following:

Pakistan has a population close to 185 million (the Central Asian nations and Afghanistan together have less than 100 million) and a significant section of Pakistan's manpower is skilled and is fully qualified to adapt to today's technologies. Before the founding of Pakistan in 1947, part of the land area that is now Pakistan was one of the main grain-producing centers of the Indian subcontinent under the British Raj, producing especially wheat. Pakistan is the fourth-largest cotton producing nation in the world, behind China, India, and the United States; in 1947 it already had state-of-the-art textile mills and nearly a dozen textile mill equipment manufacturers.

Unlike the Central Asian nations, it has a major seaport, Karachi, and a long coastline. Through the Arabian Sea, the Persian Gulf, and the Indian Ocean, Pakistan has access to Africa, Southwest and Southeast Asia, and East Asia. However, over decades, the country was exploited by Western nations as a bulwark against the Soviet Union in the Cold war era and later recruited as an "ally" to "fight" the terrorism of Islamic extremists. Islamic extremists and drug traffickers infiltrated the state at almost every level. As a result, Pakistan's economy has stagnated and its social structure has been weakened. China, like many other countries, noticed this development and became concerned.

Pakistan's security problems and its consequent instability also pose a serious threat to China's thinly-populated Xinjiang province, where some Uyghur Muslims—not many—have taken up arms against the Chinese authorities under the banner of the Turkistan Islamic Party or East Turkistan Islamic Movement, seeking a separate nation for the Uyghurs.

The Uyghur jihadis were trained, armed, and sheltered by al-Qaeda, ISIS, and Afghani/Pakistani Taliban, some analysts say. According to Nodirbek Soliev, a specialist in terrorism in China, Russia, and Central Asia, these jihadis "have shown their efforts and intentions to strike at China's overseas interests. To meet its growing demand for critical energy and mineral resources, China, through its state-owned enterprises, has been investing or promised to invest heavily in a number of conflict-affected countries such as Afghanistan, Pakistan, and Iraq."

China also noted that Pakistan's geographical location is a valid reason to engage with the country to achieve success in its BRI projects to its west and southwest. It noted that Pakistan has the crucial manpower, an industrial base, food security, and geographical links to China, India, Iran, Afghanistan, and most importantly, is endowed with a long coastline on the Arabian Sea. China recognized at the outset that just running a transport corridor and building a port would not be sufficient to establish a stable Pakistan. What was required, it envisioned, was to revitalize its decrepit industrial base by building power plants and electricity transmission infrastructure, upgrading its even more decrepit railroad, and linking its western and southern provinces to the densely populated major production centers of the eastern province of Punjab (see **Figure 12**) with a grid of roads and rails.

Culture Conflict, Topography, Disunity

The vital importance of such a grid can easily be seen when Pakistan's ethnic divides—corresponding to geographic and topographical differences to a great extent—are considered. Although Pakistan is almost 100% Muslim, it suffers from hostility across ethnic and sectarian divides. The sectarian differences include subdivisions within the Sunni (77%) and Shi'a (20%) populations. The ethnic differences correspond to the four major languages—Punjabi, Sindhi, Baloch, and Pashto—which correspond in turn to the four major provinces: Punjab, Sindh, Balochistan, and Khyber-Pakhtunkhwa (KPK), where the people, more often than not, identify themselves by their ethnic and provincial background.

Punjab is agrarian, gifted with rivers and fertile

Figure 12
Provinces of Pakistan

land, and is somewhat similar in its east to the adjacent topography across the border in India.

Sindh, bounded on its south by the Arabian Sea, is desert-like and very short of fresh water.

The two western states, Balochistan and Khyber-Pakhtunkhwa, abut Afghanistan and Iran, and are dominated by two major mountain ranges. The Federally Administered Tribal Areas (FATA)—one of the least accessible regions of Pakistan—lie to the west of Punjab (see map) in which the Safed Koh Range and the Waziristan Hills form a barrier between Pakistan and Afghanistan.

It is easy to see that in addition to the cultural identities and languages that separate the peoples of the different provinces, the country's topography has so far prevented the integration of the country.

Power and Transportation

Pakistan is a power-starved nation. With a population close to 185 million, Pakistan's installed electrical power generating capacity is only 21 GW. That is about half of the electric power consumed in Thailand, with a population of about 70 million people. Pakistan's power generation is also highly erratic. During the period of extreme heat in summer, media reports indicate that actual power generation goes down to about 15 GW.

It was evident to China that with such a low power-generation base, developing an economic corridor to stabilize Pakistan would require a large infusion of power production capacity. CPEC has allocated a major part of its funds to power generation and transmission. As of now, projects that would add 10.4 GW of electric power capacity have been started, or are being negotiated. Feasibility studies and negotiations are also on for another 7 GW of power production as part of the CPEC.

The numerous power plants under construction, in negotiation, and being studied for feasibility, include coal-fired, hydro, wind, and solar projects. There is no nuclear component, even though Pakistan has produced nuclear weapons for decades. The CPEC Portal (http://www.cpecinfo.com) organizes information on these projects and tracks their progress. They are distributed across the four provinces and Pakistan-occupied Kashmir.

The power projects were designed and located to enhance Pakistan's industrial and commercial sectors. Although some are not on any of the CPEC routes, they are not altogether isolated from them. But the transportation projects were primarily designed to tie into the CPEC routes or to other roads leading to Gwadar Port. The transport corridor development projects at an advanced stage of completion include the following:

- Karakoram Highway Phase II (Havelian-Thakot Section), 120 km
- Karachi-Lahore Motorway (Sukkur-Multan Section), 392 km
- Upgrade of Main Line 1 Railroad (Multan-Lahore Section, 339 km; Hyderabad-Multan Section, 749 km; Kemari-Hyderabad Section, 182 km)

A few other road projects are now under negotiation, including the following:

- Khuzdar-Basima Highway (N-30), 110 km
- Karakoram Highway Phase III (Raikot-Thakot Section), 280 km
- D.I. Khan-Quetta Highway (N-50), 533 km

The CPEC is also developing the area around Gwadar Port. The CPEC Portal notes: "As part of the China-Pakistan Economic Corridor, and by extension, that of the Silk Route Initiative, Gwadar holds pivotal importance. The port city of Gwadar is a hub of connectivity for the Corridor and an indispensable interchange for the Silk Route.... The China-Pakistan Economic Corridor, however, plans not to limit Gwadar to a connecting port only, but to enrich it as an economic hub that will cater to the local population by improving their livelihoods. Projects planned for the Gwadar Port City aim at capacitating Balochistan to its full economic, social, technical, and energy potential, and closely integrating it within the economic framework of Pakistan and China." Among the major projects around the port that have been completed or are under construction—or are about to be launched—the following are of significance:

- Gwadar Eastbay Expressway, 19 km, connecting Gwadar Port to Mehran Coastal Highway
- Gwadar Eastbay Expressway II, 19 km, connecting Eastbay Expressway I to New Gwadar International Airport
- Gwadar New International Airport
- Gwadar Free Zone
- Gwadar Smart Port City Master Plan

Enthusiasts and Saboteurs

The successful implementation of the CPEC, and making it secure, could mean a sea-change in the troubled region that includes Afghanistan, Pakistan, and the Indian-administered part of Jammu and Kashmir. A network of economic, trade, and transport connectivity that runs through Pakistan into Afghanistan, Iran, and Central Asia, and is bolstered by China and India, could turn the entire area into a major economic hub. This is recognized by most of the countries that can participate in this network when complete.

Iran has already shown a great deal of interest. Iranian President Hassan Rouhani, in a meeting with Pakistan Prime Minister Nawaz Sharif, on the sidelines of the UN General Assembly in September 2016 in New York City, expressed a desire to be part of the CPEC, lauding Prime Minister Sharif's vision that is translating the CPEC into reality. Connectivity projects were recognized by both countries' leaders on that occasion as vital to the progress of the region. Russia and Afghanistan have also expressed their desire to become a part of the CPEC. The Afghan ambassador to Pakistan, Dr. Omar Zakhilwal, during an interview with Radio Pakistan, said, "CPEC is a great project that is equally relevant to Afghanistan, like Pakistan," Pakistan's *Express Tribune* reported, October 15, 2016.

On December 26, 2017, in the first-ever such trilateral meeting, Chinese Foreign Minister Wang Yi hosted the first China-Afghanistan-Pakistan Foreign Ministers Dialogue in Beijing, with Afghanistan Foreign Minister Salahuddin Rabbani and Pakistan Foreign Minister Khawaja Muhammad Asif. Wang Yi proposed to extend China's $57 billion investment in the CPEC project to Afghanistan.

Wang pointed to Afghanistan's urgent need to develop and improve people's lives, saying that China hoped to synergize its development strategy for Afghanistan, with the intention to help facilitate a wide and inclusive political reconciliation process in Afghanistan, led and owned by the Afghan people.

Russia's ambassador to Pakistan, Alexey Y. Dedov, was quoted by India's *Times News Network*, December 19, 2016, as saying that Russia and Pakistan have held discussions to merge Moscow's Eurasian Economic Union project with the CPEC. Dedov said Russia "strongly" supported CPEC, because it was important for Pakistan's economy and regional connectivity. Some Central Asian countries, such as Tajikistan and Kazakhstan, have made similar endorsements.

The CPEC faces resistance in Balochistan. The corridor's western route, which leads directly to Gwadar Port from Dera Ismail Khan (D.I. Khan on the map, Figure 11), runs through a vast area where insecurity prevails. There are hostile forces, largely based in Balochistan, that openly oppose the construction of the CPEC and are involved in sabotaging efforts to bring in foreign investments and to integrate Balochistan with the rest of the country. Balochistan has been volatile since Pakistan was founded, and some Balochis remain committed to secession. Many years of instability in Afghanistan, which borders Balochistan, and the associated increase of terrorism in the area, have added to the insecurity. During the construction phase, this insecurity poses a threat to those working on CPEC component projects, especially Chinese workers and technicians. Islamabad is aware of these problems and has assured China that it will provide protection for them.

It has also asked Beijing to put in place procedures to maximize the effectiveness of security arrangements by ensuring that Pakistani security officials have prior knowledge of the movement of Chinese personnel in any insecure construction area. Pakistan has established a Special Security Division (SSD) of nine composite infantry battalions (9,000 personnel) and six civilian armed forces wings (6,000 personnel), headed by Major General Abid Rafiq, to provide security for the CPEC throughout the country.

Protect Domestic Manufactures

In addition to security concerns, Pakistan's small and medium-size industries have expressed fears that they may come under pressure because of cheaper and plentiful imports from China, further facilitated by the fully operational CPEC. In November 2016, a Pakistan news daily, the *Express Tribune*, quoted Atif Iqbal, Executive Director of the Organization for Advancement and Safeguard of the Industrial Sector, who pointed out that the Free Trade Agreement with China has not been favorable to Pakistan. "It is imperative for the government of Pakistan to keep in mind all these factors while negotiating the second phase of the FTA with China," he said. He is of the view that in talks with China, some leverage should be provided for Pakistan's products, to enable local industry to compete.

Why India Is Reticent in Joining the Belt and Road Initiative

Despite China's invitation to India to join the China-led Belt and Road Initiative (BRI), India has kept its distance. However, in April 2018, following an informal meeting between the Chinese President Xi Jinping and Indian premier Narendra Modi at Wuhan that lasted two days, the two leaders agreed to cooperate in the regional connectivity and joint projects. News reports indicated that China and India agreed to cooperate in joint projects in Afghanistan. The projects had not been identified yet as of June.

Also, what emerged from the meeting is an agreement by the parties to work on realizing the Bangladesh, China, India, and Myanmar (BCIM) Economic Corridor, which has not progressed over the years. The BCIM Economic Corridor includes four priority fields: infrastructure, constructing of connectivity, cooperation in development of industrial parks, and opening of cooperation on international finance and the formation of a systematic mechanism.

Officially, India's Modi government has presented two reasons why it has not joined the BRI. First, India opposes the China-Pakistan Economic Corridor (CPEC), a major part of the BRI in India's neighborhood, entering Pakistan from the Chinese province of Xinjiang through the northwestern Gilgit-Baltistan area of Jammu and Kashmir, a disputed territory which New Delhi claims belongs to India, but has remained under Pakistan's occupation since 1948. India's Foreign Ministry Spokesman Gopal Baglay told the media that "no country can accept a project that ignores its core concerns on sovereignty and territorial integrity."

Pointing out the other reason why India stayed away from the BRI, India's Foreign Office spokesman said in a statement, "We are of firm belief that connectivity initiatives must be based on universally recognized international norms, good governance, rule of law, openness, transparency, and equality."

Seemingly, China has begun to acknowledge the first of India's two objections. On November 17, 2017, speaking at the Centre for Chinese and South-East Asian Studies in the School of Language at Jawaharlal Nehru University in New Delhi, China's Ambassador to India Luo Zhaoh said that China may consider alternative routes through Jammu and Kashmir to address India's concerns regarding the CPEC that passes through Pakistan-administered Kashmir. "We can change the name of CPEC. Create an alternative corridor through Jammu and Kashmir, Nathu La pass or Nepal to deal with India's concerns," he said on that occasion.[8]

On India's second objection, it is evident there exists enough room to sort out the differences. Discussion on this at the highest level with the intent of a give-and-take negotiating attitude, the second objection can be overcome. However, at what level India's participation in the BRI will take place does not depend entirely on the outcome of the negotiations between the two countries. New Delhi has no intent to coattail the China-led BRI. It has its own connectivity requirements and has begun working on some of those.

To begin with, India is in the process of developing the Chabahar Port, located on Gulf of Oman in the southeastern Iranian province of Sistan-Baluchistan, and a free trade zone along with the 500-km rail-linkage between Chabahar and Zahedan, an Iranian city close to Iran-Pakistan border. This transport-link has the potential to benefit three countries—Iran, India, and Afghanistan—immensely. A highway link between Zahedan and Zaranj, a town in Afghanistan's Nimruz province, already exists.

These projects, when completed, will provide Iran an opportunity to develop its sparsely populated, and underdeveloped Sistan-Baluchistan province to grow and prosper, allow industrial development in the free trade zone, and ease pressures on the already-crowded Bandar Abbas port, situated in the Strait of Hormuz and about 700 km west of Chabahar. It will also strengthen Iran's trade and economic cooperation with India and Afghanistan in the coming years. In essence, Iran's long-term plans ensure turning the Chabahar Port into a transit hub for immediate access to markets in the northern part of the Indian Ocean and in Central Asia.

In addition to India's westward connectivity move through Iran, Afghanistan, and Central Asia, bypassing Pakistan, India is in the process of developing transport linkages in its east. This project, labeled as the "Act East" policy by the Modi administration, will eventually link India to Thailand and beyond.

The official statement issued by the Modi government on this regard says: "India's Act East Policy focuses on the extended neighborhood in the Asia-Pacific region. The policy which was originally conceived as an economic initiative has gained political, strategic, and cultural dimensions, including establishment of institutional mechanisms for dialogue and cooperation. India has upgraded its relations to strategic partnership with Indonesia, Viet-

---

8 "China proposes alternative routes for CPEC via J&K, Nepal," Kallol Bhattacherjee, *The Hindu*, November 18, 2017.

nam, Malaysia, Japan, Republic of Korea (ROK), Australia, Singapore, and Association of Southeast Asian Nations (ASEAN) and forged close ties with all countries in the Asia-Pacific region."

India's one major achievement in its Act East policy so far is developing a sea-link with Myanmar over the Bay of Bengal, connecting India's Kolkata port with Sittwe on the coast of Myanmar's Rakhine state, to link up more effectively with the southern states of India's northeast. Sittwe, a deep-water port that can handle ships with up to a 20,000-ton displacement, was built by India and is part of the Kaladan multi-modal project launched by India and Myanmar through a bilateral agreement in 2008. Before the project, Sittwe's capacity was limited to ships of about 300-ton displacement.

The project involved dredging the River Kaladan from Sittwe to Paletwa—a 158-km stretch—to improve its navigability; building an inland terminal at Paletwa where cargo will be shifted from barges to trucks; and constructing a 129-km highway linking Paletwa to the Indian border. During the project development, India discovered that the Kaladan River is unnavigable beyond Paletwa, and this meant that the road from Lawngtlai had to be extended up to Paletwa. The road will have two segments: one links Lawngtlai to Zorinpui in Mizoram along the border, and the second is a 109-km stretch from Zorinpui to Paletwa that is scheduled to be completed by April 2019.

"Delhi brought the multi-modal transport project to the Myanmar government in 2003. It then took five years for the two sides to enter into a framework agreement, and it was only in 2010 that construction work began. It was originally due to be completed in July 2013. Several more deadlines were set and missed.[9] Sittwe port was completed in 2017, but it will be more than another year before the multi-modal project is fully operational.

Notwithstanding India's lethargy—and Myanmar's instability-related hesitancy in completing all construction projects—the Kaladan multi-modal project, when it becomes fully operational, will be a successful input to India's Act East policy. Besides being a direct and hassle-free trade route with Myanmar, the opening of the Kaladan waterways reduces the distance between Kolkata, the largest city and port in eastern India, and the capital cities of India's border states of Nagaland, Manipur, Mizoram, and Tripura by more than half. The distance between Kolkata and Sittwe is roughly 539 km, and people and products from Lawngtlai would have to travel only 650 km to reach Kolkata, as opposed to the current Aizawl-Silchar-Siliguri-Kolkata route of approximately 1,700 km. Thus, the maritime transport network will reduce the dependence on the Siliguri corridor.[10]

Another project that would link India with Myanmar—and eventually Thailand, and beyond—is the India-Myanmar-Thailand trilateral highway. The 1,700-km highway is designed to take off from the India-Myanmar border town of Moreh (in Manipur) and pass through several Myanmar towns, including Tamu, Kalewa, Yargyi, Monya, Mandalay, Meiktila, and Myawaddy, finally reaching Mae Sot in Thailand. The four-lane highway is part of the proposed ASEAN East-West Corridor. According to officials, there is also a plan to link this road with Trans Asian Highway-1 that runs from Japan (via ferry) to Turkey, where it connects with the European highway ("MEA directed to monitor trilateral highway project," *Financial Express*, September 9, 2016).

The India-Myanmar-Thailand trilateral highway is nowhere near completion, yet another victim of India's inertia. According to a Joint Task Force meeting among the three countries in September 2012, the highway was scheduled for completion in 2016. But the completion target has been pushed back routinely since then; and, recently, fully operational status has been set at 2020.

In addition, during his visit to India in the first week of April 2018, Nepal's Prime Minister K.P.S Oli signed a number of agreements with India, two of which are connectivity-related. One of those is to link up Nepal's railroad with India and expedite railroad projects within Nepal.

India will build a strategic railway link between Raxaul, a town in the Indian state of Bihar border-

---

9 "The Trouble with India's Projects in Myanmar," Sudha Ramachandran, *The Diplomat*, September 21, 2016.

10 "Kaladan Multi-Modal Project in Myanmar," Papori Phukan, *Manipur Online*, December 19, 2010.

ing Nepal, and Kathmandu, Nepal's capital, to facilitate people-to-people contact and bulk movement of goods. They agreed to construct a new electrified rail line, about 140 km long, to be financed by India, connecting the border town in India to Nepal. Within Nepal, the stretch of railway lines from Jayanagar to Janakpur/Kurtha and from Jogbani to Biratnagar Custom Yard will be completed in 2018, and work on the remaining stretch of the ongoing rail link projects (Jayanagar-Bijalpura-Bardibas and Jogbani-Biratnagar) will be taken up as a priority.

The second infrastructure project, linking landlocked Nepal to the Bay of Bengal through India's inland rivers, has also been signed. The plan to develop inland waterways will give Nepali cargo access to the sea and boost its trade. Although further details on the inland waterways have not been made public at the time of writing, there exists the Kosi Study Agreement, signed in 1997 between the governments of Nepal and India to conduct a detailed study of the 165-km Kosi Navigation Canal, linking Chatara in Nepal with the seaport, through the Indian rivers the Ganges, Bhagirathi, and Hooghly.

If and when China and India can resolve the Indian opposition to the CPEC route, India may raise other concerns about the BRI. For instance, India considers that the South Asian nations, such as Bhutan, Nepal, Bangladesh, Sri Lanka, and Maldives, are not only neighbors of India, but depend on India for its security. To inter-link these countries with China, without having formal consultations with India about these projects, New Delhi considers to bring into question China's intentions, and could be endangering India's security. A formal consultation regarding the South Asian nations' connectivity, New Delhi believes, will lead to cooperation between China and India in making these projects more beneficial for all the participating neighboring nations.

In addition, in Pakistan, China is well on its way in development of the Gwadar Port, the southern extremity of the CPEC. Located at the mouth of the Strait of Hormuz, Gwadar opens up bulk trade access to the Persian Gulf, southwest Asia, Central Asia, and the Indian Ocean. In 2007, following completion of the first phase of Gwadar's development by China, Islamabad had signed a long-term agreement with PSA International of Singapore for development and operation of the tax-free port and duty-free trade zone at Gwadar. China Overseas Ports took over control of the development in 2013 under a 40-year deal that assigns ownership of the facilities to Pakistan with the Chinese firm designated the long-term operator.

India is also concerned that China may eventually develop a naval base at Gwadar Port, which would be a matter of serious security concern for India.

Resolving these issues is important not only for peaceful relations in the region, but also to facilitate India's important role in the global New Silk Road process.

Kunming Initiative

Regional collaboration among nations can create the opportunity to eradicate abject poverty. That is one of the operative principles in the Kunming Initiative for a transport corridor traversing extremely poor parts of India, Bangladesh, and Myanmar, and connecting them with major cities.

The political climate for cooperation to implement the Kunming Initiative—now known as the Bangladesh-China-India-Myanmar (BCIM) Economic Corridor—has greatly improved since China's President Xi and India's Prime Minister Narendra Modi have come to power. The corridor is a major part of the New Silk Road. It will link Kunming, the capital of China's thriving Yunnan province adjacent to Myanmar, with Kolkata—formerly called Calcutta by the British—a once great, eastern Indian port city that urgently seeks revival. It will pass through Mandalay, in Myanmar, and Dhaka, the capital of Bangladesh (**Figure 13**).[11]

A major segment of this route is what was called the Burma Road—from Lashio in Myanmar to Kunming in China, as shown in **Figure 14**—built by the

---

11 The proposed BCIM Economic Corridor from Kunming to Kolkata might run via Chuxiong-Dali-Baoshan-Dehong (all in China's Yunnan province) to Namhkan-Lashio-Mandalay in Myanmar, Imphal in India's Manipur state, Silchar in India's Assam state, and Karimganj-Dhaka in Bangladesh. Namhkan is on the China-Myanmar border and Lashio is about 100 km south of Namhkan. Different versions of a free trade area connecting Kunming and Kolkata have been floated for more than fifteen years. Discussions were often been stalled or abandoned due to unresolved Sino-Indian conflicts. See Ramtanu Maitra, "Three Eurasian Superpowers Forge New Deals for Security," *EIR*, November 1, 2013.

Figure 13
Planned Route for the Bangladesh-China-India-Myanmar Economic Corridor

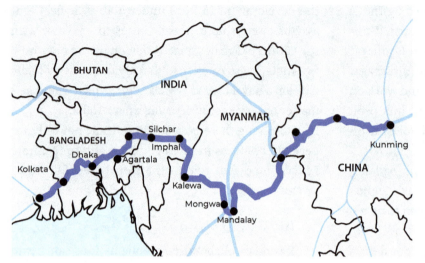

British in 1937-1938 during the Second Sino-Japanese War to supply the Chinese, while Myanmar was still a British colony.

The BCIM project continues the process of breaking the isolation of Southeast Asia from South Asia, and South Asia's isolation from Central Asia and beyond, set in place by the British Empire and other imperial powers over more than two centuries. The project involves upgrading sections of the existing 3,380 km (2,100 mile) road and possibly also building high-speed rail from Kunming to Kolkata.

In January 2015, China proposed the high-speed rail line as part of the BCIM Economic Corridor. Li Jiming, Vice Secretary-General of Yunnan province, told India's Economic Times, June 18, 2015: "The proposal has been discussed with India and other countries. It will be beneficial for all of us as it will facilitate trade and people-to-people contact. We could fund the project through the Asian Infrastructure Investment Bank and other agencies," such as China's Silk Road Fund. There is as yet no formal agreement.

As for the highway, only two segments of around 200 km each—Silchar to Imphal in India, and Kalewa to Monywa in Myanmar—are in need of urgent repair, according to Jin Cheng, Chief Counsel in the Foreign Affairs office of Yunnan province, in an interview with *The Hindu*, June 16, 2016. The rest of the route is in fairly good condition, he said.

At present, those associated features that make a multi-modal transport route into a true economic corridor—such as power production and transmission, water infrastructure, industrial development, and the building of new cities—are not part of the international planning, but are open to the planning of the individual governments.

Origins

Rehman Sobhan, an eminent Bangladeshi economist and founder of the Centre for Policy Dialogue in Dhaka, urged the development of multi-modal transport along this route based on sound economic reasoning. In 1999, the first meeting of representatives from the four countries took place, hosted by the Yunnan Academy of Social Sciences, and the Kunming Initiative was born. These were largely not representatives of the governments. But nothing was done; the governments were not interested.

Now conditions have changed, and the engine is ready to rev up. The project moved from back-channel talks to talks among the four governments at the first intergovernmental meeting held in December 2013. At that meeting, it was decided that each country would provide a country report on the Economic Corridor focusing on objectives of the corridor, scope and elements, principles and modalities of cooperation, and framework of cooperation. China, India, and Bangladesh have produced and shared their reports, but because of political uncertainty, Myanmar has lagged behind. All four reports are to be the basis of a single, agreed document at a meeting in Kolkata that has not yet been scheduled.

Countervailing Winds

An earlier project—just to connect Myanmar to India—illustrates considerations that have sometimes prevented governments from embracing such corridors. In 2005, Indian and Chinese survey teams began mapping out plans to rebuild the Stilwell Road (also called the Ledo Road), named in honor of U.S. General "Vinegar Joe" Stilwell of World War II fame and built with a large contribution of African-American troops in a multi-national effort (see Figure 14). China did all of the reconstruction work, paving dozens of miles with granite stones packed into earth.

India, however, did not move. Why? Observers have offered several reasons for India's reluctance at the time. Much of India's northeastern region has been made unstable by the secessionist Naga tribes with backing from foreign non-governmental organizations (NGOs) and British intelligence. New Delhi feared that rebuilding the road would ease the way for these hostile forces, including drug smugglers, to enter India's troubled area to fan the flames. There were also fears that the Chinese, who had earlier aggressively sought to take over trade in Myanmar, would use the Stilwell Road to also flood the markets in the northeastern region of India.

But in 2016 the prospects for progress improved, as China adopted the BCIM Economic Corridor as one of the six central corridors on the New Silk Road Economic Belt. Chinese investors were gearing up to join India's "Make in India" campaign by setting up factories in West Bengal.

But this major development by itself would not have provided the Kunming Initiative the necessary boost if other regional developments had not begun to take shape. In particular, the China-Pakistan Economic Corridor and the Chabahar Port development in Iran, both covered in separate sections of this report, signal the breakdown of the isolation of Southeast Asia, South Asia, and Central Asia from each other, progressively set in place by the British Empire over the past 200 years and more. To make that

Figure 14
Rail Connecting to the Ledo and Burma Roads

breakthrough, what was needed was the rise of China and India as formidable economic powers, seeking to spread their capabilities across Asia. Even Asia's island nations in the Far East, such as Japan, and the "island" nation of South Korea, have begun to move their focus west to join this development process.

Developments in the BCIM Region

For the region of the BCIM economic corridor, perhaps the most important milestone was the April 2014 agreement between China and India to establish a "strategic and cooperative partnership for peace and prosperity." These two most populous Asian nations, both economic giants, were already in close collaboration on the world stage, being members of the BRICS and of the associated banks that are oriented to infrastructure development. Both India and Pakistan also became full members of the Shanghai Cooperation Organization (SCO) at their June 2017 meeting in Kazakhstan, strengthening the institutional connections to overcome historical conflicts between the two Asian giants. The 2017 Doklam crisis on the China-India border once again stalled progress on issues like the Kunming Initiative, but the resolution of that crisis promises another move forward.

On the ground in South Asia, other major changes have taken place, or are in the process of taking place. Myanmar, at the junction between South Asia, China, and Southeast Asia, is now emerging from its isolation and stagnation after decades of military rule. The new government could play a major role by taking advantage of Myanmar's junction status to mobilize the BCIM project.

Meanwhile, developments between India and Bangladesh hold promise for unprecedented economic gains through new, multi-modal connections. There have been decades of virtual stagnation in bilateral relations, resulting from the walls erected by the British Raj's departing ugly kick that divided the subcontinent and killed millions. Bangladesh had been carved out of India; and India, which surrounds Bangladesh on three sides, was left with a very long route "up and around" for travel between peninsular India and its easternmost states. But on November 1, 2015, after the signing of an agreement, a cargo vehicle carrying a car and goods made the first successful trial run from Kolkata through Bangladesh to Agartala, capital of the Indian state of Tripura, reviving a route closed since Independence in 1947, and cutting the travel distance by a thousand kilometers.

The trial run came four-and-a-half months after South Asian transport ministers signed, on June 15, 2015, the landmark Bangladesh, Bhutan, India, Nepal (BBIN) Motor Vehicles Agreement for the Regulation of Passenger, Personnel, and Cargo Vehicular Traffic among their countries. The rail connection from Agartala to Kolkata through Bangladesh, which is still in the planning stage, will cut the rail distance between the divided areas on India from the current 1,590 km through Indian territory, to 499 km through Bangladesh.

India's 'Look East' Policy

But of course, as the BBIN agreement indicates, it is not all about efficiently connecting one part of India with another. In early January 2016, Nirmala Sitharaman, one of India's Ministers of State, speaking at Srimantapur in western Tripura state along the Bangladesh border, said: "The Indian government led by Prime Minister Narendra Modi is keen to develop all types of connectivity with all neighboring countries, including Bangladesh, to boost trade, economy, and people-to-people relations.... The government has taken steps to develop road, rail, water, and air connectivity with the neighboring countries. With good physical linkages, India wants to further develop all types of relations with the adjoining countries."

This is a clear statement of what India has long been projecting, a "Look East" policy, conceived in the early 1990s, which has now become a priority. Sitharaman was in Srimantapur to inaugurate an Integrated Development Complex for the India-Bangladesh border, that has modern facilities for customs and immigration, a banking and currency exchange facility, a warehouse, and public utility services.

India now proposes to expand its maritime trade by developing Bangladesh's Payra Port in the Ganges-Brahmaputra Delta. "Talks are on between our foreign ministry and [Bangladesh]. Dhaka also wants us. We have sent a team there for studies," said India's Shipping Minister Nitin Gadkari, a key negotiator for Chabahar Port with Iran, according to the Press Trust of India.

India-ASEAN

India's Prime Minister Modi took a major step forward in his "Look East" and "Act East" policy in the last week of January 2018, by inviting all ten heads of state from the ASEAN nations to be guests at India's 69th National Day on January 26. Speaking to the ASEAN leaders on January 24 in Delhi, under the theme "Shared Values, Common Destiny," Modi called for closer economic cooperation and expanded trade.

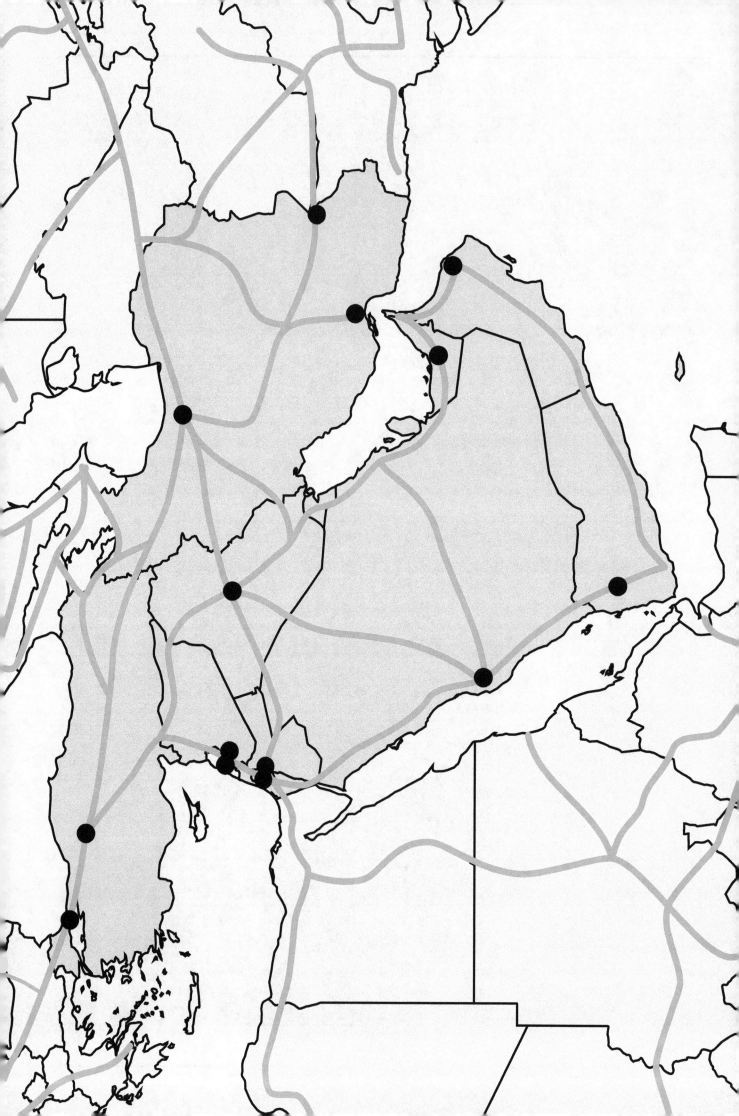

"The tragedy of war is that in its course, horrors occur, especially when it rages on for many years and is in fact a proxy war instigated from the outside.... Therefore, it is all the more urgent now that all neighbors of the region ... put large-scale reconstruction of the entire Middle East on the agenda."

SOUTHWEST ASIA

Reconstruction for a New Renaissance

Since 2014, the Southwest Asia region has been exposed to some of the most dangerous existential threats in its recent history, leading to the near disintegration of major nations as Iraq, Syria, and Yemen. The combination of regime-change policies pursued by the Anglo-American and NATO powers since 2003, and the simultaneous expansion of terrorist groups such as Al-Qaeda and its offshoot, the Islamic State in Syria and Iraq (ISIS), in many parts of this region was only stopped by the direct military intervention of Russia in cooperation with the national armies of Syria, Iraq, and Iran, succeeding, finally, in largely eradicating these groups from Syria and Iraq in late 2017.

Parallel to the Russian intervention, China continued to play the constructive role of bringing the economic benefits of the Belt and Road Initiative (BRI) to the region. Chinese President Xi Jinping's January 2016 visit to Saudi Arabia, Egypt, and Iran can be regarded as an economic and strategic turning point in West Asia. In his meetings with his counterparts and in his speeches, President Xi invited these nations to join the BRI, making it clear that this region has to build the foundations for a new modus operandi of peace through economic development.

Xi's visit came at one of the darkest moments in the history of this region: three wars have been raging simultaneously, in Syria, Iraq, and Yemen, and many other nations, such as Egypt, Libya, Turkey, Lebanon, Kuwait, and Saudi Arabia, were targeted by terrorist activities.

This region has unique characteristics: It lies at the confluence of three continents, through which a great portion of world trade passes; it contains 44% of hydrocarbon reserves in the world, holds trillions of dollars in foreign currency reserves, and has a population of 400 million, most of whom are youth and children; and it has the greatest cultural and ethnic diversity in the world, with some of the oldest civilizations taking root here. All these advantages, however, have been turned into disadvantages due to geopolitics. The win-win philosophy of the New Silk Road offers a harmonious exit from the current state of conflict, toward peace and prosperity.

President Xi's visit also came one week after the Chinese Foreign Ministry issued the first ever comprehensive Chinese political paper on the Arab world, focusing on the necessity of economic cooperation, building basic infrastructure projects along the New Silk Road, and promoting nuclear power and industrial development as the key elements to stabilize and resolve the various crises in the region. This visit and the economic, cultural, and trade agreements that were signed between China and the three countries President Xi visited created an atmosphere of optimism and openness toward the idea of the New Silk Road.

Some nations of the region continued to pursue their national development plans, in spite of the destabilizing political and military factors, keeping their internal development in tandem with the BRI. These nations are Iran, Turkey, and Egypt.

Iran

Iran took advantage of the partial lifting of international sanctions following signing of the nuclear agreement (Joint Comprehensive Plan of Action) with the P5+1 powers to continue the process started in 1996 to connect Russia and Central Asia to the Gulf and Arabian Sea; connect India to Central Asia and Russia; and most importantly, playing its natural role as a key component of the Economic Belt of the New Silk Road (i.e., the "Belt" in the Belt and Road Initiative announced by President Xi Jinping in 2013).

The first direct freight train from the eastern Chinese province of Zhejiang arrived in Tehran in February 2016, passing through Kazakhstan and Turkmenistan. This 9,300-km route cuts freight time from the same origin in China to the Iranian Gulf port of Bandar Abbas by 30 days, compared to the sea route across the Indian Ocean.

In late December 2017, China launched a $1.7 billion credit line for the electrification of the 926-km railroad from Tehran to the eastern city of Mashhad, which is part of the Economic Belt project. According to news reports, $1.5 billion was allocated by the Chinese Exim Bank, and the rest by China Export and Credit Insurance Corporation (Sinosure). The electrification project will be carried out by China National Machinery Import and Export Corporation, otherwise known as CMC. The project is expected to take up to 48 months and raise the speed of the line from the current 160 kph to 200 kph, cut down pollution, and increase the railroad's transport capacity. The route is already double-tracked and both tracks will be electrified. This is part of the Iranian plan to electrify all railways in the country by 2025, at which time the railway network will be expanded to 25,000 km of modern rail. The Exim Bank of China has so far provided $8.5 billion in loans to projects carried out in Iran.

The first high-speed railway (HSR) to be built in Iran will extend from the capital Tehran to Isfahan, passing through the Imam Khomeini International Airport in the south of the city and Qom. In July 2017, the Iranian daily *Financial Tribune* announced that China will provide the $1.8 billion for the financing of this 409-km HSR line. Iran has signed a contract with China Railway Engineering Corporation (CREC) to build this line, which is planned to become operational in 2021 with a speed reaching 350 km/h. Work on this line was first started in 2015, but was hindered by economic and political complications before the lifting of the sanctions.

In August 2017, German industrial giant Siemens and the Iranian state-backed conglomerate Mapna signed a major memorandum of understanding for the import and manufacture of locomotives and power plants in Iran. According to the agreement, Iran will buy Siemens-produced locomotives and rail cars for the Tehran-Isfahan HSR line. In return, Siemens will build a locomotive manufacturing plant in Iran to be run by Mapna, according to Iran's Press TV. A $3 billion credit line will be extended from Germany to finance the agreement. According to Iran's Deputy Minister of Road and Urban Development Asghar Fakhriyeh-Kashan, the agreement included a license for manufacturing F-class gas turbines in Iran, under which more than 20 gas turbines and associated generators will be produced for use in Iranian power plants. Iran is intending to invest the equivalent of $25 billion in the expansion and upgrading of its railway sector.

The International North-South Transport Corridor

Another major transcontinental infrastructure project in which Iran is playing a key role, is the International North-South Transport Corridor (INSTC), which is heralded by India, Iran, and Russia to create a direct transport and development corridor between the Indian Ocean and Northern Europe. Among the key components of the INSTC is a deep-sea port in Chabahar in southeast Iran on the Gulf of Oman, including an industrial zone, and railways and highways extending from Chabahar through the Iran railway network to the northeast of the country and the Caucasus nations of Azerbaijan, Armenia, and Georgia to Russia and the Baltic Sea. Another line passes through the Central Asian nations Turkmenistan, Uzbekistan, and Kazakhstan along the east coast of the Caspian Sea and further north to Russia's Trans-Siberian railway network. One major side-effect of this project is the extension of this corridor to Afghanistan.

India is the most enthusiastic partner in this project, and has supported the building of the Chabahar port and industrial zone financially and technically. Geopolitical arguments about India's aim to compete with China's Silk Road and the China-Pakistan Economic Corridor (CPEC) are rendered meaningless because the two projects will eventually complement each other, and bring development to the entire region. India is interested in this project, because waterborne transport to the Black Sea and Russia takes about three weeks, while the railway system through Iran to Russia requires only one week. However, the saving of freight time is not the most interesting aspect of this project, but rather the value this "development corridor" carries with it for the development of the regions of eastern Iran, Afghanistan, Central Asia, and the Caucasus, and creating a potential market for Indian industrial exports in addition to valuable imports of minerals.

Iran's part in the project is connecting its north-south railway network to Russia via the Caucasus region through Azerbaijan and Armenia in cooperation with Russia. On March 3, 2017, the first train crossed the bridge built over the Astaracay River, which forms the border between Iran and Azerbaijan. The railway between Astra in Azerbaijan and Rasht in Iran is the last missing piece in the INSTC.

In August 2017, Indian Union Minister of Ports Nitin Gadkari informed reporters at an event in Iran that the civil work at Chabahar port developed by India was complete, the Indian government was ordering $63 million worth of mechanized equipment and cranes, and the port would be operational in 2018. After meeting with Iranian President Hassan Rouhani, he said, "now, we are building a railway line in Iran. From Chabahar, we can go to Afghanistan, Uzbekistan, and Russia."

In August 2017, India Global Ports Limited (IGPL) applied for permission to run the Chabahar port in the interim, while Iran had already completed the construction of the jetty, and said it would build two new terminals, one for containers and another for multi-purpose ships. In October 2017, IGPL started constructing the terminals after placing orders for the construction equipment. On October 29, 2017, the first shipment of wheat was sent from India to Afghanistan through the Chabahar Port.

Iran is also actively extending its railway networks to its neighbors to the east and west. Westward, a railway project extending from Mashhad through the eastern Iranian city of Khaf to Hera in Afghanistan was completed in March 2018. This will be a major boost for landlocked Afghanistan's connectivity with the Indian Ocean on the one hand and with the Mediterranean and Europe on the other. Afghanistan has vast mineral resources that are underdeveloped, and lacks means of exporting them to neighboring countries and world markets. At the same time, the rebuilding of Afghanistan—when and if it takes place—will require the import of large quantities of machinery and technologies by land routes. To the east, Iran completed its section of the connection to the Iraqi southern port city Basra in 2016, extending the railway from its southern city Ahwaz to Khorramshahr on the Iraqi border. In addition, another railway line is being built to connect to the central part of Iraq from Kermanshah to Jalawla on the Iraqi border. This will allow Iran to connect to Syria and the Mediterranean through Syria (see Syria reconstruction section below).

Turkey

The political and military destabilizations that have been raging in the region have not discouraged Turkey from taking bold steps toward transforming its infrastructure platform to world-class standards. The promotion of the BRI by the Chinese government since 2013 has further encouraged Turkey to raise its stakes in this transcontinental project, because Turkey forms a key component of the Economic Belt of the New Silk Road, and is a natural bridge between Asia and Europe, the Black Sea and Northern Europe with the Indian Ocean, and the Caspian Sea and Central Asia to the Mediterranean. Turkey and Iran were connected together by a railway in 1998, forming a complete land-bridge from China to the Mediterranean. Iran had built a missing link to Central Asia in 1996 as it completed the Mashhad-Sarakhs railway on the border with Turkmenistan.

Some of the most spectacular developments were launched in the rail and power sectors. Turkey is developing the first network of national high-speed rail in the region.

In March 2013, then-Prime Minister Recep Tayyip Erdogan inaugurated the HSR line between Eskisehir (300 km south of Istanbul) and Konya (400 km further south). The Eskisehir-Ankara HSR line was completed in 2009, and a direct Ankara-Konya line was completed in December 2010. The Istanbul-Eskisehir line was inaugurated by Erdogan in 2014, thus connecting the administrative capital Ankara to the historical capital Istanbul.

This section also connected Istanbul to Konya in the south. Another key component of the Turkish HSR is the east-west HSR line from Ankara to Izmir on the Mediterranean. This line is under construction, and is planned to start commercial passenger traffic by early 2019. To give an empirical appreciation of the importance of the HSR network for Turkey, the Ankara-Izmir line will be cutting down the current travel time of 14 hours by road to just 3.5 hours. It will also take another route connecting other cities that are not on the main road route, such as Manisa, Usak, and Afyonkarahisar, to Ankara, thus cutting the distance between Izmir and Ankara from 824 km to 624 km.

The majority of the locomotives and rail cars are provided by the French Construcciones y Auxiliar de Ferrocarriles (CAF) and the German Siemens. Construction of several of these HSR lines, such as the Ankara-Istanbul line, were carried out by a consortium comprising China Railway Construction Corporation (CRCC), China National Machinery Import and Export Corporation, and Turkish companies Cengiz Construction and İbrahim Cecen Ictas Construction.

Turkey plans to build a 3,500-km high-speed railway and 8,500 km fast track by 2023, when the country marks its centennial anniversary, according to the Turkish railway authority (TCDD). In total, the TCDD is intending to invest $42 billion to expand the national Turkish railway network from the current 12,532 km to 25,000 km by 2023 and further to 31,000 km by 2035.

In December 2017, Transport, Maritime Affairs, and Communications Minister Ahmet Arslan confirmed that the ministry is looking to complete the HSR line between Ankara and Sivas in the east of the country by late 2018 or early 2019, before eventually integrating it with the Baku (Azerbaijan)-Tbilisi (Georgia)-Kars (northeast of Turkey) railway. This line, which was inaugurated in October 2017, is an important part of the middle section of the BRI and an important link for landlocked Georgia and Azerbaijan. Armenia is not yet part of this corridor, because historical and current disputes with Turkey and Azerbaijan have prevented economic cooperation. However, Iran and Russia are aiding Armenia by including it in the INSTC. The ongoing Ankara-Sivas HSR project will be integrated into the Baku-Tbilisi-Kars project through the Sivas-Erzincan and Erzincan-Erzurum-Kars high-speed rail lines.

A Bridge Between Two Continents

To enhance its role as a key component of the BRI and a bridge between Asia and Europe, the Turkish government increased its investments in connecting its own European and Asian parts across the Bosporus Strait.

The Yavus Sultan Selim Bridge, a 2,164 m suspension bridge on the easternmost edge of the Bosporus Strait, carries eight motorway lanes and a double-track railway. It was inaugurated in September 2016. This is the third bridge over the Bosporus following the Bosporus Bridge (the first Bosporus bridge, completed in 1973) and Fatih Sultan Mehmet Bridge (the second Bosporus bridge, completed in 1988). The construction of the latest bridge was started in 2012 by a consortium composed of the Turkish İçtaş company and the Italian Astaldi construction company.

The Yavus Sultan Selim Bridge over the Bosporus Strait, opened for traffic in September 2016.

The total cost of the project was $2.5 billion.

The Marmaray rail tunnel is the largest under-construction project in the region. It is expected to be complete this year (2018). It is composed of a 1.4-km immersed tube tunnel at a depth of 60 m below sea level in the Bosporus Strait, making it the world's deepest immersed tunnel. It contains two tunnels with Standard Gauge Rail for commuter and freight trains, connecting the European and Asian parts of Istanbul. The total length of the line is 13.5 km. Construction was started by a Japanese-Turkish consortium consisting of the Japanese Taisei Corporation and the Turkish Gama Endustri Tesisleri Imalat ve Montaj.

Although the tunnel itself was completed in 2008, the project was delayed due the slow construction of new underground stations and discovery of ancient cities dating back to the Byzantine era and even an 8,000-year-old settlement. The major part of the $3 billion credit was provided by the Japan International Cooperation Agency (JICA) and the European Investment Bank (EBI). The Turkish Transport Ministry added the freight operations to the railway capability with a pronounced intention to facilitate transportation between Asia and Europe along what they dubbed "The Iron Silk Road."

The Eurasia Tunnel is another major connector of the European and Asian sides of Istanbul. It is a road tunnel that was opened for traffic December 2016. It is a 5-km, double-deck tunnel with two lanes for vehicles in each deck, helping travellers to cross between the two continents in a few minutes, at a depth of 106 meters under the seabed in the western end of the Bosporus Strait.

Turkey is also planning to dig a 45-km canal, to provide another connection between the Black Sea and the Mediterranean. Turkey's Transport Ministry has announced the route for the proposed Kanal Istanbul. According to Turkish media reports, the canal will start from the Kucukcekmece Lake near the Marmara Sea in the southern part of the European side of the city. It will pass through the districts of Avcılar and Basaksehir before reaching the Black Sea in the Arnavutköy district north of the city. The purpose of the new channel is to relieve congestion in the Bosporus, which is the world's narrowest strait used for international navigation, and to offer a safer route for the 10,000 oil tankers that make the passage each year.

In September, President Erdogan said he hoped work would begin before the end of 2017 or early in 2018, but no concrete work has been launched yet at the writing of this report (June 2018). Global Construction Review reported that the scheme has attracted the attention of South Korea's builders, who earlier this year won a $5 billion project to build a 3.6-km suspension bridge over the Dardanelles Strait. On December 6, Korean President Moon Jae-in discussed the project with Binali Yildirim, the prime minister of Turkey, GCR reported. The final route for the 60 billion-Turkish Lira ($15.6 billion) canal project was selected after studies on five alternate routes.

Power

Turkey continued to invest in its power sector with large-scale construction of hydropower plants in several parts of the country. In addition, in 2016, it resumed its cooperation in the field of nuclear power and gas with Russia, after a short period of tension resulting from the Turkish intervention against Russia's military anti-terrorist efforts in Syria, including the shooting down of a Russia jet fighter by the Turkish Air Force in November 2015.

One of the largest hydropower projects is the entire southwest Asia region is the South Anatolia Project (GAP in Turkish abbreviation) which was launched in the 1980s. It is an integrated agro-industrial regional development plan covering nine provinces (Adıyaman, Batman, Diyarbakır, Gaziantep, Kilis, Siirt, Sanlıurfa, Mardin, and Sırnak) which are part of the Tigris and Euphrates basins. The project centers on the development of the hydropower potential for industrial and agricultural development—14 dams have been constructed in the Euphrates basin, the largest of which is the Ataturk Dam (completed in 1992), and eight dams in the Tigris basin including the Ilisu Dam which was completed in 2016. The GAP has been a source of concern for the downstream countries in Mesopotamia, Syria and Iraq, which are almost totally dependent on the flow of these two rivers. Negotiations for water sharing agreements were ongoing in the 1990s, before the invasion of Iraq in 2003 and the destabilization of Syria beginning in 2011 disrupted them. Turkey, however, continued construction of the dams and discussions are slowly coming back on track—with Iraq at least.

The hydropower plants of the GAP provide 22% of the country's annual consumption, with a total installed capacity of 8,000 MW. The modern irrigation systems created by the GAP, which covers 1.8 million hectares, more than doubled the country's irrigated farmland, increasing the production of cotton, a strategic product for the country's textile industries, from 150 million metric tons to 400 million in southeastern Turkey alone. The increase in productivity in this region made it a key factor in Turkey's trade balance. In 2002, total exports from the region were $689 million and total imports stood at $773 million. In 2010, total exports from the GAP region reached $4.166 billion, while imports reached $3.167 billion. Since 2004 the GAP region has been a net exporter.

To diversify its increasing energy needs, Turkey resorted to imports of natural gas from Russia. In 1997, the two countries signed an agreement to build the first underwater gas pipeline across the Black Sea from Bergovaya in Krasnodar Province in southern Russia to the Turkish port of Samsun in northern Anatolia. The project, Blue Stream, was completed in 2002, but not inaugurated until 2005. Blue Stream has been delivering 14 billion cubic meters (bcm) of Russian natural gas to Turkey per year on average.

In 2014 Russian President Vladimir Putin proposed to build a second and larger pipeline across the Black Sea to the European side of Turkey, with the additional function of extending it to Greece and southern Europe for export of Russia gas to European markets. This project, called Turkish Stream, was finally agreed on in October 2016. The pipeline starts at the Russian coastal city Anapa and runs 910 km offshore, reaching Kırklareli Province near the Turkish-Bulgarian border in northwestern Turkey. The projected capacity of the pipeline is 30 bcm/year, of which 15 bcm/year will be for the Turkish market and the rest to be exported to Greece and farther into Europe. The initial cost of the pipeline, which is backed by Russia's Gazprom, is $12 billion. Construction on the offshore section was started in March 2017.

Nuclear Power

Nuclear power is another field of technology which Turkey has announced its willingness to utilize, in order to back its development process into the future and reduce dependency on imports of fossil fuels. Turkey and Russia agreed in 2010 to build the first nuclear power plant in Turkey, in Akkuyu in Mersin Province on the Mediterranean. It will include four 1,200 MW pressurized water reactor units, with a total capacity of 4,800 MW, and whose construction will cost $20 billion, which will be provided by the Russian side. On April 3, 2018, President Putin and President Erdogan witnessed via videolink from Ankara the groundbreaking ceremony for Unit 1 of the plant. The Akkuyu power plant is being built by the Russian Atomstroyexport, a subsidiary of state-owned Rosatom, on a build, own, and operate (BOO) basis, allowing Rosatom to sell power generated by the plant for 15 years to recoup the cost. Rosatom will gradually transfer the ownership to a consortium of Turkish companies. "We expect to build and launch Unit 1 of the Akkuyu nuclear power plant within a shorter timeframe," Putin said after meeting with Erdogan on September 28, 2017. Construction of the power plant began in March 2018, and is planned to be completed (or at least the first unit) in 2023, which is the centennial anniversary of the founding of the Turkish Republic.

A second planned power plant will be built in Sinop on the Black Sea coast in the north of the country, and will have the same capacity as the Akkuyu plant. The power plant in Sinop will be built by a Japanese-French consortium composed of Japan's Mitsubishi Heavy Industries and French Areva. The agreement to build the plant was signed in May 2013 by then Turkish Prime Minister Erdoğan and his Japanese counterpart Shinzo Abe. Of the financing of the $16 billion project, 49% will provided through loans by the Japanese government, while 51% will be provided as equity owned by Mitsubishi Heavy Industries and trading house Itochu (30%) and French power utility GDF Suez (21%). The agreement is based on a build, operate, transfer (BOT) basis, according to which Turkish power utilities will acquire ownership of the minority share. The investment will be repaid through sales of electricity over a period of 20 years.

China is also becoming a partner of Turkey in the nuclear technology sector, although no projects are yet agreed on; the Sino-Turkish nuclear agreement is still in its initial phase. In 2012 a preliminary agreement was signed between the Turkish and Chinese governments for cooperation in development and use of nuclear technology for peaceful purposes. In the Summer of 2016 the agreement was ratified by the Turkish Parliament, and a formal agreement was signed between the Turkish Minister of Energy and Natural Resources Berat Albayrak and Chinese National Energy Administration Director Nur Bekri in June 2016. Nuclear technology-related websites report that in 2014 China's State Nuclear Power Technology Corporation (SNPTC) and Turkey signed an agreement of exclusivity to build a third nuclear power plant in Turkey.

Development of a professional national nuclear technology cadre is also one of the priorities of the Turkish government. According to the Turkish Energy Ministry, every year as many as 600 students are sent to Russia for nuclear energy education. "In particular, Turkish students will be employed in different fields from engineering to managerial level in the Akkuyu Nuclear Power Plant Project after approximately 6.5 years of training, including internship in the plants in Russia," the ministry states.

It is obvious that Turkey is "going east" to get help to fulfill its development goals. The direction of the types of investments Turkey has been making points to the fact that Turkey is riding the wave of the New Paradigm of the New Silk Road toward industrialization. Instead of pursuing its bid to become a member of the EU, making it the poor man of the disintegrating EU living off aid and tourism, Turkey seems to have chosen a much better approach of becoming the wealthy man of the Southwest Asian region, based on a large-scale, future-oriented agro-industrial development process.

Egypt

While Egypt is naturally an African nation, its geographical, economic, and political position makes it necessary to become an Afro-Asian nation. Egypt is a key nation of the so-called Middle East region, and has positioned itself to be the bridge not only between Asia and Africa, but also between Asia and Europe through the Maritime Silk Road. Since 2014, Egypt has been adopting policies of integration with the Belt and Road Initiative, but within a nationally-defined development strategy, also called Egypt Vision 2030.

New Suez Canal and Industrial Zone

On August 6, 2015, the New Suez Canal was officially inaugurated in a ceremony attended by numerous world leaders. This occasion celebrated the successful completion of a full bypass system for constant two-way traffic along the canal, a system that was built in one year and financed entirely by domestic resources. Construction began on August 4, 2014, and was completed in July 2015.

The Suez Canal, originally built over the period 1859 to 1869, reduces shipping distances by up to 8,900 km, and provides passage to nearly 20,000 ships per year, generating more than $5 billion in annual toll revenue. The New Suez Canal doubles the potential daily ship traffic, from approximately 50 to approximately 100 vessels; shortens the southbound transit time by 7 hours; and reduces by approximately 7 hours the time vessels spend waiting to use the canal.

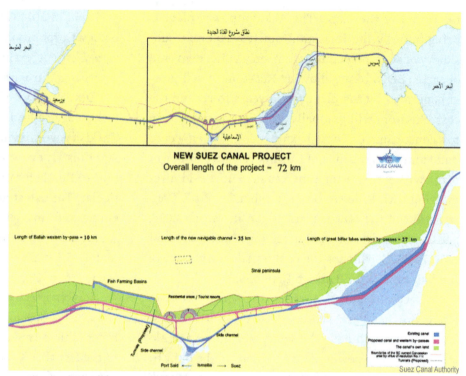

The New Suez Canal (in magenta, bottom image) is shown in the context of the existing Suez Canal. With the new construction, two-way traffic is possible along the length of the canal.

Not simply an isolated project, the Suez Canal is part of a broader regional development plan, including a 200 square kilometer industrial zone at Ain Sokhna, a technology center at Ismailia with one million jobs, the construction of seven tunnels underneath the canal, and the building of new power and desalination infrastructure at Ain Sokhna. In addition, the Suez Canal Container Terminal (SCCT) at East Port Said, one of the largest container terminals and transshipment centers between the Indian Ocean and the Mediterranean, is now being expanded. The SCCT is located at the mouth of the Suez Canal on the Mediterranean and at the confluence of the continents Asia and Africa. When Phase II of the terminal is completed, it will be able to handle 5.1 TEUs/year, making it the largest such terminal in the Mediterranean.

Because of its proximity to the canal and to other transportation, power, and desalination infrastructure, the Suez Canal Corridor is the site of planned investment of EGP 50 billion ($3 billion) for industrial, agricultural, and technical development.

Extension to Asia

Running under the Suez Canal will be four double tunnels for motorway transport, and two for rail, connecting the Egyptian Delta with Sinai in the "Asian" part of Egypt, where significant industrial zones, new cities, and agricultural projects are planned. This is

This graphic from the Suez Canal Area Development Project shows the planned upgrades and developments meant to accompany the construction of the New Suez Canal. The canal area is much more than a through-route for transit; it is an opportunity for development that can take advantage of its proximity to this major world transport artery.

Bridging Asia and Africa: Hypothetical route of the King Salman Bridge, connecting Saudi Arabia with Sinai, Egypt, at the Strait of Tiran in the south of the Gulf of Aqaba. There are also proposals to build a tunnel under the strait, but feasibility studies have yet to be conducted.

also part of the Egyptian government's plan to change the demographic imbalance in the country, whose 90 million people live and work on a thin strip of land on the banks of the Nile, constituting only 5-7% of the total land area of the country.

The development of Sinai also includes building a transport corridor to West Asia, through Saudi Arabia and Jordan. A bridge/causeway across the southern end of the Gulf of Aqaba, at the Strait of Tiran, to connect to Egypt and Africa, was under study by the Egyptian government of former President Hosni Mubarak in 2009. A new agreement between Egypt and Saudi Arabia in 2016 put this project once again on the implementation table.

This project will bring great benefits to both countries, but also greatly enhance Sinai's role as a transcontinental bridge and a major transport and industrial center between West Asia and North Africa, and between the Red Sea and the Mediterranean.

New Administrative Capital

The government of Egyptian President Abdel Fattah El-Sisi has also launched a project to build a new administrative capital. The New Administrative Capital will be located 40 km southeast of the current capital Cairo, on the road from Cairo to the Suez port city. It is intended to house all the key government institutions and financial centers. According to Egyptian Minister of Housing, Utilities, and Urban Development Mostafa Madbouli, the size of the city will be 714 square kilometers, double Cairo's area. It will be founded on a state-of-the-art underground infrastructure system for transit, power, water, and sewage. Work on laying the foundations and building the infrastructure began in May 2016. The New Administrative Capital, future home to 6.5 million inhabitants, will be connected to Cairo and Suez by a standard-gauge railway, a monorail system, and in the future, by a high-speed rail line. It will be closer than Cairo to the growth region in the New Suez Canal Industrial Zone.

Work on the New Administrative Capital was officially launched by President El-Sisi on October 11, 2017. On that date, an agreement was signed for construction of the section of the city housing the government ministries and a major business center with some of the highest towers in Africa. The contract was awarded to the Chinese construction company China State Construction Engineering Corporation (CSCEC). China's planned investment in the new capital is expected to reach $11 billion. While China will play a significant role, the majority of the construction works in the rest of the city are being conducted by Egyptian companies, governmental and private, such as Almokawloon Al-Arab.

This new city will relieve strain on the historical capital, Cairo, whose population has grown to 18 million, and is currently projected to reach 40 million by 2050. There are a dozen new cities that are being constructed outside the greater Cairo region to draw urban development away from the city, which has become one of the most congested cities in the world. The aim of the government is to restore Cairo as a historical and cultural capital of the nation.

Egypt Reclaims the Desert

Just a few weeks following the announcement of the New Suez Canal project by President El-Sisi, Prime Minister Ibrahim Mahlab announced, on August 30, 2014, that the Toshka Project was to be revitalized to become a national development project. Seventeen years after its launch under former President Hosni Mubarak, and several years after its near abandonment by former governments, this key project for reclamation of Egypt's Western Desert, the largest such project in the world, may become operational. The proposal entails transferring water from Lake Nasser (the lake created by the Aswan Dam) to the Western Desert to reclaim and cultivate 1.5 million feddans (roughly 630,000 hectares), and to build new urban and agro-industrial centers. The main pumping station, the key component of the project and the largest in the world, was installed in 2005, and a 50-km main canal was built to the Toshka Depression.

At the time of its abandonment in 2008, the project had cost $1 billion. Speaking during a tour of the Toshka region, Prime Minister Mahlab said a thorough study will be conducted to reassess the project, which proposes large infrastructure and road networks. Such a mega-project should not be neglected, said the prime minister; this would enable Toshka to become a real urban community, and help revitalize the entire region. The Toshka Project is the keystone of the New Valley Project, which includes the integration and development of the series of oases, starting from the East Oweinat Oasis deep in the southwestern desert near the border with Sudan and Libya, extending northeast into Toshka, and continuing north through the oases of the New Valley Province (Al-Dakhla, Al-Kharja, and Farafra), northeast to the Bahriya Oases, and ending in the Siwa Oasis in the northwest of the country.

The Development Corridor is defined by this chain of oases and the feature they have in common, the world's largest groundwater aquifer, the Nubian Sandstone Aquifer System, beneath them. This massive body of fresh groundwater, which extends below Chad, Libya, Sudan, and Egypt, has enormous quantities of water that can be made available for many decades.

Some scientists, such as Dr. Farouk El-Baz, the celebrated American-Egyptian space scientist and remote sensing expert who is now one of the scientific advisors to President El-Sisi, argue that such aquifer systems are not simply fossil and finite, but are subject to continuous recharge from precipitation over mountain ranges in the African desert. In addition, these areas are rich with minerals and metal ores such as phosphate, iron, and cobalt, which could become a basis for expanded industrial activities, in addition to agriculture. This Development Corridor

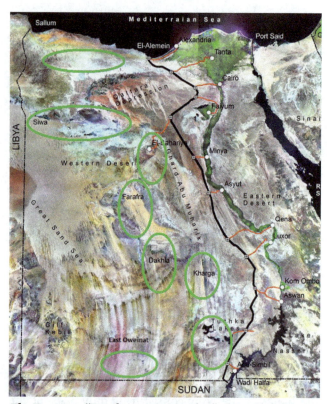

The Egyptian "Development Corridor," also called the New Valley Project, was designed by Dr. El-Baz. This image is developed by Dr. El-Baz. The green zones are superimposed by Hussein Askary to outline the chain of oases extending along the Grand Nubian Sandstone Aquifer zone.

includes the following:

- 1,200-km super-highway to be built using the highest international standards, from west of Alexandria to the southern border of Egypt
- Twelve east-west branches from the super-highway, with a total length of approximately 800 km, to connect it to high-density population centers along the way
- A railroad for fast transport parallel to the superhighway
- A water pipeline/canal from the Toshka Canal to supply freshwater
- An electricity line to supply energy during the early phases of development

This Egyptian corridor can easily be extended southward to Sudan, and all the way to the Equatorial Lakes. The navigational potential of the river can be maximized as part of this corridor.

Revival of the Egyptian Nuclear Program

Egypt has recently revived its nuclear power program and the first nuclear power plant will be built in the Mediterranean port city of Al-Dabaa, in western Egypt, with work scheduled to start in 2018. Russia's State Atomic Energy Corporation (Rosatom) has signed a memorandum of understanding with Egypt, according to which the Russian Exim Bank will finance the construction of the plant.

According to the draft agreement, Russia will loan Egypt the $25 billion needed to finance the building and operation of the plant. According to the Egyptian media reports, Egypt is to pay the loan back at an interest rate of three percent annually, with instalment payments beginning in 2029.

The agreement between Egypt and Russia includes the training of Egyptian engineers and researchers in Russian facilities. An agreement was finalized in 2017. President El-Sisi is personally overseeing the progress of this strategic development. The Al-Dabaa nuclear power plant will include four reactors with total capacity of 4,800 MW.

The agreement includes building nuclear fuel storage facilities through which Rosatom will provide fuel for the 60-year operational period. Rosatom will also manage nuclear waste, maintenance, and operations for 10 years, after which Egyptian engineers and experts will be operating the plant.

Syria's Reconstruction

Following the recent victories achieved by the Syrian army and its allies, Russian and Iran, against the terrorist groups that have been controlling large swaths of the territories of the country, discussions about the reconstruction of the county emerged strongly in 2016. The Syrian government has stressed that it will open up to the Belt and Road Initiative and head east to work with Russia, China, and the BRICS nations as a priority for the reconstruction process.

In 2015, the Schiller Institute had made a specific proposal for the reconstruction of Syria along the lines of the New Silk Road strategy. It was presented to the highest levels of the Syrian government in 2014 and again in 2016. The proposal, called Project Phoenix, consisted of three major sections:

1. How to mobilize the physical, intellectual, and moral potential of the nation for reconstruction

2. How to finance reconstruction (through a national reconstruction bank)

3. How Syria can benefit from connecting to the New Silk Road project

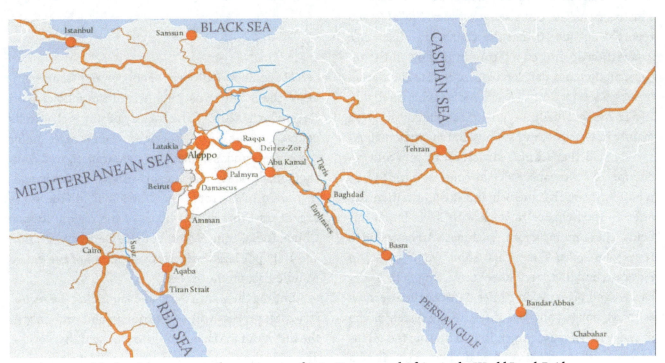

Syria's geographical position connects the continents of Asia, Europe, and Africa in the World Land-Bridge.

III. PROGRESS REPORTS

Left: Dr. Bouthaina Shaaban, Political Advisor to the President of Syria, and Foreign Minister of China Wang Yi. Shaaban in her visit to China in November 2017, stressed Syria's support to the BRI and called on China to participate in the reconstruction process in Syria. Right: Dr. Shaaban (center), with the Schiller Institute's representative and co-author of Project Phoenix Ulf Sandmark (right) and Talal Moualla (left) in August 2017.

In August 2017, a large Chinese business delegation, comprising representatives of 50 enterprises, participated in the 59th Damascus International Fair. According to *Sputnik* news agency, Qin Yong, the deputy chairman of the China-Arab Exchange Association, stated that this delegation also planned to visit Damascus, Homs, and Aleppo, and to meet with local officials to discuss investment opportunities on a wide range of reconstruction projects. Qin said discussions are "primarily focused on restoration of the power supply systems in Syria." Prior to this visit, a July 9 forum in Beijing was dedicated to Syria's reconstruction. The Chinese newspaper *Global Times* reported on July 10 that the China-Arab Exchange Association sponsored a forum in Beijing on the reconstruction and development of Syria. The Syrian Ambassador to China, Imad Moustapha, said that "Syria has gradually begun its rebuilding program mainly in energy, water supply, and manufacturing."

He said that China's structural reform and reduction of "overcapacity" can connect with Syria's rebuilding, and that the Belt and Road Initiative also offers a good chance to work with Syria in various fields. Hua Liming, a former Chinese Ambassador to Iran, told *Global Times* that China would invest in Syria's rebuilding, very likely attracting both state-backed and private companies. "Infrastructure such as roads, houses, and the water supply system is the primary investment target. Rehabilitating the oil industry would be the second goal," Hua said. He said that the unstable situation puts obvious restraints on reconstruction, but the process will begin in any case. Sputnik, in its turn, reported that there is a plan under discussion to create a Chinese-Syrian industrial park for 150 companies, costing $2 billion and creating 40,000 jobs.

Ulf Sandmark, of the Schiller Institute, also attended the Damascus International Fair and held meetings with Syrian officials, as a representative of the Schiller Institute, following up on the discussion of Project Phoenix and Syria's connection with the BRI.

Conclusion

Helga Zepp-LaRouche, Founder and Chairwoman of the Schiller Institute, stated the following on December 17, 2016: "The tragedy of war is that in its course, horrors occur, especially when it rages on for many years and is in fact a proxy war instigated from the outside, and those horrors produce a never-ending chain of horrors. Therefore, it is all the more urgent now that all neighbors of the region, Russia, China, India, Iran, Egypt, but also Germany, France, and Italy put large-scale reconstruction of the entire Middle East on the agenda."

Ending the war in Syria and launching the reconstruction process will be a turning point, not only in the history of Syria, but of the region and the world—directing the world toward peace and development.

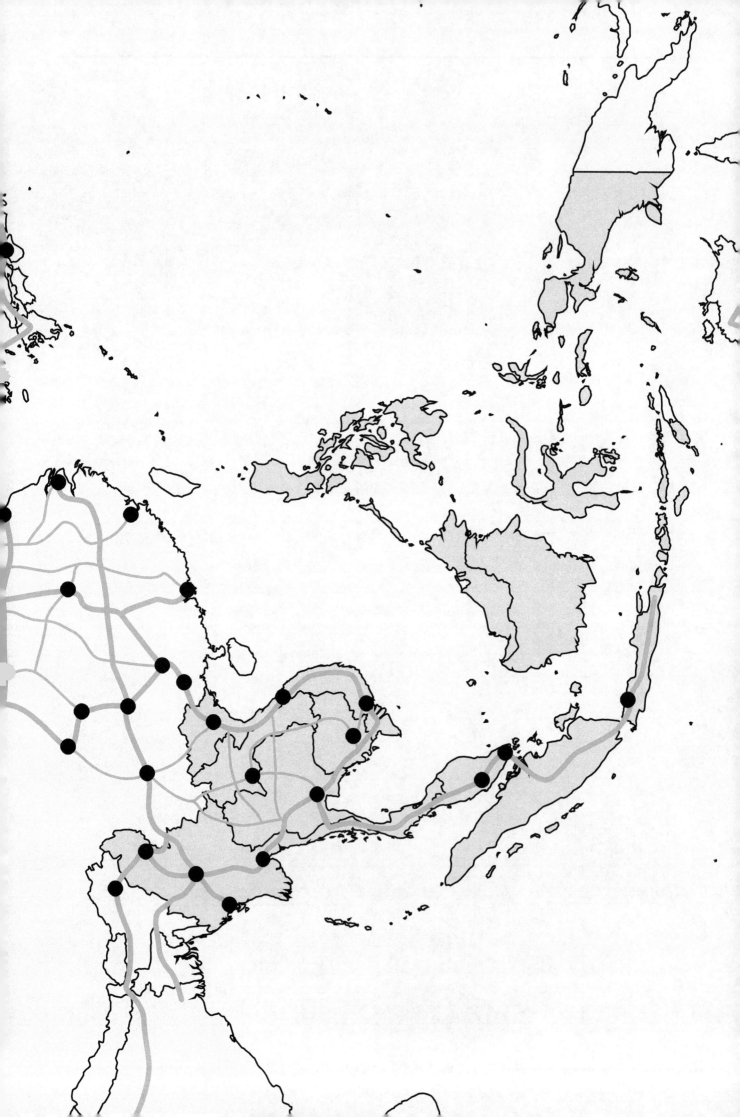

"With President Trump's highly successful visit to Asia in November 2017, there is no longer any reason to maintain the 'with us or against us' mentality.... The nations of Asia are ready and willing to welcome the United States as a partner with China, ... creating a new paradigm for mankind."

China's Belt and Road Transforming
SOUTHEAST ASIA

Southeast Asia has throughout history been multiply connected with China. Many of the ethnic identities across the region have roots in Chinese ethnic groups which migrated over land and by sea across Southeast Asia. Chinese merchants and traders have operated for millennia throughout the region. In the 14th and 15th Centuries, the great Chinese Treasure Ships, under the command of the Chinese Muslim Admiral Cheng He, plied the waters of Southeast Asia on their journeys to Africa and the Persian Gulf.

In an interview with *EIR* in 2014, former Malaysian Prime Minister Mahathir Mohamad said of Admiral Cheng He: "He is a remarkable leader, a remarkable man. He came with very powerful forces—not to conquer, but to establish diplomatic relations with countries. China never attempted to conquer countries.... This contrasts with the first Portuguese—with Vasco da Gama, Afonso de Albuquerque ..., who came here in order to conquer. The Portuguese arrived in Malacca in 1509. Two years later, they conquered Malacca. The Chinese had been in Malacca for many, many years before that, and never conquered Malacca, although they had so many Chinese in this country who could have formed a fifth-column for them. But they never tried to conquer. So there is this difference between Cheng He and the Portuguese and the other Europeans. Cheng He established friendships."

Despite occasional, relatively minor conflicts on land and sea, the relations between China and the nations which now compose the Association of Southeast Asia Nations (ASEAN—Thailand, Malaysia, Indonesia, Singapore, Philippines, Cambodia, Myanmar, Laos, Brunei, and Vietnam) have in modern times been, as Dr. Mahathir expressed, peaceful and cooperative. China's Premier Zhou Enlai and India's Prime Minister Jawaharlal Nehru formulated the "Five Principles of Peaceful Coexistence" in 1953, which were subsequently adopted at the historic Bandung Conference in 1955—the Asia-Africa Conference of formerly colonized nations of Asia and Africa, the first such meeting without the presence of the former colonial rulers.

With China's emergence from the Cultural Revolution in the 1970s, and its "opening up" to the West, its relations with Southeast Asia also developed rapidly. The vast infrastructure projects launched across Southeast Asia under the impetus of China's Belt and Road Initiative—as also in Africa, Central Asia, and South America—are breathtaking in scope and his-

III. PROGRESS REPORTS

Chinese President Xi Jinping (center left) and Indonesian President Joko Widodo. Xi announced the 21st Century Maritime Silk Road before the Indonesian Parliament in 2013. Widodo, who took office in 2014, has promoted Indonesia as the Global Maritime Axis.

torically unprecedented. New high-speed rail lines, ports and power projects, as well as soft infrastructure such as schools and hospitals, are transforming the economies across the region. The 21st Century Maritime Silk Road was in fact announced in Indonesia, the largest of the ASEAN economies, during a speech to the Indonesian Parliament by President Xi Jinping in 2013, to address the island nations and coastal nations of Southeast Asia, South Asia, Africa, and the Middle East.

The ten ASEAN nations are quite diverse, with vastly different languages, cultures, religions, standards of living, and ethnic makeup. They have therefore adopted a policy of consensus for all of their policy considerations—that the divisions among themselves cannot be the basis of policy making, but only those policies which address the common aims of all can be adopted.

In 2000, following the Asian financial crisis of 1998, ASEAN joined with China, Japan, and South Korea (the ASEAN+3) to create the Chiang Mai Initiative, to pool currency reserves as mutual protection against any recurrence of the speculative attacks which had devastated the real economies of Thailand, Malaysia, Indonesia, and the Philippines in the 1998 so-called "Asian crisis"—which Lyndon LaRouche had then identified as the first ramification of a global financial meltdown.

But desperately needed investments to address the infrastructure deficit in the region, made worse by the 1998 crisis, were at best piecemeal, coming primarily from Japan and South Korea, with some funding from the Asian Development Bank (ADB) and the World Bank.

By 2014, the ADB estimated infrastructure needs in the region to be at least $800 billion annually, compared to total World Bank lending internationally of $50 billion annually, and to ADB lending of about $10 billion. Thus when Xi Jinping initiated the Asian Infrastructure Investment Bank (AIIB) in 2014, fifty-seven countries signed on, becoming the founding members at the opening in 2015.

The degenerate Obama administration in Washington refused to join, claiming that the AIIB was not up to the "high standards" of the Western banking system, apparently oblivious to the irony of that statement following the near collapse of the entire system in 2008, and the continuing generation of huge speculative bubbles throughout the system. The Obama administration pressured the other G-7 nations to stay out, and Japan conceded, but France, Germany, Italy, and the UK all signed up.

Adding up the capacity of the new investment banks and funds set up under China's initiative, China intends to invest more than $1 trillion in development projects along the New Silk Road. In reviewing the projects underway or being discussed in the Southeast Asian region, we see that this burst in

The ASEAN Plus Three

productive activity across the region is also spurring other nations to expand their investments into this booming economic environment, especially since this development of infrastructure lifts the entire productive platform of the region.

High-Speed Rail

Until now, there has been no high-speed rail in all of Southeast Asia. China is now building high-speed rail lines in Indonesia, Laos, Malaysia, and Thailand, with projects under discussion in several other ASEAN countries. The aim is to connect all of mainland ASEAN via rail, with north-south and east-west lines, connecting northward to China and westward to India and Europe. Eventually there will be bridges to Indonesia as well, and separate rail lines in the Philippines.

The first approved project was in Indonesia, with a contract to connect Jakarta to Bandung, the third largest city, with a 150-km high-speed rail line. There was fierce competition between China and Japan for the contract, and the bid by the Japanese was better in terms of overall costs. The difference was that Japan, like all investors from the West, demanded host-government guarantees on the loans, whereas China did not.

Indonesia had learned from the massive 1998 speculative attack on its currency by George Soros and his fellow speculators, that providing government guarantees to powers that control international finance and international trade can be a death sentence for the economy as a whole. The Indonesian currency was devalued to one-third of its former value by speculators: Loans denominated in U.S. dollars, guaranteed by the government in dollars, tripled overnight in terms of Indonesia's own currency, through no fault on the part of Indonesia. While the country has achieved significant progress since that time, it is still paying the price for those unequal contracts.

China thus won the bid for the Jakarta-Bandung rail line. Construction on the $5.5 billion project began in February 2016, although it has been stalled over land acquisition issues. The line will cut travel time from three hours to 40 minutes. He Huawu, China Railway Corporation's chief engineer, said: "This is the first international cooperative project in which China has brought its entire industrial chain model to another country. The complete high-speed railway operation system includes technology, operations, equipment, and construction that will be used as a reference for other international projects in the future." China's Ambassador to Indonesia, Xie Feng, described it as a landmark in the implementation of the One Belt One Road Initiative.

Pan-Asian Railway

The next project to be launched was a north-south line through land-locked Laos. This is the first stage of a high-speed rail connection along the Pan-Asian Railway (**Figure 1**), from Kunming in China's Yunnan Province, through Laos, then to the ports in Thailand, and on to Malaysia's capital, Kuala Lumpur, and Singapore. Two segments of this route, in Laos and Thailand, are underway, and a third, in Malaysia, is expected to be launched soon. Japan is also bidding on the segment from Kuala Lumpur to Singapore.

Construction began on the Laos segment, a 420-km route costing about $6 billion, at the beginning of 2017. An amazing 60% of this segment will be bridges and tunnels, with a designed speed of 160 km/h. The project also includes construction of many new roads through the forested rural areas in the north, as well as new power lines, connecting regions which have never had electricity, to the nation's power grid.

The first step in the construction process was the clearance of unexploded ordnance left over from the U.S. war on Indochina, which had dropped more bombs on the three Indochina nations (Vietnam, Laos, and Cambodia) than had been dropped in all wars in the world throughout history up to that point.

There was some concern in Laos about the large number of Chinese workers—about 100,000—involved in this rail project and other Chinese projects in Laos. Laos, however, has only 6.5 million people, with an education system largely oriented to agriculture. While it is true that much of the work on the railroad will be done by Chinese, the many Laotians who will participate will be acquiring skills which

III. PROGRESS REPORTS

Figure 1
Pan-Asian Railway (Segment)

will be valuable for future projects. The two governments also agreed that no more than 10% of the unskilled labor, and 20% of the skilled labor, with some exceptions, will be Chinese, and that the permits for Chinese workers will be limited to two years, or four years at most.

The Laos segment terminates in Vientiane, near the Thai border, where traditional rail lines connect over the Friendship Bridge to Thailand's Nong Kai and then go on to Bangkok. But this traditional line will eventually be replaced with high-speed rail, to Bangkok and then to the southeast to connect to the Eastern Economic Corridor ports and industrial zones at Map Ta Phut in Thailand's Rayong Province, near Cambodia.

Construction began on the first part of the Thailand segment in December 2017. Prime Minister Prayuth Chan-ocha signed a contract with China while attending the BRICS Summit in Xiamen in September 2017, as one of five invited guests to the Summit. The $5 billion agreement will see a 252-km line constructed from Bangkok to Korat (Nakhon Ratchasima) in the Northeast of Thailand (called Isan), about half way to the Laos border. Prime Minister Prayuth would like to make Korat the economic hub of the Mekong region, with rail lines extending north through Laos to China, but also running east and west, connecting to Cambodia and Vietnam in the east and to Myanmar in the west. This visionary plan involves integrated water management, upgraded agriculture and industry, upgraded airports and river ports, and tourism. The Northeast is the most populated but poorest region of the country, subject to floods and droughts every year.

There is a beautiful irony in Prime Minister Prayuth's vision for Korat. The city was once a major hub for the U.S. war on Indochina in the 1960s and 1970s, with a massive U.S. airbase which sent Phantom jets to bomb and napalm Vietnam, Cambodia, and Laos. Under this new vision, the city of Korat will instead be a hub for the industrial and agricultural transformation of the region into modern industrial nations. This is the character of the New Silk Road.

Malaysia-Singapore

The next phase of the Pan-Asian Railway, which is expected to be launched relatively soon, is the high-speed rail connection between Kuala Lumpur and Singapore (**Figure 2**). The plan was agreed to by Malaysia and Singapore in July 2016, with an intention to begin construction in 2017, completing construction in 2026.

Chinese President Xi Jinping and Thai Prime Minister Prayuth Chan-ocha. China is building the first two legs of the Pan-Asian Railroad through Laos and Thailand.

SOUTHEAST ASIA

Figure 2
Malaysia High-Speed Rail

However, the bidding for the construction is still open, with China, Japan, South Korea, and France all showing interest. China is deeply involved in Malaysian development and is the leading bidder, but it is not certain. China's Ambassador to Malaysia, Dr. Huang Huikang, told *The Star* (Malaysia) in July 2017 that China would give the best terms, and would complete the project in five years rather than ten, as proposed by the other bidders. The 350-km line will be built to have a speed of 300 km/h, running four times per hour, at a cost of $11 billion.

China is now building another rail line in Malaysia, called the East Coast Rail Link (Figure 2). The east coast is far less developed than the west coast, so this line will facilitate a major transformation of the region. The route will connect Port Klang on the Malacca Strait, Malaysia's largest port, through Kuala Lumpur to the east coast, then turn north along the coast to Kota Bharu and Tumpat in Kelantan Province, close to the Thai border.

Prime Minister Najib Razak broke ground for the project in August 2017. The total length of the project is 688 km, with 50 km of tunneling for several underground sections, at an operating speed of 160 km/h and a cost of $13 billion.

The largely unexpected defeat of Prime Minister Najib Razak by former Prime Minister Dr. Mahathir in the May 2018 elections, and the opening of investigations into large-scale corruption in the Najib administration, has caused the rail projects to be put on hold, as Prime Minister Mahathir has pledged to renegotiate the projects. He has, however, assured China that relations will remain strong and Malaysia's participation in the Belt and Road Initiative will continue.

Lancang-Mekong Cooperation

Another inter-regional development project under the Belt and Road Initiative is the Lancang-Mekong Cooperation (Lancang is the name of the Chinese portion of the Mekong). The Mekong is the last major river in the world to remain undeveloped, due to colonial divisions and then decades of colonial wars. It was not until 1995 that there was enough agreement among the Southeast Asian Mekong nations (Thailand, Vietnam, Cambodia, Laos) that a Mekong River Commission was established.

That Commission, however, was heavily influenced by anti-development environmentalist ideology. Earlier efforts to design a model based on Franklin D. Roosevelt's Tennessee Valley Authority (TVA), with hydro-power projects, industrialization, and city building, were replaced with conservation measures, efforts to prevent dam construction, and typical IMF/World Bank measures providing minimal help to poor peasants and fishermen while keeping them in a state of backwardness, with no infrastructure development.

A parallel organization launched by the ADB in 1992, the Greater Mekong Subregion (GMS), bringing in Myanmar and China's Yunnan Province as participants, was far more development oriented. Three main economic corridors were developed, building roads connecting the member nations and providing credit for development along the corridors. More than $18 billion has been invested by the GMS, and nearly double that amount is planned for 107 projects in the pipeline.

With the emergence of the Belt and Road Initiative, China has taken measures to expand the vision and the planning for the region. The Lancang-Mekong Cooperation organization was founded in 2015, comprising all six countries along the river. On March 10, 2017, the Chinese secretariat of the Lancang-Mekong Cooperation was opened in Beijing. Foreign Minister Wang Yi said at the ceremony that 45 projects had already been approved and will be completed by the end of 2017, in the areas of connectivity, energy, cross-border economy, water resources, and agriculture. Water control is a primary concern, to counter floods and droughts—in March 2016, China opened the floodgates on the Lancang River dams for a period of two weeks, releasing massive amounts of freshwater into the Mekong basin, to help alleviate a drought in Southeast Asia brought on by the El Niño.

China is now carrying out the second-phase renovation of the Lancang-Mekong channel, through dredging and rock removal, to facilitate more boat traffic along the river. Plans include building cross-border industrial clusters along the river: China has already developed several industrial parks in the Mekong countries, including the Long Jiang Industrial Park in Vietnam, Saysettha Comprehensive Development Zone in Laos, Cambodia's Sihanoukville Special Economic Zone, and the Thai-Chinese Rayong Industrial Zone. They are establishing agricultural cooperation platforms and programs of poverty reduction across the region.

China is also the leading builder of dams in the world, with the majority of its hydropower projects in Southeast Asia (and many in Africa). The Laos government will start work this year on the $2.3 billion Pak Beng hydropower scheme on the Mekong River in Laos, being built by China's Datong Overseas Investment Company. It is the third of up to 11 dams that Laos is considering for the Mekong (**Figure 3**). Work has begun on two other large projects being built by the Thais and the Malaysians in Laos. The export of electricity to its neighbors is a major source of income for the country.

Opposition to the dams from Cambodia and Vietnam has been largely mitigated, but the international anti-development non-governmental organizations (NGOs) are frantically trying to stop their development. In Myanmar, a large-scale hydropower project

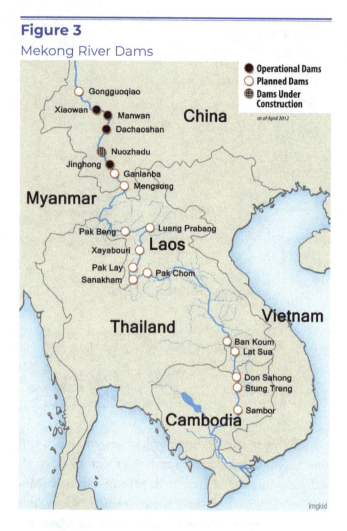

Figure 3
Mekong River Dams

undertaken by China, the Myitsone Dam in the far north of the country, was scheduled to be completed by 2017, and would have been the fifteenth largest hydro project in the world. It was suspended in 2011 due primarily to the international anti-dam NGOs' instigation of opposition from portions of the regional population, and China has reluctantly concurred in shutting it down.

But Chinese companies are nonetheless building other dams in Myanmar, including a 7,100 MW dam in the Shan State, built by China's Three Gorges and Sinohydro, together with Thailand's national power company EGAT. A smaller project is being built in the Karen State by the same partnership. These are both areas of separatist insurgencies over the history of Burma/Myanmar independence from the British, so providing water control and electricity for development will be crucial to the success of the government's efforts to bring peace to the country.

Bilateral Projects

Philippines

The Philippines was largely left behind in the New Silk Road process under the former government of Noynoy Aquino. Following directions from the Obama Administration, Aquino allowed the country to be a pawn in Obama's confrontation with Russia and China, going so far as to file for arbitration under the UN Convention on the Law of the Sea (UNCLOS) against China over contested sovereignty claims in the South China Sea. Despite winning the toothless arbitration, in which China refused to participate, the victory for Aquino (and Obama) simply encouraged Philippine voters to reject Aquino's chosen successor in the May 2016 election, electing instead the current President Rodrigo Duterte. Duterte had denounced Obama for trying to provoke a war, and called for cooperation with China's New Silk Road development program—development which was sorely lacking under U.S. tutelage.

Duterte and his Cabinet secretaries immediately began negotiations with China and Russia on economic and military cooperation. Duterte declared his administration to be "The golden age of Philippine infrastructure," calling his program "Build, Build, Build," with a target of $38 billion to be raised through taxes, foreign and local loans, and official development assistance (ODA) from bilateral partners. China has indicated its intention to provide $9 billion in loans and grants for government-to-government projects, and the possibility of $15.3 billion more in joint ventures and investments by private companies over a six-year period.

In September 2017, a delegation under Duterte's Finance Secretary, Carlos Dominguez, visited Beijing, where it arranged a set of infrastructure projects in two phases. The first phase includes two major bridges in Manila, for which construction is scheduled to begin immediately. Other priorities are a major water control and dam project to supply water to Manila; a Chico River irrigation scheme in the north of Luzon; an elevated expressway in Davao City (Duterte's home town) in Mindanao; an industrial park; two drug rehab centers; bridges connecting several islands in the Visayas; an agriculture technical center; and reconstruction of Marawi, the city in Mindanao that was seized by ISIS-linked terrorists in May 2017, and where fighting continued until October, when the government forces eliminated the last of the terrorists. The fighting left more than 1,000 dead and displaced more than 300,000.

Many of the proposed projects have been on the books for decades, with promises from the World Bank and others that never materialized. These new projects will likely be funded by the AIIB, China's Exim Bank, or China's Silk Road Fund, perhaps with support from the ADB. The AIIB has also recently agreed to co-finance a flood control project in Manila, together with the World Bank and the government.

The Philippine government has also begun to "test the debt market" in China by issuing yuan-denominated bonds there ("Panda bonds"), beginning in November 2017.

With the new momentum in the Philippines, Chinese private sector companies are opening up new investments in the country, in infrastructure projects and in manufacturing, including aviation, energy, iron and steel, and shipbuilding. China's Huili Investment Fund Management Company is planning a $2 billion world-class integrated steel mill, while Liaoning Bora is launching a joint venture in oil refineries and an oil storage terminal, worth $3 billion.

The Duterte government is open to renewing joint oil and gas exploration with China in the South

Philippine President Duterte and Chinese President Xi.

Figure 4
Mindanao Rail Project Proposal

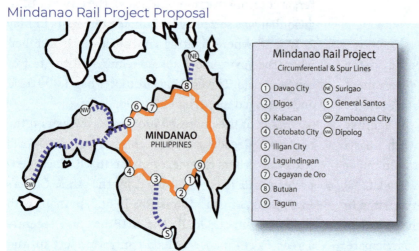

China Sea, now that both sides have returned to the earlier policy of Deng Xiaoping—that sovereignty issues should be put aside while the two nations cooperate in joint development.

Chinese investment has also spurred Japanese business to show increased interest in infrastructure and industrial investment in the Philippines. Although no agreements have been reached as yet, there is intense discussion with China on two major rail projects in the Philippines. The first is a high-speed rail connection between Manila and the Clark Air Base, formerly a U.S. military facility, now an international airport. China had been contracted to rebuild that rail line in 2003, but the contract was terminated by the Aquino Administration in 2012, under pressure from Obama. Clark Air Base is only 58 miles from Manila, so a high-speed rail connection would make it a viable alternative international airport for the capital city, whose only international airport is horribly overcrowded.

Chinese Vice Premier Wang Yang led a forty-person delegation to a forum in Mindanao in March 2017 on a proposed Mindanao railway project (**Figure 4**) connecting the major cities of the largest, and poorest, Philippine island—an 830-km project estimated to cost $4.2 billion. Wang said China would conduct a feasibility study on the project.

Lyndon LaRouche has always considered the Philippines to be the critical nation in Asia for bridging the divisions of East and West, having a tradition in both Eastern and Western cultures. He has long promoted ring rail and industrialization for Mindanao as a central feature for unleashing the Philippines' potential for development.

Mindanao has been the site of independence movements based in factions of the Muslim (Moro) community, as well as of terrorist movements instigated by Saudi-backed Wahhabis connected to al Qaeda and ISIS. China's intention in its Belt and Road Initiative is not to avoid areas of instability, but rather to consider instability as a motivation to invest, as a means of achieving peace through development. Other port and airport development projects in Mindanao are also under consideration.

Most important, the legacy of the Bataan nuclear plant is under discussion with China, Russia, and others. The nuclear plant stands unused as a symbol of the regime change carried out against nationalist President Ferdinand Marcos in 1986 by then U.S. Secretary of State George Shultz and the emerging neoconservative movement in the United States. The nuclear plant, the first in Southeast Asia, was fully completed and ready to turn on, when foreign-funded, green NGOs repeatedly stalled the project, until the Washington-orchestrated coup shut it down completely. The subsequent government nonetheless paid for the entire project, leaving the nation energy deficient, while paying exorbitant energy rates even today.

The Philippine LaRouche Society has led a lonely campaign to restore the plant, and to use small, modular nuclear reactors to furnish energy to the many islands making up the Philippines. Now, finally, the issue is on the table. Here too, China, as well as Russia, can play leading roles. A Russian nuclear team has already inspected the plant, and has concluded that it is possible to restore it to working condition.

Indonesia

In addition to the high-speed rail China is building to connect Jakarta and Bandung, referenced above, China is engaged in infrastructure development projects across the huge Indonesian archipelago of more than 18,000 islands, which are home to the fourth largest population in the world. Pak Rosan Roeslani, the Chairman of the Indonesian Chamber of Commerce and Industry (KADIN), told a Washington, DC audience in October 2016 that nearly every infrastructure construction project in the country had a Chinese name connected to it.

The former President of Indonesia, Susilo Bambang Yudhoyono, who served from 2004 to 2014, hosted two large Infrastructure conferences in Washington during his term, presenting a master list of projects which were essentially shovel-ready, if foreign funding and construction capacity could be arranged. He estimated the country needed about $450 billion per year in infrastructure to restore the nation's economy. He came up essentially empty handed on both trips. The United States has invested in mining and oil exploration, but for any infrastructure investments, it demanded government guarantees of the sort that had killed Indonesia when the speculators drove its currency down in 1998. As reported above, this is what killed the Japanese bid for the Jakarta-Bandung rail contract. It is to Yudhoyono's credit that he refused to accept the unequal terms, but in the process, he ended up with virtually no new infrastructure, except from China.

The U.S. share of foreign direct investment in Indonesia has collapsed from 8.3% in 2013 to under 2% in 2016, despite Obama's pledge of greater support to Asia, and especially to Indonesia, where he spent part of his childhood.

Xi Jinping's 2013 announcement in Indonesia of the 21st Century Maritime Silk Road recalled the historic Chinese Treasure Ships of the 14th and 15th Centuries under Admiral Cheng He—referenced above by Malaysia's former Prime Minister Mahathir. The world's largest ships of that time, and the largest armadas, had sailed to Indonesia as part of their exploration, which took them to India, Africa, and through the Red Sea to Egypt, and perhaps even to Italy, it has recently been learned.

In 2014, current Indonesian President Joko Widodo was elected, and quickly arranged a meeting with Xi Jinping. Speaking at the East Asia Summit in Myanmar in November 2014, Jokowi (as he is known) announced his vision of Indonesia as the "Global Maritime Axis" of the new paradigm emerging in the world. "Indonesia realizes that a substantial transformation is taking place in the 21st Century," he said. "The center of gravity of the geo-economic and geo-political world is shifting from West to East. Asian countries are on the rise. As the world's largest archipelagic state with its strategic location at the crossroads of the Indian and the Pacific Oceans," Jokowi said, "Indonesia must assert itself as the Global Maritime Axis." Clearly, this coincides with Xi's vision of the 21st Century Maritime Silk Road.

China has built a number of bridges and ports across the nation. The 5.4-km Suramadu Bridge, which connects Surabaya in East Java with the island of Madura, was completed in 2009, long before the Belt and Road Initiative began. It is the longest trans-oceanic bridge in Southeast Asia. Since the launching of the Maritime Silk Road, China has rapidly expanded investment, increasing it five-fold during 2016, becoming the second biggest investor (after Singapore) by the beginning of 2017, including investment in more than 1,200 industrial, mining, and infrastructure projects. The chief of Indonesia's Investment Coordinating Board, Thomas Lembong, said: "China's rate of investment growth means it is only a matter of time before it takes over first place." Projects under discussion include integrated infrastructure development in North Sumatra, and a new harbor and nuclear industry construction in North Kalimantan.

Myanmar

In Myanmar, China is building a deep-sea port in Kyauk Phyu in western Rakhine state, near the Bangladesh border, which is the terminus of the oil and gas pipelines constructed through Myanmar to Kunming, completed in 2015 (**Figure 5**). Trial operations began that year on the 771-km pipeline, but the first deliveries of Mideast crude were delayed until April 2017.

The pipeline carries 22 million tons of crude annually, with Myanmar taking 2 million tons annually. PetroChina opened a new, $4.4 billion state-of-the-art oil refinery in Anning, near Kunming, in June 2017, with the capacity to refine 13 million tons of crude from the Myanmar pipeline. The gas pipeline was completed in 2013, before the crude oil pipeline,

Figure 5
Myanmar-Kunming Gas Pipeline

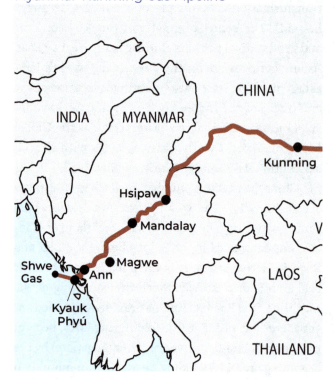

and began supplying gas to China that year, providing about 5% of China's natural gas consumption.

In December 2017, China announced the intention to develop a China-Myanmar trade corridor, along the route of the pipelines, leading to the Kyauk Phyu port. Together, the port, a connected industrial zone, and the potential trade corridor will transform the region economically.

This is the region of the Rohingya crisis, which reached catastrophic proportions in late 2017, as an estimated 600,000 ethnic Bangladeshi Muslims fled to Bangladesh to escape the violence. As of this writing, China is cooperating with Myanmar and Bangladesh to arrange the return of those who wish to return to their homes in Myanmar. China considers the development projects, creating thousands of new jobs, as the crucial means to achieve a long-term solution to the ethnic tensions between Buddhists and Muslims and the emergence of an armed movement by the so-called Arakan Rohingya Salvation Army, set up by Saudi Wahhabi-trained elements within the Rohingya population. That armed group attacked multiple Myanmar police outposts in August 2017, sparking the violence.

Vietnam

In Vietnam, despite political and military conflicts with China over centuries, China (including Hong Kong, Taiwan, and Macau) is nonetheless the largest foreign investor, with more than $56 billion in nearly 5,000 projects, mostly in manufacturing.

With a rapid, 7% growth rate, Vietnam is suffering from severe traffic congestion and air pollution in its two major cities, Ho Chi Minh City and Hanoi. The government is committed to resolving the problem through major urban rail projects in both cities. Interestingly, this has generated a model of useful competition and cooperation between China and Japan.

The Ho Chi Minh City Urban Rail Project consists of six lines, at an estimated cost of more than $20 billion. Japan is the major funder, with participation from the ADB, the European Investment Bank, Korea, the German Bank for Reconstruction, and the Spanish government.

The Hanoi Urban Rail Project, on the other hand—with nine lines at an estimated cost of more than $31 billion through to its targeted completion in 2050—is being funded and constructed primarily by China, although Japan and France are also involved. The first line is scheduled to open in 2018.

ASEAN-China

To detail all of the Belt and Road projects launched in Southeast Asia would be beyond the purpose of this report. A few general points in conclusion will suffice.

China has become the leading trade partner of all ten of the ASEAN nations, by a wide margin in most. Even the wealthy states of Singapore and Brunei are rapidly expanding their economic cooperation with China. In Brunei (the fifth wealthiest nation per capita in the world), China is building a $3.5 billion oil refinery, while China Telecom is expanding the Sultanate's cell phone networks, and a Chinese electric car factory is being constructed. Singapore, which for several years now has been the largest foreign investor in China, is now also the largest Chinese investment destination in Asia.

The Cat Linh-Ha Dong urban railway project in Hanoi, Vietnam, seen on March 28, 2017, is being constructed by China Railway Engineering Corporation.

Other major projects across ASEAN should be mentioned:

In Malaysia, one of the leading recipients of Chinese Belt and Road investments, a new port facility, called Malacca Gateway, is being built south of the current port Klang on the Malacca Strait, while a new bridge to Penang from the Malay mainland is also under construction.

In Cambodia, a Chinese industrial zone with more than 100 industries is in operation at Cambodia's only deep-water port, Sihanoukville, while more than 30 Chinese agricultural and agro-industrial projects are in place elsewhere in Cambodia, including rubber and rice facilities.

Northern Laos is now supporting extensive banana production facilities built by the Chinese.

In Thailand, the historic effort to build a canal across the Kra Isthmus in southern Thailand, connecting the Pacific and the Indian oceans, has recently been given new life due to China's Belt and Road Initiative. Friends of the LaRouche movement in Thailand, led by Pakdee Tanapura, have fought for this great project for more than 30 years. They have recently won support from leading figures in the Thai military, the Privy Council, and business layers, who joined together in a forum in Bangkok on September 11, 2017, with representatives from China, Japan, and other nations, to encourage the government to adopt the program. Chambers of commerce of multiple nations with offices in Thailand joined forces to sponsor another conference supporting the Kra Canal on February 1, 2018.

If the project is adopted by the Thai government, it will almost certainly be one of the projects that will benefit from Japanese Prime Minister Shinzo Abe's intention to co-finance Silk Road projects with China, since Japan and China will both greatly benefit from the canal.

The new middle class in China is also the source of nearly half of the tourism in the region, which is a significant source of income in the beautiful Southeast Asian countries.

The picture is clear. The Anglo-American effort, heightened under the Obama Administration, to divide Asia along the old Cold War lines—forcing nations to declare either for the United States or for China—has collapsed. Obama's attempt to isolate China economically with the Trans-Pacific Partnership (TTP) was already failing, but has been finished off by President Trump. The ASEAN proposal for a Regional Comprehensive Economic Partnership (RCEP), based on fair trade and equality among all the Asian nations, has been fully supported by China and is now coming close to implementation. Geopolitics, based on the idea that one nation can gain only at the expense of others, is being dumped into the garbage pail of British imperial history, as Xi Jinping's win-win approach to

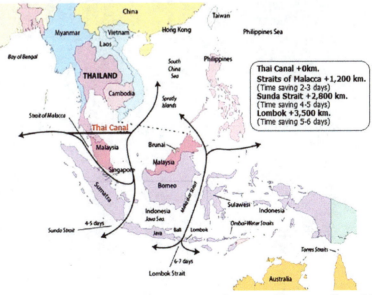

"Kra Canal—New Gateway to the Maritime Silkroad." http://kracanal-maritimesilkroad.com

achieve a common destiny based on shared interests is bringing the world together for the common good.

With President Trump's highly successful visit to Asia in November 2017, there is no longer any reason to maintain the "with us or against us" mentality of the Bush/Obama years, or of the Cold War. The nations of Asia are ready and willing to welcome the United States as a partner with China, as part of the New Silk Road, creating a new paradigm for mankind.

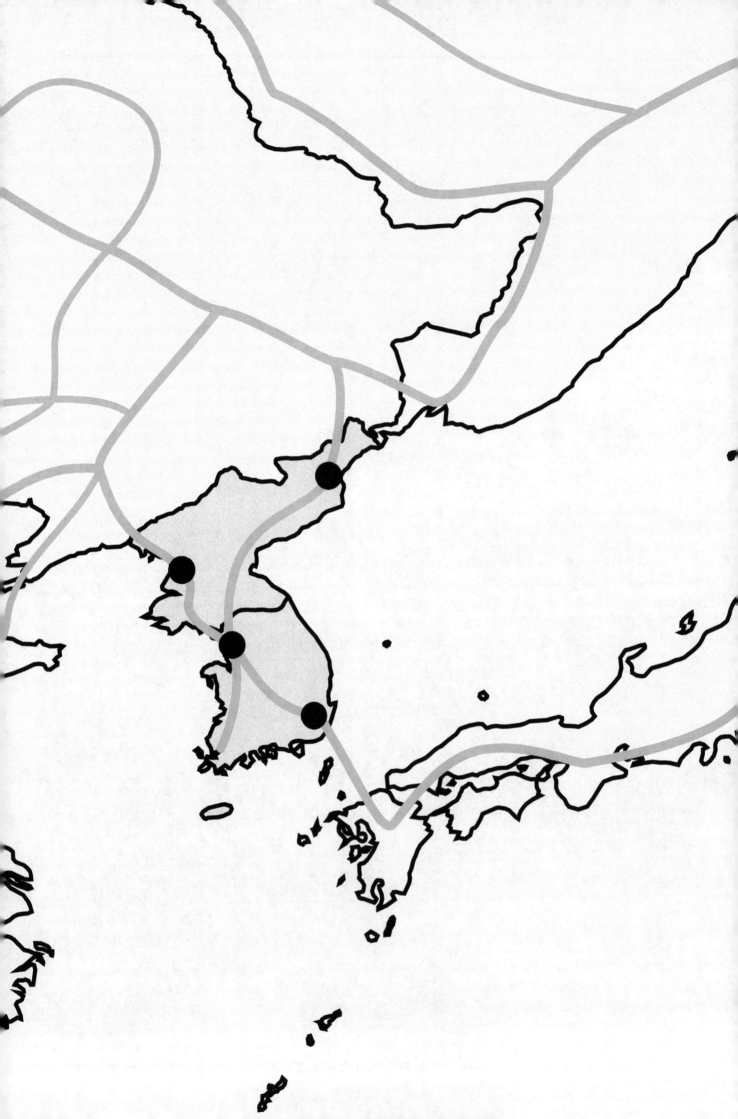

"If there has ever been a case proving that 'peace through development' is not only the surest means to break through deep seated conflicts, but the only means, it is the long-festering impasse on the Korean Peninsula."

The Silk Road—The Necessary Solution to the Crisis on
THE KOREAN PENINSULA

The date June 12, 2018, will long be remembered for the historic summit between President Donald Trump and Chairman Kim Jong-un. It marks more than the "beginning of the end" of the 68 years of hostility and near-war conditions on the Korean Peninsula—it marks the coming together of the entire Asian continent, with full U.S. support, in the spirit of the New Silk Road. The extraordinary transformation taking place could not have been possible without the close cooperation between the United States under President Trump and China, Japan, South Korea, and Russia. It is not coincidental that just two days before the summit, Trump had insisted to his fellow members of the G7 that Russia must be brought back in, making it again the G8, if the leaders of the Western nations were to remain relevant in the changing world environment.

This historic Trump-Kim meeting took place just days before the publication of this report. On April 27, 2018, Chairman Kim and South Korean President Moon Jae-in had set the process in motion with a meeting in the Demilitarized Zone (DMZ) separating North and South Korea, which could mark the beginning of the end of the British imperial manipulation of "hotspots" as cockpits for war, keeping the major

President Trump and Kim Jong-un meet for the first time on June 12, 2018, in Singapore.

powers of the world divided, to the benefit of the lords of the bankrupt London/Wall Street financial empire.

If there has ever been a case proving that "peace through development" is not only the surest means to break through deep-seated conflicts, but also the only means, it is the long-festering impasse on the Korean Peninsula. In fact, the crisis over the question of North Korea's effort to develop nuclear weapons had been solved once, then sabotaged, and then nearly solved again, only to be sabotaged a second time.

THE WORLD LAND-BRIDGE | 167

We are now on the verge of a third attempt to resolve the problem. The crucial difference in this current potential solution is that, for the first time in modern history, the United States, China, and Russia (under Presidents Donald Trump, Xi Jinping, and Vladimir Putin), the three leading powers in the world, are close to reaching full agreement—not only in regard to the North Korea issue, although they are in general agreement in that regard—but more importantly in regard to the necessity that these three great powers work together in resolving all the problems facing mankind, and in particular in cooperating in the historic global development process initiated by China, the Belt and Road Initiative (BRI). The ongoing, desperate effort by British intelligence and their assets in the United States to overthrow the presidency of Donald Trump is evidence of their terror of losing their most fundamental division of the world's major powers, that between the United States—as the "dumb giant" enforcer of the British Empire—and Russia and China.

Only if North Korea believes that these great powers are in fact ending the geopolitical division of the world into East vs. West, and cooperating with each other in the development of prosperous agro-industrial nations in every part of the world, only then will Pyongyang have reason to believe that the United States will not repeat the criminal destruction that was imposed upon Iraq, Libya, and Syria under British and American direction. Only then will they believe an American pledge that there would be no invasion, no regime change, and no forced reunification against the regime in Pyongyang following a denuclearization agreement.

And these conditions are very close to being realized, as *EIR* has insisted, despite the threats of war which were being issued by both Trump and Kim over the past year. China and Russia are, by their own standards, enjoying the closest friendship and cooperation in history. The United States under President Trump has rejected the Cold War policies of confrontation with Russia and China which nearly triggered a global nuclear war under the regimes of George W. Bush and Barack Obama. It is precisely this rejection of British geopolitics which is the cause of the hysterical anti-Russia campaign by the oligarchical forces in the U.S. and Europe, and the effort to remove President Trump from office.

The steps toward dialogue initiated by North and South Korea in the opening days of 2018 have a clear model for a workable solution to the crisis, and toward eventual reunification, in the "Agreed Framework" of 1994, negotiated by Kim Il-sung and his son Kim Jong-il with the Bill Clinton Administration, in cooperation with the South Korean government. The North froze operations on its plutonium-producing 5 MW reactor in Yongbyon, and stopped construction on two other reactors, in exchange for two 1000 MW light water reactors, whose construction was to be carried out by South Korea and Japan. International Atomic Energy Agency (IAEA) inspectors were allowed into North Korea and oil was to be supplied to the North while construction of the nuclear plants proceeded. Discussions were to proceed toward a peace treaty between the United States and North Korea (there was only an Armistice ending the Korean War in 1953).

This plan was terminated after President Bush and Vice President Dick Cheney took office in 2001. Nonetheless, President Kim Dae-jung continued negotiating with the North, and even succeeded in opening up the DMZ and reopening rail lines across the DMZ in 2002 (**Figure 1**). An effort by China to keep the discussion open, known as the Six Party

Figure 1

In September 2002, the fences and mines on the DMZ separating North and South Korea were partially removed and the rail line connecting the divided nation partially restored. Pictured is the first train to cross the DMZ. The "Sunshine" effort was short lived.

Talks, were also sabotaged by the Bush regime and shut down entirely under the Obama Administration.

It can only be concluded that the rejection of development, in favor of confrontation and sanctions, achieved its purpose—North Korea returned to nuclear weapons development and is now a nuclear-armed state. This served the Bush and Obama administrations with a justification for the massive deployment of nuclear armed land and naval forces, including THAAD missile defense systems and nuclear armed offensive missiles, in a ring around China and the Russian Far East in Asia. Such massive forces are recognized by Beijing and Moscow as being far beyond what would be needed to contain North Korea, but rather are aimed at China and Russia, dramatically altering the balance of forces in the region.

Nonetheless, the concept of achieving peace through a development process which addressed the needs and interests of all sides was demonstrated by the 1994 Agreed Framework. Today, North Korea is a nuclear armed state, although knowledgeable experts in the West concur that they would never use these weapons unless attacked, because the result would be the obliteration of the country and the regime.

The other difference today is the existence of the Belt and Road Initiative. The win-win premise of the New Silk Road Spirit guiding the BRI provides the motivation for a new agreement, one which addresses the development and security needs not only of North Korea, but also of the other nations of the region. As demonstrated in other sections of this report, the development of the Russian Far East and the Arctic region are the "New Frontier" for mankind on Earth, while Russian President Putin has pronounced his open invitation to all nations to join in the process.

It is self-evident that the technological expertise of Japan and South Korea must play a significant role in the development of the Russian Far East, and both nations have declared this intention. What is often overlooked, is that the highly skilled work force in North Korea would be, and must be, another crucial input to the process. The cooperation of Japan and South Korea with Russia in this great undertaking would go a long way to ending the tensions between these nations, left over from the wars of the past. If the United States were also to participate in this process, by fully joining the New Silk Road, Xi Jinping's vision of a "Community of Shared Future for Mankind" would be within reach.

Rason—Russia-South Korea-North Korea Cooperation

In November 2013, President Putin visited Seoul, meeting with then-President Park Geun-hye. President Park's "Eurasian Initiative," calling for binding European nations together by linking roads and railways across Eurasia to achieve what she called the "Silk Road Express," included solving the North Korea crisis, building a rail connection from Pusan to Rotterdam, as Lyndon LaRouche had long advocated as the cornerstone of the New Silk Road. President Park had asserted that a "Korean Bonanza" awaited the successful peaceful reunification of the two Koreas.

A major agreement at that 2013 Putin-Park Summit was for the development of a three-way agreement between Russia, North Korea, and South Korea, in a joint project centered on the Rason port and Special Economic Zone in North Korea, at the mouth of the Tumen River near the joint border between China, Russia, and North Korea. Russia was reconstructing the rail connection from Vladivostok to the Rason port and building a docking facility at the port. (China also upgraded a highway from Jilin Province to Rason and constructed its own docks, providing an outlet to the sea from China's landlocked northeast provinces.)

The agreement provided for three huge South Korean corporations—Hyundai Merchant Marine, POSCO (the state steel company), and Korail (the state rail company)—to form a consortium with Russia and North Korea centered on Rason, with each owning about one-third of the consortium. By 2015, three shipments of Russian coal had been transported by rail to Rason, loaded on South Korean ships from Hyundai Merchant Marine, unloaded in South Korea, and loaded on Korail trains for shipment to POSCO steel mills (**Figure 2**). This was the first industrial investment in North Korea outside the industrial park in Kaesong near the border between

III. PROGRESS REPORTS

Figure 2
Russian Coal to the Korean Peninsula

The model for cooperation: The Russia-North Korea-Hyundai Merchant Marine-KORAIL-POSCO Consortium. Starting in 2014, Russian coal was shipped to Rason in North Korea by rail, then to South Korea by Hyundai Merchant Marine, then to POSCO steel mills by KORAIL.

North and South Korea, where South Korean manufacturers hire North Korean labor. The Rason consortium was precisely the kind of structure which could potentially serve as a basis for vast industrial cooperation between North and South Korea, engaging Russia and potentially also China.

In fact, a similar consortium of POSCO and Hyundai Merchant Marine was established with Chinese companies in Hunchun, a Chinese city just north of the North Korean border and about 50 km from Rason. The logistics and distribution center planned to expand as the Rason hub developed—a win-win-win for Russia, China, and both sides of the Korean Peninsula.

In February 2015, a memorandum of understanding (MOU) was signed in Moscow between RusHydro, Russia's largest hydropower producer, and the South Korean government-owned K-Water, to work jointly on projects in the Russian Far East, and eventually also in North Korea. Russia's Minister for the Development of the Far East, Alexander Galushka,

told *Yonhap* that North Korean officials had agreed with their Russian partners, including RusHydro, on implementing trilateral projects with Seoul.

President Park took another bold step toward her vision of Eurasian integration in August 2015, attending the 70th anniversary of the victory over Japan in World War II in Beijing. Pictures of President Park standing together with Presidents Xi and Putin at the reviewing stand went viral around the world, causing consternation in the Obama White House, as President Obama was mobilizing sanctions against Russia over the Ukraine coup and preparing for war with China over the South China Sea.

Then in February 2016, President Obama struck. After the next North Korean missile test—a test which anyone in their right mind would know was a certainty as long as Obama continued with his military "Pivot to Asia" and military exercises which practiced invasions and "decapitation" operations against the North Korean regime—Obama succeeded in pressuring President Park to scrap all cooperation with the North. The entire Kaesong operation was closed overnight, doing as much damage to South Korean industry as to North Korea.

The Rason consortium was not immediately shuttered, but with shipments from the North forbidden to dock in South Korea, that too was soon aborted. South Korea was also coerced into agreeing to the deployment of U.S. THAAD missiles in the South, even though President Park had previously been very hesitant to agree. It is obvious that the high-altitude missiles have little to do with defending against a potential attack from North Korea (which is only 30 miles away from Seoul), and everything to do with the X Band radar systems which come with the THAAD system, and which see deep into Chinese and Russian territory.

President Park was impeached and removed from office in December 2016, not because of the self-destructive moves against cooperation with Russia and China on North Korea issues, but due to corruption. In the following election, the population voted in the opposition candidate, Moon Jae-in, as President, who took office in May 2017, pledging to restore the "Sunshine Policy" initiated by President Kim Dae-jung in 1998, for opening up dialogue with North Korea.

Korean President Park Geun-hye, Russian President Vladimir Putin, and Chinese President Xi Jinping on the podium at Tiananmen Square in September 2015, for the Victory Parade celebrating victory over Japan in 1945.

With the elections of Donald Trump and Moon Jae-in, both the U.S. and South Korea were committed to creating friendly relations with Russia and China. It is precisely this cooperation in development which creates an environment in which the North Korea issue can be resolved. President Moon attended the Third Eastern Economic Forum in Vladivostok in September 2017. At a press conference after a meeting between Presidents Moon and Putin, the Russian President said:

> It is telling that in the first six months of 2017, bilateral trade [between Russia and South Korea] increased by almost 50 percent, reaching $10 billion.
>
> More than 600 South Korean companies operate in Russia, and investment from South Korea in the Russian economy exceeds $2 billion…. Korean businesses are highly interested in stepping up cooperation with Russia, something that was confirmed at the Eastern Economic Forum by the presence of a high-profile delegation of almost a hundred business leaders representing 50 companies….
>
> Today Mr. President and I have agreed to stimulate the operation of the joint investment and finance platforms with the aggregate capital of $1 billion and to create a portfolio of promising projects, primarily for the Far East, where we can make use of the opportunities offered by the priority development areas and the Free Port of Vladivostok.
>
> During our talks, the Korean partners confirmed their interest in creating a free trade zone with the Eurasian Economic Union. It has been decided to continue expert consultations on this issue. We also expressed satisfaction with the successful development of our energy cooperation. South Korean companies are involved in the Sakhalin-1 and Sakhalin-2 projects. We are discussing the possibility of increasing the delivery of liquefied natural gas. Fifteen tankers will be built at South Korean shipyards to transport the products of the Yamal LNG plant.
>
> **I would like to say that Russia is still willing to implement trilateral projects with the participation of North Korea.** We could deliver Russian pipeline gas to Korea and integrate the power lines and railway systems of Russia, the Republic of Korea, and North Korea. The implementation of these initiatives will be not only economically beneficial, but will also help build up trust and stability on the Korean Peninsula. We see the advantages of the potential involvement of South Korean companies in the construction of infrastructure facilities in Russia, including the modernization of Far Eastern ports and shipyards and the joint development of the Northern Sea Route. **Mr. Moon Jae-in and I agreed on the importance of stepping up regional ties. The first meeting of the Russian-Korean Forum for Interregional Cooperation is expected to take place in … 2018.** [emphasis added]

Speaking at the same Vladivostok Summit, President Moon called on Russia to join with South Korea to immediately launch "nine bridges" between the two countries, including natural gas development and pipelines to deliver it to South Korea, railroads, seaports, electricity grids connecting the countries (perhaps through underwater cables, until the time that North Korea joins the process), shipbuilding, labor cooperation, agriculture, fisheries, and development of the Arctic. Clearly, each of these provide a basis for integrating North Korea into this historic development process.

It was reported by *Yonhap*, following the Moon-Kim Summit of April 27, 2018, that President Moon had presented Kim with a detailed proposal for joint development projects between the North and the South, and linking to their huge neighbors to the north, China and Russia.

Extremely strained relations between South Korea and China followed the deployment of the THAAD missiles in South Korea in 2017, which had been arranged between Obama and the previous Park government. President Moon was politically unable to prevent the deployment, although he had campaigned against them. Unofficial sanctions were implemented against South Korea by China, restricting Chinese tourism to South Korea and boycotting some of the huge South Korean business presence in China.

The Belt and Road Initiative was not being applied in Northeast Asia, despite the fact that the Silk Road process is precisely the means for resolving the crisis. Nonetheless, as Putin indicated, Russia and South Korea proceeded with their own Silk Road concepts as a basis for drawing North Korea into a win-win development process.

However, China-South Korean relations thawed in October 2017, when China agreed to restore relations in order to strengthen cooperation across the region, while retaining China's objection to the THAAD missiles. Moon visited Beijing in December 2017 with more than 300 top executives of Korean companies. Following his summit with Xi Jinping, President Moon said:

> At the summit, President Xi and I agreed to actively look for ways of actual cooperation between China's One Belt, One Road initiative with South Korea's New North and New South policies. I am confident a link between the One Belt, One Road initiative and New North, New South policies will lead to peace and joint prosperity in the region and become a strong wave that spearheads the development of all of humanity.

Also, officials from the South Korean Ministry of Strategy and Finance toured Northeast China in late 2017 to study the progress of the Belt and Road initiative and seek cooperation areas.

With Trump's highly successful visit to Japan, South Korea, and China in November 2017, his meetings and phone calls with Putin (despite "Russia-gate" raging within the United States), and with Japan's Prime Minister Shinzo Abe declaring in December that Japan would co-finance projects along the New Silk Road with China, all the pieces were in place for a breakthrough in the North Korea issue. The hard-line tactics expressed by Trump against North Korea, and the fact that Russia and China voted with the United States at the United Nations on multiple sanction regimes against Pyongyang, certainly placed enormous pressure on Pyongyang. But the North Korean perspective must also be considered.

First, Kim Jong-un has repeatedly said that his intention in developing a nuclear capacity is purely as a deterrent against any possible U.S. attack. The most recent missile tests, he declared, provide his regime with the necessary capacity to retaliate against the U.S. homeland (whether this is true or not is not clear).

Second, and most importantly, the collaboration between the United States and China, and Trump's refusal to capitulate to the Russia-gate hysteria, continuing his open cooperation with President Putin, provides Kim Jong-un with a basis for believing that all the key partners in the dialogue are sincere, and that perhaps the pledge issued by former Secretary of State Rex Tillerson—that there would be no invasion, no regime change, and no forced reunification—was in fact Trump's intention, and that the U.S. could be trusted—at least to begin talking.

The opening of talks between North and South Korea, beginning with cooperation in the Winter Olympics in South Korea, followed by President Trump's meeting with Kim Jong-un, has the neo-conservatives pulling their hair. The hope for a long-term solution is far from certain, but if U.S. cooperation with China and Russia continues and expands, there is no longer a reason for the North Korean crisis to continue to exist. It was, and always has been, a surrogate conflict between the East and the West. If that artificial British Imperial division of the world no longer exists, the basis for the division of Korea disappears, and a solution can be found based on the common interests of all sides.

Figure 3 shows the rail connections that would link South Korea, through the North, to Russia and China, and thus extending the New Silk Road from Pusan to Rotterdam. Russia, South Korea, and North Korea would also like to construct oil and gas pipelines along the rail routes. The issue of reunification would necessarily wait for the development in North Korea to reach a stage in which the standards of living in North and South were at least comparable. President Moon's "New Economic Map" for South Korea is predicated on the concept that "economic unification is the path to survival." Even before the recent summits, President Moon was proposing building "three economic belts," which he called: "the energy-resource belt in the East Sea; the industry-logistics and distribution-transportation belt in the West Sea; and the environment-tourism belt at the Demilitarized Zone."

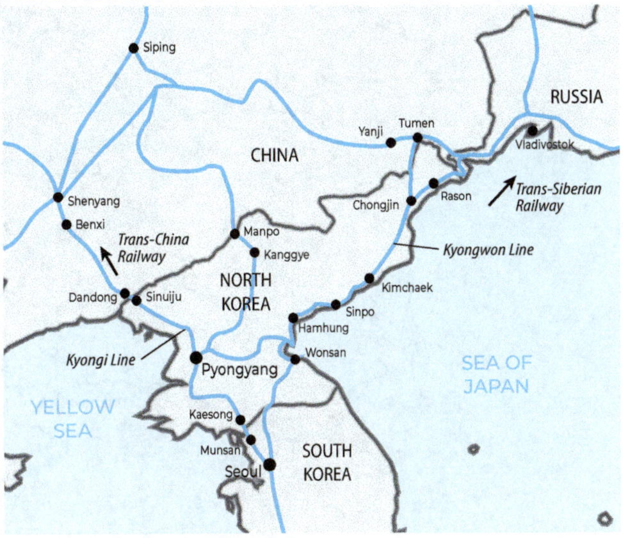

These are clearly plans which incorporate economic cooperation with the North, drawing on four-way economic development projects with the two Koreas, Russia, and China. With backing from the Trump Administration, the path to ending the Korean division is within sight.

Figure 3
North-South Korea Rail Connections

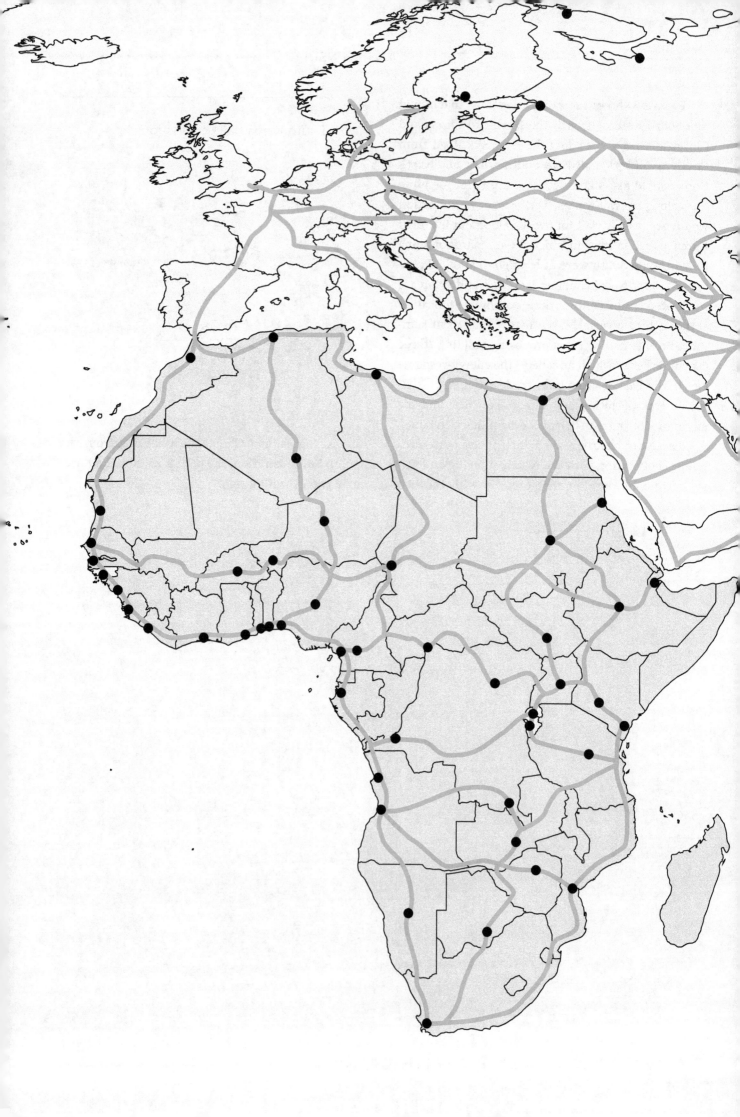

"With the Belt and Road Initiative impact of creating conditions for all necessary factors to come together—land suitability, seeds, inputs and reliable water, along with mechanization—the prospects in Africa are revolutionary."

The New Silk Road Reaches
AFRICA

A Continental Vision

In May 2014, while on a tour to several African nations, Chinese Premier Li Keqiang projected an optimistic vision of Chinese-aided industrial and infrastructural growth for the African continent. His tour started in Ethiopia, ended in Kenya, and included Angola, China's biggest African trading partner, and Nigeria, its third-biggest. Contrary to frustrated and nervous reporting in Western media and think tanks, Li was not on a shopping spree for raw materials.[1] Rather, he advocated an increase in Chinese industrial investment in Africa, and Chinese-aided infrastructure construction, policies that will raise standards of living, and propel Africa into a new economic platform.

Speaking at the African Union headquarters in Addis Ababa, Ethiopia, on May 5, Li emphasized that one of China's goals is to fulfill the dream of connecting all African capitals with high-speed rail, to boost pan-African communication and development. Li emphasized that China has developed world-class technologies in this field.

This is the first time that a leading nation has advocated a plan for extensive industrial and infrastructural development of Africa, since Lyndon LaRouche initiated a study in 1979 calling for the rapid development of infrastructure, including a continent-wide rail network, ambitious water projects, nuclear power, and industrialization.

China has taken the lead in building transport and power infrastructure throughout Africa. One of the most significant outcomes during Li's tour was the signing by the China Railway Construction Corp of a $13.1 billion deal with the Nigerian Ministry of Transport to build a coastal railway in Nigeria, from Lagos to Calabar, reported by the May 10 *People's Daily Online* to be one of the largest foreign railway projects China has ever signed.[2] The report cited the

---

[1] See, for example, the commentary by Dr. Alex Vines, published by the British Chatham House, "Premier Li Keqiang in Africa: The Importance of Angola for China."

Another, more hostile article in the *New York Review* of Books, titled "The Chinese Invade Africa," stated: "Groups such as Human Rights Watch have detailed labor abuses and shown how China's limits on free speech at home have been exported abroad, especially to dependent states in regions like Africa. The economic ties are sometimes portrayed as under-the-table deals cut between Beijing and corrupt leaders in Africa. Instead of helping to build civil society, these deals are said to hurt Africa's long-term interests, reinforcing the tendency of corrupt elites to secure resources at a low price."

[2] Lu Yanan, "China and Nigeria sign a $13.1 billion rail deal." http://en.people.cn/business/8623229.html

III. PROGRESS REPORTS

Left: Chinese Premier Li Keqiang speaking at a joint press conference together with East African leaders in Nairobi on May 11, 2014. Right: President of Kenya Uhuru Kenyatta inaugurates the Mombasa-Nairobi Standard Gauge Railway.

head of the Railway Bureau of Nigeria, who said that the company will build a 1,385 km single-track line for trains that will run at up to 120 km per hour. The Lagos-Kano Standard Gauge Railway was officially opened in July 2016, and work on the Lagos-Ibadan section began in March 2017.

Another major development was the agreement reached in Kenya on May 11, 2014 between the Chinese delegation and the leaders of the East African Community (EAC), to build a $3.8 billion rail link between Kenya's Indian Ocean port city of Mombasa and the capital, Nairobi, as the first stage of a line that will eventually link Uganda, Rwanda, Burundi, South Sudan, and Ethiopia. Under the terms of the agreement, the Exim Bank of China provided 90% of the cost to replace the crumbling British colonial-era line, the "Lunatic Express," with a 609.3 km modern standard-gauge railway. The remaining 10% is Kenya's responsibility. Construction began in late October 2014 with China Communications Construction Company as the lead contractor, and the line was completed nearly a year ahead of schedule, in May 2017.

The new Mombasa-Nairobi (Kenya) line has cut passenger travel time from twelve hours to around four. The signing ceremony for this rail-line agreement was attended by Premier Li, Kenya's President Uhuru Kenyatta, Uganda's President Yoweri Museveni, Rwanda's President Paul Kagame, South Sudan's President Salva Kiir, and high-level representatives of Burundi and Tanzania. "This project demonstrates that there is equal cooperation and mutual benefit between China and the East African countries, and the railway is a very important part of transport infrastructure development," Premier Li said. Kenyatta hailed the booming relationship with China, calling it one "based on mutual trust," and saying Kenya "has found an honorable partner in China." President Museveni took a shot at Western powers saying, "We are happy to see that China is concentrating on the real issues of development. They don't give lectures on how to run local governments."

This agreement is just one of a series—there are similar agreements with Nigeria, Angola, and Tanzania, for railway, port, power generation, and industrial projects—that China has signed to connect Africa to the Belt and Road Initiative (BRI) and build development corridors that can propel the economies of Africa into the 21st Century.

Another landmark achievement in Africa was the completion of the Addis Ababa-Djibouti 750 km electrified Standard Gauge Railway in October 2016. It connects land-locked Ethiopia and its 90 million population to world transport routes and the Maritime Silk Road through the Port of Djibouti. Construction was started after an agreement was signed in 2011 between the Ethiopian Railway Corporation and the Chinese construction corporations China Railway Engineering Corporation (CREC) and China Railway Construction Corporation (CRCC).

The project was financed with a $3 billion loan extended by the EximBank of China. This railway is part of a very ambitious Ethiopian plan for industrialization, the Growth and Transformation Plan, which includes a national railway network connecting the major cities of the country; the development of five major industrial zones; and water, power, and agricultural projects.

China in Africa: Dispelling Myths with Facts

A June 2017 report by the global consultancy McKinsey & Company revealed stunning facts about China's level of economic engagement with Africa, and refuted many myths about that involvement. The report, titled "Dance of the Lions and Dragons,"[3] is based on surveys of 1,000 Chinese firms in eight African countries.

The study reported the following:

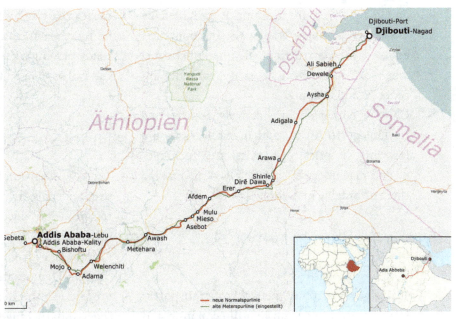

The 750 km Addis Ababa-Djibouti railway.

- China's involvement in Africa far exceeds the estimates provided by Chinese official statistics.
- In the past two decades, China has become Africa's largest economic partner, with annual goods trade in 2015 reaching $180 billion, compared to the other large partners of Africa: India ($59 billion), France ($57 billion), United States ($53 billion), and Germany ($46 billion). Trade has been growing at approximately 20% per year.
- Chinese foreign direct investment has grown even faster over the past decade, with an annual growth rate of 40%.
- China is also a large and fast-growing source of aid.
- China is the largest source of "construction financing for many of Africa's most ambitious infrastructure developments in recent years."
- Ten thousand Chinese firms are active in Africa. Around 90% of these firms are privately owned, contrary to the reports that giant state-owned firms are the dominant ones.
- A third of these firms are involved in manufacturing, handling an "estimated 12% of Africa's industrial production—valued at some $500 billion a year in total."
- Contrary to allegations of Chinese grabbing of African natural resources, the study shows that the activity of these firms is not focused on exporting goods out of Africa, but rather producing to meet the growing demand in Africa itself.
- In infrastructure, Chinese firms handle 50% of Africa's internationally contracted construction market.
- The common perception of Chinese firms bringing hundreds of thousands of Chinese laborers to Africa, rather than employing locals, is refuted. Among the 1,000 Chinese companies surveyed, 89% of the employees were African, adding up to nearly 300,000 jobs for African workers. Projecting these figures to all 10,000 Chinese firms in Africa, this suggests that Chinese-owned businesses employ several million Africans.
- Furthermore, 44% of the managers at these firms are Africans.

---

3 McKinsey & Company, *Dance of the Lions and Dragons: How are Africa and China engaging, and how will the partnership evolve?*, June 2017.

- Some form of skills training is provided by 64% of the Chinese employers. In companies engaged in construction and manufacturing, where skilled labor is a necessity, half offer apprenticeship training.
- Chinese companies are actively transferring technology to Africa, and in many cases are lowering the prices of sophisticated technology and machinery by as much as 40%, making them affordable in Africa.

African Transport Network Integration

Africa requires a robust network of transportation infrastructure to develop its full economic and social potentials. On average, intra-African trade volumes are only one-tenth the trade with nations outside Africa. A transportation grid that serves to integrate the nations of the continent, rather than optimize for trade flows with coastal ports, is therefore essential.

There are several axes of intra-African transport integration envisioned by the member states of the African Union, including, for example, the Trans-African Highway (TAH) network[4] (see **Figure 1**). The proposed North-South axes include the following:

- Alexandria-Cape Town
- Tripoli-Windhoek
- Algiers-Lagos
- Tangier-Abidjan

Four east-west axes are proposed:

- Port Said-Tangier
- Djibouti-Dakar
- Mombasa-Lagos
- Lobito-Beira

If regarded as "development corridors" rather than simple trade routes, these lines will become the backbone of Africa's industrialization. Furthermore, rather than highways, the overall integration should be built around high-speed rail, with highways and roads playing a secondary and supportive role. Africa's railways need to be standardized using Standard Gauge Rail (SGR).

High-Speed Rail

The intention to use standard gauge in the plan to connect all African capitals by rail, is evident in the rail projects that China has completed and is building, such as the Djibouti-Addis Ababa (Ethiopia), Mombasa-Nairobi (Kenya), and Benguela Railway (Angola-Democratic Republic of the Congo [DRC]) projects. In the near future and as soon as possible, the standard-gauge railway network will necessarily need to be supplemented by a separate high-speed rail network for passengers, freeing each network from the constraints of the other. One of China's most brilliant undertakings in its recent development process, was the separation of freight from passenger transport on its railway system. High-speed wheeled rail service will have to be followed by the development of magnetically levitated train networks, bringing the connectivity between the different parts of Africa to much higher speeds, shorter transit times, and thus much higher levels of productivity.

So far, that is what is planned for the high-speed rail project, the joint African Union-China plan for the African Integrated High Speed Rail Network (AIHSRN), for freight and passenger traffic.[5] In 2016, a contractor was being sought for a Detailed Scoping Study for the AIHSRN. By May 2017, the routing structure had been finalized (but not made public) after meetings of African and Chinese experts, and the AIHSRN Project Implementation Unit had been provisionally set up under the New Partnership for Africa's Development (NEPAD) Planning and Coordination Agency in Johannesburg. (NEPAD is the technical body of the African Union.) The next step is a comprehensive feasibility study, for which preparatory work is underway, according to an African Union progress report.[6]

---

4 Source: African Development Bank: https://www.afdb.org/fileadmin/uploads/afdb/Documents/Project-and-Operations/00473227-EN-TAH-FINAL-VOL2.PDF

5 African Union, "Towards the African Integrated High Speed Railway Network (AIHSRN) Development" [late 2016], Part B.

6 African Union, "Progress Report on the Implementation of Agenda 2063 First Ten-Year Implementation Plan" (May 2017).

Figure 1

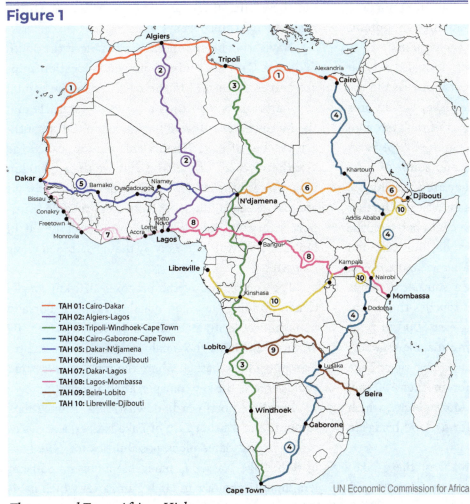

- TAH 01: Cairo-Dakar
- TAH 02: Algiers-Lagos
- TAH 03: Tripoli-Windhoek-Cape Town
- TAH 04: Cairo-Gaborone-Cape Town
- TAH 05: Dakar-N'djamena
- TAH 06: N'djamena-Djibouti
- TAH 07: Dakar-Lagos
- TAH 08: Lagos-Mombassa
- TAH 09: Beira-Lobito
- TAH 10: Libreville-Djibouti

The proposed Trans-African Highways

and the development of pre-requisite skills." According to the agreement, China will form a group for "Sino-Africa cooperation in railway and high-speed railway, which will integrate the resources of financial institutions, railway construction companies, and railway operation management companies."

At the January 2018 African Union heads of state meeting, African Union Commissioner for Infrastructure and Energy Abou-Zeid Amani reiterated the African Union's commitment to the AIHSRN.[8]

Among surface modes of transport, rail has the greatest potential for speed and transport efficiency. A continental rail network will be instrumental in improving Africa's economic potential.

On October 5, 2016 the African Union Commission (AUC) and the government of China signed a Five-Year Action Plan (FYAP) in the Addis Ababa headquarters of the African Union, committing to work together toward realizing, over a longer time span, the AIHSRN, developed as part of the African Union's Vision 2040 for Railway Revitalization in Africa as a flagship component of the African Union's continental Agenda 2063. According to a press release issued by the AUC,[7] the two sides will collaborate "in supporting and facilitating cooperation between African and Chinese enterprises, particularly in local enterprise supplier development and development of advanced manufacturing across the African continent, transfer of technology, capacity-building for local manufacturing and content, as well as education

Riparian Navigation

With a length of more than 6,800 km the Nile is the longest river in the world, more than twice the length of the Rhine–Main–Danube–Black Sea river and canal system that stretches from Holland to Romania and passes through 15 European nations. The Nile River's basin interfaces in the south with the region of the African Great Lakes in East Africa.

The river itself has two sources, the Blue Nile and the White Nile, which join together at Khartoum in Sudan. Lake Tana, located at an elevation of 1,829 m in the high mountains of northeastern Ethiopia, is the source of the Blue Nile River, which passes through steep mountain valleys, entering eastern Sudan, and flowing northwest to join the White Nile at Khar-

---

[7] "African Union Signs Agreement on Africa's High-Speed Railway Network," October 10, 2016.

[8] "AU Affirms Commitment to African Railway Revival: Commissioner," January 27, 2018, Xinhua. http://www.xinhuanet.com/english/2018-01/27/c_136927926.htm

toum. From Khartoum, the Nile continues north to the Mediterranean. Because of the high mountains and cataracts, the Blue Nile is not navigable.

The source of the White Nile is in Uganda, at Lake Victoria. This lake, the largest in Africa and the world's second-largest freshwater lake, has an area of 68,800 km². Lake Victoria is part of the system of the African Great Lakes which form the East African Rift. These lakes lie to the west and south of Lake Victoria. From north to south, they are Lakes Kyoga, Albert, Edward, Kivu, and Tanganyika, and further south, Lake Malawi. They form a chain between the Nile and Uganda, the DRC, Rwanda, Burundi, and further to Kenya and Tanzania, Malawi, and Zambia.

Lake Tanganyika continues a southerly course for more than 600 km, where it touches the northeast corner of Zambia. Traveling east 300 km from that point, moving along the Tanzania–Zambia border, one reaches Malawi and the northern tip of Lake Malawi, which stretches south for another 600 km, coming into direct contact with Mozambique, which also lies on the Indian Ocean, to form a land-bridge to Southern Africa.

Unlike the American Great Lakes, these lakes are not linked with man-made canals. Nonetheless, they lie in some of the most fertile regions of Africa, and therefore form centers of economic development in themselves. While already serving as local waterways, they must be seriously upgraded with the addition of navigation aids and construction of modern ports, and integrated into the network of roads and railways as part of the north-south and east-west transport networks.

From the White Nile's source near Jinga, on the northern shore of Lake Victoria in Uganda, it flows north, where it is joined by rivers to the east and west of the basin. It then passes the South Sudan border at Nimule, continuing north, where it joins with the Blue Nile at Khartoum. From here the Nile River flows through Lake Nasser, crossing into Egypt after the break caused by the Aswan High Dam, to Cairo, the broad delta region, and finally into the Mediterranean. Unfortunately, the Nile is not navigable for its full length, and the challenging topography would make achieving full navigability extremely difficult, but these difficulties can easily be overcome with a multi-modal transport system.

Navigation begins on the White Nile at the South Sudanese Capital of Juba, from which location ships can travel northward to the north Sudanese capital of Khartoum, after which a series of cataracts and the Merowe Dam prevent navigation until the southern reaches of Lake Nasser. This section, called the "southern reach" of the Nile, is more than 1,700 km long. For South Sudan, which is devoid of railways and paved roads, the river is its most reliable transport artery. Its improvement would greatly aid in building the roads and railway that are needed along its path.

The completion of the proposed 370 km Jonglei Canal, avoiding the Sudd marshes between Bor and Malakal, would dramatically improve navigation. By draining the Sudd, the canal would transform the region into a breadbasket, where the river-canal system could serve as the key transportation artery.[9]

Heading northward, downstream from Khartoum, to the southern tip of Lake Nasser, a series of cataracts and dams block possibilities for Nile navigation. Lake Nasser is navigable along its 550 km length, until the Aswan High Dam, after which navigation once again becomes possible for another 1,200 km to the Mediterranean.

In February 2017, the Egyptian government launched the Naval Linkage Project or Nile Corridor, in cooperation with NEPAD, to create a transport network extending from Lake Victoria to the Mediterranean.[10] The 6,800 km network will be part of a multi-modal transport system integrating river, rail, and road modalities in the ten African countries of the Nile Basin. According to Egyptian media reports,[11] Egypt signed a feasibility study contract with a German-Belgian international consultancy office, using $650,000 in funding from the African Development Bank, after having completed a $500,000 pre-feasibility study in May 2015.

---

9   For more detail about the Sudd, see chapter 9 of *Extending the New Silk Road to West Asia and Africa*, Schiller Institute, 2017.

10   "Lake Victoria, Mediterranean Sea Navigation Line Linking Project," State Information Service, Egypt. http://sis.gov.eg/section/0/5245?lang=en-us

11   "Egypt Heads Project to Connect 10 African Countries through Nile Shipping Line," Egyptian Street, February 13, 2017.

The Rhine and Danube Rivers, connected by the 171 km Main Canal, form a key transport artery in the heart of Europe, extending for more than 4,000 km. Connecting the Zambezi River, Lake Malawi, Lake Tanganyika, the Great Lakes, and the Nile can create an 8,000 km navigable river transport system connecting the Indian Ocean at Mozambique with the Mediterranean in Damietta.

Africa rivers and lakes
Lizardpoint.com
© Lizard Point Quizzes

East Africa's Economic Corridors

As mentioned above, China and the East African Community (EAC) plus Ethiopia have had advanced plans for the construction of a number of development corridors.

A combination of two ambitious regional infrastructure projects, the East African Railway Master Plan and the Lamu-South Sudan-Ethiopia Transport (LAPSSET) Corridor, can revolutionize the economies of this region and Africa. In 2007 a special study of the East African Railway Master Plan, commissioned by the EAC countries and produced by the Ottawa, Canada-based infrastructure consulting firm CPCS Transcom, proposed building a vast network of railway lines in the region.

The final report of the study states: "The railways of Kenya, Uganda and Tanzania play an important role not only in the economic development and social environment of these countries, but they also provide an access to the ports of Mombasa and Dar es Salaam for the landlocked countries of southern Sudan, Rwanda, Burundi, eastern Democratic Republic of the Congo and Zambia. They are critical for these countries, ensuring the transport of goods at competitive rates, supporting the development of industries and the creation of jobs, and providing safe and efficient transport of commuters and passengers."[12]

The study focuses on three existing transit corridors and extending them to the landlocked nations (**Figure 2**): The Northern and Central Corridors, from the East Africa Railway Master Plan, and the LAPSSET corridor. The map also shows the Djibouti-Addis Ababa railway, completed by China in 2017.

This plan remained dormant, like many other African projects that have been denied support and financing from the West. However, China's initiatives have revived these plans. Realizing this plan will make East Africa one of the largest workshops in the world in the coming years, with new industries, economic zones, and trade centers branching out from the main projects. China will be building standard-gauge railways simultaneously in several of these countries.

Take as an example a specific project in Uganda, part of the Northern Corridor of the EAC. The Exim-bank of China is providing the financing for the $2.9 billion standard-gauge railway from Malaba on the Kenyan border to the Ugandan capital Kampala. This railway is a key element of the EAC. The announce-

---

12 East African Community Information Repository. (http://repository.eac.int/bitstream/handle/11671/1631/Final%20Report.pdf?sequence=1&isAllowed=y)

ment was made by Ugandan President Yoweri Museveni in July 2017.[13] This project was delayed due to Ugandan concerns regarding Kenya's priorities in completing its national projects, such as the Mombasa-Kenya railway, before considering the connection to Malaba and Uganda. In 2013, the state-owned China Harbor Engineering Company (CHEC) signed an $8 billion contract with the Ugandan government for upgrading and expanding its railway network. It will build a standard-gauge railway, from Malaba on the border with Kenya to Kampala (east-west line), and from Malaba to Gulu, going on to Nimule on the border with Sudan (southeast-north line). From there, the network is to extend to Juba in South Sudan. In addition to building the rail system itself, the contract includes consideration for the long-term maintenance of the project: the CHEC will work closely with the Ugandan Army's Engineering Brigade, and will also construct a polytechnic school in Uganda for continuous training of army officers in technical and engineering skills.

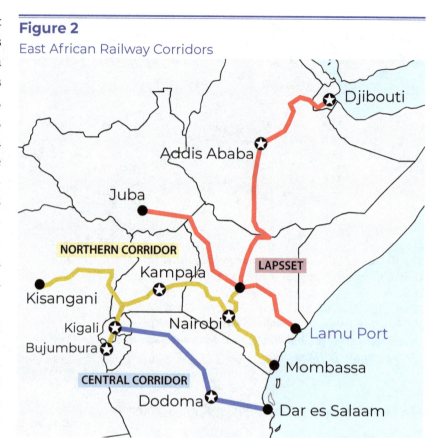

Figure 2
East African Railway Corridors

The Lamu Corridor

The Lamu Corridor, officially known as the Lamu Port-South Sudan-Ethiopia Transport (LAPSSET) Corridor, is a regional transport infrastructure project that will integrate landlocked South Sudan and Ethiopia into the East Africa transport network. The project is supervised by Kenya, and a LAPSSET governmental authority was established in 2013 by a Kenyan presidential decree.[14] The project is also part of the Kenya Vision 2030 plan for long-term development. Prior to the establishment of the LAPSSET, agreements were made with Ethiopia to build a standard-gauge railway from Isiolo in Kenya to Addis Ababa. Another agreement was made with South Sudan to build a road and oil pipeline to facilitate exports from landlocked South Sudan to Ethiopia and to international markets through the port at Lamu.

The project includes several components:

- A three-berth-deep seaport at Manda Bay, Lamu, Kenya
- A standard-gauge railway from Lamu to Juba (South Sudan) via Isiolo, with a branch from Isiolo to Addis Ababa via Moyale
- A two-lane motorway (Lamu-Isiolo-Juba and Isiolo-Moyale-Addis Ababa)
- Oil pipelines (South Sudan-Lamu and Ethiopia-Lamu), giving South Sudan an alternative to exporting its crude oil through northern Sudan to the Red Sea port of Port Sudan
- An oil refinery at Lamu
- Fiber-optic cable
- Three airports (at Lamu, Isiolo, and Turkana)
- Three resort cities (Lamu, Isiolo, and Turkana)

The Lamu Corridor, one of the largest infrastructure projects in Africa, is estimated to cost $24.5 billion, and will be funded primarily by the govern-

---

13 Dicta Asiimwe, "Museveni clears $2.9b China loan for Malaba-Kampala SGR," *The East African*, July 23, 2017.

14 LAPSSET Corridor Development Authority.

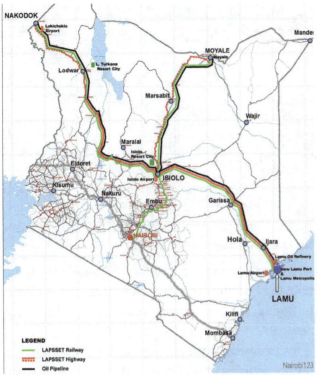

A detailed outline of the Lamu–South Sudan–Ethiopia Transport Corridor.

ments of Kenya, South Sudan, and Ethiopia. The new Lamu Port, with capacity to dock large "Cape-size" vessels,[15] will help to ease congestion at Mombasa and improve the flow of imports and exports. The leaders of Kenya, Uganda, South Sudan, and Ethiopia met in Lamu on March 2, 2012 for the groundbreaking of the Lamu Port. In August 2014, the Kenya Ports Authority and China Communications Construction Company (CCCC) signed the Lamu Port construction contract. Construction started in October 2016, and the first berth is estimated to be completed in mid-2018, with the second and third to be completed in 2020.

The Ethiopian Rail Network

Ethiopia has also been engaging Chinese companies to build its own standard-gauge railway networks. Within this decade, Ethiopia will have one of the most advanced rail networks in Africa, officially known as the National Railway Network of Ethiopia (NRNE).[16] The NRNE is part of the Ethiopian government's consecutive five-year Growth and Transformation Plans (GTP),[17] which include the massive development of its hydropower capacity, agricultural development for self-sufficiency and export, and the construction of five industrial zones in different parts of the country.

In 2011, the state-owned Ethiopian Railways Company (ERC) signed two agreements with Chinese and some European companies to build a 4,744 km rail network, which will link 50 urban centers in all the states of Ethiopia, and to towns bordering Sudan, Kenya, and Djibouti.

In December 2011, ERC sealed a contract with China Civil Engineering Construction Corporation (CCECC) to build the 339 km Mieso-Dire Dawa-Dewele railway line, which is part of the Addis Ababa-Dire Dawa-Djibouti railway project. Laying of track began in May 2014, and the project was completed in the summer of 2016, with official trial service beginning on the railway after its inauguration in October 2016.[18]

The electrified railway is 740 km long, and provides passenger and cargo transport from Ethiopia's capital to the Tadjoura Port in neighboring Djibouti. The Addis Ababa-Djibouti railway reduces travel time from three to four days by truck to only twelve hours, with a design speed of 120 km/h for passenger and 80 km/h for freight trains. The cost of cargo transport will be cut by one-third compared to transport by truck.[19]

Djibouti has become Ethiopia's main outlet to international markets since it lost access to the Eritrean Port of Assab on the Red Sea following the Eritrean-Ethiopian War that started in 1998. However, the building of this railway does not simply create a trade route, but is part of the development plan of the Ethiopian hinterland. In June 2013, India contributed to the Ethiopia-Djibouti project by providing a $300 million

---

15   "Cape size" vessels refers to very large ships that are too massive to pass through the Suez Canal—typically above 150,000 deadweight tonnage—and must instead travel around Africa, past the Cape of Good Hope.

16   Ethiopia Railways Corporation Projects, National Railway Network of Ethiopia, September 2011.

17   Ethiopia National Planning Commission, "Growth and Transformation Plan II (GTP II) (2015/16-2019/20)," May 2016.

18   Andrew Jacobs, "Joyous Africans Take to the Rails, With China's Help," *New York Times*, February 7, 2017.

19   John Aglionby, "Djibouti-Ethiopia Railway Carries Hope for Pan-African Trade," *Financial Times*, January 16, 2017.

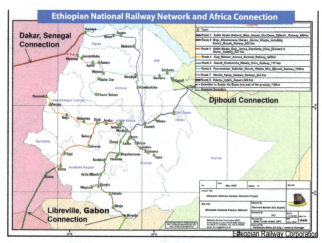

Ethiopian national railway network (left) and planned connections to neighboring countries (right).

credit line through its Export-Import Bank.

In June 2012, Ethiopian Railways Corporation and China Communication Construction Company (CCCC) had also signed a $1.5 billion agreement to build a 268.2 km railway line in the northern part of Ethiopia. The line will run from Mekelle to Weldiya. A Turkish company, Yapi Merkezi (with Swiss and Austrian subcontractors), is responsible for the construction of the railway from Weldiya to Awash (intersecting the Addis Ababa-Djibouti railway) at the cost of $1.7 billion. These two lines link the north of the country to the Addis Ababa-Djibouti line.

Sudan will be connected to Ethiopia's NRNE through two lines: one from Weldia to Matamma in the northwest, and from Weldiya eastward to Tadjoura port in Djibouti. Another line extends from Addis Ababa westward to Kurmuk in Sudan. The latter line branches at Ejaji west of Addis Ababa and continues south to Dima on the border with South Sudan and its town of Boma. Kenya will also be connected to the NRNE through a line extending from Addis Ababa southward to Moyale on the border with Kenya. The latter line is part of the aforementioned Lamu-Addis Ababa corridor.

East-West Corridors

The 4,000 km transcontinental rail corridor from Port Sudan on the Red Sea to Dakar, Senegal on the Atlantic Ocean was proposed by the Organization of Islamic Cooperation (OIC) in 2005. From its eastern terminal in Port Sudan, on the Red Sea, this northernmost transcontinental rail corridor is slated to cross Chad to its capital, N'Djamena, to go on then to Maiduguri and Kano in Nigeria, and continue to Niamey, Niger; Bamako, Mali; and finally, Dakar, Senegal.

Agreements have already been made with China for the construction of two sections of this corridor, in Chad and in Sudan.

In March 2012, Chad reached an agreement with the China Civil Engineering Construction Corporation to build the Chad portion of the rail line from N'Djamena to the Sudanese border. In 2014, Sudan and Chad reached a political agreement to link their capitals with Port Sudan. Later extensions are planned to connect Cameroon's Atlantic Ocean ports: Douala (the biggest Atlantic port in Central Af-

Mali has signed an agreement with China Railway Construction Corporation to renovate a rail line linking its capital, Bamako, to the border with neighboring Senegal. The line will cost nearly $2 billion. The project is part of a plan to upgrade the aging 1,200 km railway between Senegal's coastal capital Dakar and landlocked Mali. China Railway Construction also penned a similar agreement worth $1.26 billion with Senegal. The work on the Malian section of the project will include upgrading 644 km of rail lines and renovating 22 railway stations.

rica) and Kribi (the deepest Atlantic port in Central Africa). Construction of the Kribi deep sea port is to be financed by China. Unfortunately, rebel activities in Chad have prevented these proposals from being implemented.

On November 7, 2017, the Sudanese Railways Authority signed an agreement for a feasibility study with two Chinese companies, China Railway Design Corporation (CRDC) and China Friendship Development International Engineering Design & Consultation Company (FDDC), to be completed in twelve months, to study the 3,400 km trans-Saharan Railway that would stretch from Port Sudan to the Sudanese city of Nyala, close to the Chadian border. The Chad and Sudan lines would join at the border. The lines are to be built to standard gauge and will allow travel at speeds of 120 km/h.

The other transcontinental route, proposed by China, is a corridor from Port Lamu, Kenya to Juba, South Sudan (see "East Africa Economic Corridors," in this chapter), continuing across the Central African Republic by road and rail to its capital, Bangui, and from Bangui across Cameroon to the latter's largest port, Douala. From Douala, the Chinese proposal envisions road and rail combinations along the West African Atlantic coast to Ivory Coast and beyond.

These two east-west transcontinental corridors will connect the important West African region and Central Africa to the Maritime Silk Road, making possible city building and the establishment of industry at a rapid rate throughout both regions. The intersection of these two corridors by North-South corridors from Egypt to Southern Africa will further spur development of West and Central Africa.

This process will be augmented by another maritime corridor extension of the BRI in Kenya, from the port of Mombasa to the nation's capital, Nairobi. This component of the corridor has already been rebuilt as a standard-gauge rail line, in collaboration with China. Plans are being discussed for this corridor to be extended from Nairobi to Uganda, Rwanda, Burundi, DRC, and South Sudan to the north.

Ports Connecting to the BRI

The South Port at Port Sudan is a container port. It will have to be expanded for the northern transcontinental corridor to play a significant role in the development of Central and West Africa.

China, demonstrating its commitment to making the two corridors from Kenya viable development vehicles, is collaborating with Kenya to expand the port at Mombasa, currently Kenya's largest port, and to build the new port at Lamu, near the Somali border. Developing these two ports is necessary for the two corridors to effectively connect Africa to the Maritime Belt and Road.

The expansion of Mombasa is underway, providing an important connection into Central Africa. Kenya's Lamu mega-port is designed to connect China to a big part of Africa. The goal of the project is to connect the East African coast to the West African coast at the port of Douala, Cameroon.

The first phase of the corridor from Port Lamu is the Port Lamu–South Sudan–Ethiopia Transport (LAPSSET) corridor to Juba, South Sudan, with a spur into Ethiopia. The project includes roads, a standard-gauge rail line, airports, an oil pipeline, and oil refineries.

From Juba, the corridor will be extended across Central Africa to Douala, Cameroon, tying the BRI directly to the West African coast.

Development of West Africa

The coastal corridor into West Africa from Douala must be extended along the coast all the way to Dakar, Senegal. A third east-west railway should proceed from Conakry, Guinea or Freetown, Sierra Leone eastward between the two transcontinental corridors mentioned above, going through Abuja, Nige-

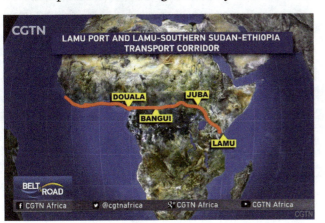

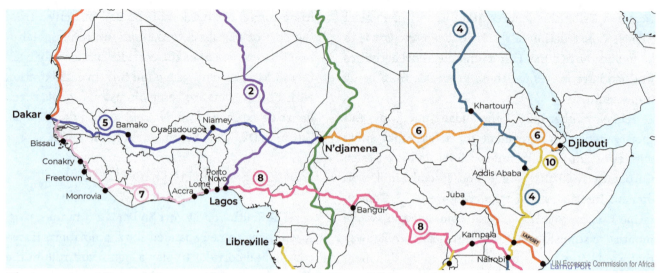

The two east-west Trans-African corridors are sections of the Trans-African Highways. The first or northern corridor runs from Port Sudan and Djibouti to Dakar (numbers 5 and 6), and the second is the Mombasa-Lagos corridor (number 8). The Lamu-Juba or LAPSSET corridor will be extended westward to become an additional east-west corridor.

ria, to Ngaoudere, Cameroon, then intersecting a future rail line from N'Djamena, Chad, paralleling the Transaqua project to the area west of Bangui, Central African Republic, and continuing into the Congo Republic and the Democratic Republic of the Congo.

Connections between these three east-west corridors in West Africa will provide the transportation infrastructure grid that will facilitate the rapid industrialization of this entire region. The Nigerian government has signed a $12 billion contract with China Railway Construction Corporation—the largest contract ever awarded to a Chinese company in Africa—to build a 1,400 km rail line through ten states, from the economic capital of Nigeria, Lagos, going through Port Harcourt, the Warri petrochemical complex, to Calabar, in southeast Nigeria. The distance from Calabar to Douala, Cameroon is only 180 km by air. A ground link will be developed to tie Douala into the West African coastal transport corridor.

In July 2016, Nigeria inaugurated its first standard-gauge rail modernization project, on a 190 km line into the more arid zone in northern Nigeria, connecting Abuja to Kaduna at a speed of 150 km/h. This line was built in collaboration with the China Engineering Construction Company.

The Nigerian government has a detailed plan for building a railroad grid that will link the sections of the country together, with benefits to be gained throughout the country.

Nigeria's port infrastructure is also being upgraded. Because there is little room to expand the Lagos port, two additional ports—Badagry and Lekki—are planned, to be built 60 km on either side of Lagos. With this development, Nigeria will be on a par with its West African neighbors, which have good port capacities, or are expanding them. The Nigerian government has awarded China Civil Engineering Construction a contract to develop a large, long-delayed hydroelectric project, at the Donga River in Tafara State. The government had been trying to develop the 3,050 MW plant for 35 years.

Earlier, Nigeria awarded a $1.2 billion contract to a consortium of China National Electric Engineering Co. and Sinohydro Group, for the construction of the 700 MW Zungeru hydropower project on the Kaduna River in Niger State, to be completed by 2020.

Given the scale of rapid industrialization, modular nuclear reactors will be needed throughout Africa.

In addition to a large population, West Africa has substantial mineral deposits that could serve as the basis for some of the heavy industry that will be established in the region.

One of the largest iron ore deposits in the world is located in Guinea, with substantial deposits in neighboring Liberia and Sierra Leone as well. These deposits could feed production of steel, a necessary requirement for building transport corridors and industrialization of the region. There are other, smaller, iron ore deposits in West Africa. The region could also be the source for partially processed iron ore to be shipped to an advanced steel production center that should be built in the DRC. The DRC is by far the world's biggest producer of cobalt, a necessary ingredient for jet engines, gas turbines, magnetic steels, and some types of stainless steel, among other uses. Chengtun Mining Group of China announced in August 2016 its intention to invest in a $60 million copper-cobalt project in the DRC.

In addition to oil and gas, West Africa also has significant deposits of gold, diamonds, coal, uranium, and bauxite.

Central African Development

Transaqua: The Centerpiece of Africa's Development

The centerpiece of Africa's future development is the Transaqua Project, which has been on the drawing boards for more than 30 years and never implemented—or rather, its implementation was prevented by geopolitical and economic warfare imposed on the Central African nations.

If mega-projects are transformative by their nature—that is, if they affect the physical, economic, social, and cultural transformation of a country, a region, or even an entire continent—then Transaqua is the perfect example of a mega project.

Transaqua is an idea for a water, transport, energy, and agro-industrial development infrastructure for west-central Africa. The design for the project was developed by the Italian firm Bonifica SpA in the 1970s with the purpose of refilling Lake Chad to its original 1950 dimensions. Neglected for 35 years, this idea was recently adopted by the countries of the Lake Chad Basin (Nigeria, Niger, Chad, Cameroon, and Central African Republic) at the International Lake Chad Conference held at Abuja, Nigeria, February 25-28, 2018.

At the conference, an initial grant by the Italian government was announced, which will allow a feasibility study to be started by the Italian engineering company Bonifica SpA and the Chinese giant PowerChina. The conference also suggested that the project be adopted by the African Union as a pan-African project and that a $50 billion fund be raised in order to finance the infrastructure. This result can in large part be credited to years of organizing by the LaRouche

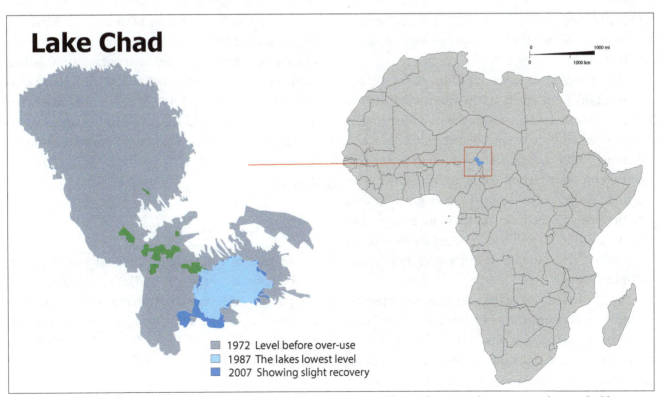

Lake Chad, upon whose waters tens of millions of lives depend, has shrunk to a fraction of its size over the past half-century.

III. PROGRESS REPORTS

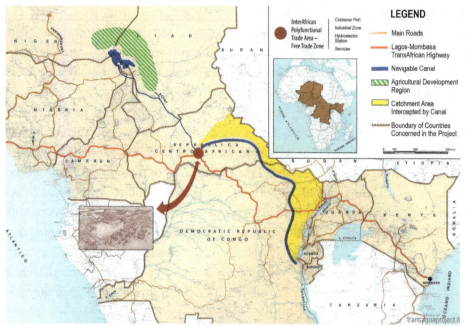

General outline of the Transaqua project. The yellow area is the catchment area of the canal (blue line) intersecting the upper, right-side tributaries of the Congo River in both the Democratic Republic of the Congo and the Central African Republic. The canal intersects the Mombasa–Lagos transcontinental transport corridor (red line), connecting the east and west of the continent.

international movement, which adopted Transaqua as a key infrastructure project for Africa at the beginning of the 1990s. Thanks to the efforts of the Schiller Institute and Transaqua author Marcello Vichi, a momentum was created that led to contacts with the Lake Chad Basin Commission (LCBC) in 2015 and to the strategic alliance for Transaqua between Bonifica and PowerChina.

The progressive shrinking of Lake Chad, which shrank by as much as 95% from about 1963 to 1998, is a major contributor to the impoverishment of the riparian population, fueling emigration and providing fertile ground for recruitment to the terrorist group Boko Haram. Refilling Lake Chad to its original size will re-create viable living conditions, jobs, and development for up to 30 million people, thereby providing a stable and developing local economy, halting emigration, and eliminating social causes for insurgency.

In 2016, at least 2.5 million refugees and internally displaced persons existed in the Lake Chad Basin countries, according to a report by Oxfam. The decisions taken at the Abuja conference are therefore an important first step toward not only stabilization of the Lake Chad/Sahel region but also the creation of a large infrastructure that will change the face of the entire African continent.

Transaqua addresses the root causes of the economic desperation that forces people living in the area to emigrate to Europe. And it gives a very concrete meaning to the proposals for launching a "Marshall Plan" to create jobs and development in the immigrants' countries of origin, mostly coming from the Sahel region.

A major article in the *People's Daily* on August 21, 2017 confirmed interest by Chinese institutions and public opinion in the great project.

The Transaqua idea is as simple as it is ingenious. Prompted by then-Bonifica CEO Francesco Curato, a Bonifica team led by Dr. Marcello Vichi began in 1972 to explore the idea of collecting enough water from the northern tributaries of the Congo River, in order to refill Lake Chad and eventually develop hydroelectric power and irrigation. Bonifica calculated that refilling Lake Chad to its original dimensions would require an annual addition of approximately 50 billion cubic meters of water. Bonifica engineers envisioned the construction of a 2,400 km system of reservoirs and canals that would collect twice this amount, totaling approximately 5-8% of the Congo River water.

Developments in North Africa

Highway Networks

As part of the planned Trans-African Highway (TAH) network of the African Union and African Development Bank, the Arab Maghreb Union (AMU) countries were supposed to undertake the construction of Routes 1, 2, and 3. (See description of TAH earlier in this chapter) Route 1 is planned to extend from Alexandria in Egypt to Dakar, Senegal. A great section of it is also known as the Maghreb Highway, a highway that passes through Libya, Tunisia, Algeria, Morocco, and Mauritania. It consists of two sections: an Atlantic highway from Nouakchott in Mauritania to Rabat, Morocco, and a Mediterranean highway from Rabat to Tripoli, Libya. The Algerian and Moroccan sections are the only ones that have been completed. The Moroccan motorway network was 1,800 km long by the end of 2016 and is run by the state-owned Société Nationale des Autoroutes du Maroc (ADM).

The Algerian East-West Highway, or A1, a six-lane divided highway of 1,216 km extending from Algeria's border with Tunisia in the east to its border with Morocco in the west, is one of the largest infrastructure projects in Africa, costing more than $11 billion. It has been undertaken by two major consortia, one Chinese (comprising the China International Trust Investment Corporation [CITIC] and CRCC) and the other Japanese (COJAAL, including Kajima Corporation, Nishimatsu Construction Company, Itochu Corporation, Hazama Corporation, and Taisei Corporation). The Chinese consortium built the western and central part of the highway, while the Japanese built the eastern section. The project was launched in 2009 and was completed in 2015 after some delays and disputes with the building consortiums.

The Algerian East-West Highway extends across Algeria from the Moroccan border to the Tunisian border (via Tlemcen, Oran, Chlef, Alger, Sétif, Constantine, and Annaba). The Tunisian section of the TAH Route 1 is not complete. The parts that are completed are, from southeast to northwest:[20]

- A1: Sfax-Tunis
- A3: Tunis-Oued Zarga
- A4: Tunis-Bizerte to the north, and further west to the Algerian border at Tabarka, with a missing link of 70 km; another missing link is from Sfax to Gabes and Ras Adjir in Libya

Trans-Maghreb High-Speed Rail

The most important event in African rail development in recent years was the launching of the construction of Africa's first high-speed railway (HSR), between Tangier and Casablanca (Dar El Beidha) in Morocco. According to the Moroccan Railway Corporation (ONCF),[21] the Moroccan high-speed railway (dubbed LGV in Morocco or TGV in France) is intended to be part of the broader plan for the Trans-Maghreb HSR network.

It is divided into two lines, from the Moroccan perspective: an Atlantic line from Tangier at the Strait of Gibraltar to Rabat, Casablanca, Marrakech, Essaouira, and Agadir; and a Trans-Maghreb/Mediterranean line from Rabat to Oujda, and then across Algeria to Tunisia and Tripoli in Libya. The completion of the Trans-Maghreb HSR line will raise the number of passengers traversing this corridor annually to 133 million by 2035, compared to the 55 million riding conventional rail today.

The Casablanca-Tangier LGV is the first of its kind in Africa. Its first phase runs 200 km; when complete in 2035, the national HSR network will cover 1,500 km. The decision to build the LGV was made in 2007 by the Moroccan government, and the project was assigned to the state-owned Moroccan rail company ONCF. The completely new section of the LGV will extend from Tangier to Kenitra just north of Casablanca; the rest of the line will be an upgrade of the existing Kenitra-Casablanca line. The planned speed of the line is estimated at 320 km/h (200 mph), cutting the travel time from the current 4-5 hours to 90 minutes. The ONCF estimates that more than 6 million passengers will use this line per year. It will have 2,500 employees when operational, but is already creating tens of thousands of job opportunities during the construction phase. In the future, the current Casablanca-Marrakech SGR line will be upgraded to LGV standard and travel time from Tangier to Marrakech will be cut to 2¾-3 hours compared to 8-10 hours today.

The project was undertaken jointly by ONCF and the French railway company SNCF. Construction was started in January 2011 and the first test runs of the Tangier-Kenitra line were conducted in October 2017. French Alstom is providing the rail cars and locomotives, and the Italian company Ansaldo STS is under contract to install the signaling and track safety systems.

---

20   Source: http://www.tunisieautoroutes.tn

21   Source: http://entreprise.oncf.ma/AR/lgv/Pages/leschemadirecteur.aspx

The Algerian East-West A1 motorway.

According to Mohamed Rabie Khlie, CEO of ONCF, "the Moroccan characteristic has always been present throughout the project, as 90% of the infrastructure construction was conducted by Moroccan engineering companies." He emphasized that the project provides a total of 30 million work days directly and indirectly for the Moroccan labor market. He added that 150 of the 250 engineers working on the project are Moroccan. Rabie, speaking at an international seminar on railway security in Tangier in April 2017, stated that 86% of the work has been accomplished, and assured the audience that the LGV would be operational in 2018.

The total cost of the Casablanca-Tangier LGV is 20 million Moroccan Dirhams ($2 billion), 25% provided the state, with the rest of the financing provided by French export credits and bank loans, and loans from Arab Gulf states.

The Trans-Maghreb high-speed rail project should be the first step for Morocco in building a world-class infrastructure construction sector, using the know-how acquired from the European companies in addition to the techniques and innovations that naturally emerge from the challenges presented by this and other promising projects.

Morocco Joins the BRI: Tanger-Med Port and Technopolis

During the visit of King Mohammed VI of Morocco to Beijing in May 2016 and his meeting with President Xi Jinping, a number of economic cooperation agreements were signed on investments, finance, and commerce.

Less than a year after that visit, an agreement was signed between Morocco and the Chinese aerospace industrial conglomerate Haite Group, to establish a high-tech industrial city near the Mediterranean port city of Tangier. The new industrial city, to be built on 2,000 hectares of land, is expected to house nearly 200 Chinese factories in the next ten years, making it "the largest Chinese industrial platform on the continent," according to *Morocco World News*.[22] The ten-year project will absorb an investment of $10 billion, contributed by the Haite Group, Morocco's largest banking group BMCE, and the Moroccan government. The Chinese companies operating in the Mohammed VI Tangier Tech City, as it is called, will specialize in aerospace, automobile, telecom, and other sectors, produced for the African and European markets, benefitting from Morocco's geographical position, developed logistics and transport networks, and skilled labor. Construction will not be carried out by Chinese companies alone, but by a Moroccan-Chinese joint venture or consortium, employing Moroccan engineers and skilled workers. Since the construction of the Tanger-Med Port, which went into service in 2007, Tangier has been transformed into a budding industrial and logistics hub. The port, located 40 km to the east of Tangier, is served by a modern railway and motorway connecting it to the Moroccan transport networks and to the rest of Africa. It also enjoys proximity to Europe, located just 15 km from Spain across the Strait of Gibraltar.

Tanger-Med I can handle 3 million twenty-foot equivalent units (TEUs) per year, with 1.6 km of container docks. Tanger-Med II is designed to handle 5.2 million containers per year with its 2.8 km of container docks. It can receive the largest Triple E class

---

22 Chaima Lahsini, "5 Things to Know About the $10 Billion Industrial City in Tangier," *Morocco World News*, March 24, 2017.

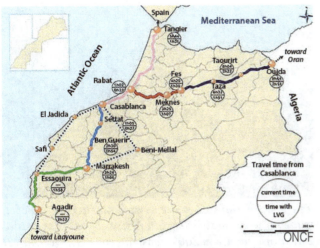

General plan of Morocco's high-speed rail network and future extensions to Europe and other African countries. The Casablanca–Tangier LGV (in pink), the first of its kind in Africa, is nearing completion.

container ships in the world (400 m overall length, 18,000 TEUs). Construction is by the French conglomerate Bouygues Construction.

The Tech City and the Tanger-Med Port will connect to Sub-Saharan Africa along the Atlantic Coast by Trans-African Highway 1, which begins at Alexandria, Egypt and terminates at Dakar, Senegal. The city and port will also use the modern rail system and ultimately the African Integrated High-Speed Rail Network (AIHSRN), with the Tangier-Casablanca LGV line, now under construction, to become a launching pad for more such development in Africa.

Algeria Joins, Too!

In March 2016, the Algerian Transport Ministry finalized an agreement with the China State Construction Engineering Corporation (CSCEC) and China Harbor Engineering Company (CHEC) to build a world-class deep-water port at the Mediterranean coastal town of El-Hamdania in the Province of Tipasa, 70 km west of Algiers, the capital. With an estimated cost of $3.5 billion, the port is being financed with a long-term loan from China. The port will include 23 docks capable of processing 6.5 million TEUs and 26 million tons of goods per annum, according to *Construction Review Online*.[23]

It will serve as a major transshipment and logistics center in the Mediterranean for freight along the Maritime Silk Road between East Asia, the western Mediterranean, and the North Sea. In addition, the port will serve a major industrial park now being constructed in the same city. The deep-water port will be completed in 2022, but will become incrementally operational beginning in 2020. The Shanghai International Port (Group) Company will manage port operations in the initial operational phases.

El-Hamdania Port will be connected to the Algerian and trans-African transport network through modern roads and railways. According to Algerian Transport Minister Boudjemaa Talai,[24] it is well-positioned as a transit port on the Mediterranean to service North Africa and Europe, as well as other locations in the Mediterranean region. He added that Mali and other neighboring landlocked countries require such a port.

The Algerian N1 Highway runs along the Mediterranean coast between Algiers and Tipasa, a little to its west, and then goes southward toward Niger. It joins Trans-African Highway 2, which extends across the Sahara, passing through Agadez in Niger and, further south, crosses the Nigerian border to Kano and finally terminates at Lagos on the Atlantic coast of Nigeria. A parallel Algerian national highway, N6, extends southward from the Mediterranean coast west of El-Hamdania Port, crossing the desert to Mali.

According to a press release issued by the Algerian Embassy in China,[25] the Algerian Minister of Foreign Affairs and International Cooperation, Ramtane Lamamra, stated in November 2016, at the African Investment and Business Forum, that "Algeria wants to seize the advantages offered by the African continent, which represents a huge reservoir of productivity, production of wealth and growth," and that "the Trans-Saharan Road (Lagos-Algiers) and El-Hamdania Port project have been conceived in this respect."

---

23 *Construction Review Online*, "China to construct mega sea port in Algeria," April 5, 2016. (https://constructionreviewonline.com/2016/01/china-construct-mega-sea-port-algeria/)

24 Ibid.

25 Embassy of the People's Democratic Republic of Algeria to the People's Republic of China, "Algiers' African Investment Forum, opportunity to focus on Africa," November 21, 2016. (http://www.algeriaembassychina.net/page_news26.php)

III. PROGRESS REPORTS

King Mohammed VI of Morocco and the president of China's Haite Group, Li Biao, at the signing ceremony for the establishment of the Mohammed VI Tangier Tech City, March 27, 2017.

Tanger-Med I and II, a deep-water Mediterranean port, is the largest container port in Africa so far. Tanger-Med I went into service in 2007; construction of Tanger-Med II began in 2009.

Hydropower, Water Management in Africa

More than 620 million people—over half of the continent's population—have no access to electricity at all.[26] Many of those that do have access to electricity are connected to a grid with low reliability and large transmission losses. Average annual electricity consumption in Sub-Saharan Africa is 488 kWh per capita, approximately 5% the average use in the United States.[27] This per capita rate of electricity use is slightly less than 60 Watts. Energy scarcity has hobbled the potential for economic growth. Efficiency is reduced by homes, businesses, and industrial facilities using low-efficiency standalone diesel electricity generation in the absence of a reliable grid. Were each African to enjoy access to an energy living standard equivalent to U.S. levels, the continent would require more than 1,500,000 MW of electricity, equivalent to more than one thousand large-scale power plants, or three dozen hydroelectric facilities equivalent in scale to the Grand Inga Dam.[28]

A number of very important dam projects are currently under construction or being planned. Sudan has recently completed the Merowe Dam in the north of the country. This is a hydropower and agriculture development program of great significance.[29] A new dam, the Kajbar Dam, is planned further north, near the border with Egypt at the Third Cataract. Two dams are under construction on the Atbara and Setit rivers, two smaller tributaries emerging from northern Ethiopia. Almost all these dam projects involve Chinese construction and financing.

However, the greatest of the dam projects in the Nile Basin, and of those under construction in Africa today, is the Grand Ethiopian Renaissance Dam (GERD) on the Blue Nile. The name of Ethiopia in the past decades has been associated with famine, poverty, and conflict. That is all about to change. Ethiopia, with a population of 105 million (October 2017), an ancient historical identity, and enormous economic potential, was not, until recently, able or allowed to realize its potential for developing its human, land, and water resources. The hydropower potential is a very clear example.

Ethiopia has more than 50,000 MW of hydropower potential, and is moving to increase its exploitation of this valuable resource for the benefit of its people.[30] Over the past 15 years, the percentage of

---

26 According to the World Bank SE4ALL database, the rate of access to electricity in Sub-Saharan Africa was 37.4% in 2014.

27 Avila, N., Carvallo, J. P., Shaw, B. and Kammen, D. M., The energy challenge in Sub-Saharan Africa: A guide for advocates and policy makers: Part 1: Generating energy for sustainable and equitable development. Oxfam Research Backgrounder series, 2017. (https://www.oxfamamerica.org/static/media/files/oxfam-RAEL-energySSA-pt1.pdf)

28 This figure is used for illustrative purposes only. The total hydroelectric potential of Africa is far less than 1,500,000 MW.

29 Hussein Askary, "Sudan's 'TVA': A Development Model for All of Africa," *EIR*, April 24, 2009. (http://www.larouchepub.com/eiw/public/2009/2009_10-19/2009_10-19/2009-16/pdf/36-40_3616.pdf)

30 Ethiopian Electric Power External Relation Directorate, "Ethiopian Electric Power: Facts in Brief," 2017. (http://www.eep.gov.et/wp-content/uploads/2017/09/english-layout-F-and-B-min.pdf)

the population with access to electricity has doubled, from 13% in 2002 to 27% today.[31] The completion of the Gilgel Gibe III Dam and Power Station has increased installed national hydropower generating capacity from 2,000 MW to 3,800 MW. Another 6,000 MW will be added to the grid by the GERD whose construction was launched in 2011 by then-Prime Minister Meles Zenawi and was 60% complete by 2017.

A lesson can be learned from the financing methods of these projects. While the World Bank and other Western-controlled institutions have refused financing for the dams, Chinese state banks have provided credit, including for the purchase of the power generation equipment and electrical components. But the major financing has come from Ethiopia itself. Showing the power of a national credit-based alternative, the GERD is being financed by nationally emitted bonds available only to Ethiopian citizens at home and abroad, in addition to special taxes. This is the same method used by Egypt to finance the New Suez Canal project.

Neighboring countries are also being solicited to contribute to the financing of the dam, in return for delivery of electricity. Djibouti is so far the largest purchaser of GERD bonds, but Egypt and Sudan have not contributed, pending a political and technical decision to be reached through a tripartite special committee studying the impact of the dam on the latter two nations.

The dam will be 150 m high and 1,800 m long. It will have two power houses, one on either side of the spillway. The left and right power houses will each contain eight 375 MW generators. Supporting the dam and reservoir will be a 5-km-long, 50-m-high saddle dam. The dam's reservoir will have a volume of 63 billion cubic meters (slightly more than an entire year's discharge of the Nile at the Aswan Dam in Egypt).

This is a major source of concern in Egypt, because filling the reservoir in the years following the completion of the dam—a process that will take a decade or more—could reduce the flow of the Nile by 10-15% annually.

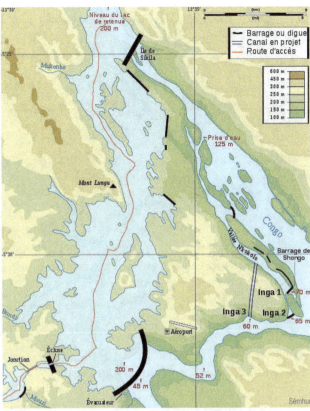

Along the Inga Falls, about 150 km from the Atlantic Ocean, the Inga 1 and Inga 2 hydroelectric dams are currently in operation. The proposed Grand Inga Dam complex is represented by the curved black line on the lower left.

Grand Inga Dam Project

The Congo River, the second-largest in the world as measured by discharge, has an enormous potential for hydroelectric production, estimated at more than 80,000 MW along the river and its tributaries.[32] This potential is focused at the Inga area, where a drop of 100 m over a very short distance provides a hydropower potential of 43,800 MW at the Grand Inga site.

This enormous electric potential dwarfs the DRC's current average consumption of roughly 1,000 MW, and will provide a reliable source of electricity for millions, both in the DRC and neighboring countries. The dam can usefully be built in a series of steps, with Inga Dams 3 through 8 adding to the current capacity of Inga 1 and Inga 2.

Although construction was slated to have begun in 2016, a July 2016 cutoff of World Bank financing put the project on hold.[33] Nonetheless, the govern-

---

31 The World Bank, World Development Indicators, accessed November 5, 2017.

32 Société Nationale d'Electricité of the Democratic Republic of the Congo, 2009 study.

33 World Bank press release, "World Bank Group Suspends Fi-

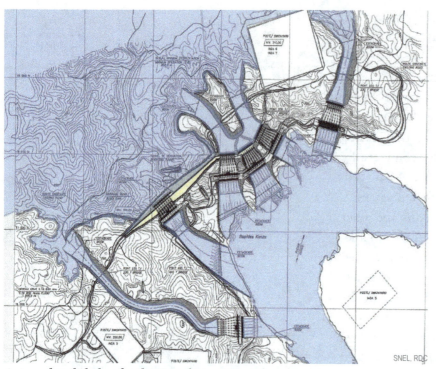
A more detailed plan for the Grand Inga Dams.

ment of the DRC has continued to pursue the implementation of this project, due to its immense value for the economy and future development of the country.

In June 2017, the Agency for the Development and Promotion of Grand Inga (ADPI-RDC) issued a press release[34] announcing that it has encouraged the two remaining bidding companies, Chine d'Inga 3 (a subsidiary of the Chinese state-owned Three Gorges Corporation) and the Spanish consortium ProInga (a joint venture of Spanish companies ACS Servicios, Comunicaciones y Energia, and Cobra Instalaciones y Servicios), to join hands and present a joint bid, rather than competing with one another. It remains to be seen whether these two major consortiums will bring their efforts together. But one thing is clear, the Congolese government and people do want this project completed, and need it for their present and future development process.

Africa's Food Security

The present-day situation of staple food production in Africa, relative to need and obvious potential, is inadequate. In recent decades, the import dependence for all types of grains (e.g., wheat, rice, and sorghum) has increased. In 1990, African nations imported 26% of their staple grain needs. In 2014, this import dependence had gone up to more than 40%. The same kind of sizable import-dependence also exists for oils and dairy products.

In recent years, African nations have come to import more than 45 million metric tons of wheat per year (representing more than 25% of world wheat traded), which accounts for around 60% of annual African wheat consumption. (Per capita wheat consumption ranges widely, from very high in North Africa, to much lower, but increasing levels in Sub-Saharan Africa.)

The prospect of increasing farmland in Africa is huge, even considering simply rainfed agriculture, with only limited irrigation. It is widely reported that more than half the world's remaining cultivable land is in Africa. Even taking into account the need to restore fertility in degraded farmland, both in use and abandoned, Africa is rich in area suitable for farm and pasture land. The total land area of Africa is 2,844 million hectares, of which, close to 900 million hectares is considered cultivable (for crops or pasture), ranging from very suitable to marginally so (depending on gradient, soil condition, and related factors). Of this potential, only some 280 million hectares are currently in agricultural use.

China's Contributions

On the question of the benefits of better seeds in Africa, hybrid rice is a model. Thanks to the introduction of hybrid rice varieties developed in China by Dr. Yuan Longping—known as the "Father of Hybrid Rice," for his breakthrough work on this in the 1970s—rice yields have dramatically risen around

---

nancing to the Inga-3 Basse Chute Technical Assistance Project," July 25, 2016. (http://www.worldbank.org/en/news/press-release/2016/07/25/world-bank-group-suspends-financing-to-the-inga-3-basse-chute-technical-assistance-project)

34 Business Wire, "Inga 3 Project: The Two Remaining Candidates Invited to Submit a Common Offer," June 13, 2017. (http://www.businesswire.com/news/home/20170613006491/en/Inga-3-Project-Remaining-Candidates-Invited-Submit)

the world in recent years, including in Africa.

For example, in Burundi, in 2016, four such rice varieties set a record for that country, for an average yield of 10,880 kg/ha—three times the typical Burundi average—and a peak yield of 13,860 kg/ha. China intends to build an agricultural technology demonstration center in Burundi to spread the gains. In China, Dr. Yuan is seeking still higher performance rice through genetic modification methods.

China's contributions to African food security were appreciated by an official of the Food and Agriculture Organization (FAO) recently, who stated that China is transforming Sub-Saharan Africa's agriculture.[35] In an interview with Xinhua at Elmina, Ghana in August 2017, Peter Atimka Anaadumba, South-South Cooperation Program Officer at the FAO African Regional Office, said that Africa has derived enormous benefits in agricultural transformation from China through its South-South Cooperation. "China is a major player when it comes to South-South cooperation in Africa. It's a major partner of FAO. When you look at the Africa region, China gave a grant to FAO in 2009 of about $30 million and recently $50 million, making it $80 million, and these funds that they provided are available to support African countries in Sub-Saharan Africa to access for them to receive technical expertise from China," he told Xinhua. "China, for example, has been working in Liberia.

Now, Liberian rice production stands at about seven million tons. We did deploy about 500 experts. We have been able to develop piggery in Liberia through insemination innovations from China," Anaadumba continued.

"When you go to Tanzania, we have South-South cooperation; there is a center of excellence in the Morogoro Region—it's been constructed by China. This center provides training for the youth. It's like an incubation center where people come and learn how to do crop management, crop budget, water management, livestock, poultry, and so on." Pointing out the Chinese contribution as key in Uganda, where rice production was on the increase, he said China is sharing their expertise and also developing aquaculture and apple production.

With the Belt and Road Initiative impact of creating conditions for all necessary factors to come together—land suitability, seeds, inputs and reliable water, along with mechanization—the prospects in Africa are revolutionary.

---

35 Source: http://news.xinhuanet.com/english/2017-08/10/c_136513553.htm

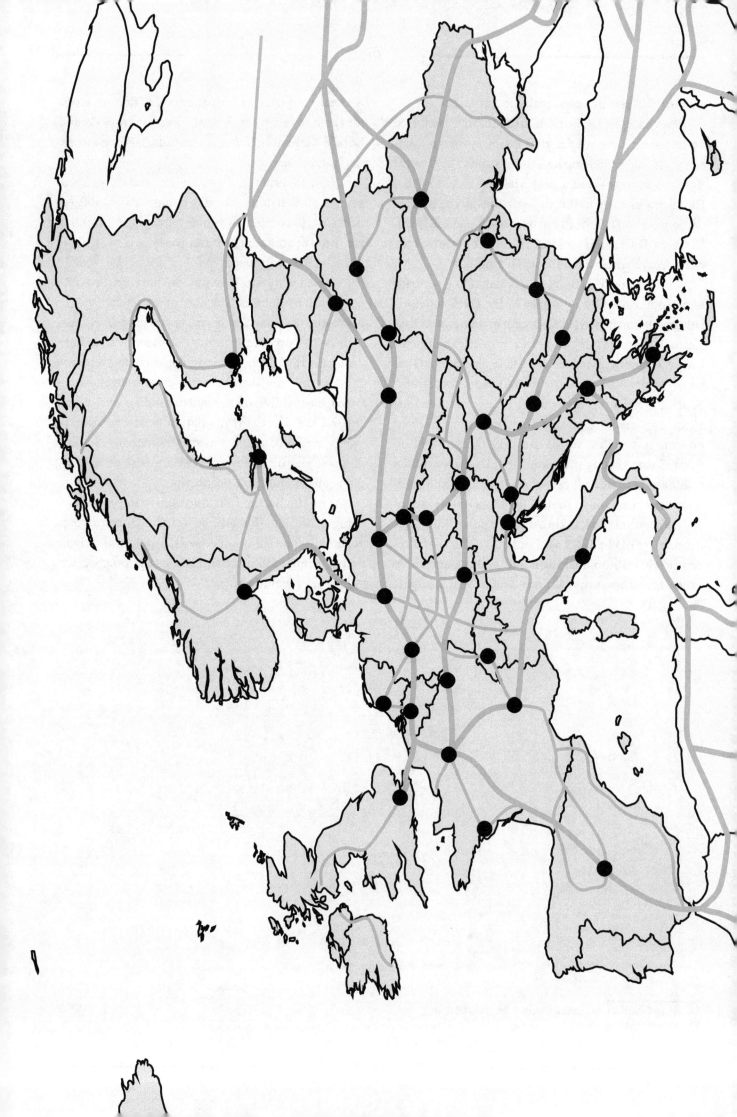

"The Paris-Berlin-Vienna productive triangle ... ranks as the economic region with the world's greatest density of productive investment, and forms the core region of the all-European magnetic train network. That will soon change ... if there is no forceful change in direction in Europe, because especially in China ... the growth of productive economies has been sharply accelerating."

EUROPE

Western Terminal of the New Silk Road

We begin our study of the European section of the World Land-Bridge with Germany, for two reasons. First, Germany is the critical component in all Europe to provide significant high-technology and capital goods contributions to the global World Land-Bridge project. Without Germany, Europe will limp along, at best.

Second, Germany today is the single biggest obstacle in all of Europe—outside of the British Empire—to the necessary shift to a New Paradigm, with its suicidal denuclearization policy, its "black zero" budget straitjacket, and its scandalous failure to keep pace with the construction of high-speed rail corridors occurring in the rest of Europe—West, Central, and East. Where high-speed rail lines from other countries reach the border with Germany, they hit a virtual brick wall: no high-speed rail connections, and in some cases, no electrified rail lines at all. **Figure 1** tells the story.

Figure 1

GERMANY AT THE CROSSROADS: TO MARS, OR TO THE MUSEUM?

The question whether Germany will continue to be counted among the leading industrial nations of the world after the middle of this century, will remain open as long as the leading elites and opinion makers of the country refuse to react constructively to the all-encompassing changes in global economic and international affairs.

Where will Germany, with its considerable potential for knowledge and technology, and its up-until-now anti-war foreign policy, focus its great hope in the coming years? Will it remain, staring into the old system and go under with it, with unswervingly loyalty; or will it take a leading role in the creation of a new system? Will it finally help to create the breakthrough for real progress in the developing countries? Will it contribute to conquering the great plagues of the past—hunger, epidemics, ignorance, and especially war and forced migration?

Germany has, in principle, everything it needs to play a constructive role, and therefore it makes a great difference whether Germany makes a contribution to a "win-win" outlook or refuses to do so.

The following contribution to this study will show what Germany and its people could do—if they only want to.

Is Germany Still Able to Compete?

Among Western nations, Germany has always created the greatest share of its productive wealth from the activity of its people. With its productive "Mittelstand" (small and medium-size firms) the German economy had something that does not exist with the same intensity elsewhere (Switzerland excepted), even in countries such as China and Korea. Engineering talent and highly qualified Mittelstand come together in a unique way in Germany, such that numerous technologies that lead the world have their origin in Germany. This German characteristic also still applies to the area of atomic energy, despite the disastrous decree five years ago to exit from the use of nuclear power without an alternative, and research and development for nuclear fusion in Germany is at the forefront with the Wendelstein-7-X in Greifswald.

The essential national centers of infrastructure and research in Germany are the Ruhr region, Baden Württemberg, Saxony, Hamburg, and Bremen. The metropolitan areas of Munich, Hamburg, and Bremen are additional important centers. Berlin was the center of the electrical industry until 1945, and it can and must be industrialized again.

Ruhr Region/North Rhine-Westphalia

North Rhine-Westphalia (NRW) is a special region in the Ruhr that has the right prerequisites to assume a leading role as producer and "idea supplier" for the reconstruction of the world economy from the bankruptcy of the monetary banking and financial system in which the world finds itself.

Duisburg-Ruhrort in NRW at the mouth of the Ruhr on the Rhine is still the largest inland port in the world, and despite the world economic crisis, handles 55 million tons of freight annually and employs more than 34,000 people. The port, Duisport, has the potential to be not only the handling center for goods produced elsewhere that pass through Duisburg, but also a great asset for goods that could be produced in the Ruhr region itself. The port can become the kernel for the reindustrialization of NRW, for establishing newer industries and employing more workers and engineers than at any time before.

Duisport Chief Erich Staake is a committed advocate of the orientation to build up the New Silk Road and for direct participation of the port in this build-up on many points between China and Europe.

There are great expectations for 2018 for the targeted completion of the southern rail line of the New Silk Road that will connect Duisburg with China via Turkey and Central Asia. Today the direct connection between Duisburg and the Chinese industrial center of Chengdu is operational with the container train "Yuxinou" making eight runs per week. Until

Figure 2

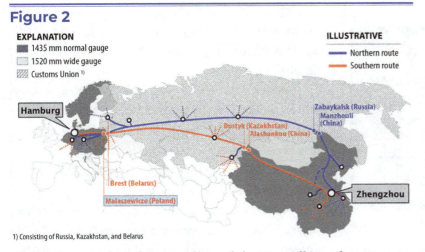

The northern and southern mainline of the New Silk Road or Eurasian Land-Bridge between Germany and China.

now the trip took 18 days by the northern route via Russia, Belarus, and Poland. With the southern route, the entire trip will take two days less (**Figure 2**).

The modernization of the transportation infrastructure will be a first step. Transport systems to locations in NRW were designed to work as fast trains on magnetic levitation (maglev), and must now finally be applied:

- The CargoCap (**Figure 3**) that was developed in Bochum could begin with an underground concrete tube route from the Opel factory there to the Duisburg port, and could transport prefabricated construction parts and other materials by standard palette cargo container made of rolled sheets, quickly, quietly, round-the-clock, and without burdening the above-ground traffic.
- At the same time, the PeopleCargoMover that was developed in Düsseldorf can be used. It is a magnetic rail system, a train system going laterally along the track, that will carry passengers and standard containers, and will be constructed on space-saving routes in the medians of the highway.

Such a system can be built not only in NRW, but also elsewhere in Europe (**Figure 4**).

This is only the first generation of maglev technology; additional systems can be developed over time, but with the systems cited here the first steps will be taken for a transportation system suited for the 21st Century.

The magnetic train infrastructure not only relieves street traffic, but also provides a safe and fast transportation system for millions of NRW citizens to get to work, school, and universities; to visit the theater and opera; and for other travel. The establishment of new industrial companies will be facilitated, at greater distances from the port of Duisburg. After the closing of the Opel factory in Bochum, the still existing skills in the workforce can be used together with the creation of highly qualified jobs for constructing new manufacturing sites for containers used in the various magnetic train systems. Goods brought to the Duisburg port can then be shipped from there via the Rhine and the other waterways, to more than 100 ports in Germany and Europe and throughout the world.

Ship transport is especially good for heavy, large-scale equipment, such as power plant components, which should be manufactured for immediate shipping in the vicinity of the port.

The Duisburg port could also be used for a newly established space industry, in which components for the space station and space vehicles, or even entire modules, could be manufactured along or near the port facilities, which can then be transported directly

Figure 3

The CargoCap is an underground transport system, on which materials of all kinds can be transported round-the-clock, quickly, with low noise, and without burdening the above-ground traffic.

Figure 4

Proposals for CargoCap connections in Europe

from Duisburg to the European space port in Kourou in French Guyana. The space industry can become a new pillar of the industry in NRW, with the perspective of the extensive mining of Helium-3 (for nuclear fusion) and other materials on the Moon, bringing into play NRW mining technology. Automatic large conveyer systems, as are seen today in brown coal surface mining in Aachen, is an example of technology that must be adapted to the lunar conditions (e.g., lower gravity, new materials, and less expenditure of energy). Perhaps many who today are training in classical industrial operations, in 20 or 30 years will be building equipment for space travel for manned missions to the Moon and Mars.

Here is the where the Ruhr region will collaborate with Bremen, whose spaceflight technical sector today already boasts 12,000 highly qualified employees at its various research centers. The modernization of inland ship connections from the Rhine to the Weser rivers, via the corresponding canal and locks system, urgently requires improvement. The great part of industrial manufacturing is best transported by water, not by train, and absolutely not by road.

There are also new construction techniques, such as those proposed by an engineering team ten years ago for a cantilever system for the PeopleCargoMover, which builds the road forward, so to speak, by a modern track-laying machine, reminiscent of the machine used in the railroad industry, that transfers the beams and rail parts and then pushes forward on the newly-built segments. If such a track-laying machine manages 800 meters for the classic train per work shift, this should also be possible in magnetic train construction. In the ideal case, a cantilever device operating round-the-clock could construct 800 km of magnetic railway in a year. The patent for this has existed for a long time in NRW, and it must now finally be put to use.

Finally, what NRW most lacks is nuclear energy. Since the hysterically motivated mothballing of the High-Temperature Reactor (HTR) in 1989 and the fast breeder in 1991, NRW has been "atom free"—an absurdity, and unprecedented for an industrial region. It is unavoidable that a higher energy requirement needs a cheap and efficient source of electrical power. Coal and natural gas are much too valuable as feedstocks for the chemical industry (e.g., plastics and fertilizers) to be burned in amounts of ten thousand tons or cubic meters for the production of electricity, while the generation of the same amount of electricity requires only a few kilograms of fuel for nuclear fission, and just a few grams for nuclear fusion. Incidentally, nuclear fission and fusion solve a transportation and disposal problem that currently exists with coal- and gas-powered plants.

NRW should not only welcome back the HTR technology that was once developed there, but is now living in exile in South Africa; but also take the plunge into nuclear fusion research, including establishing a department of plasma physics (RWTH) at the university. What the RWTH in Aachen has achieved by educating 10,000 engineers from all over the world in 100 years, can be repeated in pioneering technologies such as plasma physics in the coming decade in the Rhine and Ruhr. And NRW should be the producer of compact design HTRs, which can be built at the port of Duisburg or near it, and delivered direct to the entire world by special ships.

The industries which have to be put on a new basis include, above all, steel production, simply for the enormous need for steel for the infrastructure projects described. Not once have the 45 million tons of raw steel and 44 million tons of rolled steel been reached, which were once produced at Thyssen-Krupp and other sites in Germany, since the collapse caused by the great financial crisis in 2008. The required 100,000 new homes alone need 7 million metric tons of steel; community infrastructure (e.g., schools, kindergartens, offices, hospitals, museums, and theaters) can require three times as much steel per square meter of developed area, and the same holds for construction of research and other scientific facilities.

Construction of each 6,000 km of maglev rail track requires 10 million metric tons; one Rhine River bridge, 10,000 tons; and one 1,000 MW nuclear plant, 100,000 tons of steel. NRW alone needs more steel than is currently produced in Germany as a whole.

Admittedly, advances in productivity have played a role in reducing German steel employment from 374,000 in 1970 to just 95,000 in 2009, and where previously thousands of workers were employed, the work is performed today by highly automated equipment at the push of some buttons. Nonetheless, a doubling of steel employment is in no way an overestimate, if one considers the production capacity necessary to carry out all the projects described.

In the future, an increasing share of structural building materials can be made of high-stress and corrosion-resistant industrial fibers and ceramics, but this is not feasible for the foreseeable future. Raw iron and precursor products can of course be landed in large quantities by ocean traffic into Duisport, but the production of the sometimes very special steels for numerous uses in the homebuilding industry is still better done on site in NRW.

The reindustrialization of NRW alone could create up to two million new and highly skilled jobs, with investments in the vicinity of 40 billion euros annually.

Gateway to the Rhine, to the World—and to Outer Space

The wider industrial region around the Neckar River metropolis of Stuttgart represents an important station along the newly arising Eurasian rail lines, which stretch from the Spanish and French Atlantic Coast to the Russian Pacific Coast and the South China Sea. And from eastern Siberia this will go on to the Americas, via a rail tunnel under the Bering Strait, which is already in the pre-planning stage. Stuttgart, still today the sixth-largest German city with a considerable industrial sector, has the potential for much more, because in combination with Plochingen, it is also one of the largest German inland harbor regions.

On the precondition that the current deep economic depression, which has also brought a drop in goods transported on the Neckar, is overcome, the two harbors of the Stuttgart-Plochingen region have a growth potential of 500%—this was the forecast of a study by the previous Baden-Württemberg state government in 2011. The actual development potential may be still higher if the Neckar metropolis, an area of many advanced research centers, becomes a center for development and application of pioneer technologies such as nuclear fusion, plasma physics, isotope techniques, magnetic-levitation systems, radiology, and space technology.

The area opened up by the "Stuttgart 21" major rail project, for which many cities envy the Neckar metropolis due to its inland harbor location and great dimensions, offers sufficient space not only for planting new trees, but also for the establishment of numerous research centers and small to medium-size enterprises for the testing and application of newly developed technologies in the cited fields. In maglev rail technology, for example, development of the Transrapid has not exhausted the technological potential. The CargoCap developed in NRW offers the possibility for a system running in underground tubes, in which industrial semi-finished and finished products can be transported in magnetically guided capsules. Tunnel-boring technology today—developed by the Baden-Württemberg headquartered company Herrenknecht, among others—has been perfected to the point that tunnel equipment can be set up over a dozen kilometers away without an extensive ground surface area having to be broken. It would be possible via CargoCaps to connect a large number of industrial operations, such as goods-handling facilities, with the harbors in Plochingen and Stuttgart—this would also be the way to raise the development potential of both harbor complexes beyond the forecasted quintupling in the coming decades.

While development of the Neckar waterway has already begun (with redevelopment costs for lock and related equipment of nearly 200 million euros), with the goal of handling 135-meter ships, the rail freight aspect has been criminally neglected up to now. Freight traffic had been left out of Stuttgart 21, and should not be interjected there retroactively.

The best solution lies in the development of a robust freight variant of the Transrapid, a magnetic-levitation-driven system which makes use of the greater climbing capacity of this technology, and which, even with obviously lower speeds than for passenger traffic, in the range of 150-200 km/h (90-120 mph), is still far superior to truck freight, especially for longer distances. To build the track itself, the free cantilever method proposed by the NRW PeopleCargoMover team can be used. Once completed, the "Alb Line" would be the first section of a later continental maglev freight mainline with branches. Germany, where the maglev technology was developed, should lead in its application in great projects.

Were a magnetic-levitation rail freight line to be built in Germany, such a system could become a new export driver, because many countries have already asked for a freight Transrapid. And it makes sense to locate the first production centers for the freight Transrapid in the vicinity of the Neckar metropolis, because the Stuttgart region is a center of German auto production, and much of the machine-tool and other capabilities can readily be converted and upgraded to mag-lev freight train production. In fact, the real future of a large part of today's production of cars and trucks lies in just that direction.

The proposed science city on the grounds of the earlier Stuttgart train station compound could, in direct partnership with Daimler and its numerous medium-size suppliers, develop a palette of magnetic rail variants oriented to the type of use—for public municipal transport, private passenger and supply transportation, and industrial transport, in addition to the already existing long-distance version of the Transrapid, which itself can be further upgraded.

Magnetic rail technology can also be used to revolutionize highway traffic. Specifically on roads with rails sunk into their surfaces (similar to trolley rails in city traffic), along which the individual travel of the future will take place magnetically and automatically. Future cars and trucks would move into or out of the on- and off-ramps and into rest areas, parking areas, and emergency telephone points, and convert to operation by their own electric motors where there are no rails. The driver would program the appropriate data when starting the trip and when changing the destination while underway, in a process not very different from the use of navigation systems today.

Creating such a system is a great new challenge to research, engineering, and automotive technology, but one which can be mastered in close collaboration between the proposed Stuttgart central city science center and the still strong auto production in the Stuttgart region.

But Stuttgart and the surrounding region should also advance another pioneering field of modern technology: space technology, whose significance will clearly increase in the coming decades, as did the rapid development of air travel in the last century. Launch rocket systems of various sizes, modules for space stations, and stations on the surfaces of the Moon, Mars, other planets and asteroids; orbital or roving automated laboratories of the Curiosity Mars probe type; transport systems for resupplying materials and food; and systems for delivery of raw materials on the Moon and moons of other planets—all these will be in high demand in a serious effort of manned and unmanned space missions. The Columbus of the 21st Century will "sail" out in space to discover new worlds, and Germany, as an industrial nation with nearly 80 years of experience in the space travel technology sector, can be right up front.

The larger and more sensitive the individual modules and components, the more appropriate is transport on waterways, and after development of the Neckar is complete, the Stuttgart region will be directly linked to the rest of the world by shipping via the Rhine, the Rhine-Main-Danube Canal, and the Rhine-Rhone Canal. The motto of Plochingen Harbor, "Gateway to the Rhine and to the World," will be expanded to also read, "and to outer space."

With the development of a strong space industrial center in the region, the Neckar metropolis will be well positioned for the future, and entirely new careers and life perspectives opened for the younger generation. When the first German team is on the way to Mars, a Stuttgarter, Eslinger, or Plochinger could be there. And astronauts too will find a field of activity in the region for the training of the next generation, as Ernst Messerschmid, born in Reutlingen and astronaut in the first space laboratory operated solely by Germany, the D-1 in 1985, does today. Messerschmid was otherwise previously active in particle physics (CERN, DESY). Another great son of the city of Reutlingen was the railroad pioneer of the first half of the 19th Century, Friedrich List.

Four of the eleven German astronauts up to now come from the state on the Neckar, Baden-Württemberg, and Alexander Gerst, born in Künzelsau, in 2018 will become the first German commander of the International Space Station (ISS).

Another Baden-Württemberg astronaut, Hans Schlegel, spoke briefly in an interview on the occasion of his 65th birthday: "I have the impression that today a flight to Mars is still underestimated. We will not accomplish it in the next 15 or 20 years. It is technically possible, yes, but the will to do it must be there. Up to now our politicians see no necessity for it. If we do not change our geopolitical objectives and broaden global scientific and technological progress, human beings won't reach Mars. In the beginning space travel was rather militarily and strategically motivated. But today we can take the ISS and its operation as the role model for an international, cross-bloc collaboration. If we want to realize something like a trip to Mars, it will only work with global cooperation—thus with China, Russia, Europe, America, Japan, and other countries."

Saxony: A Great Gateway to the East

With the building of the Leipzig-Dresden railroad connection 175 years ago, Saxony opened the door for the development of the railroad network across all of Germany in the following decades; so today a Saxony contribution can be essential to the development of the rail network which plays so important a role in the Eurasian Land-Bridge. In turn this Federal state is a central interface of the newly appearing rail corridors between the China Sea and the Atlantic Coast of Europe.

Trans-Eurasia Logistics (TEL), in existence since 2008 as a collaboration of Deutsche Bahn AG with the Russian railroad RZD, has given rise to a logistics network on the line stretching from Duisburg to Beijing, so that goods can already be transported and distributed on seven rail lines across all of Eurasia:

- Three Europe-Russia lines: Moscovite, Tubetaika, and Matroschka
- Two Europe-China lines: New Silk Road and Tiger Train
- Two Russia-China lines: China-Russia Multinet and Central Asia Express

Since 2011 a train with 36 containers has run every day from Leipzig-Wahren to Shenyang in China. Initially it was merely the 8,000 parts of a BMW travelling to a new factory in China. BMW alone has built a 63,000-square-meter logistics center and created 600 jobs. But these trains can also run with 50 containers. Dr. Karl Friedrich Rausch, Chairman of DB Mobility Transport & Logistik AG, called this connection a "significant impulse for the Eurasian Land-Bridge." Vladimir Yakunin, then-head of Russian Railways, explained that because the trade volume flows primarily (in a ratio of 80:20) from east to west, he considered the Leipzig project extraordinarily welcome because it represented the first step in an improvement of this ratio.

In the context of these developments the Leipzig region can become a major European logistics center and thereby the most important gateway to the East. Such a role is much more appropriate to the character of Leipzig, a city with a centuries-old trade fair, than the role of a post-industrial consumer city as it now presents itself.

Moreover, from Dresden a Dresden-Prague-Bratislava-Uschgorod-Lvov-Kiev corridor can be created. Odessa and Crimea can be connected by it. From there, via the bridges Russia will build over the Sea of Azov, a continuation to the south Russian growth center of Krasnodar will appear, then north along the Caspian Sea and across through Kazakhstan to western China, an important second, southern strand of the New Silk Road.

Russia, whose then-Railways chief Yakunin announced in St. Petersburg on May 22, 2014 plans to build a new Trans-Siberian connection from Moscow to Vladivostok based on magnetic rail technology, will also gain a great advantage from this second route via Krasnodar. Regions all along this route will be able to profit from the fact that freight can be transported at 200 km/h (120 mph) with a container version of magnetic-levitation rail, rather than at 80 km/h (50 mph) by truck today.

Discussions are already underway in China and Russia about relying in the future more on magnetic-levitation than wheel-rail technology, and this technology should be promoted in Saxony and implemented wherever it makes sense. Görlitz, as Saxony's location for construction of rail cars, can thus become a central location for production of Transrapid trains, best together with a magnetic rail connection to Dresden, so that the trains from the Görlitz works can travel directly onto the new long-distance network and come into use on the future Dresden-Prague, Dresden-Kiev, and Dresden-Krakow lines as well as in the Berlin-Leipzig-Dresden Triangle.

Waterways Development

In the Czech Republic and Poland, building the Danube-Oder-Elbe Canal is being discussed; Saxony should get involved. At the same time as the Elbe is developed, simple regulations must be carried out by means of barrages at the latitude of Dresden, so that the water level even in the Summer months is high enough to enable through-traffic for ships year-round. This will give rise to a new framework for a resurgence of industry in all three countries—Germany, Poland, and the Czech Republic—and thus raise the productivity and living standards of their populations.

A second great water project for Saxony is the completion of the Elster-Saale Canal for freight and passenger transportation. This canal, first proposed in 1856, whose construction was stopped in 1942 due to the war, should now be finished. This requires completing the harbor and about 8 km of canal to the Saale, where a boat lift should be located. On the Saale it requires three locks be built, at Halle, Planena, and Werder (Merseburg), and a straightening be carried out at Calbe. About 1.2 billion euros could be split between the two Federal states of Saxony and Saxon-Anhalt to connect Leipzig via the Saale to the Elbe. Leipzig, with its new rail network connection to China, is already a factor in Eurasian trade. This position could be further developed by this canal and lead to a flourishing of industry in the Halle-Leipzig region as well.

Science and Research as the Motor for Industry

Participation in great projects like the New Silk Road, and thereby in the already existing programs between China, Russia, and India in such spheres as space travel, nuclear power, nuclear fusion, and magnetic-levitation technology, naturally also presupposes a science initiative for Saxony.

Saxony has core competences in the areas of nuclear physics, Transrapid, machine building, and space travel, which should be built upon. Saxony can make a decisive contribution to a new trans-Eurasian cooperation.

Superconducting technology will play a decisive role for future generations of magnetic-levitation technology. Here research approaches like those initiated in the Supratrans Project, begun at the Leibniz Institute for Solid State and Material Research (IFW) in Dresden (**Figure 5**), must be broadened and intensively supported with public funds. Russia is relying on superconducting technology for the planned new Trans-Siberian Railroad, which offers essential advantages due to its clearly higher energy efficiency and lower operating costs compared to the classic magnetic rail technology, above all for transport of freight containers. Here the Dresden research can make an essential contribution.

In addition to magnetic rail for long-distance rail, a variant of the system can be used for freight, and for passenger transport in heavily-populated cities. The development work on the Supratrans at the Dresden IFW goes in this direction and, as an innovation to the CargoCap concept already developed in Bochum, can relieve the constant traffic jams of cities.

In particular, relocating direct traffic between production companies underground, offers decisive time savings to companies whose trucks today have to spend hours daily in city traffic. As with the development of the Elbe as a through waterway for ship traffic, a CargoCap for Dresden is also a step to its future as a great inland harbor.

In addition to Mosel-Zwickau and Leipzig as great auto centers, Saxony possesses, in Chemnitz, one of the most important German machine-building centers, with tradition-rich companies such as "Union," which will receive a new surge of orders through the development of the Eurasian Land-Bridge, and can make an essential contribution to the development of industrial regions along the New Silk Road. Chemnitz University is also conducting research on high-stress plastic fibers, which will replace a large part of current construction on a steel base (e.g., bridges), as special ceramics replace metals such as copper in superconducting technology.

New impulses from construction materials development can flow into the still-new field of production with 3D printing techniques. The Fraunhofer Society in Dresden has set up a "Center for Additive Production" in which the printing process forms parts from metallic dust, ceramic, or plastic base material, as they were earlier made by casting or pressing, but which exhibit precision hardness or still better characteristics. Thus far this is the largest such facility in Europe.

In the one-time Saxony machine-casting forge of Chemnitz there are additional important core capabilities which can contribute to the development of the entire region. Improvement of the infrastructure within Saxony should ensure the full development of the Saxony Main Line (Hof-Zwickau-Chemnitz-Dresden), including connecting Leipzig and Dresden more effectively with infrastructure. These "three sisters" would then be inter-linked in a "Leipzig-Chemnitz-Dresden Productive Triangle" as the core of Saxony's overall development.

In Chemnitz, for example, Altran Technologies GmbH & Co KG shepherds innovations from development to serial production and collaborates with EADS, among others. This firm supplies the entire cable harness for Cryosat, which investigated the Antarctic, Greenland, and sea ice on its 2010-2013 circumnavigation of the Earth.

The Fraunhofer Institute for Machine Tools and Metal-Forming Technology (IWU) is a world leader in

Figure 5

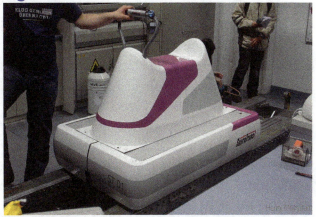

The Supratrans project of the Leibniz Institute for Solid State and Materials Research (IFW) in Dresden combines magnetic levitation with superconducting technology.

production sciences. The STFI Saxon Textile Research Institute in Chemnitz is involved in all fields of technical and industrial textiles and can play an important role in their further development.

Dresden, besides many high-technology firms (e.g., aircraft construction, precision mechanics, and apparatus engineering), has important research institutes whose importance and benefits to the Eurasian development perspective will increase greatly, for example:

- Fraunhofer Institute for Electron Beam & Plasma Technology (FEP)
- TU Dresden, Institute for Lightweight Construction and Plastics Technology
- University Center for Air and Space Travel
- Fraunhofer Institute for Machine Tools and Metal-Forming Technology (IWU)
- Fraunhofer Institute for Ceramic Technologies and Systems (IKTS)

With all these developments, a high-technology and innovation impulse would occur like that in the period of industrialization. It would thereby be possible to strengthen the already existing Saxony capacities and create new branches of industry decisive for the space travel sector and nuclear fusion. Already 28 countries are collaborating on realizing nuclear fusion in the European Fusion Development Agreement (EFDA). Among them, Germany is the only country with more than one research center.

From the Elbe to Nuclear Fusion

From many standpoints, Saxony is a location of pioneering work in several research fields, for example, in technical textiles on a plastic base, for whose future use in construction and aircraft and auto production there are great expectations. Saxony researchers also make important contributions to nuclear fusion research, such as in the new electron accelerator (ELBE) at the Dresden-Rossendorf Helmholtz Center, dedicated in February 2013, and the largest research device in Saxony with investments of 55 million euros. Saxony was already in the most advanced rank in international fusion neutronics with the predecessor institute, the "old" ELBE.

The "new" ELBE is a center for high-performance beams, which with the help of super-laser electrons, can accelerate to close to the speed of light and generate different kinds of beams, from positrons and neutrons to gamma rays. With these kinds of beams, which also include infrared light, various forms of matter and materials can be examined.

This is important for developing, for example, materials that can withstand extreme challenges, such as in the future international fusion project, the International Thermonuclear Experimental Reactor (ITER). The ELBE studies are also useful for cancer therapy and other medical applications.

In this endeavor, Saxony has its potentially best partner at its front door. In the neighboring Czech Republic important research is proceeding in all these scientific fields. With PALS, the most powerful laser in Europe, and the COMPASS Tokamak reactor in Prague, are available two research centers of international rank and reputation, whose work makes significant contributions to scientific progress.

REBUILDING GERMANY'S INFRASTRUCTURE FOR A NEW INDUSTRIAL SOCIETY

A quarter-century after reunification, Germany has lost a substantial amount of its productive capacity. Between 1991 and 2014, the number of people employed in manufacturing collapsed from 9.56 million to 7.27 million, and the percentage of people in the labor force dropped by one-third—from 24.7% to 16.8%. In addition, at least as many people depend on "Hartz-4" payments. Since 1992 the purchasing power of the German population has hardly risen at all.

That is partially the result of the ideology of globalization and free trade, which led to the relocation of production in low-wage countries—a trend which was strengthened by the erroneous way the euro was created. This is fatal, because the German economy must export in the range of 40% of its production in order to be able to import necessary raw materials and other goods. But it is also fatal because the world as a whole has a huge need for highly developed technology, a need which will be dramatically intensified as the New Silk Road's development program encompasses more and more countries.

The good news is that this obstacle potentially can be overcome, because historically, Germany's situation at the time of its industrialization was similar: When industrialization began, there were neither industrial jobs nor an educated workforce; industrialization created both. Between 1800 and 1911, the number of workers in productive sectors of the economy rose from 80,000 to 8 million. The actual motive force for this development was the construction of the rail network, which grew from 6,000 km to 24,000 km between 1850 and 1870 (**Figure 6**). Over the same period coal extraction in Prussia rose from 5 million tons to 23 million tons; steel production from approximately 200,000 tons to 900,000 tons.

Inadequate Transport Infrastructure

Today as well, the transport sector is where the greatest general impact from a technological leap can be expected. Traffic jams on the autobahns, roads in need of repair, inner cities full of parked cars, delays or even cancellations of trains and flights—whenever one travels in Germany today, infrastructure deficiencies meet the eye. This is not only a result of lack of investment and maintenance, but also of the conversion of the economy into a post-industrial society, because the traffic flow of a service economy differs considerably from that of an industrial society.

In an industrial society lots of raw materials were needed, which were often imported over long distances from abroad. Therefore ship transport is, as a rule of thumb, the most favored means of transport; where the final products were previously delivered to consumers by train, today it is mostly by truck. While warehouses for finished products can be constructed almost anywhere, the factories have been grouped in convenient places. Therefore many of Germany's old industrial regions lie on navigable rivers, while the warehouses for imports have been often located somewhere near an Autobahn, and oriented to truck transport.

There is also a big difference between an industrial and a service economy in the area of personal transportation: While factories, which are often placed in the suburbs, mostly work on the shift system, so that many people can come to and from work in a short period of time—which permits public means of transportation—there is a much more extensive (in time and space) region of coming and going among service providers; in other words, they are not so much tied to a particular place, and "come to the customers."

Also business transactions are a lot more individualized today than before. The result is that road traffic, especially automobile traffic, has become heavier, and many rail routes have been abandoned, because they are no longer "profitable."

A further aspect of the current traffic misery is that services have often been offered in small offices or business districts in the inner cities. The previous inhabitants of the inner cities have been driven out by rising rents and other factors into the surrounding regions. The result is that employees' commute to their jobs is longer, and as a rule each working family member needs his or her own means of transport. Traffic in the inner cities is jammed—to the chagrin of the driving public and residents.

Meanwhile, globalization has led to the outsourcing or closing of innumerable production facilities in Germany. Products are instead brought in by truck from abroad, which accelerates the wear and tear on the highways.

Figure 6

 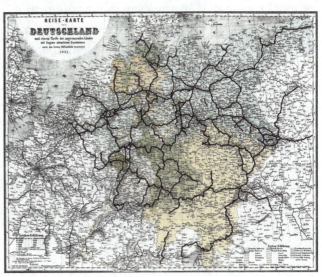

One motor for German industrialization in the 19th Century was the rapid construction of the railroad network, which grew from 6,000 km to 24,000 km between 1850 and 1870. Here are two historical maps from 1849 (left) and 1861 (right), showing the build-up of a dense network of new rail criss-crossing the country.

Investment Bottleneck

The cost to the national economy as a result of bottlenecks in transport infrastructure is estimated to be approximately several hundred billion euros a year. More must clearly be invested in maintenance and in the expansion of transport routes, yet the percentage of the Gross National Product invested in transportation has been reduced in recent years to less than half that expended in the 1970s. Capacity has been expanded much more slowly than traffic, while existing infrastructure is decaying more rapidly. A study by the German Institute for Economic Research (DIW), which compared the replacement requirement with the actual investment in the period between 2006 and 2011, said:

"The analysis shows that in the past, just under four billion euros too little per year was spent for maintenance of the transportation infrastructure. If one assumes at least this investment gap for the maintenance of transportation infrastructure in coming years as well, and takes into consideration the pent-up demand which has accumulated during this years-long period of negligence, then the additional yearly investment requirement would be at least 6.5 billion euro."

The DIW calculates the yearly replacement requirement at 13.2 billion euros—meaning that what is being done is only half as much as is necessary to maintain the transport system. Already the German national economy is hardly even in a position to finance the upkeep of the transportation infrastructure, to say nothing of the urgently needed expansion of capacity. With the increasing disrepair and growing congestion, losses from traffic tie-ups and similar problems are also increasing. The entire system is stuck in a Catch-22, from which only a decisive break from the neoliberal dogma of recent decades can rescue the country.

Reconstruction of the Transport Infrastructure

The Federal Transport Ministry is currently preparing a Federal Transportation Plan for 2030. This should include all the projects whose realization by 2030 is considered necessary or reasonable, although monetarist and environmentalist criteria usually prevail over physical-economic necessity.

Furthermore, the requirements of transport policy also change in light of the goal of reindustrializing Germany. Therefore it would be wrong to simply plan for correcting the current bottlenecks. Plans for the new transport concept must be aligned with the future requirements of the industrial society that must be reestablished.

To what extent should each transport mode be expanded? To answer this question, we must analyze the transport requirements of a reindustrialized society. The layout of the transport network is, so to speak, determined by nature: The rivers and cities already exist, and thus the placement of infrastructure for interregional transport is broadly predetermined; but the volume of transport will change, as will its composition.

To analyze the changes and establish the optimal organization for transportation, one must first differentiate between the transport of people and goods. Within personal transport one must differentiate between public and individual means of travel, short-distance and long-distance travel, business and leisure travel, and so forth. Goods, on the other hand, fall into categories such as bulk commodities (e.g., coal, sand, grain), containers, or general cargo. There is also a difference as to whether the freight has to reach its destination quickly, for example, because it is perishable. The object of transport policy must be to define the best form of transport—ship, rail, magnetic-levitated train, highway, or air—for each form of commerce, and then to optimize each transport system per se, as well as its interface with various other systems of transport.

Looking at the current transport policy from this standpoint, it is obvious that today (in addition to the generally insufficient investment in all infrastructure areas) two transport systems have been largely neglected, thus worsening the stress on transport other modes—waterways and magnetic-levitated trains.

With the shift of a large portion of goods-transport to rivers and canals, and a large portion of long-distance passenger transport to magnetically-levitated trains (such as Transrapid), the volume of traffic on other modes of transportation would be reshaped. In air travel, for example, practically all short-haul flights and many medium-haul flights could be discontinued; room would be created on the railways for general cargo and long-distance personal travel by reducing the transport of bulk commodities and short-distance passenger traffic. This, on the other hand, would take many trucks off the autobahns.

Magnetic Rail: A Technological Quantum Leap

The way German policy previously dealt with magnetic rail can only be described as scandalous. When the Transrapid test-track came on line in Emsland in 1987, it was only a few years away from being ready for commercial use; it was officially certified in 1991. Finally, over the year-end from 2002 to 2003, the first serious Transrapid commercial line came into operation—but not in Germany. Rather, it connects the Shanghai airport with the downtown of that Chinese business metropolis.

By contrast, in Germany the governments have set up the Intercity-Express (ICE), a conventional wheel-rail system, the technical parameters of which—high speed, capacity for acceleration, wear and tear, possible angle of elevation, and curve radii—clearly lag behind magnetic rail in every respect.

At the opening of the Transrapid line in Shanghai, Chancellor Gerhard Schröder pledged to also bring the Transrapid into service in Germany. Yet nothing happened; the test track in Emsland itself was decommissioned in 2011. In reality, the construction of an extensive magnetic train network in Germany would be one of the most important measures for energizing the German economy and industrializing it again.

Deutsche Bahn (German Railways) has admittedly invested a lot in the expansion of fast tracks, yet meanwhile it is nearly drowning in debt, so that important projects are in doubt. The construction of the fast track between Nürnberg-Erfurt, as the centerpiece of connecting Munich to Berlin, was even temporarily halted, before it was finally completed and put into operation in late 2017—26 years after the project was originally started. Many secondary lines have been shut down—about 10,000 km alone since reunification in 1989.

Only a technological "quantum-leap" can solve this predicament. For this, the introduction of a new technology is necessary, the magnetically-levitated train (**Figure 7**). The time is overripe for bringing the "future technology" into the present, because the technical parameters of the Transrapid are by far superior to the conventional wheel-rail systems to which the ICE also belongs.

While the Transrapid causes practically no signs of wear and tear at 450 km/hour, because the power is conveyed contact-free, the wear and tear on the wheels and rails in the wheel-rail system increases dramatically with increasing speed. In Japan the operating speed of their fast train was reduced when it became clear that the wear and tear was too great; meanwhile, there is a magnetically-levitated line under construction from Tokyo to Nagoya, which will later be extended to Osaka.

A further advantage is the clearly better power transmission through the solenoid actuator for the magnetically-levitated train: It normally takes 5 km for the Transrapid to accelerate from a stop to 300 km/hour; the ICE needs about 30 km. In practice this means that the ICE barely reaches its highest speed over the distance of 60 km between two stations, before it has to slow down, while the Transrapid can use

Figure 7

The magnetic train is clearly superior to a conventional wheel-rail system like the ICE in respect to its technological parameters—high speed, capacity for acceleration, wear and tear, possible angle of elevation, and curve radii. The picture shows the first commercial magnetic train in the world, in Shanghai.

Figure 8

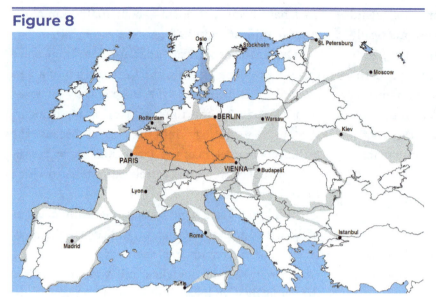

As early as 1990, immediately after the revolution in the DDR, the LaRouche movement presented the study "The Productive Triangle Paris-Berlin-Vienna" proposing a European-wide infrastructure and economic construction program.

nections extend beyond Germany. The German magnetic train network must therefore from the outset be conceived of as the centerpiece of a European-wide magnetic train network that connects all the important population centers of the continent.

The *EIR* study Das productive Dreieck Paris-Berlin-Wien (The Productive Triangle Paris-Berlin-Vienna) proposed this idea as early as 1990 (**Figure 8**). The Paris-Berlin-Vienna productive triangle, whose interior is about as large as Japan and to this day ranks as the economic region with the world's greatest density of productive investment, forms the core region of the all-European magnetic train network. That will soon change, however, if there is no forceful change in direction in Europe, because especially in China, but also in other parts of East Asia, the growth of productive economies has been sharply accelerating.

A Densely Reticulated Network

The technical parameters of the magnetic train allow most of Germany's larger cities, those with more than 50,000 inhabitants, in addition to the major cities and the commercial airports, to be connected to the network—and to travel just as fast, or faster, between metropolises than on a Sprinter-ICE, which does not stop in between them.

The magnetically-levitated lines will not run exactly parallel to the ICE tracks, but rather in many places where construction of an ICE track would barely be technologically and economically feasible. The station density of the magnetic line would also be much greater than that of the Sprinters and comparable to that of the D-trains of the 1960s. Once the magnetic rail network is completed, it will absorb most of the passengers who today use either short- or middle-range air travel, the ICE, or other fast trains. Many car drivers will also then prefer magnetic rail to the automobile. And a portion of cargo traffic can also in the future be handled via the Transrapid.

its full capabilities for a greater portion of the route. To reduce the time lost by the deceleration and acceleration, the German Railways introduced the ICE's "Sprinter"—for example, between Munich, Frankfurt, and Berlin—and gave up having intermediate stations. But with that, the number of people who could use the Sprinter to save time, shrank dramatically.

The much greater gradient angle and narrower curve radius possible with the magnetically-levitated train allows the construction of a magnetically-levitated train track over mountainous territory without appreciably higher construction costs, while the construction of a fast-train track for the ICE in the mountains is extremely expensive due to the necessary tunnels and bridges—therefore the "fast connection" of rail from Munich to Dresden was built through Erfurt and Leipzig.

The magnetic train therefore not only can go faster, but also eliminates many circuitous routes. The actual savings, however, show up in normal operations over the long term, where the magnetic train operates with one-fourth the energy of the ICE, because it does not have to overcome the wheels' friction.

The realization of a magnetic train network will only function as a system-relieving "clearance" if it is conceived from the outset as a network of all the important transport connections, and also established as quickly as possible. Many of these transport con-

The construction of a magnetic rail network will therefore cause a dramatic reallocation of volume between modes of transport: In the case of air travel, almost all short-haul flights and a great number of middle-haul flights will be cancelled in favor of the magnetic rail network. The Federal Railways will further restrict itself to local passenger and goods traffic, and act as a feeder for the magnetic rail system.

Magnetic Rail Production on the Assembly Line

It is not only rational in matters of transport policy to plan an overall network, as described above, but also economical: for example, it will be possible to plan Transrapid factories on a larger scale, so that they can cheapen the production of the magnetic rail lines. This will also make it easier to export magnetic rail. Current sites for Transrapid development, such as the Transrapid city Kassel, will experience an enormous boom.

In the 19th Century almost all the important lines of the German rail network were completed within a decade with the building techniques of that time. It should be possible to complete a similarly comprehensive network with modern methods in a similar period of time.

Mass production of the Transrapid will naturally also augment demand in the high-technology sector, and thus spark a technological revolution in the productive sector, with effects reaching far beyond the transport sector. Many technologies are currently ready for use, but either cannot or can barely be realized due to lack of demand, because they are not profitable on a small scale.

The construction of a full-blown Transrapid network would make it possible to amortize all these investments—and once they are put into effect, then they will also be at the disposal of other economic sectors.

Millions of New Jobs

A comprehensive magnetic rail network for Germany would have a track length of about 10,000 km; a magnetic rail network connecting to Eurasia would have one of at least 60,000 km. The Berlin Institute for Railway Technology has calculated that the construction of a 450-km magnetic rail track from Hamburg through Berlin to Dresden would provide work for 250,000 people for five years. The construction of the magnetic rail network within Germany would therefore create around 2.3 million jobs, of which approximately 600,000 would be in construction, if the total program were to be accomplished in 10 years (**Table 1**).

Obviously this would require far more than Germany's current industrial capacity, and countless new and young workers must be brought on and trained—also from abroad, where they then can be employed in building magnetic train lines in their home nations. And perhaps that is the most crucial aspect of such a program, because in order to become an industrial country again, Germany must very quickly attract many young people into seeking their future in industry, and train them for that. To that end, Germany must "pull itself together," and the magnetically-levitated train program is probably the most effective means to do that, because it would be a sign that Germany is orienting itself again toward the future.

Table 1
Job Creation from Construction of a Hamburg-Berlin-Dresden Transrapid Line (450 km)

Economic Sector	Jobs
Engineering, automobile, structural steelwok	53,000
Construction	53,000
Electrical Engineering	39,000
Light industry	19,000
Services	18,000
Transport, communications	18,000
Building materials	17,000
Metalworking	10,000
Chemistry	6,000
Other	17,000
TOTAL	**250,000**

Source: IFB, EIR

FRANCE AND CHINA IN THE DYNAMICS OF THE NEW SILK ROAD

In 1861, Victor Hugo condemned the sacking of Beijing's Summer Palace by "two thieves," the British and the French empires. One century later, in 1964, French President Charles de Gaulle was the first major Western leader to recognize the People's Republic of China. While Napoleon had said that China was "a giant one shouldn't awake," De Gaulle, on the contrary, underlined in 1964, "It has not to be excluded that China will become again, in the next century, what it was over the centuries, the greatest power of the universe."

In January 2018, opening his state visit to China, French President Emmanuel Macron lyrically declared in Xi'an, the Chinese gate of the Silk Road: "We are living a time where France and China can dream together." "The New Silk Roads," he said, "are reviving a vision of future civilization, to be shared."

To help this dream become reality, discussed below are some ongoing developments and some of the vast potentials still untapped for increased Franco-Chinese cooperation in the domains of financial partnerships; basic infrastructure in the areas of transportation, energy, and water management; and finally, some high-tech areas related to advanced nuclear power and health and environmental matters.

Improving Connectivity to Adapt French Transport Infrastructure to the New Silk Road Requirements

"If you want to get rich, construct a road," goes the Chinese saying. Increasing "connectivity" as leverage for global growth, is one of the key concepts of China's Belt and Road Initiative (BRI). Beyond better exchanges of people and goods, the aim of better performing infrastructure corridors and roads is to raise the economy to an increasingly higher "platform" of economic efficiency.

Such an outlook, promoted for decades by physical economist Lyndon LaRouche and currently ap-

Charles de Freycinet, French Transportation Minister, began an effort in 1878 to modernize France's ports, integrating them with inland regions and cities, and spurred an upgrading of France's steel and engineering capabilities.

plied to reality by Chinese President Xi Jinping's BRI, was also on the mind of French Transportation Minister Charles de Freycinet in the 19th Century. To reinvigorate French ports, which were lagging behind their competitors in Belgium and the Netherlands, Freycinet in 1878 engaged France in a vast effort to modernize its ports by providing them with access to a vast hinterland of regions and cities integrated by intricate networks of upgraded canals and modern railroads. It worked then, it would work again today. One of the technological spin-offs of the revamped French steel and engineering capabilities that resulted from Freycinet's plan were such proud achievements as the Eiffel tower and Ferdinand de Lesseps' Suez Canal.

"Globalization" has put transport on the front burner. While passengers and high-value-added goods travel by airplane, 90% of all other goods travel by ship. And France has the world's second largest Exclusive Economic Zone (EEZ) and the longest coastline of Europe with major ports providing access to the North Sea, the Atlantic, and the Mediterranean.

However, except for roads, French transport infrastructure is declining. While European ports saw an increase of 60% in their tonnage between 1989 and 2006, French ports only increased their tonnage by 24%. While between 1990 and 2015, Le Havre, France's largest container port, multiplied its tonnage by two and one-half times, Antwerp increased its tonnage by nine times.

In addition, due to underinvestment and privatizations, the percentage of rail freight has collapsed from 66% in the 1950s to less than 10% in 2015 and today. German railways handle three times more goods than do those of France.

According to a report of the World Economic Forum, the quality of French infrastructure has declined in a spectacular way since 2008. In six years, France fell from the fourth best ranking to tenth. The first cause is the lack of maintenance, which dropped by 33% on secondary roads. In 2014, some 72,000 bridges were structurally threatened by corrosion, according to the National Federation of Public Works. The average age of rail has increased by 30% since 2003. The required upgrading of the French ports, rail, and canal infrastructure requires rethinking integrated supply in the age of the digital revolution, i.e., the use of fiber optics, 5G IT, and robotics.

Improving the French Canal System —The Lessons of Shanghai

In that respect, France can learn some lessons from Shanghai (20 million inhabitants), which became in 2010 the world's largest port as a result of a massive upgrade of the Yangtze, the world's third longest river (6,380 km) used for inland navigation over close to 3,000 km. It has to be underlined that 58% of Shanghai's trade is with Chinese industrial centers such as Nanjing (8 million inhabitants), Nanchang (5), Wuhan (10), Changcha (7), and Chongqing (31), all of them located on the river or part of the natural hinterland of the Yangtze which contributes more than 20% of China's GDP.

Neglected during the Cultural Revolution, the rehabilitation of the waterway was part of Deng Xia-

Figure 9
Seine North Canal: Project at a Glance

oping's four reforms. Today, the "Golden Waterway Yangtze River Economic Belt" is a key component of the BRI and one of the key areas from where trains loaded with goods are leaving, heading to Lyons, France; Duisburg and Hamburg, Germany; Antwerp, Belgium; and Rotterdam in the Netherlands.

China and France could jointly develop the French canal system which is the largest in Europe. What has to be done is well known to all. First, the financing of the Seine North Canal, connecting the Seine to the Scheldt and the ports of Amsterdam and Rotterdam, should not be left to the regions alone, as is planned today, because its profitability is national (**Figure 9**).

For the rest, the ugly fact remains that nearly all rivers and canals allowing large barge traffic are dead ends. To facilitate their interconnection in France, is a plan known as the "goose claw," imagined nearly a thousand years ago by the advisers of Charlemagne, which would give a major boost to the French economy (**Figure 10**).

The plan involves connecting the following rivers: the Rhône (Lyons) with the Rhine (Basel), the Saone (Châlons) with the Moselle (Nancy), and the Saone with the Marne and therefore with the Seine (Paris). This would instantly transform Lyons into a "French Duisburg," i.e., a large inland port and intermodal transportation hub, and an ideal "terminal" for the BRI. With

Figure 10
The "Goose Claw" Plan

the new economic platform emerging from the BRI, such new transportation corridors would be ideal for the construction of floating nuclear power plants and space vessels that could be assembled along the canals.

Upgrading of Le Havre and Its Hinterland

At the same time, Le Havre and Marseille, both already hubs for Chinese investment, would need major input. Today, 87% of all goods arriving in Le Havre leave the port by truck, and only the remaining 13% via train and river. The first priority is to make the Le Havre, Rouen, and Paris (HAROPA) project an operational reality (**Figure 11**).

For Le Havre, a real "Marshall Plan" that would improve drastically the interconnections between port, railroad, and inland navigation will require:

- Direct access to the container port (Port2000) for large container push barges. This new gate requires 100 million euros.
- Rapid, full electrification of the freight rail connection going from Le Havre to the north of Paris via Serqueux and Gisors (300 million euros). Work is underway but lagging behind schedule.
- Allocation of 1.7 billion euros for several additional upgrades and extensions of the port as identified by the Union Maritime du Havre. This includes 220 million euros for the "grand canal" and 1 billion euros for the extension of the container port.
- Construction of a new fast passenger transport system connecting Paris with Le Havre via Rouen. The current plan of the national railway company SNCF for the construction of a new Paris-Normandy link (LNPN) is not a good solution. It should be replaced with a modern version of the French aerotrain invented in the 1970s by French engineer Jean Bertin. Since last year, a French start-up called Spacetrain, a division of the robotics company Vaucanson, is revamping this very promising technology known as Tracted Air Cushion Vehicle (TACV). Without wheels, the vehicles use the physical principle of "ground effect," i.e., aircushions. Gliding on a rail on pillars, the construction of such a new mode of transport would free the current rails from passenger trains and solve the deadly bottlenecks of freight transport from Le Havre to Paris.

Joint Franco-Chinese Nuclear Power Plants for the World

The Franco-Chinese cooperation on nuclear energy is already very good but can go much further. Considered to be the "the world's largest nuclear site in the making," China appears as the Promised Land for the nuclear sector. With investments in new plants and R&D on the rise, China also aims to export very soon to the rest of the world, its own Hualong ("Chinese dragon") third-generation pressurized water reactor (PWR), 100% made in China.

French cooperation in the field of nuclear energy goes back to the state visit of French President Pompidou to China in 1973. The first concrete agreement between the countries was signed in 1982 by the French state-owned Atomic Energy Agency (CEA) and the Chinese Ministry for Nuclear Power (MIN). The agreement involved construction of the first 900

Figure 11
The HAROPA Project

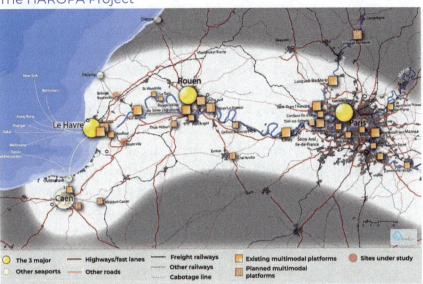

MW nuclear reactors and technology transfers. Out of this came China's first nuclear plant in Daya Bay and later Linag Ao.

Today, Franco-Chinese cooperation aims at expanding to "third-party countries." When visiting Beijing in 2016, French Minister of Foreign Affairs Jean-Marc Ayrault said that the construction of the EPR nuclear power plant at Hinckley Point (UK), built jointly by the French leading nuclear power constructor Electricité de France (EDF) and China General Nuclear (CGN), was the road to go: "It is an excellent example of what we are going to do together, i.e., getting joint contracts on foreign markets, and this in all sectors.... It is a model we are pushing all over, including in Africa and Asia," he said at a joint press conference with Wang Yi, his Chinese counterpart.

As part of the deal, which involves building a Hualong Chinese reactor in Bradwell (UK), France will help China get the certification from the UK nuclear regulators. In exchange, China will be able to export Hualong reactors to all European Union (EU) member countries. The Franco-Chinese partnership for building nuclear power stations in a "third country" is unique and considered to be a stepping stone for building joint nuclear power plants all over the planet, and in particular in Africa.

Franco-Chinese cooperation will now move onto reprocessing facilities. French President Macron's visit on January 9, 2018 included the signing of a memorandum of understanding for the construction of a nuclear reprocessing plant by the French company Orano (new name of Areva), the world's leading expert in this field. The 23 billion euro deal has still to be finalized but confirms China's choice for the "closed" cycle—reprocessing allows turning parts of burned fuel and waste into new fuel.

As a result of that choice, rapid neutron reactors (RNR), earlier known as "fast breeder reactors," are the logical next option, and another field where France, with the Super-Phénix, has much experience. At the same time, China's R&D teams are intensively exploring almost all fourth-generation reactor designs ever conceived of. As one official of the French embassy in Beijing puts it: "Even if all these projects will not be conclusive, they stimulate an accumulation of expertise by the training of a human potential which has all chances to make China a nuclear power in the 21st Century."

On top of all, during a preparatory trip for Macron's visit, France and China signed an agreement to increase substantially their cooperation on nuclear fusion by the creation of the Sino-French Fusion Energy Center (SIFFER). Already, in the framework of preparatory work for the giant ITER fusion Tokamak based in France, for which China is a major partner, cooperation had expanded with the EAST/WEST program—EAST being the Chinese, Heifei-based Experimental Advanced Superconducting Tokamak and WEST being the new name for Tore Supra, a plasma facility near Cadarache in Southern France which holds the record of the longest plasma duration time for a Tokamak (6 minutes 30 seconds) and allows researchers to test critical parts of equipment, such as plasma resistant wall components or superconducting magnets, that will be used in its successor, the ITER.

Also, the creation by EDF of the Franco-Chinese electricity partnership PFCE has created the means for small and medium-size companies to participate more easily in the Franco-Chinese nuclear cooperation by using EDF's network in China. Because France has helped China create its nuclear industry going back to 1973, China has integrated and adopted French rules and standards for design, construction, and surveillance, which created de facto a "natural" market for French technology providers.

To conclude, it should be underlined, that if the political will is mobilized, the potential for France and China to play a leading role for world development in this field is self-evident.

Other Domains of Excellence: Environmental Protection, Health, and Aging

Poverty and lack of technology are, in China and worldwide, the first cause of pollution. Some 90% of the plastics to be found in the ocean come from the main rivers of Africa and Asia, including the Yangtze. The rapid industrialization undergone by China in the past 30 years and, in particular, the largely deregulated development of the early years following the reforms, have led to massive, life-threatening pollution in the air, water, and soil.

On March 13, 2014, China's Prime Minister Li Keqiang announced an all-out "war on pollution." Between 2015 and 2020, $275 billion is to be invested in the improvement of air quality.

In this context, two French multinationals, Veolia and Suez, recognized as world leaders in water management; air, water, and soil pollution; and toxic waste, have been hired by the Chinese government to play an important role in the fight against pollution. The French de-pollution site of "Seine Aval" at Achères, which handles 70% of the water resources of the Paris region, is becoming a world attraction. Foreign delegations, including Chinese, have been touring the site. In 2011, China called on French companies to build a sewage system at Lhassa, the capital of Tibet. Built initially to recycle 50,000 tons of waste water its capacity will reach 180,000 tons in 2020. Veolia and Suez are preparing "large-scale high-performance de-pollution" systems using extremely fine filter systems.

Also notably, Sino-French Water Development, a subsidiary of Suez Environnement and of the Chinese group Shanghai Chemical Industry Park (SCIP), is on the job in Shanghai leading the SCIP, which brings together the most heavily polluting industries of the world's largest port. Part of the project involves its large R&D division, the SCIP Water Research Center (SWRc). Suez is also active in Hong Kong where the company handles the waste of the 7.3 million inhabitants of the city.

Another problem to tackle is the loss of water that occurs when traveling through the distribution pipes. While that loss is between 15% and 20% in France, it is close to 50% in Mexico, Saudi Arabia, and India, and the average loss of water in Asia stands at 40%.

Such efforts will ease pressure on water supply, but will it be enough? China, for example, currently consumes about 600 billion cubic meters of water per year, about three-quarters of its exploitable water resources. Between now and 2030, current resources will reach their limits.

New resources to be tapped include water desalination, another field of expertise of French companies. In Israel, Véolia Water, a branch of Véolia, in a joint venture with the Israeli company IDE Technologies, in 2005 opened one of the largest desalination plants of the world, the ADOM-Ashkelon Desalination Plant, which produces 70% of all the drinking water of the country. Also in Saudi Arabia, Véolia finished in 2015 a super modern desalination plant using "reverse osmosis" techniques.

French companies are also pioneers in the construction of sustainable cities in China. In the next ten years, they will participate in the construction of

The Tracted Air Cushion Vehicle design by Spacetrain is a wheel-less design which glides along the rail.

a clean quarter for 1 million inhabitants within the city of Wuhan, on the Silk Road. France is also involved in a similar project in Chengdu. Among other French companies participating in such projects, the automobile producer Renault is engaged in the production of autonomous electrical vehicles in China.

Public Health and Aging

French cooperation with China on health issues is very old. During Xi Jinping's state visit in France in 2014, the president traveled to Lyons. Besides being a terminal for Chinese freight arriving in France via Duisburg, Lyons is also the city where the headquarters of the Mérieux Institute is located. Today, it is run by Alain Mérieux, the son of Charles Mérieux who was a pupil of the great Louis Pasteur. Alain Mérieux is also the vice-president of the regional council which he convinced to develop partnerships with Shanghai.

In 1965, one year after De Gaulle recognized the People's Republic of China, members of the Mérieux family, married to the auto-producing Berliet family, went to Beijing to present the heavy trucks they were building in Venissieux in the Lyon suburb. As a result, Deng Xiaoping came to Vénissieux ten years later. But the major subject became health. In the 1970s and 1980s, Alain and his father presented their vaccine production plants to China.

The collaboration extended into diagnostics, the fight against infectious diseases, and the definition of common health programs. In parallel, Mérieux created various branches of its laboratories in China, including Mérieux Nutrisciences in Shanghaï (2009), and a high-security lab (NATO level) in Wuhan to study extremely virulent viruses, under construction since 2011.

The Mérieux Foundation, in cooperation since 2007 with the Ministry of Health of China on the prevention and control of infectious diseases, participated in the first international steering committee of the second round of the tuberculosis prevention and control project to improve the diagnosis of drug resistance to tuberculosis. In 2012, Alain Mérieux spent two weeks visiting China and participated in the Second Franco-Chinese Symposium on infectious diseases in Wuhan. Alain Mérieux and Ren Minghui, Director of the International Cooperation Office of the Ministry of Health of China, approved the medical efforts undertaken on behalf of the Uyghur and Zhuang minorities of Xinjiang and Guangxi autonomous regions.

The Pasteur Institute also is playing an important role with a division in Shanghai since 2003 and collaboration with the University of Hong Kong. This collaboration was existential in 2003 when China was hit, first by the severe acute respiratory syndrome (SARS) and then by the "Avian flu" (bird flu). A P4 laboratory has been created in China by France to deal with such highly contagious diseases. French medical specialists are already training their Chinese colleagues to reduce the overuse of antibiotics, a major cause of the development of multi-resistant forms of tuberculosis and syphilis.

China and France both must cope with an increasingly aging population. In 2017, China had already 130 million inhabitants over age 60, i.e., around 10% of total population. That proportion is expected to rise to 25% between now and 2030. In France, the proportion has already reached 20% and will continue to rise. Life expectancy figures are the same in Shanghai as they are in France, so cooperation on the subject is logical.

Already in 2015, an agreement was signed between Marc Mortureux, director general for risk prevention (DGPR), and the Chinese national center for sanitary risks and nutrition surveillance, to train French and Chinese experts in the (different) food analysis methods of both countries.

In matters of organ transplants, China is in the process of adopting the French model of specialized hospitals per region. The fact that a certain number of Chinese officials were trained in France in French hospitals is not unrelated to the enthusiasm for such cooperation. For example, Chen Zhu, minister of health between 2007 and 2013 and since then the Vice President of the Chinese National Assembly, was trained at the Paris Saint Louis hospital. Today, he is pleading for a genomics institute in Shanghai, to be created with the cooperation of the Pasteur Institute.

Financial and Industrial Partnerships

The ideal context for win-win Franco-Chinese cooperation to emerge would be after a radical overhaul of the bankrupt Western financial system. Such a reform would require a return to the "strict" banking policies of the Glass-Steagall era, protecting credit and deposits from the erratic volatility and systemic risks of the global financial speculation now threatening the world with collapse. Such an overhaul would also require, in the West, a return to the type of state credit currently used by China to "direct" its investments toward the physical economy.

However, even before that, France and China can already increase massively their industrial and financial partnerships via win-win Sovereign Fund cooperation, and extend the scope, beyond French and Chinese territory, to "third countries," especially in Africa, where investment needs in infrastructure are huge and investment opportunities are promising. On July 16, 2015, the Prime Ministers of France and China, Manuel Valls and Li Keqiang, signed a declaration in Paris, calling for joint projects in third countries. Also, France, as a founding member of the Asian Infrastructure Investment Bank (AIIB), is in a good position to co-define the projects and areas for such partnerships.

Until today, two wrong attitudes tend to prevail in the EU: either a total rejection of any cooperation, China being considered as an adversary and perhaps even an enemy; or, an "open bar" attitude of countries willing to sell their "family jewels" at discount rates to foreign government institutions. Foreign wealth funds, which are in reality run by foreign governments, are often viewed with suspicion. To break the stalemate and to promote "confidence building," France has undertaken several new initiatives to foster Sovereign Fund partnerships. For example, in 2009, it created in Paris the Long Term Investment Club (LTIC). And in 2011, the Institutional Investors Roundtable (IRR) was set up also in Paris.

Even more important, in 2014 the Caisse des Dépôts et Consignations (CDC), which is the "financial arm" of the French state, the French equivalent of the German Kreditanstalt für Wiederaufbau (KfW), created CDC International Capital (CDC IC). The idea was to create a framework for foreign capital to invest in France through what is called "Counterpart Foreign Wealth Funds." This allows foreign capital, be it, for example, Chinese, Russian, or Norwegian, to invest in sensitive economic sectors without the receiving nation losing control over its "strategic" assets or intellectual property rights. Laurent Vigier, the director of CDC IC, in a May 2017 interview, said the aim is to get people into partnerships, "not via intermediation, but in an equal-to-equal mode of relationship."

CDC IC, whose capital should rapidly be increased above the current 4 billion euros, is tasked to handle all French relationships with foreign wealth funds. In October 2016, CDC IC, together with the Russian Direct Investment Fund and others, saved the high-tech French glass maker Arc International in Northern France.

In respect to China, CDC IC also created in 2013 Cathay Capital, a joint 67 million euro "partner fund," between the French Banque publique d'investissement (BPI) and the China Development Bank (CDB). Cathay Capital is the first independent Franco-Chinese entrepreneurial fund fully registered at the French market authority agency AMF.

Most notable among a long list of financial partnerships to fund Chinese and French companies operating all over the globe, CDC IC worked out in November 2015, an equal-to-equal fund allowing one of the largest existing sovereign wealth funds, the China Investment Corporation (CIC), to invest 1 billion euros in the Greater Paris modernization project. Currently, Paris has 200 km of metro tunnels. With the Greater Paris project, currently one of the largest infrastructure undertakings of the EU, that number will double. "The Chinese have a much more optimistic vision than the French themselves," underscores Vigier.

Industrial Partnerships

The strong Franco-Chinese cooperation in the areas of aerospace (Airbus) and nuclear energy are well documented. On the bilateral level, the partnership signed at the Elysée in 2014 between global carmaker

PSA Peugeot Citroën and Chinese carmaker Dongfeng, was also a win-win benchmark.

To bring new life into PSA, the French state and the Chinese company injected 3 billion euros apiece. As a result, each partner got 12.9% of shares, the same percentage as those in the hands of the Peugeot family who created the company. The French side got the investment and access to the huge Chinese market, while the Chinese side got access to Peugeot's know-how.

Sino-French Third-Countries Investment Fund

On November 14, 2016, during Chinese Prime Minister Li Keqiang's visit to France, CDC IC and the China Investment Fund created the "Sino-French Third-Countries Investment Fund." Each partner contributed 150 million euros, and the intent is to increase its resources via leverage up to 2 billion euros in the coming years. One-third of the investments will be in Africa, one-third in Asia, and the rest elsewhere worldwide. Investment targets include industry, energy, manufacturing, industrial and retail goods, health, logistics, and infrastructure. Earlier, in April 2016, former French Prime Minister Jean-Pierre Raffarin, while attending the Beijing business forum, promoted this "trilateral" approach: "It is important to present our views and to listen to what the Chinese authorities, the French firms, and the Africans have to say," he said. "China has the capital to invest in French-speaking Africa, but having come across some problems in previous investments there, they realize they need the French partnership because they have knowledge of the language and the customs." As a sign of confidence, the fund might be headquartered in Dakar, Senegal.

According to an official of the CDC, "China wished a much more ambitious fund and was ready to put up to 50 billion euros in it, but French public finances didn't allow it." According to the French daily Le Monde, at that time French rogue financier Vincent Bolloré, heavily invested in Africa, blocked those projects, not being particularly enthused at having the Chinese "playing in France's backyard." On the opposite side, however, industrialists such as Jean-Pascal Tricoire, the CEO of Schneider Electric, the giant electricity company, or François Favier of Suez, are fully aware of the vast potentials of Sino-French cooperation in Africa and elsewhere.

THE WESTERWALD-TAUNUS TUNNEL: MAKE GERMAN RAILWAYS FIT FOR THE SILK ROAD

Is German transport infrastructure fit for integration into the New Silk Road transport corridors now emerging throughout Eurasia? The New Silk Road is already there—it is a work in progress, and already integrating the entire Eurasian land mass from Spain and Portugal to Vladivostok and Shanghai. New Silk Road express cargo trains are now coming to German cities such as Duisburg and Hamburg, and through Germany to France and Spain.

But much work is yet to be done. While there are rail connections throughout the growing network, not all are optimized for efficient and high-speed transport of goods. Speeds average a sedate 60 km per hour (37 miles per hour), and there are bottlenecks throughout the transcontinental network: An "express" train from China takes more than two weeks to arrive in many West European cities. Nonetheless, the technology exists to cut that time in half.

This report addresses one of those bottlenecks that lies in Germany and advances a solution to the problem that has been put forward by German engineers and citizens who possess the vision required for the 21st Century.

German engineers and regional citizens' initiatives have proposed a mega-project to facilitate the passage of high-speed cargo trains through the rail corridor along the Rhine Valley between Bonn and Wiesbaden. Dubbed the Westerwald-Taunus Tunnel (WTT), it entails building a 118-km tunnel from Saint Augustine (Sankt Augustin), near Bonn on the east bank of the Rhine, to Hochheim near Wiesbaden, at the junction of the Main and Rhine rivers.

It will be 50 km shorter than the existing 170-km route through the Rhine Valley. Modeled after the newly completed Gotthard Base Tunnel under the Swiss Alps, it will have double tracks passing through each of twin tunnels, allowing cargo trains to travel at speeds up to 160 km per hour (100 miles per hour), possibly unmanned.

The WTT will bypass one of the narrowest and deepest stretches of the Rhine Valley, especially between Bingen and Bonn. While this region is the most picturesque part of the Rhine Valley and has UNESCO World Heritage status, it has perhaps the most antiquated rail infrastructure in Germany. This stretch of railway is more than 150 years old and was designed for trains with an axle weight of 3 tons, not the current 23 tons, which has caused sections of the line to sink.

Yet this is the primary route for cargo trains. No fewer than 400 freight trains pass through the valley every 24 hours. While Deutsche Bahn, the German national rail company, has built a high-speed passenger line through this region, it does not carry cargo trains.

The proposed WTT is a crucial link in the emerging New Silk Road that integrates Eurasia. Moreover, the project could serve as a paradigmatic solution for the dramatic expansion of rail freight throughout Europe.

The head of an S-210 Tunnel Boring Machine used to excavate the Gotthard Base Tunnel under the Swiss Alps, shown after "breakthrough." Four such machines were used. The chisels have already been removed. The diameter is 8.8 meters (29 feet); the length of the machine is 400 meters (1,300 feet).

The Bottleneck of All Bottlenecks

Cargo trains are already traveling from Central China to West European cities, including Lodz, Poland; Duisburg and Hamburg in Germany; Lyon in France; and cities in Spain, Switzerland, and other countries. Most of these trains take one of two routes. One route begins in Chengdu, the capital of Sichuan province in Central China, where it interconnects with the Chinese network.

Traveling west from Chengdu, it goes through Kazakhstan and across Russia, through Moscow to Brest in Belarus, on to Lodz, Poland, and then continues west into Germany. A second route begins at Dalian on the Yellow Sea in northern China, where cargo from South Korea and Japan can be loaded, enters Russia at Zabaikalsk, goes across Siberia to Moscow, and then on to Lodz.

At Lodz, in the center of Poland, the trains enter the Trans-European Transport Network of corridors (**Figure 12**). These corridors were defined more than two decades ago with the aim of developing an efficient intermodal transport network linking Europe's major ports with the interior of the continent.

Now they must also serve to link Europe with the New Silk Road. For example, from Lodz, the Chinese trains can travel south to the Adriatic Sea and the Mediterranean along the Baltic-Adriatic corridor, which runs from the Polish port of Gdansk on the Baltic through Eastern Europe and Vienna to Venice on the Adriatic.

Trains headed into Western Europe travel along the North Sea-Baltic Sea corridor, which connects Tallinn, Estonia on the Baltic with the North Sea ports of Bremen, Amsterdam, Rotterdam, and Antwerp.

This corridor intersects the Rhine-Alpine corridor. In this way, an express cargo train from Chengdu via Poland, terminates at Duisburg, which lies on the latter corridor.

The Rhine-Alpine corridor links the North Sea ports of Amsterdam, Rotterdam, Antwerp, and Zeebrugge with the Italian port of Genoa on the Mediterranean. Entering Germany near Oberhausen, the route heads south up the Rhine Valley to Basel, where it divides. One branch goes through the new Gotthard Base Tunnel and the other through the Lötschberg Base Tunnel (**Figure 13**). These two tunnels under the Alps are new. Both lines continue south into Italy and terminate at Genoa.

Passing through one of the most densely populated regions in Europe and its industrial heartland, the Rhine-Alpine corridor is the most traveled in Western Europe. This same corridor links into all the major east-west corridors of Europe and the North Sea-Mediterranean corridor, which passes through the Channel Tunnel and links Glasgow, Scotland to the French port of Marseille.

The Rhine-Alpine corridor also links into the Atlantic corridor at Mannheim, Germany, where it travels west to Paris, southwest through France, and into Spain, where it branches off to the Portuguese ports of Porto, Aveiro, Lisbon, and Sines and links to

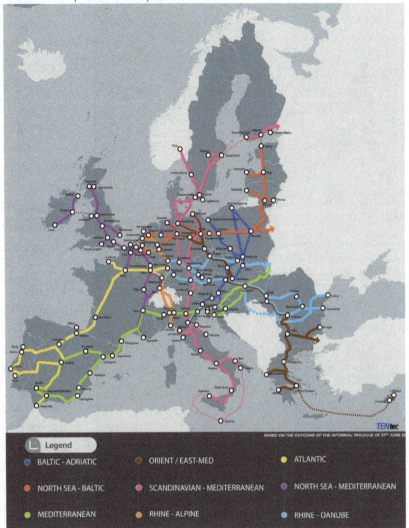

Figure 12
Trans-European Transport Network

Spain's largest port, Algeciras, on the Bay of Gibraltar.

Going east, the Rhine-Alpine corridor links into the North Sea-Baltic corridor, through which trains pass to and from China and Russia. At Frankfurt and Mannheim, the Rhine-Alpine corridor links into the Rhine-Danube rail freight corridor, which reaches the Romanian port of Constanta on the Black Sea.

It also links into the Mediterranean corridor that begins at Seville in the southwest of Spain and runs along the Mediterranean coast of Spain, France, and northern Italy; it continues eastward, passing through Budapest to reach the Ukrainian border. Thus all rail cargo coming from China and heading to points in western Germany, France, Spain, Portugal, Switzerland, and northwestern Italy must pass through this corridor.

Figure 13
The Rhine-Alpine Corridor

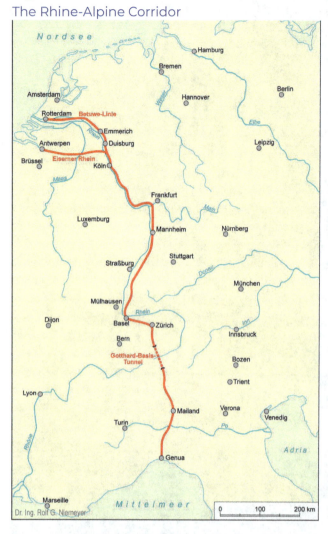

But the corridor is already heavily overburdened by the huge volumes of cargo from the big North Sea ports of Rotterdam and Antwerp, respectively Europe's largest and second largest ports.

The Rhine-Alpine corridor is the very backbone of the European rail freight network, yet its German segment is a serious bottleneck which the German government and Deutsche Bahn have so far refused to adequately address.

The New *Steel* Silk Road

The New Silk Road has to become a new, high-tech steel road employing the most advanced railway technology and operating on a separate, cargo-dedicated rail network capable of carrying cargo trains at speeds above 160 km per hour.

Transcontinental railways are often seen as the alternative to shipment by sea, but while cargo trains carry 120 containers on average, the latest container ships carry up to 18,000. There could never be enough capacity to carry this trade on rails. Nonetheless, railways do compete with ships when shipping to points in the interior of Eurasia, for example, between Germany and points in Central Asia, western China, and western Siberia.

In densely populated regions such as Western and Central Europe, railways must provide an attractive alternative to truck transport to improve efficiency. The railways must also work hand-in-hand with overseas shipping as part of the intermodal transportation system that will efficiently move cargo from Eurasia's peripheral ports to points in the interior.

Reducing current travel times of two weeks or more from Chengdu or Dalian to one week or less at lower costs, also would make railways competitive with air freight, which while faster than rail and sea transport, is also the most expensive. However, the issue is not just transporting goods from China to the European market, but rather developing the huge underdeveloped regions along these transcontinental corridors. Such development requires machinery and technical equipment.

To enable Western European manufacturers to respond to this need, a separate cargo network is required, which will enable the full development of freight-specific technologies, without having to make the compromises involved in using a single network for freight and passenger traffic. For example, on a separate network, freight trains could be run automatically without drivers. And a separate network would increase freight capacity. Eventually, magnetically-levitated train systems will be used for cargo.

To consider the requirements of such a freight-specific network across Eurasia is a task for several reports. Nonetheless, the example of the Rhine-Alpine corridor, and the WTT within it, illuminates several key issues. The creation of cargo-dedicated rail lines has begun in Europe. France and Spain have built cargo-dedicated lines along the Atlantic corridor, and other countries such as Belgium and Hungary are considering doing the same.

The Westerwald-Taunus Tunnel is proposed as an alternative to the present route on the bank of the Rhine River, shown here as it passes Burg Katz. The present rail infrastructure is more than 150 years old and has a limited load-bearing capacity for the 400 freight trains which pass through this section daily.

On the Rhine-Alpine corridor, the Netherlands is the most advanced with its cargo-dedicated Betuweroute, which runs from the port of Rotterdam to the German border at Zevenaar-Emmerich. It was begun in 1997 and opened in 2007. Built at a cost of 4.7 billion euros, the 160-km line includes 18 km of tunnels and has 130 bridges and viaducts totaling 12 km. It is designed to carry trains with an axle weight of 23 tons at a speed of 120 km per hour. Experiments will begin soon to test automatic trains without drivers.

While it carries more than 10% of the cargo volume arriving in Rotterdam, its throughput is being hindered because Germany, despite agreements, has yet to expand transport capacity from the German border at Emmerich, and throughout the rest of the Rhine-Alpine corridor in Germany.

Belgium would also like to build a freight-dedicated line from Antwerp, Europe's second largest port, to Mönchengladbach on the German border along the route of the old Iron Rhine Railway, which was closed down in the 1990s.

From the other end of the corridor, Switzerland has become a heavy lifter in rail projects. With the aim of getting trucks off of the nation's highways, it has constructed two railway tunnels that are among the longest in the world.

While these are dual use—freight and passenger trains—they have increased the efficiency of the system dramatically. The first is the Lötschberg Base Tunnel through the Bernese Alps, built below the old mountain tunnel. The 35-km tunnel has two single-track tubes. While one tube is finished and has been in operation since 2007, the second tube has not been fully completed because funds had to be transferred to the second huge tunnel project, the Gotthard Base Tunnel under the St. Gotthard Pass.

The Gotthard Base Tunnel, after 20 years of construction and the excavation of 28 million tons of rock, was officially opened in June 2016; regularly scheduled service commenced in December of that year. At 57 km (35.4 miles), it is the longest and deepest rail tunnel in the world and an inspiration for infrastructure planners throughout the globe.

Where the Vision Ends

This visionary approach ends at the German border. Under the "schwarze null" (black zero) budget policy of German Finance Minister Wolfgang Schäuble, "vision" has been banned from policy making. After almost a decade of pressure from Dutch interests in the Rhine-Alpine corridor, Germany has finally relented, but has taken the cheapest and least desirable option. Rather than building a dedicated, double-track freight line along the entire length of the corridor, it has only committed itself to building a third track along the existing passenger line that will go from Emmerich to Oberhausen, a distance of 73 km. While the third track will be dedicated to freight, it will not permit high speed and will not solve the problem along the Rhine Valley. Work is to begin this year and is scheduled to be finished in 2025, at the cost of 1.5 billion euros. But don't hold your breath.

Germany took a similar approach in the Upper Rhine Valley for the Mannheim-Karlsruhe-Basel line, where the plan has been to simply upgrade the line and lay two more parallel tracks along certain sections to support high-speed trains. Begun in the 1980s, it was expected to be finished by 2008, but still remains unfinished with no date set for completion, although the German government "hopes" it could be completed by 2030.

And this stretch of the Rhine Valley does not present great topographical challenges, because the valley is broad and relatively flat. One of its primary functions is to serve as the approach from Germany to the new Gotthard Base Tunnel. Although this is one of the most important sections of the Rhine-Alpine corridor, the upgrade is primarily for passenger trains.

Build the WTT, Establish a New Paradigm

By implementing the principle that the future of rail cargo operations must entail the establishment of an entirely new, independent rail freight network, the WTT could be the game changer that launches a new paradigm for rail transportation in Germany and the new Steel Silk Road.

Further details on the WTT project, inspired by the Gotthard Base Tunnel and drafted by D. Eng. Rolf G. Niemeyer, is available on the website www.wester-wald-taunus-tunnel.de/ It indicates that all of the technology and engineering know-how required for the project has been proven and is readily available.

The tunnel will traverse a straight line beginning at the town of St. Augustine, east of Bonn and not far from the two railway marshalling yards at Cologne. It will terminate at Hochheim near Wiesbaden, where it can connect with the rail line leading to the nearby Mainz-Bischofsheim marshalling yard. From there, various rail lines go south along the Rhine-Alpine corridor, and there are also connections to lines going east and west. The route will be 50 km shorter than the old 150-km Rhine Valley route (**Figure 14**).

An alternative is to have the line terminate near Wiesbaden-Schierstein on the other side of Wiesbaden, where it could link with the line to Mainz-Bischofsheim from further down the Rhine. The former configuration would be 118 km long and the latter, 107 km.

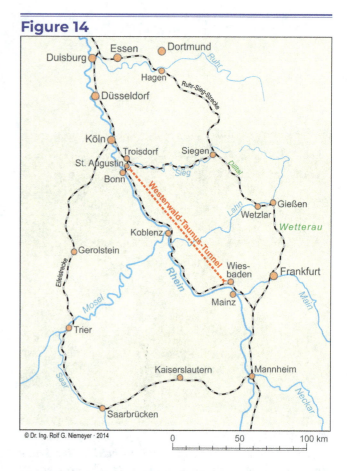

Figure 14

The tunnel must cut through the Rhenish Massif (Rheinisches Schiefergebirge), the geological formation that includes the Westerwald and Taunus ranges, and will use the Gotthard Base Tunnel configuration—two tracks passing through each of two parallel tunnels, with connecting tunnels between the two for emergencies and maintenance operations.

The tunnel will be in two segments, one under the Westerwald and the other under the Taunus range. Eight boring machines similar to the ones used on the Gotthard Base Tunnel could operate simultaneously, working from both directions on each parallel pair of tunnels in each segment. Assuming a construction cost of 45 million euros per kilometer (2012 estimate), the tunnel alone will cost an estimated 5.3 billion euros. Adding the rail lines, technical equipment, and signaling system, the estimated total cost is 10 billion euros.

The current traffic through the Rhine Valley is 400 freight trains per day, and the tunnel will enable a large increase. Modern signaling technology is so good that it will permit more trains per day (720 per track, 1,440 per day) than is practically feasible given other constraints. The projected cost of the WTT compares with the 177-km Cologne-Frankfurt high-speed rail line, begun in 1995 and finished in 2002, which parallels Germany's A3 Autobahn and costs 6 billion euros.

Too expensive? The promoters compare the cost to the "rescue" of German banks, pointing out that the rescue of WestLB, the German Landesbank, cost taxpayers 18 billion euros, while the rescue of IKB Deutsche Industriebank, HRE-Hypo-Real East, and others cost a total of 74 billion euros. They might have added the European bank bailout that was camouflaged as the Greek bailout, which cost more than 250 billion euros.

Using tunnels for a rail freight network would be very attractive along other sections of the corridor that pass through high-density population centers, both for safety and to permit high speed. It is about time that a few railway tunnels were built to improve a rail network that is, in part, more than 150 years old.

THE FUTURE FOR CENTRAL AND EASTERN EUROPE: THE DANUBE-ODER-ELBE WATERWAY

One of the projects which could prove to be of decisive significance for the further economic and political development of Central and Eastern Europe is the Danube-Oder-Elbe (DOE) link, a river and canal system which would enable direct shipping traffic between the Danube, Oder, and Elbe rivers.

A general plan for this project was created in 1990-1991 by the Ecotrans Moravia (EM) firm, and was published as a study under the title: "The Danube-Oder-Elbe Waterway - Yes or No?" (further referred to in what follows as the DOE Study). The plan at the time was to complete the overall project by 2018 in several stages, and thus lay the basis for a rapid modernization and development of industries in the Czech and Slovak Republics, intending that 30 integrated port and industrial zones would be created or developed on the Elbe, Moldau, Oder, Morava, and Danube, as spearpoints of this development in the overall context of the project. But the Czech Republic itself lacked the means and the hoped for support from the EU did not materialize.

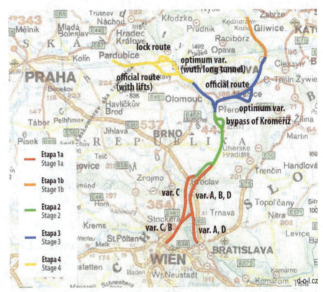

A schematic of the DOE corridor, with stages and variants.

After 25 years of attempts by the Czech government to realize this project, at all levels of the EU, which nonetheless scarcely moved it a single step forward—only feasibility studies for the Czech parts of the project were produced—now with the recent visit of Chinese President Xi Jinping, an agreement for a feasibility study of the Danube-Oder-Elbe Canal has been signed between Sino Hydro Corp and DOE Europe SE.

Naturally the project will be driven primarily by the participating governments of the Czech and Slovak Republics, to improve economic conditions in these two countries. But the project will also unfold wide-ranging effects beyond the borders of these nations, and therefore the canal should have been integrated from the beginning into the Trans-European Transport Network of the EU.

From the Chinese point of view the project today is part of the BRI; it is a component of the efforts to improve and shorten the lines of communication and connection from the Mediterranean Sea to Northern Europe. In this framework, China is also supporting the creation of the Danube-Morava-Axios-Aegean Waterway to the Greek port of Thessaloniki, and the development of rail routes from the Greek port of Piraeus to Belgrade—on the route from Piraeus to Thessaloniki, Chinese locomotives are to make possible speeds of up to 250 km/h (150 mph)—and from there on to Bucharest. Chinese firms have already finished building a new Danube River bridge in Belgrade.

A Long History

A look at the history of the DOE project will help make it possible to appreciate the wide-reaching impact of the Danube-Oder-Elbe project.

Already in the 14th Century, Kaiser Karl IV had the vision of a navigable connection between the Oder and Danube rivers. Connecting the Danube, Oder, and Elbe by navigable canals was first conceived of in the 18th Century, and prepared as Lothar Vogemont's detailed plans for the construction of a navigable canal, which were taken up again at the beginning of this century.

In the 18th Century the ulterior motive was to deepen, through this project, the economic interdependencies within the Hapsburg monarchy, and thereby to counter centrifugal nationalist forces. In this incarnation, the current DOE was only the northern branch of an overall project whose southern branch would have traversed Hungary, Croatia, and Slovenia, connected the Danube with the Adriatic, and thus also connected the various peoples living in this region with Vienna.

Construction began in some locations near Vienna, but the First World War and subsequent division of the Habsburg Empire prevented continuation of the work. Later, a better transport connection of Czechoslovakia to the West was not in the interest of the Communist government, and especially not in the interest of the final decision makers of the government in Moscow.

The latter was set, above all, on a close meshing of Czech and Slovak industrial production with the Soviet Union, and such a connection would not have been made by the waterway, so only the railroad connections were built. The fact that it was certainly desired to send Soviet ships into the satellite nations but that the Soviet Union was not prepared for the converse, admitting ships from these nations into Soviet territory, also played a role. Thus the proportion of ship traffic in the total transport volume inside the COMECON was 7.7%, while in Western and Central Europe it was 35%.

Only at the end of the 1960s were the plans for the DOE link again taken up and revised, but only small parts of it realized—primarily where the need for river basin management made necessary the building of barrages and locks. In contrast to the old plans, which envisaged operating ship traffic via side canals, and thus essentially not impacting the flow of the river, the Communist plans were based on a complete canalization of the rivers involved, i.e., on the erection of chains of barrages, which guaranteed a sufficient water depth to shipping.

The plans presented by Ecotrans Moravia provided for linking together the already navigable stretches of the rivers by side canals, to preserve the ecologically valuable meanders of, above all, the Morava River. Here one is building on the experience of the construction of the Main-Danube Canal.

International Waterway

But revision of the plans was also made necessary by the increased demands of ship dimensions since the 1960s. It is now intended that ships with a draft of up to 2.8 m will be able to use the waterway—and a later redevelopment to 3.5 m is under consideration. The locks will be 190 m long and 12 m wide. Thus the DOE will meet all the requirements for use as an international waterway: Ships of 2,500 metric tons and pusher units of 2,950 metric tons barge loading will be able to travel on it.

Table 2 shows that the distances for inland ship travel between southeast Europe and northern Ger-

Table 2

Comparison of Distances and Numbers of Locks on the Alternative Routes via the Rhine-Main-Danube, the Danube-Elbe, and the Danube-Oder Waterways

Route from Vienna to: via:	ROTTERDAM	BREMEN	HAMBURG	SZCZECIN (Poland)
RHINE-MAIN-DANUBE	1,662 km/100% 65/0	1,784 km/100% 86/0	1,910 km/100% 82/0	2,132 km/100% 89/0
DANUBE-ELBE	1,631 km/98% 53/-12	1,293 km/72% 74/-12	1,153 km/60% 68/-14	1,193 km/56% 73/-16
DANUBE-ODER	1,795 km/108% 66/+1	1,475 km/81% 85/-1	1,317 km/69% 79/-3	989 km/46% 69/-20

** *The top line in each row gives the kilometer distance in each case; first the absolute distance, then in percentage of the route length as it is currently. The bottom line gives the number of locks and the change relative to the current route.*

many will be distinctly reduced by the DOE from what they are currently (on routes via the Main-Danube Canal). Thus, for example, the Vienna-Hamburg trip would be reduced by 40%, the link to the Baltic Sea via the Danube-Oder Canal by 54%.

Comparing the route parameters, one sees that the individual partial sections of the DOE are comparable with those of the Main-Danube Canal (**Table 3**), but some have clearly more favorable relationships; e.g., the individual route sections are distinctly longer on average. The two ship lifts in the course of the canal between the Morava and the Elbe, which each have a greater height differential of more than 100 m, make possible a relatively low number of locks, so that the transport times remain very low despite a relatively greater height differential.

Above all, the connections from the Balkans region to the North and Baltic Seas are shortened, even compared to the Main-Danube Canal on the Vienna-Rotterdam stretch (Table 2). But the advantage of the DOE over the Main-Danube Canal lies not in the shorter route length alone. Because the two peak points of the DOE are not as high as the peak points of the Main-Danube Canal, ships do not need to be lifted as far.

Ship lifts are planned at Pecikov and at Zalsi, conditioned by the topography, which will hoist ships up 100 m and 109.5 m, respectively. The greatest lock height is 30 m. Thereby fewer locks are necessary, the average length of the individual canal section is greater, by about 7 km compared to the Main-Danube Canal (Table 3). Thereby the traffic will need distinctly shorter trip times.

In case of blockages of ship traffic by repairs to lock equipment or due to damage, the two routes can be used alternatively. This does not mean, however, that the profitability of the Main-Danube Canal will drop due to this "competition"; quite the contrary. The two canals open up different regions; they will

Table 3

Comparison of Route Parameters of the Main-Danube Canal with Those of the DOE Partial Sections

Section	Main-Danube	Morava	Morava-Oder	Morava-Elbe
Length	171 km	172 km	161.1 km	149.8 km
Height Differential	243 m	124 m	171 m	394.2 m
Highest Point	405 m	224 m	275 m	395 m
Locks	16	11	12	8
Average Queue Length	10.6 km	17.2 km	13.4 km	18.7 km
Average Stage Height	15.2 m	12.4 m	14.25 m	43.6 m

Figure 15

With a connecting waterway from the Danube at Vienna to the Elbe and Oder rivers, a productive inland shipping route will arise on the eastern leg of the "Paris-Berlin-Vienna Productive Triangle."

function as mutual feeders. The through traffic, bringing goods from the Balkans to Rotterdam (or the reverse) plays only a quite subordinate role compared to the terminating traffic, which is heading for terminals on short sections of the waterway or linking them together. Because many routes for inland ship traffic will then become shorter than they are today, in these cases it will be more cost-effective to transport goods by ship than by other transport means.

For inland ship traffic—and, as later discussed, for the railroads—the DOE will create a shorter connection between the metropolitan areas of Vienna, Prague, Dresden, and Berlin. It forms the eastern axis of the "Paris-Berlin-Vienna Productive Triangle" (**Figure 15**). The Prerov-Ostrava stretch connects industrial Upper Silesia, the most important industrial region of Poland, with the eastern part of this Triangle.

Island Position

For the industrial areas of the Czech Republic and Slovakia the DOE means, primarily, connection to the international waterway network. Up to now these regions have occupied a kind of island position; the Elbe and the Moldau are very well developed from Usti up to Prague and Kolin, and permit traffic year-round with drafts up to 2.2 m. But there the Elbe, on the German stretch between the Czech-German border and Magdeburg, has only low water flow regulation; cross-border through traffic is often largely—and shipping operation entirely—impossible for periods of two months.

As long as this situation is not remedied on the German side, the Czech side is forced to conduct their transport by other means for a large part of the route. And as long as the polemics of the self-proclaimed "environmental guardians" are more respected on the German side than the actual facts, and as long as austerity is more valued in the Finance Ministry than economic viability, it will remain unremedied. Thus a basic improvement of the Elbe is not envisaged in the Federal Transport Routes Plan.

Therefore in Phase 1 of the project the connection along the Morava to the Danube will be made in the Czech Republic, as is now ongoing with Chinese support. The Slovakian government supports the project; Austria appears to be holding back up to now, apparently on environmental protection grounds.

Of all the great European rivers, only the Oder is more poorly developed today than the Elbe. Poland is interested in deepening the Oder from Szczecin to Breslau, to make it accessible to larger ships; the connection to the Danube-Oder-Elbe Canal would then be made via the Gliwice Canal. But even here there is still much to be done—not least, because here Germany, as the riparian state of the Oder, must also come on board. Thus for the foreseeable future, the Danube is the only internationally significant river touching Czech economic space and normally offering adequate operating conditions for inland shipping.

One could argue that in light of this situation the DOE is not a reasonable project, because it could be expected to tie only one of its three ends to the European waterway network. The planners of the DOE see this precisely the other way around, however. They argue that just because the development of the Elbe and Oder is stalled, connecting the Elbe to the Danube via the DOE is the only opportunity for their countries to enlarge the use of inland shipping on their own, and thereby to overcome the island position with regard to river transport.

At the same time, realization of the DOE ups the pressure on the German and Polish governments to get to work on their side of the Elbe and Oder, which in turn would further augment the benefits of the DOE.

The DOE as Development Corridor

As shown in the "Berlin-Paris-Vienna Productive Triangle" study, the benefits of infrastructure projects increase if they are combined in development corridors. The planners of the DOE have come to the conclusion that much cost could be saved if, from the outset, the building of a canal were conceived

Figure 16

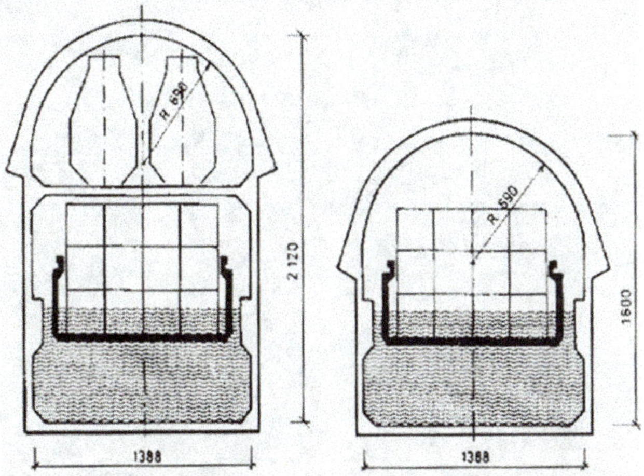

Construction plan of a tunnel which can be used in common by ships and a railroad.

of simultaneous with building a Prague-Bratislava (Pressburg) high-speed rail connection immediately parallel to the canal, which is necessary in any case. In that way, undergrade crossings or bridge construction would not have to be done twice.

Tunnel construction is even planned in such a way that trains and ships can travel in one tunnel (**Figure 16**). The large curvature radii necessary for high-speed trains is also advantageous for inland ship traffic.

But lower construction costs are not the only argument for proceeding in this way. Along with the shipping route, a corridor will arise in which it will be much easier to settle industries, because the transport costs drop for raw materials in particular. Combining the canal with a high-speed rail line strengthens the impact of the waterway as a motor of economic development, because then express freight and passengers can travel as well.

Industrial Development Along the Canal

The DOE project is a good example of how to develop an industrial corridor. Along the waterway there are 30 industrial port zones planned in connection with the building of the canal (**Figure 17**). The model for these industrial and trans-shipment hubs is the port of Nuremberg, built at the beginning of the 1970s as a "greenfield site," and where today 8,300 people are employed in 260 businesses on 833 acres.

Figure 17

Plans for industrial and infrastructural development in the region along the Danube-Oder-Elbe waterway.

Some of these 30 industrial zones are already growing, and in total should give work to more than 30,000 people. The canal itself will employ about 5,600. Some 7,400 workers are needed for the construction, and another 37,000 supply jobs will appear.

One particular aspect which will come into effect with the realization of the DOE, but is not further mentioned in the study, is the fact that the construction process also will lead to the modernization of the supply industries. The higher productivity of the modernized industries enlarges purchasing power in the country, while simultaneously the better traffic conditions lead to a reduction of costs.

The project now appears, finally, to be underway with the help of China.

Notes:

1. *The Danube-Oder-Elbe Waterway – yes or no?*, Ecotrans Moravia, Prague, 1991.

2. *Das Produktive Dreieck Paris-Berlin-Wien. Lokomotive der Weltwirtschaft [The Paris-Berlin-Vienna Productive Triangle. Locomotive of the World Economy]*, EIRNA, Wiesbaden, 1990.

3. *Hamilton's Nationalbank Heute [Hamilton's National Bank Today]*, EIRNA, Wiesbaden, 1992.

THE NEW SILK ROAD AND THE ROLE OF 16+1 IN CREATING A NEW ECONOMIC MIRACLE FOR EUROPE

In addressing more than 1,000 entrepreneurs from 16 Central and Eastern European Countries (CEEC) and China at the Economic and Trade Forum before the annual 16+1 CEEC Leaders summit in Budapest in November 2017, Hungarian Prime Minister Victor Orban said: "If Europe shuts itself in, it loses the possibility of growth. We 16 have always been open and would always like to remain so. We always saw cooperation with China as a great opportunity." Orban added: "European resources are in themselves insufficient. For this reason we welcome the fact that as part of the new economic world order, China sees this region as one in whose progress and development it wants to be present." Hungary understands President Xi Jinping's Bel and Road Initiative (BRI), he said, as a "new form of globalization, which does not divide the world into teachers and students, but is based on common respect and common advantages."

Chinese Prime Minister Li Keqiang in his speech presented an ambitious program for increased China-CEEC cooperation by "docking" the BRI with the development strategies of the CEEC, in the words of Xinhua. "Our aim is to see a prospering Europe," he said, adding that the closer ties with the 16 countries, which includes 11 EU members, will "usefully comple-

EUROPE

Figure 18
Intermodal Transport Corridors Across the CEE Countries Linking Europe with the Belt and Road

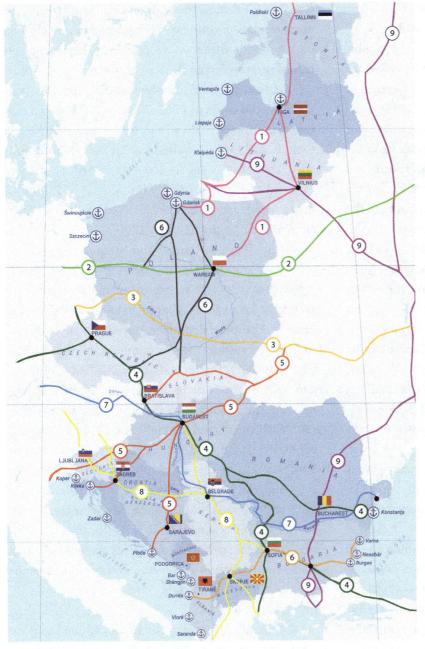

their place in this volume and expand their presence on the huge Chinese market."

Prime Minister Li said that the Budapest summit—the fifth anniversary of 16+1 Leaders' conferences—provided the basis to review achievements and draw a new blueprint for the future. Besides calling for accelerating key connectivity projects such as the Hungary-Serbia high-speed railway, Li proposed expansion of production capacity building, through the joint building of "economic and trade cooperation zones and creating an industrial chain, value chain, and logistics chain featuring closer integration, stronger drive, and wider benefit." He also called for the promotion of cooperation between small and medium-sized enterprises (SMEs), a subject extremely important for all CEE nations, which urgently want to develop their own high-technology industry Mittelstand and other productive facilities.

Indeed, China's Silk Road strategy has opened a new perspective for the nations of Central, Eastern, and Southeastern Europe, to contribute to the establishment of a productive future of all of Europe and Eurasia. The 16 CEE Countries are a crucial bridge, due to their geographical location, for making the infrastructural and economic development of Eurasia through the New Silk Road/BRI

ment" EU-China relations. He pointed out, that the 19th Party Congress developed new guidelines and perspectives for a more open and prosperous China, thus opening more and greater opportunities to all countries in the world. The Prime Minister estimated China's imports over the next five years should total $8 trillion, as it has moved from a phase of high-speed growth to high-quality growth, which "will surely create opportunities for all countries in the world…. We hope the Central and Eastern European countries find

infrastructure projects work, spanning Europe from north to south, between the huge Russian market and Western Europe (see **Figure 18**). The New Silk Road is not only generating an entire new Eurasian network of cross-continent infrastructure and trade ties, but also opening the opportunity for CEE Countries to re-industrialize their national economies and fulfill their productive potential, in agriculture, machine-building, high-technology, and research (e.g., in the nuclear sector).

This prospect was presented by the Schiller Institute after the fall of the Berlin Wall in 1989, in its programs for the "Productive Triangle Paris-Berlin-Vienna" and the "Eurasian Land-Bridge" to many conferences in Eastern Europe and the Balkans (e.g., in Poland, Hungary, Slovakia, the Czech Republic, Croatia, Bosnia, and Serbia). The program called for productive state credit on the model of Germany's postwar Kreditanstalt für Wiederaufbau (KfW) and Alexander Hamilton's National Bank principle. This would finance the construction of European and Eurasian infrastructure corridors, with high-speed connections (such as a Transrapid link from Berlin via Warsaw to Moscow and a maglev network among the main cities of Western and Eastern Europe), the upgrading and new construction of waterways, and the use of the most modern energy technologies (such as the safe high-temperature reactor and the development of nuclear fusion power), with the goal of a dramatic increase in productivity. The Schiller Institute also proposed a comprehensive "Marshall Plan" for the Balkans (the natural bridge to the Middle East, Asia, and Africa), with reconstruction and infrastructure in the context of the Eurasian Land-Bridge. This policy was designed to create long-term peace through economic development.

Instead, during the International Monetary Fund (IMF)-led monetarist "shock therapy" in the early and late 1990s after the fall of Communism in Eastern Europe and Russia, a huge wave of privatizations and deregulation was pushed through, leading to the impoverishment of many of these nations and the closing down of industrial facilities. The geopolitically-instigated wars in the Balkans after 1990 created devastation, with economic reconstruction prevented by dictate of IMF, World Bank, and EU institutions.

While European transport corridors were defined already by the 1994 European Transport Ministers Crete conference, these projects did not get off the ground or only to an insignificant degree. Only with the EU expansion incorporating Eastern countries after 2004, did things slowly start to move. But still today, the Trans-European Transport Network can be best described as patchwork, with current EU funding not providing for an integrated, high-priority approach.

Even if countries such as Hungary, Poland, and the Czech Republic for the past few years have profited from EU funding for their national infrastructure plans, the EU uses those financial commitments to pressure nations into political submission on various issues, under threat of stopping already-agreed-on infrastructure financing.

Another shock hit the region with the effects of the financial crisis of 2007-2008, which led to a further diminishing of already scarce EU investments. By then, it had become quite clear to many CEE Countries, that they could no longer rely just on meager EU funds nor just on private investment by European firms, which had opened production facilities in Eastern European countries after 1990.

While Western Europe and Brussels clung to the old financial globalization policies of the past, imposing vicious austerity measures on member states to save a bankrupt trans-Atlantic banking system, many Eastern European countries looked for other opportunities to restart their economies. In this period, China initiated the format 16+1 with CEE Countries and held its first official meeting in Warsaw, Poland in 2012. The 16 nations include the Baltic states (Estonia*, Lithuania*, and Latvia*), the Central European countries (Poland*, Czech Republic*, Slovakia*, and Hungary*), and the countries of Southeastern Europe and the Balkans (Albania, Bosnia-Herzegovina, Bulgaria*, Croatia*, Macedonia, Montenegro, Serbia, Slovenia*, and Romania*). It is significant for China, which also has special historical ties to some of the nations, that eleven of these very diverse countries are EU members(*), and thus provide access to the EU internal market.

Cooperation between the 16 and China since has intensified and expanded to various degrees, in the areas of investment, transport, finance, science, education, and culture, with a huge future potential.

Transnational and Eurasian transport and logistics are defined as a key feature of CEEC-China cooperation: In May 2016 the 16+1 Secretariat for Logistical Cooperation was inaugurated in Riga, Latvia, during the first China-CEEC Transport Ministers meeting, preceding the Riga conference of Leaders in November 2016. The "Riga Declaration" supported cooperation of the ports on the Adriatic, Baltic, and

Black Seas and along the inland waterways ("Adriatic-Baltic-Black Sea Seaport Cooperation").

Next, in Warsaw, the Secretariat for Maritime Cooperation was opened in October 2017, during the second meeting of 16+1 Transport Ministers. Discussions focussed on the huge cooperation potential of Adriatic, Baltic, and Black Sea ports and the long overdue development of inland waterways in CEECs in order to enhance overall multimodal connectivity in Central and Eastern European nations as a crucial gateway for China-Europe infrastructure and economic cooperation.

In terms of new credit mechanisms for projects, at the most recent 16+1 Leaders summit in Budapest, Hungary, in November 2017, the China-CEEC Interbank Association was inaugurated, for which the China Development Bank will provide $2.4 billion. Prime Minister Li Keqiang announced at the summit, that China also will provide another $1 billion for the second phase of capitalization of the China-CEEC Investment Cooperation Fund, most of which is to be channeled to CEE Countries' projects. The fund plans to invest 10 billion euros in the CEEC region, a crucial source of credit for real economic development. Also, by now, Poland and Hungary are full members of the AIIB, while Romania was accepted as a prospective member in May 2017.

Once the EU's geopolitical maneuvering against China (and Russia) can be overcome, there is no limit in unleashing the full productive potential of this region, for Europe and beyond. Existing instruments such as the EU-China "Connectivity platform" could be immediately used to synchronize and expand transport infrastructure grids in all of Europe, which is becoming very necessary in any case, given the growing rail transport connections between China and Western Europe.

Central, Eastern, and Southeastern European nations thus finally should be able to concentrate on real development of their nations, instead of being misused as a geostrategic "cordon sanitaire" or military staging area against Russia. China's initiative for the New Silk Road has created, along with the opportunities to cooperate with the Eurasian Economic Union, a long-term peace strategy for Eurasia and beyond. This second chance after 1989, cannot be missed.

Baltic Countries

Exports of the Baltic countries to China are mostly timber, furniture, machinery, electronics, and mineral products. While the economies of the three Baltic states are small, they are in an ideal position in terms of transport and infrastructure for the Silk Road and Northern Europe, including for sea and rail traffic. In May 2016, Latvia established the China-CEEC 16+1 Logistics Secretariat in the harbor city of Riga and hosted the first China-CEEC 16+1 Transport Ministers meeting.

In November 2016, the Fifth Leaders Meeting of 16+1 took place in Latvia's capital, Riga. The Riga Guidelines, which were issued there, focussed on the importance of transport and logistics. At the summit, two Baltic countries, Latvia and Lithuania, and Bulgaria and Croatia signed a memorandum of understanding (MOU) on "Port and Harbor Industrial Park Cooperation."

Latvia was the first Baltic country to sign an MOU on linking with the BRI during the visit of Chinese Prime Minister Li Keqiang in 2016, and five agreements were signed bilaterally on SMEs, transportation, and logistics. Latvian ports in 2016 handled almost 20% of all cargo volume in the Baltic Sea, while Latvian railways are the fifth largest railway service provider in the EU. The transport and logistics sectors contribute about 10% of Latvia's GDP. China is Latvia's second largest trade partner outside the EU after Russia and the main trade partner in the Far East.

Also, during the 2016 Riga 16+1 summit, the first trans-Eurasia container train between China and Latvia arrived in Riga from Yiwu, after a journey of more than 11,000 km on the China-Russia-Latvia route, in a record time of four months after the Letter of Intent was signed between SJSC Latvia Railway Group and China Railway on the establishment of container train traffic.

Latvian Rail, a state-owned rail infrastructure group of companies, and China Merchants China-Belarus Commercial and Logistics Cooperation also signed an MOU on cooperation and development of marine and rail transport, especially with regard to the Chinese-Belarus Industrial Park "Great Stone" and development of traffic between China and Scandinavia.

There are more projects in the pipeline, which will place the Baltic countries in an extremely advantageous situation, starting with the $3 billion "Arctic Ocean Railway," a project from the Kirkenes harbor in Norway to Rovaniemi (Finland), which would open the northeastern passage along the Siberian coast for goods from China and through the Finnish rail network to the Baltic states, Poland, and the entire infrastructure network developed by the CEEC+1 nations. This includes the plan to build an undersea tunnel between Helsinki, Finland and Tallinn, Estonia (Fin-Est Link) by 2050 and link it with the Rail Baltica project from Estonia to Poland. Rail Baltica is an EU Trans-European Transport Networks (TEN-T) project about to start construction in 2019 on the main 500 km section from Kaunas to Tallinn. The tunnel will create a region of one and one-half million people out of the two capital cities Helsinki and Tallinn. Potentially these two capitals could link up with St. Petersburg in Russia with its 5.3 million inhabitants to form the biggest city region in Northern Europe around the Finnish Bay (see **Figure 19**).

These two projects would be integrated with the planned 3.6 billion euro Rail Baltica high-speed rail line (from Tallinn to Poland) and link into Western Europe's rail networks, enabling a direct link from Helsinki to Berlin and beyond. A Rail Baltica Global Forum took place in April 2018 in Tallinn, Estonia.

Chinese President Xi Jinping met in Beijing on January 10, 2018 with parliamentary leaders of the three Baltic nations (Estonia, Latvia, and Lithuania) and the Nordic countries (Finland, Norway, Iceland, and Sweden), to discuss more high-level exchanges and deeper cooperation in the context of the BRI in order to facilitate improved interconnectedness between Asia and Europe.

Poland

During his second trip to Europe, in June 2016, Chinese President Xi Jinping paid a state visit to Poland, which is a key transit country for rail freight from Asia to Europe, and major international transport routes cross there from east to west, to Northern Europe as well as potential routes from the Baltic Sea toward the Adriatic.

Figure 19
Arctic Ocean Railway and Connections

Polish President Andrzej Duda and President Xi agreed on upgrading relations to a "comprehensive strategic partnership." China and Poland are one another's main trading partner in their respective regions, and their bilateral trade in 2015 reached $17 billion.

The two presidents signed 40 agreements and MOUs during the visit, especially in the areas of construction, raw materials, energy, finance, and science. President Duda said he hoped that Poland, with its port at Gdansk and its major freight terminals for rail traffic, will become China's "gateway to Europe."

This perspective has developed quite well: As of 2017-2018, the Polish capital, Warsaw, is now host to three 16+1 offices for coordination of regional cooperation with China—the contact mechanism of the Investment Promoting Agency, the 16+1 Business Council, and the Secretariat of Maritime Issues.

On October 25, 2017, the Second Meeting of 16+1 Transport Ministers and the 16+1 Business Forum were held in Warsaw, with attendance by the AIIB. At this occasion, Polish Prime Minister Beata Szydlo stressed the mutual benefit for all participating countries and citizens in the development of seaports and coastal areas, as well as the waterways of the entire region. Poland wants to develop its overall road, railway, air, maritime, and inland waterway transport, she said.

The Polish government has also decided to build a central port in Gdansk, with deep-water terminals that allow for servicing the largest ships proceeding to the Baltic Sea. At the 2017 Transport Ministers meeting, the Vice President for COSCO Shipping Europe, Wang Songwen, called the Port of Gdańsk, "China's future gateway toward Central and Eastern Europe." The reloading of goods at this harbor, according to him, has increased to such extent that capacity expansion and support is needed from a highly specialized railway or road transport network. Other Polish ports, including Szezecin, Swinoujscie, and Gdynia, also are experiencing new records in overall handling of imported and exported goods.

Poland also plans to restore the navigability of the Vistula and Odra (Oder) rivers and to include Polish rivers in the international waterway system. Poland is very interested in the connection of the Danube-Oder-Elbe Canal to the Oder River and an upgrade of the Oder as a waterway. Thus, a continuous connection would come into being from the Baltic port of Szczecin via the Oder and the canal to the Danube and thereby to Central and Southeastern Europe, leading to the Black Sea. (Unfortunately, Germany, the other riparian state along the Oder, wants to designate this as a conservation area and rejects an upgrade. If Germany shows no willingness to cooperate, Poland could build a lateral canal along the Oder.)

In rail transport, the number of Chinese trains entering the territory of Poland amounts by now to several hundred per year, with Poland cooperating with Belarus, Germany, Kazakhstan, China, Mongolia, and Russia in providing container freight services between China and Europe, among the routes the Chengdu-Europe Express Railway from Sichuan via the Polish city of Lodz, since April 2016, with connections to Kutno, Poland. The Polish government intends to allocate 16 billion euros for development and modernization of its rail network.

Also, an integral part of the rail modernization strategy will be the Central Communication Port Solidarity (CPK) in Baronow, central Poland (between Warsaw and Lodz), a multimodal transport hub, including a new large airport, which will be linked directly with air cargo carriers, and to a good railway connection with the main line network, including international corridors. The CPK will be able to handle loads arriving from Asia, particularly China, and will thus serve as a vital distribution center for Central, Eastern, and Southeastern Europe, providing unique synergies between cargo and rail. Total projected costs amount to about 8.3 billion euros, for which Poland needs strategic investors.

Poland also has a great scientific tradition, to which President Xi referred to in an article in the Polish newspaper *Rzeczpospolita* before his 2016 state visit, citing the scientists Copernicus and Marie Curie, as well as the composer Frederic Chopin, as individuals who had made great contributions to the progress of humanity, and are well known and respected in China.

President Xi also pointed out that Poland was situated along both the ancient Silk Road and the old Amber Road ("Gold of the North"), which led from the Baltic states in the north via Poland to Venice in the south. The Chinese President ended his article with the comment: "China and Europe need to follow the trend of the times, toward peace, development, and win-win cooperation. We should deepen our strategic cooperation, expand communication and coordination in international affairs, and build a new type of international relations with win-win cooperation and a shared future community for all mankind."

Czech Republic

The Czech Republic is very interested in becoming a leading transport and logistics hub for China and Central and Eastern European countries. A 16+1 forum on aviation is planned for 2018 in Prague. Direct flight connections to Beijing, Shanghai, and Chengdou have greatly enhanced economic exchange and tourism, and direct connections to two more destinations will be added in 2018.

At the 16+1 Leaders Meeting in Budapest, Hungary in November 2017, Czech Prime Minister Bohuslav Sobotka reported that export of Czech goods to China grew year-on-year by 29%.

Chinese President Xi Jinping chose the Czech Republic for his first state visit to a CEE nation, when he came to Prague in March 2016. Czech President Milos Zeman and President Xi signed an agreement on strategic partnership, which underscored the importance of the Czech Republic as an "entry point" for China's One Belt, One Road Silk Road plan into the Central and Eastern European countries and beyond into the EU.

President Xi stressed China's interest in promoting mutual development, including in nuclear power and Silk Road infrastructure. Nearly 30 economic agreements were concluded, including in the financial sector. China's CEFC Energy Co. and Hengfeng Bank Co. established a fund with 1.1 billion euros for investments in Czech industry. Other agreements pertained to cooperation in, for example, nuclear power, aviation, agriculture, and healthcare. The Czech automaker Skoda (a VW subsidiary) announced it will invest $2.5 billion in China over the next five years. Chinese investors in turn committed almost $4 billion in investments to the Czech Republic.

Following President Xi's state visit, Prime Minister Sobotka attended the Local Leaders Meeting of 16+1 platform representatives and the summit of 16+1 Health Ministers in Suzhou in June 2016. During the visit, Chinese-Czech cooperation in aviation, healthcare, and the financial sector was strengthened, with 22 memorandums signed.

An important project that was negotiated during President Xi's 2016 visit was the Danube-Oder-Elbe Canal, which the Schiller Institute had called for back in the 1990s as part of the "Productive Triangle" (**Figure 20**)

For 2019, Chinese Prime Minister Li Keqiang has been invited to Prague, to celebrate the 70th anniversary of establishing Czech-Chinese diplomatic relations.

Figure 20

The waterway connections over the Rhine, Main and Danube will provide transportation across all of Europe, from Rotterdam to the Black Sea. This is shown here integrated with the LaRouches' "Productive Triangle" proposal.

Hungary

On January 19, 2018, the newest China-Europe freight train route was opened between China's eastern port city of Xiamen to Budapest, carrying about $3.5 million worth of goods, including electric products, clothes, and construction materials. The train takes 18 days to travel the 11,595 km and will operate on a weekly basis.

Hungary-China relations have increased steadily in the context of the 16+1. In 2014, Chinese Prime Minister Li Keqiang visited Hungary on the occasion of the 65th anniversary of diplomatic relations between the two countries and the 10th anniversary of their Friendship and Cooperation Agreement.

As of 2017, Hungary has the highest level of exports to China and the highest volume of investment by China in the CEE region. From 2015 to 2016 the value of bilateral trade rose by 8.2% to $7.1 billion. The Eximbanks of China and Hungary have signed an agreement on the second phase of the CEE Investment Bank Cooperation Fund, and the Hungarian Eximbank will have access to a credit line of $500 million for economic projects in Hungary (such as a chemical project loan, private agreements on a large thermal project, or sale of textile products).

The strategic highlight of Hungarian-Chinese cooperation is the Budapest-Belgrade railway modernization, a crucial element in the Chinese Sea-Land Project from the Greek harbor of Piraeus into Central and Eastern Europe, which the EU has tried to block from its beginning, questioning its compliance with EU law. Immediately after the 16+1 Leaders Meeting in December 2017 in Budapest, the public procurement tender was issued by the Hungarian government. Prime Minister Orban has referred to the Chinese role in the planned reconstruction of the railway line between Budapest and Belgrade, the capital of Serbia, as the "flagship project" of China's increased presence in the region, asserting that the rail line could become the fastest sea-land transport route to Western Europe for China's New Silk Road. The cooperation for this project involves China, Hungary, Serbia, and Macedonia, to link up with the port of Piraeus in Greece. It also includes a customs agreement among them, to ensure the free flow of goods.

Hungary has also developed into an important financial center for Chinese-European relations: In 2015, the Bank of China opened its first European RMB clearinghouse in Budapest. In May 2017, Hungary's Minister of National Economy Mihaly Varga held meetings on financial cooperation in Beijing and participated in a conference on finding new financial instruments for BRI projects. And in June 2017, Hungary became the second country in the CEEC region after Poland, to join the AIIB at the Bank's Annual General Meeting in South Korea.

On November 29, 2017, the Asian Financial Cooperation Association (AFCA), which was founded at the BRI Forum in May 2017 in Beijing, held a meeting, jointly organized with the Hungarian Banking Association, in Budapest. Also, the Shanghai Gold Exchange will launch its third office in Budapest.

Another important area of cooperation is agriculture. Hungary, Romania, Bulgaria, and other Eastern European countries have an enormous agricultural potential, but the EU's agricultural policy in the service of international cartels has steadily reduced their capacities since their accession to the EU. China, however, is extremely interested in agricultural products from Hungary and other CEE countries, including grain and processed foodstuffs. Hungary and China have established a joint working group to bring about this cooperation.

Serbia

Serbia is located at an important junction of the Silk Road Economic Belt and the Maritime Silk Road of the 21st Century, which has opened completely new perspectives for the revival of its economy. Serbia has become a leader in joint projects and investments by China in the infrastructure and energy fields, already resulting in a 1% GDP growth in 2016.

The strategically most important project for this Silk Road dynamic is the construction of a nearly 400-km new high-speed railway from Belgrade to Budapest, which will shorten the travel time from eight hours to less than three. In Serbia, the total length is 184 km. Goods from Central and Eastern Europe will reach Greece and its port at Piraeus on new railway lines crossing Hungary, Serbia, and Macedonia.

On November 28, 2017, works commenced for the first part of the Serbian-Chinese agreement to build the railway for the 34.5-km Belgrade-Stara Pozava section in the presence of Serbian Prime Minister Ana Brnabic and Wang Xiaotao, representing the National Development and Reform Commission of China. Modernization of the section of Novi Sad to the Hungarian border has been ongoing already.

Preceded by the visit of President Xi Jinping to Belgrade in June 2016 and the upgrading of the China-Serbia strategic partnership agreement (2009) to a "strategic comprehensive partnership," at the Riga summit in November 2016, Serbia and China signed commercial and financing deals worth a combined 734 million euros for infrastructure projects.

These include construction of highway sections of pan-European Transport Corridor 11 (highway E-763 Belgrade-Bar, Montenegro and further to Bari, Italy), with the Chinese Eximbank providing the funding. Another 207-million-euro deal was signed with Power Construction Corporation of China for continuation of works on the ring around Belgrade, which includes the construction of 22 bridges and four tunnels.

Among important industrial investments, China's Eximbank is financing construction of the third block of the thermal power plant Kostolac B and reconstruction of the thermal power plant Nikola Tesla, near Belgrade. Very important, the purchase of the more than 100-year-old Smederevo steel plant by the Chinese Hesteel Group several years ago saved the company and the jobs of its 5,000 employees. This particular investment was key for an overall increase of industrial activity in the Serbian economy and for the growth of GDP of 1% in 2016. Also, there are discussions about the intention to buy the Serbian Copper and Gold Mining Company in Bor, with a delegation of the Chinese Xijing Mining Group visiting Serbia in early 2018. This is one of the largest copper mines in Europe, employing about 5,000 workers.

A particularly symbolic project for Serbia and China is the Mihailo Pupin Bridge over the Danube in Belgrade, built by the China Road and Bridge Corporation (CRBC), which was finished in December 2014. Connected to this are further plans for building a Danube port, a road-railway bridge over the Danube, and industrial parks along the Danube. Construction of a water purification factory for Belgrade has been agreed upon.

China has also prepared a feasibility study for the Serbian section of the canal from the Danube to the Aegean Sea—the Danube-Morava-Vardar/Axios-Aegean Canal—which Milena Nikolic presented in October 2014 at a conference of the Schiller Institute in Germany. With its long historical friendship to China, Serbia became the first country in Central and Eastern Europe to sign an agreement on mutual visa abolition at the Riga 16+1 summit in December 2016.

Accompanying this, the Bank of China opened its branch in Serbia in January 2017, with operations extending over the entire Western Balkan region, for further contributions to China's BRI through its financial services in the region. In March 2018, President Xi accepted a new invitation to visit Serbia.

Romania

In 2013, the second 16+1 Leaders Meeting took place in Romania's capital, Bucharest. In 2015, China and Romania signed an MOU for joint development of the Silk Road Economic Belt within the framework of the Romania-China Joint Intergovernmental Commission for Economic Cooperation. In May 2017, Romania's application for membership in the AIIB was accepted. The Romanian Ministry of Foreign Affairs greeted the decision, underlining that it signified "recognition of Romania's ability to participate in promoting the financial institution's objectives to support infrastructure and economic development projects. At the same time, it highlights Romania's relevance in the context of the current efforts of the European and Asian countries to strengthen connectivity between the two continents, to which the AIIB gives special importance."

Three Pan-European corridors (north-south and east-west) cross Romania—Corridors 4, 7 (Danube waterway), and 9. For this important Black Sea country, the development of harbor and transport infrastructure is one key aspect of its national policy, as outlined in a government priority document up to the year 2030.

The seaport of Constanta, the only Black Sea port at the mouth of the trans-European Danube River (2,860 km), plays a key role in the flow of goods between Asia and Europe. Romania expressed its intention to develop this harbor for all transport modes, river, rail, and road, thus strengthening the country's strategic position as a center of intermodal transport between the Far East and Europe. The port of Constanta also offers a multimodal connection between ports in the Baltic Sea and the Adriatic Sea.

With current capacity of more than 100 million tons per year and facilities for tankers of 165,000 dead weight tons (DWT) and bulk-carriers of 220,000 DWT, goods are transferred from high-sea vessels to river vessels and reach ports upstream in EU and non-EU member countries, via the Danube-Black Sea Canal. Of the Danube Basin, 29% is located in Romania, before reaching the Black Sea coast. Romania calls this waterway the "Blue Highway," on which goods for Europe coming via the Suez Canal can reach markets in Western Europe without having to cross the entire Mediterranean Sea (see Figure 20).

In another example of Romania-China cooperation, China General Nuclear Power Corporation is involved in negotiating the construction of two additional nuclear power units of the Cernavoda power plant in southeast Romania. Nuclear energy provides almost 20% of Romania's electricity. The project, two 700 MWe CANDU-6 reactors, is worth 7 billion euros and will be the largest so far between China and CEE Countries. A letter of intent was signed in November 2013 during the visit to Bucharest by Chinese Prime Minister Li Keqiang. During this visit, numerous bilateral agreements were signed, including an MOU on the peaceful uses of nuclear energy.

Bulgaria

Bulgaria, which holds the EU presidency in the first half of 2018, will host the next 16+1 Leaders conference in its capital, Sofia, at the end of 2018. Its geographical location, linking Europe, Asia, and African nations, is one of the greatest advantages of this Black Sea nation, to cooperate with China's BRI plans. It can become part of the Europe-Caucasus-Asia Transport Corridor with the connection between the Georgian and Bulgarian (as well as Romanian) seaports—from Poti in Georgia to Varna and Burgas in Bulgaria, and Constanta in Romania. The connection to the Danube River route for cargo transport to Central Europe is ideal.

Bulgaria also can take part in the planned high-speed rail connection from Northwest China via Central Asia, Iran, and Turkey via the Bosporus to Bulgaria, and with a further extension to Central Europe through Serbia and Hungary.

Several corridors of the Pan-European transport network (IV, VIII, IX, and XII – Danube) cross Bulgaria, which has many transport centers, such as the intermodal hubs of Sofia, Burgas, Varna, Gorna Oryahovitsa, and Plovdiv airport; the railway terminals of Sofia, Plovdiv, Gorna Oryahovitsa, Ruse, and Dragoman; and inland waterways and the seaports of Varna and Burgas.

In November 2017 a logistics hub for e-trade in agricultural products between CEECs and China was started in Plovdiv's Trakia Economic Zone (TEZ), with more than 100 Chinese companies opening their warehouses. Plovdiv is Bulgaria's economic capital. The TEZ industrial and commercial zone has existed since 1995 and includes six major industrial zones in the region of Plovdiv, with more than 140 Bulgarian and multinational companies operating in it. It has received targetted state support since 2015, and in 2017 it expanded into the districts of Haskovo and Burgas, thus covering all of southern and southeastern Bulgaria. In October 2017, the third working meeting of 16+1 regional governors took place in Plovdiv under the title "Plovdiv: The oldest city on the Silk Road." Regional governor Zdravko Dimitrov stressed the need for a railway line from Plovdiv and Bulgaria along the Silk Road.

At the Suzhou 16+1 Leaders Meeting in 2015, Bulgaria formally joined the One Belt, One Road Initiative, with the participation of Prime Minister Boyko Borisov, after several joint 16+1 activities had taken place in Bulgaria. The Association for Cooperation in Agriculture between China and CEE Countries was established in Sofia in June 2015, and in November of the same year Sofia hosted the Second Ministerial Forum on Cultural Cooperation in the 16+1 format.

Like other CEE Countries, Bulgaria also places a lot of emphasis on internal and external infrastructure development, to upgrade its productivity, and make full use of its industrial and agricultural potential. This includes cooperation with its neighbor Romania, on issues such as Danube bridges, and efforts to finally bring about full realization of Pan-European Corridor 8, which links the Black Sea and Adriatic Sea via Bulgaria, Macedonia, and Albania.

It also includes the Sea2Sea Corridor, a link from the Black Sea to the Aegean, and the establishment of the Black Sea Highway, for which China has announced interest, according to Prime Minister Borisov. To realize these important regional, national, and transnational projects, cooperation between China and EU partners will be crucial.[1]

---

1 References and further background: "Bulgaria's Contribution to the B&R Initiative in the context of the geopolitical state of the Balkans," Marian Tian, Ph.D., speech at Schiller Institute conference, Bad Soden, November 2017. https://www.larouchepub.com/eiw/public/2017/eirv44n49-20171208/25-28_4449.pdf

"The participation of Bulgaria in the Initiatives of the 'New Silk Road' - Achievements and Challenges," Mariana Tian, Ph.D., in: Belgrade conference, July 2017: Initiatives of the New Silk Road - Achievements and Challenges, Institute of International Politics and Economics, Duško Dimitrijević, Huang Ping (Eds.), Belgrade 2017. http://16plus1-thinktank.com/u/cms/cepzh/201712/13095430sus8.pdf

Albania

Participation in the New Silk Road by land, water, and air is of strategic importance for Albania. Albania has drafted a 15-year plan for national development, including modernizing infrastructure throughout the country and connecting with today's New Silk Road. The goal is to develop the entire country, for which China's assistance and the 16+1 format will be crucial.

Chinese investment increased from $87 million in 2015 to $760 million in 2016. Chinese companies including Huawei, Geo-Jade, Hilong, and others are investing in communications, oil and drilling industry, mining industry, and energy. The Chinese company Everbright bought Albania's "Mother Theresa" international airport in April 2016. In less than one year passenger traffic increased by 10% and two new lines were opened, one to Holland and one to Hungary. The Chinese market will be further opened to Albanian agricultural products, raw materials, and medicines.

At the 16+1 economic forum between China and the CEE Countries in Suzhou, China, on November 24-25, 2015, contracts were concluded for infrastructure development, trade, agriculture, tourism, and cultural exchange between China and Albania, Serbia, Montenegro, Bosnia-Herzegovina, and Macedonia.

For Albania, a further result of that China-CEEC forum was a special agreement between the city of Shantou in China, a starting point of the Silk Road, and the Albanian port city of Durres on the Adriatic. The port of Durres is to be modernized and expanded with the assistance of Shantou, creating a new period of prosperity for this port and the region.

Also, the China Pacific Construction Group (CPCG) has agreed to invest $1.72 billion in the construction of a modern highway through Albania and Montenegro, in a "public-private partnership." This highway is 280 km long and runs through very mountainous terrain in both countries. The Adriatic-Ionian Motorway, which will connect Albania, Montenegro, and Croatia, is very important for the Balkan region as a whole.

The Albanian government, under Prime Minister Edi Rama, wants to build up Albania from the ruins of the past. The construction of a modern "Via Egnatia" (which linked ancient Rome with Constantinople) and the project of the New Silk Road are important components of Albania's development policy.

Note:

An overview on important infrastructure connections and potential projects, including in those CEE Countries which have not been mentioned, may be found at:

http://ceec-china-maritime.org/blog/strategies-for-the-development-of-intermodal-transport-of-the-central-eastern-european-countries-with-regards-to-the-silk-road-initiative/

GREECE AND CHINA ARE PARTNERS IN BELT AND ROAD INITIATIVE

The future of the economies of Greece and of all the Balkan countries lies in taking advantage of their geostrategic location in the eastern Mediterranean, to make them the economic development gateway to Eurasia to the northeast, Southwestern and Southern Asia to the east, and Africa to the south. For Greece, this is an historic role. For the Balkans, this is a critical mission, to serve as a corridor of peace and development, and to uplift an area, stretching from the north Adriatic, eastward through Ukraine, and southeastward across to Southwest Asia.

On June 19, 2014, Chinese Prime Minister Li Keqiang met in Athens with Prime Minister Antonis Samaras of Greece, after which Li announced specific joint projects, but stressed overall that the two ancient civilizations of the East and West—China and Greece, respectively—enjoy a glorious history and culture. They made special contributions to civilization, and now they will collaborate on the future. Specifically, they will build the port of Piraeus into a regional transit center and gateway for trade to all Europe.

This Greek-Chinese cooperation on the Belt and Road has deepened even further under the government of Prime Minister Alexis Tsipras, who attended the Belt and Road Forum in Beijing in May 2017.

China and Greece formed a Strategic Partnership in 2006, and in 2017 the two countries launched the Greece-China Action Plan 2017-2019 with the aim of combining the BRI with Greece's Growth Strategy.

The principal intercontinental vectors of this region's connections are evident in the 1997 east-west "three corridors" on the Eurasian Land-Bridge. The Balkan peninsula is at the Mediterranean Basin juncture of these routes, and with full inter-modal development for trade and transit—rail, road, waterways, air, ports, and sea—the critical geo-position of Greece and the Balkans can be maximized for the benefit of all.

First, consider these intercontinental corridors more closely; next, look in brief at a few of the priority regional corridors across the peninsula itself. Greece and the Balkans connect to the north, into the full Eurasian east-west land-bridge development corridor. To the west, via the Rhine-Main-Danube Canal, there is the connection to the international ports of Antwerp, Rotterdam, and Hamburg. To the east, via the Danube corridor, there are links into the Black Sea Basin. This continues eastward to the Dnieper River, the Volga-Don Canal, and deep into central Asia and western Siberia, via the Caspian Sea. Greece and the Balkans will thus be integrated into the trans-Eurasian rail corridors spanning the landmass.

Greece and the Balkans also connect to the east/southeast by railway corridors leading into Turkey, across the Anatolian peninsula, then branching eastward into South Asia, through Iraq and Iran, to the Indian subcontinent. This Anatolian peninsula overland route also proceeds southward through the trans-Jordan, across the Sinai, into north and east Africa. The connections by sea in the Mediterranean and outward worldwide are self-evident, but an entirely new horizon of transportation and trade has come into view now that the capacity of the Suez Canal has been doubled.

Peninsular Corridor Priorities

A quick overview of the priority transportation/development routes and regions across the Balkans and Greece can be obtained by starting with the picture more than 20 years ago, of what were identified as "priority corridors" for modernized rail lines (and implied, related road, water, and other infrastructure), stipulated by transportation ministers at the March 1994 Second Pan-European Transportation Conference on the island of Crete. There were ten European corridors designated, of which four traverse Greece and/or the Balkans. **Figure 21** shows a May 1994 European Community Transport Infrastructure map, from the Crete meetings, presenting an "Outline Plan for a European High-Speed Train Network—2010." Besides a high-speed rail line shown for Greece, vector-arrows elsewhere in the Balkans show the direction of other routes to be worked out.

III. PROGRESS REPORTS

Figure 21
Outline Plan for a European High-Speed Train Network

As for the Balkans, only Greece has completed anything close to a high-speed rail line capable of speeds of 200 km per hour. Among the other countries, including Romania, Bulgaria, Serbia, Hungary, the Former Yugoslav Republic of Macedonia (FYROM), Croatia, Montenegro, and Bosnia and Herzegovina, some have plans for high-speed rail projects, but these nations are currently only in various stages of upgrading and rebuilding old lines, some of which permit speeds of only 20 km per hour. A noted example of a high-speed project is the link between Budapest and Belgrade, which will be built and financed by Chinese companies.

While the EU seems satisfied with its pace of taking decades to accomplish projects that in China take a few years, Europe should be welcoming China's involvement. One proposal put forward by the Schiller Institute was for Europe to create a European Infrastructure Investment Bank that would team up with the AIIB to help finance these projects. European financing should be supporting the capabilities within the region itself for these projects. The Czech Republic, Romania, and Poland already have train manufacturing capability while others, such as Greece, have high-level civil engineering capacities.

The specific Balkans priority transportation links, as first proposed at the 1994 Pan-European conference, out of the ten designated corridors are:

Corridor 4. On the major west-east link across Europe, going from Berlin to Istanbul (Berlin/Nuremberg-Prague-Bratislava-Gyor-Budapest-Arad-Craiova-Sofia-Istanbul), there must be branch links between Sofia and Thessaloniki.

Corridor 5. On the major west-east link between northern Italy and Ukraine, there are important branch links into the Balkans. The main corridor is Venice-Trieste/Koper-Ljubljana-Budapest-Uzhgorod-Liviv, extended through Rijecka-Zagreb-Budapest and Ploce-Sarajevo-Osijek-Budapest.

Corridor 8. The Adriatic Sea to the Black Sea, from Albania to the ports of Varna and Burgas on the Black Sea (Durres-Tirana-Skopje-Sofia-Plovdiv-Burgas-Varna).

Corridor 9. Going from Greece to Moscow, beginning at the easternmost Greek port of Alexandroupolis to Dimitrovgrad-Bucharest-Chisinau-Lyubaskeva-Kiev-Moscow.[2]

Corridor 10. From Salzburg to Thessaloniki (Salzburg–Ljublijana–Zagreb–Belgrade–Nis–Skopje–Veles–Thessaloniki). The ancient Roman Via Egnatia, from the Adriatic to the Bosporus, is a priority redevelopment route.

These are not merely transportation corridors but also constitute development corridors that will integrate the entire region.

---

[2] Corridor 9 goes north from Alexandropolis through Bulgaria, Romania to Kiev in Ukraine. From there, one branch goes northwest to the port of Klaipeda in Lithuania on the Baltic and the other branch goes northeast to Moscow where it can connect to the Arctic, thus providing a corridor linking the Baltic, the Arctic, and the Aegean.

EUROPE

China Is Greece's Partner

When the Berlin Wall fell in 1989 and the collapse of communism ensued throughout Eastern Europe and the Soviet Union, Greece had the ambition of becoming the transport, energy, telecommunications, and even financial hub of Southeast Europe, a region including the nations of the former Yugoslavia, Romania, Bulgaria, Hungary, and even extending into Ukraine and Russia. Greece's strategic location at the foot of the Balkan peninsula made the port of Piraeus the region's natural outlet to the eastern Mediterranean, Asia, and Africa. As an EU member, Greece could help usher the new nations into the EU.

The realization of this ambition required a first-class infrastructure, which at that time Greece sorely lacked. The port of Piraeus, while Europe's tenth largest port and largest passenger port, was in need of modernization. Its railways where antiquated. The north-south trunk line between Athens and Thessaloniki was not electrified nor fully double tracked. The port of Piraeus, although less than 10 km from Athens, was not linked to the railway network.

Athens' airport was not only antiquated but its location had become a fully built-up section of the greater Athens metropolitan region, making it impossible to expand. Athens, a city of 4 million people, had neither a subway nor even a streetcar network. Nor did it have a regional railway network linking the outlying Athenian suburbs. Greece was not fit to be any kind of hub; nonetheless, Greece took it upon itself to build the first-class infrastructure it required.

By the end of the last century Greece began to implement a revolution in transportation infrastructure. It began the huge task of double tracking and electrifying the main Athens-Thessaloniki north-south trunk line which required building entirely new lines with numerous viaducts and tunnels, including the Balkans' longest railway tunnel, the 9-km Kallidromo twin tunnels, completed in 2018. In 2013 the link between the Piraeus container port with the main north-south line was completed.

After almost two decades this north-south line has just been completed and should reach full operations by June 2018. It has reduced passenger rail times between Athens and Thessaloniki from 6 hours to 3.5 hours. Passenger trains can reach speeds of more than 200 km per hour while freight rail can now achieve speeds of up to 120 km per hour.

Greece's railway planners had hoped this project could have been integrated simultaneous with the building of high-speed lines from Thessaloniki and Belgrade and then on to Budapest, and another to Sofia, but those countries could not secure financing, and the EU was unwilling to back them.

Greece also built a fully integrated suburban rail, subway, and streetcar network that for the first time unified the entire Athenian metropolitan region. The highway network was also upgraded.

A new airport was built northeast of the city where sufficient area was available for future expansion. Moreover, the Piraeus container terminal, which is now owned by China's COSCO, was built by the Greek government.

While the EU should have been a more than willing partner in this enterprise, which would have turned Greece from being at the end of Europe into a gateway to Europe from the rising economies of Asia, its aid did not go much beyond various amounts of co-financing Greece was entitled to under EU entitlement programs.

A small part of the newly completed Athens to Thessaloniki double-track high-speed railway. Behind and above the new double line is the old single line railway.

Moreover, the rest of the region went into a steep economic decline through the "shock therapy" policies forced upon them by the IMF and the EU as a requirement for integrating into the so-called Western economic systems.

Thus most of the financing had to be raised by Greece itself on the international financial markets. When those markets collapsed in 2008 Greece found itself caught in a catastrophic debt trap. Its so-called European partners, desperate to save the bankrupt banks of the Eurozone, forced Greece to take on more than 300 billion euros of debt.

Nonetheless, in 2008 Greece won a real partner, China. That year China's COSCO signed a 35-year lease to operate Piraeus Container Terminals (PCT) 2 and 3, thus creating a strategic partnership between the two countries which has had unprecedented and positive consequences for Greece. The number of containers handled by the PCTs went from 880,000 a year to nearly 4 million, and is expected to expand to 6 million by 2019 and to 7.2 million by 2022.

Greece has become an integral part of the revolution China is creating in maritime transport though developing very large container ships, to carry its huge trade from Asia to Europe, Africa, and the west coast of North and South America, which now pass through the Suez Canal and the Mediterranean. For forward-thinkers like the Chinese it was easy to see the potential of using Greece as a transshipment hub for cargoes to and from Eastern and Central Europe as well as the broader eastern Mediterranean.

A case in point is the ever-increasing number of cargo trains traveling between China and Europe. While cargoes from China include consumer electronics and other consumer goods cargoes, trains on the return trip are carrying technical goods, especially automobile parts from Germany destined for China's automobile industry. While Germany imported 1.5 billion euros worth of goods by rail from China in 2016, it exported a total of 4 billion euros to China.

Thus over the next decades trade flows between East and West will be increasingly dominated by goods related to industrial supply chains as the nations in Africa and Asia become fully industrialized and integrated into global industrial supply chains.

Turning Piraeus into the Rotterdam of the Mediterranean

Greece's partnership with China was not enough to forestall the economic catastrophe inflicted on Greece by its so-called "partners" in the EU; nonetheless, the Greek-Chinese partnership has yielded positive results. This partnership has developed along logical and beneficial lines.

The 35-year lease China signed in 2008 for Container Terminals 2 and 3 was worth 831 million euros over the period of the lease. Between 2009 and 2016 COSCO's Piraeus Container Terminal has generated more than 1 billion euros in taxes and salaries. Despite fears to the contrary, COSCO did not dismiss any workers and has only brought seven Chinese managers from China. COSCO has already invested 300 million euros in upgrading the terminal with new cranes capable of unloading the largest of container ships and is completing works within the terminal which were still under construction when their lease began.

In 2016 COSCO invested 280 million euros for a controlling 51% of the Piraeus Port Authority and will invest another 88 million euros by 2021 to expand its holding to 67%. The agreement calls for China to invest another 350 million euros in upgrading the port over the next 5 years. Already the cruise ship terminal has been substantially upgraded.

The port of Piraeus proper, which lies to the east of the Container Terminal, serves as a gateway for travelers to and from Greece's innumerable islands where a substantial portion of the Greek population resides and travel via ferries. It is this traffic that accounts for the fact that Piraeus is the largest passenger port in Europe. It has been in the process of upgrading for more than a decade with new subway and streetcar lines having been constructed or in the process of being completed. The port itself has been in a slow process of upgrading for some time.

With fresh energy and funds, COSCO has already submitted for approval a master plan for the development of the port. This includes a new passenger terminal and two major hotels as COSCO has promised to encourage tourism from China itself.

The Container Terminal at the Port of Piraeus

The expansion of the Container Terminal and its massive throughput creates economic potentials in many directions. Initially containers arriving in the port were transferred to smaller ships for transshipment to other smaller ports while other cargoes were transferred north via truck and road transport. None were shipped by rail. The opening of the rail link to the main north-south line in 2013 saw thousands of containers ship by train. With the recent opening of the railway system to private cargo train operators, three new firms have been founded to carry on this trade.

Through its contacts in China, COSCO has convinced major companies with production in China, such as HP, Sony, ZTE, and Huawei, to use Piraeus as its port of entry for its products destined for Central and Eastern Europe.

This new rail traffic has given renewed life to the Thriasio logistics center created north of Athens where the junction of the rail line from Piraeus connects into the main north-south trunk line. This has now attracted investment from Greek logistics companies including the Greek ETVA BIPE – Goldair consortium. COSCO, in cooperation with Trainose, the recently privatized railway operator now owned by Italian State Railway, has expressed interest in establishing a logistics center there as well.

Greek shipping companies control the largest fleet of cargo ships, including tankers, bulk carriers, and container ships, in the world. Therefore, in former times, Greece had a vibrant shipbuilding and repair industry which served ships not only for overseas trade but also for the substantial local ferry and fishing industry. This industry has been in decline for decades.

One important reason for the shipbuilding and repair industry decline is that Greek shipowners have established a very special relationship with China. Their ships carry much of the oil and bulk cargoes China imports. Many of these ships are now built in Chinese shipyards with credit from Chinese banks. Many of the ships in the COSCO fleet are on lease from Greek shipping companies.

Another important reason for the decline is the EU competition rules which have allowed shipbuilders in Germany and northern Europe into the Greek market.

In response to the Greek government request that COSCO aid in reviving this industry, China has responded through operating three new floating dry docks, Piraeus I, II, and III, which promise to help revive the repair industry as more ships use the port. Piraeus III arrived in Greece in March 2018. Almost 250 meters long the Piraeus III can accommodate ships up to 80,000 tons.

Greece has numerous other ports. Thessaloniki, Greece's second largest port in Greece's second largest city, is a major regional port and serves as an outlet to the Eastern Mediterranean for all of Eastern Europe. It has been recently privatized to a consortium that includes Deutsche Invest Equity Partners of Munich; Belterra Investments, controlled by the Russian Ivan Savvidies group; and CMA CGM Terminal Link, the port division of CMA CGM, a French company which is the world's third largest container shipping company. The consortium intends to increase the throughput of the port from 350,000 to 550,000 containers, while CMA CGM, taking a lesson from COSCO, intends to use the port as a hub for the entire Balkans.

Two other ports are Kavala and Alexandroupolis, on the Aegean to the east of Thessalonki. Although far smaller than Thessaloniki, they are strategically located as the termination of the TEN-T Corridor 9 going north from these ports along a line, Dimitrovgrad-Bucharest-Chisinau-Lyubaskeva-Kiev-Moscow.

The Greek and Bulgarian governments have signed agreements to construct the Sea2Sea railway link between the Black Sea and the Aegean, thus relieving the congested Bosporus. The project will link the Greek Aegean ports of Thessaloniki, Kavala, and Alexandroupolis with the Bulgarian Black Sea ports of Varna and Burgas as well as the river port of Ruse on the Danube. The two governments will be seeking EU financing. Discussions are taking place to bring Romania and Serbia into the project.

The ports also lie on an east-west axis known as the Ionian/Adriatic Intermodal corridor. The Pan European Plan (Corridor 7 described above) traces the priority route for modernized rail, to connect this region into Eurasia. On the Adriatic coast of Greece is the port of Igoumenitsa, one of the most important ports in the region.

There is a project underway to further develop the link between the port of Taranto, Italy's second-largest, and Igoumenitsa, and then through the Egnatia Odos Motorway, across northern Greece, linking it with the ports of Thessaloniki, Kavala, and Alexandroupolis, and then with Istanbul. Thus it would provide access to all the Balkans, including Albania, the FYROM, and Bulgaria. To the south, there is the port of Patras on the northwestern tip of the Peloponnese, with its recently completed South Port, strategically located to serve the new traffic flows from the enlarged Suez Canal.

Three Game Changing Canal Projects

There are three major canal projects on the drawing boards that could serve as a transportation game-changer in a region stretching from Eastern Europe and the Eastern Mediterranean deep into Central Asia and China. These include two already mentioned elsewhere in this report. One is the Danube-Oder-Elbe Canal project. Through the Oder the project will connect the Baltic with the Danube and through the Elbe the North Sea port of Hamburg to the Danube. While already begun by the government of Czechoslovakia prior to World War II, it remains on the drawing boards despite widespread interest in Poland and the Czech Republic.

The second project is the Danube-Aegean Canal that would form a link between the Danube and the Aegean through connecting the Morava River in Serbia with a canal to the Vardar-Axios River that runs through the FYROM and down into Greece entering the Aegean to the west of Thessaloniki (**Figure 22**). The China Gezhouba Group Company Ltd, which is already building power stations in Serbia, has completed a feasibility study.

Figure 22

The Danube-Aegean Canal

Up until now the Danube River east of Austria has been under-utilized because it is like a 1,000-km highway between two cities without any intervening exits or entrances. The ability to ship cargoes through highly economic inland waters will quickly capture the attention of Chinese and other interests.

The port of Piraeus and other Greek ports will be able to transship cargos to the Baltic and North Sea. For landlocked countries such as the Czech Republic and the FYROM, the prospect of inexpensive water transportation will enhance their economic development.

In addition, there is a third project on the drawing boards that could create a new east-west economic corridor. This is the proposed Eurasian Canal connecting the Caspian Sea and the Black Sea through a canal built through the Russian Caucasus. (See separate section below on details of the canal.) The opening of this maritime corridor will serve to further integrate the landlocked Central Asian countries into the greater Eurasian economy.

In ancient times Greece's wealth stemmed in large part from its intercourse with Asia via the ancient Black Sea Silk Road route. These projects will renew that ancient role. It will open opportunities to Greek engineering and construction firms which are already active in the Middle East and Africa.

Energy

Greece also aspires to become an energy hub between Europe and Asia, but Greece's creditors have not been very cooperative in this effort. The EU and the Obama Administration moved to block the South Stream Gas Pipeline project and later the Turkish Stream project because both were sponsored by Russia's Gazprom.

TAP at a Glance

The EU and the United States only support the Trans-Adriatic Pipeline (TAP), which will transport Caspian natural gas to Europe via the Trans-Anatolian Pipeline (TANAP) at the Greek-Turkish border and across northern Greece, Albania, and the Adriatic Sea before coming ashore in southern Italy to connect to the Italian natural gas network. It is designed to bring gas from Phase II of the Shah Deniz Gas Field—which has yet to produce gas, although production was scheduled for 2018. Nonetheless the pipeline project has already started.

While South Stream and the European side of Turkish Stream have been blocked, the Turkish connection between Russia and Turkey will be finished by 2019 and might very well enable Russian gas to be transported through the Turkish part of TAP and then into Europe.

While the international creditors who are overseeing the crushing bailout forced upon Greece have put unrelenting pressure of the Greek government to privatize government energy enterprises, they have failed to address the serious energy issues Greece faces, not the least of which is electricity production for Greece's islands. Many of these islands have diesel-powered generators, which is the most expensive form of electricity production.

Diesel is also unreliable, as witnessed in recent years by the island of Rhodes, which suffered extensive blackouts when one of its diesel generators broke down. The solution which the Greek government has embarked on is to create an inter-island electricity network linking the islands together and with the mainland.

In 2017 China Grid International Development Ltd bought a 24% holding in Greece's state power grid corporation, ADMIE. Later the same year the two companies signed an MOU whereby the former is committed to aid in securing fresh capital to finance a 2-billion-euro ten-year investment plan, which includes connecting Greek islands, including Greece's largest, Crete, to the mainland's grid via undersea cables.

The China Machinery Engineering Company also signed an MOU to build a second lignite-powered power station alongside the existing Meliti power station owned by Greece's state power company PPC.

The EU has thrown up roadblocks against both projects as violating the European competition rules, claiming that the Chinese companies have the same owner, i.e., the Chinese government. The other issue is that the EU and its financial institution will no longer support any lignite power stations. This is being used to block lignite power projects throughout the Balkans which Chinese companies have expressed serious interest in.

While Greece has no plans for nuclear power stations, Bulgaria and Romania do.

Bulgaria has a long history of nuclear power. Its Kozloduy Nuclear Power Plant, on the Danube, manages two Russian-built VVER-1000a nuclear power reactors with a total output of 2,000 MWe. Both units are being upgraded and their operating life extended. A third 1,000 MW unit is in the planning stage using parts from the terminated Belene project. The latter project, which was also being built by Russia's Rosatom, was terminated under pressure from the EU, forcing Bulgaria to pay 600 million euros to Rosatom for canceling the project.

The current government is pro-nuclear and wants to expand nuclear power production which already accounts for 35% of Bulgaria's power, through reviving the Belene project. On March 16, 2018, Bulgarian Energy Minister Temenuzhka Petkova announced that the China National Nuclear Corporation (CNNC) has expressed an interest in investing in a 2,000 MW nuclear power project at Belene which could cost 10 billion euros. In February 2018, Bulgarian Prime Minister Boyko Borissov suggested Belene be built as a pan-Balkan project.

Greece, which is already in the process of interconnecting its power grid with Bulgaria, had in the past expressed interest in such cooperation.

Romania has one nuclear power station at Cernavoda operated by the state's Nuclearelectrica. It has two reactors using Canada Deuterium Uranium (CANDU) technology. The government is currently in negotiation with China General Nuclear Power Corporation (CGN) to build two more reactors, which will give the station a capacity of 1.4 GW.

CNNC and Canada's SNC-Lavalin, which owns CANDU technology, have had a longtime cooperation agreement; the latter has already built a large CANDU reactor in China. CNNC has signed an agreement for two next-generation CANDU nuclear reactors to be built in China. The companies are now teaming up to build reactors in third countries. An exclusive and binding agreement has been signed with China Nuclear Power Engineering Company, a subsidiary of CGN, to cooperate on the construction of the two units, both of the CANDU-6 type.

Romania could be one of the "third countries," making for a "win, win, win" opportunity for China, Canada, and Romania. The CANDU technology uses recycled spent uranium, making these plants ideal counterparts to the Rosatom VER-1000 nuclear power plants that exist in Bulgaria and other East European countries.

Greece as a Center of Science and Technology

By far the most important resource of Greece is its well-educated young people. Yet under the brutal austerity policies forced on Greece by its creditors it is suffering the highest youth unemployment rate in Europe. This has caused a serious brain drain. Greece finds itself spending hundreds of millions in euros educating its population in its world-class universities only to see these young engineers, scientists, medical doctors, and technicians leaving for Germany, France, the United States, and even China to seek employment.

Acutely aware of this crisis the Greek government wants to promote Greece as a center of learning, as well as science and technological development. This includes creating new university programs in the English language to turn Greece into an international educational center. Under the BRI Greece could play a crucial role as an educational and training center for students from Africa, Asia, and the Middle East.

The Greek government is promoting Greece as an excellent location for international companies to establish research and development centers. Its fine weather and living conditions and strategic location within reach of the rapidly developing economies of Asia, Africa, and Europe make it an attractive location.

Greece's National Technological University of Athens (NTUA) is among the best of Europe and is only one of several such technical universities located in major cities throughout the country. Linked to these universities are National Research Institutes dedicated to specific fields of research. In addition, the government, in cooperation with the private sector, has created technology parks alongside these

The National Center for Scientific Research "Demokritos," including the Technology and Science Park of Attica "Lefkippos."

universities and research centers, call "incubators," where success in the laboratory can be spun off into technologies for the economy.

An important case in point is the National Center of Scientific Research "Demokritos," which is linked to NTUA. It was founded in the 1950s as the Nuclear Research Center "Demokritos," with a boost from the U.S. Atoms for Peace program, from which it received an experimental reactor. The founding of this institute initiated a wave of repatriation of scientists at the time, who had been conducting research abroad because of the lack of opportunities in Greece. Today, with the BRI initiatives, this science mission can be resumed to proceed with achievements never before imagined.

"Demokritos" founded the Technology and Science Park of Attica (TE.S.P.A.), "Lefkippos," in September 2009, located at its campus in Aghia Paraskevi of Attica, where several spin-off companies and private research centers are already in operation.

In February 2018 the U.S. electric vehicle manufacturing company Tesla announced it was opening a small research hub at "Lefkippos" under the initiative of three young Tesla engine designers, all Greek citizens who are graduates of NTUA. They, like tens of thousands of young well-educated Greeks, emigrated to the United States to work at Tesla's California headquarters. They include Constantine Laskaris, Tesla's chief engine designer, and Konstantinos Bourchas and Vasilis Papanikolaou, who are research engineers at Tesla's electric motor design department. The center will initially employ ten Greek engineers and scientists who will be conducting research related to electric motors.

Greece's Deputy Minister for Education and Research, Konstantinos Fotakis, said the opening of the Tesla research center "marks the beginning of a new type of investment in the country: research-based investments innovation and knowledge intensity.... It should be stressed that synergies between foreign and Greek companies that focus on 'knowledge intensive' activities and innovate, promote the new production model that the government has shaped for the country and is based on the Knowledge Economy.... We are very happy to welcome all the talented Greek engineers who will return to work on our side. Opportunities for significant research and development partnerships are being created for both the Center's research teams and the thirty more innovation companies already operating in the Park."

"Lefkippos" is one of such parks which also include the Epirus Science and Technology Park (E.TE.P.I.) in Ioannina; Thessaly Technology Park (TE.PA.ThE.A.E.) in Volos; Thessaloniki Technology Park, in Thessaloniki; Crete Science and Technology Park (ETEP-K), on the island of Crete; Lavrio Technology and Culture Park, near Athens; and Patras Science Park S.A., in the city of Patras.

The ancient Hellenes were the original "Peoples of the Sea," as immortalized by Homer's Iliad, but today, that legacy can be expressed by transforming a nation of seafarers into a nation of spacefarers.

For example, the Elefis Shipyard not only builds state-of-the-art vessels, rail cars, and other craft, but also built the Delta-Berenike, a self-propelled special purpose vessel that is being used as a stable platform to build the Cubic Kilometer Neutrino Telescope, one of only four that exist in the world today. It has been erected at a depth of 5,200 meters on the Mediterranean seabed, the deepest point in Europe.

The site of the telescope is 17 km off the coast of the Peloponnese. The headquarters of the project is in the small city of Pylos on the Bay of Navarino. Ancient Pylos, which is a few kilometers from the modern city, is the location of the palace of Nestor, of Iliad fame, giving the name Nestor to the project.

Greece's potential of moving to the front lines of the world extraterrestrial imperative took a big step forward on March 19, 2018 when, under the initiative of Digital Policy and Media Minister Nikos Pappas, the Greek government officially founded its first space agency, the Hellenic Space Organization.

"The establishment and operation of the Hellenic Space Organization will be one of the most dynamic features of our course toward the modern digital economy of the future," Secretary General of Telecommunications and Post Vassilis Maglaras said on March 19 in an interview with the Athens-Macedonian News Agency. "Greece is already actively involved in the European Space Agency and must be able to exploit the opportunities arising from its participation in these European organizations for the benefit of its businesses, research, and all economic sectors," he said. He added that the establishment of a space organization and the attempt to organize the wider space sector is not an unnecessary luxury but an absolute necessity.

There is discussion within Greece's aerospace sector for Greece to develop its own capacity to build satellites. It already has the skilled scientists, technicians, and engineers, many of whom are working in other countries. Within this context discussion has already begun on the possibility of building a space launch center on the island of Crete, Europe's southernmost point closest to the equator.

With China's BRI, this science mission can be resumed to proceed with achievements never before imagined.

EURASIA CANAL

National economies without direct access to the sea or through river and canal waterways are always at a serious disadvantage. A glance at the most productive region in Europe, the "Productive Triangle Paris-Berlin-Vienna," shows it is integrated with a dense network of autobahns, railways, and interconnecting river and canal networks providing for efficient and inexpensive transportation for bulk cargoes including mineral ores, chemicals, hydrocarbon products, and less time-sensitive containerized cargoes.

A glance at the map of Eurasia reveals its vast land-locked central region as its least developed. The geographical situation is similar to the North American continent where the Great Lakes reach almost halfway across the continent. These vast inland waterways began to be connected to the open seas first by the Erie Canal, followed by linking all the lakes with a system of canals and locks, which was ultimately followed by the creation of the St. Lawrence Seaway enabling 28,000-ton ocean-going ships to reach the lake port of Duluth, Minnesota, almost halfway across the continent. This process of development took more than 150 years to complete but in the process helped industrialize the United States and Canada.

The Mediterranean, Black, and Caspian Seas similarly stretch halfway across Eurasia and bring together three continents—Asia, Africa, and Europe. While the former two are connected through the Dardanelles and Bosporus, the Caspian is connected only through the very low capacity and inconvenient Volga-Don Canal in the Russian Federation. The remedy is to cut a ship canal across the Russian Caucasus through the Russian Federation's Republics of Kalmykia and Dagestan, the Stavropol krai, and Rostov oblast, along the Kuma-Manych depression linking the Caspian with the Sea of Azov and on to the Black Sea. It was a mere 18,000 years ago that this depression served as a strait, the Manych Strait, connecting the two seas (see **Figure 23**).

The Tsar's engineers dreamed of building such a canal and the engineers of the Soviet Union, under orders from Joseph Stalin, began the construction of

Figure 23
The Eurasia Canal

the Kuma-Manych Canal in 1932. Work stopped because of the outbreak of World War II and after the war the project was downgraded to an irrigation canal, and completely halted in 1989 by the environmentalists in the government of Mikhail Gorbachev. While much of the canal still exists, it is in very poor condition.

During his annual national address in April 2007 Russian President Vladimir Putin called for modernizing the Volga-Don and Volga-Baltic canals, for which he proposed the government "examine the establishment of an international consortium to build a second section of the Volga-Don Canal. This new transport artery would have a significant impact on improving shipping links between the Caspian and the Black Seas.

"Not only would this give the Caspian Sea countries a route to the Black Sea and the Mediterranean, thus providing them with access to the world's oceans, it would also radically change their geopolitical situation by enabling them to become sea powers." This proposal was called the Volga-Don 2 Canal.[3]

Speaking at a conference of foreign investors in the same year, on June 15, 2007, the President of Kazakhstan, President Nursultan Nazarbayev, proposed the construction of a Eurasia Canal through the Manych Depression, declaring, "We need different routes: naturally, these commodities—oil and gas—will follow the routes that will prove to be economically sound for us. The construction of a new 'Eurasia' shipway from the Caspian to the Black Sea can become a landmark project.... This canal would be a powerful outlet for the entire Central Asia seaward across Russia."

The two presidents soon met on the subject, resulting in the commissioning of a feasibility study comparing the two projects which was carried out with financing provided by the Eurasian Development Bank. The study subsequently concluded that a ship canal through the Manych Depression was economically feasible and would also benefit the development of the Russian Caucasus, providing employment and improving the region's agricultural potential.

In 2009 Nazarbayev recruited the support of China in the project, and in August 2009 during an official visit to China the Head of the Russian Republic of Kalmykia, Kirsan Ilyumzhinov, a political ally of President Putin, signed a letter of intent with the Chinese corporation Sinohydro for its participation in the building of the Eurasian Canal, which also resulted in a preliminary feasibility study.

The 2008 financial crisis, and the failure of the Russian government to come to a decision led to both the Volga-Don 2 project and the Eurasia Canal to be frozen, despite the keen interest of Kazakhstan. In the meantime the EU, as part of a bid to isolate Russia, organized in 2001 the Intergovernmental

---

3 http://en.kremlin.ru/events/president/transcripts/24203#sel=156:1:L,156:1:L

Lock No. 14 on the Volga-Don Canal

Commission TRACECA of all the former Central Asian Soviet Republics including Azerbaijan, Armenia, Georgia, Kazakhstan, Kyrgyzstan, Moldova, Tajikistan, Ukraine, and Republic of Uzbekistan as well as Bulgaria, Romania, and Turkey. China and Russia were not included.

The absence of Russia obviously signaled that the EU and the West did not support the Eurasian Canal, instead opting for developing a road and rail corridor, through mountainous Azerbaijan and Georgia. Because the rail and roadways already exist, it also means minimal investment while it does not solve the basic problem that would be addressed by a new waterway.

The Belt and Road Initiative Can Make the Difference

In 2013 Chinese President Xi Jinping launched what is now known as the Belt and Road Initiative, thereby opening new potential for the realization of this project. In Russia, the former head of Kalmykia, Kirsan Ilyumzhinov, has embraced the BRI, and on November 11, 2016 presented the proposal for a transport corridor called "Eurasia" at the "Eurasian Economic Integration" conference in Moscow where the Eurasia Canal was featured. Moreover the strengthening of ties between Putin and Xi could induce Russia to take more action on the project.[4]

Not insignificant was a short study, "The Eurasia Canal as a Factor of Economic Prosperity for the Caspian Region," published in the Kazakh journal Geography, Environment, Sustainability (Vol. 10 No. 1, p. 33-41). Its authors were Nuraly Bekturganov of Kazakhstan's Academy of Natural Sciences and Arasha V. Bolaev, advisor to the President of the Russian Academy of Sciences.[5]

The two authors correctly asserted that China's BRI and its commitment to rapidly develop its western regions has dramatically shifted the situation. They assert, "The Eurasia Canal construction project is consistent with the spirit of the One Belt One Road initiative, as the route 'western China – Kazakhstan – Caspian Sea – Eurasia Canal – Black Sea' will be the shortest between China and the European Union."

The region of Central Asia that forms the "market" for a canal can easily encompass more than a billion people. The riparian countries alone including Kazakhstan, 18 million; Uzbekistan, whose western border is a mere 200 km from the Caspian, 32 million; Turkmenistan, 5.7 million; Iran, 80 million; Azerbaijan, 10 million; and of course Russia, where a sizable portion of its 165 million citizens live. Afghanistan, 35 million; Tajikistan, 9 million; and Kyrgyzstan, 6 million, also would benefit from the canal.

The city of Urumqi, capital of China's most western region, Xinjiang (population 24 million), is almost equal distance between the eastern shore of the Caspian Sea and China's eastern sea coast.

In effect, all cargoes destined to and from the Mediterranean, thus including Europe, Africa, and even the east coast of the Americas, would benefit.

According to the above authors freight transportation capacity will need to increase to 75 million tons over the next decade. The current capacity of the Volga-Don Canal is less than 15 million, the vast majority of which is taken up by Russian cargoes. Ships larger than 5,000 tons cannot pass through it.

With oil reserves of 24-26 billion tons, the region accounts of 6-10% of world reserves, and with 8.3 trillion cubic meters of gas reserves and exports of 25 to 50 million tons per year, the transport of hydrocarbons through such a canal would benefit. While pipelines can transport oil and gas, refined products are best transported by ship.

---

4 http://kirsan.today/en/analytics/item/1175-ilyumzhinov-s-project-the-new-silk-road.html

5 http://ges.rgo.ru/jour/article/view/273/270

Cargoes from the region not associated with hydrocarbons is estimated at 20 to 25 million tons. The vast majority of this cargo is transported by rail and road. Much of region's exports are bulk cargoes, including 4.5 million tons of grain exports from Kazakhstan alone. The region is rich in mineral resources, which are expensive to extract and transport due to lack of water transport.

A Eurasia Canal would clearly lead to a dramatic increase in freight transport due to cargoes from China and other countries that would normally ship via China's east coast ports or by rail. A research study by Sinohydro found that 24 to 30 million tons of Chinese cargoes that would otherwise be transported through Chinese ocean ports would be diverted to the canal by 2030 and 43 to 51 million tons by 2050.

In terms of viability, for comparison the highly successful Rhine-Main-Danube Canal transports 6 million tons a year, and the more comparable St. Lawrence Seaway, 40 to 50 million tons.

Revolutionizing Navigation on the Caspian Sea

The revolutionary potential of the BRI in Central Asia demands a solution that will also revolutionize maritime transport. The largest ships plying the waters of the Caspian are no larger than 10,000 to 13,000 tons, the so-called river-sea class, primarily because that is the largest size for ships capable of navigating the Russian inland waterway network.

By contrast, ships up to 100,000 tons, the maximum size ship that can traverse the Bosporus Straits and Dardanelles, operate in the Black Sea.

Initial canal proposals called for a canal with the limited parameters for the river-sea ships of the 10,000 to 13,000 ton class.

The author of this report and Bekturganov and Bolaev concur that a canal should be modeled after that of the Great Lakes and St. Lawrence Seaway which can accommodate ships as large as 20,000 to 26,000 DWTs, so-called Seawaymax or Handysize. This class of ship is far more cost-effective in carrying cargoes to transshipment ports on the Black Sea, especially at the port of Constanta at the entrance of the Danube-Black Sea Canal, where cargoes can be transferred to barges and enter the European inland waterway network. They could also sail direct to the ports of the Mediterranean and the Seven Seas.

The parameters of such a canal would require a two-way channel and locks to accommodate ships 226 meters long, 24 meters wide, and 7.15 meters draft. At a required length of 750 km it would not be much longer than the 600 km St. Lawrence Seaway, including the canals and locks connecting the five lakes.

Moreover the topography of the Kuma-Manych Depression is almost ideal for canal construction and would require far fewer locks than the Great Lakes and St. Lawrence Seaway (15) and the 172-km Rhine-Main-Danube Canal (16).

The Caspian Sea is 27 meters lower than the Azov and Black seas. The watershed between the Azov Sea and the Caspian Sea has an elevation of 27 meters on its western slope and 54 meters on the east slope.

This compares to the watershed between the Main and Danube rivers which require lifting ships 176 meters. The Eurasia Canal would require three shipping locks of low pressure on the western slope, and three of average pressure or six of low pressure on the eastern slope.

Up until now it has been proposed to use the remains of the old Manych ship-irrigation canal which

Handysize bulk carrier vessel COPAN in Bosporus waters

includes the Manych River and a series of artificial lakes and reservoirs which would have to be connected and deepened. There is also the issue of supplying water for the canal, which would require the erection of dams and possible water transfer from the Volga.

Bekturganov and Bolaev suggest building an entirely new construction parallel to the old structures. Such a cement-lined canal would allow for better management of water resources that could be integrated in a regional system of optimal management of water resources to improve the ecosystem and benefit the industry, agriculture, and fisheries sectors.

The costs of the canal are estimated anywhere between $4.5 billion to $17 billion, depending on the design parameters. This cost must be measured against the huge benefits that directly affect not only the vast region of Central Asia and China, but also well beyond as a new development corridor stretching from the Mediterranean and through the Black and Caspian Seas is created.

The decision for the United States and Canada to jointly develop the St. Lawrence Seaway took 50 years before construction started, primarily because of opposition from vested interests including railway companies and ocean port operators—not cost. It took strong leadership by President Dwight D. Eisenhower to finally overcome the resistance of those interests and get the project off the drawing boards.

There also vested interests blocking the Eurasia Canal, the most serious being the EU and Western interests that continue a policy of isolating Russia and view the BRI as a threat to what are old imperial interests. Once these are overcome, and they will be overcome, a new path will be opened to integrate Eurasia.

ITALY: BUILD THE MEZZOGIORNO, AND A NEW RENAISSANCE

On May 14, 2017, speaking after Chinese President Xi Jinping at the Belt and Road Forum in Beijing, Italian Prime Minister Paolo Gentiloni declared that the BRI is "perhaps the most important infrastructure modernization project underway in the world today."

Gentiloni added that "bringing the Chinese economy closer through this gigantic infrastructural operation is enormously interesting to Italy, not only for our government but also for our universities and public and private businesses." Gentiloni stressed that Italy has strong cards to play in building a European terminal of the Maritime Silk Road.

Many hoped that negotiations with the Chinese would start again, after they had been interrupted in 2011, to develop southern Italy (the "Mezzogiorno") as a terminal for the Maritime Silk Road, but this did not occur. Instead, the Italian government chose to offer as terminals the northern Italian ports of Genoa, Venice, and Trieste, whose connections to northern and eastern Europe are already quite developed, and therefore involve a minimal effort in investments.

This is, however, a strategic mistake. Italy will fully exploit its geographical position only if it develops its Mezzogiorno regions, which are today a burden for the national economy. Italy's Mezzogiorno, with a population of 20 million, includes the regions of Molise, Campania, Basilicata, Puglia, Calabria, and the islands of Sicily and Sardinia.

Whereas northern Italy is as productive as Germany, its southern part is exactly one-fourth less productive than the north. Accordingly, whereas official unemployment in the north is around 10%, in the Mezzogiorno it is more than 25%. Youth unemployment is more than 50%.

And yet, the geographical position of southern It-

Figure 24
Strait of Messina Bridge and Tunnel to Tunisia

aly offers the potential for a reversal of this situation, turning a depressed region into a booming economy. The Chinese understood this when, in 2010, they chose the deep-sea port of Augusta, Sicily, as a potential European terminal for maritime trade between Asia and Europe. Meetings had taken place in 2010 between representatives of the Sicilian government and Chinese officials, including party leaders, sovereign funds and banks, and the Chinese ministry for the commercial fleet in Beijing.

The very idea alarmed then U.S. Secretary of State Hillary Clinton, who raised the issue with Italian Foreign Minister Franco Frattini. Nevertheless, negotiations between the Italians and the Chinese proceeded, and a delegation led by the Chinese Trade Minister travelled to Augusta and Catania to discuss technical aspects.

Augusta is a deep-sea port (22 m at its deepest point), but needs to be upgraded in its port infrastructure, especially in view of the planned doubling of the Suez Canal. The Chinese offered to entirely finance the upgrade, in exchange for a long-term lease. They demanded, however, that what they called "the stable connection with the European hinterland" be built.

What they meant by that is a bridge over the Messina Strait between Sicily and the Italian mainland (**Figure 24**), including upgrading railway lines to and from the bridge.

Thus, Augusta would become fully efficient as a base where Chinese ships would unload their freight, load new freight, and continue from there. At that time, under the Berlusconi government in Italy, construction of the bridge was starting, although part of the financing issue had not yet been clarified. A large part was supposed to be financed with private capital, to be repaid through toll revenues.

The Chinese offered to help finance the bridge, so that tolls would be reduced to a minimum. A meeting took place between representatives of the Chinese Railways, government officials, and the Società Stretto di Messina (the Messina Bridge Authority).

The Chinese also offered to build an intercontinental airport in Sicily, to be a base for Africa trade. The Italian counterpart, which included central government officials and the contractors for the Messina Bridge Authority, agreed with the project.

But in December 2011, the EU toppled the Italian government and installed a technocratic government led by Mario Monti, with the mandate of imposing austerity policies. One of the first measures Monti announced was the cancellation of the Messina Bridge project, arguing that there was no money in the budget.

Springboard for Development of North Africa

To foster a rebirth of the Mezzogiorno, its geographical role in the center of the Mediterranean, and its potential land connection from central Europe through the Italian peninsula to Africa, must be considered. From its northeast to its southernmost point, the island of Lampedusa, the Italian "boot," stretches for 1,291 km as a natural bridge between Northern Africa and Central Europe. It is 140 km from the coast of Tunisia, and 70 km from the Albanian coast. There are projects to connect at least one of these two distances through an undersea tunnel.

Italy is the only country belonging to "Southern Europe" that has a self-subsisting industrial capacity, able to provide capital goods for itself as well as other countries. Italy has the second-largest manufacturing sector in Europe, after Germany. The problem is that this industrial base is concentrated in northern Italy, and partly in central Italy, whereas southern Italy is underdeveloped. Italy's industrial potential is now blocked by its loss of sovereignty. The euro system vetoes the creation of credit for development, and forces industrial companies to outsource production. These two main problems must be eliminated by re-establishing monetary and credit sovereignty, and protective measures of commerce. If this is done, Italy can go back to the FDR-style methods used in the postwar reconstruction, and use its large scientific and industrial potential to develop its southern region, while helping to develop neighboring countries, such as Greece, Spain, Portugal, and Northern Africa.

By extending its capacities in the Mezzogiorno, northern Italian industry will enjoy the unique advantage of being closer than any competitor to its export markets. Italy's Mezzogiorno must become the production site for capital goods for itself and for the entire Mediterranean region.

Here are the main projects to be implemented.

Energy

Energy is the main deficit item in the Italian trade balance. Italy imports 78% of the energy it consumes, as electricity, and as fuel for industrial and domestic consumption. Of its electricity, 12% (43 TWh) is imported from France, Switzerland, and Slovenia. Of the electricity produced domestically, 66% (230 TWh) comes from imported natural gas; coal accounts for 18%, and oil, 16%.

This causes energy prices for production to be on average 30% higher than for Italy's industrial competitors. To stay in the market in today's insane system of free trade and globalization, Italian producers are thus pressured to reduce labor costs. Due to this and to high rates of taxation (more than 50% of the gross wage), Italian wages are among the lowest in Europe.

The energy problem is the result of the demolition of Italy's nuclear capability which, in 1966, was the third-largest in the world after the United States and Great Britain. In 1987, when that capability was shut down, Italy was the technology leader in Europe in this area. A solution to Italy's energy problems will come through a massive return to nuclear energy.

Italy's nuclear tradition goes back to Enrico Fermi, the father of the first nuclear reactor in the world, built in Chicago in 1942. Enrico Mattei built the first Italian commercial reactor in 1958. After the first oil crisis in 1973, Italy had four active nuclear plants and the government pushed a plan to build six new reactors. A massive British-led economic and political assault against Italy, using the newly-born environmentalist mob, brought the Italian nuclear program first to a stop, and then to a shutdown, with a national referendum conducted in 1986 under the emotional shock of the Chernobyl accident.

When the government resumed a nuclear program, planning to build eight new plants in order to achieve 25% of its electricity from nuclear, the same forces organized another referendum in 2011. It turned out that the referendum coincided with the Fukushima accident following the Japanese tsunami in February 2011. The massive Goebbels-like media propaganda campaign resulted in another plebiscite against nuclear energy, and the nuclear program was cancelled.

New nuclear reactors can and must be built in southern Italy, starting with one per region—Campania, Basilicata, Puglia, Calabria, Sicily, and Sardinia. With a mixed system of European Pressurized Reactor (EPR) and High-Temperature Reactor (HTR) complexes, production of about 10 GW can be achieved with the first shot. Anti-seismic and other considerations will lead, in some cases, to building the plants on floating platforms off the coast.

At the same time, four plants can be built in central and northern Italy, in Trino Vercellese, Latina, Caorso, and Montalto di Castro, on the same site as the old plants, for a total capacity of about 16 GW. In a second phase, this capacity can be doubled.

Although due to the nuclear moratorium, Italian industry has not built any nuclear plants since 1987, companies such as ENEL, ENI, and Ansaldo (Finmeccanica Group) have continued to participate in international consortia, so that the know-how has been maintained. This means that Italy could start exporting nuclear technology after the first phase of its own nuclear program is completed.

Transportation Networks

A revolution in freight transport is indispensable in Italy, and will produce a great boost in productivity. Currently, only 10% of commercial goods are moved by rail, 0.1% on barges, and 0.6% on coastal waters, despite Italy's 7,750 km of coastline. The huge remainder goes by truck on the roads, with a great expense for gasoline and rubber, and creation of massive traffic congestion. Producers do not use rail because it is slow and inefficient. It takes a container less time to go from Milan to Berlin than from Palermo to Rome. An effort to change this involves upgrading the rail network, making it faster and more efficient.

Currently, Italy is completing its sections of three Trans-European corridors of high-speed rail that connect most of the country's major cities—Corridor 6 (Lyon-Kiev), Corridor 1 (Berlin-Palermo), and Corridor 24 (Genoa-Rotterdam). The Milan-Salerno part of Corridor 1 (**Figure 25**), which involved major engineering work in its Bologna-Florence Apennine part because of 73 km of tunnels, is already functioning. The Turin-Venice section of Corridor 6 (**Figure 26**) is being completed. The Milan-Genoa section of Corridor 24 (**Figure 27**) is scheduled to be ready by 2020.

Figure 25

The Italian sections of Corridors 6 and 24 are opposed by environmentalist groups, which are often violent, and backed by the media. The environmentalist mobilization against the Turin-Lyon section, which includes a new 57-km-long tunnel under the Alps, has degenerated into violent clashes with the police and against the construction site. In the past years, as prosecutors in Turin arrested insurgent leaders, they discovered two former members of the Red Brigades terrorist group.

The same groups oppose the new Genoa-Milan high-speed project. Those corridors, once completed, will provide modern and fast connections between the ports of Genoa, Venice, and Trieste, which the Italian government has offered as terminals for the Maritime Silk Road.

Once implemented, however, these three lines will not be sufficient. Italy has 55.4 km of rail per 1,000 square km, about half the density in Germany (94.5 km). Italy has 238 km of rail per 1 million in-

Figure 26

Figure 27

habitants, as compared to 481 in France and 412 in Germany. The high-speed section is currently 13 km per million inhabitants, as opposed to 16 in Germany, 30 in France, and 35 in Spain. Furthermore, of the conventional lines, only half of the total 22,935 km are electrified, and 9,213 km are single tracked. The latter case dominates, for instance, in Sicily.

These figures, however, supplied by the national railway company, do not reveal that a large portion of the secondary lines is in a state of decay. This involves commuter line connections among minor centers. Thus, an effort to modernize the Italian railway system means double-tracking the single-tracked lines, electrifying half of the current network, and doubling it on a national scale.

Italy's strategic goal still is to develop its Mezzogiorno. In the Mezzogiorno, railway lines must be quadrupled, and high-speed rail lines must be extended beyond the current southern terminal, Salerno, to the tip of the "boot," and over the future Messina Bridge, to Palermo.

From Palermo, the line will be continued to the small town of Pizzolato, in the province of Trapani, where an undersea tunnel will connect with Capo Bon, in Tunisia. The bridge over the Messina Strait will be a major engineering enterprise. At 3.3 km, it will be the longest single-span suspension bridge in the world (**Figure 28**). The bridge will connect the cities of Messina and Reggio Calabria, creating a single, large urban conglomerate, with more than 2 million people. This urban center will be connected by high-speed line to Central and Northern Italy, to Central Europe, and, via the same line and the Sicily-Tunisia tunnel, to North Africa.

Part of this center, on the Calabrian side, is the deep-water port of Gioia Tauro, which could become, together with Augusta in Sicily, the main port receiving cargo ships coming from the Suez Canal. Currently, 30 million 20-foot-equivalent-unit (TEU) containers per year move through the Mediterranean, and Italy handles fewer than 4 million, 3 million of which are handled in Gioia Tauro.

At least 20 million TEUs head to Gibraltar, circumnavigate the Iberian Peninsula, and dock in Rotterdam in order to reach Central Europe. It would be much easier to unload the freight in Southern Italy, put it on a train, and ship it to the North, but this is not convenient now because of the inefficiency of the rail connection. (A similar plan is underway with the Chinese-backed port of Piraeus in Greece.) After Sicily and Calabria ports are efficiently connected via rail, starting by making the current conventional rail efficient, while building a high-speed connection to Salerno, freight would take 30 hours or less to reach Berlin, as opposed to the current time of one week.

High-speed rail must be extended over the Messina Bridge to Palermo and beyond, so that Corridor 1 can be extended all the way into Africa This will be achieved with the undersea tunnel and a bridge to Tunisia, the former a project of the Italian national research agency ENEA and the latter an idea by Enzo Siviero called TuneIt.

The Experience of the Cassa per il Mezzogiorno

The Fund for the Development of Southern Italy (Cassa per il Mezzogiorno), established in 1950, is still today a model for the development of southern Italy and other underdeveloped regions of the Mediterranean area. Thanks to the Cassa, the development of Italy's Mezzogiorno took off, going through a decade (1950-1960) in which, for the first time, the income of southern families grew at the same rate as the income of northern families.

Private land ownership, the idea of the "independent farmer," appeared in southern Italy only in 1950, with the De Gasperi[1] land reform that distributed 30% of the latifundia to farmers. The Cassa was fundamental in ensuring that the new farmers would get credit and means for productive improvements, including irrigation, seeds, machines, and livestock.

In the 1950-1960 decade, the Cassa was flanked by the role of the state conglomerate IRI in building infrastructure and industries throughout Italy, and by the state oil company Ente Nazionale Idrocarburi (ENI) in providing cheap energy through the discovery of large gas reservoirs in the northern Po plain. The steady 7% yearly growth was called an "economic miracle"; inflation was defeated, and for a short time, even became negative. The national currency, the lira, was recognized for its stability. In 1959, full employment was reached.

By 1975, when the role of the Cassa was abruptly downsized through the devolutionary introduction of regional governments that took over jurisdiction of long-term investments, the Cassa per il Mezzogiorno had created 2 million hectares of irrigated land; built 62 dams, 52 aqueducts, and numerous sewage systems; modernized 20,000 km of roads, and built 6,000 km of new ones; electrified railway lines; and started numerous industrial centers. However, the job was only half done.

Following the model of the Tennessee Valley Authority and the New Deal projects for the Appalachian region in the United States, the Cassa was given un-

A sign detailing a road construction project of the Cassa per il Mezzogiorno

precedented technical competence and power, including funding to finance a ten-year program that was drafted and executed by the Cassa itself, under approval of a special government committee composed of the Minister for the Mezzogiorno, and the ministers of the Treasury, Finance, Public Works, and Labor.

In addition to the long-term projects, which the Cassa leaders drafted with an integrated approach, new projects could be adopted yearly, according to the changed situation. The Cassa's structure allowed it to move funds it had earmarked for a project, to another project, if priorities changed. Local authorities were forced to collaborate with the Cassa and put their competencies at its disposal. As the Cassa's longtime president, Gabriele Pescatore, often said, the aim of the Cassa was to create "a process of self-subsistent capital accumulation."

The regional devolution meant a shift from a unitary integrated approach for infrastructural development of the entire Mezzogiorno, to local approaches and views, breaking up the unitary vision and ending the development process, which degenerated into localism and clientelism.

Today, the original approach of the Cassa per il Mezzogiorno must be revived to foster a rebirth of southern Italy and provide a locomotive for the entire Italian economy—and that of all the Mediterranean.

---

[1] Alcide De Gasperi (1881-1954) served as prime minister during 1945-53; and as foreign affairs minister and interior minister before that.

Figure 28
Strait of Messina Bridge and Italy-Albania Connection

The distance between the coastlines is about 155 km, and will be reached by five tunnels constructed between four intermediate artificial islands that will be built with the excavated material. There would be two tunnels in each direction, plus one service tunnel. On the surface, a bridge will be built using the Messina bridge as a module. The tunnel will provide a fast commercial railway route to export capital goods for the development of North Africa, not only from Italy, but also from Central Europe.

Another tunnel and/or bridge could be built between Italy and Albania, connecting the port cities of Otranto and Valona (**Figure 28**). There is no concrete plan yet, although Italian and Albanian authorities have talked about it in the past. This would connect the newly created European-African landbridge with the Via Egnatia corridor, thus creating a short cut for a Balkan-African connection.

Waterways

Italy has a poor internal waterway system. Basically, only the Po River is partially navigable, along with a network of channels in the Veneto-Emilia Romagna region that go back to the time of the Republic of Venice.

And yet, the Lombardy region is studying plans for making the Po entirely navigable from the Adriatic coast to Milan.

At the same time, a major waterway could be opened in northeast direction, connecting the Adige River with the Inn River, creating a waterway that goes from Venice to Passau, connecting the northern Italian network to the entire central European waterway system. The project, developed by the Tyrol-Adria AG company, foresees a canal-tunnel between the Inn River in Austria and the Adige in Italy, which come within 70 km of each other on the plain.

The tunnel-canal would be 78 km long, and would be large enough to allow the passage of barges of the EU Class V. Water would be pumped into the tunnel, creating an artificial current that would push the ships, thus avoiding the use of engines and pollution of the tunnel. The energy for pumping the water is produced by hydroelectric plants built along the Inn.

SPAIN AND PORTUGAL: THE WORLD LAND-BRIDGE'S BRIDGE TO AFRICA AND IBERO-AMERICA

At the Belt and Road summit in Beijing in May 2017, Chinese President Xi Jinping suggested to the Prime Minister of Spain, Mariano Rajoy—who was one of the few European heads of state wise enough to attend that summit—that Spain could serve as a kind of bridge of the BRI to Africa and to the nations of Ibero-America, with which Spain has a long historical connection. Not only Spain but also Portugal, which together form the Iberian Peninsula, have eagerly taken up Xi's proposal, and over the past year have been actively working out the specific projects and proposals to make that perspective a reality.

As Spain's then-Economics and Trade Attaché in Beijing, Javier Serra Guevara, argued in a February 2016 policy paper, Spain should not view its role in the global project as merely a Western terminus of the Belt and Road, "but should propose itself as a hub to link that corridor with the north of Africa and Latin America." Portuguese Economics Minister Manuel Caldeira Cabral likewise told the First Sino-Portuguese Economic Forum, held in Portugal less than two weeks before the May 2017 Beijing Belt and Road Summit, that Portugal is ready to play the part of a "pivot country, which builds bridges between Asia and Europe, as well as a port of entry to Europe."

The Iberian Peninsula is in fact the natural geographic interface of the Silk Road Economic Belt, which now stretches from the Pacific to the Atlantic across the Eurasian land mass, with the Maritime Silk Road, which will extend westward across the Atlantic Ocean to Ibero-America, the Caribbean, and the United States, as well as southward to Africa. Two critical points for that interface will be the Spanish port of Algeciras, located at the mouth of the Mediterranean Sea and currently the busiest port in the Mediterranean, and the Portuguese port of Sines on the Atlantic.

As part of that full integration of Spain and Portugal into the BRI, those nations will develop major projects in the following areas:

Rail: Spain and Portugal will build high-technology industrial corridors on either side of some 15,000 km of new, high-speed rail lines (including magnetically-levitated systems) that will crisscross the Iberian Peninsula, and link up with the World Land-Bridge in southern France.

Strait of Gibraltar Tunnel: A 40 km tunnel built under the Strait of Gibraltar, from Spain to Morocco, will allow European rail corridors to be connected to future North African rail systems. This will be a project on the scale, and of the significance, of the Bering Strait tunnel and the Darién Gap project because, like them, it will link an entire continent into the World Land-Bridge.

Water: Spain will dust off existing, viable water transfer projects, such as the Ebro River project, to transfer about 1 cubic km of water per year to the semi-arid Mediterranean coast, and it will also produce some 1.5 cubic km of fresh water yearly with nuclear-powered desalination plants.

Nuclear Energy: In addition to the nuclear plants needed for desalination, Spain will build modern nuclear power plants to produce about three times the 7,500 MWe per year that the country currently gets from its eight aging nuclear plants. This will allow Spain to rid itself of the economically destructive (and scientifically incompetent) emphasis on wind and solar power, which has been imposed on it by the British Empire's fascist Greenie movement, led by the World Wildlife Fund (WWF). (Where is Don Quixote when we need him?)

Space Science: The Canary Islands is an ideal location for a new Euro-African space center, including a major satellite-launching facility and related science city. This will be coordinated with critical work being carried out in Greece, Italy, and other nations on earthquake precursor detection and other endeavors involved in the Strategic Defense of Earth program, in furtherance of the common aims of mankind.

This will not be the first time in its history that Spain will play a catalytic role at the crossroads of co-operating civilizations. Under the personal guidance of Alfonso X, "The Wise," King of Castile and Leon during 1252-1282, the Castilian capital of Toledo was built into Europe's most important scientific center of the time, and became the nexus for the transmission of the Greek Classics and the highest achievements of the Arab Renaissance into continental Europe. Alfonso was especially known for his work in astronomy, and for his Toledo school of translation, which brought together the outstanding scholars of the world's three major monotheistic religions—Islam, Christianity, and Judaism—to render the most advanced religious and scientific texts of each culture, into the languages of the others. It is past time for a new "Alfonsi Era."

For its part, Portugal launched a virtual "Apollo Project" of mastery of deep sea voyaging and navigation under the direction of Prince Henry the Navigator in the first half of the 1400s. Prince Henry's "School of Sagres" and its successors, worked in intimate collaboration with Florence during the high-water mark of the Florentine Renaissance during the same years. Paolo dal Pozzo Toscanelli, one of the greatest figures in that Renaissance, provided the world map outlining the lands to be found by sailing west across the Atlantic, to Portugal in the 1470s, right at the time Columbus was washed up on Portuguese shores after a shipwreck. Columbus studied the map and entered into correspondence with Toscanelli, in the course of more than 15 years he spent absorbing the most advanced knowledge of Portuguese seafaring, before transferring his services to the Spanish court of Isabella and Ferdinand.

The Iberian Bridge

Both Spain and Portugal are already taking steps in the right direction.

When President Mariano Rajoy went to Beijing to participate in the Belt and Road summit in May 2017, he took his Development Minister and Secretary of State of Trade with him. His main message at the forum and in his bilateral meetings with Xi and Prime Minister Li Keqiang was that Spain's world-class infrastructure, engineering, and construction companies want to participate in building the Belt and Road in other countries, from Asia to Ibero-America. (Spain's large infrastructure companies do 73% of their business abroad, because Spain's domestic economy is, in physical economic terms, moribund.)

Work began immediately on developing this trilateral cooperation. The Spanish Confederation of Employers' Organizations (CEOE), China's Chamber of Commerce and Investment in Spain (CCINCE), and China's Embassy in Spain sponsored a forum in Madrid on June 1, 2017 to present "Business Opportunities for Spanish Companies under the Belt and Road Initiative," where 200 representatives of Chinese and Spanish companies participated. Spanish State Secretary for Commerce Marisa Poncela opened the forum by telling the businessmen that "all the tools of the State Secretariat for Commerce are available" for Spanish participation in the BRI. Spain wants to have not only a land connection by rail, she said, but also "the maritime connection between China and Europe to end in Spain, in our ports, Barcelona, Valencia, in all of our ports on the Mediterranean, or even beyond, in our country."

Three weeks later, a cooperation agreement was signed between the Spanish and Chinese Chambers of Commerce, at a Spain-China Business Forum in Madrid. Numerous agreements for joint business cooperation were reported to have been discussed by the more than 100 Chinese and Spanish companies participating, with metallurgy, aeronautics, construction engineering, shipbuilding, and railroads identified as among the priority areas of Spanish interest in the BRI.

Later in 2017, China's National Development and Reform Commission (NDRC) and Spain's state trade promotion agency, ICEX Spain Trade and Investment, organized a forum in Beijing in December on "Opportunities for Cooperation in Equipment, Engineering and Infrastructure" to discuss strategies for joint work in third countries, as part of the New Silk Road. Attended by representatives of 50 Chinese and Spanish companies, the aim of the seminar was to get Spanish and Chinese companies to work together, instead of competing with each other, Jose

Luis Kaiser, Director General of Spain's Secretary of State for Trade, told Spain's news agency, EFE. "We always have the idea that the large consortia of Chinese and Spanish companies compete for great infrastructure projects worldwide, but we think that they are complementary, both because of geographic specialization and because of technology, and therefore we are looking for them to work together," Kaiser said. Each can provide needed regional "know-how" to the other, he said, pointing out that Spanish companies are not very active in Southeast and Central Asia, but have a lot of experience and presence in Ibero-America.

Spain: Debating the Mission

In February 2018, Spain's Foreign Ministry issued a report summarizing the findings of a multi-ministry study on "A Strategic Vision for Spain in Asia, 2018-2022." The report points to the opportunities for Spanish engineering and infrastructure companies in the New Silk Road, but adds the recommendation (Point Four), that a "Spanish New Silk Road Strategy be prepared, with the participation of all public and private actors with an interest in the initiative, so that everyone can contribute to this strategy, as regards their respective areas of activity."

A national debate on a Silk Road strategy could transform Spain. Participation in the New Silk Road offers Spain a much bigger opportunity than simply more business for its multinational companies abroad, as important as that is.

The great issue before the Spanish people is how to revitalize the nation's physical economy. According to official statistics, 16% of its labor force of 23 million (Spain's total population is 46.3 million) are still without work, as of the first months of 2018, with 35.5% of its under-25 working-age youth unemployed. Peninsular Spain enjoys one of the largest land areas in Europe, yet it has one of its lowest population densities. Instead of the booming population growth it requires to fully develop, Spain's total population is still below what it was in 2010, while the median age of its people, at 43.6 years, is higher than in 2010. Spain is in desperate need of the jobs, upgraded infrastructure, industrial growth, agricul-

Figure 29
Iberian Peninsula: Atlantic Rail Corridor

tural modernization, and new cities required for it to begin its own national rejuvenation, as China has done for its more than 1.4 billion people.

Spain's more farsighted autonomous communities (regions), port authorities, and national businesses are already turning to China's Belt and Road as the hope for their future.

The northeastern autonomous community of Aragón is exemplary. On December 20, 2017, it celebrated the success of months of travel back and forth to China, with the arrival of the first transcontinental container train from Zhengzhou, China at the intermodal terminal in its capital, Zaragoza, which is already the second largest dry port in Spain (see **Figure 29**). Located in the interior of the country, officials are promoting this rail connection to China, a branch of the Yiwu-Madrid rail route, as an excellent choice for shipping food and agricultural exports to China and countries along the way, among other features. Zaragoza's mayor and officials from Aragon's government were on hand for the arrival of the first shipment, and spoke proudly of being "pioneers" and having "put Aragon on the map." Local newspapers headlined that "Aragón Is Now a Regular Part of the New Silk Road."

The ports of Valencia and Algeciras have likewise been working hard to position themselves on the New Silk Road. Both have invited Chinese delegations to inspect their facilities and invest in their development, and they have sent officials to participate in major international port conferences in China. A leading official from the Algeciras Bay Port Authority spoke at the Third Maritime Silk Road Port International Cooperation Forum in China's Ningbo Port in July 2017, "laying out to attendees the possibilities which the Algeciras port offers as a logistical partner for African and European markets," while the head of the Port Authority of Valencia told the "International Forum on the Belt and Road Port Cities" in Tianjin in December that the port of Valencia, a terminus on the Ancient Silk Road, "is ready to take advantage of the opportunities that come hand in hand with the new Silk Road."

The prospects for national business offered by the Silk Road inspired Valencia's Businessmen's Association to lead a spirited national mobilization to demand the national government commit the resources required to finish the Mediterranean corridor, a railway running from the border with France down to the port of Algeciras on the Strait of Gibraltar in the south, passing through Barcelona, Valencia, Alicante, Murcia, and Málaga along the way (described later in this chapter). Meetings in four regions involving hundreds of businessmen culminated in a heated October 3, 2017 meeting in Madrid of more than 1,500 businessmen and civil society representatives who insisted the rail line be completed on time and as planned, as a double-tracked, high-speed rail line with separate tracks for passenger and freight.

Portugal's Links to the Belt and Road Initiative

Portugal has had a keen interest in playing a leading role in the Maritime Silk Road from the outset. Since its audacious sea-faring days of the 15th and 16th Centuries, "the sea has always been in Portugal's DNA," as the President of Portugal's Friends of the New Silk Road Association, Prof. Fernanda Ilhéu, often notes.

Now Portugal has finally won its several-year fight for recognition that it also must be connected to the land-based New Silk Road economic corridors. For the Iberian Peninsula to serve its proper role as a bridge in the BRI, those corridors must not end in Spain, but continue on to Portugal. Both nations gain from the connection.

Portugal's participation in the BRI was the centerpiece of Prime Minister Antonio Costa's five-day official visit to China in October 2016. Lisbon had been a key port on the maritime routes between China and Europe in centuries past, and today Portugal seeks to revive that role through the BRI, he emphasized. Costa signed an MOU with his Chinese counterpart, Li Keqiang, on expanding third-party cooperation between their nations. Both leaders also spoke at the Fifth Ministerial Conference of the Forum for Economic and Trade Cooperation between China and Portuguese-speaking countries, held in Macao, which is now functioning as a gateway for cooperation between China and Brazil and Portuguese-speaking countries in Africa, in particular.

As part of Costa's visit, the state Portuguese Investment and Foreign Trade Agency (AICEP) signed an MOU with Haitong Bank and China Development Bank to form a consortium to interest Chinese companies in upgrading and expanding the industrial and logistics zone at Portugal's Sines Port.

Sines, a deep-water port on the Atlantic located some 55 km south (by road) of Lisbon, is pivotal to Portugal's participation in the BRI. Appropriately, Sines was the birthplace of Portuguese explorer Vasco da Gama, the first European to sail around the southern tip of Africa and on to India and further east at the turn of the 15th Century.

Portugal was represented at the May 2017 Belt and Road Summit by then-Secretary of State for Internationalization Jorge Costa Oliveira. While in Beijing, he told Xinhua and Lusa news agencies that Portugal proposes to contribute to the BRI through two big projects, and the first is to establish an Atlantic Ocean route of the Belt and Road through Sines port. The port's importance is enhanced now that much larger ships can go through the expanded Panama Canal, he said, but he emphasized that for Sines to function as "the meeting point" between the Silk Road land routes and the Atlantic, the Chinese rail line from Chongqing to Madrid must continue onto Sines, and that requires significant upgrading of Portugal-Spain rail connections.

The second project identified by Costa Oliveira is that of connecting Portugal's electrical grid to that of Morocco and all North Africa, through an undersea interconnector. The idea was initiated by China, whose State Grid electricity utility is a major investor in Portugal's state electricity company. This project remains in the stage of feasibility studies.

When China's top parliamentarian, Zhang Deijiang, chair of the National People's Congress's Standing Committee, visited Portugal during July 10-12, 2017, Prime Minister Costa again identified Portugal's role as a crossroads for the Belt and Road relating to other developing countries. At a ceremony with Zhang to celebrate the upcoming inauguration of direct flights between the two countries on July 26, Costa noted that Portugal is already a great hub for Brazil and Africa. Sines Port occupies a "crucial position to become, for the maritime routes, an essential part of this initiative," he specified. "With the opening of these routes to the East, Portugal can become a strategic hub for doing what Portugal and the Portuguese have always done throughout its history: unite peoples, unite cultures, open routes, open doors."

Portugal's participation in the Maritime Silk Road took another step forward with the eight-day visit to China by Portugal's Minister of the Sea, Ana Paula Vitorino, at the end of October 2017. She was accompanied by representatives of 39 Portuguese port and related companies and industries hoping to concretize $2.5 billion in Chinese investments in expanding container and other facilities in the ports of Sines, Lisbon, and Leixoes, as well as in areas of "blue biotechnology," oceanic aquaculture, and marine industry. At high-level seminars and in her meetings, Vitorino reiterated that "Portugal wants to declare itself a global logistical hub in the Atlantic area," and "double the value of the blue economy," to become one of the five most sea-related economies in the world. She described Portugal as "a necessary stop on north-south Atlantic routes ... [and] a required crossing point in east-west routes."

Among other agreements reached, Vitorino and her Chinese counterpart, State Oceanic Administration Director Wang Hong, signed an Action Plan outlining collaboration on research and commercial projects as part of an expanded "blue economy" partnership.

A few weeks later, on November 24, Chinese and Portuguese public companies signed an MOU for a joint partnership to build rail and road projects in Portuguese-speaking countries in Africa, with the possibility of doing the same in Brazil. The MOU was signed at AICEP's Lisbon headquarters between IP Engenharia/Grupo Infra-estruturas de Portugal and China Tiesiju Civil Engineering Group/China Railway Engineering Corp.

Shao Gang, vice-president of the Chinese group, reported that a joint commission of Portuguese and Chinese companies would draw up a timetable in January 2018 for the implementation of joint projects in the Portuguese-speaking African countries of Angola, Mozambique, Cabo Verde, São Tomé and Principe, and Guinea-Bissau, "projects that each country will most need to develop and stimulate the local economy," as Jornal de Angola reported on November 27.

In March 2018, the first steps were taken to close the biggest gap on the Portuguese side of the project: building the stretch of high-speed rail required to connect the Sines port on the Atlantic with Badajoz, Spain, from there to Madrid, and then on to China and everything in between. In recognition of the importance of this project, Prime Ministers Antonio Costa and Mariano Rajoy joined in holding a ceremony in the Portuguese town of Elvas on the border of the two countries to mark the launching of the public tender for construction of the 94-km rail line from the town of Evora, southeast of Lisbon, to Elvas, near the Spanish border, and the start of construction of the 11-km stretch from Elvas to Caia, which is dubbed the "missing link" between the central Portuguese-Spanish rail systems (see Figure 29). Construction of the larger stretch of rail is scheduled to commence in March 2019, with work on the entire project to be completed by early 2022.

In his remarks, Costa emphasized that this is the largest stretch of rail line to be built in Portugal in the past 100 years; it will reduce the cost of shipping between the Sines, Setúbal, and Lisbon ports in the center of the country by 30%, and reduce the time of transport by 3 hours and 30 minutes, shortening the distance by 140 km. This corridor, which is part of the EU's South International Corridor, "will not only link all of the Iberian meseta to the Atlantic, but it will allow all of Europe to benefit from the deep-water port closest to the Panamanian Canal," Costa added.

Costa pointed to the benefits for both sides of the border which will be connected now by decent rail. Alentejo in Portugal and Extremadura in Spain—both among the poorest regions in each country—will "have the opportunity of having logistics platforms and production platforms, because we will be more connected with Europe and the Atlantic," Costa said. Rajoy called the rail projects Portugal is undertaking "excellent news" for Spain, because it will better the "day-to-day lives" of citizens of both nations.

Like Spain, Portugal has not recovered from the 2007-2008 crisis, and urgently requires the radical transformation of its physical economic platform that participation in the Belt and Road can bring. Since that time, Portugal's total population has dropped to just under 10.3 million people, down from a high of more than 10.6 million in 2010, and its median population age has risen to 44.4 years, higher even than Spain's. Unemployment of its under-25 working age youth is still higher than 21%.

Here the Friends of the New Silk Road Association (ANRS), the think-tank dedicated to fostering Portuguese cooperation with the Belt and Road set up in December 2016, is working on some exciting ideas. Its annual report, issued in December 2017, summarizes the work of various working groups it has set up to develop proposals for how Portuguese participation in the Belt and Road can develop Portugal's economy as a whole.

The ANRS working group on transportation, logistic platforms, and industrial parks, for example, is preparing a general development plan for the region between the ports of Sines and Setúbal, located approximately 130 km to the north of Sines by road. The plan focuses on increasing port capacities, logistical platforms, and industrial and tourist development zones in that area. They propose that the effort be connected to the development of the broader Lisbon to Évora area, which will benefit from the rail connection to the Spanish border discussed above, and to the creation of an aeronautics industry-centered "development hub" in the region between Évora and Beja, where a modern but still-underutilized new airport is located. And that, in turn, will lay the basis for drawing up a general plan for technological development in the entire Setúbal-Sines-Évora region.

Another taskforce is working on ideas for how Portugal can best develop the science and advanced skills and technologies required to exploit the rich mineral deposits lying offshore of its continental territory and around its Azores and Madeira islands in the Atlantic. Proposals include creating research centers dedicated to ocean sciences, robotics, nano-technologies, and related R&D.

Spain's Rail Sector: Building on Strength

As can be seen from the above overview, both Iberian nations are moving in the right direction of working with the BRI. But far more ambitious projects can and must be undertaken, as indicated below.

One of the few bright spots of Spain's physical economy is its rail sector, in terms of existing infrastructure as well as world-class engineering and production capabilities. High-speed trains now run on 3,240 km of track in Spain, with significant additional lines under construction.

Spain already has the second largest network of high-speed rail lines in the world, after China, as **Table 4** demonstrates.

The existing plan of the Spanish government—which can never be executed within the euro straitjacket—aims for having 10,000 km of high-speed track by 2020.

Historically, Spain has had a gauge (1,668 mm) different from most of Europe (1,435 mm, also called the UIC gauge), which has created major bottlenecks requiring, until relatively recently, transfer of passengers and freight at the French border. Portugal's slightly larger gauge of 1,774 mm is inter-operable with Spain's, so the two are often referred to as the "Iberian gauge." This is also a major problem as you move east into Ukraine, Belarus, and Russia, which have a third gauge (1,520 mm).

The very raison d'être of the World Land-Bridge, especially as maglev and other high-speed rail lines come online, demands a solution to this problem. New lines can and should be standardized, but interim solutions to link existing rail networks of different gauges are also required.

EUROPE

Table 4
High-Speed Rail Lines (km)

Country	Existing	Under Construction	Total
1. China	25,000	16,155	41,155
2. Spain	3,240	1,800	5,040
3. Germany	3,038	330	3,368
4. Japan	2,765	681	3,446
5. France	2,647	670	3,317
21. United States	45	0	45

Rather than transferring passengers and cargo between trains (and switching out locomotives), which is highly inefficient, there is now technology, pioneered by Spanish companies, to automatically change the gauge of the existing axles while the cars are in motion (at about 15 kph). This requires axles specially constructed for this purpose.

Spain's Talgo company pioneered work internationally in this area, developing the first commercial application of a track changeover system in 1969. A second Spanish company, CAF, developed its own system in 2003. Other countries now producing similar systems include Poland (SUW 2000, in 2000), Japan (in 2007), and Germany (Rafia, no commercial application yet).

There are a number of Spanish companies involved in high-speed rail today, including Talgo, Renfe, CAF, AVE, and others. CAF recently signed contracts for building five high-speed rail lines in Turkey. And Talgo has built and runs rail lines in Kazakhstan, Argentina, the United States, and the Portugal-Spain-France-Switzerland-Italy corridor in Europe.

They also recently sold 17 cars and one locomotive to Russian Railways, which will now be able to run continuously between Moscow (standard gauge) and Berlin (UIC gauge). Existing high-speed rail lines also link Berlin to Paris and Perpignan, and from there they will go under the Pyrenees Mountains through a new tunnel, to Figueras on the Spanish side, and down to Barcelona and Madrid.

In 1988, Spain decided to construct all of its new high-speed rail corridors at the European (UIC) gauge. There are currently four principal high-speed corridors: Madrid-Barcelona, Madrid-Valencia, Madrid-Valladolid, and Madrid-Sevilla/Málaga. As **Figure 30** shows, the existing lines in Spain are in the form of radial spokes with Madrid at the center.

What is required instead is a network which crisscrosses the entire peninsula and extends into Portugal. As noted above, two key terminuses of these networks will be the ports of Algeciras in Spain and Sines in Portugal, which will serve as key links to the Maritime Silk Road. Their corresponding rail corridors can be referred to as the Mediterranean corridor and the Atlantic corridor, which are described in turn.

Mediterranean Corridor

This corridor begins in Hungary and ends in the south of Spain, at the port of Algeciras, which is the number one port of the Iberian Peninsula in terms of traffic and cargo. The high-speed rail line would run from the border with France, through Barcelona, Valencia, Murcia, Cartagena, Almería, Granada, Málaga, and finally Algeciras. Only parts of it have been constructed so far (see **Figure 31**). The greatest population centers are to be found in Barcelona and Valencia. This project has a number of key features. First, it connects Spain with the rest of Europe. Second, there is a parallel corridor which goes to the center of the coun-

Figure 30
Spain: High-Speed Rail Lines

Figure 31

Spain: Mediterranean Rail Corridor

try, to Zaragoza, Madrid, Toledo, and Sevilla. In this way, there is access to the ports of the Mediterranean that in turn provide access to Africa and Asia.

Work is already underway on the Murcia-Almería route, which will provide a rail connection between the eastern coast and the southern, Andalusian coast of Spain. In that way, a direct high-speed connection would exist from the port of Algeciras all the way to Paris. This area has about 38% of Spain's population and an equal percentage of its employed labor force, concentrated in the cities of Valencia and Barcelona. However, between 75-80% of the employment in those cities is in the service sector. The situation in Andalusia is even worse, with more than 80% of employment provided by the service sector.

Industry, on the other hand, is concentrated in Castellón, to the north of Valencia, and in Girona, which is on the border with France. About 16% of those employed in that area work in the manufacturing sector. Further south, in Almería, there is significant agricultural potential—that province has the largest number of agricultural workers in the country. However, given the semi-arid conditions in the region, a significant increase in agricultural production will require an increase in the supply of fresh water for irrigation.

This area of Spain will see an increase in the demand for steel, copper, and cement, among other industrial inputs needed for the construction of the Strait of Gibraltar tunnel, and for the cooperation agreements with the nations of the north of Africa, to link Europe with the Transaqua project in central Africa. Therefore, it is likely that the logistical terminals of Sevilla and San Roque (near Algeciras), which will be critical for the transportation and storage of materials for these projects, will need to have their capacity significantly increased.

Similarly, given that the Algeciras port is already at or near capacity (an expansion is under discussion), the ports of Almería and Málaga will also need to be expanded and developed. All along the corridor, steel will be supplied from the Valencia region, which historically has had a tradition of steel production. The region of Aragón, which lies north of Valencia and stretches up to the border with France, is one of the areas of Spain with significant machine-tool production.

Atlantic Corridor

The Atlantic rail corridor (Figure 29) links the ports on the Atlantic Coast of the Iberian Peninsula—such as Sines and Porto, in Portugal, with the Spanish ports of Bilbao in the north and Algeciras in the south. Currently there are studies underway to build a high-speed rail link from Sines to Madrid, which would be crucial to extend the westernmost terminus of the New Silk Road from Madrid to Lisbon and Sines, and for shipment of maritime cargo from there to the Americas and Africa, as well as to allow for the shipment of products from Atlantic ports in the Americas and in Europe, by rail across the Iberian Peninsula. This would allow for reducing maritime shipping through the Strait of Gibraltar, and avoiding future congestion in that passage.

Another connection which is under study is Bilbao-Pamplona-Zaragoza-Valencia—that is, a Cantabrian-Mediterranean corridor. The June 2017 purchase by the Chinese port and shipping giant COSCO of controlling shares in Noatum Portus, a Spanish company which currently operates the ports of Bilbao and Valencia (as well as a half-dozen additional port facilities in the country), a purchase valued at EU203 million, opens up great possibilities in this regard. About 50% of Spain's population resides along the Atlantic corridor, including the cities of Vizcaya and Asturias in the north, Cádiz and Sevilla in the south, and Madrid in the center of the country. A large part of the country's capital and intermediate goods production comes from this area. For example, some 35% of the country's foundry and smelting activity occurs in Asturias, on the north coast of Spain. Metalworking is concentrated east of that, in the Basque country.

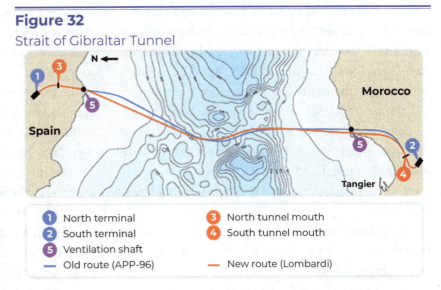

Figure 32
Strait of Gibraltar Tunnel

1 North terminal
2 South terminal
3 North tunnel mouth
4 South tunnel mouth
5 Ventilation shaft
— Old route (APP-96)
— New route (Lombardi)

The Gibraltar Tunnel

The southernmost point of this network in Spain is Algeciras. From here, a new high-speed rail line will be constructed to Tarifa and Cádiz; Tarifa will be the Spanish terminus of a tunnel with high-speed rail going under the Strait of Gibraltar to Tangiers, Morocco, and from there will link to the entire African leg of the World Land-Bridge.

The idea of a tunnel was first proposed in Spain in 1930, and since that time, various options have been considered, including a fixed bridge (ruled out because of the impossibility of building supporting pillars in 300 m or more of water), a floating bridge (discarded because of the strong cross-currents in the strait), and a tunnel bolted to the seabed (not viable, because of the strong currents and the seabed's instability in that region).

In 2003, Spain and Morocco agreed to explore the construction of a fixed tunnel, and in 2006, their SECEGSA (Spain) and SNED (Morocco) state companies hired the Swiss tunnel engineering company Lombardi to draft a design for the project. In 2009, the Lombardi proposal was presented to the EU—after which absolutely nothing has been done, because the entire Eurozone and world financial system is collapsing.

The Lombardi plan considered the option of a bridge at the narrowest point between the two continents (14 km), but because the seabed there is a very deep (900 m), it was discarded as impractical. The selected route instead runs at a more western point, from Tarifa, Spain, to Tangiers, Morocco, a route where the sea floor is "only" 300 m deep—which would make this the deepest undersea tunnel in the world. The length of the tunnel would be about 40 km (see **Figure 32**). It would consist of two tubes for train lines for passengers and freight, with an emergency or service tunnel running between them.

Lombardi estimated that it would take about 15 years to build, given the engineering problems to be solved—including the fact that it would run through a highly active seismic area (the Azores-Gibraltar Transform Fault), and difficulties in the stratification of the seabed there, described as a virtual "cocktail of sand, stone, and mud that make for a digger's nightmare." In fact, engineers have had to invent new boring methods just to drill exploratory holes, given the rock formations and the fierce underwater currents. For purposes of comparison, the Channel Tunnel is 50 m below sea level and 49 km long. The Bering Strait Tunnel would be at about the same depth (54 m), and run 85 km in total, but it would make use of the Big Diomede and Little Diomede islands as "stepping stones," making the longest stretch only about 35 km long.

Once completed, and linked to high-speed rail lines, SECEGSA/SNED calculate that it would take 1.5 hours to get from Casablanca to the tunnel terminus in Tangiers; 30 minutes to cross to Tarifa, Spain;

under 3.5 hours to then get to Madrid; and then 2.5 hours more to get to Barcelona. In other words, it would take less than 8 hours to get from Casablanca to Barcelona. The joint SECEGSA/SNED website summarizes their concept of the project as follows: "The Fixed Link through the Strait of Gibraltar can be considered the decisive connection between two continents and two great seas, which will articulate a heretofore unknown system of transportation between Europe and Africa and the Mediterranean surroundings."

As part of this project, it would be appropriate to return Gibraltar to Spain, from which the British stole it in the 1700s.

On the Morocco side, the Strait of Gibraltar tunnel will link up with high-speed rail lines in North Africa. The French are already helping to build high-speed rail lines in Morocco, and the entire North Africa rail project is a perfect area for French-Spanish cooperation.

. . . and on to Other Planets

Achieving these ambitious projects on planet Earth, however, depends on inspiring coming youth generations with mankind's true mission, his extraterrestrial imperative. The scientific breakthroughs, and the related cultural optimism, that is so sorely lacking today, will only come with such a focus and mission.

With that in mind, our Marshall Plan for the Mediterranean Basin will also construct a world-class Euro-African spaceport and associated science city on the Canary Islands. This location—100 km off the western coast of Morocco, at the same latitude as the United States' Cape Kennedy—is ideal for such a project.

There is, in fact, already advanced scientific work underway in the Canaries. The Canary Islands are the site of a number of observatories, the latest and biggest of which, the solar telescope GREGOR, was inaugurated on May 21, 2012 on Tenerife. There, on the plateau at the foot of the 3,718-m-high Teide volcano, the telescope, Europe's biggest, is being run by a consortium of researchers from the Kiepenheuer Institute for Solar Physics, Astrophysical Institute Potsdam, Institute for Astrophysics Göttingen, Max Planck Institute for Solar System Research, and other international partners, that began constructing the GREGOR solar telescope there in 2000.

Scientists at GREGOR do not look directly at the Sun; this is done using electronic detectors, such as spectrographs, polarimeters, interferometers, and cameras. GREGOR's rotating-fold mirror deflects the bundled beam generated by the adaptive optics system to the various instruments. Their purpose is to measure various physical solar parameters with an unprecedented level of precision, in particular, the Sun's magnetic field, and in doing so, reveal small structures down to a scale of 70 km—an astounding resolution capacity, given that the Sun is located approximately 150 million km from Earth.

Tenerife is already the site of numerous astronomical observatories, and will become the site of a larger scientific complex, a space city, which will be connected to the existing airport by a maglev train—especially because the area is mountainous and not suited for traditional train systems.

A feasibility study for a maglev track connecting the south and north of the island has already been performed by the German Railway Research Institute in Berlin.

The island of Lanzarote, a lava-dominated landscape that strikingly resembles the surface of the Moon and of Mars, could serve as a testing site for coming Euro-African space missions—mankind's true destiny.

"The entire economic geography of the Americas can be upgraded through a construction process, of realizing continental corridors, hubs, and areas of concentrated development, in the mutual interest of all concerned.... The principle involved is to build for tomorrow."

The Future of
THE AMERICAS
Lies with the New Silk Road

IBERO-AMERICA LEADS THE WAY

Introduction

The Belt and Road summit held in Beijing on May 14-15, 2017 was a strategic turning point for the world, launching the next stage of China's Belt and Road Initiative (BRI) as the dominant global paradigm. It was also particularly significant for the nations of Ibero-America and the Caribbean, because it was there that President Xi Jinping and other Chinese leaders announced explicitly that they intended to extend the BRI, also known as the New Silk Road, to all of Ibero-America and the Caribbean. This was a question that lay heavily on the minds of many of the leaders of the region, who had been taking careful note of the enormous success of the Chinese economic model at home and abroad, and were wondering how they could get on board.

The way President Xi put it in his bilateral meeting with Argentine President Mauricio Macri at the Beijing summit was: "Latin America is the natural extension of the new 21st Century Maritime Silk Road."

A "Policy Paper on Latin America and the Caribbean" issued by the Chinese government on November 24, 2016, had already laid out the highlights of China's view of what such proposed cooperation would look like, but it was only at the BRI summit on May 14-15, 2017 that the doors were formally flung open.

This came in confirmation of what *EIR* and the Schiller Institute had been insisting on for years, and then most emphatically in an international video-conference keynoted by Schiller Institute founder Helga Zepp-LaRouche, held on May 6, 2017, just a week before the Beijing BRI summit, under the title: "The Future of the Americas Lies With the New Silk Road." The event drew some 500 participants to simultaneous live meetings held in six cities in three countries: Peru (Lima and Pucallpa), Mexico (Mexico City, Querétaro, and Hermosillo), and Guatemala City.

Ibero-America and the Caribbean had experienced a period of great optimism and bilateral and multilateral agreements on specific great projects consistent with the BRI, during the July 2014 BRICS summit in Fortaleza, Brazil and its immediate aftermath. These included commitments to such great, *game-changing* infrastructure projects as:

- The construction of a South American trans-continental railroad with leading Chinese participation (either the Brazil-Peru route, or the Brazil-Bolivia-Peru route, or better still, both)
- A Grand Inter-Oceanic Canal in Nicaragua, to be carried out by HKND, a leading Chinese private company
- Chinese assistance in the construction of a high-speed Mexico City-Querétaro rail line and other critical rail projects in Mexico, including across the Isthmus of Tehuantepec
- Science city and other advanced technology projects, including nuclear energy, in Argentina, Bolivia, Ecuador, and elsewhere

With such projects on the horizon, the prospect for finally ending the poverty which besets 200 million out of the population of 600 million in Ibero-America and the Caribbean, seemed within reach.

But the region soon entered a period of delay and suspension of most of these projects, as a result of de facto political coups d'état in Argentina (December 2015), Brazil (May 2016), and Peru (July 2016). The "Lava Jato" corruption scandal, demanded by Wall Street and the City of London, and then concocted and promoted by their handymen in the U.S. Department of Justice and State Department, has been the principal instrument used to implement these regime-change policies to attempt to forestall the arrival of the BRI in Ibero-America and the Caribbean.

Earlier, in November 2014, Mexico's stated intention of working with China to construct key rail corridors in the country was stymied by the direct intervention of the Obama White House, Wall Street, and the City of London.

As a result, few of the BRICS and BRI great projects have actually gotten off the ground in Ibero-America to date, especially as compared to other regions such as Asia, Africa, or even Europe.

However, the prospects for the integration of the nations of Ibero-America with the BRI improved dramatically with the June 12, 2017 decision by Panama to establish diplomatic relations with the People's Republic of China (PRC), and its announcement only five months later at the November 12, 2017 summit between China's President Xi Jinping and Panama's President Juan Carlos Varela that Panama was joining the BRI, as a platform for all of Ibero-America to do the same. This decision was "an act of heroism" which will "go down in history," President Xi stated at the time, and it is already having far-reaching political impact in other nations across Ibero-America and the Caribbean.

The same point was emphasized by Zhao Bentang, head of the Chinese Foreign Ministry's Department of Ibero-American and Caribbean Affairs, in commenting on the Xi-Varela meetings: "Panama is the newest of our circle of new friends. It is well-positioned in terms of geography, logistics, and openness. It can naturally become a connection in the 21st Century Maritime Silk Road for Ibero-America and the Caribbean.... This good beginning in relations with Panama will also provide new energy to China's relationship with Ibero-America."

It is noteworthy that Panamanian authorities in no way view their emerging relationship with China and the BRI as something antithetical to their long-standing historical ties with the United States. Less than a week after his national television broadcast announcing the establishment of relations with the PRC, President Varela paid a four-day visit to the United States to meet with President Trump and members of his cabinet. Speaking before the Inter-American Dialogue in Washington, D.C. on June 21, Varela defended his decision on relations with China enthusiastically, at the same time that he emphasized that Panama is a strong U.S. partner, which plays an important regional role in Central America, particularly working with other nations on dealing with security issues in the "Northern Tier" of El Salvador, Guatemala, and Honduras, which has been invaded and overrun by drug gangs.

Three months later on September 17, the last day of Chinese Foreign Minister Wang Yi's visit to Panama, the local press reported on a speech delivered a few weeks earlier by an official from the Economics Unit of the Panama Canal Authority, Eddie Tapiero, in which he stated that the Chinese Belt and

Figure 1
Next Phase of Expansion of the World Land-Bridge Network

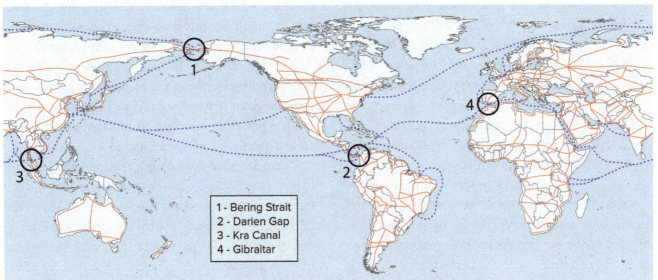

Road Initiative "will change the world in the coming years.... The United States as the main partner of all countries in Latin America needs to be part of the Initiative. With all the players working toward the same goal, the countries will achieve a balance in their strength and stability in the long term."

Panama, with its recent (June 2016) expansion of the Panama Canal, is indeed at the crossroads of the extension into the region, not only of the Maritime Silk Road, as the Chinese government has put forward, but also of the Silk Road Economic Belt, as *EIR* has long proposed. This will require the construction of high-speed rail lines through the Darien Gap on the Panama-Colombia border, as well as the Bering Strait tunnel connecting Alaska and Russia. These two great projects will allow high-speed rail corridors to extend northward from South America's southernmost region of Tierra del Fuego, to pass through the Darien Gap, traverse Central and North America, and from there travel through the Bering Strait tunnel, to link up with the Eurasian component of the World Land-Bridge (see **Figure 1**).

If the gates to Ibero-America's involvement in the Belt and Road were opened at the May 2017 summit in Beijing, and a first step was taken by Panama a month later, then it can be said that many of the nations of the region enthusiastically began walking through them at the late January 2018 China-Community of Latin American and Caribbean States (CELAC) Foreign Ministers meeting in Santiago, Chile. As China's Foreign Minister Wang Yi stated at the China-CELAC Economic and Trade Cooperation and Business Forum, reporting to that gathering of businessmen from Latin America and the Caribbean (LAC) and China, the just-concluded China-CELAC Foreign Ministers meeting had "agreed to jointly build the Belt and Road." Wang also said that "during the meeting, the Foreign Ministers issued a special declaration on supporting and participating in the Belt and Road Initiative."

However, as important as the Panama and CELAC political breakthroughs were, it is the future role of Brazil in the BRI that remains the decisive regional factor for all of Ibero-America and the Caribbean, given its economic and political specific gravity. The Lava Jato coup in that country must be reversed, and a government committed to serious economic development come into power, for full regional integration with the BRI to succeed.

Methodological Considerations

Before turning to evaluate the status of the various "game-changer" BRI projects in the Ibero-America and Caribbean region—both those already being promoted under the BRI, as well as those that *EIR* and the Schiller Institute have identified as crucial for the region—a brief methodological note is required. By *"game-changers,"* we mean those projects which uniquely cause an upshift of the technological platform of the nations involved, to bring about the most rapid possible advance of the productive powers of labor. "Game-changers" are those projects which break out of the paradigm of zero-sum game economics, and embody the win-win approach characteristic of Lyndon LaRouche's science of physical economy—and of Xi Jinping's Belt and Road Initiative.

To properly evaluate proposed infrastructure projects—or the economy in general for that matter—it is necessary to reject the use of GDP and related monetary measurements of the economy as a valid metric of actual economic performance. We rely instead on the approach to the science of physical economy elaborated by Lyndon LaRouche, and his proven metric of Potential Relative Population Density (PRPD) (see Section II of this Special Report).

GDP is a metric that works only for economic systems which function as a *zero-sum game*. In fact, it was designed for just that purpose, and to help bring about such an unfortunate result. There are two distinct methodological flaws with GDP (and all related monetary measures). First, it fails to distinguish between productive and unproductive economic activity. Is $100 million invested in derivatives speculation or building whorehouses in Las Vegas really economically equivalent to $100 million invested in high-speed railroad infrastructure or nuclear energy? Perhaps the most egregious example of this problem is the International Monetary Fund's (IMF) demand that illicit drug cultivation be counted as part of GDP, as that institution stated in writing in a report to the Colombian government in 1999.

The second flaw with GDP, as with any monetary measurement, is that it employs a fixed metric to try to measure a process which is characterized by non-linear transformations in the very basis of measurement itself. Specifically, no fixed metric can take into account scientific and technological advances which transform the physical economic parameters themselves of the economy. And yet it is precisely such innovations, such *game-changers,* which are the driver of actual economic development.

Lyndon LaRouche solved this problem with a set of scientific discoveries in the middle of the 20th Century, which are uniquely designed for the *win-win* economic processes which are the result of man's unique creativity. Man's creative innovations are reflected in increases in the average physical-economic productivity of labor in the economy, which in turn permits rising Potential Relative Population Density—the power of a society to continuously advance from generation to generation.

The elaboration of such a non-monetary metric to evaluate physical economic processes requires the mathematics of Bernhard Riemann (1826-1866), the detailed development of which is beyond the scope and purposes of this report. However, LaRouche himself provided a useful summary statement of his approach in his 1982 book, *Operation Juárez*, written after LaRouche's historic 1982 meeting with then Mexican President José López Portillo:

> Economics is essentially a study of the principles by means of which a people is able to produce the material preconditions for its own continued existence. It is these physical-economic issues which are fundamental; monetary matters, such as currency, credit, banking, and debt, are a subordinate issue....
>
> Therefore, we take as our first measurement in economic science a quantity we call potential relative population-density. How many people can be sustained per square mile, by means of nothing but the production of members of the society inhabiting the land?... The correlative of advances in potential relative population-density of society, is increase in the per-square-mile quantity of usable energy-supplies consumed by the society. This is the basic measurement of energy-flux-density we employ: kilowatts per square mile of usable consumption of energy by society.... What economic science seeks to define is an institutionalized policy, through which successive advances in both potential relative population-density and energy-flux-density are accomplished....
>
> This progress, this increase in potential relative population-density, occurs as an advancement in applied technology. It occurs in the form

of more or less continuous changes in the manner in which people work....

We measure work, therefore, as a second-order partial-differential expression, within a total potential-function for society. We measure the rate of rate of change of technology of production for the society as a whole; we treat the rate of rate of change of each part of the total division of labor as a partial-differential expression in the potential-function for the technological advancement of the society as a whole. This potential function corresponds to potential relative population-density.

Whence this change, this rate of rate of change?

The source of this rate of rate of change for the potential function, is the creative powers of the human mind.

Therefore, in analyzing and comparing various proposed projects, the question is *not* which projects return the highest rate of financial profit, or even of GDP value added; but rather which projects induce changes in the technological platform and raise the productivity of labor of the society most rapidly and sustainably—a process which cannot be measured monetarily. Only in this way can poverty finally be eliminated, as China has demonstrated.

A good example of the approach that should be taken, which is particularly relevant for raw materials-producing nations but has broader significance as well, can be called the "Mutún Model." This refers to the agreements that were reached in 2017 between China and Bolivia to develop Bolivia's enormous iron ore (and manganese) deposits at Mutún, in the southeast corner of the country. Emphatically included in the accords is downstream processing of the iron ore, including establishing the country's first steel-producing plant. Bolivia's dream has always been to use its significant natural resources to leverage its own advanced industrial development, but for decades controlling international financial interests have refused to permit that. Now, with China's participation, it will occur.

China's Ambassador to Bolivia, Liang Yu, was emphatic in an October 2, 2017 interview with the Bolivian daily *El Deber*, that China intends to "energetically" help Bolivia, in any way Bolivia wishes, to develop into a prosperous, industrial nation at the center of a prosperous and developing South America. "Expanding cooperation on such areas as productive capacity, mining and energy, infrastructure, the development of highways, airports, railroads and hydroelectric plants, and collaboration and exchanges in such areas as aerospace, telecommunications, science and technology, and protection of the environment, will drive the development of Bolivian industrialization; the value-added of Bolivian products will increase, and its capacity for autonomous development will advance," Ambassador Liang told the daily. He cited in particular, the contract signed for China's Sinosteel Equipment and Engineering Co. to build a steel complex near Mutún. Sinosteel's contract is to build an iron ore concentration plant, a pelletizing plant, a direct reduction plant, and a steelworks with a continuous caster and a rolling mill, such that Bolivia can become largely self-sufficient in sponge iron, structural steel, and "long products" (bars, rods, beams, and rails).

Ambassador Liang rightly called the Mutún steel complex "a gigantic step for the industrialization of Bolivia." Eventually, Bolivia will become a steel exporter, after the second phase of the project is completed, including construction of the necessary logistical capabilities for export (roads, bridges, railways, and port infrastructure).

This type of cooperation at the cutting edge of science and technology will find an appreciative response throughout the region, as it has in Bolivia.

The Silk Road Economic Belt

Inter-Oceanic Rail Corridor

At the July 2014 BRICS summit, China, Brazil, and Peru signed an agreement to build an inter-oceanic railroad to connect the Atlantic and Pacific coasts of South America, to open up the interior of the continent to development, and to establish connectivity across the Pacific with China and the Asian components of the BRI. The precise route was not specified, but was left open depending on feasibility studies that were to be conducted. Although most

Figure 2
South America Great Rail Projects

subsequent official Chinese statements have indicated support for the so-called Northern Corridor (e.g., São Paulo-Santa Fé do Sul-Cuiabá-Porto Velho-Pucallpa-Saramirisa-Paita), the possibility has also been left open for Chinese participation in the Central Bioceanic Rail Corridor, which would traverse Bolivia as well as Brazil and Peru (e.g., São Paulo-Santa Fé do Sul-Santa Cruz-La Paz-Mollendo) (see **Figure 2**).

The Schiller Institute, which proposed such transcontinental high-speed rail projects as far back as the late 1980s (see *Ibero-American Integration: 100 Million New Jobs by the Year 2000!*, Schiller Institute, 1988), and reviewed the basic technical considerations of each route, has repeatedly argued that *both* options are viable, and that preferably both should be built. The Northern Route, although longer in total length (some 8,000 km), has the distinct advantage of using the lowest pass of the entire Andes mountain range near Saramirisa (the Abra Porcuya Pass at 2,137 m, or 7,000 ft, above sea level). The Central Corridor has to deal with greater engineering challenges, such as for tunnel and bridge construction and train braking technologies, given the geological formations and soil types of the higher Andes pass, but it has the technical advantage of being substantially shorter in length (about 3,755 km). In addition, the Central Route has the distinct political advantages of integrating more countries in the rail project per se (i.e., Bolivia), as well as offering ready possibilities for linking to the Great Waterway project of the Paraguay and Paraná river systems, which connects Paraguay, Argentina, and Uruguay in the broader great project as well. (In fact, the China-backed Mutún project in Bolivia involves shipping of iron ore and steel southeast-wards to the Atlantic coast, by a combination of rail and water transport.)

The internationally orchestrated 2016 regime-changes in Brazil and Peru, however, stalled out *both* options. The Temer government in Brazil has ruled out the Northern Route, using the specious environmentalist argument that it would traverse the Isconahua Reserve and otherwise "endanger" the Amazon's eco-system. The Brazilians have not formally ruled out the Central Corridor as of this writing, but they are at best spinning their wheels, with no manifest intention of actually proceeding with the project.

On the Peruvian side, the government of Boston banker Pedro Pablo Kuczynski (PPK), which was finally driven out of office in early 2018, argued against *any* major inter-oceanic rail project, while agreeing to meetings with their Bolivian and Brazilian counterparts on the Central Corridor, which predictably went nowhere.

This has left the Evo Morales government in Bolivia, which unlike the PPK and Temer governments is fully committed to the BRI global policy, to engage in extensive regional and international diplomacy to try to get Bolivia included in an inter-oceanic rail project. Morales has found significant interest among private sector companies in Germany and Switzerland in particular, but without China's central involvement, and with Brazil and Peru's de facto sabotage, the Bolivian proposal has tended to devolve into a project that would simply "upgrade" existing antiquated rail lines in Bolivia and elsewhere—not the kind of game-changer project that had been agreed upon at the 2014 BRICS summit.

North-South Rail Corridors

But it is not only the east-west inter-oceanic rail corridors that are required; there are also critical north-south rail corridors that must be built.

Such north-south corridors will help open up the interior of the continent to development, and link each and every nation of South America to the World Land-Bridge. One such rail line will preferably run along the eastern slope of the Andes Mountains, and not along the more populated Pacific Coast to the west of the Andes, in order to help open up the interior of the continent to development. And a second one will hug the Atlantic coast of the continent, connecting Brazil, French Guiana, Suriname, Guyana, Venezuela, and Colombia with the Darien Gap project. As Figure 2 indicates, today there are no rail lines whatsoever, connecting the nations that lie between São Luís, Brazil and Caracas, Venezuela. (It should be noted that Figure 2 is not meant to be a full representation of all rail lines to be constructed in South America, but only an indication of the principal continental corridors which will then be supplemented by the respective national rail grids.)

Additional north-south routes would traverse Brazil's Amazon region. At the 2014 Fortaleza BRICS summit, China and Brazil reached an agreement to open bidding for foreign, including Chinese, companies, to participate in the construction of one critical segment of the overall South American rail project: the "T"-shaped Palmas-Campinorte-Anapolis/Campinorte-Lucas route in central Brazil. The importance of that segment within the overall project presented by *EIR* is clear from Figure 2. The northern terminus of Palmas is a stone's throw from the famous Carajás project in the middle of the Amazon jungle, one of the world's largest (and purest) iron ore deposits, which is now connected by rail only to the Atlantic port of São Luís. Once built, the western rail terminus of Lucas would then be halfway to the Brazil-Peru border.

Our proposed rail route across the northern coast of South America roughly follows that for existing and proposed highways in the region. In all cases, bridges will have to be built across border rivers where none now exist, and areas where the borders are disputed will also have to be traversed—a condition which applies to *all* of the relevant borders: Venezuela-Guyana, Guyana-Suriname, and Suriname-French Guiana. In addition, a southern spur from Georgetown, Guyana to Boa Vista and Manaus, Brazil will also be constructed, to link the coastal area to the very heart of the Amazon—Manaus being a major inland port on the Amazon River.

Of particular importance in this rail corridor along the northern coast of South America, is the stretch linking Brazil's São Luís/Alcântara with Cayenne (French Guiana), Paramaribo (Suriname), and Georgetown (Guyana). Two game-changer projects are directly involved.

Downstream Industrialization of Raw Materials: the Mutún Model

The rapid development of the productive powers of the labor force in countries whose economies are today largely extractive (e.g., Suriname and Guyana), will be achieved by the application of what we have referred to as the Mutún Model. High-value-added downstream metals-processing capabilities will be developed in those countries—such as transforming bauxite into alumina and then into aluminum—along with the infrastructure required to support that, including rail, electricity generation and transmission (aluminum production in particular is notoriously energy-intensive), and industrial processing plants. Over time, more advanced industrial activities of metal-working and metallurgy will be developed, along with the domestic skilled labor force required to support such activities.

This same approach applies to Caribbean island nations with similar economic characteristics where extractive sectors are predominant, such as Trinidad and Tobago, Jamaica, and Barbados.

Take the case of Suriname. Colonial economic policies in lesser developed countries (LDCs) have famously been described as doing little more than exploiting unprocessed raw materials, building a railroad to transport them to a port, and exporting them to pay the foreign debt. That is pretty much what happened in Suriname as well both before and after its 1975 independence from colonial power Holland—except they never even built a railroad! Or rather, they built one which was never used, and was then overgrown by the jungle.

Suriname is a sparsely populated nation (a little more than a half-million inhabitants), half of whom live in the coastal capital of Paramaribo. Having gained political independence from Holland in 1975, economic sovereignty has proved far more elusive. The country has remained a significant producer of gold and bauxite, but the latter has only been smelted down into alumina for export, but no aluminum plants have ever been built in the country. In the late 1970s, a plan to achieve some measure of domestic value-added production was envisaged in the West Suriname Plan. Between 1976 and 1978, a one-track railroad was constructed between newly discovered bauxite deposits in the Backhuis Mountains and a smelter in Apoera, with plans to also build a hydroelectric plant on the Kabalebo River (see **Figure 3**). But Dutch development funds were abruptly cut off in 1980, apparently for political reasons, and the rail line was never used and has now been completely overrun by the jungle. Not only does that 100-km rail line need to be re-built, but a national east-west network needs to be built to begin opening the country's interior to exploration and development.

Neighboring Guyana faces a similar situation. Its economy is heavily dependent on exports of bauxite and gold, as well as rice and sugar. In addition, Exxon-Mobil has just confirmed the existence of major oil deposits offshore, which are expected to be commercially available by the year 2020. Guyana once had a coastal railroad, but it was abandoned in the 1970s. Likewise, the flagship Amaila Falls Hydro project, which was to have been built by Chinese compa-

Figure 3
Suriname

nies, first was put on hold by the incoming Guyanese government in 2015, and then was cancelled outright in 2017—after the China Rail Construction company had already completed the access road, bridges, and other site infrastructure. The project was to have been Guyana's first major hydroelectric plant, tripling the amount of electricity available today in the country.

China is clearly favorable to such an approach. The November 2016 Chinese Foreign Ministry's "Policy Paper on Latin American and the Caribbean" stated:

"China wishes to expand and deepen cooperation in the fields of energy and resources with Latin American and Caribbean countries based on the principle of win-win cooperation and sustainable development.... Cooperation will be extended to downstream and supporting industries such as smelting, processing, logistics trade and equipment manufacturing, so as to improve added value of product ... which will cover the whole industrial chain, so that the two sides can complement each other, increase local employment, upgrade the level of industrialization, and promote local economic and social development."

Figure 4
The Carribean Basin Belt and Road

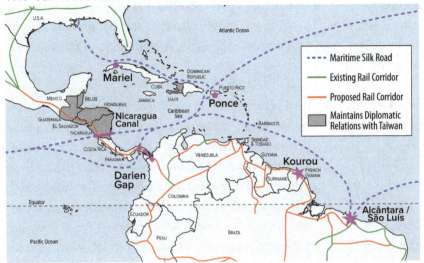

Space Science Cooperation

A second project in this area which will be a game-changer for all of Ibero-America and the Caribbean, is fostering a renaissance of coordinated space launches and other space science activities at the two existing launch sites nearest to the Equator of any on the planet: the European Space Agency's site at Kourou, French Guiana; and the Brazilian Space Agency's site at Alcântara, Brazil (see **Figure 4**). The center at Kourou is located at a mere 5.3 degrees (575 km) north of the Equator; and Alcântara is even closer, at 2.3 degrees (267 km) south of the Equator. The significant advantages of such locations for launching satellites into geostationary orbit are well known. The coastal location is another significant advantage.

The center at Kourou is the launch site for the European Union's space program, as well as for some Russian launches—precisely the sort of international cooperation required. The center at Alcântara, however, has been plagued by various problems. On August 22, 2003, an attempted launch of a VLS-1 rocket ended tragically, with an explosion which killed 21 Brazilian technicians. Brazil did recover and successfully launched its first rocket into space a little over a year later, and it has subsequently carried out a number of successful launches. But budgetary and related constraints have also limited its development. Brazil had established a strong working relationship with Ukraine for launches from Alcântara, but that has suffered as well with the foreign-sponsored coup in that country.

Nonetheless, a concerted international effort in this area of advanced science—one in which China is also well-positioned to participate and help—is crucial to providing a science-driver for all the nations of South America and the Caribbean Basin, and pull the labor force of the entire region into their orbit.

Brazil and Argentina are the most advanced in space activity among the nations of the region, and clearly have a decisive role to play. In terms of the Caribbean Basin per se, in addition to Cuba and Costa Rica, where significant initiatives have been taken in the area of space science, perhaps Trinidad and Tobago is the nation which currently has a labor force most suited to rapid participation in this area of scientific endeavor, because of its significant oil and petrochemical activity and the training it has provided to a stratum of local workers.

China's 2016 "Policy Paper on Latin America and the Caribbean" weighed in clearly on this matter:

"China will actively explore the expansion of its cooperation with Latin American and Caribbean countries in high-tech fields such as information industry, civil aviation, civil nuclear energy and new energy, to build more joint laboratories, R&D centers and high-tech parks, support innovative enterprises and research institutions on both sides to carry out exchanges and cooperation, and promote joint research and development.... China will pay full attention to the role of space technology as a driving force for the scientific, technological, and industrial development of Latin American and Caribbean countries, and promote sustainable development in science and technology and the economic fields."

The Darien Gap

The Darien Gap project is another key component of the Silk Road Economic Belt in Ibero-America and the Caribbean, one vital to linking the entire region to the World Land-Bridge. The region involved is some 150 kilometers in length, covering the border area between Colombia and Panama. It is generally considered to be impenetrable (although, if truth be told, it is today overrun by the FARC narcoterrorist drug cartel, among others). The Pan American Highway, for example, extends down through all of Central America and Panama, until it reaches the Darien Gap, and goes no further.

The highly qualified American rail engineer Hal Cooper has specified an appropriate rail route to finally bridge the Darien Gap (see **Figure 5**):

> The Darien Gap railway connector would be approximately 85 to 95 miles (136 to 152 km) long, and could go by either a central lowland route, parallel to the uncompleted Pan American Highway, or by an elevated hill and mountain route to the east of the Pan American highway.... [The former route would run] through thick tropical rain forests in parallel to the Chucunaque and Tuira Rivers where heavy rainfall, thick jungles, insects and snakes, plus frequent flooding, would be major problems over much of the year.... The alternative eastern mountain route would go over the Serranía del Darién Mountains to the Atlantic drainage side over relatively gentle grades through rolling hills with maximum elevations of 1,500 to 2,000 feet (455 to 610 meters) through heavy tropical forests....
>
> A significant challenge would be involved no matter what routes were chosen. The western lowlands route would be shorter in length, but would go through flood-prone areas with heavy rainfall, and would have to be built through a national park. The eastern highland route would be longer, but would be able to avoid much of the flood-prone areas, and would probably not need any tunnels, and would not have to be built on an elevated causeway.... [Regardless], there are some advanced construction techniques which have been developed that can be used for building into those types of land. The best example to look at is the Atchafalaya Causeway of Interstate 10, between Lafayette and Port Allen, Louisiana. Port Allen is just west of Baton Rouge. This area has swampland over the entire distance. The Atchafalaya Causeway is a perfect example; it's about 35 miles long. It's up on pilings, and it's about 40 feet above the water, and you just drive on it. You can just build something like that. Just build one of those causeways over the Darien Gap and the Tumerando Swamp, and put railroad tracks on it.

The 'Taiwan Gap'

There are many political problems to achieving the above great projects, but one merits special mention. And that is that 9 of the 17 countries internationally that still maintain relations with Taiwan rather than the People's Republic of China, which reflects a profound geopolitical anachronism, are located in the Caribbean Basin region. Five of them are in Central America: Nicaragua, El Salvador, Honduras, Guatemala, and Belize. Another four are in the Caribbean: Haiti, Saint Kitts and Nevis, Saint Lucia, and Saint Vincent and the Grenadines. (A tenth is the South American nation of Paraguay.)

The five Central American countries pose a particular problem. Their rejection of the One China policy makes it impossible to fully incorporate them into the BRI, for reasons often stated by the Chinese government. Specifically, it will not be possible under these conditions to extend the proposed rail corridor through those countries, to link up the entire South American rail grid with Mexico, North America, and from there to the Bering Strait tunnel and the Eurasian Land-Bridge. In that sense, the difficulty to be overcome to create such an integrated rail network is not only the Darien Gap between Colombia and Panamá, but also what we might call the "Taiwan Gap" stretching from the northern border of Costa Rica up to Mexico's southern border (see Figure 4).

There are hopeful signs, however, that this problem can soon be resolved, and quickly, as those five countries observe the highly positive benefits that Panama is receiving from establishing diplomatic ties with the PRC, and joining the New Silk Road. It is also useful that responsible Chinese authorities have been frank and explicit about this matter.

As China's Chargé d'Affaires in Panama, Wang Weihua, told *La Estrella de Panamá* in an August 8, 2017 interview: "Panama, by making the decision to establish relations with China, gave an example to the rest of the countries and islands in the Caribbean that

Figure 5

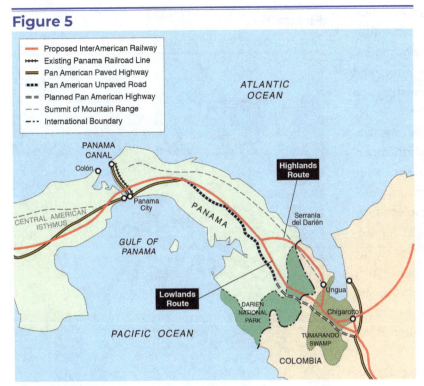

do not yet have diplomatic relation with China. Panama has given them a great example."

Wang explained that China's desire is to not only build a high-speed rail line from Panama City to the border with Costa Rica, but to further construct the corridor all the way into Mexico.

The Maritime Silk Road

The Caribbean Basin lies at the crossroads of maritime traffic linking Eurasian economic activity with the entire Western Hemisphere (see Figure 1). This will become a fulcrum of the region's integration with the BRI and its resulting development, by taking full advantage of the newly-expanded Panama Canal (especially with Panama's recent adherence to the BRI), and by:

- Constructing the even larger Nicaraguan Grand Inter-Oceanic Canal, which will permit the passage of the world's largest bulk cargo and container ships, significantly shortening shipping distances and times from South America to China.
- Developing the deep-water port of Ponce, Puerto Rico, which lies directly on the principal shipping routes from Europe and Africa to the Panama and Nicaraguan canals, and can serve as a connection point for cargo traffic to U.S. Gulf and Atlantic Coast ports, as well as to the Caribbean nations. The fact that Ponce, Puerto Rico is part of the United States is particularly important to help integrate the United States into the Caribbean Basin Belt and Road project, and into the global BRI more generally.
- Finishing construction of a deep-water port and industrial development zone in Mariel, Cuba, which is especially well-suited to include Cuba's relatively skilled labor force, and its significant hydrocarbon and other raw materials deposits, into the BRI.

The Iberian nations of Spain and Portugal have both stressed that they have a special role to play in the extension of the BRI into Ibero-America and the Caribbean, because of cultural and language affinities and long-standing economic ties, as well as the natural shipping routes connecting Europe with the Americas, which can readily extend the Maritime Silk Road into the region. The Chinese government has also stated that they are promoting the extension of the Maritime Silk Road into Ibero-America and the Caribbean.

The Chinese Foreign Ministry's 2016 "Policy Paper" also stressed China's role in this regard:

"[China will] promote the connectivity of infrastructure in Latin America and the Caribbean.... China will strengthen cooperation on technical consultation, construction and engineering, equipment manufacturing, and operation management in the fields of transportation, trade logistics, storage facilities, information and communication technology, energy and power, water conservancy, housing and urban construction.... China will support its strong enterprises to participate in major resources and energy development projects and infrastructure construction projects in Latin American and Caribbean countries and, using these projects as the basis, to build production lines and maintenance service bases in the region for construction materials, non-ferrous metals, engineering machinery, locomotives and rolling stock, electric power and communication equipment, with the purpose of reducing costs for resources and energy development and infrastructure construction in Latin American and Caribbean countries."

The evident advantages of establishing water-borne commerce routes connecting South America, the Caribbean Basin, and North America were recognized as far back as the 19th Century, and probably earlier. One of the first systematic studies of the potential was made by the German scientist Alexander von Humboldt (1769-1859), who envisioned the physical integration of South America's three great river systems (the Río de la Plata, the Amazon, and the Orinoco), the development of cross-Caribbean sea routes, and their connection to the Mississippi River system in the United States (see **Figure 6**).

The essentials of that proposal remain totally valid today, and need only be supplemented with canals crossing the Central American isthmus, to open up an entirely new dimension of cargo shipping from Europe and the Atlantic coast of South America, across the Pacific to the booming economies of China and the rest of Asia.

The Nicaraguan Grand Inter-Oceanic Canal

The expanded Panama Canal is an excellent development for global physical economic trade and development, but it by no means eliminates or even diminishes the importance of the planned Grand Inter-Oceanic Canal in Nicaragua. The Nicaraguan Canal's construction has run into delays of various sorts, due to the opposition of internationally-financed indigenist and environmentalist groups, and the difficulties arising from the fact that Nicaragua still maintains diplomatic relations with Taiwan, rather than the PRC. Some informed sources believe that Panama's decision to rectify that problem will create the conditions in which other area nations, including Nicaragua, may soon decide to do the same. The Grand Inter-Oceanic Canal project would be enormously beneficial to Nicaragua and the entire region, generating in the range of 200,000 jobs, while doubling Nicaragua's GDP.

Figure 6
The Humboldt Maritime Silk Road

On the technical side, the need for the Nicaraguan Canal is evident. Post-Panamax ships have maximum dimensions of about 336 meters and 13,000 twenty-foot equivalent units (TEUs); but today's largest cargo ships, including the Triple E class, reach 400 meters in length and can carry up to 25,000 TEUs, which cannot go through the expanded Panama Canal but will be able to traverse the new Nicaraguan Canal.

Or consider the matter from the standpoint of shipping bulk cargo, such as iron ore. Brazil today exports some 330 million tons of iron ore, or 25% of total world exports, largely to China. The Brazilian government announced at the end of 2014 that it was investing to increase its output of iron ore by 50% over the next five years. Brazil's Vale do Rio Doce, which handles the enormous Carajás iron ore mine in northeastern Brazil, has already placed orders with various Chinese and South Korean shipbuilders for 35 new cargo ships, each with a maximum capacity of some 400,000 deadweight tons (DWT)—way more than current cargo ships handle. Although DWT and TEU are not strictly convertible metrics—DWT measures tonnage; TEU measures volume—industry standards estimate about 14 tons per loaded TEU. That means each of Vale's new cargo ships is roughly the equivalent of a 28,000 TEU container vessel.

These new ships will be too large to go through the expanded Panama Canal, and even the expanded Suez Canal. But they can be handled by the Nicaraguan Canal. This strongly suggests that the current preferred trans-Atlantic maritime shipping route for such super-large ships from São Luís, Brazil (which is Carajás's principal port for exports, and notably right across the São Marcos Bay from the Alcântara launch site) to Shanghai, China, will instead go westward, once the Nicaraguan Canal is in operation, proceeding through that canal and across the Pacific, directly to Shanghai. The current route, according to maritime shipping experts, takes an estimated 36 days to cover 22,800 km; the new route will be a shorter 20,500 km and take only 32 days—a saving of more than 10%, which is highly significant in physical-economic terms, given the magnitudes involved (see **Figure 7**).

A Deep-Water Port in Ponce, Puerto Rico

Ponce, located on Puerto Rico's south coast, lies on one of the main shipping routes from Europe to the Panama Canal (and the planned Nicaraguan Canal), through the Mona Passage. Ponce's Port of the Americas is a potential hub for the biggest cargo ships, with "spoke" routes for somewhat smaller ships going from there to ports across the Caribbean and on the Gulf and Atlantic coasts of the United States (see Figure 4). The government of Puerto Rico has invested more than $285 million in upgrades to the port, including dredging the entrance channel and berths up to 50 feet, and it is now the deepest port on the island, and one of the deepest in all the Caribbean. In addition, two super Post-Panamax ship-to-shore cranes and 4,400 linear feet of quayside have been installed.

The development of Ponce as a super-port is also important as part of any viable plan to reconstruct the island after the 2017 hurricane damage—the other elements being replacing the entire power grid, building rail lines (there are now none on the island), and expanding the San Juan international airport, already the busiest in the Caribbean.

A Deep-Water Port in Mariel, Cuba

This project parallels and complements the Ponce port project. Mariel lies on Cuba's northern coast, just west of Havana, and as such is directly on major shipping routes connecting South America and the entire Caribbean Basin to New Orleans and other major U.S. ports (see Figure 4).

Cuba's Deputy Foreign Trade Minister, Antonio Carricarte, announced on October 31, 2017 at the China Pavilion at the Havana International Fair, accompanied by Chinese Ambassador Chen Xi, that Cuba hopes to become a regional hub as part of the Belt and Road Initiative, so that the BRI can extend throughout Ibero-America and the Caribbean. Specifically, Carricarte said, Cuba's goal is to become a maritime and air transport center for the entire region, particularly in the Mariel Special Development Zone. "This goal for our country can connect us with China's Belt and Road, for the purpose of extending that noble goal to the Caribbean and Latin America," he said.

The fact that our proposal for the Caribbean Basin Belt and Road involves nations still plagued by border disputes, and more broadly the participation of such disparate nations and language groupings—South and Central American nations, Caribbean nations, the United States, and the European Union—is a fact which some might consider a weakness and vulnerability, but it is actually one of its greatest strengths. The Caribbean Basin can be a microcosm of the kind of cooperation that is required for the global success of the BRI.

Mexico Rail Projects Derailed

The Enrique Peña Nieto government in Mexico was one of the first in Ibero-America to announce its intention of working with China on a number of key rail corridor projects which, had they not been sabotaged, would have marked the de facto incorporation of Mexico into the broader BRI-BRICS/Ibero-American alliance for development which emerged out of the July 2014 BRICS summit in Fortaleza, Brazil.

Figure 7
São Luis to Shanghai Maritime Routes

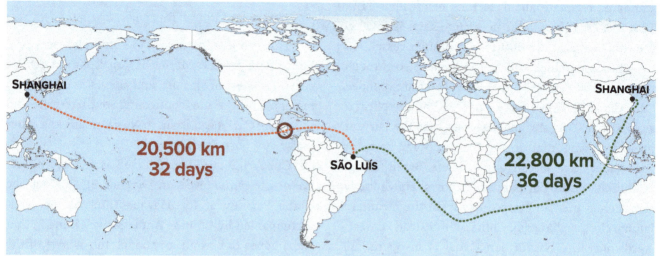

For Mexico, such development projects are the only physical-economic basis for breaking the country free of the Dope, Inc. coup d'état which Barack Obama and his British controllers orchestrated in Mexico in 2009, and of reversing the decades of looting under the IMF and the Bush-Salinas North American Free Trade Agreement (NAFTA) which las left the country at death's door.

On November 3, 2014, Mexico's Communications and Transport Secretary, Gerardo Ruiz Esparza, announced that a consortium led by China Railway Construction Corp (CRCC) had won the contract to build Ibero-America's first high-speed rail line, from Mexico City to Querétaro (see **Figure 8**). The 130-mile route was to have trains traveling up to 186 mph, making the trip in just under an hour. Construction was expected to begin before the end of 2014, with the line open for business in 2017, and daily passenger traffic of 27,000 people expected.

CRCC was the only final bidder for the project when other international companies—including Siemens of Germany and Bombardier of Canada—had to withdraw because they could not pull together a financing package in time. The CRCC-led consortium, which included four Mexican construction companies and the French company Systra, was backed by financing from China's Eximbank for 85% of the cost of the project, which was some $3.74 billion.

It was widely expected that China would win the bidding; what is significant is that the award was made official on the eve of Mexican President Enrique Peña Nieto's November 8-15, 2014 trip to China and Australia, which included participation in the Asia Pacific Economic Cooperation (APEC) and G20 summits and a state visit to China. In late October 2014, there was a flurry of reports that the Peña Nieto trip had been cancelled, when the President's office temporarily withdrew a request to travel that they had presented to the Mexican Senate, as required by the Constitution. According to reliable Mexican intelligence sources, the Mexican government had come under intense pressure from the Obama White House to cancel the trip, as well as from domestic forces also opposed to the prospects of deepening cooperation between Mexico and China, and all of the allied BRICS nations.

In addition to the Mexico-Querétaro high-speed rail line, Peña Nieto was expected to finalize a number of other projects with China, including a major rail line covering the route Nayarit–Ciudad Juárez, Chihuahua to El Paso, Texas. That area of northwestern Mexico is currently controlled by the drug trade, which can only be defeated by bringing development to the area. This rail link is also critical for connecting the cross-Pacific Maritime Silk Road to a new deep-water port in the state of Nayarit, and to a high-speed rail line into the United States, and to the broader World Land-Bridge.

A third, strategically important Trans-Isthmus rail corridor was also agreed upon, connecting the

Figure 8
Proposed Mexico-China Rail Project

port city of Coatzacoalcos on the Gulf of Mexico, with the port of Salina Cruz on the Pacific. This corridor is often referred to as a "dry canal," because with intermodal transfers at the ports, it is expected to function much as the Panama Canal does today. This trans-isthmian project harkens back to the projects and policies of the great Mexican President José López Portillo (1976-1982), a friend and ally of the American statesman Lyndon LaRouche.

Faced with the prospect of a reawakening of López Portillo's policies and political networks in Mexico, and of the BRI establishing itself right on the U.S. doorstep, the Wall Street and City of London banking crowd went wild. They howled their objection, and used a well-publicized alleged "corruption scandal" to force Mexico to revoke the announced Querétaro-Mexico City high-speed rail contract on November 6, 2014—only two days after it had been officially announced.

The Economist, the flagship magazine of the City of London financial oligarchy, celebrated Peña Nieto's capitulation in a November 8, 2014 column: "It was a good sign on Nov. 6 when, in an unprecedented move, Mr. Peña ordered the overturning of a controversial award of a $3.75 billion railway tender because it lacked transparency," *The Economist* gloated.

Immigration and Drugs

Given the region's geographic and political proximity to the United States, it is vital to include the United States in the Caribbean Basin Belt and Road process in particular, as well as the broader global BRI effort. To do that, it is important to stress that the connection of the region to the BRI is not a threat to the United States, but is actually the key to addressing a series of vexing problems of great concern to the United States, which have no available workable solution outside of the BRI. The two most salient such problems are: the vast flows of illegal immigrants into the United States from the region; and the related issue of the enormous, often dominant role of the drug trade in the area.

The immigration issue is best understood from the standpoint of LaRouche's concept of Potential Relative Population Density. The nations of the Caribbean Basin region, as with Mexico, today have levels of physical-economic activity (i.e., PRPD) which are significantly lower than their existing populations. This means they currently lack the economic power to maintain their existing populations at an acceptable standard of living. This in turn has led to sharp deficits in multiple physical-economic parameters, and it is also reflected in the sizable illegal and (to a lesser degree) legal emigration which occurs, especially to the United States. The remittances which these millions of individuals send home to their families are often their only means of survival.

Consider **Table 1**, which shows cumulative emigration to the United States from Central America and Mexico, as of 2015. The case of El Salvador is exemplary, and perhaps the most dramatic: more than 20% of native-born Salvadorans have emigrated to the United States, fleeing economic devastation, violent drug-running gangs which control large parts of the country, and natural disasters such as earthquakes. However, when one also considers second- and third-generation Salvadorans who were born in the United States, the total is almost 35% of the 2015 Sal-

III. PROGRESS REPORTS

Table 1
Emigration from Mexico and Central America
(population in millions, as of 2015)

Country	Population	in U.S. (1st gen.)	%	in U.S. (1st-3rd gen.)	%
Mexico	125.9	11.5	9.1%	35.8	28.4%
Guatemala	16.3	0.9	5.5%	1.4	8.6%
Honduras	9.0	0.6	6.7%	0.9	10%
El Salvador	6.3	1.3	20.6%	2.2	34.9%

vadoran population. In other words, had El Salvador had a vibrant, functional economy over recent years, they would currently have a population living at home about one-third larger than today—and the so-called "immigration problem" in the United States would be that much more manageable. The point is underscored when one considers Honduras, Guatemala, and (especially) Mexico as well. Bringing the vast development potential of the Belt and Road Initiative into this region, will create the economic conditions in which populations that are today driven to emigrate from their homelands will be able to find productive work and a dignified life for themselves, with the prospect of an even brighter future for their children and grandchildren.

A closely-related problem is that of the drug trade, which has largely taken over the economies of Mexico and Colombia, and many of the Central American countries in between (as well as a number of Caribbean islands). A full discussion of this matter would take us well beyond the scope and intention of this report, but suffice it to say that there can be no solution to the drug problem in the Caribbean Basin region (as in other parts of the world, such as Afghanistan), without a solid economic development policy which can guarantee a livelihood to the millions of peasants, and also urban youth, who today see no alternative to conscription into the drug mobs.

The Belt and Road thus offers the best hope to the nations of the region to solve this problem, and retake their national sovereignty back from the international drug-running apparatus that has stolen it from them. The BRI is thus also critical to aid the United States in properly addressing the drug problem on its southern border.

New Science Cities

On the occasion of Chinese President Xi Jinping's state visit November 17-18, 2016, Ecuadorean President Rafael Correa hailed China's financing of the Yachay "City of Knowledge"—Yachay is the Quechua word for "knowledge"—as "what I consider the most important project in our country's history, not because of its dollar amount, but because of its significance: the City of Knowledge, Yachay, which includes a world-class university, dedicated to fostering innovation and the development of the hard sciences."

China's Export-Import Bank, the China Gezhouba Group Company (CGGC), and the IZP Group are some of the Chinese entities building and financing the Yachay project which was launched in March 2014, and is the first {planned} city built in South America since the 1960 construction of Brazil's capital, Brasilia. China's backing, and more recently Russia's, is emblematic of these nations' commitment to cooperating with Ibero-American countries to accelerate their economic development by advancing their scientific and technological capabilities. Because Yachay is intended to serve as a regional hub for a variety of scientific, technological, and trade activities, China views it as a key component of the One Belt, One Road perspective.

Ecuadorean experts and participants explain that Yachay's goal is to create a new generation of scientists and engineers dedicated to building "a new economy based on knowledge, science, and technology," the Andes news service reported in July 2017. Many of the scientific, industrial, and agricultural entities operating there are directly linked to the improvement of Ecuador's economy, and the benefits this will bring to its population, in terms of jobs, education, medical care, improved food production, and access to advanced technology.

In an August 2015 interview with Radio Universidad de Chile, Yachay's Technical Manager, Fernando Cornejo, emphasized the *international* nature of the project, with academics, students, and researchers from 54 countries involved. In addition to the Yachay Tech University, all of Ecuador's 12 national research institutes will be located there, along with an industrial park, the Superior Technological Institute, 37 high-tech companies, schools, hospitals, agro-industrial enterprises, and much more. The project, Cornejo underscored, is "an emblematic project of Unasur" (Union of South American Nations), designed to expand knowledge and development of science and technology throughout South America, to help it achieve its "second Independence."

Nor is China the only nation involved in Yachay. Russia's St. Petersburg Vaccine and Serum Institute announced November 13, 2017 that it had signed an agreement with Ecuador's Foreign Ministry, to provide $30 million to build a vaccine and serum-production plant there, similar to the Mechnikov Vaccine Production Plant it has already built in Nicaragua. Russia provided $14 billion of Mechnikov's total $21 billion investment, offered technology, and trained Nicaraguan personnel at the St. Petersburg Institute. When fully operational, the Mechnikov plant will supply vaccines to Central America, the Caribbean, and other Ibero-American nations. The Yachay plant will supply the domestic and regional market, and the St. Petersburg Institute has announced it will reinvest all profits in continued scientific research and development.

Bolivia also plans to build a "City of Knowledge" like Yachay in the city of Cochabamba, which is still in the planning stages but has already gotten a financial commitment from China's Huawei Co. to build a laboratory that will train professionals and university students in telecommunications and information technology. Russia's nuclear energy agency, Rosatom, is also financing the construction of a state-of-the-art Nuclear Research and Development Center in La Paz, that will benefit the entire region.

The Bolivian Public Works Ministry's official overseeing the Cochabamba project, Ariel Torrico, told the daily *El Dia* in a November 1, 2015 interview, that the Cochabamba site will be a planned city from start to finish, to include all services and equipment "to house scientists, teachers, and researchers." Areas of research include petrochemicals, agro-industry, information technology, telecommunications, alternative energy sources, and hydrocarbons, among others.

With laboratories, housing, research and educational facilities, and recreational areas, the project aims to "exploit national knowledge to the maximum," Torrico said, "and prevent human capital from leaving the country."

Cornejo explained that the principle guiding the Yachay project is that *"we have changed the neoliberal conception of knowledge as a finite good, to one of knowledge as an infinite good that can be shared, is open and collaborative."* Knowledge, he continued, "is linked to independence." The challenge for Latin America, he said, is to transform itself into "a producer of knowledge." He emphasized that a project of Yachay's magnitude could only be carried out by the State, not the private sector. "It implied thinking big, in [terms of] megaprojects that would have a direct influence on the productive sector." It also implied "a change in the mentality of the Ecuadoreans and Latin Americans since a change in the productive matrix [of society] can only occur with a change in the cognitive matrix."

Chile under the government of Michelle Bachelet (who left office in March 2018) has also been a leading voice in Ibero-America for full integration with the BRI, especially in terms of science, technology and innovation. As Chile's former ambassador to China Fernando Reyes Matta put it in a November 17, 2016 statement to Xinhua, "it's time for Latin America and Chile to discover the meaning of the word 'innovation.'" The fundamental principles of China's development model, he said, "are related to the development of advanced science and technology." Latin America, he asserted, must develop "the ability to create knowledge."

President Bachelet herself, in a November 20, 2016 interview with Xinhua, stressed that "science, technology, and innovation" are top priorities in Chile's bilateral relationship with China, and pointed to the importance of China's offers to help build various rail and other bi-oceanic corridors across South

America—a subject she had also emphasized to Chinese Premier Li Keqiang during his May 2015 visit to Chile. In this context, she pointed to the possibility of connecting the two countries via an underwater fiber-optic cable "which would be a bridge to the rest of Latin America ... important for both countries' integration is what we can do in the Latin American region," she said.

Conclusion

The key to success in an undertaking of the magnitude of fully integrating the nations of Ibero-America and the Caribbean with China's Belt and Road Initiative, is often to overcome centuries of deep-rooted pessimism and conviction that things will never really change, and thereby unleash the kind of optimism which can drive the campaign forward to success. It is often wise, for just that reason, to take the worst, most intractable problem and show that it can be solved. China has taken an approach of that sort in the development of Africa, with highly encouraging results—for Africa and the world.

For Ibero-America and the Caribbean, that same approach translates into what China is undertaking in Haiti. There is no country in the region that is poorer, has less infrastructure, worse health and sanitation conditions, lower literacy rates, greater unemployment, and has endured more natural disasters, than Haiti. They have been promised international aid time and again, and they have never received more than crumbs—certainly not enough to end the cycle of poverty and underdevelopment. Haiti, not surprisingly, suffers from pervasive pessimism and even cynicism about such promises of help—as do the other nations of the region when they hear about help for Haiti.

China's offer to help bring Haiti out of the Middle Ages is thus of importance that goes far beyond that island's 10 million inhabitants. On August 25, 2017, Ralph Youri Chevy, mayor of the Haitian capital, Port-au-Prince, formally accepted a $4.7 billion proposal from China's Southwestern Municipal Engineering Design and Research Institute to renovate and rebuild that city, including its port, over the next three years, providing all the infrastructure required to modernize the capital and uplift its impoverished population.

Haiti has never recovered from the effects of the January 2010 earthquake that killed 250,000 people, injured tens of thousands more, and wiped out what little infrastructure existed.

Now all of that will begin to change, in Haiti and across the region.

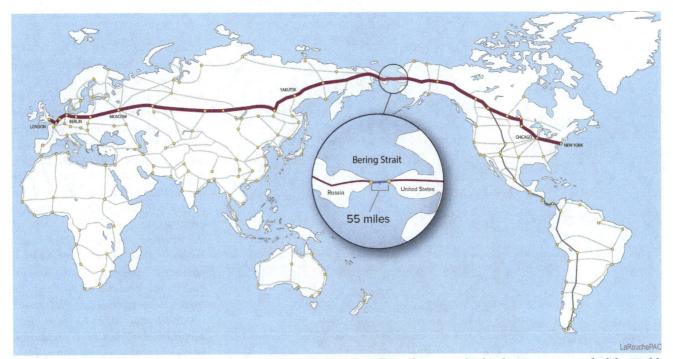

The Bering Strait connection—with North America as a keystone—will revolutionize the development potential of the world.

NORTH AMERICA – JOIN THE FUTURE!

The outstanding feature of the continent of North America, as of nearly two decades into the 21st Century, is the degradation of its physical and social economic condition, compared to both past periods of its own development, and to the advancement now underway through the New Silk Road, across Eurasia, Africa, and as of 2018, in South America. From train wrecks, to wildfires, storm devastation, demographic devolution with soaring death rates from drugs and despair, and waves of desperate migrants, the North American picture is stark.

Across the board, what is called for are projects to either renew, or initiate new physical infrastructure, and cultural and scientific activity to restore the development process; and in addition, to come to the aid of reconstruction in war-ravaged regions of Southwest Asia and other points of need. Why and how this has been obstructed in the United States, is explained elsewhere in this report (see Section V). The first moves on the continent, toward the New Silk Road and development, are coming from the south, from the collaboration between China and Panama, and plans in South America and the Caribbean.

To begin with, the far northwest of North America remains unlinked with Asia and the New Silk Road, which requires only a tunnel under the Bering Strait, an engineering feat technically achievable years ago; and then full rail connections into Canada, into the Lower 48 States and Mexico, through the Darien Gap and southward. Back in 1942, a 2,000+ km route was surveyed by the U.S. Army Corps of Engineers, but it was never built. There is no rail connection between Alaska, Canada, and the Lower 48 to this day.

Beyond that, North America has other unrealized prospects, in its span from the Arctic, the world's new frontier, to the Sub-Tropics. The development perspective embodied in Land-Bridge corridors, presents vast opportunities for population growth, productivity, and happiness on this continent, if the obvious programs are undertaken to immediately stop the inaction and decline, and to act on the great potential. A few key geographic patterns illustrate this point.

Overall, as of 2018 there were only 543 million people in North America (including Central America). In terms of land area per person, this is 0.04 km² per capita (**Figure 1**), which is very spacious, in contrast to Europe, with a population of 743 million,

Figure 1
North America Population Density, 2000

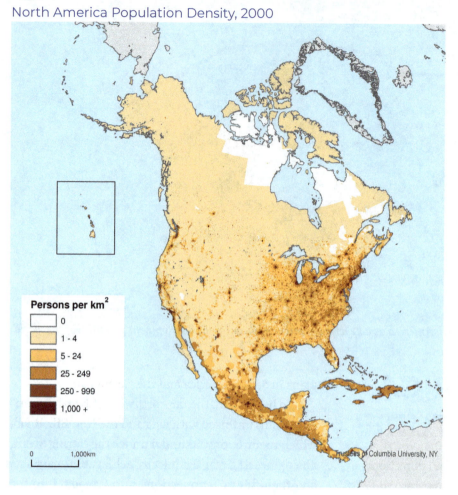

The large land area of North America has a relatively low population of 545 million people. Two striking features of the continent are the sparse settlement densities in western United States, and in most all of Canada. Of the 37 million people in Canada, two out of three live within 100 km of its southern border with the United States—an area accounting for barely 4% of the nation's total land. New land-bridge development corridors—especially spanning mid-Canada, and running north-south along the continent's western High Plains, will create the conditions for new cities, agro-industry, and vast population growth. Infrastructure for reliable water in the dry west is critical. The Canadian "growth latitudes" are on a par with the historic, high-density population concentrations of northern Europe.

giving 0.006 km² per capita; or in contrast to the nation of China, with 1.423 billion people, for 0.007 km² per capita. Canada, with a small population of fewer than 37 million, and a large land area, has 0.25 km² per capita, one of the highest ratios of land area per person of any nation, far exceeding the world average of 0.017 km² per capita. The United States has 0.028 km²; and Mexico, 0.015 km².

A look at the physical geography of the continent shows obvious challenges to be met: mitigating the extensive western deserts, dealing with the Arctic, and providing defenses against floods, Tropical storms, and the Pacific Rim tectonic activity. There are programs of R&D and infrastructure, long overdue for action, to meet these and other challenges.

Figures 2 and 3 give a snapshot view of the situation. First, land and water. The extent of the western area defined by low rainfall is shown, which includes four deserts, in what has been historically called the "Great American Desert." Figure 3 presents a schematic of the "North American Water and Power Alliance (NAWAPA)," a continental-scale water diversion program, first proposed in the 1960s, and then thwarted to the present day. The concept is simply to move water from relative abundance in the northwest, to places of need in the south, and ameliorate conditions along the way. Also in order, are installations to provide plentiful water through nuclear-powered desalination. Mostly needed along the coast, such infrastructure is also important for inland sites, where underground water is plentiful, but impure. Most importantly, research is underway on promising new systems of inducing increased rainfall, through ionization, where atmospheric vapor patterns are present and conducive for precipitation.

Figure 4 shows the North American physical terrain, and **Figure 5** shows priority routes for high-speed rail. What is depicted is the North American

NORTH AMERICA – JOIN THE FUTURE!

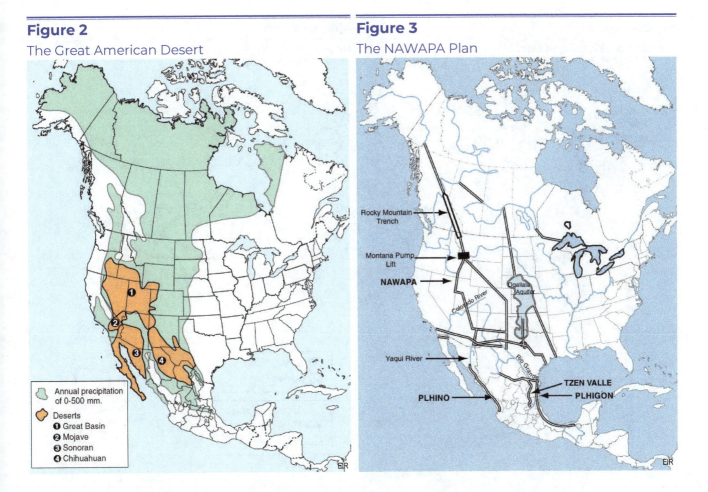

Figure 2
The Great American Desert

Figure 3
The NAWAPA Plan

section of the north-south Land-Bridge Corridor running along the "spine" of both continents of the Western Hemisphere, from Alaska, through western Canada and the United States into Mexico, and southward through Central America, then proceeding to the farthest point of South America. The entire economic geography of North America can be upgraded through a construction process, of realizing continental corridors, hubs, and areas of concentrated development, in the mutual interest of all concerned. The map indicates selected priority rail-centered corridors. For many of these routes, and interconnected cities, the challenge is to upgrade the existing infrastructure systems, from their outmoded condition. In other cases, construction is needed, for completely new transportation links, towns, industry, and agriculture.

The principle involved is to build for tomorrow. President Abraham Lincoln acted on this principle throughout his life. He spoke of the value of modern infrastructure, using the expression of his times, "internal improvements." In 1862, in the middle of wartime, he signed the Pacific Railway Act, which mandated the first trans-continental railway, linking the Pacific and Atlantic Coasts.

This was accomplished in 1869. In 1832, in Lincoln's first campaign for public office (for the Illinois General Assembly), he addressed the voters about the need for a railroad along the Illinois River: "Time and experience have verified to a demonstration, the public utility of internal improvements. That the poorest and most thinly populated countries would be greatly benefitted by the opening of good roads, and in the clearing of navigable streams within their limits, is what no person will deny.... No other improvement that reason will justify us in hoping for, can equal in utility the rail road."

Figure 4
North America Elevation Map

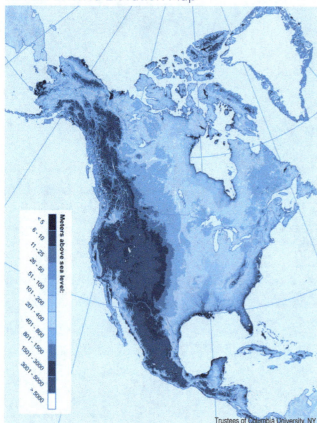

Trustees of Columbia University, NY

Figure 5
Priority Rail Routes and Connections

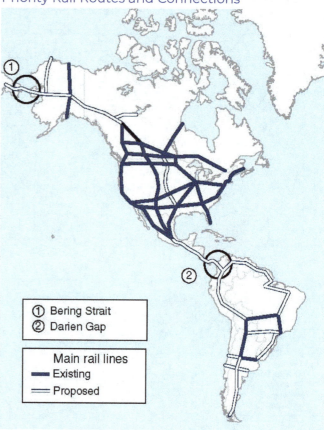

UNITED STATES – ACTION NOW

There is no justification for continuation into the mid-21st Century of the hardship and worsening condition of the American people. The causes can be eliminated. This means putting an end to the breakdown of infrastructure, reversing the takedown of industry and subversion of agriculture, ending the cultural decay, and stopping the spread of dope and death. It also means ending the wrongful foreign policy of geopolitics and regime-change warfare, which destroys whole nations, and recycles young Americans into danger and death.

Details of each area of activity to transform the U.S. economy—power, water, transportation, health, disaster defense, science, and culture—are described below. What is required is a policy shift, for the government to resume acting, as it states in the Preamble to the Constitution, to "promote the general welfare" (see "Four Laws for the New Paradigm," Section V of this Special Report).

An important impetus for this shift was embodied in the package of economic friendship deals between the United States and China, made during the "state visit-plus" by President Donald Trump to Beijing, hosted by President Xi Jinping, in November 2017 (see map and box).

The 37 business accords, amounting to more than a quarter-trillion dollars, signed at that time, included statements of intent and contracts for Chinese investment into projects, and purchases of U.S. products, both immediately and over the next two decades. As the specifics in the figure show, the deals covered many regions and types of manufacturing and agriculture (e.g., aircraft, electronics, soybeans, and beef). Energy is the biggest sector, involving collaboration in three top energy states. More than two-thirds of the $253 billion of 2017 business accords between China and the United States were for Chinese

The 2017 Trump-Xi $253 Billion 'Big Deals' for China-USA

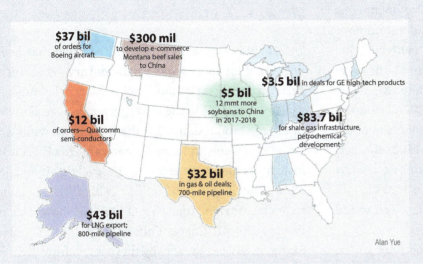

In November, 2017, commitments totaling $253.5 billion were made by China for 37 "big deals" of U.S. imports, and investments into U.S. economic activities, over the period 2018 to 2038. President Donald Trump and President Xi Jinping witnessed the November 9 signing ceremony in Beijing, on Trump's "state visit plus." *China Daily* headlined it, "Sino-U.S. Ties at 'New, Historic Starting Point,'" in *China Watch*, Washington, D.C. November 29.

Major Gas and Oil Infrastructure and Petrochemical Industry

West Virginia. $83.7 billion in projects for the development of shale gas in the tri-state region, involving pipeline infrastructure, a new storage hub in the state, and petro-chemical manufacturing. China Energy Investment Corp., Ltd. signed the 20-year deal with the state, which can become the second petro-chemical center of the U.S., after the Gulf Coast.

Alaska. $43 billion of investments to build a new 800-mile gas pipeline (North Slope south to Kenai Peninsula), and agreements for China to import Alaskan LNG were signed by Sinopec, the China Investment Corp., and the Alaska Gasoline Development Corp., a state entity.

Texas. A $32 billion package of new, and already agreed-upon deals were set, involving the energy sector. Among the elements: a 700-mile pipeline from the Permian oil and gas fields in West Texas, to the Gulf Coast. Houston-based American Ethane Company signed a $26 billion contract with China's Nanshan Group for supplying ethane gas over a 20-year period.

Aviation and Electronics

Washington. $37 billion to Boeing Co. (headquarters, Chicago) from orders and investments by China Aviation Supplies Holding for 300 aircraft over the coming years. Boeing's largest factory is in Everett, Washington, which, with factories in other states, will produce 260 narrow-body 737s, and 40 wide-body 787s and 777s.

California. $12 billion in orders to Qualcomm were made by three Chinese firms (Xiaomi, Oppo, Vivo), for the purchase of semi-conductors over the next three years.

Indiana. $3.5 billion in deals were made by General Electric Company with Chinese buyers, for GE to supply aviation and power generation components. Headquartered in Boston, GE has factories in many states, including, especially, engine manufacturing sites in Indiana, Ohio, New Hampshire and Alabama.

Agriculture

Illinois. $5 billion in increased commitments by China to buy U.S. soybeans over the 2017-2018 marketing year were made between Chinese buyers and the U.S. Soybean Council (based in Missouri). The top five soy states are Illinois, Iowa, Minnesota, Nebraska and Indiana.

Montana. A $300 million deal was made between the Montana Stockgrowers Association and the Chinese giant e-retailer, JD.com, for the company to invest $100 million in a new feedlot and packing plant in the state, and to buy $200 million of cattle, for marketing "Montana" brand beef in China. This deal came on top of a growing volume of U.S. beef exports to China, which were resumed in Summer 2017 after China lifted a 2003 ban.

promotion of oil and gas infrastructure and sales: West Virginia ($83.7 billion), Alaska ($43 billion), and Texas ($32 billion). The projects include a new 800-mile gas pipeline in Alaska, a 700-mile pipeline in Texas, and in West Virginia, new underground gas storage and a petro-chemical industry center.

Although these projects are limited in scope and their technological platform, there are nonetheless three aspects to the historic 2017 Trump-Xi deals which are important for the momentum of the United States into a New Paradigm. First, the personal friendship cemented between the two leaders amounts to an open door for the United States to join in the New Silk Road for development, which would benefit all nations.

Second, the increased economic activity in the United States, associated with the China-U.S. 2017 deals, sparked a sense of optimism in otherwise bleak parts of the country, hard hit by economic decline and pessimism. Following the announcements in Fall 2017, regional leaders spoke of this explicitly. West Virginia Gov. Jim Justice called the $83.7 billion Memorandum of Understanding (MOU) between his state and China Energy, "incredible."

He said at a press conference, that this "is the right thing for our citizens. It gives us hope, it gives us jobs, it gives us real life." Alaska State House Speaker Rep. Bryce Edgmon said of his state's $43 billion MOU with Sinopec and Chinese Investment Corp. (CIC), "A pipeline project will bring jobs, investment and, perhaps most importantly, a renewed sense of hope that Alaska's best days are ahead of us, not behind." In May 2018, Alaska Governor Bill Walker personally led a business delegation to China, under the theme, "Opportunity Alaska: China Trade Mission."

Third, the new deals imply restored prospects to advance energy modes to higher levels for the United States, China, and worldwide. China's new collaborative projects for gas infrastructure in North America are part of its international involvement in the high-tech development of fossil hydrocarbon resources, while at the same time, China is fully backing the expansion of nuclear fission power, and as early as possible, fusion energy. With this policy, the nuclear age can supersede the fossil fuel era altogether, not just in "fuels and energy," but as a fundamental advancement in chemistry, medicine, biology, and in all respects.

Power Up the United States

The power profile of the United States has been degrading for more than a half-century, by all measures, from the stagnant level of electricity use per capita after 2007, to the lowering technological mode of energy production, with the increase of wind, solar, and biofuels, relative to nuclear. This is seen in historical context, in terms of the leveling off and decline of nuclear fission, and the lack of advancement to nuclear fusion. The chart (**Figure 6**) shows this in its depiction of "Energy Flux Density" for the United States, in kW per person, by fuel source, from 1780 to after 2000.

According to 1960s projections, nuclear power by the 21st Century would be providing an increasing share of a rising level of energy throughput per capita in the economy. Instead, the expansion of nuclear power has been thwarted well into the 21st Century, relative to government-backing for the very lowest modes of energy production—wind, sun, and biofuels. After commercial nuclear power got underway in the 1960s (with the first commercial reactor in 1956 in western Pennsylvania), the number of commercial nuclear reactors, which had been anticipated to surpass 200 by the 21st Century, instead reached only 104 at maximum. As of 2015, this number dropped to 99, with only two more units expected to come on line by 2020, and another two possible. Plus several of the 99 existing plants are slated for early shutdown.

This situation reflects the combined impact of the Wall Street principle of financial gain, above the public good, which was unleashed through "deregulation," and also the subversion of the country by "greenism"—the policy of lowering modes of production and consumption, in the false name of benefiting the environment.

There is less power per person overall in the U.S. economy. As of 2010, the throughput per capita, in BTUs, was 310 million per year, far down from the level of 350 million BTUs per capita three decades earlier.

Figure 6

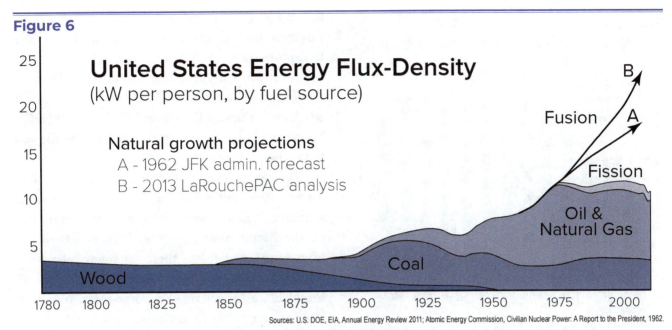

Total per capita primary power use in the U.S. from 1780 to 2010, divided by energy source. Two projections indicate what could and should have occurred under the continuation of a healthy growth process. Curve A is a 1962 projection made by the Kennedy administration, which focused on the then-coming role of nuclear fission power. Curve B is an estimation of what were possible had the Kennedy vision been pursued, followed by the development of controlled fusion (following the 1970s realization of its feasibility).

Moreover, the United States has the terrible distinction, along with Brazil and its sugar cane gasohol, of leading the world in biofuels—the use of biomass, a low energy-flux-density fuel source. As of 2015, some 40% of the U.S. corn crop—which itself represents one-third of the corn production of the world—was going into corn ethanol. Diesel fuel from soybeans and other oil crops is also rising. In addition to the direct loss to economic productivity, and the food supply, from this low-mode energy source, there is detriment to economic and social conditions because infrastructure and trade come to be distorted to serve the biofuels investments. For example, corn-ethanol transport must be by tank car, displacing other rail transport, because it is corrosive to existing pipelines. The corn-ethanol by-product, dried distiller grains (DDG), is heavily promoted in the livestock trade, in order to support the corn-ethanol sector.

A re-commitment to nuclear power development will uplift the entire economic base of the nation. This means orders for new fission reactors to be located at strategic sites for serving increasing agro-industrial activity, and electrified high-tech transportation. It also means starting a crash program for harnessing nuclear fusion. International collaboration is essential.

As the world goes nuclear, an orderly phase-out of the fossil fuel mode (as an energy source, and shift to industrial feedstock) can then proceed, including the wind-down of the hydraulic fracturing sector, and eventual setting aside of the liquefied natural gas dependency internationally.

What is at stake, is not just fuel, electricity, or power in a limited sense, but entering a whole new era of mankind's enhanced capacities in the nuclear age, for manufacturing, agriculture, medicine and basic chemistry, and science itself, all the while looking outward into space.

Provide Water

Total water use in the United States, for all purposes, has been falling in absolute volume for some 30 years (**Figure 7**). This reflects the shrinkage of economic activity of all kinds, from irrigated agriculture, to manufacturing, and the lack of infrastructure to increase supply. Although water use efficiency has improved in some cases, this is not a significant factor behind the trend of declining water usage. In

Figure 7

Trends in Population and Freshwater Withdrawls by Source, 1950-2010

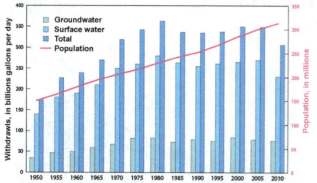

The U.S. total fresh water usage (for all purposes) has been decreasing for several decades, reflecting both the decline in economic activity, and the lack of infrastructure to increase supply.

2010 (the last year for which estimates are available) the total national water use was calculated to be 355 billion gallons per day (Bgal/d), which was 13% less than in 2005, and down from previous highs. Water for irrigation, one of the largest categories of water use, fell by 9% from 2005 to 2010.

The impact of the lessening water use throughout in the United States has been disguised in recent decades by the import of large amounts of "virtual" water in the form of increasing imports of food and manufactured goods, for example from Mexico, under the Wall Street so-called free trade system.

The approach required for a growing economy is to act on the principle that natural resources are man-made. In the case of water supply, there are three areas of water infrastructure for urgent consideration for action—some of which involve transferring existing fresh water supplies, while others involve making entirely new fresh water. First, conveyance of water from areas of surplus to areas of scarcity. The continental-scale project design for this, the North American Water and Power Alliance (NAWAPA), was first put forward in the 1960s, and backed by Congress at the time (see Figure 3). Although in essence the concept is a scale-up of the highly productive "California Water Project" (begun in 1961; completed in 1997), which collects water in northern California, and re-distributes it to the dry central and southern parts of the state, the NAWAPA proposal was thwarted under the combined impact of fake environmentalism and fiscal fanaticism, i.e., calling infrastructure-building "too expensive." In brief, the idea was to capture some 10-15% of the run-off now going to the Arctic, of the McKenzie/Alaska River Basin in the Yukon and Northwest Territory, and re-direct it southward, through the natural defile in British Columbia, and through man-made channels all the way to northern Mexico.

The second means of increasing water supplies, likewise feasible for decades, is through nuclear desalination. There is an obvious priority need for this on the Pacific coast, to serve cities, and their dry hinterland. In addition, there are many inland water-short areas, with large volumes of underground, brackish water, suitable for large-scale de-salting. The problem on the Atlantic coast is salt water intrusion. Florida is a national priority for nuclear desalination. As a peninsula, it has many sites where salt water intrusion is a problem, given the drawdown of Florida's wells over centuries of settlement, and the fact of its underlying karst geology.

Third, there are good prospects for enhancing rainfall, based on recent work in understanding the impact of ionization, in the presence of atmospheric vapor formations. Positive experimental results have been achieved to increase rainfall at locations in Australia, the Persian Gulf, Mexico, and elsewhere, warranting large-scale trial implementation in, for example, California. Its coast and dry inland is periodically hit by the "Pineapple Express" phenomenon—an atmospheric river going over the state from origins in the Pacific near Hawaii.

In addition to increasing the volume of water available in the economy, there is an urgent need to upgrade the aged distribution system. There are some 1.9 million km (1.2 million miles) of underground pipes, many of which are at or near the end of their service lifespan (which can be 75 to 100 years or more). The period of peak replacement and repair was after World War II, then investment declined. An estimated 240,000 water main breaks were occurring yearly in the 2010s. Looking ahead to 2050, work is needed to replace about half the pipes, and otherwise to build infrastructure to serve new growth areas, according to the American Waterworks Association, which has a timeline proposal for how to do this.

Figure 8
Proposed 42,000-Mile Network of High-Speed Rail

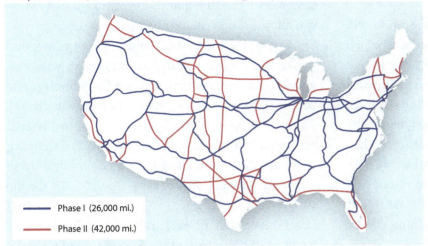

In blue, the proposed first 26,000-mile phase of a new electrified and high-speed rail grid, concentrating on the most heavily-traveled lines. In red, the second stage of building out to 42,000 miles. This proposal includes the addition of three north-south high-speed corridors in the Great Plains, from the Mexican to Canadian borders, the most obvious missing element of the current transportation system of the United States. The Alaska Railroad corridors would connect these continental rail lines to the Bering Strait Tunnel to Russia and on into Eurasia.

Transportation: Rail Connectivity, Water Navigation

Connectivity across the United States through railroads has been declining steadily since its peak in the 1920s, and more rapidly in recent years. The rail grid—once the primary mode of intercity freight transport, carrying three-quarters of the nation's freight during World War II—has been systematically dismantled, beginning in the post-war period, and accelerating after the rail industry was deregulated in the 1980s. As of the early 21st Century, the remaining aging rail infrastructure, in varying states of disrepair, is heavily clogged with diesel trains carrying coal, oil, ethanol, and sand for hydraulic fracturing, frequently to the exclusion of such essentials as farm inputs and commodities. The vestigial passenger service is no better, as seen in the long delays, frequent breakdowns, and wrecks.

The United States must immediately launch a crash project to rebuild, expand, and modernize its dilapidated rail grid. The priority continental rail corridors required are shown in the North America introduction. Within the Lower 48 states, the needed lines are shown on the "High-Speed and Mag-Lev" map (**Figure 8**), and described in the caption, in terms of a two-phase plan to build 42,000 miles of modern, electrified rail. The idea is for the first phase of improvement to concentrate on upgrading the currently most heavily travelled lines—about 26,000 miles—to modern high-speed standards. The next phase is to build out the full grid to some 42,000 miles. With modern high-speed rail (more than 150 mph) and magnetically levitated, or maglev rail, with average speeds of 250 mph, goods and people can be efficiently and safely moved at speeds two to three times faster than on the outmoded and congested existing rail and highway systems.

The proposed 42,000-mile project will require an enormous mobilization of industrial production to supply the necessary goods and materials, as well as advanced workforce training to create the necessary skilled labor needed to complete such a task (**Figure 9**).

Currently less than 1% of the existing U.S. rail network is electrified, and the tracks of the freight rail system absolutely cannot support high-speed or even

Figure 9

REQUIREMENTS FOR 42,000 MILES OF ELECTRIFIED RAIL

10,000 locomotives	**1,000** power substations	**15.5 million tons** high-tensile steel	**22 million tons** cement	**50 gigawatts** power production

moderate-speed travel by passengers or high-value freight (the average speed of a freight train today is less than 25 mph).

Therefore, the new high-speed rail system will require its own electrified track, each mile of which requires 370 tons of steel, 535 tons of cement, and a mile of electrical transmission line. All of this will need to be produced, as well as the rolling stock for the train itself, including modern, aerodynamically designed, electric locomotives. To provide for all this, the decades of deindustrialization must be reversed, and a national mobilization called for, to reindustrialize the formerly productive areas of the nation. It is an area in which cooperation with China can be particularly productive.

The U.S. waterway system—ports, inland and coastal channels—is long overdue for refurbishing, also allowing for improved integration with a modernized, full rail grid. There are about 25,000 miles (40,000 km) of navigable inland waterways, including the 3,000 miles (4,800 km) of the "Intracoastal" system, which runs along the Atlantic Seaboard and Gulf of Mexico. For some 12,000 priority channels, the Army Corps of Engineers has responsibility, including in particular for the 191 active lock and dam sites, involving 237 lock chambers. But for decades, the Corps has lacked the resources for proper refurbishment, so that, as of nearly 2020, more than half of these structures will be more than 50 years old, and at the end of their engineering lifespan. The number of incidents of breakdown and closure of locks and dams on U.S. rivers increased seven-fold over the period 2005 to 2015, amounting to days of wait-time on the rivers. In addition to modernizing this existing system—critical to such inland ports as Pittsburgh, Chicago, and Minneapolis—building water supply systems in the dry Southwest, through NAWAPA, can allow for new inland channels and depot cities.

Expanding the number and capacity of seaports is likewise on the agenda, in integration with rail, air, and roadway systems, to serve flows of cargo and people in new patterns related to a growing world. The legacy pattern of seagoing cargo is highly concentrated in a very few ports. As of the 21st Century, there are 260 coastal and inland ports, but only 18 major ports handle 75% of cargo, by value. Of the top 10 U.S. seaports in cargo value, six are on the Gulf Coast (three each in Texas and Louisiana), two on the Pacific coast, and two on the Atlantic. Upgrading the capacity of more ports, and especially upgrading chosen ports to New Panamax capacity, is in order.

Corridors, Links, Hubs

The national high-speed rail grid must be seen in the context of the re-conceptualized economy, and world of which it will be a part. An economy whose profit derives from physical production and scientific discovery, will have a much greater need to transport industrial materials and manufactured (including intermediate) goods. At the same time, an advancing economy will have less need, in the nuclear era, to haul around coal and oil (accounting for more than half of all U.S. rail tonnage at the beginning of the 21st Century). The U.S. pipeline system—currently chaotic, and in some places dangerous—can be expanded and made coherent with national improvements.

An artist's conceptual view of the North American entrance to the Bering Strait Rail Tunnel (left) and the proposed new Central North American corridor (right), to connect the Bering Strait tunnel through the High Plains states, into Mexico.

Moreover, development will be furthered along new and existing transportation corridors and hubs, and new links. These are defined not only in terms of national boundaries, but span the entire Western Hemisphere, Eurasia, and the world over. Three priority U.S. examples make the point of how the whole must be conceptualized.

Intercontinental Link: Bering Strait Tunnel. The gap between Alaska and Siberia can be closed by 85 km (52.8 miles) of tunnels under the Bering Strait, linking rail systems of the Americas and Eurasia. Some 3,000 km (1,865 miles) of new railway in Eurasia and more than 1,000 km (620 miles) in North America, are required to complete the connections grid.

The Russian Railways Strategy for 2030 calls for building a railway to the Bering Strait, in Chukotka, from the existing Baikal-Amur Mainline (BAM). By 2014, the first leg had been built, from the BAM to the bank of the Lena River opposite Yakutsk. On the Canadian and U.S. side, no progress has been made. Transportation engineer Hal B.H. Cooper, Jr. has laid out the basic parameters, in a study for the Canadian Arctic Railway Corporation. The route for a rail line from Alaska, through Canada, to the Lower 48 states will be 2,280 km (1,417 miles) long, if it follows the survey for a direct route, mapped out in 1942 by the U.S. Army Corps of Engineers.

The idea for such a Bering Strait crossing dates from the 1800s, with renewed interest in recent years. In April 2007, a conference was convened in Moscow by Russia's Council for the Study of Productive Forces (SOPS), to promote the start of feasibility studies. Papers were given by advocates from Russia and China, and by former Alaskan Governor Walter Hickel. A paper was also presented from Lyndon LaRouche.

New Corridor: Central North America Land-Bridge Corridor. This proposed continental north-

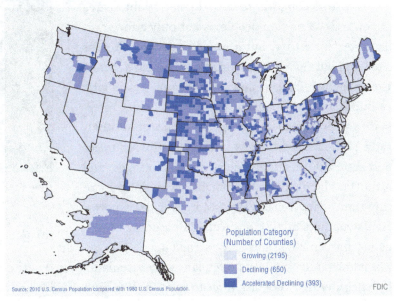

Figure 10

Approximately One-Third of U.S. Counties Lost Population Between 1980 and 2010

south rail and utility corridor, connecting with the northwest and Bering Strait Tunnel, is to run from the Canadian prairies down through the U.S. High Plains states, into Mexico and southward. It was long contemplated, but only lesser links were built for north-south rail traffic. The concept is illustrated on the artist's depiction of the "Central North American Land-Bridge Corridor." A proposed route is indicated in Figure 8 in the earlier section, "Ibero-America Leads the Way" ("Proposed Mexico-China Rail Project"), in which such a corridor could be constructed east of the Rocky Mountains, and carry multiple utilities—rail, highway, electricity, gas, water.

This development corridor can provide, along with new, reliable water supplies, the basis for economic expansion of the entire Great Plains, with the creation of a new landscape of farm fields and cities, home to new industrial, cultural, and scientific centers. Coupled with policies supporting diversified, high-technology family farming—instead of enforced agriculture monoculture—this area is set for dramatic population growth. This will reverse the decades-long de-population trend in the Western Farmbelt, which is shown in **Figure 10** for 1980-2010.

World Hub: New York City – Transportation Modernization

New York City, whose tri-state metropolitan area is home to 22 million people, is not only a foremost Trans-Atlantic City, but a world metropole. Yet its aged and outmoded transportation base has reached the stage of danger and breakdown. Systematic re-building and expansion is required for its interstate and urban rail service, to interconnect Manhattan and the other boroughs and surrounding counties and states, with safe, modern tunnels, bridges, and airports. The overburdened highways no longer can function in any reliable way. Moreover, transportation structures of all kinds were damaged by Hurricane Sandy in 2012, and only patched up, neither replaced nor fully fixed. In 2017, plans were circulated by a Schiller Institute task force to relevant local and Washington, D.C. bodies, including the Metropolitan Transportation Authority, New York City Transit Authority, and others. The "New York City Transportation Infrastructure Proposal"[1] covered the main features of what is required; for example, new tunnels to Manhattan, under the Hudson and East Rivers, as shown on the maps from the report.

A New Industrialization – Re-Enlist the Workforce

The volume of physical inputs needed—from steel to aggregate—for the vast construction involved in building new, large-scale infrastructure, factories, and machinery across the United States and North America seems impossible to provide, given the decrepit state of the nation. But with a mobilization approach to reviving the former concentrations of heavy industry—especially the Great Lakes Rust Belt, as well as the other idled production centers, e.g., Birmingham, Houston, Baltimore, and the Quad Cities—and creating new industrial centers, the goal becomes achievable. A key element for start-up, is collaboration with the heavy-industry leaders of the Belt and Road process—China and Japan (which is becoming increasingly involved in the BRI).

New York City's main rail hub, Penn Station, is one example of the city's overcrowded and broken down transportation infrastructure, which is in desperate need of systemic rebuilding and expansion.

The Chinese government, besides floating the idea of financial investment into U.S. infrastructure projects, has stressed its readiness for joint work on the heavy manufacturing side, for example, in rail rolling stock. After the first meeting of President Xi Jinping and Donald Trump, in April 2017, China issued a White Paper ("Research Report on China-US Economic and Trade Relations," May 25, 2017, Ministry of Commerce of the People's Republic of China), which outlined ways it stood ready to engage in manufacturing and infrastructure projects. It is notable, that in the context of this kind of China-U.S. collaboration, suddenly, the concept of there being "overcapacity" of steel production in Asia, the Americas, and Europe, disappears. There is a scarcity, not a glut, when measured against the inputs needed for the projects which must proceed.

Two aspects stand out in this "new industrialization" process—advanced industrial R&D, and re-enlisting the American workforce. First, this is the opportunity for the application of the most advanced kinds of heavy industry and machining techniques, and prioritizing research on still newer modes. For example, in steel-making, there is the necessity for scale-up of ore-to-iron plasma furnace methods. Initial research and trials in such methods in the Mesabi Range, and in Pittsburgh, were thwarted over the past three decades of casino, anti-development Wall Street policies. In machining, there is still room for advancements in digital, plasma, and e-beam tools.

---

1 Hal B.H. Cooper, Jr., Jason Ross, and Richard D. Trifan; Schiller Institute, New York, July 2017.

Robotics and artificial intelligence potential applications are wide open.

Second, at the center of the "new industrialization" of the United States, is the priority to re-enlist the workforce in productive life. There are three aspects of the mobilization to engage the working age cohort of the total U.S. population (325 million, as of 2018). First, most obviously, is to provide jobs for the currently unemployed, which number has fluctuated in the range of 16 million people (at the "official" labor statistics figure of 3% to 5% unemployment) as of the mid-2010s. Second, for the 150 million-plus people officially considered currently employed, the nature of their work must be upgraded. Millions of workers are doing unproductive and part-time labor, many of them struggling to survive on multiple jobs. Finally, there is the vast number of people who are in the category of "not in the labor force" at all (that is, not working and not looking for work). This number exceeded 94 million people as of 2015. Since the turn of the 21st Century, this category of "not looking for work" soared by 37% from 2000 to 2015, while the general population as a whole grew by 14%. It is de facto disguised unemployment, and reflects the terrible breakdown in the U.S. economy.

The challenge to transform work and people's lives may seem staggering, but the key is, to get the process going. Launch the priority projects described in this report, along with programs for R&D, education, and skills, along with all the required rehabilitation and health treatment needed from the scourge of opioids, drugs, and despair. The take-off will occur. There are key precedents—as in the 1930s "New Deal" systems, and the vast leap in production during World War II. The mightiest factor of all will come from new optimism and high morale.

Agriculture – The Astronaut Farmer

The U.S. farm and food sector has been caught in a bad paradox well into the 21st Century. Some of the world's highest technological practices are to be found at locations throughout the U.S. food chain, and in Canada and Mexico, from farm fields and barns, to the dinner plate; but at the same time, the overall organization of agriculture and the food supply has been degraded over decades of the "free" (rigged) trade era, to the point that rural areas are suffering depopulation and poverty. Instead of having prosperous farm counties, with family-scale farms and food processing, and modern transportation, the agriculture sector, over the 1970-2018 half-century, has trended to mega-farms and livestock operations, controlled in various ways (e.g., concentration and commodity speculation) by a small cohort of giant corporations and related banks. Large areas of monoculture—from soybean fields, to apples—have come to typify U.S. production.

Of the 2.1 million farms in the United States (from small three hectares in size, to multi-thousands of hectares), 10% produce 77% of the value of U.S. farm commodity output (as of 2016). For example, 40 mega-hog farm operations produce two-thirds of all the pork in the United States. Half of the raw milk produced in the United States comes from 1,200 mega-milk cow operations. Likewise, food processing is extremely concentrated. Walmart in 2018 opened its first directly owned and operated mega-milk processing facility in Indiana. Four cattle-slaughtering companies account for more than 80% of beef processed.

At the same time, some basic commodity sectors were shifted abroad (frozen and fresh vegetables and fruit), shutting down whole regions of U.S. farming, while the United States became increasingly import-dependent for many foods in the daily diet. Once-active local farm communities are now ghost towns, with decaying farmsteads, drug epidemics, and high suicide rates. Where there are jobs in the mega-livestock and food processing operations, the pay is low, and conditions harsh, despite some of the world's highest technology in use. Displaced foreign labor—legal or not—is the rule.

This downgrade in physical production has been imposed by financial deregulation of all kinds, in particular, the ending of the concept of "parity" pricing for farmers, which had given security to the public food supply; the furtherance of commodity speculation, and unregulated trade; the ending of anti-trust enforcement, and similar practices. This kind of de-regulation was the inherent nature of the North

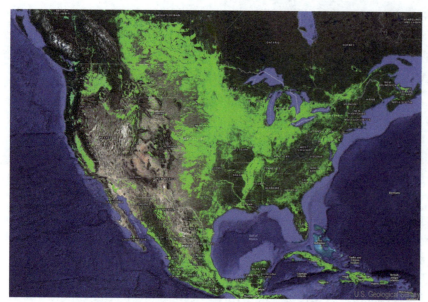

In November 2017, the U.S. Geological Survey, using Landsat satellite imagery, issued new maps of croplands worldwide. Large parts of North America are yet open to agricultural use, given new connectivity and water, in the western and northerly regions.

American Free Trade Act, beginning in 1995, which served to benefit Wall Street, but harm the entire continent. There is no way to make NAFTA "better," while the Wall Street principle governs.

Thus, U.S. agriculture capacity has remained significant in terms of output potential, but degraded in its patterns of production in terms of social and ecological costs. This can all be put right with agriculture policy changes to benefit the population of the United States, and at the same time, that of Mexico and Canada, and internationally. There is a "win-win" way ahead for agriculture. Three areas of policy are involved.

First, continue the advanced scientific and high-technology-based practices, that can be called the "astronaut farmer" approach. The name refers in particular, to the use of satellite guidance and data-analysis systems, but more generally to all the R&D applications affecting agriculture production, from seed genetics, to drones, to aeroponics. The way is wide open for international collaboration on this, especially in the new agriculture zones developing in Africa.

Second, unwind the detrimental NAFTA and other "free" (rigged) trade practices, which served no nation's farmers nor population, only the Wall Street/City of London financial networks of speculators and mega-corporations. Concretely, this can mean such new patterns of activity on the continent, such as fostering resumed corn production in Mexico, while transforming the corn and soy monoculture areas of the United States, into more diversified crop and animal operations, new industrial centers and towns, with special support for young farmers and the most advanced education. While U.S. soybeans are useful for China's livestock production, China is steadily increasing its own output of animal rations, and the United States can start working on diversifying the current soybean base area, as well as contribute to international food chain needs elsewhere, in win-win trade deals.

Third, support farmers and rural areas in the course of this, by reestablishing the principle of parity pricing. This means that the price farmers receive for their output, must cover, or bear relation to, their costs of production, with some decent profit, in order to provide stability and future food output potential. As of 2018, this was again under discussion in Washington, D.C. in terms of reactivating the 1930s parity pricing mechanism called the Commodity Credit Corporation (CCC). These measures will enable farmers to support a family, and set up the conditions for dramatically increasing the number of smaller, but very high-technology farming enterprises. Not only restoring the social fabric of rural life, these measures will result in farmers making creative innovations in agro-science itself.

Public Health and Medicine

Much is required to be done in the United States in the area of "soft" infrastructure, especially healthcare. Medical services across the United States have been decreasing as measured in the decline of modern ratios of hospital beds, staff, and natal and other specialty units per 1,000 people. These services were originally built up to the highest standards, beginning in 1946, with the Hospital Survey and Construction Law, popularly called the "Hill Burton Act," after its bi-partisan co-sponsors, Senators Lister Hill (D-Alabama) and Harold Burton (R-Ohio). From that time until about the 1980s, the nationwide hospital bed ratio, for example, was extended in most all 3,000 counties, to reach the standard of 4 to 6 beds per 1,000 people (more or less, depending on rural or urban settings).

Then, with the introduction of Wall Street finance principles of de-regulation, privatization, and other practices, the ratios of all kinds deteriorated, to the point today where large areas have no hospital at all, no physicians, nor diagnostic or emergency equipment. The number of beds per 1,000 persons has fallen from a national average of 4.5 in the mid-1970s, down to under 3, by 2000. The number of community hospitals has fallen from more than 6,000 in the 1970s, down to 4,840 in 2016.

The "Hill Burton" principle, of seeking to provide infrastructure for health care for all, is still the valid standard to govern action. As in the original post-WWII law, surveys can determine where construction of new hospitals, or expansion of existing facilities, needs to be undertaken, and Federal grants can work with other financing, to see this through.

The same principle applies in public health, that is, that infrastructure sufficient to the task must be built up, for everything from providing laboratories to test for food safety, to capacities for deterring disease vectors. Insect-borne diseases have soared in the United States, given the take-down of insect control systems.

For example, the number of officially reported cases of illness from ticks, fleas, and mosquitoes alone tripled from 2004 to 2016. States and localities have customarily conducted anti-insect measures, but they lack the resources. A survey of more than 1,000 of such local programs found that, as of 2015, 80% reported serious deficiencies in ability to conduct basic services.

Figure 11

IHNC Lake Borgne Barrier

This structure, about 26 feet high, and 1.8 miles long, was built from 2008 to 2013, under supervision of the U.S. Army Corps of Engineers, to protect New Orleans, about 12 miles to the west, from sea surge. The barrier already worked perfectly in 2012, when it was activated for the first time, to defend against Hurricane Isaac, which brought a 15 ft storm surge. It was activated in 2017 during Hurricane Nate. The Inner Harbor Navigation Canal Lake Borgne Surge Barrier is located at the confluence of the Mississippi River Gulf Outlet, and the Gulf Intracoastal Waterway.

Disaster Defense

The most obvious call to action for a New Silk Road paradigm of nation-building, comes from the need to defend against disasters, and to swiftly rebuild when there is damage. This has been posed dramatically for the United States by repeated hurricanes. For example, in 2017 came the terrible succession of storms in late Summer and Fall—Hurricanes Harvey, Irma, and Maria—that hit Texas and the Gulf Coast, Florida, and across the Caribbean. More than 90 million people were severely hit by disasters.

To begin with, there are coastal sites appropriate for barriers against sea surge. These include such locations as New York City; Jacksonville, Florida; Houston, Texas; San Juan, Puerto Rico; and New Orleans, Louisiana. The sole instance of the United States building a sizable infrastructure project in recent decades, is the case of the sea wall built to protect outer New Orleans after Hurricane Katrina in 2005. The 1.8-mile Inner Harbor Navigation Canal (IHNC) Lake Borgne Barrier (**Figure 11**) was completed in 2013, but is an isolated example. Since its first use against Hurricane Isaac in 2012, which sent up a 15-foot-high surge, the Lake Borgne Barrier has repeatedly protected New Orleans from storms.

These kinds of barriers, plus inland defenses as well, including levees, run-off catchment and diver-

Figure 12
Puerto Rico Before and After Hurricane Maria

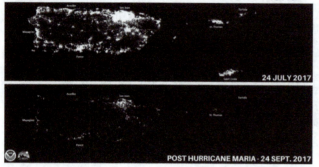

sion systems, flood impoundments, and other structures, must proceed. In the case of Southeast Texas, there are proposals on the books since the 1960s, for a system of reservoirs, integrated with a Southeastern inland canal to convey water safely to the Rio Grande Basin, none of which was built.

Puerto Rico's situation pulls the whole picture together of what the United States must do across the board. Hurricane Maria (September 16-October 1, 2017) devastated the island, including knocking out the entire system of electricity generation and distribution, which already was aged and under-par. Satellite photos document the sudden blackout (**Figure 12**). What rebuilding means, apart from interim contingency measures for diesel generators and the like, is to construct a modern, nuclear power generation base and modern distribution system. Here there is a role for the Small Modular Nuclear Reactor

Aerial view of Ponce, Puerto Rico's second largest city in 1999, showing shoreline features before expansion began on facilities for the Rafael Cordero Santiago Port of the Americas. With a channel depth of 15 m, Ponce is well-positioned to be a mega-port for the Maritime Silk Road, strategically located near the Mona Passage, where the Atlantic Ocean comes into the Caribbean Sea.

(SMR). For example, there are designs for light water-cooled SMRs, in the range of 300 MWe or less. Advanced designs feature non-traditional coolants, such as salts, liquid metals, and helium.

In addition to Puerto Rico's dramatic power crisis, the 2017 Hurricanes Irma and Maria hit every other infrastructure sector on the island, which likewise was already outmoded and in decay, from the 38 dams on the rivers—classified as "high hazard potential"—to the inadequate water supply, and lack of rail transport. Prior to the storms, there existed no railroad at all, only a 10-mile Tren Urbano light transit system serving San Juan, Guaynabo, and Bayamon. For decades, Puerto Ricans had been leaving their homeland, largely for the U.S. mainland. The population fell by 334,000 in the 15 years from 2000 to 2015, down to 3.47 million.

Building anew all needed infrastructure sectors in Puerto Rico, adds up to a new homeland of productivity, and even a special link in the world Silk Road chain. One unique opportunity is to build up Ponce, what was Puerto Rico's second largest city, to take its place on the world Maritime Silk Road. Ponce had already seen itself as the "Port of the Americas."

Science and Culture

Science activity is critical for leading the way for the world New Silk Road drive, and gaining success from its momentum. The decades of defunding and constraining advanced R&D—often under the euphemism of imputed gains from privatization and competition—must stop, especially for the frontier fields of plasma and nuclear fusion investigation, and space. The principles of public good from science are still applicable today, which were stated explicitly in the National Aeronautics and Space Act of 1958 (Public Law #85-568), which launched the U.S. space effort. In its Declaration of Policy and Purpose, the Act asserted that the "general welfare and security of the United States" required space activities. The study of phenomena in the atmosphere and space contributes to "the expansion of human knowledge." Congress mandated NASA to take measures for: "The establishment of long-range studies of the potential benefits to be gained from, the opportunities for, and the problems involved in the utilization of aeronautical and space activities for peaceful and scientific purposes." The details of what must be done in the United States today, in collaboration internationally, are given in Section V.

The demotion of NASA by the so-called privatization of space activities is a guarantee for failure.

In addition, the "soft" infrastructure in place for other areas of investigation must be restored to full functioning. The obvious networks include the system of U.S. National Laboratories, the R&D capacities of the traditional land-grant universities, the U.S. Department of Agriculture, and the hospital and university-based biological and medical research assets.

But beyond these measures, which are self-evident, the most pressing intervention required is for the general public to gain an active outlook of interest and delight in knowledge—the defining quality of mankind. One of the greatest challenges is what to do about the "lost generation" of young people who have grown up, and come into adulthood during the years of the presidencies of George W. Bush and Barack Obama, between 2001 and 2016, and thereafter. With high youth unemployment, large numbers of young Americans have never experienced anything remotely resembling meaningful or productive work, let alone creative thought.

Add to this the impact of the pervasive "entertainment" culture and effect of social media on young people, who have no grounding in seeking truth, beauty, and compassion. The results are that millions of individuals lack a sense of self-worth, and purpose, through no fault of their own. Add to this, the scourge of drugs, and the situation is desperate.

An immediate measure to take, is to ban dope, and move to shut down the source—the banks as well as the narco-networks involved. Beyond that, are social conditions which cannot be reversed overnight, but there are measures and precedents that can have a crash mobilization effect for preparing people to gain the skills and sense of future, in a new, growing economy.

One ready contingency is to activate apprenticeship programs, which can be scaled up through trade unions and vocational education centers. In West

Young cadets of the Navy Junior Reserve Officers' Training Corps (NJROTC) are shown learning how to operate equipment at their training center, taught by a Chief Machinery Repairman. Such education programs from the military, from trade unions, and schools, linked with national AmeriCorps and state-level CCC-programs (Community Conservation Corps) can be massively scaled up to both upgrade personal skills and productivity, and accomplish needed work projects of all kinds.

Virginia, plans were raised in 2018 to add an extra year of high school, for skill-training, looking ahead to a new petro-chemical manufacturing center in Appalachia.

Nationwide, a modern Civilian Conservation Corps (CCC) will be very successful, based on the model of the CCC instituted under President Franklin Delano Roosevelt in the Great Depression. From 1933 to 1942, more than three million youth were employed in all kinds of projects, from land reclamation to construction, all the while learning skills, and a sense of purpose in the course of the work and training. We can add music, history, science, and other programs.

Today, the type of CCC projects can be determined by the requirements for the United States to join the New Paradigm, providing a template for much of the shovel-ready work to be taken up: clearing ground for new rail lines, a new electricity grid, new industrial zones and port capacity, and new science centers.

A skeleton organization for a modern CCC is adaptable from the VISTA/AmeriCorps system, where, on a much smaller scale, young people currently deploy for disaster relief, cleaning parks, improving public health, and other projects.

The Schiller Institute Community Chorus performs at New York City's Carnegie Hall on June 29, 2017.

'Manhattan Project'

A national rallying point for the shift of the United States to a New Paradigm for restoring national and international development, is what is known as the "Manhattan Project," of the Schiller Institute, centered in the New York City/New Jersey area. In the Fall of 2014, statesman Lyndon LaRouche called for focusing activities there, to conduct conferences, webcasts, concerts, and other interventions in the policy direction of the nation, to restore it to a pathway of cultural, economic, and scientific advancement.

A core part of this mobilization is the choral process, in which a Manhattan-based community chorus is growing, and serving as a national choral movement to inspire and embolden people to become part of the mission to restore the United States to a level of principle and goodness, and to experience singing and beauty.

LaRouche pointed to the potential in the Manhattan region-at-large, for many from among the 22 million people in the region, to respond and mobilize on matters of principle. Manhattan can boast of the legacy of Alexander Hamilton (1757-1804), the brilliant leader of the new Republic, whose economic programs (see Section V) were critical to the new nation, and ultimately the world, to successfully understand and combat the British Empire system, of looting and conflict. The connotations of "Manhattan Project" also refer to the success of nuclear scientists in the mid-20th Century, to harness atomic power.

Lyndon LaRouche spoke of his new initiative, as a cultural combat force against the lingering Wall Street/City of London anti-development system. He said in November 2014, "If you establish the principle of Manhattan as being a rallying point for the nation as a whole, a rallying point based on principle, based on a passion into which people are captured, then you can beat the enemy!"

CANADA – GATEWAY TO THE AMERICAS

Although after five years Canada still had not responded to Chinese President Xi Jinping's 2013 invitation for nations to join the Belt and Road Initiative (BRI), it did take a step in this direction by becoming a member of the Asian Infrastructure Investment Bank (AIIB), the first North American country to do so. The decision was announced in Beijing on August 31, 2016, during Prime Minister Justin Trudeau's eight-day first state visit to China where he met with Chinese Premier Li Keqiang and President Xi Jinping, and later attended the China-led G20 Summit in Hangzhou, China.

Canada has had significant positive ties with China historically which should be built upon to establish a closer cooperation between the two nations, clearing the pathway for Canada to join the BRI. Canada is the geographic gateway—along with the U.S. state of Alaska—for linking the Western Hemisphere to the World Land-Bridge, and is positioned as a frontline nation for the new Arctic frontier of development.

It was Justin Trudeau's father, then-Prime Minister Pierre Trudeau, who in 1968, showed the extraordinary foresight to begin the negotiations which led on October 13, 1970, to Canada establishing diplomatic relations with the People's Republic of China, one of the first Western nations to do so. Even earlier, in the late 1950s and early 1960s, Canada's wheat sales to an isolated "Red China" played a major role in helping them to overcome famines, while providing Canadian farmers a much needed export market. In the late 1980s, Canada provided the feasibility study for China's Three Gorges Dam, which when built in 2008, finally freed China from the threat of deadly annual flooding in the Yangtze River Basin, while providing the capacity to generate 18 GW of electricity. In 1996, Prime Minister Jean Chrétien arranged Canada's sale of two CANDU nuclear reactors to China, laying the basis for future cooperation in this area which still exists today.

The rail division of Canada's Bombardier Inc., Bombardier Transportation, one of the world's largest rail equipment manufacturers, now headquartered in Berlin, Germany, was the first foreign train maker to form a joint venture, technology-sharing agreement in China. Through such technology-sharing joint ventures, Bombardier, as well as other nations' train builders such as Kawasaki Heavy Industries, Alstom, and Siemens, have benefited by the ability to upgrade their own high-speed rail technologies to meet the huge demand for mobility in China; while giving China, beginning in 2006, access to state-of-the-art high-speed rail technologies. The fact that in more recent years China has introduced its own even more advanced high-speed rail designs should not be seen as a downside, because foreign train makers still have many opportunities in China, and the world is wide open for rail connectivity. Bombardier Transportation's Chinese joint venture, Bombardier Sifang (Qingdao) Transportation Ltd (BST), was awarded a contract in 2017 to produce five eight-car high-speed train sets with an operational speed of 250 km/hr for the Nanning Railway Bureau in the Guangxi Zhuang Autonomous Region of southern China.

Despite such political and economic ties, Canada has lagged behind many other countries in developing a forward-looking relationship with China, the world's fastest-growing economy, and the BRI. In addition, China and Canada have cultural ties. For example, Canadians of Chinese ancestry make up 5.1% of Canada's population (2016 Census), and China is the leading source of foreign students studying in Canada.

Instead of assuming its geo-strategic position in the Americas, Canada has so far been limited in its forward role, and captive to circumstances. There are two obvious aspects. First, as a member of the British Commonwealth, Canada has been restricted and harmed by the City of London's anti-development policies. Second, Canada is adjacent the United States, which has been in decline, and holding back from the world New Silk Road.

Canada, with fewer than 37 million people, is surrounded by three oceans and bordered only by the United States, which for more than a century has been the world's leading economy, but now is in retreat. Two-thirds of the Canadian people live within 100 miles (160 km) of the United States border on a tiny fraction of Canada's territory. These are generally the regions accessible today by ocean shipping to Atlantic and Pacific ocean ports, and by inland maritime navigation up the Saint Lawrence River-Great Lakes Seaway, together with areas which were opened up for settlement by the two transcontinental railroads built in the late 19th and early 20th Centuries. Canada's primary modes of transportation by water, road, and rail have extensive connections south into the United States, the destination of three-quarters of Canada's exports, and source of more than half of its imports of merchandise. Although most of the population lives in, and much of the economic activity takes place in, southern Canada, both depend to a significant degree, directly or indirectly, upon extraction and processing of natural resources which are increasingly located in central Canada or the Canadian Arctic. And in this case, water, road, and rail connections into these resource-rich areas are sparse or, in many areas, nonexistent.

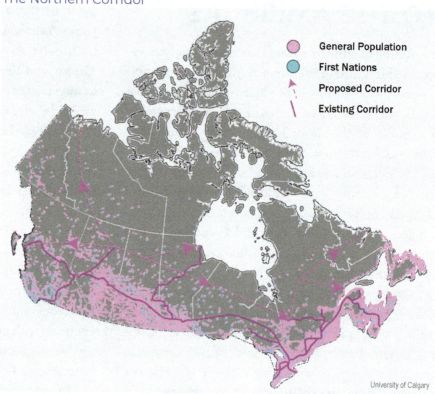

Figure 1
The Northern Corridor

Among the features of what Canada's participation in the BRI would mean, are initiatives in three areas: connectivity, the Arctic, and collaboration in key development areas internationally, especially nuclear. In turn, these efforts define significant increases in the manufacturing and agriculture sectors, and an exciting future of population and settlement expansion in Canada's vast and beautiful territory.

Connectivity

Canada has two unique prospects for dramatically new rail corridors, in addition to the rail connectivity expansion needed throughout its existing, limited rail grid, which is oriented almost entirely along the Canada-U.S. border. First, the Bering Strait rail tunnel link with Asia, after traversing the U.S. state of Alaska, then proceeds into Canada, enabling not only the long-overdue direct line into the Lower 48 U.S. states, thence through Mexico, and Central and South America, but opening up vast areas for agro-industrial development across Canada.

This gives new life to the proposals which have been around for decades for a "Canadian Northern Corridor" (**Figure 1**) multi-modal belt across the nation's north and near-north. In the 1960s, this idea was proposed by Major General (Retired) and author Richard Rohmer; it was then known as the "Mid-Canada Corridor." Simultaneously with the BRI corridors now stretching across Eurasia, there has been renewed discussion in Canada on the trans-Canada corridor concept. A study group exists at the University of Calgary School of Public Policy and Center for Interuniversity Research and Analysis of Organizations, Montreal (CIRANO), and the concept has been taken up in Ottawa over 2016-2017. Although much of the support for the idea derives from the desire to build infrastructure to access the vast mineral wealth of Canada, the merits of the "Northern Corridor" are in no way limited to that. There are exciting challenges, for example, establishing agriculture, through

Figure 2

Selected Canadian cities, towns, ports and remote communities in relation to Arctic shipping routes

innovative practices for northern-latitude farming, using new methods to overcome the harsh continental weather patterns, and poor soils common on the Canadian Shield.

Although details are not worked out, the idea is for a 7,000-km infrastructure corridor to cross Canada, accommodating rail and roadways, pipelines, electricity transmission, and communications. The Calgary group issued a study in 2016 of their review of essential preliminaries, including rights of way. Also of note in this light, is Novaporte, a proposed mega-container facility at Port of Sydney, Nova Scotia, which would be the first deep-water port on the east coast of North America designed specifically to accommodate the largest container ships in the world (18,000 plus TEUs), allowing trans-Atlantic shipping a two-day shorter trip compared to the Port of New York/New Jersey. In April 2016 China Communication Construction Company was retained to prepare the feasibility study.

One of the more compelling examples of what Canada's participation in the BRI would mean is the case of Newfoundland and Labrador, the last province to join Canada in 1949. Although its Port of St. John's would allow an even shorter trip for trans-Atlantic shipping than Nova Scotia's ports of Sydney or Halifax, the province's only railroad, 1,500 km of narrow gauge track linking St. John's with Port aux Basques 550 km to the west, was abandoned in 1988. The province is proceeding with a pre-feasibility study for a 17-km tunnel under the Strait of Belle Isles at its narrowest point linking the island of Newfoundland to Labrador. Although the plans call for a shuttle train to replace the current ferry service, perhaps rebuilding the Newfoundland Railway to modern standards and linking it with a rail tunnel, or bridge, to Labrador could finally connect the province to what should become a new system of passenger and freight rail services for the entire country.

Arctic Frontier

The population and productivity growth implied in this "Northern Corridor" vision, goes right along with Canada's participation in Arctic Silk Road activity (**Figure 2**). In transportation terms, a proposal exists for connecting an expanded national Canadian rail grid, to the Arctic Ocean coast in the north. The line would run from Hay River, Northwest Territories, the northernmost stop of the Canadian National Railway on the banks of Great Slave Lake, northward down the McKenzie River Valley, reaching the coast at Tuktoyaktuk, in the Northwest Territories. This is analogous to the Arctic Circle connections now in Russia and Scandinavia (see section on the Arctic Silk Road). In addition, the Port of Churchill, Manitoba, Canada's only deep water Arctic port with a connection to the Canadian rail system, needs to be revived. Although it is only open four months of the year, the "Arctic Bridge" shipping route between the Port of Churchill and Murmansk, Russia offers a significantly shorter connection between North America and Russia than the conventional route through the Saint Lawrence Seaway.

Nuclear

As a legacy of Canada's participation in the Manhattan Project of World War II, Canada became the second nation to control a nuclear fission reaction, in September 1945. After the war in 1946, an English physicist, Dr. Wilfred Bennett Lewis, took charge of the Canadian National Research Council's nuclear research facilities at the remote Chalk River, Ontario site along the Ottawa River. When the federal Crown corporation, Atomic Energy of Canada Ltd. (AECL), was set up in 1952, Lewis became the Vice President of Research and Development and took up the task of designing a distinctively Canadian approach to the design of a nuclear fission power reactor. As a result of a partnership between AECL, the Hydroelectric Power Commission of Ontario (Ontario Hydro), and Canadian General Electric, the CANDU reactor was born: a Canadian-designed reactor using heavy water (deuterium oxide) to moderate the nuclear fission process and natural uranium (as opposed to enriched uranium) as the fuel.

Since the first CANDU prototype, the 20 MWe Nuclear Power Demonstration (NPD) reactor, came online in 1962 in Rolphton, Ontario, to be followed six years later by the first full-scale power reactor, the 220 MWe Douglas Point reactor in Kincardine, Ontario, Canada's nuclear fleet has expanded to 19 reactors, mostly in Ontario, which provide 13.5 GWe of power capacity, and generate 15% of Canada's electricity. An additional 12 CANDUs have been exported to Argentina (1), China (2), India (2), Pakistan (1), Romania (2), and South Korea (4). India has also built 16 indigenous pressurized heavy water reactors (PHWR) modelled on the CANDU design, and Siemens has built two PHWRs in Argentina. Of the 449 nuclear power plants currently operating worldwide, the vast majority (382) are light water reactors, but the 49 PHWRs have a significant role to play in meeting the demands for reliable baseload electricity generation.

Canada's nuclear sector has undergone a dramatic restructuring in the period since June 2011 when the federal government of Prime Minister Stephen Harper arranged the sale of AECL's commercial reactor division to Candu Energy, a wholly-owned subsidiary of the Montreal-based international engineering company SNC-Lavalin Group, for C$15 million plus C$285 million in future royalties earned through the sale of new reactors. Candu Energy has focused on completing the design for the 740 MWe Enhanced CANDU-6 flagship reactor, while it pursues new build opportunities and the highly specialized task of refurbishing the fleet of 31 aging CANDUs in Canada and around the world.

On September 22, 2016, during an official four-day visit to Canada by Chinese Premier Li Keqiang, SNC-Lavalin Group announced that they had signed an agreement in principle to create a joint venture with China National Nuclear Corp. and Shanghai Electric Group Co. Ltd to design, market, and build the Advanced Fuel CANDU Reactor (AFCR). China's interest in the technology comes from the fact that they currently have 38 nuclear plants, with 20 more nuclear plants under construction, and more in the planning stage—almost all of these are light water reactors—but only limited supplies of uranium. One AFCR reactor would have the ability to reuse the spent fuel from four light water reactors to generate an additional six million MW-hours of electricity annually without needing any additional natural uranium fuel. The joint venture would also open the possibility of exporting the technology to other parts of the world.

AECL's Chalk River Laboratories, now Canadian Nuclear Laboratories (CNL)—which is still government owned but now managed by the Canadian National Energy Alliance, representing a group of experienced nuclear engineering and management firms including CH2M Hill Canada, Fluor Government Group Canada, Energy Solutions Canada Group, SNC-Lavalin, and Rolls-Royce Civil Nuclear Canada—is undergoing a major transformation.

CNL's National Research Universal (NRU) reactor, one of the largest and most versatile high-flux research reactors in the world, and a major source internationally for radioisotopes for medicine and industry, closed down on March 31, 2018 after 60 years of operation. The Canadian Nuclear Isotope Council, a coalition of Canadian science, healthcare, and nuclear sector organizations, has been formed to ensure Canadian production of critical radioisotopes such as

Figure 3

Terrestrial Energy's Integral Molten Salt Reactor (IMSR): The Replaceable IMSR Core Unit

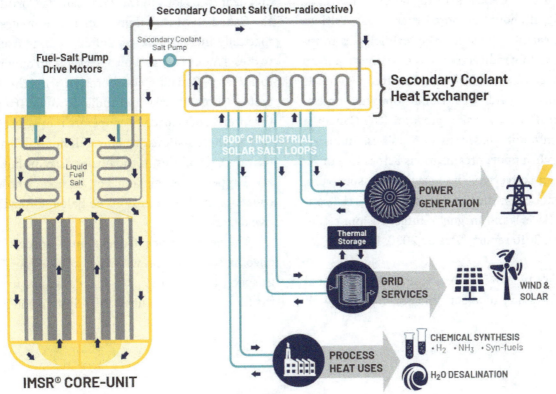

cobalt-60 and molybdenum-99 through alternative routes using commercial power reactors, research reactors, or particle accelerators across Canada.

The federal government is providing a C$1.2 billion investment over ten years to "strategically consolidate and modernize" the Chalk River site, with the construction of an Advanced Nuclear Materials Research Centre complex and other infrastructure and facilities to support the nuclear research needs of the Canadian government and the science and technology needs of the Canadian and global nuclear industry. CNL has four broad application-driven science and technology development programs: energy, including extension of the life of existing reactors, fabrication of advanced nuclear fuels, deployment of small modular reactors (SMRs), and decarbonization of the transportation sector; health, including radiobiology research and targeted alpha therapy; safety and security; and the environment, including decommissioning nuclear sites and radioactive waste management.

In June 2017, CNL issued a *Request for Expressions of Interest in CNL's Small Modular Reactor Strategy,* which received 80 responses—from Canada (51), UK (11), United States (9), Europe (5), China (1), Japan (1), Brazil (1), and one other country. The responses included 19 expressions of interest to build a prototype or demonstration reactor at a CNL site, spanning a wide range of SMR concepts. Canada's nuclear regulator, the Canadian Nuclear Safety Commission (CNSC), is involved in pre-licensing vendor design review (VDR), an optional service to assess a nuclear power plant design based on a vendor's reactor technology, for ten SMRs with capacities in the range of 3 to 300 MWe. For example, the Canadian company Terrestrial

Energy announced in November 2017 the completion of the first phase of CNSC's pre-licensing VDR for their Integral Molten Salt Reactor, a 400 MWt (190 MWe) modular design which they expect could be ready for deployment in 2026 (**Figure 3**). Other VDR applications which CNR has received include those for NuScale Power's 50 MWe self-contained integral pressurized water reactor and Westinghouse's eVinci micro-reactor, capable of providing heat and power from 200 kWe to 25 MWe and process heat up to 600 degrees Centigrade, which would be suitable for remote communities, mining sites, and industries in Canada's north and near-north.

Finally, it should be noted that CNL's Tritium Handling Facility which has the technologies to remove this mildly radioactive isotope of hydrogen (an ideal first generation fusion fuel) from a CANDU reactor's heavy water feed, can also provide crucial support for Canada's fusion program. The Canadian fusion community based in universities, industry, and research support organizations across five provinces has an active program covering the spectrum, from magnetic confinement (tokamak), inertial confinement (laser), and magnetic target fusion, as described in a 2016 report, "Fusion 2030: Roadmap for Canada."

Canada's bid to become a leading international test bed for small modular reactors, together with the capabilities of its fusion community, can help to accelerate the delivery of reliable, low-cost power and heat to regions in the Mid-Canada Corridor and the Canadian Arctic where transportation costs dramatically increase the cost of everything from food to diesel fuel, because it also serves as an opportunity to increase Canada's collaboration with the United States, China, Russia, and India. It would truly be in the interest of Canada to cooperate more closely with each of these nations, all of which not only have significant capabilities in the nuclear sector, but which also happen to be the Four Powers upon whose close collaboration the success of the Belt and Road Initiative depends.

The next step lies in deepening Canada's already ongoing collaboration with each of the Four Powers in space, to chart the path for mankind's future on the Moon, Mars, the entire Solar System and beyond.

"As with the other corridors of the New Silk Road, it is not only that the 'Northeast Passage'—as Europeans have called it— through the Arctic along the Russian coastline is a better means of travelling from Asia to Europe, but that the entire region along the way can be developed in the process."

THE ARCTIC

The Ice Silk Road

Russia and China are escalating their efforts to develop one of the last, relatively untouched frontiers for mankind on Earth—the vast expanse of the Arctic's rich resource base. While Russia's huge coastline on the Arctic Ocean will be the primary base of operations, China is also heavily engaged in building the infrastructure needed to make the exploitation of these resources feasible. As with the other corridors of the New Silk Road, it is not only that the "Northeast Passage"—as Europeans have called it—through the Arctic along the Russian coastline is a better means of travelling from Asia to Europe, but that the entire region along the way can be developed in the process. In addition, the development of means for human occupation of these regions, and the extremely harsh conditions that must be overcome, provide a test-tube basis for preparing for human habitation on the Moon, Mars, and beyond.

A major physical driver for this initiative is the fact that the Northeast Passage (also called the Northern Passage) has become increasingly viable due to the receding of the Arctic ice cap. While the green movement is quick to claim that manmade climate change is responsible for this recession of the Arctic ice cap, the Russian government and Russian scientists (among others) have proven that this is a cyclical phenomenon unrelated to carbon—and indeed, very beneficial to mankind. Not only is trade facilitated by this recession, but Arctic resources are also rendered more accessible—if the world chooses to take advantage of the new circumstances. A fleet of nuclear-powered icebreakers is being expanded to facilitate this trade, while also preparing for a future cyclical expansion of the ice cap.

According to no less an authority than Dmitri Mendeleyev, it was Russian Tsar Peter the Great (1672-1725) who commissioned Vitus Bering's expedition that discovered the strait between the Pacific Ocean and the Arctic, and sought a Northeast Passage. Mendeleyev himself, in a November 1901 memorandum to Finance Minister Count Sergei Witte, "On the Exploration of the Arctic Ocean,"[1] proposed to lead an expedition, in hopes of breaking through the ice and establishing a passage. He considered the shortening of the sea lanes to be a means of advancing civilization and industry, including the development of Russia's Arctic Ocean coast.

In the space age, Mendeleyev's mission must lawfully be expanded to an even higher one, appro-

---
1 See *EIR*, January 6, 2012.

priate to mankind's role as a citizen of the Solar system. In addition to linking the two hemispheres of the globe, the Arctic region is, and has been called, mankind's "window to space," a laboratory for exploration of the causes of climate and weather, and for devising means to meet the challenges of cosmic radiation in its dynamic interaction with our planet. Such a laboratory, like the ITER program for nuclear fusion, requires international collaboration among the scientists of all the world's major nations.

The Northeast Passage has just as long and dramatic a history as does the elusive Northwest Passage in the opposite hemisphere—or more so, considering the argument by India's Bal Gangadhar Tilak, in *The Arctic Home in the Vedas* (1898), that Indo-European civilization began with people who lived and studied the stars along this coastline.

Under the World War II Lend-Lease program, 120 ships brought 450,000 million tons of materiel from American West Coast ports to the Soviet Arctic via the Northeast Passage, for forwarding to the Eastern Front. Fifty-four of them docked in Tiksi at the mouth of the Lena River, 13 rounded the Taymyr Peninsula to reach Yenisei River ports, and one continued westward to Arkhangelsk on the White Sea. Of all these Northeast Passage ports, only Murmansk in the far northwest is classified as "ice-free" year-round. Reinforced ship hulls and icebreaker escorts are the rule.

The Northeast Passage went dormant after the break-up of the Soviet Union, as state-subsidized winter provisioning of its port towns ceased. Following the preliminary announcement of a new Arctic policy in 2001, a major Russian government report in 2009 termed the Arctic a "strategic resource base of the country," requiring upgrades to social and economic infrastructure, a heightened military presence, and cooperation among northern nations in utilizing the region's resources.

The Russian Geographical Society (RGS) is a leading institution for the Arctic. Since 2009, its president has been Sergei Shoygu, now also Russia's defense minister. The RGS initiated periodic "Arctic—Territory of Dialogue" conferences in 2010, attended by President Putin and leaders of other Arctic Ocean littoral countries.

The coastal Northeast Passage is undisputedly in Russian waters. Encompassing several shipping lanes varying in length from 2,200 to 2,900 nautical miles (4,075 to 5,370 km), it is a shorter trip between Seoul and Rotterdam by 6,400 km, compared to sailing south of Eurasia and through the Suez Canal (**Figure 1**). It is less than half the distance.

One Belt, One Road, One Circle

Hu Angang, a leading Chinese economist at Tsinghua University, coined the term "One Circle"—referring to the encirclement of the entire Eurasian landmass by the completion of the Northeast Passage—to go along with the "One Belt, One Road." Beside reducing shipping time, the resources waiting to be developed—waiting only for the human race to develop the technologies needed to facilitate such development in a harsh environment, in a manner acceptable to human habitation—include vast deposits of gold and other minerals, as well as an estimated 30% of the world's undiscovered natural gas and 13% of undiscovered oil, according to the U.S. Geological Survey.

While issues of sovereignty apply to the resources near the borders of the Arctic nations (Russia, United States, Norway, Finland, Sweden, and Denmark), the vast territory of the Arctic is mostly outside of territorial waters, and is thus subject only to the United Nations Convention on the Law of the Sea (UNCLOS), which allows only joint development of the resources under consensus agreements.

Governing this process is the Arctic Council, comprising the six Arctic nations, with others present as observers, including China. China considers itself a "near-Arctic" state, and points out that the region holds "the inherited wealth of all humankind." The last biennial summit of the Arctic Council took place in Juneau, Alaska in March 2017, where Finland took over as president for the current two-year term.

On his way to visit President Trump in Florida in April 2017, President Xi Jinping stopped in Finland to discuss Finland's role in the Belt and Road, but he also arranged for Finland to represent China in meetings of the Arctic Council. The deliberations of the council have thus far quite successfully avoided

Figure 1

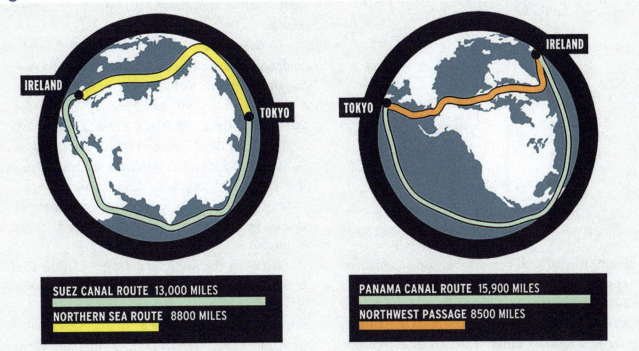

efforts to introduce geopolitical conflicts.

In fact, the U.S. collaboration with Russia, as also in the space program, has been both friendly and mutually beneficial, despite the fact that the U.S. sanctions on Russia under the Obama Administration in 2014 essentially shut down extensive investments by Exxon and other oil companies in the Russian regions of the Arctic—to the detriment of both parties.

Despite good intentions by many U.S. institutions, the United States has cut off cooperation with the leading player in the Arctic, and has few resources to pursue its own interests. The United States, for example, has a grand total of one functioning ice-breaker, while Russia has 40, and is in the process of building or ordering (primarily from South Korea) the construction of dozens more.

In June 2017, President Putin oversaw the christening and naming of the world's largest liquefied natural gas (LNG) icebreaker tanker in St. Petersburg, the *Christophe de Margerie*, built for Russia by South Korea's Daewoo Shipbuilding and Marine Engineering Corporation. Clearly not intended for military purposes, the ship was directly deployed to the Yamal Peninsula on the Arctic, at the northern end of the Ural Mountains. This region holds huge natural gas deposits that are being developed by a consortium including Russia's Novatek, France's Total, and the China National Petroleum Corporation. The ship is the most modern tanker of a high-ice class, and will become the flagship in a fleet of 15 similar vessels. The Yamal project aims to produce 16.5 million tons of LNG a year.

Russia is also building a Northern Latitude Railway to connect Yamal with the Ural regions to the south and the nation's transportation arteries, ensuring year-round transport of the region's mineral resources.

In another major development zone, that of the Arkhangelsk region south of Murmansk, near the Norway and Finland border, China's Poly Group Corporation is planning a $5.5 billion development project, involving a new deep-water port and a rail connection to the south (the Belkomur rail project, **Figure 2**). The intention is to ship coal, fertilizer, oil, and other goods from Siberia and the Urals to Arkhangelsk via the Arctic, and then south by rail. Igor Orlov, the governor of Arkhangelsk, estimates that the project will generate 40,000 jobs when it is completed in 2023.

Chinese high-speed rail technologies, developed for the high-altitude Tibet railway and the relatively high-latitude lines in northeastern China, will be

Figure 2
The Belkomur Rail Project

relevant. Russia itself opened the world's northernmost conventional railway, on the Yamal Peninsula, in 2010. On January 26, 2018, China released its first "Arctic Policy White Paper," presenting a plan for a "Polar Silk Road." Chinese enterprises are encouraged to participate in infrastructure development for these routes and conduct commercial trial voyages.

Besides opening the new trade route and the development of Arctic resources, China is in discussions with Finland, Japan, Russia, and Norway about building a 10,500 km fiber-optic cable from China along the Arctic Circle, which would create the fastest data connection between China and Europe.

Scandinavia and the Polar Silk Road

The easternmost port in Norway is Kirkenes, which Finland would like to connect to the famous home town of Santa Claus, Rovaniemi, in Finland to the south, which is now the northern end-station of the Finnish railways. The 3 billion euro Arctic Rail project would open up a major mining region in northern Finland and Sweden to rail transport, a region whose product could be shipped out north to the Atlantic and the Polar Silk Road, instead of via the Baltic Sea.

Kirkenes would also make the polar route itself more economical, because the ice-protected ships classed for going through the Arctic are more expensive than need be, when used on the open sea to the west. Kirkenes would offer unloading of the ship cargo for further transport south by rail to continental Europe.

In the south of Finland, there is a Finnish-Estonian plan to build an undersea railway tunnel between Helsinki, Finland, and Tallinn, Estonia. A first feasibility study financed by the EU is expected in 2018, on construction of this "FinEst Link" by 2050.[2] In November 2017, Finnish IT billionaire Jan Vesterbacka called for building this 80 km tunnel in just five years, by bringing in Chinese technology and financing. The tunnel would create a region of one million people out of the two capital cities. Its cost is estimated at 13 billion euros.

Together, the Arctic Rail project and the FinEst Link are looking to China for financing. The two projects would be integrated with the planned 3.6 billion euro Rail Baltica high-speed rail line, which will run from Tallinn to Poland, and there link into Western Europe's rail networks, enabling a direct rail link from Helsinki to Berlin and beyond.

NATO member Norway has promoted cooperation with Russia for the development of its "High North," where the exploitation of the energy resources in the Barents Sea was pioneered by the Norwegian oil companies. Norway has been a leading promoter in Europe of Arctic development, hosting the world's largest-ever conference on the Arctic, with 3,000-3,500 participants from all over the globe, on January 21-26, 2018, in Tromso, Norway, more than 200 miles north of the Arctic Circle.

The Finnish initiatives to take part in the development of "a global transport system" has brought Sweden to join Finland (and the World Land-Bridge) in pushing for an extension northwards of the EU TEN-T corridor called the Scandinavian-Mediterranean (ScanMed) which ended at the Swedish capital Stockholm. Infrastructure Minister Tomas Eneroth announced February 21, 2018 that Sweden has submitted a request to the European Commission to extend ScanMed to northern Sweden by an additional 1,000 kilometers to Haparanda, on the border with Finland.

---

2 http://www.finestlink.fi/en/

At the same time Finland requests from EU that the corridor continues through Finland to Turkku, Helsinki, and then to the Russian border. In this way the Scand-Med corridor in Sweden and Finland will form a horseshoe railway corridor called the Bothnian Corridor, on both sides of the Baltic Sea (**Figure 3**).

The Arctic Ocean Railway will be a link from the Northern Sea Route to both horseshoe legs of the Bothnian Corridor. So both Finland and Sweden/Denmark can become main rail trunk lines of container traffic from the Northern Sea route to Continental Europe.

The Nordic Triangle between the capital cities Copenhagen, Oslo, Stockholm, and Helsinki was also integrated in the EU ScanMed Corridor. Also in the planning stage is the Fehmarnbelt tunnel between Denmark and Germany.[3] The project was approved on the Danish side in 2015, while approval is expected from Germany in 2018. The 18 km road and rail immersed tunnel will be the longest of its kind in the world and the biggest infrastructure project in Northern Europe, costing an estimated 7 billion euros.

China's Interest in Scandinavian Infrastructure

The Hongkong-based company Sunbase, representing a Chinese consortium, offered to build a new harbor in a fjord called Lysekil, north of Gothenburg on the Swedish Atlantic (North Sea) coast, in November 2017. It would have the capacity to receive the biggest container ships in the world, which currently have no harbor deep enough in Sweden. This harbor would also be an early stop in Western Europe for the Polar Silk Road. The new harbor would have a berth 1,800 meters long and 1,000 meters wide. The plan includes a new bridge, new roads and railways, a terminal for cruise ships, and urban development. It would be a huge investment in a nation starved for decades

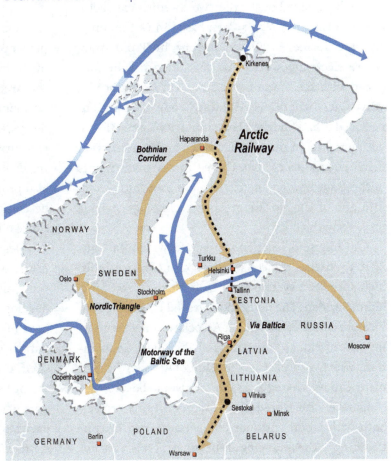

Figure 3
Scandinavian Transport Corridors

of infrastructure development and jobs. It has been welcomed by the city administration, so the Chinese have been asked to present a more detailed plan.

However, the harbor offer has met a storm of protests from the major media, and by some locals and security analysts. In the geopolitically charged climate of Russia-bashing in Sweden, not only Russia, but also China is being attacked for allegedly having colonial and military interests in connection with port development projects internationally. The Belt and Road Initiative is attacked as a policy to project Chinese military and political domination. The participation, in July 2017, of Chinese naval units in military exercises with the Russian fleet in the Baltic Sea, has been highlighted in this debate.

The result was that the Chinese consortium announced its decision to pull out of the project on January 30, 2018. This Swedish China-bashing is very ill conceived, as it could deter Chinese interest in building much needed Swedish high-speed railway systems.

---

3 https://femern.com/en

It could also imperil the huge Chinese investments in the Swedish auto sector. Two Chinese industrialists have bought the two Swedish car factories in this region, Volvo Cars, based in Gothenburg, and the former Saab car factory in Trollhattan, where electric-powered cars for China will be produced with the brand name Nevs. On December 27, Volvo Cars owner Geely Holding Group of China, announced it had bought a large minority share (15% in voting rights) in the Swedish truck and construction machine producer Volvo. These Chinese investments in these automotive industries have brought Sweden into one of the world's greatest technology-sharing projects with China.

A Chinese delegation visited Norway in January 2018 to discuss the construction of a Chinese-built, high-speed rail system from Oslo, Norway, to Stockholm, Sweden. The delegation was led by Huang Xin, vice president of the China Association for Promoting International Economic and Technical Cooperation, which is a part of the China Overseas Investment Union. Huang Xin said: "We would be happy to cooperate with Norway and Sweden in this project, both with labor, with our competence, and in contributing to the financing of the project." It is a part of "the Chinese strategy for international investments in infrastructure." The project would cost about $20 billion, reducing the travel time to 2.5 hours from nearly 6 hours. The current railway was built in the 19th Century, with very little improvement since.

Denmark a Global Maritime Hub

Scandinavian shipping to China is dominated by Denmark and its global container shipping company, Maersk. On January 22, 2018, the Danish Minister of Business, Brian Mikkelsen, announced a plan to develop Denmark into a Global Maritime Hub by 2025. The plan, called Blue Denmark, will develop the maritime industry in all parts of the nation.

Denmark is already the most China-oriented nation in Europe. Bilateral trade has increased steadily since the 2008 "strategic partnership" between the two nations. Denmark has the highest proportion of China's trade, 6%, among the Nordic nations, especially because of shipping services from Maersk.

Nuclear Power for Arctic Development

Russia plans to build several floating nuclear power plants, each with two 35 MW nuclear reactors of the type used on icebreakers, for deployment on the Arctic coast. The keel of the prototype, the *Academician Lomonosov,* was laid in 2007; after several delays, it is now scheduled to be towed from St. Petersburg to the port of Pevek on the Kamchatka Peninsula in Russia's Far East, in November 2019. China also projects that its first floating nuclear plants will be completed by 2020, for use on islands and offshore oil rigs.

Despite the U.S. sanctions, which cut off western sales to Gazprom and Rosneft gas and oil projects, Russia has proceeded to implement its plans for developing the Arctic region. In April 2017, Rosneft began drilling in the Khatangsky Krai region in the Laptev Sea—the northernmost drilling on the Arctic shelf. President Putin said, at the ceremony opening the project, that this was the "start of work to develop a whole oil and gas province, which preliminary data suggest contains a vast quantity of energy resources."

There are no port facilities at the site—drills, accommodation modules, and other equipment had to be shipped from Arkhangelsk, 3,600 km away. The project was preceded by Rosneft setting up a research base a year earlier near the site. Future drilling is planned in the Kara Sea and the Barents Sea, beginning in 2019. It is expected that by 2050, between 20 and 30% of Russia's crude oil will come from the Arctic.

China set up its first research station in the Arctic in 2004, the Yellow River Station in Svalbard, the Norwegian islands halfway between Norway and the North Pole, operated by the Chinese Arctic and Antarctic Administration. The Polar Research Institute of China is now setting up the Aurora Observatory in Iceland, in partnership with the Icelandic Centre for Research, with the stated purpose of furthering the "scientific understanding on solar-terrestrial interaction and space weather by conducting polar upper atmosphere observations, such as auroras, geomagnetic field variations, and other related phenomena, and outreach to the public." Another research station is being planned in Greenland.

In September 2016, the Russian-Chinese Polar Engineering and Research Centre was established by the Russian Far Eastern University and the Chinese Harbin Polytechnic University, with the aim of promoting industrial development in the Arctic, including ice-resistant platforms and frost-resistant concrete appropriate for the regional climate conditions.[4]

A Window to Space

Proximity to the Earth's magnetic pole and the geomagnetic fields defines the Arctic as the junction between the Earth and galactic radiation, an ideal place for exploring the causes of climate and weather, and meeting the challenges of cosmic radiation in its dynamic interaction with our planet. The Arctic has been called a "window to space," because of this position as one of Earth's two invisible polar portals through the atmosphere, receiving an influx of extra-terrestrial radiation of which the Aurora Borealis is only the visible, beautiful fringe.

Russia is expanding the Northern Federal Arctic University, in Arkhangelsk, as a center for training Arctic development specialists. Establishment of an Arctic Research Center, to conduct inter-disciplinary Arctic studies under the auspices of the Russian Academy of Sciences, is also proposed for the Arkhangelsk Region.

At the September 2011 "Arctic—Territory of Dialogue" conference, Russian architect Valeri Rzhevsky's plan for a new facet of the "window to space" was exhibited. Then-Prime Minister Putin viewed the three-dimensional design of a "wonder city" in the Arctic, which would pioneer ways for humans to live in environments far removed from those of Earth. The project is called Umka, a word suggesting "cleverness" (and the name of an enterprising polar bear character in a Soviet-era animated cartoon).

The site of the domed, self-sustaining city is Kotelny Island, between the Laptev Sea and East Sibe-

The International Space Station looks down over a stunning aurora—the interaction of Earth's atmosphere with the cosmic environment.

rian Sea, some 400 km northeast of the Lena River delta. It is 1,500 km from the North Pole. The giant dome is designed to contain life-support systems, modeled on those of the International Space Station.

With power from a floating nuclear power station, Umka will have a regulated, temperate climate, in which air circulation and the biological cycles of all plants and creatures within are interdependent. Circulation of oxygen and plant growth-stimulating carbon dioxide will be contained under the dome, minimizing contact with the frigid outside environment.

Fish farming, in waters slightly warmed by the nuclear power plant, will help to supply food. All waste will be recycled or reduced to less than ashes. Recreational facilities will lessen psychological strain on Umka's human residents, helping them adjust to living in an enclosure. The Umka design has been submitted to all five Arctic littoral nations (Canada, Denmark/Greenland, Norway, Russia, and the Unit-

A model of the proposed Arctic city, Umka

---

[4] See "Emerging Chinese-Russian cooperation in the Arctic," SIPRI Policy Paper No. 46, June 2017. (https://www.sipri.org/sites/default/files/2017-06/emerging-chinese-russian-cooperation-arctic.pdf)

ed States). With a footprint of 1.2 km x 800 m, and 5,000 residents, the population density of Umka will approach Hong Kong's 6,350 inhabitants per square kilometer. Those first 5,000 residents of the city might be scientists, engineers, and workers primarily focused on the requirements of oil platforms and mining companies, but scientific researchers living in Umka will also plumb the rich Arctic depths of undiscovered knowledge for the biological and physical sciences. The Umka project is best appreciated from an extraterrestrial standpoint. At 75° N latitude, there are strong winds, and temperatures sink below –30°C—the same temperature as in lunar lava tubes. These hostile conditions provide an opportunity to develop and apply technologies that will be needed at the frontiers of space exploration.

IV. TRANS-ATLANTIC AT THE CROSSROADS

"The Trump Administration at the start of 2018 stood before the challenge of joining in this new economic paradigm, or continuing to play along with the geopolitics which have left the American economy and labor force in such straits."

THE UNITED STATES
Strategic Relation to the New Silk Road

While the economic opportunity of China's Belt and Road Initiative has become a major policy factor for nations all over the world—and often referred to by informal shorthand as the "New Silk Road"—there is little discussion any longer of an earlier, United States State Department policy formally called "The New Silk Road" when it was launched under the Obama Administration and Secretary of State Hillary Clinton in 2010. The Obama State Department said in 2016, "The New Silk Road initiative was first envisioned as a means for Afghanistan to integrate further into the region by resuming traditional trading routes and reconstructing significant infrastructure links broken by decades of conflict." Its central objective was the provision of energy and electricity from oil and water power in Uzbekistan and Tajikistan to Afghanistan, which was to become a trade "hub."

In formal terms the policy still existed at least to the end of that Administration, and the World Bank was convinced to offer $400 million in funding for the CASA-1000 high-voltage transmission project, which is still committed though no construction has occurred. A simple comparison of this, to China's investment/commitment of roughly $100 billion to infrastructure development in Pakistan, Kazakhstan, Iran, and Turkey; billions of dollars more to the ASEAN nations; and more still to India's development of Chabahar Port and the "North-South Rail/Road Corridor" through Iran to continue through to Russia to Europe, shows why the State Department's "New Silk Road" has become irrelevant.

This forgotten initiative expresses perfectly the now decades-old problem of U.S. economic diplomacy: An attempt to seize influence, particularly at the expense of Russia and China, by rhetorically promoting trade while having no capacity or intent to invest in new infrastructure that would develop trade, and relying on American military forces operating abroad to make U.S. policy work.

This is the strategic position President Donald Trump inherited after running a Presidential campaign which opposed the free trade and environmentalist/climate change policies that have stymied development, renounced regime-change wars, pledged to build a new economic infrastructure, rejected the free trade deals of international finance, called for international cooperation with Russia, extolled revived and expanded space exploration, and criticized Wall Street's stock market "bubble."

THE UNITED STATES

Left: Presidents Trump and Putin meet in Helsinki, Finland for their first official summit, July 16, 2018. Right: President Xi and Peng Liyuan take President Trump and the First Lady on a tour of China's "Forbidden City," November 2017.

U.S. strategy during the 50 years its economy declined in productivity, became simply that of being the dominant, and then the sole military superpower. This reached the level of the post-1990 "neo-conservative" doctrine that no national power in the world could be permitted even to approximate American military strength.

Under this geopolitical doctrine, the United States has often been a "dumb giant" manipulated by British governments—abetted by their French collaborators—into perpetual wars. It has been pushed into the shocking series of regime-change wars of the Bush and Obama Administrations in Iraq, Libya, Syria, Afghanistan, Yemen, and—by "irregular warfare" means—Ukraine. All of these have had Russia, and China, as their ultimate targets for confrontation.

With the British all-out confrontation with Russia through dubious "chemical weapons attack" claims in early Spring 2018, President Trump has been forced to choose between his clear intent for strategic cooperation with Putin's Russia, and demand that he support more wars—from the same British intelligence-instigated forces trying to drive him out of office.

American financial dominance, and trade dominance of the largest U.S.- and Europe-based multinational banks and corporations have also been seen as required by this strategy, and pursued through the World Trade Organization (WTO) and by "trade agreements" that cede the sovereign authority of many nations to those of Wall Street- and London-centered banks and corporations.

But here, too, it is actually London which has become the world's dominant financial center in recent decades, with now 25% of all financial activity in the world taking place on UK territory, 19% in the United States; 50% of all financial derivatives activity centered in London against 25% on Wall Street. Particularly since Britain's 1986 "Big Bank" financial deregulation, London has had the whip hand in breaking down bank separation and regulation in America and making Wall Street's banks the risky giant casinos they are today.

Again, Donald Trump became President vowing to end this strategic paradigm, and to make America first by virtue of rapid economic revival and progress, rather than claiming America is first due to its military power. This would require cooperation on strategic issues with the other great powers, specifically with China and Russia, and India as well. Whether President Trump can see this as actually economic and scientific cooperation—the Belt and Road Initiative, joint space exploration—remains a question. Only once since President John F. Kennedy's assassination and the late 1960s' disappearance of funding for the American space exploration program, has an industrial frontier potentially opened. It appeared with President Reagan's Strategic Defense Initiative adopted from the initiative of Lyndon LaRouche.

But Reagan could not secure funding for the SDI to any significant degree, particularly those elements based on new physical principles, and despite the military initiative's impact on the Soviet Union's breakup as LaRouche had forecast, laser, relativistic beam,

Figure 1
The 50-Year Disappearance of U.S. Infrastructure
(Annual Investment as % of GDP)

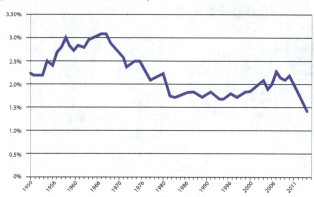

Figure 2
NASA Budget History (% of total budget)

and plasma technologies did not enter industry even in the United States. The collapse of the Soviet Union only made the United States far more militarily dominant, and even less motivated to maintain its economic and industrial infrastructure; since that time the pessimism of its population is turning steadily to anger and even despair.

Measurements of a Broken Paradigm

What President Donald Trump's administration now confronts, and has been unable to change in his first year in office, is a strategic and economic policy paradigm which he clearly knows is broken, and for which the new paradigm of the Belt and Road Initiative offers a cooperative way out, toward "making America great again." Trump throughout 2017 was under a fierce attack intended to drive him from office, and originating within intelligence and security agencies of Britain and the United States because Trump rejects confrontation with Russia and China and opposes regime-change wars. But even within his own administration, almost no leading official will admit the metrics of what the United States has become:

- The United States has not had a national credit institution to pursue new infrastructure platforms and industrial breakthrough technologies, for 70 years since the end of the work of President Franklin Roosevelt's Reconstruction Finance Corporation's crucial part in winning World War II. It has not had a capital budget for 40 years, and has the greatest difficulty addressing infrastructure voids which have become life-threatening on a significant scale, as with the repeated hurricane devastations during this century. **Figures 1** and **2** give an idea of this.

- The proportion of the United States workforce engaged in goods-producing work of all kinds—manufacturing, construction, mining, power generation and distribution, transport—has fallen to 13% of the workforce (20,200,000 workers) from 31% (25,100,000) in 1979 (**Figure 3**).

- The real productivity of the American workforce, measured as total factor productivity or "technological productivity," has fallen dramatically since 1970 (**Figure 4**); and as the OECD and leading economists have noted with great surprise, has continued to fall despite the advent of the essentially labor-intensive "IT revolution." During a significant later portion of this 45-year period, by contrast, total factor productivity of China's workforce has grown at 3% annually or higher, even as its rapid economic growth has drawn it near to the United States in the total size of its economy.

Figure 3
Workforce Employed in Goods-Producing Industries

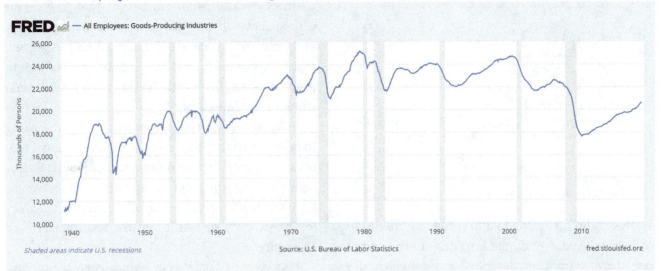

- The rate of family formation among the increasingly "deindustrialized" American population has dropped precipitously, a concomitant of rising economic and cultural pessimism. The rate of family formation was approximately 80,000/year during the decade of the 1970s in the United States; it has been approximately 50,000/year in the 21st Century thus far.

- The American life expectancy has shockingly dropped during 2015 and 2016, according to the National Health Statistics Agency, a phenomenon not seen in other industrialized nations and not seen in the United States for 55 years. More tellingly, life expectancy at age 65 is still rising steadily; it is falling life expectancies and rising death rates among Americans in the prime working ages which are causing the overall declines. The phenomenon of "deaths of despair" from drug and alcohol addiction and suicides has become undeniable; and the more than tripling of drug overdose deaths since 2000 has become an issue verging on panic in many states. Overdose deaths rose another 21% in 2016, to 63,400 nationally.

As the United States has deindustrialized, there has been a 45-year secular decline in real wages of workers, per hour and per week. **Figure 5** shows the long slide in average weekly wages.

Given the many claims by U.S. Republican elected officials that the lowering of corporate taxes legislated at the end of 2017 will cause real wages to rise substantially, the past 40 years of history shows no such thing. Following the significant reductions in tax rates during the first administration of President Ronald Reagan, a previously slow decline in real wages became a more rapid fall during 1985-1996. Another round of tax cuts in the first year of the George

Figure 4
Total Factor Productivity in the U.S. Economy
(Annual Growth by Decade)

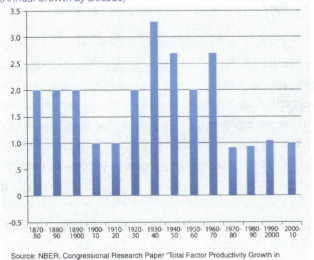

Source: NBER, Congressional Research Paper "Total Factor Productivity Growth in Historical Perspective", 2013

IV. TRANS-ATLANTIC AT THE CROSSROADS

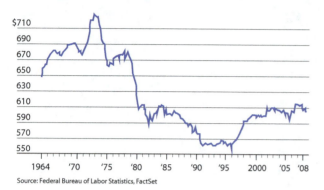

Figure 5
Real Wages Struggle
Average weekly earnings of U.S. workers in 2008 dollars, since 1964

Source: Federal Bureau of Labor Statistics, FactSet

W. Bush Administration in 2001 produced no rise in real wages. And overall, the long drop in the corporate share of taxation, described above—which also reflects increasing ways and means of tax avoidance by larger corporations—has seen an equally long decline in real wages.

The 2017 tax cuts were authorized by a resolution which called for the U.S. deficit and debt to be increased by $1.5 trillion through lowering tax revenue. Were the $1.5 trillion in new debt, instead, taken by a new U.S. national infrastructure bank or a revived Reconstruction Finance Corporation from the Franklin Roosevelt era, the resulting targeted investments in new, high-technology infrastructure would in fact raise real wages, skilled productive employment, and productivity.

That is just one part of the prospect, or paradigm, which the Belt and Road Initiative offers to the United States, if President Trump is defended from the "deep state" attempts to remove him, and actually adopts such a strategy. It would obviously also involve a new perspective on revived American space exploration as a cooperative venture with other spacefaring nations, and the prospect of new scientific breakthroughs in nuclear fission and fusion technologies.

Raising Profit Rates as 'Strategy'

The dramatic lowering of corporate tax rates in the United States at the end of 2017 was presented to, and by, President Trump as "strategic," because it will attract capital into the United States from other countries to which it has gone, giving those countries "unfair advantage" over the United States. In the 21st Century "Washington consensus" this has meant China, above all; and China's central bank immediately realized, upon the U.S. tax cuts being legislated, that China would have to take regulatory measures to prevent capital flight into the U.S. stock markets and similar speculation.

The idea of cutting corporate taxes and seeking to raise corporate profit rates as an international economic strategy, merely reflects the geopolitical strategic thinking which defines any major nation whose economy is growing more rapidly than that of America, as an adversary with "antithetical interests," or an enemy.

Completely fact-averse claims often try to support this geopolitics; as for example, the claims of circles in and around the Trump Administration and throughout Congressional groups of both parties, that China and even Germany are "manipulating their currencies" downward, even as the dollar has fallen against both the euro and the renminbi.

In the event, the very large increases in profits reaped by many banks and major U.S.-based multinational companies in 2018 since the tax cut, are turning out to be no match—even in the stock markets—for the impact of rising interest rates on the immense and overleveraged U.S. corporate debt bubble. Another financial crash is threatening, one which would immediately increase the potential for a global trade war and hot war showdown with Russia and China.

Need To Abandon Geopolitics

President Trump has rejected the adversaries/enemies rhetoric, and instead described China and Russia, for example, as "rival powers." This, however, still countenances and perpetuates geopolitics. A break with geopolitics—adopting the idea that major national powers should be partners in policies which keep peace, promote development of third countries, and advance science and technology for the common aims of mankind—is the strategic concept the United States needs the President and Congress to adopt. With that concept, the hollowed-out formerly industrial economy of the United States can be revived, provided with modern infrastructure platforms, and actually "make America great again."

During the President's trip to Asia and particularly his visit and summits in China in November 2017, he engaged directly with the "New Silk Road" policy, as well as with China's ancient and modern culture, and negotiated economic cooperation on the highest level.

The trip was immediately followed by announcement of a stunning investment by major Chinese banks and corporations into West Virginia, more than $80 billion committed to create new industries in the third-poorest, most opiate-addicted, and heretofore most pessimistic state. Other state and local elected officials in the United States are ignoring the geopolitical "Washington consensus," as West Virginia's officials did, and dealing directly with China in pursuit of economic development.

Houston's mayor and Texas' governor, for example, arranged in late 2017 for significant investments in transportation and energy infrastructure and the entry of major Chinese infrastructure-logistics firms into U.S. business through Texas. China wants to invest in American infrastructure projects, as does Japan, including using their large holdings of U.S. Treasury securities to do so.

These are the potentials if Trump is able to follow through on the beginning made in his 2017 summits with China's President Xi Jinping. The most crucial shift in U.S. strategic thinking actually required at the start of 2018, is to recognize that a financial crash of the London- and Wall Street-centered trans-Atlantic banking systems is threatening immediately. Section V of this report deals with this threat in detail. The denial of it by U.S. elected officials originates in British geopolitics. It contrasts sharply with the recognition of the threat by China's leaders.

Both President Xi Jinping and former Finance Minister Lou Jiwei have repeatedly warned that the 2008 financial/economic collapse in those banking systems was not "solved," and have warned of another explosion of the global financial system. China's 2017 Central Party Congress even formed a new national body tasked with preparing to face such a crisis, and elevated that body to the highest national level.

We discuss the measures necessary to deal with this financial crisis—"LaRouche's Four Laws"—in Section V of this report. China's investment strategy prioritizing new technologies and new economic infrastructure platforms at home and abroad, along with its regulation of its banks on the Glass-Steagall principle, places China's banking system in a better position—once again—to avoid financial collapse which is stalking the trans-Atlantic region. It underpins the Belt and Road Initiative as a strategy, as well as a "win-win" offer of credit and know-how.

The Trump Administration at the start of 2018 stood before the challenge of joining in this new economic paradigm, or continuing to play along with the geopolitics which have left the American economy and labor force in such straits.

"Many ... in Europe are attracted by projects along the New Silk Road.... The main obstacle they face is the reluctance of the top policy-making elites ... to join hands with China and formulate a larger design for a genuine European contribution to the New Silk Road."

WILL EUROPE FINALLY JOIN THE NEW SILK ROAD?

Many cities, regions, industrial companies, and other economic and scientific institutions in Europe are attracted by projects along the New Silk Road. Many also view the New Silk Road as an opportunity to finally revitalize infrastructure development plans that have gathered dust for decades. The main obstacle they face is the reluctance of the top policy-making elites in the European Union (EU) bureaucracy, many governments, and associated think tanks and related academic institutions to join hands with China and formulate a larger design for a genuine European contribution to the New Silk Road, create financial institutions equipped with sufficient funds to promote big projects, and make definite steps into the new paradigm of development and cooperation. Instead, the political energies of Europe's elite are wedded to the old paradigm of financial speculation and disinvestment which is to blame for the outbreak of global crisis in 2007-2008, and that elite has been neither capable nor willing to draw any constructive conclusions from that crisis.

Germany in particular, is way behind in efforts to be fit for the New Silk Road: its rail freight sector is outmoded, for example, running on the Middle Rhine Valley route through tunnels that are 150 years old at average speeds of maybe 60 km/hour—not competitive today. Germany's rail connections to neighboring countries need to be electrified, so that the procedure of changing from electric- to diesel-driven locomotives on the German side is overcome. Duisport, Germany's main destination for rail freight from China, meanwhile handles 26 freight container trains per week, but the freight transferred to trucks already causes quite some congestion on nearby highways and roads.

How Duisport will handle five times as many trains, which is the target that China envisions for 2020, remains unsolved. The non-investment attitude of the German government is the pattern for all infrastructure in the country: highways, roads, bridges, waterway locks, rail. In many cases, railway bridge construction dates back to pre-World War I. This attitude invalidates a lot of the constructive efforts made in Germany's neighboring countries to upgrade their transport infrastructures. This creates an impossible, and intolerable situation, because Germany is at the center of nearly all important north-south and west-east transportation routes in Europe. The "Europe" that German policy-makers prefer is one that does not spend any money for bigger projects, but instead pumps more and more revenue into covering budget deficits.

A Widening Division

But aside from the EU elites, the reality is that Europe is divided: Particularly in the eastern and southwestern parts of the continent, where hopes that membership in the EU would give them economic and infrastructural development after the fall of the Iron Curtain in 1989 have been betrayed, policy-makers have begun to look for alternate partners. Instead of waiting for another one or two decades for concrete commitment by the EU to promote real economic development in their countries, leading officials of economic and political institutions in eastern and southeastern Europe have stated their intent to work with China; some EU member governments there, such as those in Greece, Bulgaria, Hungary, and Poland, in the course of 2017 and early 2018 have even shown interest in becoming active partners in the New Silk Road development.

Government-level attendance was visibly higher from Europe's East and Southeast, than from Europe's West, at the mid-May 2017 Belt-and-Road Summit in Beijing. And, located at the center of western, eastern, and southeastern Europe, Austria has opened up to the New Silk Road since the new government in Vienna was sworn in on December 21, even taking the lead among European nations so far in stating strong commitment to take an active role in the Belt and Road Initiative in its official government program.

One of the tragedies in Europe's West is that Germany even signed a promising document on the eve of the early July 2017 G20 Summit in Hamburg on cooperation with China in hydropower and other infrastructure projects in Africa, but loyalty to the EU Commission's stonewalling against China and loyalty also to its own budget-cutting ideology has prevented the German government from acting on that document. Thus, news on bigger projects in Europe carried out in cooperation with China will continue to come from the East and Southeast of the European continent, for the time being. It may be hoped though, that in the course of 2018, the West of Europe will wake up to the opportunities that are offered by the New Silk Road.

Reason for such hope was provided at the start of 2018, with diplomatic breakthroughs achieved during the 3-day (January 8-10) visit to China of French President Emmanuel Macron, who there proclaimed his intent to create an alliance of cooperation between Europe and China appropriate for the 21st Century in the framework of the New Silk Road. "I am thus ready to work to the announced objectives," Macron said in a speech in Xi'an. "The programs of road, railway, airports, maritime, technological along the silk roads can bring elements of response to the deficit in infrastructure, especially in Asia, and to create perspectives in sectors such as transport, water management, wastes, durable cities, green economy. The bringing together of our financial resources, public and private, for trans-border projects can reinforce the connectivity between Europe and Asia and beyond the Middle East and Africa, contribute to better integrate, structure, open up by trade and growth." During Macron's China visit, the Agence Française de Development and the China Development Bank signed a contract on this cooperation perspective.

Similar cause for optimism came in March 2018 when the Italian Foreign Ministry signalled interest in seeing the "Transaqua" project, originally designed by Italian engineers some 30 years ago, finally being realized. At a conference in Abuja, Nigeria, an initial grant by the Italian government was announced for a feasibility study of "Transaqua," to be carried out by Italian and Chinese companies. However, in neither the French nor the Italian case, have substantial new funds yet been assigned for new projects in Africa— this owed to the same outdated pro-austerity loyalty shown also in Germany. The dynamic with which the year 2018 has begun, however, offers the potential of things to change also in Western Europe.

New Momentum in the Balkans

For Southeast Europe, Prof. Mariana Tian (Bulgaria) and Dr. Jasminka Simic (Serbia), at the November 25-26, 2017, Schiller Institute international conference held in Bad Soden, Germany, presented the

Left to right: Mohammed Bila (Lake Chad Basin Commission), Andrea Mangano, Marcello Vichi, and Claudio Celani, discussing plans for Transaqua in the Rome Bonifica office, summer 2015.

perspective of grand infrastructure development in their region, focussing on "Pan-European Corridors" 5, 8, and 10. These highway and railway corridors were originally defined by European experts and signed into an official document at a 1994 conference in Crete, at which all European governments were participants, but little has been done by "Europe" to turn these projects into reality. However, these transport corridors were much in the forefront of news about the "16-plus-1" summit held in the Hungarian capital Budapest on November 28-29, 2017, by the 16 eastern and southeastern governments and the government of China. Although numerous projects had been in discussion between these 16 countries and China before, that summit clearly opened doors for much bigger things to be put on the agenda and gotten underway in the near future.

The Serbian government was the first to enter the new era concretely with a ceremony on November 29, attended by Prime Minister Ana Brnabic, for the start of construction in Belgrade of Serbia's section of the first high-speed rail route between Budapest and Athens which will connect Hungary, Serbia, Macedonia, and Greece. The President of Macedonia followed a few days later with the news that his country had been invited by China and Serbia to build the Macedonian section of that same route. The Bulgarian Prime Minister after the end of the Budapest Summit announced on national television that it had been agreed that work to complete Corridor 8—the highway connecting the Adriatic Sea and the Black Sea via the territory of Albania and Bulgaria—would begin soon. Two weeks after the Budapest Summit, commitment was signalled from Greece and Serbia to begin work on the long-overdue Vardar-Axios canal. And a few days later, the announcement was made from Poland for the first international New Silk Road conference on rail freight, sponsored by Nunner Logistics and held in March 2018, in the southern Polish city of Wroclaw. One should also note the fact that on January 8, Hungary began work on 55 km of railway track modernization along the Budapest-Hatvan route, which is a section of the Pan-European Corridor 5 (See Section III, "Europe," Figure 21).

Poland Looking Eastwards, and To Its Own Development

This contribution by Poland is the more important, because a week after the Budapest Summit the country got a new Prime Minister who is committed to put an end of the neo-liberalist era of economics that has dominated in the country since 1989, and to launch a program of national infrastructural and industrial development, along with a reorganization of the banking sector so that it will serve the development of the real economy and family incomes. Although the new Prime Minister, Mateucz Morawiecki, did not explicitly point to China, it is apparent that his ambitious program of economic revival for Poland will hardly be funded by the bureaucrats of the European Commission which views politicians like him as an enemy of the neo-liberalist dogma that dominates the EU bureaucracy. The biggest nation in Europe's East with its 40 million citizens, Poland will no longer listen to the discredited advice coming from the unproductive EU bureaucracy, but instead open up more and more to active cooperation with the Chinese.

A clear warning shot against the Eurocrats in Brussels was delivered by Morawiecki during a visit to Berlin February 15, 2018, during which he called in a speech for a "Europe of equal chances" which would put an end to the "colonialist practices" of western investors taking over most of Poland's economy when the Poles naively opened their borders wide to "Europe" after the fall of the Iron Curtain. Whether that

Polish dynamic will lead to a formal break with the EU, like the British "Brexit," is not certain yet, but many observers would not rule out that such a break might indeed occur in 2020 after the next national elections in Poland. The Eurocrats in Brussels already are sounding the alarm over the fact that Poland shows a clear intent to work much closer in the future with the three other states of the "Visegrad Group"—the Czech Republic, Slovakia, and Hungary—on realizing an economic agenda which is more in concordance with the genuine national interest of these four states.

New Silk Road Issue Resonates with Austria

A comparably very promising situation has developed in Austria. Petty party interests and frictions had driven the government there into a crisis at the end of April 2017, the direct result of which had been that Austria called off the participation of its transport minister, Joerg Leichtfried, in the mid-May Belt-and-Road summit in Beijing. The abrupt cancellation of the China trip by Leichtfried, who earlier had come out in favor of his country joining the Silk Road, kept Austrian politics paralyzed until the mid-October early elections. Angered by this development, leading officials of Austrian industry and transport associations launched a strong lobbying effort for the next government to state a clear commitment to active cooperation with China's New Silk Road. A week after the Austrian elections, a delegation led by leaders of the country's national chamber of industry and of the state railway company, left for a several-day tour of China. There, they not only signed a cooperation agreement with their respective partner institutions on the Chinese side, but also stated at press briefings that they expected the new government of Austria to give "clear priority" to a New Silk Road orientation, otherwise the latter's dynamic would bypass the Austrian economy. Remarks like these, and a big conference of the industry chamber on the New Silk Road in Vienna on November 21, 2017, created the required environment for the two winners of the early elections and future coalition partners OVP and FPO to state in their government program a clear commitment to working with China:

"Austria lies in the middle of Europe and thus through its geographic location alone represents an important hub. This position can have an additional enormous benefit from a stronger development of the trans-European nets. We must make sure that big supraregional and geostrategic infrastructure projects like for instance the planned Silk Road project or the broad-gauge as well, do not bypass Austria but that we are a part of it as a hub."

This refers in particular to the extension of the Russian Trans-Siberian Railroad's broad gauge from Kosice in eastern Slovakia to a new huge logistics complex near Austria's capital Vienna, a distance of 400 km. Discussed for many years, this project alone will create 140,000 permanent jobs, but a much broader engagement of Austria's industry and engineering capacities in projects of the New Silk Road in all of Europe's East and Southeast is envisaged as well. This was stated clearly by Johann Strobl, CEO of Austria's Raiffeisen International Bank, who in a year-end interview criticized the EU's China-bashing views against the "16-plus-1" summit. He said there is no reason to be alarmed over China's increased role in eastern and southeastern Europe: "This is good news. Financial means from outside that flow into Eastern Europe improve the economic potential of the region. Being a bank specialized on Eastern Europe, we are benefitting from that." The EU should change its attitude viz. China, Strobl added, and "simply face the challenges and find constructive solutions with which the differences in views can be bridged."

China has taken positive notice of the most recent changes in Austria, and during an event on the New Silk Road organized by the Austrian Society for Transport Sciences (ÖVG) in Vienna on January 31, Ambassador Li Xiaosi directly called on his hosts to make constructive proposals for joint projects, and to even join the "16-plus-1" format, turning it into a "16-plus-1-plus-Austria." To that, a spokeswoman of the Austrian foreign ministry said that the Chinese proposal would be carefully studied, once presented officially.

The first concrete steps in the realization of the New Silk Road transport connection were made at an international railway conference entitled "Strategic Partnership 1520: Central Europe," held in Vienna, February 20-22, 2018, during which Russian Railways

WILL EUROPE FINALLY JOIN THE NEW SILK ROAD?

Austrian President Alexander Van der Bellen (right), Austrian Railways CEO Andreas Mattae (left), and others inspecting the first China-Europe freight train that arrived in Vienna from Chengdu on April 27, 2018.

CEO Oleg Belozerov and Austrian Railways CEO Andreas Mattae signed an agreement on an integrated Eurasian railway corridor. The 250 delegates at the event included the CEOs of railway companies from 24 countries. An accompanying agreement also was signed by the Russian and Austrian transport ministers, Maxim Sokolov and Norbert Hofer, respectively.

Under the Russian-Austrian agreements, the parties committed the railway companies and transport agencies of Austria, Slovakia, and Ukraine to construct a 1,520-mm-wide-gauge, 400-km new railway line from Kosice (Slovakia) to Vienna, including an international logistics center in the twin-city region Vienna-Bratislava. Kosice currently is the end point of the Russian gauge grid. The project is to be carried out by the Breitspur Planungsgesellschaft mbH, a joint venture established in 2009 which involves Russia, Ukraine, Slovakia, and Austria and is registered in Austria.

This will allow uninterrupted rail freight service from the Kazakh-Chinese border to central Europe on the Russian broad gauge, with an annual capacity of 1 million containers, with freight trains reaching a frequency of several hundred weekly. The logistics hub alone will create up to 140,000 jobs, and broader industrial and other economic initiatives sparked by the project along the new rail route are expected to create more than 600,000 jobs.

Concerning the funding of the roughly 7 billion euros required for the broad gauge extension, Austrian Transport Minister Norbert Hofer hinted that "investors from Asia" will be interested in the project, which will be completed by 2033.

The central plenary session of the Vienna conference proceeded under the theme, "Eurasian Corridor and New Silk Road: Towards Each Other," discussing ways to achieve higher interoperability between the Chinese and European standard gauges of 1435 mm and the Russian gauge of 1520 mm. Austria's railway CEO Andreas Matthae said at the Vienna event: "The further development of the Eurasian Railway-Land-Bridge will not only ensure that Europe and Asia come closer to one another, but will also boost economic progress in the participating regions." Matthae has been one of the leading proponents of Austrian constructive cooperation with China's New Silk Road strategy.

Alexander Misharin, First Deputy General-Director of the Russian railway company, said in Vienna: "The Project OBOR [One Belt One Road] will not only consolidate a unified gauge in the transport systems ... and promote the emerging of a united Eurasian economic area. The cooperation with the Austrian Federal Railways (ÖBB) is an important step toward a cooperation beneficial for both sides, for the industry as well as for the population of both countries."

And Clemens Foerstl, CEO of the OEBB freight daughter firm RailCargo Austria AG, in his concluding speech at the Vienna conference, declared: "We are glad to note that the New Silk Road and the extension of the broad gauge railroad to Vienna are not seen as two different projects but rather as the common objective to advance Eurasian rail transport. Austria welcomes and supports the development of rail infrastructure in the Eurasian corridor.... The Russian-Austrian agreement is a milestone in our efforts to establish the Eurasian Transport Corridor." A follow-up conference to this one in Vienna was announced for Sochi, Russia.

V. WITHOUT LAROUCHE'S 'FOUR LAWS,' FINANCIAL CRASH MEANS CHAOS

"The development of the new economic paradigm is threatened not only by war but by the incalculable danger of a new international financial crash, equal or worse in economic effects than that of 2007-08."

DANGER OF A NEW FINANCIAL CRASH
without Glass-Steagall Bank Regulation

The development of the new economic paradigm is threatened not only by war but by the incalculable danger of a new international financial crash, equal or worse in economic effects than that of 2007-08. The ability of the City of London and Wall Street to stop Glass-Steagall bank separation laws from being enacted in the United States and Europe since the 2008 crash, is the reason for that danger and the Achilles' heel of the trans-Atlantic financial system.

The runaway effects of a decade of major central banks' post-2008 furious issuance of cheap debt into banking systems, combined with the lack of Glass-Steagall bank separation which has seen the "universal banks" become immensely larger and more complex over 20 years, have brought the trans-Atlantic countries' banking systems, centered on Wall Street and London, to the point of another meltdown.

And what Japan's former IMF Director Daisuke Kotegawa has recently explained as the "financialization" of those economies since the mid-1990s has fostered 20 years of low growth, low productivity growth, and loss of industrial strengths, making the huge reinflated debt bubbles even more ready for collapse.

In December 2017 as the Federal Reserve very gingerly implements its fourth small increase in short-term interest rates over two years, it and the European Central Bank, Bank of England, and Bank of Japan appear to face Scylla and Charybdis. Junk-rated firms and sub-prime consumer debt are so overextended due to the 9-years' ocean of cheap central bank money, that higher interest costs will doom them to default. But the longer the central bankers keep pumping the cheap debt out, the greater the overvaluation of such bank assets, producing intense "reverse leverage" when they start to fall.

Accurate 2007 Forecast Ignored

In its March 19, 2007 issue, 18 months before Lehman Brothers failed, Founding Editor Lyndon LaRouche's *EIR* magazine published a 10-page analysis as its cover story, "How U.S. Mortgage Crisis Can Trigger Global Crash." Analyzing the exposure of the post-Glass-Steagall megabanks of the United States and Europe, to the securities and derivatives related to the then-$11 trillion mortgage bubble, *EIR* warned of the blowout which would accelerate over the following 18 months, leading to full-blown global bank panic. Members of Congress and others in leading positions in the United States denied the forecast as impossible.

A decade earlier, the Glass-Steagall Act had been eliminated after it had preserved banking system stability against panics and crashes for 60 years. In early 2007, the idea that this deregulation was bringing on a general financial crash within less than 10 years, was dismissed out of hand. *EIR* Editor-in-Chief Lyndon LaRouche's July 2007 proposal to stop the coming crash with emergency legislation, combining Glass-Steagall bank reorganization with a national moratorium on home foreclosures, was kept out of Congress by Wall Street, despite broad constituency support.

Again the choice was posed in 2009-10: Restore Glass-Steagall to prevent this from happening again, or accept universal banks, using huge deposit bases as the basis for securities speculation, as inevitable, and simply draft some rules to "limit" it. Thus far, the wrong choice has again been made.

Corporate Debt Bubbles Buckling

Now another, perhaps worse collapse is looming, this time not from mortgage securities and derivatives, but primarily from the Wall Street and City of London megabanks' exposure to an even larger bubble in speculative corporate debt, which is showing alarming patterns of defaults.

The debt of U.S. non-financial corporations has more than doubled in seven years, reaching more than $14 trillion—$11 trillion owed to banks and the rest to "shadow banks" such as money market mutual funds, pension funds, and similar funds. **Figure 1** shows the extraordinary rate at which the banks' portion—only—of that debt bubble grew, leading into the 2008 crash and after it, up through mid-2015.

European non-financial corporations' bond market debt is now at about 1.8 trillion euros, but has grown by roughly 750 billion euros in 2016-17

Figure 1
Non-Financial Corporate Debt

alone. The European Central Bank (ECB) has bought a thousand bond issues totaling 120 billion euros of corporate bonds, and in fact now is exposed to the potential large bankruptcy of the Steinoff AG multinational. The ECB has driven corporate junk bond rates in Europe down to the range of 2%, lower than the yield on 10-year U.S. Treasury bonds, an absurd and dangerous situation.

Feeding the explosion of corporate debt has been the vast money-printing of the central banks of the United States, UK, Japan, and the Eurozone: their $15 trillion in lending facilities to big banks, with effective zero interest rates, has been combined with roughly $14 trillion in capital and liquidity infusions by buying bonds from the big private banks.

Just as dangerously, the large corporate borrowers, especially in the United States, have been using the vast accumulation of debt primarily to raise stock market values of their own companies and others they target for takeovers—and not for business capital investment, which has been persistently low. In some years since 2013, some 80% or more of this borrowing has been used by larger corporations for "financial engineering"; that is, buying their own stock to drive it up, or buying other companies' stock in mergers and acquisitions which have the same effect. Approximately $4 trillion has gone into driving up stock market indices, while betting on them; another $4 trillion into dividends to stockholders. But total non-financial corporations' profits have not increased since 2011; and in the three years 2013-15, they fell.

Therefore debt leverage has jumped up. Morgan Stanley bank itself published a detailed research note on April 20, 2017 which reported that the ratio of non-financial corporate debt to cash-from-operations is at an all-time high of 3.2:1 (2.7:1 is the highest it has ever been before, the bank reported). Companies have low and falling "interest coverage," or ability to even pay interest from earnings—coverage levels like those in the 2001 recession and the 2008 crash (**Figure 2**).

The IMF 2017 Global Financial Stability Report found that in the United States, the debt service to income ratio of non-financial corporations had risen quickly from 37% in 2014, to 41% in 2016. With debt flying up relative to operating cash, and profits declining, companies can keep servicing debt only by borrowing more. Those corporations have $7 trillion more debt than at the 2008 crash, but $3 trillion less equity invested in them.

In that report, the IMF made the startling forecast that any sudden interest rate rise in the United States economy would result in 20% of more of American non-financial corporations being brought to default—a default rate higher than any reached in the mortgage sector prior to the 2008 bank panic. Shortly after that, on June 5, a report by the British Association of Business Recovery Professionals, or bankruptcy experts, found that just a one-quarter-percent rise would trigger defaults by as many as 80,000 businesses, one in every 25.

And this was rising rapidly; in September 2016, the Association had found that just one in 100 companies would be knocked out by a quarter-point rate rise. And it said 96,000 companies—about one in 20 across the UK—cannot repay their debt; "they are only able to pay interest on their borrowings." This is what the Federal Reserve and other central banks face in trying to inch up short-term rates.

In the same period as the IMF and British Association warnings, *Handelsblatt* on May 8, 2017 and the London *Financial Times* on May 30 published articles by bank researchers noting that a 2008-like debt crash could be near, triggered by an unrepayable U.S. corporate bubble. *Handelsblatt* wrote, "A surge in corporate loans, especially in the United States, could unleash a new global financial crisis.... Companies worldwide took up $3.7 trillion (3.37 trillion [euros]) in new debt in the capital markets last year. The last time a similarly high [relative] level was reached was in 2006—just before the beginning of the last major financial crisis.

It is a loud warning signal.... The United States could once again become the trigger and possibly the epicenter of the next crisis." And it blamed the Federal Reserve's and European Central Bank's zero-interest and qualitative easing.

The *Financial Times* piece, by author Dombisa Moyo and financial editor Gillian Tett, was headlined "Global debt woes are building to a tidal wave." But it placed most of the weight of danger on debt bubbles in the United States. "U.S. companies have added $7.8tn [trillion] of debt since 2010 and their ability to cover interest payments is at its weakest since 2008.... Growth in the United States and Europe is very slow, and any recession will cause a nasty shock to the system."

Figure 2
Average Interest Coverage Ratio
(ratio of EBIT to interest payments)

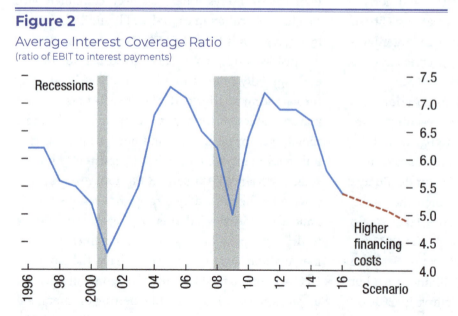

The End of the Bubble

Total debt securities in the U.S. economy are, as of the IMF's Global Financial Stability Report, 2017, at 220% of GDP, whereas in 2007 at the height of the last (mortgage-centered) bubble, they reached 180% of GDP. Total debt in the economy, as of the IMF's Global Stability Report, 2018, approximated $70 trillion, some 350% of GDP.

But the banks decided during 2017 to put the brakes on new credit, indicating that they are aware this bubble has rolled over its top and is headed for big trouble. Corporate debt growth levelled off in the United States in 2017. Growth in total U.S.-based banks' credit has suddenly dropped from 4.5% to 2-3% annually; commercial and industrial lending growth stopped entirely in early Summer 2016 and as of November 2017 was just 0.7% above the November 2016 level.

Bloomberg reported already on April 26, 2017: "Total loans at the 15 largest U.S. regional banks declined by about $10 billion to $1.73 trillion in the first quarter, compared with the previous three-month period, the first such drop in five years.... A slump in commercial and industrial lending sapped growth." One example from American Banker April 25, involving Fifth Third Bank, a large Cincinnati-based regional, was reported as follows: "The withdrawal from auto lending was said to be a conscious choice to reduce lower-return auto originations to improve returns on shareholders equity, while the decline in C&I [commercial and industrial—ed.] lending was described as a deliberate exit."

The default rate for all non-financial corporations has jumped from 3.0% at the start of 2016 to 5.0% at its end, averaging 4.2%, the highest since 2009. The default rate for "high-yield" (i.e., subprime) corporate debt had more than doubled in a year to 6% at the end of 2016 (**Figure 3**). And the corporate "subprime" debt bubble—junk bonds and leveraged loans—approximates $2.5 trillion in the United States alone. Subprime mortgages never exceeded $1.5 trillion in debt. Standard and Poor's said 162 U.S. companies defaulted on $239.8 billion in debt in 2016, more than double the $110.3 billion total for 2015. Again, this was the highest since the economic collapse year 2009. Defaults have gone still higher in credit card and auto loan debt, and are above 25% in student loan debt.

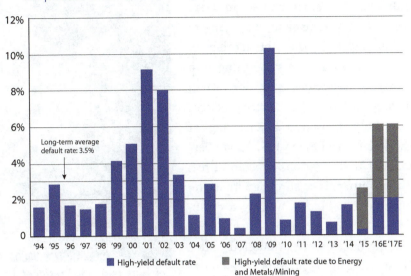

Figure 3
Corporate Debt Default Rate

As the corporate debt bubble in the United States reached its peak and threatened to begin the collapse, its composition shifted strongly in 2017 toward "junk debt"—that is, junk bonds and leveraged loans, or loans to already over-indebted companies essentially allowing them to pay interest—with this junk or subprime component of corporate debt growing by $800 billion in 2017 alone. A further shift was away from commercial and industrial lending to real estate debt. At the same time, consumer debt suddenly started growing rapidly after generally shrinking since the 2008 crash. The Bank of England reported November 9 that consumer debt in the UK was growing at a nearly 10% annual rate; credit card, auto loan, and student debt all grew sharply in the United States in 2009, while default rates on these categories also rose. Subprime auto debt, for example, has higher default rates in 2017 than subprime mortgage debt did in 2007.

But the rates at which these categories of the debt bubble were growing, were not as fast as the rates at which they were being securitized by the major banks, and the new debt securities sold to mutual funds, pension funds, individual investors, and so on. Here too, the biggest banks were trying to get out and dump the debt on other investors. They did the same thing with mortgage securities and derivatives during 2007 and 2008. These practices were fully exposed in 2011 hearings of then-Sen. Carl Levin's U.S. Senate Permanent Investigations Subcommittee. Their return is a sure sign that the huge debt bubble is nearing a crash, and a securitization practice which lending banks were prohibited under Glass-Steagall regulation. Re-enacting Glass-Steagall now would stop this dumping of toxic waste all over the world, which was the hallmark of the 2007-08 crash and the reason lawsuits continue to this day pitting investors all over the world against their financial advisors and major bank issuers of securities and debt derivatives.

On June 6, 1933, President Franklin Roosevelt signed the Banking Act of 1933, more commonly known as the Glass-Steagall Act, into law, thus separating commercial banking from investment banking, and creating the Federal Deposit Insurance Corporation (FDIC) which provided protection for commercial banks only.

In the Fall of 2017, then-German Finance Minister Wolfgang Schäuble warned in the *Financial Times* on October 8 that "spiraling levels of global debt and liquidity present a major risk to the world economy," because of "bubbles forming due to the trillions of dollars that central banks have pumped into markets." Schäuble also warned that the risks in the Eurozone were becoming greater, because the balance sheets of its major banks are weighted down by masses of non-performing loans from the 2008 financial collapse.

William White, former Bank of International Settlements (BIS) chief economist and now head of the OECD Review Committee, had warned already at the end of 2016 that the condition of global debt bubbles was "worse than 2007," and had particularly blamed the refusal across the European banking systems to write down or write off bad debts. Now the BIS itself, in its quarterly financial report December 2, warned that unstable financial bubbles were far too large and that the Federal Reserve and Bank of England had failed in their efforts to cut off higher-and-higher-risk debt, by raising rates.

In November 2017 the U.S. corporate and "emerging market" junk debt markets started to buckle, with European corporate junk next to go. The superinflated prices in the $2.5 trillion "junk debt" part of the $14 trillion U.S. corporate debt bubble was unable to withstand even the small and slow interest rate increases being dripped into the financial system by the Federal Reserve. In the third week of the month average yields jumped up to 3.8% from 3.3% in U.S. junk; a near-record $6.7 billion flowed rapidly out of junk bond investment funds, according to the Novmber 18 *Wall Street Journal*. The paper quoted an analyst, "We're seeing huge outflows from mutual funds and ETFs, so it's triggering this domino effect." In the telecom sector, which has about $400 billion of this debt, average interest rates rose faster, from 5.2% to 6.4%. The *Financial Times* posted an article November 15 headlined "Contagion worries rise after junk-bond sell-off." And at that point a *Wall Street Journal* report of November 16 on Europe's unpayable corporate debts informed that "10% of the companies in six Eurozone countries including France, Germany, Italy and Spain are zombies, according to the [European] Central Bank's latest data—they are incapable of paying even the interest on their debts."

The crash of South Africa-based international retail conglomerate Steinhoff S.A. thus occurred at a bad time, in the second week of December 2017. Steinhoff lost 80% of its share value and was immediately downgraded into deep junk debt by Moody's. The firm represented $21-23 billion in loss exposures of banks led by Citigroup, Bank of America, HSBC, and BNP Paribas, and ironically, the European Central Bank itself, which had bought Steinhoff bonds from banks as part of the 1000 issues purchase described above, supposedly to backstop against exactly this kind of event.

The gigantic bubble of corporate debt used for their own stock-buying, mergers and acquisitions, financial engineering, and general Wall Street-pumping, is made more unpayable, and more dangerous, by the continuing lack of economic growth, productivity growth, or growth in business capital investment in the trans-Atlantic economies.

Despite the extreme descriptions by Wall Street and London financial analysts of the amount of debt in the Chinese economy, this financial crash is threatening from the universal banks of Europe and the United States. The structure and practices of these banks are a critical part of the incalculable danger of a bank panic worse than 2007-08.

Some 35% of the assets of the 12 largest U.S.-based banks are securities, although they are supposed to be commercial banks receiving deposits and making loans. The nominal derivatives exposure of these banks has grown to $265 trillion, 30% more than their exposure 10 years ago and 12 times U.S. GDP. The five largest Chinese public commercial banks, by contrast, have very little exposure to the derivatives markets, accounting for less than 3% of global derivatives contract issuance despite their size and extremely large issuance of credit. They do not own securities broker-dealers or other kinds of "non-banks" and investment firms.

For this reason—regulation according to the Glass-Steagall principle (**Figure 4**)—these banks are far better able to handle non-performance of loans, defaults, and bankruptcies, and Chinese regulators have been able to crack down on credit creation of "non-banks" by about 40% in 2017 without harming the state-owned commercial banks.

The purpose of the latter, has been to lend, on a very large scale, for the creation of new, productive infrastructure and other physical-economic assets— as is the purpose of commercial banks in the "American System" tradition, and also very large government credit institutions in U.S. history such as the Reconstruction Finance Corporation of President Franklin Roosevelt's administrations.

Until Glass-Steagall was abandoned in the 1990s, there were no U.S.-based "megabanks" or "universal banks"; none held more than 6% of the total assets in the banking system as a whole. From the late 1990s

Figure 4

GLASS-STEAGALL
SEPARATE LEGITIMATE COMMERCIAL BANKING *from* SPECULATIVE INVESTMENT FUNCTIONS

Under Glass-Steagall standards all banking institutions are forced to choose between either commercial or investment banking.

Productive functions of banks will be federally protected, while other, worthless, speculative functions are left out to dry.

NEW GLASS-STEAGALL LEGISLATION

DERIVATIVES • CARBON SWAPS • CDO's & MBS's • EXOTIC INSTRUMENTS

TRASH

INFRASTRUCTURE • LOANS TO SM. BUSINESS • MORTGAGES • PENSIONS

ALL SPECULATIVE ACTIVITY MUST BE PURGED FROM OUR ECONOMIC SYSTEM
&
VITAL COMMERCIAL AND DEPOSIT BANKING FUNCTIONS ARE PROTECTED

the Wall Street banks exploded in size, and this has continued since the 2008 crash, so that now just six banks hold two-thirds of the deposits and assets in the entire banking system. They also exploded in complexity: A New York Federal Reserve study of 2012 showed that whereas in 1995 the largest bank holding companies typically had 100-300 subsidiaries, by 2011 they each had 2,500-4,000 subsidiaries, vehicles for every manner of securities and derivatives speculation. The derivatives markets themselves exploded in size under the impact of this deregulation, from nominal values totaling about $70 trillion in 1997 to more than $700 trillion in 2008. These derivatives markets would have brought all the biggest U.S.- and Europe-based banks to bankruptcy at once in late 2008, had not governments bailed most of them out. After the crash they accumulated, on average, 30% more derivatives exposure.

Today, as a result, these megabanks are still greatly overleveraged, as has been repeatedly emphasized—in the face of further deregulation campaigns—by the most credible American bank regulator, Federal Deposit Insurance Corp. (FDIC) Vice-Chairman Thomas Hoenig. Hoenig has reminded that the major banks lost, on average, more than 6% of their total assets during the 2007-08 meltdown, and had very large derivatives losses; therefore the "European level" (Basel III) of a 5% capital ratio is completely inadequate, and so is the 6% target ratio under Dodd-Frank in the United States. The 5,500 or so non-systemic "community banks" in the United States, for example, have an average capital ratio of 16%, and almost none have any derivatives exposure at all.

The Adam Smith Institute in the UK, which did an analysis of the mid-2017 Bank of England "stress tests" of the biggest British bank, made the same point: The stress tests are not modelling even the degree of asset losses the big European banks took in 2008-11, although a corporate debt bubble on the verge of crashing now is considerably larger than the mortgage bubble which blew up a decade ago. And many of the universal banks in the United States and Europe went on failing these mild central banks stress tests right up to the 2017 round.

The FDIC's Hoenig holds that because these are still universal banks, mixing lending and Federal deposit insurance with the whole spectrum of securities speculations, they should be compelled to maintain a capital ratio of 10% of all their assets, including the full value at risk in their derivatives exposure.

Banking experts truly familiar with the practices of these universal banks—especially their multitude of investment banking and broker-dealer units—point out that the collateral backing which regulations like the Dodd-Frank Act are requiring for the banks' speculation and trading, are similar to backing which the same banks thought they had provided for these speculations before the crash. They were wrong. When the liquidity in credit markets froze, not just those particular speculations, but all assets plunged, because it was so difficult to sell them, or to make interbank borrowings against them.

Precisely because they were universal banks, all involved in similar speculations and trades, and completely interconnected in doing so, they suffered losses across nearly all their units and what seemed like "capital fortresses" were swept away, leaving them insolvent. As Federal Reserve Chairman Ben Bernanke acknowledged to the Financial Crisis Investigative Commission in 2011, all but one of the 12 largest, most interconnected universal banks based in the United States became insolvent at once in September 2008. They would all have failed without hundreds of billions in Federal bailouts and more hundreds of billions in liquidity loans from the Federal Reserve.

This is the nature of the kind of general bank panic and financial crash which was avoided for 60 years due to the success of U.S. Glass-Steagall bank regulation, which was copied in the post-War decades by many European countries.

Moreover, even one of the authors of the Volcker Rule, U.S. Sen. Jeff Merkeley of Oregon—who has adopted sponsorship of the 21st Century Glass-Steagall Act—has acknowledged that the complexity and opacity of these megabanks' trading activities made it impossible to determine whether the Volcker Rule has worked or not. The Volcker Rule had been put forward by its sponsors as "the modern version of, or substitute for, Glass-Steagall." It has failed as such.

The fact that in 2017, with a debt crash looming, only China of the major nations protects its commercial banks with Glass-Steagall-type regulation, is a major factor in the gravity of the threat of financial breakdown and the economic collapse which followed the last crash.

Even at this moment to stop the megabanks' practice of transferring the risk from this huge mass of endangered debt and derivatives, to depositors by "bail-in," to investment funds by securitization, and to taxpayers, Glass-Steagall must be restored in the United States and Europe. This critical situation underlies the sudden appearance of high-profile attacks on Glass-Steagall in leading media of New York, London, and Washington, DC during 2017. All of the attacks date from the April 5 introduction of the U.S. Senate 21st Century Glass-Steagall Act, and the reporting that its sponsors had received some form of encouragement from President Trump's head of the National Economic Council, Gary Cohn. The attacks on Glass-Steagall, in number, volume, and tone have become indicative that the City of London and Wall Street, knowing the signs of an approaching financial crisis, are arrogantly—perhaps suicidally—determined to stop the bank breakup which could prevent it.

See following two-page spread on LaRouche's 1995 Triple Curve and collapse forecast.

V. WITHOUT LAROUCHE'S 'FOUR LAWS,' FINANCIAL CRASH MEANS CHAOS

LaRouche's 1995 Triple Curve:

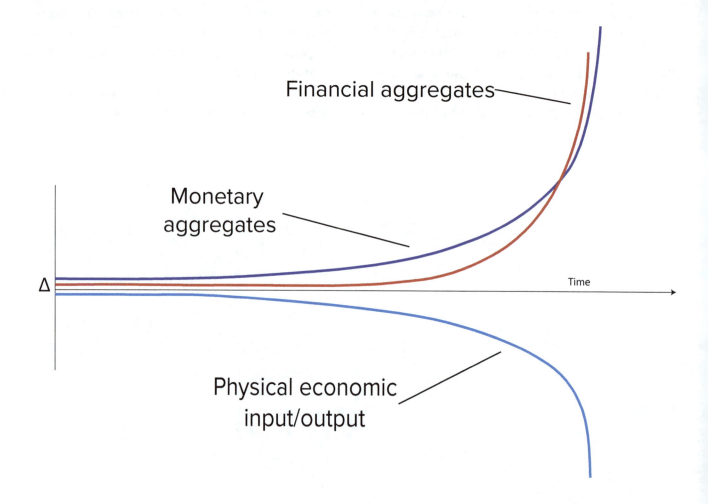

"The **top curve** is a hyperbolic, self-feeding growth of financial aggregates — what might be called 'shareholder values,' nominal shareholder values as accountants would account for them, or the equivalent. The **second curve**, which is the monetary expansion, both by Treasuries and Central Banks, which was feeding the money-flow in, to help pump up the growth of this financial bubble. Then the other tendency, the **third curve**, which I dated from 1971, is the accelerating decline in real physical output and consumption, in terms of productive potential per capita and per square kilometer."

—*Lyndon LaRouche, January 2002*

A Forecast of the Trans-Atlantic Collapse

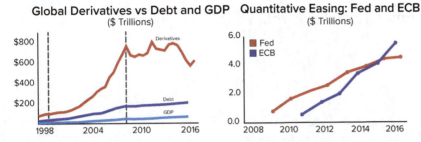

Global Derivatives vs Debt and GDP ($ Trillions)

The explosion of derivatives in the 1990s signaled the beginning of a self-doomed feeding frenzy based not on investments and growth of the real economy, but purely speculative bets on its "performance." Derivatives are essentially legalized gambling. They have hijacked the flow of investments away from the real economy, and into short-term profit.

Quantitative Easing: Fed and ECB ($ Trillions)

When the derivatives bubble burst in 2007, the Fed and ECB stepped in to bail the speculators out. After seven years of Quantitative Easing (QE), when the Fed could no longer continue its frenetic 2013 pace of $1 trillion in a single year, the ECB stepped in and has continued to pump trillions of dollars of QE into the bankrupt trans-Atlantic banking system.

Total Debt & Loans vs. U.S. GDP ($ Trillions)

Another indicator of the vulnerability of the U.S. economy is the widening gap between debt and Gross Domestic Product (GDP) growth. For more than forty years, U.S. debt growth followed economic growth. But beginning in the 1990s, the growth of debt began to far outstrip growth in the economy. Today, every $1 increase in GDP is associated with a $4 increase in debt.

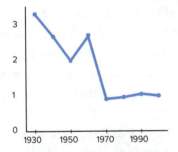
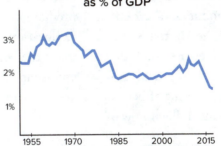
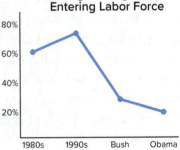

Total Factor Productivity (TFP)

Total Factor Productivity (TFP) measures the rate of growth of an economy due to technological advance, rather than the simple application of more labor and/or capital. The highest rate of growth of TFP in U.S. history, was its 3.3% annual rate of growth in the 1930s, under Franklin Roosevelt's New Deal & Four Corners infrastructure programs.

Annual U.S. Infrastructure Investment as % of GDP

In 1965, as the so-called "golden age of productivity" was nearing an end, U.S. annual investment in infrastructure was above 3% of GDP. By the mid-1980s it had fallen below 2%, and since 2005 has fallen further to 1.4%, an extremely low proportion compared to China's nearly 9% over the past 20 years, and investment rates of 5-6% in other major Asian economies.

Percentage of Eligible Youth Entering Labor Force

In the 1980s-90s, between 60-70% of newly eligible youth were entering the workforce. After sixteen years of Bush and Obama, however, 70-75% of eligible youth are *staying out* of the labor force, a shocking statistic which reflects the plight of the young generation, which is experiencing rising hopelessness and despair.

The Triple Curve depicts a typical collapse function. When monetary and financial policies are systematically decoupled from physical investments, the economy enters a breakdown process, as the physical economy collapses due to lack of investment and due to looting (such as asset-stripping, for example), and the monetary and financial systems become hyper-inflationary (generating increasingly fake assets to support the system). Shadows of this process can be seen in the above economic statistics.

"Lyndon LaRouche's 'Four New Laws To Save the USA Now'... remains today the immediate and indispensable policy necessary to launch sustained economic recovery from a decade's worsening effects of an international financial crash and following economic collapse."

'FOUR LAWS'
For the New Paradigm

Lyndon LaRouche's "Four New Laws To Save the USA Now," was authored and published in 2014. It was intended to propose economic and scientific steps which must be taken by the United States. However, it remains today the immediate and indispensable policy necessary to launch sustained economic recovery from a decade's worsening effects of an international financial crash and following economic collapse.

In "The Principles of Long-Range Forecasting" in 1998, LaRouche had written:

> The potential increase of the potential relative population density of a society is bounded by the number of valid ... discovered principles known, and thus available to be expressed, in the form of applicable new technologies of individual and social practice.
>
> However, the realization of the benefits of discovery and proliferation of scientific and technological progress, is conditional upon the way in which social relations define the communication of [these] validated products of cognition...

LaRouche's "Four Laws" specify principles of credit—in this case, *re*discovered; of technological productivity; and of nuclear science and human space exploration which nations must master and implement to avoid another general financial breakdown and establish a new paradigm of economic progress and cooperation. He described them as follows:

> The economy of the United States of America, and also that of the trans-Atlantic political-economic regions of the planet, are now under the immediate, mortal danger of a general, physical-economic chain-reaction breakdown crisis of that region of this planet as a whole....
>
> The only location for the immediately necessary action which could prevent such a genocide throughout the trans-Atlantic sector of the planet, requires the U.S. Government's decision **to institute four specific, cardinal measures which must be fully consistent with the specific intent of the original U.S. Federal Constitution,** as had been specified by U.S. Treasury Secretary Alexander Hamilton while he remained in office:

Table 1
China Real (Inflation-Adjusted) GDP Growth*

Year:	1985	1987	1989	1991	1993	1995	1997
Growth*:	105	170	200	220	250	420	500
1999	2001	2003	2005	2007	2009	2011	2013
600	700	850	1020	1320	1630	2000	2280

*based on 1980 = 100; source: IMF

1. The immediate re-enactment of the Glass-Steagall law instituted by U.S. President Franklin D. Roosevelt, without modification as to principle of action.
2. A return to a system of top-down, and thoroughly defined, national banking.
3. The purpose of the use of a Federal Credit system, is to generate high-productivity trends in improvements of employment, with the accompanying intention to increase the physical-economic productivity, and the standard of living of the persons and households...
4. Adopt a fusion-driver "crash program" ... [for scientific breakthroughs in fusion science and space exploration].

In this section we elaborate these actions as necessary for making the New Silk Road into the World Land-Bridge.

1. 'GLASS-STEAGALL' BANK SEPARATION

The well-known University of Chicago economist Luigi Zingales has said that one characteristic distinguishes Glass-Steagall bank separation from all other actual and conceptual regimes for organizing and regulating banks and the financial sector. *Glass-Steagall has public support and full credibility, because it has been tested over a long period and it works*, Zingales points out. It not only works in preventing individual bank problems from spreading "contagion" into general bank panics. It also works in creating deep and reliable capital markets for business, industry, and households, based on the special and separate roles of commercial banks and investment firms.

We present one example of this point which nations all over the world should pay attention to.

During the period 1994-97, the United States Federal Reserve and Securities and Exchange Commission essentially eliminated the effect of the Glass-Steagall Act in the American financial system. They set aside some of its most important regulations and allowed commercial banks to invest more and more of their deposit bases and profits into securities and derivatives markets, and into credit support of securities firms of all kinds. Finally in 1999 the U.S. Congress repealed Glass-Steagall entirely and allowed commercial banks to acquire, merge with, and/or create, all manner of securities broker-dealers and insurance underwriting firms.

At just that same point, 1993-95, China's government acted through the People's Bank of China to create a number of large commercial banks for the first time, and put those large public commercial banks under a regime of bank separation, not permitting them to engage in securities broker-dealing or to acquire securities firms or "shadow banks."

It subsequently severely limited these commercial banks' ability to create or deal in financial derivatives, so that although these banks are now among the world's largest financial companies by assets, they are extremely small actors in the notional $550 trillion world derivatives markets.

Thus, China put its large commercial banks under a Glass-Steagall regime.

Which regime has *worked* to create a large and dynamic capital (credit) market for business investment, infrastructure building, overall economic growth? The Chinese economic path since those mid-1990s actions is shown in GDP growth in **Table 1**. Even leaving aside the lack of the cavernous plunge in 2008-10 seen in so many economies around the

V. WITHOUT LAROUCHE'S 'FOUR LAWS,' FINANCIAL CRASH MEANS CHAOS

Figure 1
US GDP Growth Year on Year

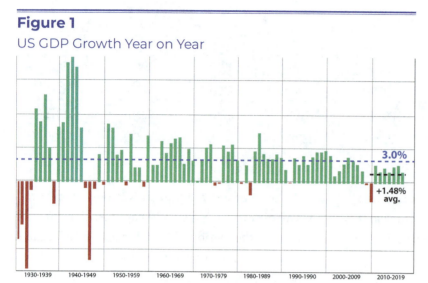

world, China's growth, if anything, inflected upward in the mid-1990s from an already fast pace, and sustained it.

The U.S. economic path since casting aside Glass-Steagall regulation is shown by GDP growth in **Figure 1**. Again, even considering only the years in which there was positive economic growth, its impulse since the 1990s has been lower than any decade in 80 years, and steadily falling from the 1990s to the 2000s to the 2010s. The only thing growing rapidly during the past 25 years has been the Wall Street banks, which have become true megabanks for the first time and control two-thirds of the banking system's assets among just six banks.

And in terms of the annual rates of GDP growth themselves, China's have been approximately three times as high, even as its economic product has become comparable to that of the United States.

(European governments which during 1945-55 had imitated the United States's original Glass-Steagall Act, had all repealed their Glass-Steagall laws by the late 1980s' "Big Bang" complete deregulation of City of London banking. **Figure 2** adds the UK and Eurozone to the United States, and shows the effect is the same.)

As already shown in the previous section of this Special Report, since 2008 even an estimated $14 trillion in newly printed capital pumped into the trans-Atlantic banks by the "quantitative easing" programs of the Federal Reserve, European Central Bank, and Bank of Japan have not been able to revive lending and business capital markets under "post-Glass-Steagall" banking.

In the U.S.-based banks, deposits increased by $3.5 trillion to $11 trillion, $4 trillion in newly printed "quantitative easing" capital was provided, along with nearly $10 trillion more in temporary liquidity assistance. Yet loans and leases from the banks rose only from $7.3 trillion in 2008 to $8.3 trillion at the end of 2015, according to Federal Reserve data. Some 35% of assets of the largest U.S. commercial banks are now reported to be securities—leaving aside derivatives exposure.

The same effect, during the period from the 1990s to today, shows (**Table 2**) when comparing U.S. and Chinese total factor productivity, or labor productivity which results directly from technological progress (these figures are those of the OECD; other estimates differ slightly in amount but not direction).

An International Necessity

The issuance of large masses of credits among countries for large-scale and modern new infrastructure platforms requires, first, "Glass-Steagall" bank separation and regulation by the nations involved. Without such legislation being urgently reinstated throughout the trans-Atlantic nations, the major banks of the United States and Europe are facing another crash. Warnings of a debt crash with any significant rise in interest rates have been issued during

Figure 2
Economic Growth UK - EU - US

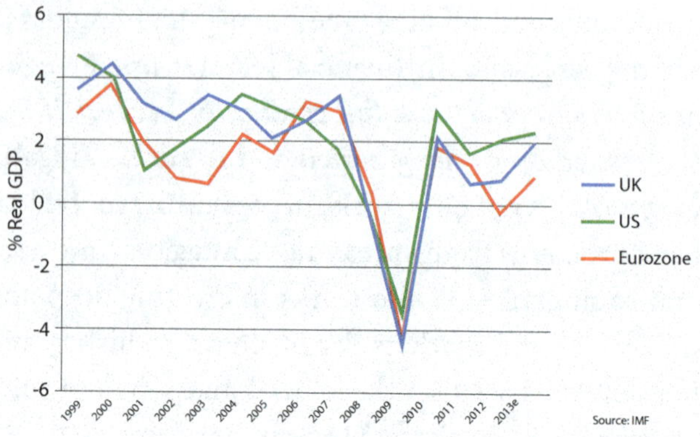

Table 2
Annual Total Factor Productivity Growth, 1985-2015

Years	United States	China
1985-1995	1.85%	2.3%
1996-2004	1.75%	3.9%
2005-2015	0.7%	3.3%

2017 by the Bank for International Settlements, the IMF, and by national agencies such as the Bundesbank, as well as private forecasters led by *EIR* Founding Editor Lyndon LaRouche.

Most dangerously, the huge new bubbles of corporate and household debt are aggressively being securitized and re-securitized with derivatives by large banks, which shift increasingly illiquid debt onto other investors by this means—a means prohibited to commercial banks under Glass-Steagall regulation.

Furthermore, productivity "driver" projects on a national or global scale have always been done by national credit. If such credit is issued directly to banks (private or national) which are plugged into securities markets and offshore profit centers, or have large parts of their asset books in high-risk securities and derivatives activities, the credit will likely be wasted.

If nationally chartered *commercial banks* have been protected, regulated, and kept out of securities market speculation, those banks will participate in the infrastructure driver projects by vigorous private lending.

What Does Glass-Steagall Bank Regulation Mean?

As the introduction to the original 1933 American legislation stated, the intention was "to provide for the safer and more effective use of the assets of banks, to regulate interbank control, and to prevent undue diversions of funds into speculative operations, and for other purposes." Investment banks were forced to completely separate their activities from commercial banks, and because only commercial banks were federally insured, the speculative holdings made by (non-banks) were not, and their fictitious "assets" could now be written off.

A Glass-Steagall Act's regulations basically have four components. First, the requirement that commercial banks, investment banks or broker-dealers/ funds or similar entities, and insurance companies (able to underwrite insurance as well as sell it) be entirely separate from one another, and not share directors, ownership, or management. Nor can a commercial bank's deposit base be used in loans to create, expand, or support investment banks or securities broker-dealers.

Second, the definition of a significant range of securities and derivatives activities as "not sufficiently closely incident to banking as to be proper to it," and therefore not permitted to commercial banks.

Third, the provision of Federal deposit insurance exclusively to support commercial banks and their depositors.

Fourth, the prohibition of transferring any but the highest-rated securities, within a holding company, onto the books of a Federally insured commercial banking unit, or otherwise causing low-quality securities to be backstopped by government funds intended to safeguard customer deposits.

More important, was the greater conception encompassing Glass-Steagall known to then-U.S. President Franklin Roosevelt, that the physical productivity of the nation, in food production, transportation, and technology levels, per person and per square land area, was the absolute primary concern, and had to

The U.S. Supreme Court in 1971 (Camp vs. Investment Company Institute) *ruled that the Congress's intent to protect commercial banks from the temptation to throw deposits into high-risk, high-yield securities was a legitimate national interest, and that the Glass-Steagall Act was the United States's primary banking regulation.*

remain free from financial manipulations by speculative financial entities.

Roosevelt took an emergency approach to halt the compound economic crisis then, and paired Glass-Steagall with numerous other measures to stop farm foreclosure, restore employment, and return security to the banking system. In later years, Roosevelt was an original voice in the movement for global economic progress now sweeping the planet, as seen in his role in the creation of the Bretton Woods financial system for secure long-term economic development for every nation; his push for the independence of former British, French, Dutch, Belgian, and Portuguese colonies; and efforts to enforce these countries' rights to self-development, in productive growth and by scientific and cultural contributions. He wanted an alliance of the strongest countries on the planet, which would secure the ability for weaker countries to develop.

For more than 60 years after its passage, under Glass-Steagall organization of the commercial banking system, no U.S. bank failure triggered failures or bailouts of other banks. But within a decade of the removal of Glass-Steagall regulation, Federal Reserve Chairman Ben Bernanke had to testify (to the Financial Crisis Investigation Commission) that as of September 2008 all but one of the 12 largest banks operating in the United States were insolvent at the same time—a condition never seen before, even in 1931-33. And the same condition obtained across banking systems in Europe; the largest, most complex, most interconnected "universal banks" were nearly all bankrupt.

Without Glass-Steagall, Recurring Bank Panics

The disingenuous claims that Glass-Steagall enforcement would not have avoided the global financial crash of 2007-08, can be dismissed. The financial institutions whose failure set off the collapse were not—as so often claimed—those overleveraged institutions which lacked a connection to a large commercial bank. Rather, they were those overleveraged institutions which were not bailed out by governments.

In the United States, for example, the financial institution widely known to be most bankrupt in 2007-08 was Citibank—the very "destroyer of Glass-Steagall" through its 1998 merger with Travelers Insurance. Citigroup survived only through a massive series of government bailouts of its capital assets totaling more than $400 billion, not including short-term liquidity loans from the U.S. Federal Reserve. At the other extreme were the investment firm failures Bear Stearns and Lehman Brothers, frequently described as "independent" of any commercial banks and therefore not subject to Glass-Steagall regulation. Both, in fact, leveraged their capital up to 40:1 with various forms of debt borrowed from JP Morgan Chase and other commercial banks, which would not have been permitted were Glass-Steagall in effect. Bear Stearns was bailed out when it collapsed by the Federal Reserve, making an absorption by JP Morgan Chase possible; Lehman was not bailed out, and so became one major trigger for the global crash.

The two real alternatives were: Glass-Steagall bank separation; or, huge and indiscriminate taxpayer bailouts of the largest financial institutions.

All of the various "alternatives to Glass-Steagall," in which regulators attempt various schemes of "ring-fencing" divisions of banks, have the same fatal disability, and will not produce sound commercial banking. The much-invoked "bank bail-in" schemes are the most disastrously unworkable; they have triggered increasingly dangerous plunges in the value of whole ranges of bank securities each time they have been tried, from the "Cyprus template" to the most

President Bill Clinton repeals Glass-Steagall by signing the Gramm-Leach-Bliley Act in 1999. A number of those still in Congress who voted for Gramm-Leach-Bliley call it the single worst legislative mistake they have ever made.

recent Monte dei Paschi and other Italian bank hybrid bailouts/bail-ins. Worse, they have impoverished investors in bank securities, who are very numerous in some nations' banking systems, and led to wealthier investors and funds gambling on the high returns of bank securities which *are made to be bailed in and become worthless when the bank has a crisis.*

In all the "alternatives," the large bank holding companies (or whatever agencies try to resolve them into when insolvent) remain responsible for capitalization of all their operating subsidiaries. This capitalization either is taken from the commercial bank division, in violation of the ring-fencing scheme; from a large public taxpayer bail-out in a crisis; or, in the "bail-in" scheme, from both. "Bail-in" simply attempts to expropriate creditors' assets and depositors' money, and besides being chaotic and actually potentially triggering runs on banks, it represents deadly economic austerity.

Reinstating Glass-Steagall

Lyndon LaRouche and his political movement have been organizing for the restoration of Glass-Steagall bank separation since 2008, and there have been moves to put bank separation back in force in numerous countries since then. Against intense opposition from Wall Street and the biggest London-centered banks, legislation to restore the Glass-Steagall Act is being sought across the trans-Atlantic countries.

In the United States, bills to reinstate the Glass-Steagall Act now have bipartisan support in both Houses of the U.S. Congress: Senate bill S-881 with nine sponsors and House of Representatives bill HR-790 with 59 sponsors, one of two such bills in the House. Both major political parties put reinstatement of Glass-Steagall in their platforms during the 2016 Presidential election.

In Italy, nine bills to enact Glass-Steagall bank regulation have been introduced in both the Senate and the House of Delegates, and have broad support across all but the current governing party. Glass-Steagall bills have come close to passage in the British Houses of Lords and Commons, and actually passed in the lower Houses of both the Swiss and Danish Parliaments.

At the first sign that an oncoming new financial crash is upon these nations, these moves to restore Glass-Steagall bank separation will rapidly gain strength. But will that be too late? As the prominent American bank regulator Thomas Hoenig (vice-chair of the Federal Deposit Insurance Corporation) has frequently warned the U.S. Congress and others, the time to break up the now-immense "universal banks" is *before* they crash again; when these banks are in crisis, it will be much more difficult to do so.

The cycle of recurring bank panics must be broken now. It is clear that reinstating the Glass-Steagall Act in the United States, its originator, will lead quickly to the passage of similar legislation in many European countries.

2. FINANCING THE WORLD LAND-BRIDGE: 'HAMILTONIAN' NATIONAL CREDIT AND NATIONAL BANKS

A well-regulated—Glass-Steagall regulated—system of nationally-chartered commercial banks does not in itself create economic growth, although a deregulated speculative casino of a banking system can destroy it in cycles of debt-bubble expansion followed by collapse.

What is necessary to create sustained growth is *credit* issued and directed to support and raise the productivity of the nation and its workforce. Above all, this means credit to make possible building new economic infrastructure at high levels of technology—such as high-speed and highly connected transportation systems, high-energy power sources, multi-modal ports, etc.—and credit to enable entrepreneurs to exploit creative changes in production. What is at stake is the answer to the constant complaint of elected officials all over the world when necessary "great projects" are discussed: "How will this be paid for?"

The most powerful answer for this question, thus far today, is being given by China's Belt and Road Initiative, where such "great projects" in scores of nations are being funded by partnerships with China's large state-owned commercial banks issuing large volumes of new credit.

But the greatest leap in modern history, in understanding and directing national credit to foster productivity and individual creativity, was made 225 years ago by the first United States Treasury Secretary Alexander Hamilton, and a few of his closest collaborators such as the revolutionary financier Robert Morris.

Hamilton's method of generating productive national credit was realized in national Banks of the United States in the early 19th Century, in President Abraham Lincoln's creation of a new currency and national banking system for the last third of that Century, and in President Franklin Roosevelt's extraordinary use of $50 billion in credit ($600 billion today) issued by the Reconstruction Finance Corporation (RFC) to recover from the Great Depression and win World War II.

The results were extremely successful in every case, in terms of sustained national economic growth and breakthroughs to new "platforms" of infrastructure, technology, and productivity.

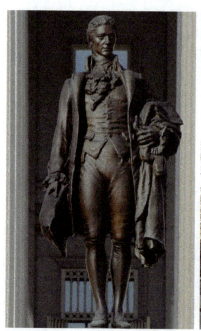

The Philadelphia headquarters of the Second Bank of the United States, 1816-36, one of the extremely successful American national credit banks based on Alexander Hamilton's methods, from Hamilton's First Bank of the United States in 1791 to Franklin Roosevelt's Reconstruction Finance Corporation. Today the building is a museum, and the United States has no such national credit source. Hamilton's credit concepts are successfully reflected in China's rise.

Today both China and Japan use strategies of national credit creation which are similar to those of Hamilton and of Franklin D. Roosevelt, although with their own characteristics. The United States, however, has abandoned Hamiltonian methods of credit since Roosevelt's death. It has not had a national credit and lending institution since the RFC ended operations in 1957; it has not had a national "infrastructure mission" since the Apollo Project to travel to the Moon. It clearly lacks any means or policy, to fund President Donald Trump's often-repeated promise of $1 trillion in new rail, road, port, and airport infrastructure—even though both China and Japan clearly want to support this by investments in new infrastructure in the United States. America actually needs not $1 trillion, but $5 trillion or more in new infrastructure investments. Its Congress is postponing even the obviously urgent reconstruction funds for the states and territories devastated by hurricanes in 2017.

So the United States must create a Hamiltonian national credit bank in order to participate in the Belt and Road Initiative and the new infrastructure development banks set up by the BRICS nations, simply in order to meet America's own needs for long-overdue new infrastructure. It is also urgent that the nations of the Middle East and North Africa use Hamilton's method to create a regional infrastructure development bank so that the "New Silk Road" of infrastructure development can fully expand throughout that region.

Hamilton's and LaRouche's Credit System

Alexander Hamilton not only founded America's first national bank in 1791; he had earlier co-founded two of its first four private commercial banks. These were banks of a new kind, commercial banks whose *only* business was to, as Hamilton said, "concentrate the savings of the country and place them at the disposal of those best able to use them productively," through lending. Hamilton's partner in the Bank of New York was an ancestor of President Franklin Roosevelt, who during his own university days studied his ancestor's work; so FDR as governor and President did

A drawing of work building the Erie Canal, perhaps the most important single infrastructure project in American history, during the period of functioning of the Second Bank of the United States.

not merely "accidentally" take up Hamilton's methods of credit.

Hamilton's view was not only that such well-run private commercial banks were a blessing to the nation, but that the national government needed a national bank to coordinate its important national purposes with an expanding number of private banks.

The most important of those national purposes, Hamilton said, was fostering individual invention and creativity of the population, which he understood was the basis of national wealth. In his reports to Congress on public credit, a national bank, and manufacturing, he wrote:

> Public Credit … is among the principal engines of useful enterprise and internal improvement.… As a substitute for capital, it is little less useful than gold or silver [then considered the only "capital"–ed.], in agriculture, in commerce, in the manufacturing and mechanic arts.
>
> Public utility is more truly the object of public banks, than private profit. And it is the business of Government, to constitute them on such principles, that while the latter will result, in a sufficient degree, … the former be not made subservient to it.
>
> To cherish and stimulate the activity of the human mind, by multiplying the objects of enterprise, is not among the least considerable of the expedients, by which the wealth of a nation may be promoted.

Hamilton amazed his President and military commander George Washington, by: first, successfully exchanging distressed, non-performing debt of the Continental Congress and the individual states for new, long-term debt of the new United States funded by specific revenues; second, quickly raising the value of that newly funded debt up to par by 1790; third, successfully exchanging that debt in turn, for stock in a Bank of the United States capitalized at $10 million; and fourth, issuing a new national currency from that Bank, which effectively allowed the nation's debt to be used as sound money.

With each new adoption of Hamiltonian national banking in American history, the investments in new infrastructure and new industries became more expansive. Hamilton's first national bank invested in development of water power for industry, ironmaking, canals, etc. The Second Bank helped launch the first American railroad building, more important canals and ports, steam power, coal mining. President Abraham Lincoln's "Greenback" system created new continent-wide railroads—for war and for transcontinental travel and freight—as well as an expanded and revolutionized coal industry, a steel industry, a merchant marine, a national education system for scientific agriculture, the beginnings of electrification, and so on.

EIR historian Anton Chaitkin has shown[1] that each surge in industrial growth and technological revolution in American history has been linked directly to the application of Hamilton's principles—often called "the American System of economy"—by American governments. Senator and Secretary of State James G. Blaine's great economic history of the 19th-Century United States demonstrated exactly the same conclusion.

Lincoln, after a 20-year period in which banking and currency had fallen into chaos and the nation was splitting apart, successfully organized a new national system of commercial banks which—along with individual citizens—purchased newly issued national debt fully funded by new tax revenue. Those chartered banks held the government debt as their reserve capital, placed it at the Treasury, and circulated a new Treasury currency ("Greenbacks") based on it, again effectively making government debt circulate as sound money. The new Greenback currency funded the expansive investments Lincoln launched into creation of infrastructure and industry, which propelled the United States to the world's leading industrial power by World War I. The fact that those banks were prohibited by Lincoln Administration regulations from securities broker-dealer activities—the "Glass-Steagall principle"—was essential.

In the process, Lincoln's Administration demonstrated how large a volume of new, funded debt can be issued to and raised from a nation's own citizens, commercial banks, and other institutions, for purposes of creating national credit for important projects, even when a nation is cut off from international borrowing as the United States was in 1861. Many nations today can take heed of this principle. It was shown in 2016 by Egypt's successful and very rapid borrowing of approximately $8 billion from its own citizens exclusively, for the major project of building a second channel for the Suez Canal.

President Franklin Roosevelt, through the Reconstruction Finance Corporation, expanded the nation's electric power generation by 50% in a decade, dramatically increased its agricultural productivity, lifted millions out of poverty in the Southeast of the country, and in mobilizing for World War II created entirely new industries such as aluminum production, multiplied the national production of machine tools by hundreds of times, and more.

EIR Founding Editor Lyndon LaRouche revived the "American System of economy" which was based on Alexander Hamilton's life's work, and has carried it forward to a greater understanding of the impact of technological advance upon successful and sustainable economic growth.

In 1976 LaRouche's proposal for an International Development Bank (IDB) was adopted by the nations of the Non-Aligned Movement in conference at Colombo, Sri Lanka. In 1982, after meeting and collaboration with then-President of Mexico José Lopez Portillo, LaRouche in his book Operation Juárez spelled out how individual nations could cooperate with the IDB.

---

1 "Leibniz, Gauss Shaped America's Science Successes," EIR, February 9, 1996.

- Loan of government-created credit (currency notes) must be directed to those forms of investment which promote technological progress in realizing the fullest potentials for applying otherwise idled capital goods, otherwise idled goods-producing capacities, and otherwise idled productive labor, to produce goods or to develop the basic economic infrastructure needed for maintenance and development of production and physical distribution of goods....
- In each republic, there must be a state-owned national bank, which rejects in its lawfully permitted functions, those private banking features of central banking associated with the Bank of England and the misguided practices of the U.S.A.'s Federal Reserve System....
- No lending institution shall exist within the nation except as they are subject to standards of practice and auditing by the Treasury of the government and auditors of the national bank. No foreign financial institution shall be permitted to do business within the republic unless its international operations meet lawful requirements for standards of reserves and proper banking practices under the laws of the republic.
- The Treasury and national bank, as a partnership, have continual authority to administer capital controls and exchange controls, and to assist this function by means of licensing of individual import licenses and export licenses, and to regulate negotiations of loans taken from foreign sources....

In the 1980s LaRouche inspired Ronald Reagan's adoption of the Strategic Defense Initiative to develop "new physical principles" to shoot down nuclear missiles; LaRouche then organized strongly, though ultimately unsuccessfully, for Reagan to adopt a Hamiltonian national credit strategy so as to spread these new laser and beam technologies into both the industrialized and the developing world economies.

Had Reagan adopted Hamiltonian credit policies as LaRouche urged, not only could we have achieved actually effective anti-nuclear missile defenses, but

FDR's recovery plan depended heavily on infrastructure construction, financed by such agencies as the TVA and the Reconstruction Finance Corporation. Here, construction work at the TVA's Douglas Dam in Tennessee, June 1942.

also global economic progress would have contributed to putting the threat of world war permanently on the shelf.

But LaRouche forecast that the Soviet system would collapse within five years of its refusal to cooperate on new strategic missile defense technologies with Reagan's United States—this did in fact occur. LaRouche then, in numerous meetings and events in Russia during the 1990s, recommended that Russia adopt "the Chinese system" of national credit and new infrastructure building, though this did not occur.

For more than forty years LaRouche and his wife, Schiller Institute Founder Helga Zepp-LaRouche, have held conferences and met with heads of state and other leaders all over the world to promote those national programs and "great projects" of infrastructure most important for raising the productivity of nations' economies.

Today the LaRouches' concept of nations cooperating to issue joint national credits for high-technology "great projects" of new infrastructure across the world, has finally been launched by China's Belt and Road Initiative, stretching to more than 60 nations.

Lyndon LaRouche's movement proposes the United States Congress now urgently create a Hamiltonian Third Bank of the United States, as sketched in **Figure 3**. This will bring the United States into cooperation with the Belt and Road, or "New Silk Road," and bring that New Silk Road into the United States

Figure 3
A Third National Bank—How to Turn U.S. Debt into Credit for the Real Economy

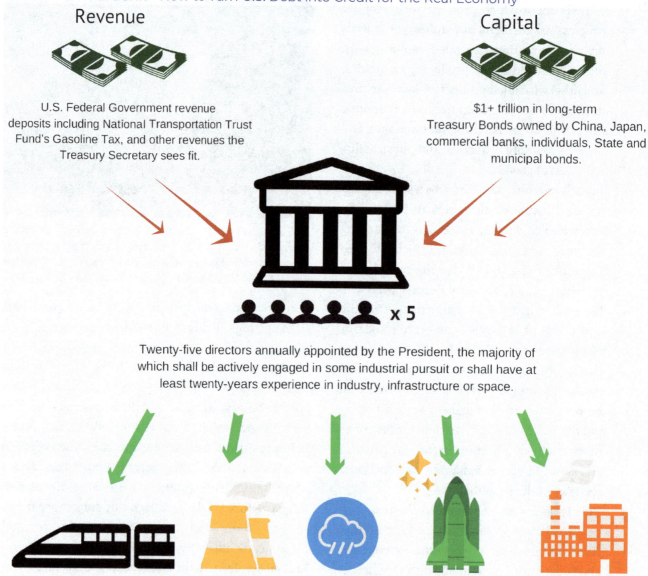

to build the new economic infrastructure, from high-speed rail corridors to flood-prevention sea-gates, which it so badly needs.

Here once again, as in Alexander Hamilton's successful Bank plan and its successors, holders of U.S. Treasury debt voluntarily subscribe that debt to become shareholders in a Bank of the United States. Private commercial banks, which hold considerable excess reserves in the form of Treasury securities, would become a major part of the shareholders. In this respect the Bank's structure would resemble that of the Federal Reserve Bank but with *entirely opposed intention*—that of a commercial lending institution to major national, regional, and local infrastructure projects and new branches of industry, as opposed to a rarified investment bank whose only "clients," by policy, are the biggest money-center banks of Wall Street and the City of London.

But the new Bank would also expand international cooperation—and the Belt and Road Initiative—because China and Japan have U.S. Treasury securities holdings in excess of $1 trillion each, and both wish to invest in new infrastructure development in North America.

Proposed legislation circulated to Members of the U.S. Congress by LaRouche's associates reads:

"Section II. Responsibilities and Authorizations

"**(a)** By this legislation, the Congress authorizes the creation of a public corporation to be called the Bank of the United States, which is authorized to: provide credit for major national projects of infrastructure, including surface transportation and ports, national intercity high-speed rail transport, water management and supply, drought prevention, flood prevention and storm protection, electrical energy production and distribution, and space exploration; make loans to agencies of the United States authorized for such projects; enter joint ventures with agencies of other nations mutually to provide credit for major international projects of new infrastructure; provide credit to state and municipal capital projects by purchase of municipal bonds as issued; discount bank loans to businesses participating in such projects; and cooperate with the United States Export-Import Bank to provide trade credits to businesses engaged in international infrastructure projects."

Japan's 'Second Budget'

Clearly such U.S. legislation to create a Bank of the United States would effectively create a "second national budget" or "capital budget" consisting of credit for building of new infrastructure and introducing new technologies to industry. The Reconstruction Finance Corporation (RFC) of President Franklin Roosevelt was the last such credit system the United States had.

Japan, which invests in new infrastructure projects through a program similar to Roosevelt's RFC, has now publicly indicated it will join in cooperation with China on the Belt and Road Initiative. At a reception of the December 4-5, 2017 Sino-Japanese Entrepreneurs and Former High-level Officials Dialogue in Tokyo, Japanese Prime Minister Shinzo Abe said: "I believe Japan will be able to cooperate well with China, which has been putting forward its 'One Belt, One Road initiative' in a free and open Indo-Pacific region…. Meeting robust infrastructure demand in Asia through cooperation between Japan and China will contribute greatly to the prosperity of Asian people, in addition to the economic development of the two countries."

In Japan, the predominant credit institution funding new economic infrastructure is the Fiscal Investment and Loan Program (FILP)—an institution very similar in operation to the Reconstruction Finance Corporation of President Franklin Roosevelt's administrations.

The FILP loaned infrastructure credits, according to its own 2017 report, of more than 20 trillion yen (approximately $200 billion) in 2016, which was a typical year. The FILP is funded by investments from the Postal Savings system (i.e., by citizens), from commercial banks, from pension funds, and from some privatized former government monopolies such as NTT. Its bonds pay slightly more than Japanese government bonds.

Crucially, the FILP has been called "a second budget for Japan"; in other words, a national capital budget. Its credit is also designated as "fiscal loans." The FILP makes loans to those government agencies which carry out infrastructure projects, whether they receive additional tax revenue, or not. The government agencies in turn lend to contracting companies on the projects, to local infrastructure utilities, and so forth. The FILP may also make international infrastructure loans.

Japan's capital budget for infrastructure projects comes in significant part from a Fiscal Investment and Loan Program very similar to the American Reconstruction Finance Corporation of the period 1933-57.

A Southwest Asia/Africa Development Bank

It is also urgent, in order that rapid reconstruction can proceed with the end of 25 years of war devastating the Mideast and that the new China-led infrastructure building in Africa can be maximized, that the economically stronger nations in this region should form a Southwest Asia Regional Development Bank. The purpose: To create credit to cooperate in new infrastructure projects with the new international development banks led by the Asian Infrastructure Investment Bank (AIIB), the New Development Bank, China's public commercial banks, and Japan's infrastructure credit facilities. Roughly $200 billion can be taken as a baseline level for the Bank's equity and borrowed capital combined.

The nations forming the regional development bank should provide a basic share of its equity capital, at least 20% of the total stock, in the form of new full-faith-and-credit bonds issued by their Treasuries, and back those bonds by dedicated future tax revenues which are to make the payments on the bonds to the Bank. The Bank will have other revenues directly and indirectly related to the infrastructure projects it invests in and the economic expansion around these projects; but the "sinking fund" for the Bank's stock dividend payments should be identified in advance and be independent of this future expansion, to ensure the soundness of the Bank's liabilities.

The founding nations will offer stock in the Bank directly to their citizens and to their private banks in order to subscribe the other 80% of the equity capital. This will include banks or citizens who already hold bonds issued by their governments, subscribing those bonds to the Bank in exchange for its stock—which will increase the future payments of the governments to the Bank.

The regional development bank should be authorized to issue bonds to the public as well, including internationally, in order to reach its targeted capitalization with the help of borrowed capital. But the goal should be to meet the original capitalization entirely by stock subscriptions of the governments, citizens, and private banks of the countries forming the Bank. The Bank's stock must be a long-term investment.

The regional development bank will issue loans exclusively to agencies assigned to carry out important infrastructure developments, whether those be local government agencies or agencies created for the purpose of the project. It will conduct discounting activities with private banks only as those banks make loans to contractors and service providers on the projects, and only as necessary for those loans to flow. It will also buy and/or syndicate infrastructure bonds issued by regional governments and local governments for approved projects.

Cooperation with International Development Banks

The recent important emergence of new international development banks for non-austerity-conditioned, infrastructure-specific lending—the BRICS New Development Bank and the Asian Infrastructure Investment Bank (AIIB) initiated by China—open up potentials for credit agreements not seen since the Bretton Woods Conference. The critical great projects or "infrastructure platforms" proposed here require cooperation among several nations, including credit cooperation among the major economic powers providing the bulk of capital goods and industrial products for these projects—but *not* supranational direction.

Extending the New Silk Road to West Asia and Africa will require more credit for major projects than can be created by a new development bank for the region. It requires international project lending as well. This is clearly true for the great reconstruction efforts needed in areas which have been subject to wars.

It is also shown by the long-term, low-interest international credits recently extended for the nuclear power complex at El-Dabaa in Egypt, for example, or the new Kenya Standard Gauge Railway. A Southwest Asia/Africa Regional Infrastructure Bank will provide proportional matching funds for such major projects or assist national development banks in doing so; and it will facilitate the conversion of international project loan funds into national currencies (also essential to prevent capital flight and/or speculation).

A Southwest Asia/Africa Regional Infrastructure Bank will be able to develop credit agreements for major projects in cooperation, for example, with the Export-Import Bank of China at low, government-to-government interest rates, if that country's companies are involved in providing capital goods and logistics; and could develop similar agreements with the AIIB, New Development Bank, or the Silk Road Fund. Such credit partnerships will minimize the need of the Regional Infrastructure Bank to borrow capital by issuing bonds on international capital markets at higher rates.

If the United States and Japan were now to join both the AIIB and the Belt and Road Initiative, an international combination of powerful development banks would be capable of acting like an International Development Bank with capital in the trillions.

A Southwest Asia Regional Infrastructure Bank will be able to act as an arm of this combination of international development banks, and the mediator between them and national banks of the nations of Southwest Asia and Africa.

Public-Private Partnerships Cannot Substitute

It is only when the funding of new infrastructure by public credit fails, as it has for decades in the United States and Europe, that "public-private partnerships for infrastructure" become a subject of constant proposals in the financial media and from governments. Such partnerships with private investors have worked only when they are used to feed and complement larger-scale public infrastructure developments with more local developments, as with connecting major high-speed rail lines into secondary cities and light rail systems. In those cases the public investors are typically municipalities and the private investors typically larger locally-active companies which want to develop and modernize the infrastructure around them; such public-private partnerships have become common in China's burgeoning urban areas.

"PPPs" have not often attempted to build substantial new economic infrastructure; when they have taken over infrastructure previously publicly built, particularly in the United States, their special corporations have usually failed, sometimes going into bankruptcy and forced public bailout more than once.

A June 17, 2017 *New York Times* article, entitled "World Offers Cautionary Tale for Trump's Infrastructure Plan," discussed a broad academic study of such partnerships, compared to public funding of infrastructure. The paper reported that countries which had placed emphasis on PPPs had bad results to show for it. "In India, politically connected firms have captured contracts on the strength of relationships with officialdom, yielding defective engineering at bloated prices. When Britain handed control to private companies to upgrade London's subway system more than a decade ago, the result was substandard, budget-busting work, prompting the government to step back in. Canada has suffered a string of excessive costs on public projects funneled through the private sector, like a landmark bridge in Vancouver and hospitals in Ontario."

Public funding, the *Times* reported, had been far more successful. "By contrast, China has engineered one of the most effective economic transformations in modern history in part through relentless investment in infrastructure, traditionally financed and overseen by an unabashedly powerful state." The authors report that China has invested an average of 8.6% of its GDP into new infrastructure projects for 25 years, 1992-2016. This has worked, with rapid and efficient development of projects and high productivity; and large amounts of private investment in industrial development—both from within and outside China—has followed.

Credit for serious new infrastructure development, from new rail and road corridors to nuclear power complexes or major water management and water supply projects, must be at interest rates in the 2-4% range, and must be for terms approximating the prime operating life of the project. Because new economic infrastructure platforms are not low-risk investments, private capital cannot create such credit even if it has no intention to loot the public or speculate on real estate and commodity values. Public infrastructure banks, able to look to long-term increases in general productivity and economic growth for the return, can do so.

3. CREDIT FOR INCREASED PRODUCTIVITY

The purpose of the use of a Federal credit system, is to generate high-productivity trends in improvements of employment, with the accompanying intention to increase the physical-economic productivity and standard of living of persons and households.

"Productivity" is given in everyday government statistics as the national product—or the product of an economic sector—divided by the total hours worked by employed persons in that national economy or sector. This definition of productivity does not show the advances or regressions in the power of an economy to provide for the general welfare of its people, because it does not account for whether the calculated "product" is useful in any way, nor whether it is being produced more or less efficiently than in a previous period of the same economy. Worse, this measure is shown to be nearly useless by the fact that in periods of sudden mass unemployment—such as the year 2009 in the United States and some European economies—this "productivity" rises sharply; amidst economic collapse, the few still employed are producing more "product" per capita than before.

Lyndon LaRouche's economic method takes productivity to be reflected in the degree of free energy which an economy can produce, over and above maintaining the living standard of the employed population, producing and maintaining modern capital goods including infrastructure against attrition, and providing for those employed in non-goods-producing occupations or not employed. The measures of such free energy, and of the "energy of the system" which it exceeds, are market baskets of consumer goods and services of all kinds, and "market baskets" of existing and/or new-technology capital goods and infrastructure.

Over the longer run, such productivity is fundamentally reflected in what LaRouche years ago named "potential relative population density." Greater productivity increases the highest *potential* level of population density per square kilometer of an economy, at the same or higher living standards and cultural levels, *relative* to the degree of improvements that economy has made to land, infrastructure, and production technologies.

To quote a further specification of this by LaRouche more than 30 years ago:

> Taking the society (economy) as a whole, this net increase [in productivity and free energy—ed.] is the outcome of some increase in average level of technology of the economy as a whole. This may be accomplished either by introducing new, more advanced technologies, or by replacing obsolete capital stocks with competitively modern capital stocks, or by increasing the average level of productivity of the entire labor force through productive employment of significant portions of the unemployed, or some combination of these measures. All things being equal, in the longer run, it must be based on introduction of more advanced technologies.

Most crucially, this is a function of the introductive of new economic infrastructure built with higher levels of technology, on the scale of regions, nations, or even the connectivity relations among continents and seas. LaRouche's notes on this in 2010:

> Man as a creator in the likeness of the great Creator, is expressed by humanity's creation of the "artificial environments" we sometimes call "infrastructure," on which both the progress, and even the merely continued existence of civilized society depends.
>
> The level of achievable productivity depends upon raising the "platform" through revolutions in infrastructure, on which successful general advances in potential relative population densities depend. Without those advances in basic economic infrastructure, merely particular technological progress, locally applied, will fail in its attempted performance of the truly vital mission of physical economic program....

The constant herald and measure of rising productivity, as LaRouche emphasizes, is rising *energy*

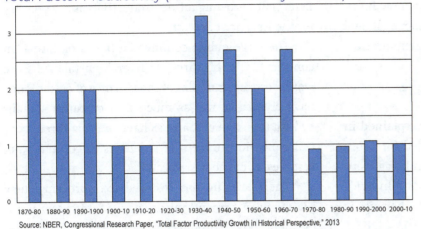

Figure 4
Total Factor Productivity (Annual Growth by Decade)

Source: NBER, Congressional Research Paper, "Total Factor Productivity Growth in Historical Perspective," 2013

flux-density of technologies used to produce power and for industrial processes; that is, the capacity to concentrate a growing amount of energy in a relatively small apparatus through which it flows in order to perform work. The potential energy-density of fuels themselves contributes to this—see the chart in the following section of rising energy density of fuels over human history, to the peaks of nuclear fission and fusion fuels—as does the efficiency in converting energy to power or work, because this tends to make the apparatus or "power plant" smaller for the same power output. The radical advances of energy flux-density in industrial work, can be seen in the dramatic difference in tolerances and smoothness of a metal cut made by a laser, as opposed to one made by a diamond saw. The energy flux of the laser is both much greater, and applied on a far, far smaller cross-section.

An Example of Technological Productivity

A physical-economic example of this definition of productivity—one which sprawls across the 20th Century as China's example has dominated the 21st to date—is the "golden age of American productivity" centered in President Franklin Roosevelt's terms in office, clearly resulting from his administrations' extraordinary building of new economic infrastructure. **Figure 4** shows this upsurge as measured by sustained, extremely high rates (2-3%) of annual growth of "total factor productivity" in the U.S. economy, which is the estimated economic growth caused by technological advance, over and above all other growth factors.

The highest annual rate of growth of productivity in America's history, occurred in the periods in which the greatest investments were in new infrastructure which required new technologies—rail and road, and later space transportation technologies, electric power technologies, water management and flood control technologies, and communications. These periods are the decades after the American Civil War in the 19th Century, and the decades of the 1930s to 1960s in the 20th Century.

The U.S. Commerce Department's National Bureau of Economic Research wrote in a 2005 report, "Sources of Total Factor Productivity Growth in the Golden Age": "This was due to the very strong growth in electric power generation and distribution, transportation, communications, civil and structural engineering for bridges, tunnels, dams, highways, railroads, and transmission systems; and private research and development."

Roosevelt's New Deal built roads, rails, airports, and bridges across the country; it increased national power generation by 50% by building large-scale, high-efficiency, and high-power-rating (online performance) hydroelectric installations; and it established national laboratories for research in frontier areas such as atomic fission and aerodynamics. Private companies' engineering capabilities were challenged to perform this extraordinary building and responded with research and development and technological breakthroughs.

New, more advanced infrastructure was the driver of productivity. Technological productivity growth was also fairly good in the 1920s, the graph shows—new technologies like the internal combustion engine, radio, and telephone were spreading—but not comparable to the decades which followed.

In the 21st Century thus far, it has been China's technological productivity growing at rates near or even above 3% annually, according to studies by the same U.S. agency and by the OECD; and for the same reason, very high investments in building new infrastructure, transportation connectivity above all, and in frontier energy technologies and space exploration.

Productive Credit and Money

The issuance of national credit, as explained in the prior section, is targeted, or intended for those improvements in infrastructure platforms, agro-industrial technology, and also household and individual productivity as through education—otherwise it cannot be called *credit*.

The "big three" central banks of the United States (Federal Reserve), Europe (European Central Bank), and Japan (Bank of Japan) have shown dramatically, over the past decade, the difference between credit, and simple creation of new money. These central banks have created, by rough estimates, $13-14 trillion equivalent in money since late 2008 (by "quantitative easing" programs), and have additionally issued temporary liquidity loans to banks in the many trillions of dollars equivalent.

But none of that money—new currency and electronic entries—has been created for an economic purpose, nor for a trade purpose. It has all been created for a strictly financial purpose: Providing the largest banks in the Trilateral countries enough capital and liquid reserves to survive massive losses and bad debts, and to resume and expand investments in whatever markets or securities those banks saw fit. Claims that the creation of this vast quantity of money in this way, would cause banks to restore and then dramatically increase their lending—thus claiming a general "economic purpose"—have proven to be untrue in Europe, the United States, and Japan. Most of the money which has not simply become excess bank reserves—the majority of it—has gone instead to investors in the form of dividends, and stockholders in the huge rises in market prices, and to large corporations which in turn used it to buy their own stock.

Credit is also issued in the form of currency and electronic entries. Credit issued by governments is a debt those governments assume, but when issued for purposes of a more productive nation, it is a debt which will be "paid back" with a large amount of interest by the greater overall productivity of a future generation. Essentially, growing future productivity is the security for the issuance of *credit*.

The large public commercial banks of China, in contrast to the "big three" Trilateral central banks, are world-leading examples of the issuance of credit. They have created nearly as much new currency—"money"—in the form of loans, as have the "big three" central banks in the form of securities prices and bank reserves, over the past decade.

Their lending has fostered extraordinary new platforms of transportation, navigation, water management, power production, agricultural production, and scientific research in the Chinese economy; and they have now extended and committed roughly $300 billion since 2014 in additional credit for infrastructure projects outside China through the Belt and Road Initiative. The result has been an extraordinary 8-10% of GDP invested in economic infrastructure for 20 years, and the near-complete eradication of rural poverty which once entrapped 6-700 million Chinese. Moreover, accounting studies like those of PricewaterhouseCoopers have estimated that these banks' credit has created in excess of $10 trillion in new physical capital assets dominated by intercity and urban infrastructure, in China and increasingly in the Belt and Road countries.

The lack of such new infrastructure and industrial assets associated with the extraordinary growth of corporate and household debt bubbles in the trans-Atlantic countries since 2010, is why we assess a general financial crash coming on in those economies. This is not the case for the large amounts of new credit created by China's public banks and international development banks and funds.

The Principles of New Infrastructure

Energy-flux density and power: When higher levels of power per capita and per square kilometer can be created at the same relative physical costs to society, the cost for existing applications is lowered, new processes with higher total power requirements become economical, and new physical reactions, as-

Figure 5

A High-Temperature Gas-Cooled Reactor

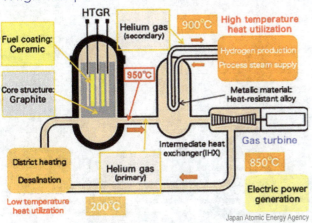

Japan Atomic Energy Agency

sociated with new domains of physical chemistry, become possible. In the past, this process was demonstrated when the new principles of electromagnetism replaced the simple motion of steam engines; or in production, when previously enormously expensive materials, such as aluminum, became easy to mass produce.

It is seen in the potential—given enough reliable electric power—of computer controlled machining, electron-beam welding, laser cutting, and electric-discharge machining. Conversely, when the technological level of an economy stagnates, the resources defined by that level of technology become "finite" and are gradually depleted by continued use. Then the development of higher levels of power per capita allows the creation of new resources.

This next level requires a long-delayed nuclear power revolution. This involves vastly expanding the installation of nuclear power plants, and, in particular, a crash effort for mass production of cheaper and safer fourth-generation nuclear fission reactors (including the medium-term development of the thorium cycle).

There are productive innovations on the immediate horizon. The introduction of high-temperature gas-cooled reactors (see **Figure 5**), developed in concept four decades ago, will not only be inherently safe but will make possible energy-efficient and inexpensive desalination of salt and brackish water, the production of hydrogen for fuel, generation of easily available process heat, and reliable electric power.

Another innovation is the deployment of floating nuclear power stations for special uses. Decades ago, Westinghouse Corp. was at work on this concept, at its facilities in Jacksonville, Florida, for quick deployment off the coasts of developing regions in need of abundant reliable power. However, this initiative was thwarted during the years of casino economics. Now Russia and China have active construction programs for floating nuclear plants.

Russia's first one will be installed at the Arctic Circle town of Pevek, in Chukotka in Summer 2019. In April 2018, the *Akademik Lomonosov* left the shipyards in St. Petersburg, Russia, under tow to Murmansk, where two on-board reactors will be fueled before it proceeds to its final mooring in the Far East.

China expects to launch its first floating nuclear plant in 2019-2020. These kinds of small barge-mounted units in the range of 50-75 MW will offer ready power not only for Arctic towns, but also for a range of needs including port operations and construction, restoring power after natural disasters, and quickly introducing flexible electric power supplies in regions which lack electrification.

The full picture of nuclear needs and capacities is

The Akademik Lomonosov *is shown departing the Baltic Shipyard in St. Petersburg in April 2018, under tow to Murmansk, where the two nuclear reactors on board will receive nuclear fuel, and then be towed to Pevek, Chukotka for installation in Summer 2019. The barge's two nuclear reactors can produce up to 70 MW of electricity, enough to serve 100,000 people.*

V. WITHOUT LAROUCHE'S 'FOUR LAWS,' FINANCIAL CRASH MEANS CHAOS

Construction of the Norris Dam, part of the Tennessee Valley Authority system. The dam was completed in 1936.

presented in Volume 1 of The New Silk Road Becomes The World Land-Bridge, in Section II, "Expand Nuclear Power for the World's Survival." As the sub-title to that 2014 report states, "Much of the world lives in virtual darkness, lacking the electricity essential for modern life; but world leaders are not prioritizing the solution to the problem."

In the four years since that was written, the governments of China and Russia, in collaboration with India, South Korea, and others, have made a priority of pushing ahead with commitments for nuclear power plant construction. China, for example, has 28 reactor projects in the works within its own borders, and additional projects abroad. Russia is collaborating on nuclear power plants in Egypt and elsewhere.

However, the United States and Western Europe continue to go backward on nuclear fission capacity. The consequences of this go beyond the harmful impacts confined within their own national boundaries.

What is required internationally, is many times over the current 450 nuclear power plants in operation worldwide, which account for only 11% of total electricity used. Humanity needs not only more electricity, but the productivity only possible from fully "going nuclear" with fission energy, in order to create the worldwide conditions of industrial might, and human ingenuity to lift off into a totally new domain of a fusion energy era. This is discussed in Law Four below, "A Crash Program for Fusion Power, Plasma Technology and Space."

Water: Increasingly since the breakthrough represented by the Tennessee Valley Authority, water management projects for flood control and irrigation have also been power projects, providing electricity with very high energy-conversion efficiency and reliability. As construction technologies have advanced, the potential geographical scope for surface water management has expanded. A prime example is the Three Gorges Dam project on the upper Yangtze River, completed in 2012.

Among the most important such infrastructure undertakings now pending in the world is in Africa: the long-planned Transaqua Project, to recharge the disappearing Lake Chad, by diverting a small percentage of the massive freshwater resources of the Congo Basin, to transform productivity and population potentials throughout the Sahel and central Africa (see Section III of this Special Report). *EIR* and the Schiller Institute have promoted the launching of this combined water management/irrigation/transportation/power infrastructure project for many years, and it is now coming closer to realization as a result of the Belt and Road Initiative.

Another potential project of the same scope and importance is the North American Water and Power Alliance (NAWAPA) plan, designed and engineered already by the 1960s, and discussed in the North America section of this report. Above all, the agricultural productivity of the entire western, dry, and partially desertifying portion of the North American continent would boom with NAWAPA, by conveying southward, 5-10% of the abundant fresh water run-off of the Alaska/Yukon hydrological district of the northwest (much of which currently flows unused into the ocean with little productive economic or biospheric application).

However, the inherent constraint associated with such river diversion projects come from dry spells and natural variations in weather patterns, which can reduce water availability and, therefore, hydroelectricity output and supply for irrigation.

Two advanced technologies relieve any such constraints entirely. They constitute direct intervention into higher levels of the Earth's water cycle itself, not simply reconfiguring surface run-off—desalination (providing freshwater directly from the oceans), and weather modification with atmospheric ionization technologies (tapping the freshwater resources of the sky). The "Dimensions of the Water Cycle" graphic shown here illustrates this point (**Figure 6**).

Because the process of desalting sea water (or brackish inland water) is energy intensive, nuclear-powered systems are in order. Several nations have good designs, and there are many successful operating nuclear desalination plants, with long records. The challenge is to scale-up the programs to not only relieve the growing number of water-short regions, but to provide abundant water for increased economic activity to spur productivity and progress. As of 2018, only an estimated 350 million people worldwide were served by desalinated water, and most of that was produced by limited, expensive non-nuclear power sources.

The power to increase rainfall with weather modification will be greatly enhanced with new kinds of technologies using electrically-induced ionization of the atmosphere to accelerate water vapor condensation and increase precipitation (or reverse the process where precipitation is not desired).

The principle involved mimics the way galactic cosmic radiation controls key aspects of climate change through influences on cloud formation. The techniques have been tested and successfully demonstrated in Mexico, Russia, Australia, Israel, the United Arab Emirates, Oman, and in other locations.

Thus, through infrastructure, mankind creates "natural" water resources. A full report on these technologies, and the status of world water supplies, is given in "The New Silk Road Becomes the World Land-Bridge, Volume I" in the chapter entitled "Solve the World Water Crisis," and its appendix, "Initiatives for Nuclear Desalination."

Figure 6
Dimensions of the Water Cycle

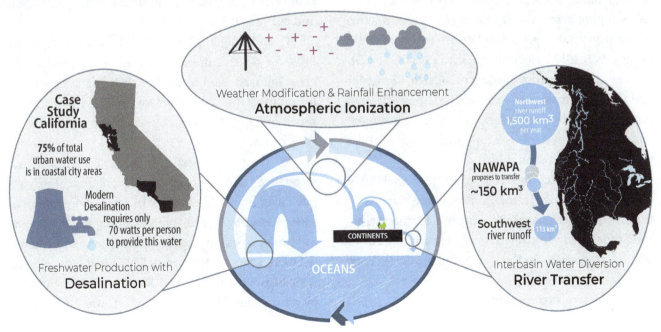

V. WITHOUT LAROUCHE'S 'FOUR LAWS,' FINANCIAL CRASH MEANS CHAOS

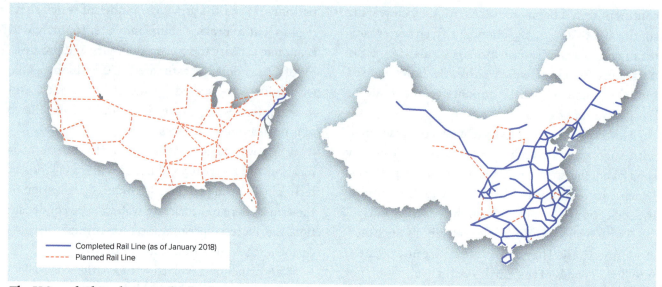

The U.S. and China have similar land areas, yet China has more than 100 times as much high-speed rail (16,000 miles), with a network of 30,000 miles planned by 2020. In the graphic, blue lines depict currently existing high-speed rail, and red lines depict potential future routes. While in China these future routes are already on the books and slated to be built, in the U.S. they remain only proposals.

In water management, it is equally important to develop advanced *storm and coastal flood protection* technologies, which have been thus far limited to relatively few countries and selected urban areas. The United States's recent history with powerful hurricanes provides a dramatic example. Not only economic productivity, but thousands of lives and hundreds of billions of dollars of wealth have been needlessly thrown away in the devastation of cities which could have been protected. The city and metropolitan area of New Orleans has been protected by large modern sea-gates, new levees, and a powerful pumping system—only after Hurricane Katrina killed nearly 3,000 people and destroyed whole areas of the city in 2005. Not only America's East Coast cities, but those all across the Gulf of Mexico, in Mexico and Central America as well, need the protection of modern sea-gates and dykes, as well as many more dam/reservoir systems to stop the flooding of those cities by tropical storm rains.

These projects are postponed in the United States, due to costs in the billions—only because of the lack of a national credit institution for infrastructure—and then reconsidered only after hundreds of billions in wealth, and priceless human lives, once again have been lost.

The lesson is true worldwide.

Transportation: A modern high-speed and magnetic levitation rail system does more than increase speed and convenience of transportation. It changes the entire physical-economic space-time characteristics of the economic system. More extensive areas become accessible in less time, ensuring more diverse population centers and encouraging healthy growth of population; manufacturing capabilities are increased (especially in the building and operation of the high-speed/maglev lines!); agricultural regions can be economically accessible to the individual or productive process; the social interchange of ideas and cultures is encouraged.

Transcontinental rail corridors are still to be built for South America, Africa, and Australia. The great Eurasian landmass is finally being spanned now by multiple rail corridors for freight which moves much more quickly than by sea, much more cheaply than by air.

As these corridors become standardized and electrified, making high speeds possible, Eurasian passenger lines will develop. In Africa, the new high-speed Kenya Standard-Gauge Railway is one of many rail projects developing and leading toward a Djibouti-Dakar Transcontinental. All this is the developing fruit of the great Belt and Road Initiative initiated by China, the "New Silk Road" toward which the war-ravaged Mideast nations are looking for reconstruction as well.

On the cross-continental scale, the 55-mile crossing of the Bering Strait by high-speed rail and road—opening the shortest route from Beijing and Northern China to America's Midwest—must be in the near future. This will integrate the North American continent into the modern rail systems now being built across Eurasia. It will be associated with the crossing of the North American continent from North to South by rail for the first time, and ground transportation finally through Central America's Darien Gap to South America.

Just further in the future, advanced systems of vacuum tube transport could provide supersonic access between select regions.

4. A CRASH PROGRAM FOR FUSION POWER, PLASMA TECHNOLOGY, AND SPACE

Currently, the world population is 7.6 billion people. Had the great progress and momentum in nuclear fusion research during the decades following World War II been allowed to continue, the world population today would be in the range of 20-25 billion people, living longer, healthier, and more productive lives than those relatively few in the most technologically advanced nations today.

In 1954, then-head of the United States Atomic Energy Commission Lewis Strauss said of ongoing efforts to achieve fusion power:

> Our children will enjoy in their homes electrical energy too cheap to meter. It is not too much to expect that our children will know of great periodic regional famines in the world only as matters of history. Will travel effortlessly over the seas and under them, and through the air with a minimum of danger and at great speeds; and will experience a life span far longer than ours, as disease yields and man comes to understand what causes him to age.

Such is the natural optimism which accompanies—then and now—the potentialities of a fusion platform.

Humanity has now reached a point where shifting to a platform of fusion power and plasma technology is no longer an optional step. Thermonuclear fusion will completely transform the conversion of energy into power and useful work, and thereby transform human economies and the productive capacities of individual human beings.

A human race that wants to explore the solar system and the galaxy will need fusion power to do so—a trip to Mars powered by fusion propulsion will take just a few weeks. Nations that want such high-quality power and heat, that we will produce the materials and pure isotopes we need from scrap and waste, and cut and shape anything easily, can only achieve that with plasma technologies. A world that wants unlimited energy indefinitely, wants fusion energy. And a human race that wants to eliminate pollution from the production and use of power and heat energy, needs fusion power to do it.

The revolutionary discoveries of the early 20th Century revealed an immense potential, altogether beyond chemical reactions: the fundamental equivalence of matter and energy, as expressed in the domains of fission, fusion, and matter-antimatter reactions. Each in this series of reactions operates at successively higher energy densities, and the entire set is orders of magnitude beyond the entire successive set of chemical reactions in the creation of power for work.

Control of these reactions enables the increase in what Lyndon LaRouche has termed the energy-flux density of the economies, as measured in the rate of energy use and efficiency of energy conversion

Table 3
The Energy Density of Fuels

Fuel Source	Energy Density (J/g)
Wood*	1.8×10^4
Petroleum (Diesel)*	2.7×10^4
Coal (Bituminous)*	4.6×10^4
H_2 and O_2*	1.2×10^5 (only H_2 mass considered)
Uranium-235 (Fission)	3.7×10^9
Deuterium-Tritium (Fusion)	3.2×10^{11}
Matter-Antimatter	9.0×10^{13}

combustion

to power of applied technologies, such as the energy concentrated in the beam of a laser used for metal cutting, compared to a power saw. Energy-flux density can be measured as the energy use per person and per unit area of the economy as a whole. This increasing power is associated with qualitative changes through the entire society—new technologies, new resources, higher levels of living standard, and essentially new economies (see **Table 3**).

For example, at the founding of the United States, the wood fire- and water wheel-based economy of the time provided an estimated 2,400-3,000 Watts (W) per capita. Thus, each member of that economy represented a potential application of energy up to 30 times greater than a fire-less society. By the 1920s, the increasingly coal-powered United States had a per-capita power use of 5,000 W, meaning every individual in the economy expressed nearly twice the power of members of a wood-waterpower-based economy. This supported the powered machinery, transportation, and early electricity generation that transformed life alongside the development of modern chemistry.

By 1970, the per-capita power rate in the United States, which now made extensive use of petroleum, natural gas, hydroelectric, and limited applications of nuclear power, had reached 10,000 W per capita, another doubling over the level 50 years prior. Thirty years later, per-capita power had reached 11,000 W; since 2005, however, this measure of individual human productive power has fallen slightly.

In each of these transitions, the previous fuel declined in use as a power source, allowing non-combustive uses—wood for construction and petroleum for plastics and other petrochemicals—while the array of resources expanded. In today's electromagnetic, and partially nuclear economies, rare earth minerals have become resources, the excellent fusion fuel of helium-3 on the Moon is being eyed by the Chinese space program, and the future, truly fusion-based economy will be able to process mineral deposits far below the quality of ores exploited successfully today.

Given these power transitions, it is no surprise that per-capita electricity consumption and per-capita wealth are so closely correlated, as seen in **Figure 7**.

The potential of a fusion-powered economy would approach 40,000 W of power per capita within a generation. Such potential drives home how unacceptable the current world average of only 2,400 W per capita (similar to the United States at its founding) truly is.

A Multi-Nation Crash Program

The United States and China have the task of leading the world into an entirely new level of capabilities of the human race, on Earth and in space: fusion power and plasma technologies. Other nations, such as the Republic of Korea and the Federal Republic of Germany, have very advanced experimental fusion power devices; and many nations will contribute

Figure 7
Electricity Consumption vs. GDP, Per Capita

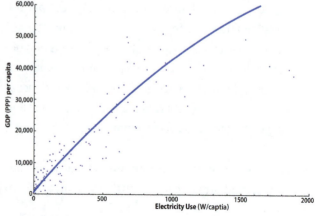

critical designs and breakthroughs for sustained generation of controlled fusion power.

But to make these breakthroughs and create a successful reproduction of the fusion process which drives the stars, requires a true crash program which joins the urgent work of large numbers of scientists, engineers, and machinists for a common objective. Some 135,000 such highly talented people made the breakthrough to nuclear fission in the United States's 1944-45 "Manhattan Project," for example. And Project Apollo, the American mission to the Moon, employed 400,000 skilled people and 20,000 industrial companies for several years.

But in no country thus far, has the number of scientists and engineers working on fusion power exceeded a few thousand at the very most. America invested the equivalent of more than $25 billion current dollars in the Manhattan Project in two years; its fusion research funding has never exceeded $450 million/year and recently is far below that. Scientists knew quite well back in 1979, when the U.S. Congress passed legislation promoting fusion research, that such merely investigative levels of funding and manpower could and would never conquer fusion power (**Figure 8**). China, on the other hand, is leading the world in resources invested in fusion experiments. It is the only major nation whose fusion power program funding level is growing rapidly; it is getting experimental results accordingly, and aiming at operating a first, relatively lower power demonstration fusion reactor in less than 15 years.

But opening the fusion technology era of mankind will take more than funded research. It will take very large concentrations of electrical power, applied to create the demonstration "platform" from which fusion will vault us up to a much higher "platform" of unlimited, easily controlled and directed power for every kind of human work and adventure.

For example, the ultra-short laser pulse used in laser-fusion experimental work at Lawrence Livermore Laboratory, is given 500 million megawatts of power for a small fraction of a second, compressing a tiny capsule of deuterium fuel which could produce even greater amounts of power. In "tokamak" and other magnetic fusion experimental reactors, the heating of light gases into plasmas and the operation of strong magnetic fields which compress the plasma to cause fusion, require application of large amounts of electrical power. Aggressively conducting dozens of such experiments simultaneously—the characteristic of a scientific crash program—will need very large capacities for completely reliable, high-voltage electrical power.

As an example, the United States increased national electric energy generation and use by 150% in a single decade 1935-45—using particularly a great surge in hydroelectric power capacity—making possible a tremendous 1944-50 concentration of manpower, experimentation, and demonstration of new technologies including atomic power, but also aluminum production, pure chemical and medical isotope production, new levels of computing power, and electronics manufacturing (see **Table 4**).

Today, American power generation has not risen since 2005; but what was done then, can be done again at a higher level. China, for its part, now has the world's highest level of power generation at 5,500 billion kWh/year. Given its population, its power generation per capita is still well below the level of the United States, but its power generation per square kilometer is significantly above it.

All the countries involved should rapidly increase their nuclear electric power production, as the driver for other sources, and the driver for the breakthrough of a crash scientific program to demonstrate and then achieve fusion power. Once the breakthrough to continuous, controlled fusion reactions is

Figure 8
Fusion Funding Regimes

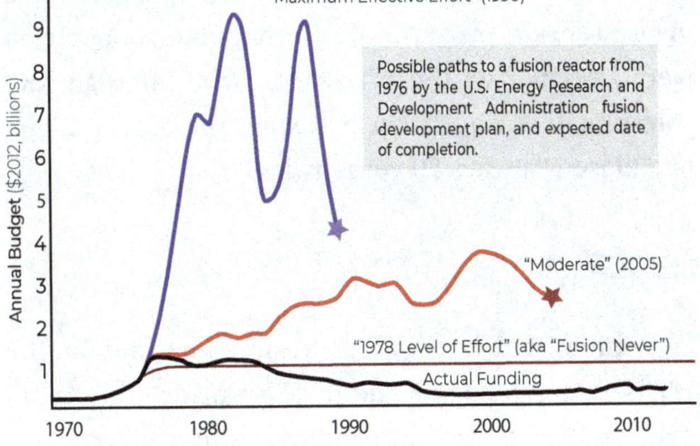

"Maximum Effective Effort" (1990)

Possible paths to a fusion reactor from 1976 by the U.S. Energy Research and Development Administration fusion development plan, and expected date of completion.

"Moderate" (2005)

"1978 Level of Effort" (aka "Fusion Never")

Actual Funding

credit: Graphic design by Geoffrey M. Olynyk, incorporating 1976 projetions from U.S. ERDA, "Fusion power by magnetic confinement: Program Plan," Stephen O. Dean

Table 4
Power Production Leading to Mastery of Nuclear Fission, United States, 1930-1950

Year	Electric Power Generation (kWh)		
	Per km²	Per Capita	Per Productive Worker
1930	30,000	650	6,000
1935	33,000	700	7,300
1940	47,000	1,100	8,000
1945	73,000	1,600	10,500
1950	94,000	2,050	13,100

made, this large "investment" in electrical power will be "paid back" many times over for the indefinite future. But it will also have great benefits in itself.

What will this mean?

- Power for high-speed freight and passenger rail systems; a great deal of electrical capacity, generation and distribution, which must be of a high energy density and complete on-line reliability, is demanded by a system like China's now nearly 20,000 km of high-speed rail.
- Power for higher quality industrial machines, tools, and processes, featuring the use of lasers and the production of very high purity chemical isotopes.
- Power to lift, pump, and move water over distances to where it is needed.
- Power to desalinate salt and brackish water efficiently at very high temperatures, relieving drought and desertification conditions.
- Power for industrial expansion, especially in high-value-added industries.
- The ability to develop nuclear propulsion for spacecraft, of much higher specific moment—and therefore, speed—than chemical propulsion.
- The potential to develop plasma technologies—such as plasma steelmaking, plasma metal-cutting, and "fusion torch" materials purification—even before fusion power itself is demonstrated.
- The potential of achieving fusion power breakthroughs within 15 years.

Fusion: Mastery of the Cosmos

There are many challenges to be overcome as we tame the fire of fusion. A fusion reaction is the uniting of two light nuclei (e.g., hydrogen) into one, which results in a tremendous release of energy in the form of electromagnetic radiation and high-energy particles. We can capture that energy to produce electricity, heat for industrial processes, and many other advanced applications, such as rocket propulsion.

In the most basic terms, for two nuclei to get close enough to fuse, they must overcome the Coulomb barrier, created by the tendency of two similarly-charged particles (in this case, the positively charged nuclei) to repel one another. This requires a tremendous input of energy. A successful, energy-producing fusion reaction—one which yields more energy than was required to bring it about—requires that the fuel is confined at a high enough density and temperature, and for a sufficient time, such that the energy being given off heats the fuel without further external input. In the process of trying to make this happen, plasma instabilities and other surprising behaviors of the fusion fuel have disobeyed our mathematical formulas, and challenged our assumptions about the characteristics of matter and energy.

Today, stunning new breakthroughs are being made by the impressive fusion efforts which have been developed around the world (**Figure 9**). If a vigorous crash program of international cooperation were initiated within a new win-win paradigm, we could finally bring to fruition what the old paradigm had placed "always 50 years away."

Leadership in the EAST

China, which began its fusion program in the 1970s, has developed one of the world's only tokamaks (a type of fusion machine) using advanced superconducting magnets, the Experimental Advanced

Figure 9

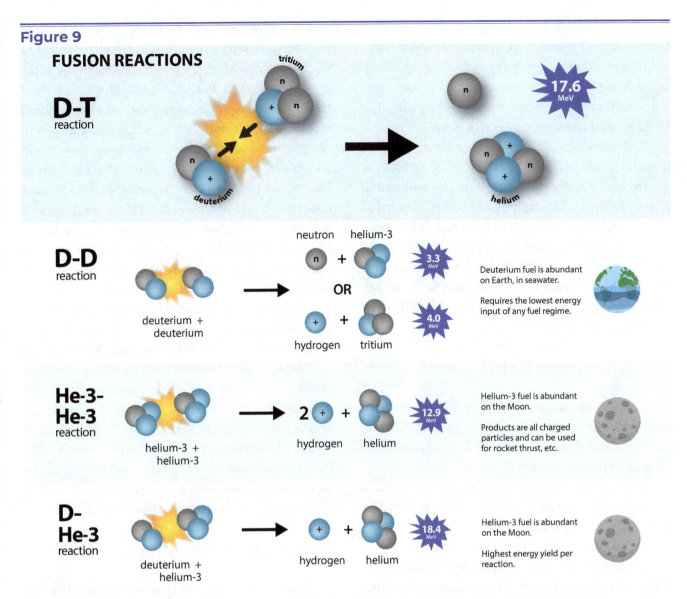

FUSION REACTIONS

Superconducting Tokamak (EAST) housed at the Institute of Plasma Physics in Hefei. China is the only nation today which is increasing its domestic fusion budget, and it has the intention of graduating 1,000 fusion scientists by 2020 (there are currently more than 350 Master's and Ph.D. students studying fusion in Chinese universities).

In February 2016, it was announced that with recent upgrades, scientists were able to maintain a plasma in the EAST tokamak at 50 million degrees (over twice the temperature of the Sun's core) for 102 seconds, setting a new record for plasma creation. The goal is to sustain a plasma for 1,000 seconds, at twice the temperature. Professor Luo Guangnan, deputy director of the EAST project, said, "It is a milestone event, a confidence boost for humanity to harness energy from fusion." In November 2016, another record was set, maintaining a plasma of 50 million degrees for 60 seconds in a "high confinement mode," nearly double the previous record.

These advances were not accomplished alone. Scientists in the United States, at General Atomics in San Diego, collaborated with their Chinese colleagues on the experiment, and have even begun operating the tokamak remotely for a "third shift," during the nighttime in China. The cooperation is viewed as very valuable on both sides. "We have made a very good start of international collaboration in fusion research between China and the U.S., and we are very proud to be a pioneer in this field," said Dr. Xianzu Gong, of China's Institute of Plasma Physics.

The recent achievements have bolstered confidence to move forward with the next step toward fusion energy, the Chinese Fusion Engineering Test

Reactor (CFETR), for which approval is expected in China's next Five Year Plan. This facility will be dedicated to solving the remaining engineering challenges, such as the need for new materials, before moving ahead with a demonstration power plant. The CFETR could come online as early as 2025.

Promising work is emerging in other parts of Asia. In December 2016, a record of 70 seconds of plasma high-density mode operation was achieved in Korea's KSTAR tokamak, breaking its prior record of 55 seconds, set in 2015. KSTAR is one of only three advanced superconducting tokamaks in the world (another is Japan's JT-60 SA), and began operation in 2008. Major upgrades over the next few years are intended to allow work that would lead to a demonstration power reactor, KDEMO.

Achievements in the West

Deindustrialization and geopolitics have held back scientific progress for decades in the West, but glimmers of real optimism appear in the fusion laboratories of Europe and the United States.

At the Max Planck Institute for Plasma Physics in Greifswald, Germany, the Wendelstein 7-X, the largest stellarator in the world, went online in 2014. The stellarator is a design for a fusion machine based on a different concept than the more common tokamak, and may avoid many of the plasma instabilities which challenge the basic tokamak designs.

In February 2016, the Wendelstein 7-X began its experimental operation, and in December released a report that the very complicated geometry of its stellarator is accurate to within 1 part in 100,000. In March 2018, new upgrades of five additional "trim" coils, designed to improve the machine's operation, were declared successful. The 2016 analysis of the Wendelstein 7-X stellarator's geometry and the 2018 uprades were completed with collaboration from the U.S. and other fusion programs, all of which show great excitement at what can be learned from this unique approach.

In the United States, fusion work has made experimental breakthroughs in national laboratories and universities despite virtually no funding. On September 30, 2016, the last day of its operation due to budget cuts, the Alcator C-Mod tokamak at the Massachusetts Institute of Technology set a new world record, achieving a plasma pressure (one of the key parameters in an energy-producing fusion reaction) of 2 atmospheres, surpassing its own previous record. The Alcator device, a high-magnetic-field compact tokamak, is of a unique design, and could be readily restarted with restoration of funding. Dale Meade, formerly of Princeton Plasma Physics Laboratory, said of the work, "This is a remarkable achievement that highlights the highly successful Alcator C-Mod program.... The record plasma pressure validates the high-magnetic-field approach as an attractive path to practical fusion energy."

However, breakthroughs continue. In March 2018, scientists at MIT announced new developments in advanced high-temperature supeconducting magnets—four times as strong as those currently in use—with which they (via Commonwealth Fusion Systems) intend to develop a prototype compact fusion reactor within 10 years.Similarly, a division of Lockheed Martin secured a patent in February 2018 for a non-tokamak compact reator, small enough to be mounted on a truck, which would produce 100 MW of electricity. They aim to have a prototype in 2019.

Fusion Is a Space Platform

Fission and fusion power will allow us to live and work in other places in the Solar System, and to transform them in a way that is impossible with chemical power alone (see "Applications of Fusion Plasmas and Technology" at the end of this section).

The process will begin on the Moon, which is a rich depot for fusion fuel. For billions of years, the Sun via the solar wind has been depositing helium-3, an isotope of helium, onto the surface of the Moon, where it is held within the upper layers of the lunar soil. Helium-3 is very rare on Earth, but estimates are that there are 1 million tons of helium-3 on the Moon, enough to power civilization on Earth at current levels of consumption for millions of years.

Helium-3 is an ideal fuel for controlled fusion. Fusion of deuterium and helium-3 releases more energy than any other regime (see Figure 9), and unlike other fuel combinations, the products of the reaction are almost entirely charged particles—which can be controlled with a magnetic field. This means that they can be used to produce electricity directly and efficiently, and also can provide thrust in fusion rockets. With nuclear power we can maintain work and industry through the 2-week lunar nights. Nuclear rockets can power flight to distant bodies like Mars in weeks, as opposed to 8 months with chemical fuels.

With fusion power, we will upshift the human species to one which can extend its existence and activity throughout the inner solar system, and perhaps beyond. Immediately, we have the potential for international cooperation in exploration and development of the Moon and cislunar space. Such a program would involve new discoveries in high-energy physics, biology in the space environment, and fission and fusion power.

China has taken leadership on lunar missions in the past decade, inviting cooperation from other nations, and will soon place a lander and rover on the far side of the Moon. Mankind has never landed on the lunar far side in any way. Its unique geology promises to tell us more about the history of the development of our Solar System than anything we can access on Earth. Setting up a very low frequency radio astronomy observatory there will give us a glimpse into features of the Solar System, Milky Way galaxy, and far distant galaxies which are simply impossible to see from Earth or Earth orbit.

The spinoff technologies generated by expanding human dominion first to cislunar space, then to the orbit of Mars, and then to the entire Solar System, have the ability to lift every nation out of poverty, feed every child, cure diseases, and render the tools and causes of war obsolete. The commitment of space-faring nations to space exploration will be the embodiment of the new paradigm. Human beings are a space-faring species, with a mission to discover and understand who we are as mankind in the universe.

The great German-American space pioneer Krafft Ehricke, designer of upper-stage rockets for America's space program during its great growth, understood that the industrial development of the Moon and beyond is an extraterrestrial imperative (see **Figure 10**).

Ehricke wrote in 1970:

> Space opens new horizons beyond Earth and offers new beginnings in ways we can manage this precious planet. It offers noble aspirations, opportunities for creative action, for bringing the human family closer together and contributing to a better future for all.

Figure 10
The Development of Cislunar Space

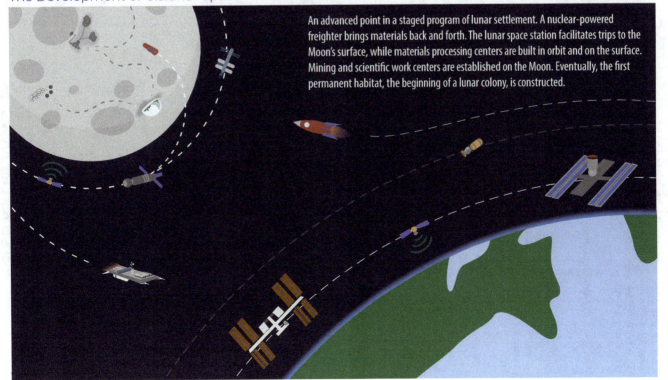

An advanced point in a staged program of lunar settlement. A nuclear-powered freighter brings materials back and forth. The lunar space station facilitates trips to the Moon's surface, while materials processing centers are built in orbit and on the surface. Mining and scientific work centers are established on the Moon. Eventually, the first permanent habitat, the beginning of a lunar colony, is constructed.

TRANSMUTATION

With the high-energy products of fusion reactions, we can transmute elements, manufacturing specific isotopes to serve specific purposes. Short-lived medical isotopes can be manufactured on-site. Isotopically-pure materials such as steels for construction, or diamonds and silicon for industrial purposes, can be stronger or better conductors than isotopically-mixed materials.

medical

construction

industry

for more, visit:
lpac.co/forging-fusion
lpac.co/fusion-torch
lpac.co/world-mine

FUSION TORCH

Plasmas inside fusion reactors reach temperatures of millions of degrees, hot enough to vaporize any material, breaking it down into its constituent elements. In the 1960s, Eastman and Gough developed a design for the fusion torch, in which any feedstock, from material from landfills to scrap metal to dirt, could be turned into plasma, and the constituent elements separated and harvested. We could then mine landfills for our commonly used resources, or easily harvest resources from low-grade ore.

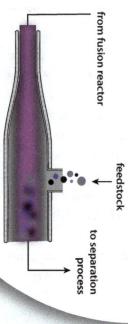
from fusion reactor → feedstock → to separation process

PETAWATT LASER

The petawatt (quadrillion watt) laser, originally developed for laser inertial fusion, is many orders of magnitude more powerful than conventional lasers. When used for industrial purposes, it can vaporize the target material while transferring little to no heat to the surrounding material—a non-linear leap in precision for cutting and machining.

Steel cut with a conventional laser (left) and petawatt laser (right).

FUSION PLASMA

FUSION ROCKETS

Plasma from a fusion reactor source is expelled by a magnetic nozzle to produce thrust. A fusion-powered rocket has a specific impulse nearly 300 times that of chemical rockets. Fusion rockets would make trips to Mars and beyond possible in weeks, rather than months.

magnetic nozzle

CHEMICAL PROCESSING

The industrial processing sector consumes over 30% of energy in the U.S. Controlled fusion reactors can provide 1) high temperature thermal energy, 2) electrical energy, 3) neutron and gamma high energy radiation, all of which can be used for chemical processing on a mass scale. Temperatures up to 3,000°C, plentiful electricity for electrolysis, and gamma and UV radiation can revolutionize or make economical mass production of heavy chemicals, aluminum, ozone, methanol, ultraviolet radiation for sanitation, water, etc.

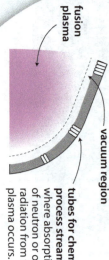
fusion plasma
vacuum region
tubes for chemical process stream where absorption of neutron or other radiation from the plasma occurs.

"The only location for the immediately necessary action which could prevent such an immediate genocide throughout the trans-Atlantic sector of the planet, requires the U.S. Government's now immediate decision to institute four specific, cardinal measures: measures which must be fully consistent with the specific intent of the original U.S. Federal Constitution..."

THE FOUR NEW LAWS TO SAVE THE USA NOW!

Not an Option: An Immediate Necessity

by Lyndon LaRouche

The following policy document was originally authored and published in June 2014. It remains the immediate and indispensable policy necessary to launch an economic recovery of the United States.

The Fact of the Matter

The economy of the United States of America, and also that of the trans-Atlantic political-economic regions of the planet, are now under the immediate, mortal danger of a general, physical-economic, chain-reaction breakdown-crisis of that region of this planet as a whole. The name for that direct breakdown-crisis throughout those indicated regions of the planet, is the presently ongoing introduction of a general "Bail-in" action under the several, or more governments of that region: the effect on those regions, will be comparable to the physical-economic collapse of the post-"World War I" general collapse of the economy of the German Weimar Republic: but, this time, hitting, first, the entirety of the nation-state economies of the trans-Atlantic region, rather than some defeated economies within Europe.

A chain-reaction collapse, to this effect, is already accelerating with an effect on the money-systems of the nations of that region. The present acceleration of a "bail-in" policy throughout the trans-Atlantic region, as underway now, means mass-death suddenly hitting the populations of all nations within that trans-Atlantic region: whether directly, or by "overflow."

The effects of this already prepared action by the monetarist interests of that so-designated region, unless stopped virtually now, will produce, in effect, an accelerating rate of genocide throughout that indicated portion of the planet immediately, but, also, with catastrophic "side effects" of comparable significance in the Eurasian regions.

The Available Remedies

The only location for the immediately necessary action which could prevent such an immediate

V. WITHOUT LAROUCHE'S 'FOUR LAWS,' FINANCIAL CRASH MEANS CHAOS

genocide throughout the trans-Atlantic sector of the planet, requires the U.S. Government's now immediate decision **to institute four specific, cardinal measures: measures which must be fully consistent with the specific intent of the original U.S. Federal Constitution,** as had been specified by U.S. Treasury Secretary Alexander Hamilton while he remained in office:

(1) The immediate re-enactment of the Glass-Steagall law instituted by U.S. President Franklin D. Roosevelt, without modification, as to principle of action.

(2) A return to a system of top-down, and thoroughly defined, National Banking. The actually tested, successful model to be authorized is that which had been instituted, under the direction of the policies of national banking which had been actually, successfully installed under President Abraham Lincoln's superseding authority of a currency created by the Presidency of the United States (e.g. "Greenbacks"), as conducted as *a national banking-and-credit-system placed under the supervision of the Office of the Treasury Secretary of the United States.*

For the present circumstances, all other banking and currency policies, are to be superseded, or, simply, discontinued, as follows. Banks qualifying for operations under this provision, shall be assessed for their proven competence to operate as under the national authority for creating and composing the elements of this essential practice, which had been assigned, as by tradition, to the original office of Secretary of the U.S. Treasury under Alexander Hamilton. This means that the individual states of the United States are under national standards of practice, and, not any among the separate states of our nation.

(3) The purpose of the use of a Federal Credit-system, is to generate high-productivity trends in improvements of employment, with the accompanying intention, to increase the physical-economic productivity, and the standard of living of the persons and households of the United States. The creation of credit for the now urgently needed increase of the relative quality and quantity of productive employment, must be assured, this time, once more, as was done successfully under President Franklin D. Roosevelt, or by like standards of Federal practice used to create a general economic recovery of the nation, per capi-

Lyndon LaRouche

ta, and for rate of net effects in productivity, and by reliance on the essential human principle, which distinguishes the human personality from the systemic characteristics of the lower forms of life: the net rate of increase of the energy-flux density of effective practice. This means intrinsically, a thoroughly scientific, rather than a merely mathematical one, and by the related increase of the effective energy-flux density per capita, and for the human population when considered as a whole. The ceaseless increase of the physical-productivity of employment, accompanied by its benefits for the general welfare, are a principle of Federal law which must be a paramount standard of achievement of the nation and the individual.

(4) Adopt a Fusion-Driver "Crash Program." The essential distinction of man from all lower forms of life, hence, in practice, is that it presents the means for the perfection of the specifically affirmative aims and needs of human individual and social life. Therefore: the subject of man in the process of creation, as an affirmative identification of an affirmative statement of an absolute state of nature, is a permitted form of expression. Principles of nature are either only affirmation, or they could not be affirmatively stated among civilized human minds.

Given the circumstances of the United States, in particular, since the assassinations of President John F. Kennedy, and his brother, Robert, the rapid increase required for even any recovery of the U.S. economy, since that time, requires nothing less than measures taken and executed by President Franklin D. Roosevelt during his actual term in office. The victims of the evil brought upon the United States and its population since the strange death of President Harding, under Presidents Calvin Coolidge and Herbert Hoover (like the terrible effects of the Bush-Cheney and Barack Obama administrations, presently) require remedies comparable to those of President Franklin Roosevelt while he held office.

This means emergency relief measures, including sensible temporary recovery measures, required to stem the tide of death left by the Coolidge-Hoover regimes: measures required to preserve the dignity of what were otherwise the unemployed, while building up the most powerful economic and warfare capabilities assembled under the President Franklin Roosevelt Presidency for as long as he remained alive in office. This meant the mustering of the power of nuclear power, then, and means thermonuclear fusion now. Without that intent and its accomplishment, the population of the United States in particular, faces, now, immediately, the most monstrous disaster in its history to date. In principle, without a Presidency suited to remove and dump the worst effects felt presently, those created presently by the Bush-Cheney and Obama Presidencies, the United States were soon finished, beginning with the mass-death of the U.S. population under the Obama Administration's recent and now accelerated policies of practice.

There are certain policies which are most notably required, on that account, now, as follows:

Vernadsky on Man and Creation

Vladimir Ivanovich Vernadsky's systemic principle of human nature, is a universal principle, which is uniquely specific to the crucial factor of the existence of the human species. For example: "time" and "space" do not actually exist as a set of metrical principles of the Solar system; their admissible employment for purposes of communication is essentially a nominal presumption. Since competent science for today can be expressed only in terms of the unique characteristic of the human species' role within the known aspects of the universe, the human principle is the only true principle known to us for practice: the notions of space and time are merely useful imageries.

Rather:

The essential characteristic of the human species, is its distinction from all other species of living processes: that, as a matter of principle, which is rooted scientifically, for all competent modern science, on the foundations of the principles set forth by Filippo Brunelleschi (the discoverer of the ontological minimum), Nicholas of Cusa (the discovery of the ontological maximum), and the positive discovery by mankind, by Johannes Kepler, of a principle coincident with the perfected Classical human singing scale adopted by Kepler, and the elementary measure of the Solar System within the still larger universe of the Galaxy, and higher orders in the universe.

Or, similarly, later, the modern physical-scientific standard implicit in the argument of Bernhard Riemann, the actual minimum (echoing the principle of Brunelleschi), of Max Planck, the actual maximum of the present maximum, that of Albert Einstein; and, the relatively latest, consequent implications of the definition of human life by Vladimir Ivanovich

Vladimir I. Vernadsky, 1911

Vernadsky. These values are, each relative absolutes of measurement of man's role within the knowledge of the universe.

This set of facts pertains to the inherent fraud of the merely mathematicians and the modernist "musical performers" since the standard of the relevant paragon for music, Johannes Brahms (prior to the degenerates, such as the merely mathematicians, such as David Hilbert and the true model for every modern Satan, such as Bertrand Russell, or Tony Blair).

The knowable measure, in principle, of the difference between man and all among the lower forms of life, is found in what has been usefully regarded as the naturally upward evolution of the human species, in contrast to all other known categories of living species. The standard of measurement of these compared relationships, is that mankind is enabled to evolve upward, and that categorically, by those voluntarily noëtic powers of the human individual will.

Except when mankind appears in a morally and physically degenerate state of behavior, such as within the cultures of the tyrants Zeus, the Roman Empire, and the British empire, presently: all actually sane cultures of mankind, have appeared, this far, in a certain fact of evolutionary progress from the quality of an inferior, to a superior species.

This, when considered in terms of efficient effects, corresponds, within the domain of a living human practice of chemistry, to a form of systemic advances, even now leaps, in the chemical energy-flux density of society's increase of the effective energy-flux-density of scientific and comparable expressions of leaps in progress of the species itself: in short, a universal physical principle of human progress.

The healthy human culture, such as that of Christianity, if they warrant this affirmation of such a devotion, for example, represents a society which is increasing the powers of its productive abilities for progress, to an ever higher level of per-capita existence. The contrary cases, the so-called "zero-growth" scourges, such as the current British empire are, systemically, a true model consistent with the tyrannies of a Zeus, or, a Roman Empire, or a British (better said) "brutish" empire, such as the types, for us in the United States, of the Bush-Cheney and Obama administrations, whose characteristic has been, concordant with that of such frankly Satanic models as that of Rome and the British empire presently, a shrinking human population of the planet, a population being degraded presently in respect to its intellectual and physical productivity, as under those U.S. Presidencies, most recently.

Chemistry: The Yardstick of History

We call it "chemistry." Mankind's progress, as measured rather simply as a species, is expressed typically in the rising power of the principle of human life, over the abilities of animal life generally, and relatively absolute superiority over the powers of non-living processes to achieve within mankind's willful intervention to that intended effect.

Progress exists so only under a continuing, progressive increase of the productive and related powers of the human species. That progress defines the absolute distinction of the human species from all others presently known to us. A government of people based on a policy of "zero-population growth and per capita standard of human life" is a moral, and practical abomination.

Man is mankind's only true measure of the history of our Solar system, and what reposes within it. That is the same thing, as the most honored meaning and endless achievement of the human species, now within nearby Solar space, heading upward to mastery over the Sun and its Solar system, the one discovered (uniquely, as a matter of fact), by Johannes Kepler.

A fusion economy, is the presently urgent next step, and standard, for man's gains of power within the Solar system, and, later, beyond.

VI. MOVING 50 YEARS AHEAD

"...The notion of sovereignty based upon a shared experience, culture, and common decision-making process broadened, such that nations understood their own populations and each other as existing in a shared world of common growth."

2068—A RETROSPECTIVE

On the Fifty Years Since the British Empire Was Defeated and the World Joined the New Paradigm

Looking back from 2068, the next generations will recognize that as the British Empire was defeated and the world joined the New Paradigm in 2018, few could have foreseen how the specific actions taken and specific policies enacted would have effects far beyond the fields those policies seemed to address. The Korean War was brought to a close, a peace treaty was signed between Russia and Japan, and U.S. and trans-Atlantic cooperation with China and Russia eclipsed the anti-Russia and anti-China ravings of the representatives of the dying British system. Engineers, contractors, and millions of workers got to work building new power plants, rail lines, water management systems, and city grids, and an increasing portion of the citizenry rejected being played against each other and against their own best future interests, recognizing instead the shared interests of humanity at large and the historically British origin of the stories seeking to maintain the status quo.

As all of these changes were made and as a great hope for the future was enkindled, only the slightest glimmerings of what these changes would bring were felt, rumbling in the background like distant thunder. Surveying the enormous political and economic changes over the preceding half-century will set the stage for understanding the greatest difference of all, a difference in the outlook of the people themselves, in the quality of their souls. People of 2068 will reflect on their present and look back on the immense change of the past fifty years:

The limited imaginations of the past, hampered by difficult economic conditions and by desires that rarely moved beyond the realm of physical comforts and pleasures, blossomed to encompass the full gamut of human conception. With the new free time afforded by the ten-fold increase in world economic output over the preceding 50 years, 2068 has become an era of music, of poetry, of community and social musical and scientific groups.

In 2068, even as industrial and logistical automation have increased productivity many-fold, the people themselves do not feel like automata. From childhood, people are raised to be creative thinkers, by an educational system that focuses on re-creating great discoveries and on knowing *why* rather than *what*. Upon entry to the workforce at an average age of 25, adults have engaged in laboratory re-creations of the greatest of discoveries (including a working through of Kepler's derivation of the planetary orbits by the age of 15), have acted out scenes from the greatest dramas, and have sung the greatest choral compositions from around the world, both classical works and the beautiful new pieces created in the flood of optimism during the 2020s and 2030s as the realization that progress would be an ongoing condition of mankind settled upon the popular sentiment.

Ending Geopolitics

The most pernicious and infantile of outlooks—that identified with the Zeus against whom Prometheus rebelled, and evolving through a continuity of empire into the British system of geopolitics—was ended in 2018. The puerile worldview that saw others' gains as one's own loss, and maintained its dominance through the promotion of military conflict, was shattered during the decade of the 2010s, with the Belt and Road Initiative of 2013 and the actions by U.S. President Donald Trump in 2018. These actions, a combination of resolving of military conflicts and joining international cooperative initiatives, along with a recognition of the British Empire as the greatest strategic enemy of civilized life, came as a result of decades of relentless organizing by the LaRouche movement, committed to bringing into being a new, world-wide renaissance.

Three-quarters of a century before that great change of 2018, the world had faced a similar opportunity. With the alliance between Russia, China, and the United States near the end of World War II, with Franklin Delano Roosevelt serving as U.S. President, the potential to wipe out colonialism seemed at hand. As the imperial ambitions of Germany and Japan were crushed, why not those of Britain, France, and their junior competitors? Why should Hitler be defeated and the Japanese invaders be driven out, while allowing Britain to maintain an Empire upon which it bragged that the sun would never set? With the unfortunate death of the ailing President Roosevelt, and his replacement by Harry Truman, this opportunity was lost. Instead of building on the victory of World War II, the Cold War was promptly launched. The misvenerated imperialist Winston Churchill, in a speech in Fulton, Missouri announced that an "Iron Curtain" had fallen and that the world was divided by competing powers.

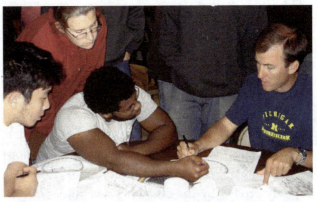

Education is to be based on re-creating the greatest discoveries of the past and present, developing students' insight into how knowledge is created. Pictured: a 2008 LaRouche movement study group working on Johannes Kepler's Astronomia Nova.

With the collapse of the Soviet Union, British cunning had enlisted American might to create a world ruled by a single hegemon: the Anglo-American alliance, along with a tightly controlled Europe. This system was challenged by Russia's recovery as an independent sovereign actor on the world stage and by the meteoric rise of China's economy and global influence. Desperate to prevent a new world of international affairs from taking hold, attempts were made to build alliances to isolate Russia and China, to drive conflict between China and India, and to turn the American people against their own interests, through an attempted coup against their elected president, Donald Trump—a British-launched coup focused in large part on frankly hysterical accusations against Russia.

In 2018, as the world stood on the knife's edge, the swelling current of hope that had shaken governments across Europe and the Americas saw a major victory in the United States. With the absolute discrediting of the plotters of the coup against President Trump, in the wake of their British origin being clearly identified by the LaRouche movement, and with the inspiration of a better future becoming manifest by a greater understanding of China's Belt and Road Initiative and of the physical economic approach championed by the LaRouchePAC, President Trump was freed to pursue his election promise of ending geopolitical war. Inspired by the wide-ranging agreement reached with North Korea, the United States went on to reach a stable relationship with

Russia, finally putting to an end the entirely unnecessary Cold War.

British machinations that had served to maintain conflict within and between colonial victims also fell by the wayside. India and Pakistan, for example, shook off the colonial outlook, as those two nations began joint military operations and initiated more and more cooperative economic development projects. Whatever animosity had existed was entirely eroded by the following several decades of cooperation for the common good, with no military conflicts during that time. Buoyed by the optimism created by these victories for the human species, and terrified by the potential of a financial market collapse—catastrophic if allowed to occur unchecked under the then-current legal framework—the United States Congress voted up reforms required to allow the United States to play a significant positive role in offering unique contributions to the new paradigm of economics spreading across the globe.

Over howls of protest from Wall Street and London, Glass-Steagall banking separation was introduced into the Congress. Predictably, several scandals erupted around relevant Members of Congress—non-stop press coverage of years-old sexual indiscretions maintained for blackmail purposes and publicized at this desperate moment. But the old levers of power seemed no longer to function, no longer to be connected to anything. Glass-Steagall passed! As similar reforms were made across the world, the potential to set a new basis for the financial system was at hand.

Recognizing that there was life after Wall Street, real economic thinking sprang to the fore. Civil engineers testified about the trillions of dollars in investments required to repair broken infrastructure. The more long-sighted scientists and economists spoke of large programs that went far beyond repairs: regional high-speed rail systems, continental water management, and greatly increased funding for the space program and for research into nuclear fusion. Such projects had always made sense, but the funding had never seemed to be available. (Of course, funds were no issue when various trans-Atlantic nations spent the better part of $10 trillion on immoral and shameful wars since 9/11.)

The desire to engage in huge endeavors, economically useful though financially unviable (not generating user or other fees capable of compensating private investors) required a new approach to economics. No longer would the system that made patently useful projects economically impossible be tolerated! Across the world, bills were passed to set up national banks for infrastructure and manufacturing, with the United States accepting the offers made by Chinese and other international investors to help capitalize the bank at a level of $2 trillion. Recognizing that dividends could be paid based on indirect profits to the bank—through a new system of taxation—the United States *as a nation* was finally able to finance great projects in the way that Franklin Roosevelt had during his administration and China had been doing to great effect for the past decade.

Like Glass-Steagall, this legislation was denounced by idiot "experts" who hadn't seen the 2007-2008 crash coming, and a new round of scandals relating to members of the relevant legislatures erupted. But the public, sick of being led by the nose from one immediate scandal or disaster to another, was able, in sufficient numbers, to recognize the longer view and reject the nostrums of these failed economists.

By throwing off the shackles of British economics, the world's economic potential was unleashed, ready to be taken advantage of through policies based on the true origin of economic growth.

Economics

While some infrastructure investments had already been planned and could begin construction almost immediately, the new opportunities associated with a mission for growth meant that planners went into overtime, less afraid to have big dreams and to put them into practice. Over the course of a year, concepts coalesced into designs and then into blueprints. With the "where's the money" problem addressed by the availability of adequate credit, the shortfalls of productive capacity required to make those plans a reality, came to the fore. It was simply not possible, with then-current industrial capabilities, to embark on the construction of the planned regional rail networks, on the model of China's Jing-Ji megaregion.

Industrial leaders were forced to become historians, as they delved into the methods responsible for the success of past explosions of industrial output. The astonishing gear-up for World War II, in which captains of industry offered their services to the government, served as a prime case study. These leaders re-learned the lessons of how, over the period of a single decade, unemployment shrank nearly to zero as output increased dramatically and as seemingly insurmountable production goals were met and surpassed. Liberated by the emergency nature of the mobilization, gains far surpassing anything considered possible under business-as-usual conditions created the materiel needed to win the war, and to assist in the physical rebuilding afterwards. At the close of the war, fully one-half of world output was of U.S. origin.

Drawing on the inspiration of such economic mobilizations in wartime and in peace (such as China's 2010s infrastructure boom), a renaissance of productivity was brought into being. By rejecting and overcoming decades of stupidity, the United States drew the inspiration and focus to achieve the needed industrial build-up to make its infrastructure renaissance possible. Millions of tons of steel and aluminum, thousands of power plants, millions of rail cars and engines, enormous quantities of cement, glass, wiring, rail—these were all required to build the needed network of high-speed rail, provide the needed power for a growing economy, and enable capital orders across industry to be realized.

As the renaissance began, a large portion (nearly two-thirds) of increased industrial output went not into residential or commercial consumption, but rather into infrastructure itself. Over the succeeding decades, new industrial technologies, made possible by the dramatically increased availability of power and materials, increased by an order of magnitude the output that could be produced per operative. Metal-on-metal machining was increasingly replaced by laser, particle beam, and plasma processing. Advancements in additive manufacturing changed the nature of industrial design itself, making it possible to produce high-strength components that before had to be created by a process of subtractive machining.

Former colonial nations began to recover from the colonial legacy. In Africa, for example, the African Union's plans for continental transportation connectivity and a growing space presence were achieved, as the economic and population growth rates on this continent led the world in the ensuing two generations after 2018. By 2068, the image of Africa as a forgotten continent, to be perpetually enmired in poverty, seemed as absurd as the only slightly older characterization of China as a nation of poor peasants.

Fusion

By far the greatest single achievement of human society over the preceding 50 years was the 2031 development of the world's first large-scale helium-3-fueled commercial fusion power plant. Through significant advancements in the space program (discussed below), helium-3 had become a viable lunar export, and the benefits of this unique fuel were rapidly achieved. This fuel's aneutronic reactions with readily available deuterium produced only charged particles, allowing power generation to finally free itself from converting heat into energy—as even the advanced thorium nuclear fission plants did. This not only doubled the plants' already enormous energy output, but radically simplified their design, dramatically reducing the physical cost of constructing and maintaining them.

Because all human economic activity depends on increasing the supply and concentration of energy, the benefits of fusion were manifold and widespread in a way that surprised even those promoting the research project. A fundamentally new relationship to materials emerged: Ocean water could be desalinated on a large scale, dramatically increasing the habitable land area of the planet by reducing the areas of unusable desert. Fusion-powered plasma torches made the processing of ores much simpler, finally eliminating the antiquated reliance on carbon-based chemical reactions to process ores into pure metal. The processing of those materials took a major step forward with the more extensive use of lasers in manufacturing.

VI. MOVING 50 YEARS AHEAD

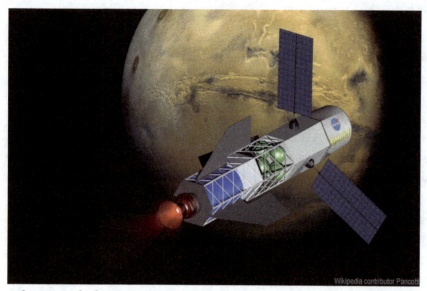

A depiction of a fusion-powered spacecraft departing Mars orbit. With the high energy density of fusion fuel, spacecraft will reach the red planet in nine days, rather than the nine months required for rockets powered by chemical fuels.

Some more mundane applications that would have seemed like wasteful extravagances a few decades earlier became commonplace improvements to the quality of life. Heated sidewalks and streets cut down on traffic accidents and pedestrian injuries in winter, and homes and businesses were kept at comfortable temperatures without worrying about energy use.

Our relationship to space was fundamentally transformed. Rather than trying to use pitifully weak chemical rocket engines to send spacecraft to other parts of the Solar System (a practice that seems as antique in 2068 as using a team of oxen to plow a field seemed in 1968), fusion engines could be fired for the duration of the flight, in contrast to the chemical rockets whose poor fuel density allowed their use only at take-off and upon arrival. This brought Mars into the neighborhood of the Earth, with a travel time of only a week or two, rather than the 9 months required for chemical rockets.

The social effects of developing fusion were possibly the most significant benefits. Energy, which had been, on the one hand, a fundamental limitation to development, as well as a maligned cause of purportedly catastrophic global warming, had become a plentiful resource, much as food had become in almost the entire world by 2023. While energy use had previously been considered almost a sinful activity, its availability was now a source of pride and a feeling of accomplishment for all people. With energy poverty eliminated, so many other problems fell by the wayside.

Space

By 2068, although the Earth would continue to be the home for the vast majority of human individuals, it was no longer as central in the consciousness of the human species. The development of fusion rockets meant that voyages to outer planets had become more routine than were flights to the moon a century earlier. After a few unsuccessful trials, a small fleet of autonomous helium-3 extraction machines were deployed to the moon to recover this valuable isotope, so essential for the modern forms of fusion. The human base on Mars had reached a necessary degree of self-sufficiency to require only the import of helium-3 and a few rare earth metals that were particularly hard to come across on the red planet. Otherwise, the scientific base (open for adventurous and well-trained tourists as well) was able to satisfy its physical needs with resources available on that planet, thanks to the processing capability of the fusion-powered plasma torch, serving as a sort of universal machine capable of processing all materials.

Great advances in space science captured the imagination of humans on whichever heavenly body they resided. The radio astronomy telescope network on the far side of the moon, established through a growing international consortium of space-faring nations, had already helped advance new hypotheses for such stubborn problems as the galaxy rotation curve, resulting in a truly new understanding that supplanted the previous "dark matter" hypothesis. Potentially threatening asteroids had been located and their orbits determined to an accuracy of over 99% by 2032, when the fusion-powered interceptor rockets were available to counter any potential threat to the planet. Around the world, Departments of Defense were greatly scaled back, and had shifted much of their attention to space. Exciting new discoveries were in the news every year or two, resulting in unexpected applied technological advancements that pleasantly surprised economic planners and industrialists.

Health

In addition to developing a greater mastery over the reaches of nearby planetary space, a voyage into the very small was undertaken as well, made possible by transferring the rejection of materialism in political affairs to an openness to new principles in biology. The assumption that all of biology would invariably be fully explained by chemical processes gave way to research into simply biological principles. Insights gained from a renewed study of the evolution of life allowed for the improvement of forms of life and of human health. As the antibiotic revolution began to show diminishing returns, a revolution in treating viruses was achieved, with a healthcare system capable of delivering truly personalized medications, such as synthetic antibodies, developed within hours by a computer and a synthesizing system, rather than by the body over a period of days. Individual viruses could be treated specifically, and HIV, hepatitis, and even the flu and common cold were finally overcome! Cancer, too, was finally understood on a holistic basis; breakthroughs in the understanding of the functioning of tissues and organisms as a whole allowed cancer to be treated in the context of its variance from healthy biology, and the primitively barbaric chemotherapy treatments of the early 2000s were almost unheard of by the early 2040s.

Health increased dramatically by a variety of causes. Some were very direct: a better understanding of diet and the wealth necessary for healthy eating, and the ample free time that the more productive economy afforded for exercise. But a major factor was the intense optimism and *joie de vivre* that had taken over humanity. The prevalence of many patterns of thought and affect previously treated as mental illnesses decreased markedly as the outer world provided ample reasons for optimism and happiness. The exciting variety of career opportunities took much of the worry out of life, and the anomie of working day after day performing unrewarding, mind-deadening labor. Surrounded by opportunities to take in (and participate in) beautiful works of culture, the inner health of people was leaps beyond what it was at the opening of the 21st Century. Happiness, pure and simple (yet also developed and refined), was as potent a medicine as many of the new developments in the treatment of disease.

Personal Relations

A new feeling of unity and shared brotherhood took increasing hold over the planet. With the shared experiences of creativity afforded by the excellent new educational system and the tackling of such common human problems as poverty, disease, and threats from space, human beings had an arsenal of experience of the common creativity and value of all human individuals. Eradicating poverty and developing a growing culture led to the nearly complete elimination of violent crime. Incarceration rates plummeted as healthy cultural traits grew and optimistic futures beckoned, and as people were increasingly seen as necessary (rather than a burden). Trust and a general feeling of friendship increased, and sociologists measured distress and anxiety as decreasing and as shifting in their source. Rather than hunger, concerns for safety, or the ravages of violent conflict, the greatest sources of worry were in the treatment of complex diseases, resolution of difficult scientific problems, and even the stress of choosing from among numerous excellent career opportunities.

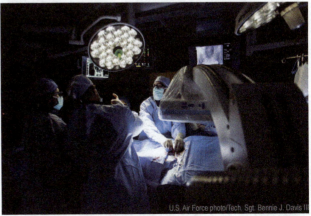

Traditional surgical medical care will be supplemented by health treatments based on creation of personalized medicines capable of addressing viruses and genetic issues.

VI. MOVING 50 YEARS AHEAD

In the musically literate culture of the future, choral societies and orchestras will be a common way for people to spend time together. Pictured: the chorus about to perform at a June 2017 celebration of musician Sylvia Olden Lee at Carnegie Hall.

While environmental conditions became excellent, with swimmable rivers, breathable air, and enjoyable hikes in parks, the anti-human thrust of "environmentalism"—the view that any changes made by human beings are inherently bad—had entirely vanished, and with it, the burden of feeling like a plague upon the planet. Freed from the foolish idea that creativity and industry were forms of "original sin," people were free to love unreservedly their human nature, free to recognize in every newborn infant a limitless potential to do good and to create new kinds of joy for the entire human race

Relations among nations changed as well. Although nations still existed, the notion of sovereignty based upon a shared experience, culture, and common decision-making process broadened, such that nations understood their own populations and each other as existing in a shared world of common growth. Some "sovereignty" issues that had plagued earlier eras (such as the Senkaku-Diaoyu Islands) were simply sidestepped through programs for joint development. The opportunities of space endeavors also demanded a reconceptualization of sovereignty and nationhood. A dialogue among the world's civilizations had developed as a matter of course—going far beyond the exchanges of food, culture, and traditional habits of the past—to a dialogue of shared effort to resolve problems and create opportunities common to all human beings.

Through it all, mankind had developed a superior recognition of its beauty and of its essential, shared, creative nature. Death held no threat to such people, confident, while alive, in their own immortality. In 2068, life itself has become a celebration of the ongoing discovery of just how wonderful humanity is!

"The Silk Road initiative, extended through the World Land-Bridge, will create economic wellbeing and restore dignity to all mankind. It lays the basis for the greatest great project humanity will pursue over the next 50 years—the exploration of space."

Earth's Next 50 Years
THE SPACE SILK ROAD

It will take two generations, and a mobilization of all nations, to bring all of humanity up to a standard of living that allows each world citizen to lead a productive life and fulfill their potential to make contributions to society. The near-term focus and deployment of resources will be on lifting up people in "Third World" nations who have suffered human deprivation under centuries of imperialist rule and financial dictatorship, and populations that are suffering the effects of man-made and natural disasters, to a productive standard of living.

As we are rebuilding the economy of Earth, through the Chinese-initiated Belt and Road infrastructure programs, under the overall global umbrella of the World Land-Bridge, mankind will be getting ready to reach out past the Earth and open a new age of scientific discovery. The Renaissance created the first Age of Exploration, leading to the discovery of the New World. The scientific and technological revolution under President Kennedy's Apollo program to conquer deep space, opened the Second Age of Exploration. Within the next 50 years, mankind will be ready to tackle profound questions in science and philosophy that only leaving the Earth will allow. That future will

The World Land-Bridge will bring light and a productive standard of living to all of the presently dark regions of the globe. Here, global electricity use can be seen from space.

depend upon creating what Chinese President Xi Jinping has called a "community of the shared future for mankind."

Few thinkers are able to "see" a half century into the future. Economist Lyndon LaRouche has created the theoretical framework with which to evaluate what policies were successful in the past, and what must be changed in the present, in order to proceed into the future. His concept of relative potential population density is the measuring stick by which

Left: Lyndon LaRouche, receiving a globe of Mars, for his 90th birthday. Right: Space visionary Krafft Ehricke saw space exploration, not as a program, but as an "Extraterrestrial Imperative."

to evaluate whether a society is progressing. If society is creating the scientific breakthroughs that introduce new technologies into the economy, it will support a growing, increasingly productive population. LaRouche has located space exploration as a fundamental science driver to unleash the creative potential of mankind, and develop the new technology platforms that will create the future.

German-American visionary, Krafft Ehricke, who made fundamental contributions to space science, technology, and engineering, also looked into the future. And he also believed that it is space exploration which is mankind's most challenging mission. What did Krafft Ehricke "see" over the next 50 years?

Earth's 'Seventh Continent'

Fifty years from now, mankind, no longer tied to the Earth, will have integrated the Moon into the Earth's economy, creating a "Seventh Continent," as Ehricke described it. With the availability of resources and manufacturing facilities in Earth orbit and on the Moon, mankind will have the potential to strike out on his own, not just by visiting and settling other planets, but also, by exercising his freedom, adding new planets to our Solar system. These "androcells" will travel freely around the Sun, able to explore all of the unique bodies in our neighborhood. Also called "planetellas," these will be city-states, developing their own independent cultures, and creating a "plurality of human civilizations." The androcells, Ehricke explained, would be "spun off" from the mother planet, and create a civilization that "is truly three-dimensional." It is "mobile, and seeks other resources, beyond the Earth-Moon system." The politically-independent city-state, will be "trading with the Earth, Moon, orbiting manufacturing facilities, and other places, forming new cultural cells of a mankind whose choice of living in space has increased tremendously, thereby adding to the plurality of human civilization." Finally, man would have cut the umbilical cord to Earth.

This three-dimensional civilization, Ehricke proposed, is not limited to our neighborhood in space, but is a precondition to future interstellar flight, particularly to "stellar migration and interstellar or galactic nomadism," a new "theater of action" even beyond our Solar system. The future is limitless.

The creation of these man-made planets, Ehricke proposed, would be preceded by the construction of a city in Earth orbit, which he called "astropolis." This city will be not only a way-station to points further out, and where the androcells will be constructed, but also will be truly a city in space, with microgravity medical treatment facilities, a university, agriculture, manufacturing, recreation, and a view of the Earth to be enjoyed by tourists and visitors, as people learn to live and work in space. Astropolis will be the port-of-call for products arriving from the Moon. Some cargo will be transferred to spacecraft headed to Mars, and some, to spacecraft delivering goods to

In the next 50 years, mankind will create whole new planets, or androcells, that can orbit the Sun, or roam among the planets.

Earth. "It is part of an era when space tourism, manufacturing based on lunar metals, and professional careers spent in space have become as much a matter of routine, as are traveling the oceans of Earth, intercontinental flights, and working or living anywhere on Earth to us," said Ehricke.

Coincident with the building of large-scale Earth-orbiting infrastructure, such as astropolis, smaller, specialized stations; unmanned manufacturing facilities; and the entire array of satellites for Earth applications, mankind would be embarked on a multi-decade project for the industrial development of the Moon. How fortunate we are, Ehricke stressed, that we have a heavenly body so close to Earth, just a couple of days' travel away, that is rich in minerals, water ice, and other resources, not the least valuable of which is the rare isotope of helium-3, which will fuel fusion reactors propelling spaceships, and powering the economy on the Earth, and on the Moon and the planets.

Krafft Ehricke created a detailed engineering design for lunar industrialization, based on the deployment in the near term of nuclear fission technologies, for the processing of mined material and the propulsion of huge cargo freighters between lunar and Earth orbits. Underground caverns would function as huge "atomic ovens" heated by nuclear fission explosions, to separate the soil into its constituent elements.

The thousands of people working on the Moon, will live in a city Ehricke called Selenopolis. He described it as a "fully developed lunar world with a large population underwritten by industry." Fusion energy would power Selenopolis, which would enable the city on the Moon to re-create the variety of climates that we have on Earth, and the mining, processing, manufacturing, and agriculture that makes the city self-sufficient. Selenopolis will, over time, become virtually independent from Earth, and Ehricke believed that it would develop its own culture, form of government, and a new civilization, with a population that considers the Moon, and not the Earth, "home."

The Extraterrestrial Imperative

But for this grand vision of the future of mankind to be realized, it will require dramatic changes in today's culture, values, education, philosophical outlook, and economic policy. Krafft Ehricke made that point in stark relief in a chart he developed in 1970, to accompany his explanation of the Extraterrestrial Imperative. The chart makes dramatically clear the consequences of the increasingly "popular" proposition that there are "limits to growth."

That is true, Ehricke explained, only if mankind is bound inextricably to the Earth, with no scientific advancement. Such a "closed world," with "limits to growth," is the practical expression of a no-growth ideology and anti-technology world view, which Ehricke saw leads to economic stagnation and regression, geopolitical and power politics, and regional chauvinism, which will ultimately lead, Ehricke warned decades ago, to extreme poverty, mass starvation, epidemics, revolutions, ecological crises, and wars.

The "open world," which is created through mankind's exercise of his power of reason through extraterrestrialization, is based upon growth, which is fostered by increases in productivity through science and technology. The extraterrestrial world view promotes international cooperation, and preserves human growth potential. These are the choices faced by mankind.

Nearly 50 years ago, Krafft Ehricke could see humanity at the branching point that we are witnessing today, and proposed that the great challenge of exploring space provides the "open world" extraterrestrial path. At the same time, Lyndon LaRouche, recognizing these threats to mankind, proposed a series of great economic development projects to reintroduce the long-buried American System of economics, based on the mobilization of the creative capabilities of man. These projects, through the New Silk Road, encompassed by the World Land-Bridge, now, after half a century, bring humanity the tools and long-term commitment to make these plans a reality.

Krafft Ehricke's lunar "settlement" will be a lunar city, Selenopolis, powered by fusion reactors, seen here under construction.

LaRouche and Ehricke shared the passionate belief that it is not for individual gain that we must discard decades of failed and destructive policies, but that each "world citizen," must take moral responsibility for the condition of the rest of humanity. Meeting the challenges of exploring and living in space will require a maturity, where the conflicts, geopolitics, pettiness, and pessimism characteristic of the current crisis are left behind. Krafft Ehricke believed that following the Extraterrestrial Imperative would "open the Age of Reason."

Space Technology for Development

Almost every nation in the world already uses space technology to increase its growth potential. Earth-orbiting satellites have connected nations, regions, cities, and otherwise isolated rural communities through telecommunications, via telephone, television, and access to information. Satellite-based communications have brought teachers to isolated rural areas, through long-distance learning, and brought medical attention where there are no medical professionals, through tele-medicine. Earth remote sensing satellites, using the unique vantage point from space, have revolutionized our ability to understand and develop our planet. Governments, industries, scientists, and farmers use data from satellites for monitoring the health of crops and tracking plant disease, measuring Winter snowfall and expected Spring melt, developing a planetary water inventory, locating underground water resources, tracking the conditions that forewarn of the spread of human diseases, locating caches of raw materials, and dozens of other applications.

Newly-developing nations begin their application of space technology by taking advantage of what the industrial countries make available, buying communication services and remote sensing images, and training their own engineers to manage such programs. But because Earth images and data cost up to tens of thousands of dollars, the next step is to buy a satellite from one of the global vendors, and own the services outright. This allows the spacecraft's operations to be maximized for the specific needs of a nation.

Satellite communications are critical to Indonesia, for example, with its 17,000 islands. In July 2017, Indonesia, where the Internet is available to only 20% of the population, has ordered two communications satellites from China. As part of the contract, Indonesian students will go to China to learn about space technology.

India has led the world in an extensive program to develop space technology for Earth applications. The GSAT-19 communications spacecraft is seen here undergoing the testing of its solar arrays.

Recently, the appearance on the space scene of cubesats, or relatively inexpensive tiny satellites, typically weighing not more than 10 pounds, has made it possible for students to take the first steps to gain spacecraft engineering and operations skills, at very minimal levels of investment. Often the tiny spacecraft are developed in groups, with the assistance of experienced industrial and scientific partners. One such project for non-space-faring nations, supported by Japan, is the "BIRDS" project. Students from Ghana, Mongolia, Bangladesh, and Japan are learning how to design, assemble, test, and operate cubesats, which will be deployed into Earth orbit from the International Space Station. Students from Nigeria, Thailand, and Taiwan are also participating.

When the skilled cadre and the appropriate high-technology manufacturing capability have been created, often with assistance from space-faring nations, engineers and technologists are ready to design their own satellites. With the nation having ownership, the service is "free" for the government and the citizens. The satellite can be operated such that it is of maximum benefit to the specific needs of the nation.

While it costs tens of millions of dollars for a country to build its own satellite, and a like amount to have it launched, it is still economically beneficial to do so. In 2011, at an international space symposium held in Cape Town, South Africa, it was reported that the cost of buying three satellite images of a country could cost as much as $40,000. One head of an African space agency described the process of paying foreign companies for urgently-needed images, as "capital flight." Such costs are contributing to more and more nations developing the capability to design, test, and build their own Earth-orbiting satellites.

But the large-scale infrastructure projects along the Silk Road and extending across the globe through the World Land-Bridge, will require an upshift, a quantum leap, in space technology, by all of the nations along the route. The projects will not be built by reviving 20th Century techniques, but will require the most advanced, high-precision engineering and industry, to build magnetically levitated trains and small, compact fission reactors, using the most advanced construction and manufacturing techniques. Space research and technology will make contributions to all of the Silk Road's great projects.

The Space Silk Road

Indicative is the role that space technology played in Egypt's recent expansion of the Suez Canal. As summarized in July 2016 by the Space Foundation, Earth remote sensing and other imaging satellites surveyed the area to determine the best route for the expansion of the canal. Radar satellites probed the water, sand, and shore to determine how to solve engineering challenges. The pinpoint accuracy of the U.S. Global Positioning System (GPS) satellite network allowed the construction plan and its progress to be mapped with great precision, guiding people and machines at the site.

The massive scale and extensive characteristics of the great projects, and the fact that they are multi-national, introduces a new necessary regional approach to the building of infrastructure, and the use of space technology to do it.

An instructive example is China's satellite navigation constellation system, BeiDou, which is in the midst of being deployed. The government space policy paper released in December 2016 specified that the Belt and Road countries would be first in line to have access to the BeiDou network, which applications include navigation for ships, mapping and surveying, and locational information for any vehicle that carries a receiver. In November 2017, the 21st and 22nd satellites were added to the constellation. The system currently can serve China and the immediate vicinity, and ten neighboring countries are participating. By 2018, the satellites on station will extend BeiDou's reach to cover all of the Silk Road nations, and when complete, in 2020, BeiDou will be a global system.

The positioning system will play a significant role in Belt and Road projects, including all transportation system modes, power distribution, aviation, mapping routes for rail and road projects, and building new cities. The satellite system has been described as the "digital glue" for the Silk Road's infrastructure projects.

A study presented in 2015, on the economic impact of the similar U.S. GPS satellite network, which only included the impact in the United States, and only on select sectors of the economy, conservatively estimated that in 2013, GPS contributed more than $68 billion to the U.S. economy. Of that, more than $26 billion was from location services for vehicles, $13.7 billion from grain-related precision farming, $11.6 billion from land surveying, and $5 billion from the guidance of earth-moving equipment.

Greatly expanding the delivery of energy resources throughout the Silk Road and World Land-Bridge regions will include the creation of networks of oil and gas pipelines, and some are already under construction. These pipelines traverse isolated regions,

When it is fully deployed, China's Beidou navigation satellite constellation will consist of more than 30 satellites, providing global coverage.

such as deserts, which makes it difficult to monitor potential problems, which can be costly and deadly.

A Dutch company, Orbital Eye, has combined satellite radar images with imagery provided by Google Earth, and can detect and locate the slightest ground movement and other potential threats to the integrity of the pipeline. It has the potential to substantially improve the detection rate of currently-used aerial inspections from helicopters, which pick up only 17% of the potential pipeline hazards.

In April 2016, Pakistan and China announced that a special remote sensing satellite will be launched to monitor the development of the projects of the $46 billion China-Pakistan Economic Corridor. The agreement calls for the Pakistan Remote Sensing Satellite to be launched in 2018.

China has proposed the creation of a "digital Silk Road" to engage international scientific cooperation of Earth observation to provide "digital backing" to the "megaprojects." The proposal was put forward at an international symposium in May 2016, attended by more than 300 experts in Earth observation from more than 40 countries along the Belt and Road. At the meeting, Guo Huadong, of the Chinese Academy of Sciences, explained that the program would provide statistical and environmental information for the Belt and Road, and support project decision making. The digital Silk Road, Guo said, will be scientific, open, and cooperative, and he welcomed more countries, organizations, and scholars to participate. Ge-

NASA's Landsat 8 satellite captured these before and after images of the expansion of Egypt's Suez Canal. The Belt and Road infrastructure projects will similarly benefit from space technologies.

ologists, chemists, geographers, agronomists, water experts, professionals with computer programming and imaging skills, and many more, will be needed by each participating country.

The thousands of miles of new rail and roads planned along the Silk Road will require dozens, if not hundreds, of bridges and tunnels, some of them in difficult terrain. The University of Nottingham in the UK has teamed up with the China Railway Group to develop a satellite-based system to monitor the structural integrity of bridges, from space. The system uses data from GPS positioning satellites, and images from Earth remote sensing satellites. Sensors are placed around the bridge and provide feedback via satellite on the slightest movement and deformation of the structure. At the same time, satellite remote sensing imagery tracks the soil conditions around the bridge, that can warn of critical problems below the surface.

Modern-day natural disasters in developing and "advanced," formerly-industrialized countries, such as the United States, where infrastructure is either in virtual collapse or does not exist, wreak havoc on buildings and infrastructure, notably power and communications, and take lives. For relief operations in Puerto Rico following Hurricane Maria, for example, American Red Cross volunteers relied on satellite communications. Small satellite receiver dishes that could be placed virtually anywhere and are mobile, using standalone power generation to operate when power grids are down, allowed more than 500 volunteers to use satellite phones to communicate with each other and their headquarters.

With a concerted effort, there is no reason why at least every village and community, if not every home, where there is no communications infrastructure, could not have a small satellite dish, to connect them to the outside world, when the land-based infrastructure does not exist or has been disabled.

Presentations at the Asia-Pacific Forum on Sustainable Development Goals, which took place in November 2016, described the Asia-Pacific as "the most disaster-prone region in the world." In 2016, natural disasters accounted for 16,000 fatalities, incurring more than $45.1 billion in direct economic damages. Meteorological satellites have for decades provided early warnings for coming storms, providing a margin of time for preparations. But for earthquakes, which have wiped out entire communities, there have been no warnings. Scientists in China, mindful that along the Silk Road, and in China itself, there are many earthquake-prone regions, are developing a satellite system, called Zhangheng, that they hope will solve scientific questions that lead to a method of providing earthquake warnings in advance. The first satellite is scheduled for launch in 2018.

Scientists have observed that earthquakes are sometimes preceded by electromagnetic disturbances in the earth. These emissions scientists plan to detect from orbit. "We don't really understand the physical mechanism behind these phenomena," says Chen Xiaobin from China's Earthquake Administration's Institute of Geology. Satellite observations could help provide an answer. The satellite constellation will be able to cover the entire globe by 2020, collecting data to study pre-earthquake electromagnetic waves. The proposal for the mission was made in 2009, a year after 70,000 people in Sichuan province were killed in an earthquake.

A commonly asked question, when advancements in space technology are being considered is, "But how much will it cost?" Lyndon LaRouche has often made the point that the U.S. space program costs citizens nothing, not even a penny. Studies on the economic impact of the 1960s Apollo program estimate the return on the nation's investment, in the form of new industries and more advanced and productive technologies, as between 10 and 14 cents on every penny spent. But measuring the benefit to the economy of space exploration in dollars provides only a pale reflection of the true effect.

The most long-lasting contribution of the Apollo program to the U.S. economy, was the enthusiasm and optimism that created a generation of scientists, engineers, and technically qualified individuals, who went on to create advancements in every field of economic activity.

The increase in productivity in the physical economy from applied space technology can be measured in specifics, such as the increased freight-miles per box car on a rail line, with the introduction of computer software developed for rocket launches. But it is more elusive to quantify the benefit of the lives saved, from the earlier detection of breast cancer, using advanced imaging technology, developed so the Hubble Space Telescope could see further back in time. Or the lives saved because hospital intensive care units have heart monitoring systems that were developed for the long-distance monitoring of the health of astronauts in space.

It is not possible to predict in advance what breakthrough technologies will be created by meeting the exploration challenges over the next 50 years, but it is necessary to assert that they will lawfully create leaps in scientific knowledge, and in increased economic productivity.

President Kennedy's Apollo program, to land a man on the Moon and return him safely to the Earth, is often described as a "crash" program. Generally, this is defined as a project done in the fastest possible time, perhaps with an unlimited amount of money. Lyndon LaRouche defines a "crash program" as having a mission with a stated national goal, which increases the rate of introduction into the economy of new technology, bringing society to a new economic platform. By this definition, China has a "crash program" in space exploration.

The Chinese Model for Space Exploration

China is pursuing a space exploration program that is a reflection, and a leading edge, of its overall national policy to create, in the near term, a "moderately prosperous society" driven by innovation. The leadership's vision is for China to become a "knowledge-based society," and a world leader in scientific advancement. China's investment being made in its space program indicates its view of the importance of the role of space exploration toward that goal.

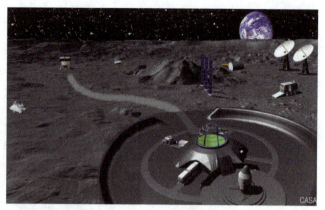

Scientists and engineers in China's space program have created this preliminary conceptual design for a lunar base, which was presented at a conference in Beijing in June 2017.

China's space program proceeds at its own pace. Contrary to popular commentary, it is not in "competition" with its space-faring Asian neighbors, India and Japan. There is no "Asian space race." Being first is not the goal of the effort. Nor is China's goal to repeat what other nations have already accomplished, but to break new ground.

From a relatively late start in civilian space applications, China's leaders decided in the early 1990s to take on a project that would present the greatest challenge to Chinese science and industry—putting a man in space. This, it accomplished in 2003. Since then, a half-dozen astronauts have lived and worked on orbit, in preparation for a space station early in the next decade. China, which under pressure from the United States has been excluded from participation in the International Space Station, has invited other countries, including the United States, to send their astronauts to the Chinese station, or even contribute their own laboratory module for joint scientific studies. The space station will be a platform for studies in microgravity, and a stepping stone to the next great challenge, which is Chinese astronauts living on the Moon.

China is pursuing a multi-step exploration of the Moon with the goal of a manned landing and, eventually, a lunar colony—the first step toward Krafft Ehricke's Selenopolis. The current China Lunar Exploration Program (CLEP) has three phases of increasingly challenging missions: orbit the Moon, land on the Moon, and return samples from the Moon. The first phase was carried out in 2007 and 2010 by the spacecraft Chang'e-1 and Chang'e-2; the second by the Chang'e-3 lunar lander and its rover "Yutu," which made the first soft landing on the Moon by any nation since 1976.

The third and last mission, called Chang'e-5, to return samples, is scheduled for 2019.

The success of China's lunar missions has opened up the opportunity of an additional mission, to take place in 2018. The Chang'e-4 mission will be the first time mankind has landed on the non-Earth-facing, or far side of the Moon. Chang'e-4 is a two-spacecraft mission: The first phase, launched in May 2018, placed a relay satellite in a far-lunar orbit, where it will be able to communicate with both the future lander and Earth. It will relay photos and data from the lander to mission control, and send commands from Earth to the lander. The second phase will be the lander, to be launched at the end of 2018, equipped with an array of scientific instruments and sampling devices—including a very low frequency radio antenna, to detect for the very first time signals from our Solar system and galaxy which cannot be detected from the vicinity of Earth.

It was reported in March 2018 that Chinese scientists are working on designs for a "phase four" of the lunar exploration program. Chang'e-6 would set up a robotic lunar research station. The south pole of the Moon is under consideration as the site. Scientists would plan to land where there is sunlight most of the year, and most likely water. This would be another "first" for China's lunar program, as no national has ever landed at a lunar pole.

The scientific study of the Moon will continue, as China establishes the first manned base on the lunar surface—the first step toward Krafft Ehricke's Selenopolis. In addition to the common resources on the Moon, such as water ice and various minerals and metals, scientists will be most interested in one particular resource: Helium-3. Rare on Earth, helium-3 from the Sun has been collecting on

Selenopolis, seen here in a re-creation of winter, will be built to spread human civilization to a new world. It will create the foundation to then go on to Mars and further reaches in the Solar System.

the lunar surface for eons. This isotope will be the fuel for the fusion economy, with an array of plasma-based technologies, and an industrial revolution that will increase productivity by orders of magnitude—and with the estimated 1 million tons on the Moon, could power human civilization for thousands of years.

In 2020, China plans to send its first mission to Mars. It will, for the first time, aim to orbit Mars, and place a lander and a rover on the surface, all in one mission. Missions to Venus and asteroids are also under consideration. And Chinese space science missions now underway are contributing to mankind's understanding of gravity waves, and the evolution and characteristics of the most energetic bodies in the universe, thus taking concrete steps forward toward Krafft Ehricke's vision of mankind fulfilling its extraterrestrial imperative, and increasingly expanding its dominion over the farthest regions of our Solar system and galaxy.

Each nation has contributions to make to what must be a humanity-wide thrust into the future. The Silk Road initiative, extended through the World Land-Bridge, will create economic wellbeing and restore dignity to all mankind. It lays the basis for the greatest great project humanity will pursue over the next 50 years—the exploration of space.

"The object must be, therefore, not a compromise among differing opinions, but a search for the higher truths, which exist as living words, on which different cultures must converge to a common purpose."

The Dialogue of Eurasian Civilizations

EARTH'S NEXT FIFTY YEARS

by Lyndon H. LaRouche, Jr., December 19, 2004

The full article by Lyndon LaRouche, from which the following excerpts are taken, was published in the January 7, 2005 edition of Executive Intelligence Review, *as well as in LaRouche PAC's March 2005 book,* Earth's Next Fifty Years. *The author's footnotes are excluded from these excerpts, but can be found in the above-mentioned publications.*

This relatively fulsome report is required by the importance and urgency of addressing what has been a poorly understood, but now immediately onrushing threat to civilization as a whole. My purpose here is chiefly to correct a menacing lack of general awareness of certain among the most urgent, and potentially deadly of the practical implications at issue in current, probably failed efforts to conduct a needed dialogue of cultures. That need is indicated by the great likelihood that the effort on behalf of that dialogue would turn out to be a catastrophic failure for mankind today, unless certain relevant, wrong, but presently popular assumptions about that dialogue were pinpointed, and some among those errors corrected by aid of some painstaking attention to detail, as I do here.

Our plan of attack in this report, must be to define the origins and nature of the present mortal threat to civilization on this entire planet, and then provide this critical assessment of the errors and options in the currently attempted use of a dialogue of cultures as an optional remedy for the present threat.

However, participation in this dialogue can not be limited to representatives of that largely failed generation which has played an increasing role, in steering the world and its respective nations into the deadly present, cultural mess produced by developments of the recent four decades. We would fail our purpose unless we also said what needs to be said, specifically, to the presently emerging adult generation, especially those of the age-interval 18-25, to whom we are implicitly entrusting the future of mankind. We must tell this young adult generation all that they need to know, and must always say these things to one another in the hearing of that entire generation of young adults into whose hands we are intending to dump the execution of the solution of this problem now looming before us.

It is, unfortunately, now customary, to attempt to conduct a dialogue of cultures with a certain pref-

Lyndon LaRouche speaks to an international audience in Washington, DC, November 9, 2004.

erence for broad generalities and sentimentalities, an agenda which avoids the controversial concreteness of attention to the who, how, what, when, and where of certain current problematic discussions, discussions which some among us might prefer to avoid, rather than resolve. In this case, excessive attention to courtesy unfortunately often avoids not only issues of "personalities" which need to be faced, but, therefore, for reasons of courtesy, also avoids needed precision in defining concrete, substantive remedies for problems which must be frankly addressed if durable progress is to occur. Concrete remedies, even if they are sometimes also controversial, are what the present situation requires, that urgently. Victory sometimes lies in the direction of a strenuous climb up the hill....

The Present Situation

There is only one way in which the members of any chosen concert of national cultures could each competently assess its own judgment about the kind of future which that concert's currently proposed choice of impulses would bring into being. That duty would be, to track, and to judge the series of those qualitative changes in the world as a whole, by which that concert's own array of impulses would actually tend to foster the new forms of the deadly conflicts which it is our presumed wish to prevent. The question so posed is: With that included consideration in view, how must we judge, and, therefore, amend, any currently proposed concert of opinion?

The task that question implies, would be, for example: to visualize the physical outcome to be expected during an estimated test-period of not less than two generations ahead: from today's birth of the child to the birth of that child's grandchild. In today's circumstances, it were probable that any attempted ecumenical agreement among nations which existing institutions would probably choose at first hand, would tend to include elements which would lead toward a result which today's descendants would have good reason to curse, two or more generations later.

That kind of ironical outcome has been, for example, the record of the attempt to form a League of Nations, which was thoroughly self-discredited in less than one generation, and which even helped greatly to bring on World War II. A similar outcome is to be seen in the work of the United Nations Organization (UNO), which has been much more useful than the League of Nations, even indispensable at some moments, but which, at the present moment, about two generations after its creation, has now, as the case of Iraq today shows, failed awfully its presumed, primary, categorical objectives of nearly sixty years ago.

As an example of the disappointing performance of the UNO, take the example of the mid- to late-1960s decision by the Anglo-American establishment, and others, to plunge into a "post-industrial" utopian future. That decision, for what was proposed as "ecological ecumenicism," which unfolded over the 1964-1981 interval, is what has been the chief cause, the key cultural paradigm used in bringing about, now most immediately, the presently threatened, self-inflicted doom of both the American and European economies. At this moment, the chain-reaction effects of that latter decision now threaten, in and of themselves, to carry the entire planet into a new dark age.

It should be obvious, that that countercultural impulse is also a deadly threat to any effort to define a "dialogue of cultures," by drowning it in what presently threaten to become its own self-inflicted contradictions. However, that is only an exemplary aspect of the larger obstacles to the success which are already internal to presently attempted dialogues of cultures. The general obstacles are chiefly of two types.

First, in general, the mistake contributed to the discussions by, at a minimum, nearly all among the relevant varieties of utopians participating in such attempts, has been, from the outset, that their characteristic assumption was, that the choice of the best agreement would be a kind of minestrone, the fruit of combining an eclectically formed array of "democratic" forms of proposal from each. It would be an agreement which sought to raise the relatively minimal objections from the pre-existing cultural and related presumptions of the others.

Under that inclination toward sophistry which is sometimes called "democracy," the crucial functional issues, the issue of the functional quality of lack of competence of some among the customary cultural impulses of the individual nation, and so forth, was not actually challenged in any efficiently scientific way. If matters are continued in that way, this would tend to become the crafting of a pact struck by the kind of competing lawyers who proceed from no common functional principle of what I shall define, below, in my own choice of argument, as natural law. Under a dialogue of cultures so ordered, the more the conflict is apparently resolved by agreement, the more it reappears in new forms in practice. Today, the common mistake is, to attempt to judge science from the vantage-point of tradition per se, rather than the urgent work of judging tradition, and sorting its good from its evils, sorting these out from the standpoint of a competent science.

The most deadly of the fallacies perpetrated in a misguided approach to a dialogue of cultures, is the notion that religion must be counterposed categorically to science.

That deadly error of assumption, respecting alleged, and, worse, widely believed conflicts between religion and science, is addressed and corrected as a special feature of emphasis in the appropriate places within this report. However, sources of mere confusion aside, the element of pure evil harbored, however inadvertently, in these referenced, inherently erring kinds of advocacy of so-called "democracy," is typified by the depravity characteristic of the existentialist irrationalism of the pro-Nazi Allen Dulles's Congress for Cultural Freedom. Merely typical of the pro-fascist quality of that Congress for Cultural Freedom, is the so-called "Frankfurt School" existentialism of the Nazi philosopher Martin Heidegger and his Jewish Frankfurt School friends Hannah Arendt, Theodor Adorno, et al., who, together with their fellow existentialists, and their allies among the American Family Foundation and its associates, combined their efforts to justify the fascism of the notorious "rat-line" and other Nazi cronies of Dulles et al., in the guise of professing to combat the cultural evils of Communism!

Thus, the effort became an attempt at compromises among cultural groups, which each assumed that a core-set of their current culturally-informed desires was considered self-evidently right. Those so duped into adapting to the Congress's characteristic irrationalism, assumed their respective, conflicting notions of "right" because, in each case, it was presented by them as existing a priori. The worst of the fascist existentialist philosophers, like Nazi Crown Jurist Carl Schmitt's one-time protégé Professor Leo Strauss, and Strauss's followers in today's George W. Bush Administration, adopted the philosophical bestiality of the combined real-life and literary character of Thrasymachus, that the power to rule arbitrarily, is the quality of lawful rightness to be claimed by a usurpatious, tyrannical regime such as Hitler's or President George W. Bush's.

Secondly, we must ask whether the question of whether the proposed result would actually work or not, might have been axiomatically excluded from serious consideration. The exclusion of consideration of this error was made, more or less, on grounds of mutual respect for the other's axiomatic, inherently mutually incoherent sensibilities. It was thus excluded on the ground that such consideration would mean passing judgment "from the outside" upon the relevant value-system of each, or at least some, among the participating parties. The worst aspect of such attempts, was the proposal that the intrinsic incoherence of the principles attributed to the respective cultural-value systems, such as the arbitrary conflict attributed to inhere in the confrontation of European and Asian spiritual values, be treated as a positive principle!

The consequence of such searches for relatively, painlessly unprincipled agreement to disagree on principle, is the result of avoiding the crucial fact, that if something is really a principle, it must be a principle in the same sense we associate the term "principle" with the physical laws of our universe.

In other words, we must understand "principle" in the way the Classical tradition of Plato and of the modern science of Cusa, Kepler, Leibniz, Gauss, and Riemann define scientific method: the way in which V.I. Vernadsky's experimental principle of the Noösphere defines a science appropriate for what must become a new, Eurasian culture. To evade a true principle, or to impose a false one such as the mass-murderous, Olympian "ecology cults" of the recent four decades, incurs efficient penalties for all mankind, as this has been shown in the Apocalyptic results of forty years to date of the influence and practice of such deluded beliefs. World Wars I and II are useful illustrations of the lawful consequences of overlooking that connection....

The greatest folly of known cultures has been the attempt to build the policies and leaderships of nations on a supposed political-cultural consensus, a so-called venerable tradition, as in the case of the continental powers which were leaders in the onset of World War I, when an oncoming crisis would have required reliance upon those kinds of hard truth, contrary to current trends, the kind of truth which exposes the deadly folly represented by an existing culture's currently prevalent cultural norms.

As an animal species is doomed by its genetic heritage, so, like an extinct species, civilizations are doomed by their stubborn clinging to the flaws embedded within relevant kinds of inherited cultural habits. Thus, ironically, often only a revolution in cultural traditions, such as the Benjamin Franklin-led American Revolution of 1776-1789, could have conserved, and did, the most precious of the political and other institutions which the English-speaking world had accumulated up to that time. So, it has been the failure of continental Europe to free itself, in a revolutionary way, from the legacy of parliamentary habits and so-called "independent" central banking systems, which has been, repeatedly, since July 1789, the source of the great tragedies, and spoiled opportunities, which continental Europe has continued to impose upon itself, repeatedly, up to the present day.

In physical science, great Classical artistry, or political statecraft, it is the application of the needed, principled exception, or otherwise known as "revolutionary" exception, such as that of President Franklin Roosevelt's return to the U.S. Constitution, the exception to the error of the currently accepted habit, which is the mark of a nation's achievement of greatness; and, it is the choice of exceptional leadership from among the most exceptional members of those professions, which makes possible the changes upon which not only greatness, but even survival of a culture depends. The beasts are vulnerable to nature's timely condemnation of their continued existence, because those species have a fixed nature; man is not a beast, except when he attempts to imitate the beasts, by adopting the beliefs, such as today's "radical ecology" dogmas, suited to one of those lower species of a culturally fixed set of genetic-like characteristics.

The draft of the Declaration of Independence is presented to Congress.

VI. MOVING 50 YEARS AHEAD

President George W. Bush and Prime Minister Tony Blair of Great Britain, June 28, 2004

It is so in religion, too. Those religious beliefs which set the existence of the Creator essentially outside the universe, a universe defined by them as a fixed set of intended rules of a playing-field, thus commit the blasphemous falsehood of denying the Creator Himself the power of creating changes from within His universe. His real universe is that in which He Himself lives. The fool's hubristic effort, to deny the Creator of the universe this power, thus also degrades the fool who accepts that denial, to adopt the likeness of a beast; he denies the existence of the human individual, the existence of that soul which should outlive that mortal body which it occupies for a bare moment of time. By denying the individual the power, and duty, to contribute willfully to improving the universe which shall outlive his momentary mortal incarnation, we would degrade the individual, in his own estimation, to a beast, and he would then behave as a variety of beast, such as Grand Inquisitor Torquemada—as, we might see again, today, is the frequently manifest result.

The discussion in the form of a "dialogue of cultures" is not only important; it is urgent. However, as history should have taught us, the danger is that the participants might go too far, too quickly, too superficially, in their adoption of attempted, and all too cheaply accepted commonplace assumptions. The danger is that the search for a new compromise, would, like the League of Nations before it, produce a quickly compromised result.

Therefore, I emphasize an outlook which I have expressed in various earlier publications. How should we attempt to estimate, beforehand, why and how no less than those two generations ahead should judge the results of our agreement to act in concert now? The implicit basis for competent foreknowledge of the competence of our choices, lies not in the experience of the past, but the competence of our experience of the future. That is the crucial paradox with which this report challenges the sponsors of any dialogue of cultures; there lies the crucial paradox menacing any attempt to shape a functional quality of common agreement from within a dialogue of cultures. The best rule-of-thumb statement of the solution for the latter, crucial paradox, is V.I. Vernadsky's systemic definition of the Noösphere....

For example: It is only typical of the delusions of many of those approaching the subject of a dialogue of cultures, that, during the immediately past decades, it is the U.S.A., and virtually it alone, which has been popularly denounced as the willful agent of world domination by a body of opinion as silly as it is widespread. For those who actually know the relevant facts about the decision-making processes, that myth is the fruit of a deadly, implicitly suicidal folly by those who seek to explain matters as simply as that.

Contrary to that popular delusion, as it is met even inside as outside the U.S.A. itself, it has been the post-February 1763 hegemony of that Anglo-Dutch Liberal system which presently controls the U.S.A. to a significant extent, as it has done increasingly since the death of President Franklin Roosevelt, and especially since the aftermath of the assassination of President John F. Kennedy which terrified the U.S. population into a state of relative numbness, as the events of September 11, 2001 did, later.

This alien influence is chiefly the Liberal system presently represented abroad by Prime Minister Tony Blair's Liberal-Imperialist Fabian crew, and, notably, by the Margaret Thatcher gang of the same pedigree before it. This is the Anglo-Dutch tLiberal system against which the American War of Independence was fought, but which has fastened itself like a parasite upon the foolish neck of the U.S.A. today, as during the regimes of Harry Truman and Richard Nixon earlier. Long before Truman, that imperial mother of the system of global oppression, the Liberal system, was served by such representatives of the

Confederacy tradition as Theodore Roosevelt, Woodrow Wilson, and, after that, by the epidemic of typically Liberal theft under Wall Street creatures such as Coolidge and Hoover.

The failure to acknowledge that set of connections, would be like the honeymooners' denying the presence of the trumpeting elephant in their marital bed. That kind of denial, in and of itself, could be the most likely cause for the assured tragic failure of any attempted global dialogue of cultures....

1. The Vernadsky Remedy

Competent science, or an actually efficient pursuit of a dialogue of cultures, proceeds always by presuming that the totality of present belief of any national culture, of any body of doctrine, contains a large ration of wrongness.

Therefore, the first principle of science should be, to consider the problem of the systemic falseness within what may be presently even a proudly defended opinion, scientific or other. This means concentrating special attention upon those special kinds of paradoxes which lie at the boundaries of any existing body of generally accepted belief, such as the boundaries separating the abiotic, living, and human cognitive systems of Vernadsky's Noösphere, in their essential character, and respective distinctions as the universal physical systems of which the known universe as a whole is comprised: that as a Riemannian quality of an integrated system.

The permission to employ this method, must not depend upon definite prior indications of any specific wrongness in currently accepted belief. Good health is not only a matter of lack of evident sicknesses, but also of detecting and preventing the existence of a kind of disease which has not yet been recognized by us as the menace it does in fact represent, as had been the case of human retrovirus disorders. This is the method by means of which we are enabled to uncover the existence of wrongness even within what has been unchallenged as generally accepted belief. It is not a mere repair-kit to be called out only when failed opinions have been detected; it is a way of thinking which must supersede all others, on all occasions.

The method of learning from our experience of the future, which I have identified in the introduction to this report, is not new. It is ancient. Notably, it is implicit, for physical science as such, in the method of Sphaerics which the Pythagoreans and Plato, among other ancient Classical Greeks, adduced from the development of astronomy by Egypt. In fact, all competently Classical currents of European scientific thought since that time, have expressed a return to that method, as a choice of means for avoiding the relevant decadent, contrary method of such as the Eleatics, Sophists, and other philosophical reductionists. This is, for example, the method of Kepler, as reflected in his tasking future mathematics to develop the kind of infinitesimal differential calculus actually developed, with unique originality, by Leibniz.

That discovery, successively, by Kepler, Leibniz-Bernoulli, Gauss, and Riemann, et al., is the demonstration of the method by which mankind achieves its discovered forewarnings, and, in this way, a certain type of experienced knowledge of the yet to be experienced future. This depends upon that Classical Greek notion of powers employed by the Pythagoreans, Plato, his Academy, et al., the notion of what we may rightly regard as a universal physical principle. Vernadsky's development of the notions of the Biosphere and Noösphere, is an example of application of the same Classical method of powers.

As I shall show in this report, that viewpoint offers the only trustworthy approach to the subject of a dialogue of cultures. The case of Vernadsky's referenced work provides such a needed point of reference for addressing the challenges of modern political-economy, by attacking those subjects from within the higher standpoint, the domain of the Sublime.

It has been usually demonstrated by all those fundamental discoveries of such powers in science, that the greatest concentration of wrongness is usually disguised as assumptions which the misled representatives of a faulty culture have been inclined to adopt as unshakeable qualities of traditional beliefs, including such as a priori assumptions. The empiricists' Cartesian set of a priori definitions, axioms, and postulates, or the Aristotelean scheme in astronomy of the Roman Empire's hoaxster Claudius Ptolemy, is typical of what is often not only an intellectually fatal error, but an outright fraud. Thus, science must always seek a vantage-point of practical existence in the universe which is located outside the frame of reference within which the suspected error of assumption may lurk, a frame of reference outside the range of the investigator's presently customary belief. For this purpose, in dealing with matters bearing upon the nature of the human individual, and mankind in general, Vernadsky's concept of the Noösphere is an extraordinarily useful, and currently most relevant point of departure for understanding the problems to be recognized and mastered in the times now immediately before us....

Vernadsky's Riemannian definition of the Noösphere presents us with a universe composed as a multiply-connected physical geometry of three experimentally distinguishable qualities of universal physical principle. Each of these three is distinguished by what Riemann points out as the unique quality of experimental method of proof associated with the discovery of any universal physical principle.

On the lowest of the three levels, the so-called inorganic, or pre-biotic, we include those processes whose known experimental proof of elementary existence neither requires, nor permits the assumption of the causative intervention by a principle of life. (We thereby consign the radical positivist opponents of such a conception of life, such as the late John von Neumann of "artificial intelligence" notoriety, to the purely inorganic ash-cans into which they have already pre-located their own existence.) The second, relatively higher level, is that of processes which occur as living processes, as the tradition of Louis Pasteur has defined the experimental approach to achieving this result. The third, is the domain defined by those cognitive processes of the creative (noetic) individual human mind, through which discoveries of universal physical principles, such as Kepler's, occur, and without which such discoveries would never occur.

The domain of combined inorganic and living processes, is the Biosphere. The domain of a Biosphere under the creative reigning power of human cognition, is the Noösphere.

All three domains of action (powers) are multiply-connected in the Riemannian sense of that term. In Vernadsky's biogeochemistry, we apply this view

Vladimir Vernadsky, 1934

to the evolving state of the planet Earth in terms of the planet's composition in terms of changing relative portion of fossils, an arrangement in which one process's waste-product is another process's capital opportunities, and the key to understanding, and mastering the so-called "raw materials" challenge of today. Such is the manifest intention governing the existence of our planet, were its self-development limited to these two terms of reference.

However, then, we intrude upon that scheme, as we, mankind, enter as an increasingly significant player, as from outside and above, in the development of the planet according to that functional arrangement.

There is no raw materials crisis of this planet, on this planet today; there is only a crisis caused by the ignorance of those modern physiocrats who create a raw materials crisis among scientifically illiterate men and women with all too much financial power for their own, or the planet's good.

Against this view, there is no competent objection; the fossils, when examined from Vernadasky's standpoint, prove it so. If no tongue could speak, the fossils will have spoken this to be the truth of the existence of our planet, from its origins to the present time. This is the Creator's expressed intention, so displayed.

The most upsetting feature of Vernadsky's view of such effects, is that it refutes all attempts to account for the human creative powers' role in ways which locate creativity within the kind of brain which belongs only to the Biosphere. On that account, a kind of creeping anxiety grips the individual who begins to grasp the implications of what I have written to this effect, here thus far. For those readers who are most sensitive, a certain uncanny prescience now lurks at this stage of my account.

We, of modern society, tend to think of ourselves as embodying all our essential qualities of life and personality, too, within the bounds of a biological process as such. Yet, as the relationship of the increased accumulation of Vernadsky's higher-ranking class of fossils to human increased power in the universe attests, there is a power, not confined to the domain of the Biosphere, which accounts for all this about our human existence. Something higher impinges upon the biological processes of the living human individual, to produce the effects we must associate with nothing other than the Noösphere. This is precisely what we experience, as in action, in the transmission of an idea, as a living word, through the indicated processes of reanimation of a mark, as bequeathed to us from an ancient Archimedes long since deceased, to be reborn in the mind of a student today.

On reflection on this, it must begin to appear to us, that all of humanity, past, present, and future, is of the character of a pulsating mass of self-development as if in a simultaneity of eternity, a simultaneity expressed as a continuity through the principled processes of reanimation expressed by living words. We are properly consoled at that point in our reflections, because the notion of spiritual actuality so implied is now scientifically clear. As in the case of the real-life, historical Jeanne d'Arc as portrayed by Schiller, the sense of a real basis for the notion of human personal immortality, rather than a childishly fantastic one, shifts the sense of self upward, away from Hamlet's fear of a bourne from which no traveller returns, and thus multiplies greatly the spiritual power of the individual to make his or her contribution to the permanent advancement of both mankind and to whatever still higher purpose a beloved—of the Creator—mankind's existence is intended to serve.

Such, in and of itself, were a great boon to a humanity so perilously burdened today with leaders rendered timid by fears of a mortality more frightening than simple death, leaders, at their usual best, if not otherwise cowardly or corrupt, whose fears of immortality make them Hamlets, or worse....

2. Vernadsky and Physical Economy

I have not proposed that we terminate the existence of money, nor do I intend to so; but, as I have said repeatedly, money is an idiot, which has no sense of what to do with itself, and, left to its own devices, has shown an uncanny impulse for finding the wrong place to go and the wrong thing to do. What I do propose, as the U.S. Federal Constitution originally prescribed, is to take away from all sources but government itself, the power to "create" (to utter) money, and, instead, to hold government accountable for the way in which the issuance and circulation of money in society is regulated. This means, to return to what was known as The American System of political-economy, as indicated by the first U.S. Treasury Secretary, and closest collaborator of President George Washington at that time, the Alexander Hamilton who was also an ally and co-thinker of President Franklin Roosevelt's ancestor Isaac Roosevelt.

The time has now come, when the existing world monetary-financial system is not only bankrupt, but hopelessly so. In and of itself, that is not the cause for gravest worry among those who really understand how the modern world works, or, at the least, how it could work even under these conditions of general bankruptcy. The serious worry should be that of the leader who knows essentially what needs to be done, but thinks, "If what I propose to be this action, is not taken, the results of not taking that action would be catastrophic for the planet as a whole," but then denies that thought almost as soon as it is thought, as Hamlet did in the Third Act soliloquy.

A concert of responsible governments, if they act while my proposed action still exists as an available option for this purpose, will simply put the entire world monetary-financial system, otherwise known as the IMF system, into receivership by governments, and provide a new world monetary-financial system, modelled, chiefly, for the time being, upon the precedents of the original 1944 Bretton Woods system. Those governments, if they are prudent, would maneuver the bankrupt central banking and related institutions in a timely fashion, maneuvering them into roles as wards of the relevant governments. The adopted policy would be to create a state-run credit-and-money system which is efficiently designed to prevent any monetary-financial crisis from triggering a general breakdown of the physical economy of the nations, or causing a breakdown in the essential mechanisms of hard-commodity forms of world trade.

There are numerous special reasons—in other words, proximate influences—why the present global monetary-financial crisis has come upon us in the way, and during the interval of time this has occurred. However, causes and cures are often asymmetrical, as now. The deeper reason for the crisis, is the choice of the system of values under which the world's monetary-financial system has been operating for about four decades. This has been a system of values which has prompted governments and other relevant institutions to use the wrong measuring-rods, the wrong formulas of management, for determining the way in which the economy has, in fact, been managed. Governments have tended to respond to statistical reports, often even wishfully contrived ones, which give indications which are either not relevant to, or even directly contrary to needed actual physical developments and conditions.

For example, there is the case, as in the U.S. now, of reporting an "improvement" in the U.S. economy, at a time that a new increment of physical general collapse in the physical economy has actually occurred, as by a foolishly optimistic reading of monetary-financial data which actually reflect an increase in unpayable indebtedness as an improvement in spendable funds. Or, by shrinking the national economy through shutting down the margin of production on which a stable national balance of accounts depends in a national economy already operating below break-even levels, The latter might be done as what is celebrated as an alleged "economy measure" to improve future national accounts, but not the real economy.

Therefore, it would be foolish to attempt to fix the economy by methods allegedly intended to cause a return to healthy function, when these methods are the same design under which that economy had failed to function successfully under such policies during some time as long as recent decades. It is often that putatively "traditional" system, that set of policies, which foolish governments and others declare that they intend to improve, which is the economic-policy system whose continuation now, in any form, would ensure an early general collapse. In this situation, the only workable solution would require us to scrap that design, and to adopt a new choice of system of values by which to guide the economy's functioning. Today, the needed new system, would not be something modelled on the precedents of recent decades, but, rather, in a large degree, a return to the still earlier set of what had been the relatively successful policies which were operative in western continental Europe, Japan, and the U.S.A., under the original Bretton Woods system at a point taken from about forty years ago, or earlier.

Since the U.S. and world economies did perform rather well under the Bretton Woods system instituted under President Franklin Roosevelt's direction in 1944, and have worked badly since that system was undermined, and then discarded during an interval between 1964 and 1982, a sane incumbent government of the U.S.A., for example, would promptly re-institute virtually all of those protectionist and related regulatory measures which had become terminated U.S. practice during the recent period of nearly four decades. That sudden reversal of the relevant kind of thinking about that policy which has dominated post-1971 legislation and related agreements, would be a change now motivated by presenting those legislators and relevant others who still needed to be convinced, with a clear view of the horror the nation would bring upon itself—thanks to their stubbornness—should they succeed in resisting these urgently needed reforms.

Those are the minimal required measures. That change to a pro-Franklin Roosevelt orientation, would be good, for a beginning; but it would not be adequate by itself. The physical condition of the world has not remained constant during the recent four decades. Our world has undergone crucial changes during the recent half-century, largely changes for the worse. Although the design of more than forty years ago was a good one, it would not be adequate to meet the challenge now immediately before the changed world today. For this reason, we must move in directions which require rethinking our notions of world and national economy in a more advanced way than needed in earlier times; we must now think in ways which correspond to the implications of Vernadsky's conception of a Noösphere.

Roosevelt, Stalin, and Churchill in Tehran, Iran, November 29, 1943

It might be argued by some, that we should introduce what might be the right system at the start, rather than reviving precedents from a successful past period. The point to be made on that issue, is that we should use a return to a relevant, tested, successful, alternative approach from past experience, such as the original Bretton Woods system, an approach which we should never have abandoned, but then, relatively at leisure, and with great care for the future over the long term, develop a thoroughly designed future system of regulation for later installation.

The policy should be, for practical political and other reasons, to act initially on the basis of the best choice of sets of precedent for regulation from a relevant earlier period of successful organizing of an economic recovery, but, then, with leisurely care work through a comprehensive system comprehension of the coherent set of principles which should shape the long-term evolution of regulation for two or more generations yet to come.

As the implications of the current importance of using Vernadsky's concept of the Noösphere for effects on global management of raw materials requirements illustrate a point, in designing the relatively permanent system of economic regulation for the time henceforth, we must recognize that we are entering into the future, into a rather poorly explored territory of long-term economic practice. Decisions which must be made, and some of them involve massive amounts of value committed over decades, will affect the entire systems of real capital formation over generations to come. For the moment at hand, the mission should be to "get started," with the view that the longer-term capital commitments should be developed with that certain thoroughness which regard for the implications of an important error require. Thus, the prospect should be that we undertake preliminary steps toward reconstruction, by adopting an immediate set of previously tested transitional reforms to this effect, with the intent to integrate those present transitional reforms into a more permanent, more long-term system at some point in the foreseeable future.

Provided we adopt that view toward which I have just pointed, certain short-term measures consistent with President Franklin Roosevelt's notions of the Hamiltonian American System of political-economy, can be considered an adequate set of short- to medium-term measures for managing a transition from the Hellish mess of the world system at this moment, to reaching the platform from which the more fundamental, long-term reforms must be launched. This should be the relevant economic perspective of a dialogue of cultures....

Therefore, if the world is going to survive this presently onrushing general monetary-financial breakdown-crisis, it will be because the kinds of reforms I have indicated above are in fact made, and that in a timely fashion. If that does not happen, then we shall have to put the matter of a politically successful dialogue of cultures off the agenda for perhaps two or more generations yet to come. If we do not open up the dialogue to put everything relevant to the outcome, including the hallowed prejudices of this or that constituency, on the table, so to speak, the present civilization will not emerge from the present crisis alive.

If the happier choice occurs as indicated, then, beyond that, there are some extremely interesting reforms in the way in which the world thinks about economy, which will have to occur, and that rather rapidly. In that case, a rational world would adopt Vladimir I. Vernadsky's defining of the Noösphere as the keystone for defining the physical-economic doctrines of management and development of all modern economies. In order to effect the necessary connections combining Vernadsky's contributions, and the structural features of modern political-economy, my own contributions to the founding of a contemporary science of physical economy would be indispensable.

That result would be a shock to many, a shock expressed by the way in which the sheaf of budgetary and other financial reports they might be holding, falls from suddenly trembling hands, to the floor, as if never to rise again.

Jaws drop. Eyes seem to glaze over. This is, indeed, a revolution! Ah, but it is a very good one, and long overdue.

Therefore, let us begin this phase of the discussion with the basics which represent the vantage-point from which to see both the merits of the Franklin Roosevelt approach, and the needed additional transition to what may be fairly identified as a Vernadsky reform of the way in which we must define a long-term view of the future economy of this planet. This use of the work of Vernadsky will prove to be of unique importance in bringing forth the now urgently needed transition from a division between European and Asian cultures, to the emergence of the presently needed true Eurasian culture.

The dialogue of cultures, grounded in an agenda of such considerations, must function as a forum of general reference for developing acceptance for that process of progress toward such an emerging Eurasian culture, progress shared as a mode of policy-shaping dialogue and agreements among sovereign nations.

That said, we now proceed, with the help of reference to the work of Vernadsky, to the most basic, underlying issue of them all: the relevance of the special, rarely understood nature of our human species, its relevance for defining any competent view of the world and national economies today.

On the Road Toward Globalization

If we compare the so-called ecological potential of various species of higher apes, and compare that evidence with a study of the conditions of life for an ape-like species on this planet during the span of the known "ice ages," the planetary potential for a species of higher ape most closely resembling mankind would be in the millions of individuals. Today we have a reported population in excess of six billions, approximately three decimal orders of magnitude greater than a form of man which would apparently approximate the requirements of a higher ape. Whence the difference?

We also have studies of the Earth's human population going back into pre-historic times, with a marked up-shift in the potential population since that Fifteenth-Century Renaissance which rose from the ashes of Europe's Fourteenth-Century New Dark Age. (See **Figure 1**.) Since that Renaissance, especially since the 1648 Treaty of Westphalia, until developments of the recent four decades, there has been an acceleration among otherwise asymmetric demographic patterns of long-term population-increase, and a tendency, coming out of Europe and the Americas, into Asia, for example, for an accompanying improvement in the physical standard of living, and the longevity of the populations.

This data is asymmetric in several respects which are of significance for our present subject of physical economy.

However, the raw data's impact is itself sufficient evidence of a great increase in the potential relative population-density of the human species since the changes in policy associated with the Fifteenth-Century birth of the modern sovereign nation-state, and

Figure 1

Growth of European Population, Population-Density, and Life-Expectancy at Birth (Estimated for 100,000 B.C.–1975 A.D.)

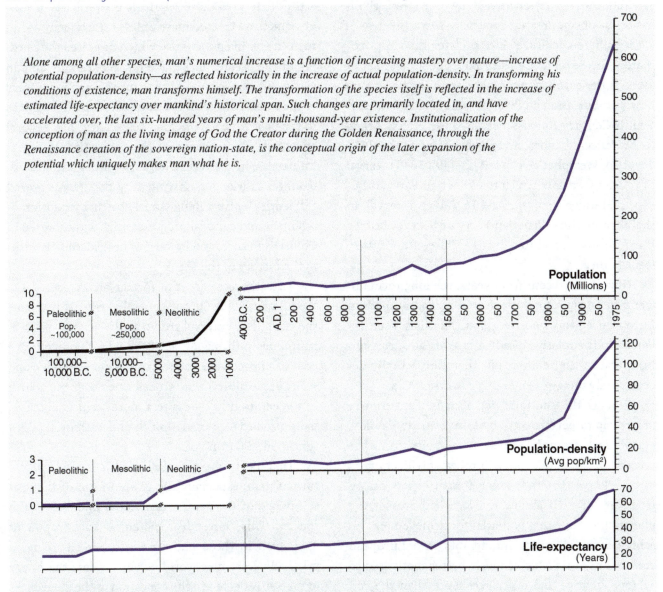

Alone among all other species, man's numerical increase is a function of increasing mastery over nature—increase of potential population-density—as reflected historically in the increase of actual population-density. In transforming his conditions of existence, man transforms himself. The transformation of the species itself is reflected in the increase of estimated life-expectancy over mankind's historical span. Such changes are primarily located in, and have accelerated over, the last six-hundred years of man's multi-thousand-year existence. Institutionalization of the conception of man as the living image of God the Creator during the Golden Renaissance, through the Renaissance creation of the sovereign nation-state, is the conceptual origin of the later expansion of the potential which uniquely makes man what he is.

All charts are based on standard estimates compiled by existing schools of demography. None claim any more precision than the indicative; however, the scaling flattens out what might otherwise be locally, or even temporally, significant variation, reducing all thereby to the set of changes which is significant, independant of the quality of estimates and scaling of the graphs. Sources: For population and population-density, Colin McEvedy and Richard Jones, *Atlas of World Population History*; for life-expectancy, various studies in historical demography.

Note breaks and changes in scales.

the rapid, science-driven changes in productive powers of labor unleashed under the impact of France's so-called dirigist (Colbertiste) policies during the middle of the Seventeenth Century.

Only during the recent forty years, has the long-term trend turned downward, a poorly understood trend which is about to overtake the poorly supported, threatened growth of some parts of the world population rather brutally, that very soon. Whence that long wave of earlier net gain?

When we review the good estimates and other statistical views of the composition of the world's population from as far back as we can trace this with reasonable accuracy, one set of facts respecting the characteristic historic differences between the demography of European and Asian cultures stands out. (See **Figure 2**.) Throughout this time, European civilization has been less populous, by a relatively great margin, than Asian.

Yet, the power expressed by European civilization has been greater, especially since the rise of Classical Greek culture since no later than approximately the Seventh Century B.C. The second set of facts, is the revolutionary increase in the per-capita power of European civilization unleashed by the Fifteenth-Century Renaissance, as these effects began to be reflected more conspicuously since the 1648 Treaty of Westphalia's close of the 1492-1648 interval of religious warfare which the Venetian Party of Europe had unleashed, over the 1492-1648 interval, in the ultramontane Venetian Party's effort to destroy the reforms introduced by the Fifteenth-Century Renaissance.

During the recent forty years, the long-term uptrend in European culture generally, and in modern European culture most emphatically, has been reversed to the relative disadvantage of European culture, and to the relative, but therefore actually deceptive advantage of emerging powers of Asia.

Whence the thus indicated periods of superiority of per-capita performance by European civilization, and whence, from the same vantage-point, came the recent forty-year decline of European civilization?

We know that individual human beings drawn from any of each among the local cultures of the planet show an equal potential for achievement, an achievement in which immigrants into European culture are often conspicuously better motivated to achieve creative and other excellence than the relatively more complacent members of the society which the immigrant has entered. All human beings have the same potential in this respect; the significant differences in potential quality of performance are cultural. The same study shows also that the dragging down of one part of a population drags down the moral level and capacity for net achievement of the relevant culture as a whole.

The root of the relative, long-term historical advantage enjoyed by European culture lies in the radiation of Greek Classical culture, in what historian Friedrich Schiller identifies as the moral and other superiority of the standpoint of the exemplary Classical figure of Solon of Athens, over the morally regrettable, decadent culture of Lycurgus's Sparta.

The core of the issue is to be seen reflected in the attitudes toward those relatively poorer parts of society which are treated more or less categorically as human cattle. Even a culture which practices the herding of the greater mass of the population as human cattle, but whose idea of the nature of man is contrary to the notion of a permanent class of human cattle, as in the post-Lincoln U.S.A. until recently, has a moral advantage which translates, through radiated cultural influences, into a rather large, potential physical advantage, as was demonstrated by the Italy-centered Fifteenth-Century Renaissance, by that explosion of scientific and cultural progress which was centered in Colbert's France, and by various crucial aspects within the history of the U.S.A.

Take the case for the former advantage of the U.S.A., relative to Europe generally, especially during the exemplary interval from the Presidency of Abraham Lincoln through that of Franklin Roosevelt. The poor of Europe who fled to the U.S. for economic and social opportunity, were transformed over the course of a generation or two, into a more fertilely creative, more productive population than had those families remained in Europe.

This has to do, essentially, with the special nature of man, especially the related form of induced self-image of the typical individual member of the society. This portends a potential catastrophe in Asia, even in those nations which are emerging as relatively great new world powers, unless the image of man as reflected in the condition of the great mass of poor, is upgraded from the status of cheap labor, to an intellectually enlightened, creatively innovative mass of the population. This task becomes, obviously, a crucial problem in the context of any global discussion of the matters of a dialogue of cultures.

It is important, therefore, to stress that the disgusting spectacle which European civilization has been making of itself, especially during the recent forty years, is not to the credit of Asia culture, but rather proof of the way in which European civilization has willfully disgraced and degraded itself by tolerating the resurgent global tyranny of the modern form of the Venetian Party.

Figure 2
Population of the World's Regions, 400 B.C.–2000 A.D.
(Millions of People)

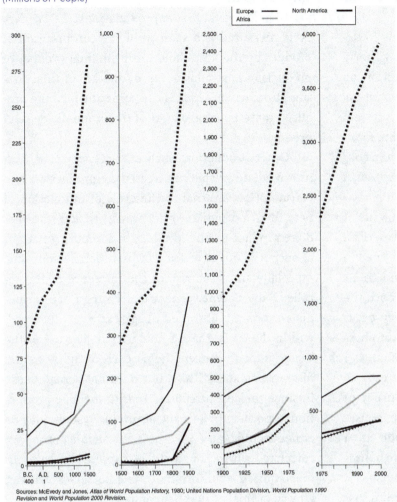

Frankly, the strongest single piece of evidence which could be presented, of the cultural and moral decadence of the U.S. population today, is the fact that that nation could be so collectively shameless as to, apparently, elect, and, worse, accept the election of a George W. Bush, Jr. as President. It has often been said, that those (persons, or nations) whom the gods would destroy, they first make mad.

Globalization is madness. President Bush is, indeed, mad.

Two great issues to be set before any competent dialogue of cultures are expressed by the considerations which I have just summarized. What is the nature of man?

How do we enable societies to purge themselves of that cultural baggage which accepts the degradation of great masses of the population to the relative status of expendable human cattle? These queries, as the Religious Society of Friends might wish to put the point, are also the key for defining the root of that moral depravity of the U.S.A. which is expressed by the presence of George W. Bush, Jr. and his crew in the U.S. Presidency.

Potential Relative Population-Density

How shall we define this factor of culture in a universal way, in a way relevant to all parts of our planet?

Implicitly, Vernadsky answers those questions in essential, if but broad terms. My own discoveries in the science of physical economy, referencing Leibniz's work, of the late 1950s and early 1960s, are an included key to solving the remainder of the questions implicitly posed by Vernadsky's contributions on this matter. I begin with certain essential reflections of my own work. I limit my report on that subject here to a summary description of some bare essentials, focused on the least technologically burdensome considerations which must be taken into account to support insight into the gist of Vernadsky's crucial contributions to the way in which the world economy must be organized and managed at this stage in the evolution of our planet.

The root value which provides the functional basis in my method of physical-economic accounting, does not involve the notion of money as a value taken into consideration for defining the economy as a physical process. Only essential physical values are taken into account as the primary factors in the physical-economic aspects of the cycle as such. Money, which should be created, issued, and controlled by sovereign government, I define, and treat chiefly in its normal role in a healthy form of modern society, as an end-result of physical-economic decisions and related actions of production and distribution within that more or less state-regulated form of organization of a national and world economy known to leading economists such as Hamilton, Friedrich List, and Henry C. Carey, as the American System of political-economy of U.S. Presidents Washington, Abraham Lincoln, Franklin Roosevelt, and some others.

Why waste effort by indulging proposals to design the perpetuation of the presently terminal form of the Anglo-Dutch Liberal form of world system, an essentially outmoded, pro-feudalist money-system, at a time when an entirely different money-system must be created, one premised on the alternate foundation of a physical-economic basis? Why try to convince an ocean liner to fly into geostationary Earth orbit?

I begin this bare outline of essential elements of the physical-economic conception of the American System, with the density of population, as defined in terms of members of family households, and count these as measured per square kilometer of both the total territory available, and as the territory occupied by the relevant residences and of relevant physical activities by members of those households. I compare the consumption required to sustain those households, with the physically efficient output of the labor performed by members of those households. The primary measurements to be made, are a comparison of the output of the work of those households to the level of consumption, by society as a whole, of the same classes of products needed to sustain those households, and also the society in which they live, that in the quality of existence of those modes of production and the expression in produced output, which latter is measured per capita and per square kilometer of relevant territory occupied by these households and the activities associated with their functions in society, and, most emphatically, in the determination of the characteristics of the economic cycle.

The mission (the expressed intention) of the productive cycle must be to increase the net, physically defined productive powers of labor per capita and per square kilometer, while raising the level of life-expectancy within that population. This notion underlies the preliminary phase of the process of conception of a potential relative population-density per capita and per square kilometer. The central notion is that, that quality of existence of the household, which improves the ratio of production to that required increase of consumption, should not fall, but will be improved anti-entropically.

In pedagogical first approximations, the primary cycle measured is a span from the consumption of product by the household until the final product of production is swallowed up by the act of final consumption, which latter is the point at which the produced material is taken out of the economic cycle of production.

Other production, such as that associated with intermediate output, is treated as production and consumption internal to the cycle of production of net "final" output. In other words, to add intermediate product to final product in computing national output is often, at least in part, double-counting, especially since the rise of the influence of the so-called Baby-Boomer generation. The cost of intermediate product is absorbed in aggregate cost incurred, within the cycle, that of final output. The use of the "value added" concept helps correct the potential discrepancy statistically, but does not actually cure it, since the cost attributed to intermediate production, especially in a financial-pricing system, may be either significantly in excess, or significantly less, correlated with what should be supplied to maintain the required equilibrium in technology-driven net growth of final output per capita.

The case of the production of inherently obsolete components, such as buggy-whips for automobiles, is only one example of the various ways in which the relevant error of assumption might be expressed.

It were better to think in physical, rather than monetary terms, of a capital ratio of intermediate product to final product, treating intermediate product, otherwise, as a capital factor of cost in the systemic cycle as a whole. The point is, that cost should be defined in respect to rates of technological progress and related productivity-rate improvements, rather than by methods of financial accounting which are more or less indifferent to these implications. We must avoid accounting methods which tend, unfortunately, to be used as a substitute for the work of serious economic-policy shaping.

In between those two end-points, the production of intermediate values occurs. These include basic economic infrastructure, which is measured approximately in square-kilometer and per-capita terms, and capital of the production cycle itself. These two classes of intermediate product are classed as capital formation, and are measured in years of useful physical life. In first approximation, the proper measurements for capital formation are essentially the following.

We begin with the span from birth to adult or equivalent functional maturity of the newborn member of society. This is the most useful unit of measurement for defining capital cycles, and is itself a capital cycle.

We are concerned to compare the useful physical life of a capital improvement for infrastructure or production with the standard period of investment represented by the development of a child from infancy to economically functional adult maturity. The functional assumption is, that the rate of net increase of the productive powers of labor should correspond to both an improvement in the standard of living within households, and the convergence of the equivalent of a school-leaving age on some optimum, such as, a proper future perspective for the U.S. today, a twenty-five-year-old school-leaving age of a qualified professional.

Overall, against the background just summarized, there are two aspects of the process, as roughly described in that manner, which bear upon what I shall now emphasize about Vernadsky's developed conception of the Noösphere.

One is that kind of improvement of the Biosphere as such which increases the productive potential of an area, as potential may be measured in (human) per-capita and per-square-kilometer terms, rather than other measures.

The second, is the qualitative and quantitative development of that portion of the Noösphere as such, which, in first approximation, is the product of cognitive, rather than biological functions/components of cumulative fossil-formation on the planet.

The general rule already implicit in Vernadsky's own portrait of the subject, is that the rate of increase of useful fossils of the Noösphere should be greater than the rate for fossils of the Biosphere, while the development of the Biosphere, per square kilometer, should be advanced.

The driver of this latter ratio is the cognitive (noetic) powers specific to the human individual. Both rates combined can be expressed as one, when we take into account the fact that the willful improvement of the Biosphere, in per-square-kilometer terms, is a product of increases in productivity which have been generated by man's creative powers.

The foregoing points on economy considered from a physical, rather than a monetary-financial standpoint, converge on a concept which I developed more than a half-century ago, which I named potential relative population-density. The term seemed to me then to be one within the practical reach of industrial engineers or comparable technicians of the productive process, while nonetheless implying the higher standpoint of relevance, a specifically Riemannian view of the process which a productive form of modern economy expresses.

Essentially: given a relevant territory, the potential productivity of the whole population relevant to that territory, as expressed in demographic terms, reflects, on the one hand, the development of the productive process, including the population and its labor-force, as such; but, the level of performance achieved depends upon the development of the territory, including the production facilities and available services, in which this activity occurs.

In the final analysis, this includes mankind's management of all of those physical processes associated with our planet which are relevant to human existence and improvement of the potential relative population-density of mankind on this planet. On this account, this view from a higher standpoint, the condition of human life on this planet today, elevates the work of Vernadsky on the concept of the Noösphere from the more limited domain of selected applications of scientific research, into being, under presently emerging planetary conditions, an indispensably determining feature of any economics practice to be taken seriously by governments and the like today.

The measure of changes which foster the implied result is the anti-entropy of the relevant current policy of practice.

These indicated factors all orbit about a single central question: the nature of man as a cognitive (i.e., noetic) being, as set apart from, and above the beasts.

VI. MOVING 50 YEARS AHEAD

Launch of STS-132 Atlantis *Shuttle, May 14, 2010*

The key is the power of hypothesizing, as defined by Plato's collection of Socratic dialogues. It is to the extent that society is organized around the role of that creative function unique to the human individual, and to the degree that the individual member of society in general is induced to cultivate, and assisted in cultivating and employing that specific creative potential within themselves, that economies may prosper, and the cultural development and improved physical well-being of the people in those societies may be promoted.

Thus, the suppression of the cognitive development within a large ration of the population, as by customary means, results in a reduced capacity for development in the population as a whole, including the relatively more "privileged" strata. The poor may not lose their humanity under such depressed conditions, but they do lose much of their potential development as human beings. The tolerance of such conditions, in the name of traditional values, is the most deadly source of weakness in any culture.

Therefore, the objective of changes in the design of the productive process itself, must be, of course, the effect of the consumption of the product. That granted, the way in which that effect is accomplished, must also mean included emphasis on the development of the human quality of the role of the human being in the productive process.

People who disdain physical labor, for example, tend to underestimate the importance of emphasis of the work-process on fostering, or tendency to dull the cognitive factor in the work and life of the operative.

We shall resume that latter line of discussion, on the role of man's creative powers in an economy studied from the vantage-point of Vernadsky's conception of the Noösphere, after now finishing up another matter about economy which must now be put away. That matter is the functional difference between a monetary system of the medieval type, which is the presently dominant form of the world's monetary-financial system today, and a modern monetary system of the type whose design is unique to the two original Eighteenth-Century constitutions of the U.S.A.

The Modern Money Economy

The gain in productivity which occurs within the bounds of that simplified portrait of a physical economy which I have given above, illustrates the basis for a real form of profit—a form of physical, rather than monetary-financial profit, of which the former may be also termed the margin of social profit which is generated within the terms of what I have described above as a rough sketch of the rudiments of a physical economy. This social profit is distinct from the fictitious form of what is accounted as financial profit, the latter attributed by standard financial-accounting practice to the implicitly feudalist fictions of a monetary-financial system on which contemporary financial-accounting practice presently relies.

There is nothing wrong with good financial accounting, especially if it is also honest. Accounting is clearly necessary in a modern economy, especially one in which high-binders such as the predatory Enron crew ran amok in the wake of the Bush family's dynastic scheming. Within the legitimate practice of that mode of accounting, the trouble usually arises in the guise of those adopted fictions whose existence and effects the credulous or simply inattentive reader overlooks. The qualitatively more serious kind of error arises when some accountants, like Professor Milton Friedman of the late Friedrich von Hayek's frankly pro-Satanic Mont Pelerin cult, parade themselves as economists, when they are only, at their least worst, financial accountants of a sort who rely heavily for their doctrines and proffered conclusions, on knowing actually less than nothing about a real economy.

Nonetheless, we must not permit the accountants, honestly qualified or not, to design the system which they employ for their trade. Rather, the accounting profession must adapt its standards of practice to the mission which the Constitution and the functions of government define as the goals and standards to be applied to the design and maintenance of accounting systems. Therefore, one of today's problems, especially under the lunatic reign of the current U.S. Bush Administration, is that we have presently very few economists qualified to provide the accountants with the mission-oriented standards of practice which the accounting profession should follow. Even those who are qualified can not operate effectively under the current reign of lunacy from the President's Executive Mansion and kindred fonts of influential opinion. Even without the added burden of that addle-headed administration, that problem of attempting to define sane standards for today's accounting practice could not be solved without overturning the rule of the presently reigning monetary-financial system.

As to the origins of today's popular monetary theory, the following point of clarification is most urgent at this time of crisis.

After my original discoveries in a science of physical economy, I engaged for a time in relevant continuing 1950s studies. I tracked the subject of the history of money and financial accounting from the interval of the rise of usury within the bow-tenure system of ancient southern Mesopotamia, through, and beyond the traffic between Mesopotamia and the Hittites, the latter a traffic which providently (for modern scholars) employed cuneiform-tablet systems (rather than perishable parchment documents) as the medium for bills of exchange which could be considered quite modern in intent and use. Against that background in samplings of ancient society, I tracked the emergence of European money systems through channels of development of those practices such as Tyre and the great usury center at the cult of Delphi, into those developments in the Roman system which have been the continuing basis for the origins of most European monetary systems. My interest included the modern forms which appeared since double-entry bookkeeping emerged in modern society from its now inherently anachronistic origins in the feudal practice of the Venetian financier oligarchy, a development which apparently occurred late during the pre-Renaissance medieval, feudal centuries of ultramontane rule.

The need for a tolerable species of money economy operating as an adjunct to a modern physical economy, arises as a by-product of the special nature of man as uniquely a creative species, in which creativity, as Vernadsky defines the noetic principle, is located as a sovereign quality of human individuals. Thus, the transfer of wealth-making in progress through the social process, requires a means by which certain functions within the process can be assisted in the special way associated with the institution of a state-created money-system. The proper function of the general management of money in a modern society, is to regulate the flow of productive activity and consumption in such a way as to foster an optimal rate of that kind of growth which can be generated only through fostering the use and development of the sovereign individual creative powers of individuals. However, to fulfill that function, the generation and flow of money must be regulated, primarily by government, so as to prevent that idiot, money, from running off in lunatic directions on its own inherently inhuman impulse, otherwise to be recognized as a usurer's greed.

The axiomatic quality of evil intrinsic to currently popularized versions of feudal and even more ancient dogmas respecting the idea of money, is the assumption that money has some intrinsic physical, or, at least moral power, a natural right of usury, which should rightly act as a physical principle of the real economy. This notion of money as "filthy lucre," is something to be regarded even as inherently Satanic in nature. Money's bad reputation on this account is warranted by the fact that Mandeville, while a colorfully nasty fellow of obviously bad personal morals, was not off the mark in insisting that money, as defined by the Anglo-Dutch Liberal outgrowth of the Venetian tradition, does depend upon something nasty from outside the real universe, a kind of "Maxwell's demon," suspect as probably from Hell, who, according to Mandeville, von Hayek, Friedman, et al., rewards a nation's promotion of vice with public benefits.

However the function of money, as it should occur in a modern nation-state economy, and in relations among such economies, must be as different from the function of money in ancient and medieval society, or in expressions of the Venetian money-system in modern economies, as men differ from monkeys. There is no intrinsically lawful law which prescribes a certain rate of interest as an inherently usurious, lawful property of money per se....

This means that we must abandon that foolish doctrine, the so-called theory taught as economics in most of our universities and other relevant locations today. We must relieve our political leaders of that alien monetarist succubus now eating at their brains. More important than that, we must free ourselves so that a sane form of economy, or economic policy-shaping, could be achieved through aid of eradicating any controlling system of thought which sought to explain an economy in terms of the free circulation of money by so-called "independent central banking systems" or their like.

The Way to Regulation, Credit, and Capital

I now turn your attention directly to the matters of economic policy-design of policies of general economic regulation, credit, and capital, in and among nations. By no means, are these matters merely peripheral to the subject of a dialogue of cultures. These are matters of life-and-death importance for most of the world's population today.

Keeping the argument to be made as simple as possible: the principle of economic regulation by governments, is, in effect the following:

Begin with the matter of the regulation of prices. In the preliminary statement on this subject now, I refer to the relative money-prices; however, the argument as to principle is based not on the actual money-price, but looks at these problems from the standpoint of a physical price.

Ultimately, after we have made reasonable allowances for needed temporary adjustments during the short- to medium-term, the price of the physical capital required for employment in producing a certain quantity and quality of product, must not fall below a level at which the price of goods corresponds to what is needed, as defined in physical terms, to cover both the continued production of goods, and the maintenance, replacement, and progressive development of the physical capital needed for maintaining and improving that quantity and quality of output over the long term of capital cycles.

This level includes the cost of maintaining households of actual and prospective operatives at cultural standards of physical income consistent with not only the work which they are to be expected to do, but the always rising general cultural level required for the population as a whole. The price of goods themselves must also include the charges to that production for the maintenance of the household of the enterprise's operatives and essential staff, and appropriate support of the government and basic economic infrastructure upon which that operation's enterprises depend.

Those and related considerations determine the base-line for estimation of what has been termed a fair price. Therefore, it would appear to follow from that, that, on principle, if the price is not fair, it is wrong. Over the long term, that must become the intended and realized effect.

However, getting to a quality and quantity of short- to medium-term performance corresponding to the delivery of that intended longer-term result, is not a simple matter. In this connection, there are considerations which the world and its nations individually must now take into account, which may have been touched upon by others, peripherally, before this time, but which are presently of crucial importance, and which must be addressed, as I do now, in a completely fresh way, that in light of the practical implications of Vernadsky's concept of the Noösphere for today's policy-making.

In the long run, any forced reduction of the prices of a nation's product below the fair price level is as insane as it is immoral. But—a rather large but—there are still some qualified kinds of permissible short- to medium-term exceptions, even required exceptions to this rule, during the relatively shorter term. I explain that point by aid of beginning now with a bit of relevant, sometimes curious sidelights, as illustrations from the history of this problem in policy-shaping. After that brief bit of pedagogically useful teasing of the reader's possible prejudices on this subject, to loosen up the discussion in this special topical area, I shall turn our attention to the meat of the matter which I have just described in broad terms. As I shall show summarily here, matters are not quite as simple as even most of the so-called experts were taught to understand: not at all.

Sometimes, nations have been compelled to choose, in what is virtually their own free choice of policy-shaping, to lower the prices paid for their goods, and wages, below fair price levels, as China has been doing, as a policy for the time of approximately the present quarter-century.

This policy of China and some other developing nations, is what a once-famous Soviet economist of the 1920s and early 1930s, Preobrazhensky, called socialist primitive accumulation. In his writings, that meant building up the Soviet industrial development of the 1920s, and perhaps somewhat beyond, through a transfer of part of the physical capital which might be generated, as at then current world prices, within the agricultural sector, as transfers to the industrial sector. This could be done through such devices as relative agricultural prices paid for domestic consumption set below what would have been the calculable relatively fair price level for net payments to the agricultural sector at that time. In China today, it is using cheap labor in China, to produce goods for sale on the world market, in order to accumulate advanced technology as physical capital investments for the China of a generation ahead.

The term primitive accumulation as used by Preobrazhensky, had been used to similar effect by the sanest and most gifted socialist economist of the early Twentieth Century, Rosa Luxemburg. Preobrazhensky used the notion of socialist primitive accumulation to distinguish the motive for such a Soviet policy from the role of primitive accumulation in the practice of imperial financier policy as reported by Luxemburg. Otherwise, the problem he addressed in this way, was neither specifically Soviet, nor peculiar to economies classified, prior to 1989, as nations with socialist constitutions. It is a commonplace challenge, and often a menace, faced by economies of developing nations, even prior to the 1971-1972 radical changes made in the world's monetary system....

There can be no competent study of economy which does not begin with focus of attention on the essential difference between man and beast. That is illustrated by the rise of the human population of our planet from the level of millions possible for the habitation of the planet by a species of higher ape, to the billions of today. This difference is the result of a factor which does not exist in any species inferior to man, that power of hypothesizing which is the foundation for the development of European civilization since Thales, Solon of Athens, and the Pythagoreans, as that power is codified for appreciation through, chiefly, the collection of Plato's dialogues.

The characteristic, corresponding physical feature of the human species' existence, is the increase of the productive powers of labor, per capita and per square kilometer, an increase which does occur, and could only occur through the fruits of hypothesizing as summarily defined by Plato's Socratic dialogues.

In ordinary discussion of economy, a useful approximation of the scientific explanation is met in the discussion of a margin of gain attributable to improved technology. Arguments of that form are often approximately true as rule-of-thumb explanations. It is only when we trace particular technological improvements back to the design of some unique proof-of-principle experimental apparatus, as Riemann defines unique experiments of that significance, that we can locate the place of a technological improvement in a way adequate for representing the relevant theory.

This development occurs within the context of what is already a self-developing universe. From the standpoint of Vernadsky's writings on the subject of the Noösphere, this development appears as self-development of, and interdependent development among the three categorical, but essentially interacting forms of physical existence, known respectively as what are, from the standpoint of crucial-experimental method, the abiotic, biotic, and noetic domains. Each of these three is a developing domain, as the famous aphorism of Heraclitus points out; but their development is also interactive. Man is a willfully self-developing, rather than fixed species (as each and all of the lower species are as a definite species), who exists by interaction with each and all of these three domains.

Modern knowledge shows that, as Heraclitus insists, and as Leibniz defines "the best of all possible worlds": nothing exists in the universe, but a quality of change which is of this anti-entropic quality....

3. A Fixed-Exchange-Rate System

Given, the presently onrushing general breakdown-crisis of the world's monetary financial system, it is not possible that civilization could continue on this planet for much longer, without an immediate return to a system of relatively fixed exchange rates among perfectly sovereign nation-states, a return to a world whose economic affairs would have been organized in a mode akin to the original Bretton Woods system under U.S. President Franklin Roosevelt. The only rational response to that crisis would be a general reorganization-in-bankruptcy of the present system, a reorganization relying upon the principled approach taken by President Franklin Roosevelt in March 1933.

Any dialogue of cultures which does not recognize the indispensable role of that responsive set of arrangements, would become the endorsement of an essentially immediate global catastrophe, that for all humanity, given the onrushing conditions of general breakdown-crisis of the world today. In the absence of the principled type of emergency measures which I have just summarized in the preceding elements of this report, a dialogue of cultures would rapidly degenerate into a minestrone of eclecticism, and the dialogue itself would, therefore, soon virtually go off the agenda of serious efforts in progress....

Therefore, before turning to the concrete features of the needed design of such a fixed-exchange-rate system, we must bring into perspective the unifying, therefore implicitly monotheistic element in the cultural basis for the possibility of a founding and existence of a truly self-subsisting system of sovereign nation-state republics on which a successful design of a dialogue of cultures would ultimately depend.

This means, at least implicitly, that the efficiently sovereign nation-state republic should not, and, under present world conditions, can not rely upon its own autonomous will, as the madmen of the U.S. Bush regime have continued to attempt to do. True sovereignty depends upon the nation's conscious, willful commitment to the common good of all nations and peoples....

That is to say, there is a natural, principled reciprocity between the humanistic notions of culture and economy, a connection rooted in that distinction of man from beast which is expressed by what I have defined, above, the function of "the living word."

Thus, to understand what must happen now, it is essential to recognize that although the institution of the modern sovereign nation-state was established in Europe only a few centuries ago, the requirement of that institution for the modern world, was already embedded as a universal physical principle, in the notion of the original, specific nature of the human being as that of an immortal personality. The fact, that the institution of the sovereign nation-state is to be seen as a very late arrival in the development of our species, reflects nothing as much as that humanity's prolonged earlier sojourn in pathetically childish states of cultural development. Consequently, the underlying challenge of a dialogue of cultures today, is the urgency of bringing the leading layers of influence of humanity as a whole out of the grip of cultural habits which have been regarded as the virtual "childhood diseases" of human culture to date.

The scientific premises for that view, which some will mistakenly regard as a debatable assertion, have already been developed to a significant degree of approximation in earlier portions of this report, especially in treating the notion of "the living word." However, we have now reached the stage in this report, at which the most crucial of the practical implications of this principle are to be made more perfectly clear, even as presented now to an audience including persons who might wish to disagree, even passionately.

The principled key to this requirement of the sovereign nation-state republic, lies, as I have just emphasized this once again, in the intersection of the universal physical principle of cognition by individuals, and the function of what I have identified as the living word, the latter as the medium of communication of ideas of universal physical, and related principles within society. That intersection defines the Noösphere as associated with the argument by Vernadsky.

For the reason of this distinction, although man has the mortal attributes of an animal (a mammal), the human individual's existence, as human rather than bestial, is nonetheless defined by, and depends for its continued existence upon the immortal aspect of man, as expressed by his cognitive powers. Despite the hostility to the idea of the existence of those cognitive powers, which, admittedly, reductionist doctrinaires have passionately denied to exist, the existence of the human species must be defined by us as the view of a human species which is to be placed, functionally, absolutely outside and above the category of animal life. It is the immortal aspect of the life of the human individual, the creative powers of the individual, the soul whose existence is to be comprehended in this light, which sets man apart from all other living species.

Therefore, the form of organization of society which is suited to the requirements of the human individual, and therefore his (or, her) species, is a form organized around the concept of what I have defined, earlier in this report, as the living word.

That is the principled basis for a successful dialogue of cultures....

The object must be, therefore, not a compromise among differing opinions, but a search for the higher truths, which exist as living words, on which different cultures must converge to a common purpose. This point may be restated here, in the following terms.

These ideas may be accessible to the speakers of a different language, or in that speaker's familiarity with a different language-culture, but the way in which they are formulated in the mind of the user finds its necessary basis in the ironies which can be generated in his or her language. However, the ideas which are valid, will be susceptible of being recog-

Russian President Vladamir Putin and Chinese President Xi Jinping, June 2016

nized, afresh, as valid in every language-culture, provided that culture is a sufficiently developed one....

We have entered into a time in which management of our planet and its conditions, is a clear imperative; but, the problems and opportunities that imperative implies do not end at the upper limit of scramjet ascent. All of the scientific and related challenges before civilized humanity today are inseparable from the growing field of extraterrestrial exploration. The existence of the Solar System is a product of a process inhering in the nature of the Sun's existence as a former solitary star. The past, present, and future conditions of life on our planet, Earth, are determined by ongoing processes of development associated with the continuing evolution of the Solar System. That system, and its relationship to the broader parts of the universe it inhabits, include matters which ought to be of concern, as either problems or potential advantages for human life on Earth.

To some degree, the scientific investigations which that perspective implies for any intelligent governments on Earth today, must lead to manned exploration, and some development of operating systems placed on relatively nearby parts of the Solar System. The development of new systems whose sheer power per capita and per cross-section of operation vastly exceed anything employed today, is also a necessary goal, for related reasons.

However, the greatest immediate practical impact of a space-oriented science-research function, will be the provision of knowledge essential for improvement and security of life on Earth. There is very little which might be developed in promotion of space research, which does not have a powerful application for human benefit back here on the surface of our planet. Hence, the principal public efforts in support of scientific research and development now, should be located in space-research-oriented programs which, by their nature, touch every area of interest for science to be practiced here on Earth.

This neither presumes, nor prohibits more or less global proprietorship over some relevant projects. It does strongly suggest limits on extending private patent rights beyond traditional categories of protection of actual inventors. In some cases, there should be setbacks of lately introduced novel kinds of proprietary claims in this area.

There must also be a more extensive sharing of access to promotion of technologies generated through cooperation among nations, or by supranational agencies. The idea of patenting of naturally pre-existing genetic types is an expression of naked financier-oligarchical rape which goes much, much too far.

The result to be expected from the rather inevitable role of space-oriented general scientific research and development, under a newly established form of fixed-exchange-rate system for the present time, would be a rapid psychological shift in outlook, toward thinking of ourselves as people living in the Solar System, rather than as huddled fearfully back in some local part of the surface of Earth. The conception of man must change to shift in that direction of self-image....

CPSIA information can be obtained
at www.ICGtesting.com
Printed in the USA
BVHW010858040419
544560BV00003B/3/P